Exam 70-640: TS: Windows Server 2008 Active Directory, Configuring (2nd Edition)

OBJECTIVE	LOCATION IN BOOK
CONFIGURING DOMAIN NAME SYSTEM (DNS) FOR ACTIVE DIRECTORY	
Configure zones.	Chapter 9, Lesson 1
Configure DNS server settings.	Chapter 9, Lesson 2
Configure zone transfers and replication.	Chapter 9, Lesson 2
CONFIGURING THE ACTIVE DIRECTORY INFRASTRUCTURE	
Configure a forest or a domain.	Chapter 1, Lessons 1, 2
	Chapter 10, Lessons 1, 2
	Chapter 12, Lessons 1, 2
Configure trusts.	Chapter 12, Lesson 2
Configure sites.	Chapter 11, Lessons 1, 2
Configure Active Directory replications.	Chapter 8, Lesson 3
	Chapter 10, Lesson 3
	Chapter 11, Lesson 3
Configure the global catalog.	Chapter 11, Lesson 2
Configure operations masters.	Chapter 10, Lesson 2
CONFIGURING ADDITIONAL ACTIVE DIRECTORY SERVER ROLES	
Configure Active Directory Lightweight Directory Service (AD LDS).	Chapter 14, Lessons 1, 2
Configure Active Directory Rights management Service (AD RMS).	Chapter 16, Lessons 1, 2
Configure the read-only domain controller (RODC).	Chapter 8, Lesson 3
Configure Active Directory Federation Services (AD FS).	Chapter 17, Lessons 1, 2
CREATING AND MAINTAINING ACTIVE DIRECTORY OBJECTS	
Automate creation of Active Directory accounts.	Chapter 3, Lessons 1, 2
	Chapter 4, Lessons 1, 2
	Chapter 5, Lessons 1, 2
Maintain Active Directory accounts.	Chapter 2, Lessons 1, 2, 3
	Chapter 3, Lessons 1, 2, 3
	Chapter 4, Lessons 1, 2, 3
	Chapter 5, Lessons 1, 2, 3
	Chapter 8, Lesson 4
Create and apply Group Policy objects (GPOs).	Chapter 6, Lessons 1, 2, 3
Configure GPO templates.	Chapter 6, Lessons 1, 2, 3
	Chapter 7, Lessons 1, 2, 3
Configure software deployment GPOs.	Chapter 7, Lesson 3
Configure account policies.	Chapter 8, Lesson 1
Configure audit policy by using GPOs.	Chapter 7, Lesson 4
	Chapter 8, Lesson 2
MAINTAINING THE ACTIVE DIRECTORY ENVIRONMENT	
Configure backup and recovery.	Chapter 13, Lesson 2
Perform offline maintenance.	Chapter 13, Lesson 1
Monitor Active Directory.	Chapter 6, Lesson 3
	Chapter 11, Lesson 3
	Chapter 13, Lesson 1
CONFIGURING ACTIVE DIRECTORY CERTIFICATE SERVICES	
Install Active Directory Certificate Services.	Chapter 15, Lesson 1
Configure CA server settings.	Chapter 15, Lesson 2
Manage certificate templates.	Chapter 15, Lesson 2
Manage enrollments.	Chapter 15, Lesson 2
Manage certificate revocations	Chapter 15, Lesson 2

Exam Objectives   The exam objectives listed here are current as of this book's publication date. Exam o'
are subject to change at any time without prior notice and at Microsoft's sole discretion. Please visit the'
Learning Web site for the most current listing of exam objectives: *http://www.microsoft.com/learning/*
Exam.aspx?ID=70-640.

MCTS Self-Paced Training Kit (Exam 70-640): Configuring Windows Server® 2008 Active Directory® (2nd Edition)

Dan Holme
Danielle Ruest
Nelson Ruest
Jason Kellington

PUBLISHED BY
Microsoft Press
A Division of Microsoft Corporation
One Microsoft Way
Redmond, Washington 98052-6399

Library of Congress Control Number: 2011929710
ISBN: 978-0-7356-5193-7

Printed and bound in the United States of America.

4 5 6 7 8 9 10 11 12 QG 7 6 5 4 3 2

Microsoft Press books are available through booksellers and distributors worldwide. If you need support related to this book, email Microsoft Press Book Support at mspinput@microsoft.com. Please tell us what you think of this book at http://www.microsoft.com/learning/booksurvey.

Acquisitions Editor: Jeff Koch
Developmental Editor: Karen Szall
Project Editor: Rosemary Caperton
Editorial Production: Tiffany Timmerman, S4Carlisle Publishing Services
Technical Reviewer: Kurt Meyer; Technical Review services provided by Content Master, a member of CM Group, Ltd.
Copyeditor: Crystal Thomas
Indexer: Maureen Johnson
Cover: Twist Creative • Seattle

[2012-02-17]

Contents at a Glance

Contents

What do you think of this book? We want to hear from you!

Microsoft is interested in hearing your feedback so we can continually improve our books and learning resources for you. To participate in a brief online survey, please visit:

www.microsoft.com/learning/booksurvey/

Chapter 2   Administering Active Directory Domain Services   35

Chapter 4   **Managing Groups**   **149**

Chapter 5   Configuring Computer Accounts   205

Chapter 7   Managing Enterprise Security and Configuration
with Group Policy Settings   317

Chapter 8   Improving the Security of Authentication in an AD DS Domain   389

Chapter 9　Integrating Domain Name System with AD DS　439

Chapter 10 Administering Domain Controllers   507

Chapter 11 Managing Sites and Active Directory Replication   557

Chapter 12 Managing Multiple Domains and Forests 605

Chapter 13 Directory Business Continuity   655

Chapter 17 Active Directory Federation Services   879

What do you think of this book? We want to hear from you!

Microsoft is interested in hearing your feedback so we can continually improve our books and learning resources for you. To participate in a brief online survey, please visit:

www.microsoft.com/learning/booksurvey/

Introduction

This training kit is designed for IT professionals who support or plan to support Microsoft Active Directory (AD) on Windows Server 2008 R2 and who also plan to take the Microsoft Certified Technology Specialist (MCTS) 70-640 examination. It is assumed that you have a solid foundation-level understanding of Microsoft Windows client and server operating systems and common Internet technologies. The MCTS exam, and this book, assume that you have at least one year of experience administering AD technologies.

The material covered in this training kit and on exam 70-640 builds on your understanding and experience to help you implement AD technologies in distributed environments, which can include complex network services and multiple locations and domain controllers. The topics in this training kit cover what you need to know for the exam, as described on the Skills Measured tab for the exam, which is available at *http://www.microsoft.com/learning/ en/us/exam.aspx?ID=70-640&locale=en-us#tab2*.

By using this training kit, you will learn how to do the following:

- Deploy Active Directory Domain Services, Active Directory Lightweight Directory Services, Active Directory Certificate Services, Active Directory Federation Services, and Active Directory Rights Management Services in a forest or domain.
- Upgrade existing domain controllers, domains, and forests to Windows Server 2008 R2.
- Efficiently administer and automate the administration of users, groups, and computers.
- Manage the configuration and security of a domain by using Group Policy, fine-grained password policies, directory services auditing, and the Security Configuration Wizard.
- Implement effective name resolution with the domain name system (DNS) on Windows Server 2008 R2.
- Plan, configure, and support the replication of Active Directory data within and between sites.
- Add, remove, maintain, and back up domain controllers.
- Enable authentication between domains and forests.
- Implement new capabilities and functionality offered by Windows Server 2008 R2.

Refer to the objective mapping page in the front of this book to see where in the book each exam objective is covered.

System Requirements

Practice exercises are a valuable component of this training kit. They allow you to experience important skills directly, reinforce material discussed in lessons, and even introduce new concepts.

Each lesson and practice describes the requirements for exercises. Although many lessons require only one computer, configured as a domain controller for a sample domain named contoso.com, some lessons require additional computers acting as a second domain controller in the domain, as a domain controller in another domain in the same forest, as a domain controller in another forest, or as a server performing other roles.

The chapters that cover AD DS (Chapters 1–13) require, at most, three machines running simultaneously. Chapters covering other Active Directory roles require up to four machines running simultaneously to provide a comprehensive experience with the technology.

Chapter 1, "Creating an Active Directory Domain," includes setup instructions for the first domain controller in the contoso.com domain, which is used throughout this training kit. Lessons that require additional computers provide guidance regarding the configuration of those computers.

Hardware Requirements

You can perform exercises on physical computers. Each computer must meet the minimum hardware requirements for Windows Server 2008 R2, published at *http://www.microsoft .com/windowsserver2008/en/us/system-requirements.aspx*. Windows Server 2008 R2 can run comfortably with 512 megabytes (MB) of memory in small test environments such as the sample contoso.com domain. However, when you begin to work with other AD technologies, such as AD Rights Management Services, AD Certificate Services, or AD Federation Services, your computers should be configured with at least 1024 MB of RAM. Although Windows Server 2008 R2 Standard edition is sufficient for most chapters, later chapters require the Enterprise edition, and we recommend installing that edition when setting up servers for Chapters 14 through 17.

To minimize the time and expense of configuring the several computers required for this training kit, it's recommended that you create virtual machines by using Hyper-V—a feature of Windows Server 2008 and Windows Server 2008 R2—or other virtualization software, such as VMware Workstation or Oracle VirtualBox. Note that although the book calls for a number of machines, you never use more than four machines together at the same time. Refer to the documentation of your selected virtualization platform for hardware and software requirements, for instructions regarding host setup and configuration, and for procedures to create virtual machines for Windows Server 2008 R2.

If you choose to use virtualization software, you can run more than one virtual machine on a host computer. Each virtual machine must be assigned at least 512 MB or 1024 MB of RAM as required and must meet the minimum processor and disk space requirements for Windows Server 2008 R2. The host computer must have sufficient RAM for each virtual machine that you will run simultaneously on the host. If you plan to run all virtual machines on a single host, the host must have at least 4.0 GB of RAM. For example, one of the most complex configurations you will need is two domain controllers, each using 512 MB of RAM, and two member servers, each using 1024 MB of RAM. On a host computer with 4 GB of RAM, this would leave 1 GB for the host. Note that each time you run a machine with the Enterprise edition of Windows Server 2008 R2, you should assign 1024 MB of RAM to it.

If you encounter performance bottlenecks while running multiple virtual machines on a single physical host, consider running virtual machines on more than one physical host.

Ensure that all machines—virtual or physical—that you use for exercises can network with each other. It is highly recommended that the environment be totally disconnected from your production environment. Refer to the documentation of your virtualization platform for network configuration procedures.

We recommend that you preserve each of the virtual machines you create until you have completed the training kit. After each chapter, create a backup of the virtual machines used in that chapter so that you can reuse them, as required in later exercises.

Finally, you must have a physical computer with a CD-ROM drive with which to read the companion media.

Software Requirements

Windows Server 2008 R2 with SP1 is required to perform the practice exercises in this training kit.

You can download evaluation versions of the product from the TechNet Evaluation Center at *http://technet.microsoft.com/evalcenter*. If you use evaluation versions of the software, pay attention to the expiration date of the product. The evaluation version of Windows Server 2008 R2 with SP1, for example, can be used for up to 60 days before it expires, but it can be rearmed up to three times, giving you up to 180 days to use the evaluation.

If you have a TechNet or an MSDN subscription, you can download the products from the subscriber downloads center. These versions do not expire. If you are not a TechNet or MSDN subscriber, it is recommended that you subscribe so that you can access benefits such as product downloads.

If you will install Windows Server 2008 R2 on a physical computer, you need software that allows you to burn the .iso file that you download to a DVD, and you need hardware that supports DVD recording.

To use the companion media, you need a web browser such as Internet Explorer 8, and an application that can display PDF files, such as Adobe Acrobat, which can be downloaded from *http://www.adobe.com*.

Using the Companion CD

A companion CD is included with this training kit. The companion CD contains the following:

- **Practice Tests**   You can reinforce your understanding of the topics covered in this training kit by using electronic practice tests that you customize to meet your needs. You can run a practice test that is generated from the pool of Lesson Review questions in this book. Alternatively, you can practice for the 70-640 certification exam by using tests created from a pool of over 200 realistic exam questions, which give you many practice exams to ensure that you are prepared.

- **Links to References**   The CD includes links to references given in this book. Use these links to go directly to references that supplement the text.

- **An eBook**   An electronic version (eBook) of this book is included for when you do not want to carry the printed book with you.

How to Install the Practice Tests

To install the practice test software from the companion CD to your hard disk, perform the following steps:

1. Insert the companion CD into your CD drive and accept the license agreement. A CD menu appears.

> **NOTE   IF THE CD MENU DOES NOT APPEAR**
>
> If the CD menu or the license agreement does not appear, AutoRun might be disabled on your computer. Refer to the Readme.txt file on the CD for alternate installation instructions.

2. Click Practice Tests and follow the instructions on the screen.

How to Use the Practice Tests

To start the practice test software, follow these steps:

1. Click Start, click All Programs, and then click Microsoft Press Training Kit Exam Prep.

    A window appears that shows all the Microsoft Press training kit exam prep suites installed on your computer.

2. Double-click the lesson review or practice test you want to use.

> **NOTE** **LESSON REVIEWS VS. PRACTICE TESTS**
>
> Select the (70-640) TS: Windows Server 2008 Active Directory, Configuring lesson review to use the questions from the "Lesson Review" sections of this book. Select the (70-640) TS: Windows Server 2008 Active Directory, Configuring practice test to use a pool of 200 questions similar to those that appear on the 70-640 certification exam.

Lesson Review Options

When you start a lesson review, the Custom Mode dialog box appears so that you can configure your test. You can click OK to accept the defaults, or you can customize the number of questions you want, how the practice test software works, which exam objectives you want the questions to relate to, and whether you want your lesson review to be timed. If you are retaking a test, you can select whether you want to see all the questions again or only the questions you missed or did not answer.

After you click OK, your lesson review starts.

- To take the test, answer the questions and use the Next and Previous buttons to move from question to question.

- After you answer an individual question, if you want to see which answers are correct— along with an explanation of each correct answer—click Explanation.

- If you prefer to wait until the end of the test to see how you did, answer all the questions and then click Score Test. You will see a summary of the exam objectives you chose and the percentage of questions you got right overall and per objective. You can print a copy of your test, review your answers, or retake the test.

Practice Test Options

When you start a practice test, you choose whether to take the test in Certification Mode, Study Mode, or Custom Mode:

- **Certification Mode**   Closely resembles the experience of taking a certification exam. The test has a set number of questions. It is timed, and you cannot pause and restart the timer.

- **Study Mode**   Creates an untimed test during which you can review the correct answers and the explanations after you answer each question.

- **Custom Mode**   Gives you full control over the test options so that you can customize them as you like.

In all modes, the user interface when you are taking the test is basically the same but with different options enabled or disabled depending on the mode. The main options are discussed in the previous section, "Lesson Review Options."

When you review your answer to an individual practice test question, a "References" section is provided that lists where in the training kit you can find the information that relates to that question and provides links to other sources of information. After you click Test Results to score your entire practice test, you can click the Learning Plan tab to see a list of references for every objective.

How to Uninstall the Practice Tests

To uninstall the practice test software for a training kit, use the Programs And Features option in Windows Control Panel.

> **NOTE COMPANION CONTENT FOR DIGITAL BOOK READERS**
>
> If you bought a digital edition of this book, you can enjoy select content from the print edition's companion CD. Visit *http://go.microsoft.com/FWLink/?LinkiD=218370* to get your downloadable content.

Acknowledgments

The authors' names appear on the cover of a book, but we are only part of a much larger team. Jeff Koch gave us the opportunity to update the first edition of this training kit and guided it through the business. Karen Szall and Rosemary Caperton, with whom we worked closely, were a dream team as always! And each of the editors did a phenomenal job of adding value to this training kit. Kurt Meyer, our technical reviewer, was extremely helpful and thorough. We are very grateful to the entire team and to everyone's efforts at making this training kit an indispensible resource to the community. We look forward to working with each of you again in the future!

Support & Feedback

The following sections provide information on errata, book support, feedback, and contact information.

Errata

We've made every effort to ensure the accuracy of this book and its companion content. Any errors that have been reported since this book was published are listed on our Microsoft Press site at oreilly.com:

http://go.microsoft.com/FWLink/?LinkID=219768

If you find an error that is not already listed, you can report it to us through the same page.

If you need additional support, please email Microsoft Press Book Support at mspinput@microsoft.com.

Please note that product support for Microsoft software is not offered through the addresses above.

We Want to Hear from You

At Microsoft Press, your satisfaction is our top priority, and your feedback is our most valuable asset. Please tell us what you think of this book at:

http://www.microsoft.com/learning/booksurvey

The survey is short, and we read every one of your comments and ideas. Thanks in advance for your input!

Stay in Touch

Let us keep the conversation going! We are on Twitter: *http://twitter.com/MicrosoftPress*.

Preparing for the Exam

Microsoft certification exams are a great way to build your resume and let the world know about your level of expertise. Certification exams validate your on-the-job experience and product knowledge. While there is no substitution for on-the-job experience, preparation through study and hands-on practice can help you prepare for the exam. We recommend that you round out your exam preparation plan by using a combination of available study materials and courses. For example, you might use the Training Kit and another study guide for your "at home" preparation, and take a Microsoft Official Curriculum course for the classroom experience. Choose the combination that you think works best for you.

Microsoft
C E R T I F I E D
Technology
Specialist

CHAPTER 1

Creating an Active Directory Domain

A ctive Directory Domain Services (AD DS) and its related services form the foundation
for enterprise networks running Microsoft Windows. Together, they act as tools that
store information about the identities of users, computers,
and services; authenticate individual users or computers; and
provide a mechanism with which a user or computer can access
resources in the enterprise. In this chapter, you will begin your
exploration of Windows Server 2008 R2 Active Directory by
installing the Active Directory Domain Services role and creating
a domain controller in a new Active Directory forest. You will
find that Windows Server 2008 R2 continues the evolution of
Active Directory by enhancing many of the existing concepts and
features with which you are already familiar.

> IMPORTANT
>
> **Have you read
> page xxxiv?**
>
> It contains valuable
> information regarding
> the skills you need to
> pass the exam.

This chapter focuses on the creation of a new Active Directory forest with a single
domain in a single domain controller. The practice exercises in this chapter guide you
through the creation of a domain named contoso.com that you will use for all other
practices in this training kit. In later chapters, you will gain experience with other
scenarios and the implementation of the other key Active Directory components
integrated with AD DS.

Exam objectives in this chapter:

- Configure a forest or a domain.

Lessons in this chapter:

Before You Begin

To complete the lessons in this chapter, you must have done the following:

- Obtained two computers on which you will install Windows Server 2008 R2. The computers can be physical systems that meet the minimum hardware requirements for Windows Server 2008, found at *http://www.microsoft.com/windowsserver2008/en/us/system-requirements.aspx* or *http://technet.microsoft.com/en-us/library/dd379511(WS.10).aspx*. You will need at least 512 MB of RAM, 32 GB of free hard disk space, and an x64 processor with a minimum clock speed of 1.4 GHz. Alternately, you can use virtual machines that meet the same requirements.

- Obtained an evaluation version of Windows Server 2008 R2. A 180-day trial evaluation version of Windows Server 2008 R2 with SP1 is available for download at *http://www.microsoft.com/windowsserver2008/en/us/trial-software.aspx*.

 REAL WORLD

Jason Kellington

Windows Server 2008 R2 supports only x64 or Itanium 2 processors; it no longer supports the x86 processor architecture. If this system requirement is not met, Windows Server 2008 R2 will not install. This is most important when upgrading pre-existing servers to Windows Server 2008 R2. Pre-existing servers based on the x86 processor architecture must be replaced with hardware based on either the x64 or Itanium 2 processor architecture.

In the most common AD DS installation scenario, the server functions as a domain controller, which maintains a copy of the AD DS database and replicates that database with other domain controllers. Domain controllers are the most critical component in an Active Directory infrastructure and should function with as few additional unrelated components installed as possible. This dedicated configuration provides for more stable and reliable domain controllers, because it limits the possibility of other applications or services interfering with the AD DS components running on the domain controller.

In versions of Windows Server prior to Window Server 2008, server administrators were required to select and configure individual components on a server to ensure that nonessential Windows components were disabled or uninstalled. In Windows Server 2008, key Windows components are broken down into functionally related groups called *roles*. Role-based administration allows an administrator to simply select the role or roles that the server should fulfill. Windows Server 2008 then installs the appropriate Windows components required to provide that role's functionality. You will become more familiar with role-based administration as you proceed through the practice exercises in this book.

Lesson 1: Installing Active Directory Domain Services

Active Directory Domain Services (AD DS) provides the functionality of an identity and access (IDA) solution for enterprise networks. In this lesson, you learn about AD DS and other Active Directory roles supported by Windows Server 2008. You also explore Server Manager, the tool with which you can configure server roles, and the improved Active Directory Domain Services Installation Wizard. This lesson also reviews key concepts of IDA and Active Directory.

After this lesson, you will be able to:

- Explain the role of identity and access in an enterprise network.
- Understand the relationship between Active Directory services.
- Install the Active Directory Domain Services (AD DS) role and configure a Windows Server 2008 R2 domain controller using the Windows interface.

Estimated lesson time: 60 minutes

Active Directory, Identity and Access

Identity and access (IDA) infrastructure refers to the tools and core technologies used to integrate people, processes, and technology in an organization. An effective IDA infrastructure ensures that the right people have access to the right resources at the right time.

As previously mentioned, Active Directory provides the IDA solution for enterprise networks running Windows. AD DS is the core component of an Active Directory IDA infrastructure. AD DS collects and stores enterprise-wide IDA information in a database called the *Active Directory data store*. The data store contains all pertinent information on all objects that exist within the Active Directory infrastructure. In addition, AD DS acts as a communication and information hub for additional Active Directory services which, together, form a complete IDA infrastructure.

Active Directory stores information about users, groups, computers, and other identities. An identity is, in the broadest sense, a representation of an object that will perform actions on the enterprise network. For example, a user will open documents from a shared folder on a server. The document will be secured with permissions on an access control list (ACL). Access to the document is managed by the security subsystem of the server, which compares the identity of the user to the identities on the ACL to determine whether the user's request for access will be granted or denied.

Computers, groups, services, and other objects also perform actions on the network, and they must be represented by identities. Among the information stored about an identity are properties that uniquely identify the object, such as a user name or a security identifier (SID), and the password for the identity. The *identity store* is, therefore, one component of an IDA infrastructure. The Active Directory data store, also known as the *directory*, is an identity store. The directory itself is hosted within a database that is stored on and managed by a domain controller—a server performing the AD DS role. If multiple domain controllers exist within an Active Directory infrastructure, they work together to maintain a copy of the data store on each domain controller. The information within this store allows Active Directory to perform the three main functions of an IDA infrastructure: authentication, access control, and auditing.

- **Authentication**   A user, computer, or other object must first verify its identity to the Active Directory infrastructure before being granted the ability to function as part of the Active Directory domain. This process of verification is typically through an exchange of protected or secret information such as a password or a digital certificate. After the authentication information has been submitted to the Active Directory and verified as valid, the user may proceed as a member of the domain and perform actions such as requesting access to shared files, submitting a print job to a printer, accessing and reading email, or any number of other actions within the domain.

Kerberos Authentication in an Active Directory Domain

In an Active Directory domain, the Kerberos protocol is used to authenticate identities. When a user or computer logs on to the domain, Kerberos authenticates its credentials and issues a package of information called a *ticket granting ticket* (TGT). Before the user performs a task such as connecting to a server to request a document, a Kerberos request is sent to a domain controller along with the TGT that identifies the authenticated user. The domain controller issues the user another package of information called a *service ticket* that identifies the authenticated user to the server. The user presents the service ticket to the server, which accepts the service ticket as proof that the user has been authenticated.

These Kerberos transactions result in a single network logon. After the user or computer has initially logged on and has been granted a TGT, the user is authenticated within the entire domain and can be granted service tickets that identify the user to any service. All of this ticket activity is managed by the Kerberos clients and services built into Windows and remains transparent to the user.

- **Access control**   The IDA infrastructure is responsible for protecting information and resources by ensuring that access to resources is granted to only the identities that should have access. Access to important resources and confidential information must be managed according to the enterprise policies. Every single object (such as computers, folders, files, and printers) within Active Directory has an associated discretionary access control list (DACL). This list contains information regarding the identities that have been granted access to the object and the level of access granted.

When a user whose identity has already been authenticated on the domain tries to access a resource, the resource's DACL is checked to determine whether the user's identity is on the list. If the identity exists on the list, the user is allowed to access the resource as specified by the access permissions on the DACL listed for that user.

- **Auditing** Monitoring activities that occur within the IDA infrastructure is referred to as *auditing*. Auditing allows organizations to monitor events occurring within the IDA infrastructure, including the access of files and folders, where and when users are logging on, changes made to the IDA infrastructure, and general functionality of Active Directory itself. Auditing behavior is controlled by system access control lists (SACLs). Like the previously mentioned DACL, every object within the IDA infrastructure has an SACL attached to it. The SACL contains a list of identities whose activity on that resource will be audited, as well as the level of auditing that will occur for each identity.

AD DS is not the only component of IDA supported by Windows Server 2008. With the release of Windows Server 2008, Microsoft consolidated several previously separate components into an integrated IDA platform. Active Directory itself now includes five technologies, each of which is identified with a keyword that indicates the purpose of the technology, as shown in Figure 1-1.

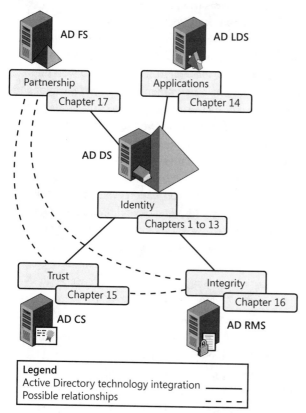

FIGURE 1-1 Integration of the five Active Directory technologies

These five technologies comprise a complete IDA solution:

- **Active Directory Domain Services (Identity)**   AD DS, as described earlier, is designed to provide a central repository for identity management within an organization. AD DS provides authentication, authorization, and auditing services on a network and supports object management through Group Policy. AD DS also provides information management and sharing services, enabling users to find any component—file servers, printers, groups, and other users—by searching the directory. Because of this, AD DS is often referred to as a *network operating system directory service*. AD DS is the primary Active Directory technology and should be deployed in every network that runs Windows Server 2008 operating systems. AD DS is covered in Chapters 1 through 13.

> *MORE INFO*   **AD DS DESIGN**
>
> For more details on planning the implementation of AD DS and information regarding AD DS design, see the AD DS Design Guide at *http://technet.microsoft.com/en-us/ library/cc754678(WS.10).aspx.*

- **Active Directory Lightweight Directory Services (Applications)**   Essentially a stand-alone version of Active Directory, the Active Directory Lightweight Directory Services (AD LDS) role, formerly known as Active Directory Application Mode (ADAM), provides support for directory-enabled applications. AD LDS is really a subset of AD DS because both are based on the same core code. The AD LDS directory stores and replicates only application-related information. It is commonly used by applications that require a directory store but do not require the information to be replicated as widely as to all domain controllers. AD LDS also enables you to deploy a custom schema to support an application without modifying the schema of AD DS. The AD LDS role is truly lightweight and supports multiple data stores on a single system, so each application can be deployed with its own directory, schema, assigned Lightweight Directory Access Protocol (LDAP) and SSL ports, and application event log. AD LDS does not rely on AD DS, so it can be used in a stand-alone or workgroup environment. However, in domain environments, AD LDS can use AD DS for the authentication of Windows security principals (users, groups, and computers). AD LDS can also be used to provide authentication services in exposed networks such as extranets. Using AD LDS in this situation provides less risk than using AD DS. AD LDS is covered in Chapter 14, "Active Directory Lightweight Directory Services."

- **Active Directory Certificate Services (Trust)**   Organizations can use Active Directory Certificate Services (AD CS) to set up a certificate authority (CA) for issuing digital certificates as part of a public key infrastructure (PKI) that binds the identity of a person, device, or service to a corresponding private key. Certificates can be used to authenticate users and computers, provide web-based authentication, support smart card authentication, and support applications, including secure wireless networks, virtual private networks (VPNs), Internet Protocol security (IPSec), Encrypting File

System (EFS), digital signatures, and more. AD CS provides an efficient and secure way to issue and manage certificates. You can use AD CS to provide these services to external communities. If you do so, AD CS should be linked with an external, renowned CA that will prove to others you are who you say you are. AD CS is designed to create trust in an untrustworthy world; as such, it must rely on proven processes to certify that each person or computer that obtains a certificate has been thoroughly verified and approved. In internal networks, AD CS can integrate with AD DS to provision users and computers automatically with certificates. AD CS is covered in Chapter 15, "Active Directory Certificate Services and Public Key Infrastructures."

- **Active Directory Rights Management Services (Integrity)**   Although a server running Windows can prevent or allow access to a document based on the document's DACL, there have been few ways to control what happens to the document and its content after a user has opened it. Active Directory Rights Management Services (AD RMS) is an information-protection technology that enables you to implement persistent usage policy templates that define allowed and disallowed use whether online or offline, inside or outside the firewall. For example, you could configure a template that allows users to read a document but not print or copy its contents. By doing so, you can ensure the integrity of the data you generate, protect intellectual property, and control who can do what with the documents your organization produces. AD RMS requires an Active Directory domain with domain controllers running Windows 2000 Server with Service Pack 3 (SP3) or later; IIS, a database server such as Microsoft SQL Server 2008; the AD RMS client (which can be downloaded from the Microsoft Download Center and is included by default in Windows Vista, Windows 7, and Windows Server 2008); and an RMS-enabled browser or application such as Microsoft Internet Explorer, Microsoft Office, Microsoft Word, Microsoft Outlook, or Microsoft PowerPoint. AD RMS can rely on AD CS to embed certificates within documents as well as in AD DS to manage access rights. AD RMS is covered in Chapter 16, "Active Directory Rights Management Services."

- **Active Directory Federation Services (Partnership)**   Active Directory Federation Services (AD FS) enables an organization to extend IDA across multiple platforms, including both Windows and non-Windows environments, and to project identity and access rights across security boundaries to trusted partners. In a federated environment, each organization maintains and manages its own identities, but each organization can also securely project and accept identities from other organizations. Users are authenticated in one network but can access resources in another—a process known as single sign-on (SSO). AD FS supports partnerships because it allows different organizations to share access to extranet applications while relying on their own internal AD DS structures to provide the actual authentication process. To do so, AD FS extends your internal AD DS structure to the external world through common Transmission Control Protocol/Internet Protocol (TCP/IP) ports such as 80 (HTTP) and 443 (Secure HTTP, or HTTPS). It normally resides in the perimeter network. AD FS can rely on AD CS to create trusted servers and on AD RMS to provide external protection for intellectual property. AD FS is covered in Chapter 17, "Active Directory Federation Services."

Together, the Active Directory roles provide an integrated IDA solution. AD DS or AD LDS provides foundational directory services in both domain and stand-alone implementations. AD CS provides trusted credentials in the form of PKI digital certificates. AD RMS protects the integrity of information contained in documents. And AD FS supports partnerships by eliminating the need for federated environments to create multiple, separate identities for a single security principal.

Beyond Identity and Access

Active Directory delivers more than just an IDA solution, however. It also provides the mechanisms to support, manage, and configure resources in distributed network environments.

A set of rules, the *schema*, defines the classes of objects and attributes that can be contained in the directory. The fact that Active Directory has user objects that include a user name and password, for example, is because the schema defines the *user* object class, the two attributes, and the association between the object class and attributes.

Policy-based administration eases the management burden of even the largest, most complex networks by providing a single point at which to configure settings that are then deployed to multiple systems. You will learn about such policies, including Group Policy, audit policies, and fine-grained password policies in Chapter 6, "Implementing a Group Policy Infrastructure"; Chapter 7, "Managing Enterprise Security and Configuration with Group Policy Settings"; and Chapter 8, "Improving the Security of Authentication in an AD DS Domain."

Replication services distribute directory data across a network. This includes both the data store itself as well as data required to implement policies and configuration, including logon scripts. In Chapter 8; Chapter 11, "Managing Sites and Active Directory Replication"; and Chapter 10, "Administering Domain Controllers," you will learn about Active Directory replication. There is even a separate partition of the data store named *configuration* that maintains information about network configuration, topology, and services.

Several components and technologies enable you to query Active Directory and locate objects in the data store. A partition of the data store called the *global catalog* (also known as the *partial attribute set*) contains information about every object in the directory. It is a type of index that can be used to locate objects in the directory. Programmatic interfaces such as Active Directory Services Interface (ADSI) and protocols such as LDAP can be used to read and manipulate the data store.

The Active Directory data store can also be used to support applications and services not directly related to AD DS. Within the database, application partitions can store data to support applications that require replicated data. The domain name system (DNS) service on a server running Windows Server 2008 can store its information in a database called an *Active Directory integrated zone*, which is maintained as an application partition in AD DS and replicated using Active Directory replication services.

Components of an Active Directory Infrastructure

The first 13 chapters of this training kit focus on the installation, configuration, and management of AD DS. AD DS provides the foundation for IDA in and management of an enterprise network. It is worthwhile to spend a few moments reviewing the components of an Active Directory infrastructure.

> **NOTE WHERE TO FIND ACTIVE DIRECTORY DETAILS**
>
> For more details about Active Directory, refer to the product Help installed with Windows Server 2008 and to the Windows Server 2008 R2 home page located at *http://technet.microsoft.com/en-us/windowsserver/bb310558.aspx.*

- **Active Directory data store**   As mentioned in the previous section, AD DS stores its identities in the directory—a data store hosted on domain controllers. The directory is a single file database named Ntds.dit and is located by default in the %SystemRoot%\Ntds folder on a domain controller. The database is divided into several partitions, including the schema, the configuration, and the domain naming context that contains the data about objects within a domain—the users, groups, and computers, for example. Depending on the environment, there may also be application partitions and a partial attribute set (PAS), also called the *global catalog.*

- **Domain controllers**   Domain controllers (DCs) are servers that perform the AD DS role and maintain a copy of the Active Directory data store, along with other data important to the domain. As part of that role, they also run the Kerberos Key Distribution Center (KDC) service, which performs authentication and other Active Directory services. Chapter 10 explains the roles performed by DCs.

- **Domain**   One or more domain controllers are required to create an Active Directory *domain.* A domain is an administrative unit within which certain capabilities and characteristics are shared. First, all domain controllers replicate the domain's partition of the data store, which contains, among other things, the identity data for the domain's users, groups, and computers. Because all DCs maintain the same identity store, any DC can authenticate any identity in a domain. Additionally, a domain defines the boundaries of administrative policies such as password complexity and account lockout policies. Such policies configured in one domain affect all accounts in the domain and do not affect accounts in other domains. Changes can be made to objects in the Active Directory database by any domain controller and will replicate to all other domain controllers. Therefore, in networks where replication of all data between domain controllers cannot be supported, it might be necessary to implement more than one domain to manage the replication of subsets of identities. You will learn more about domains in Chapter 12, "Managing Multiple Domains and Forests."

- **Forest**   A *forest* is a collection of one or more Active Directory domains. The first domain installed in a forest is called the *forest root domain.* A forest contains a single definition of network configuration and a single instance of the directory schema.

A forest is a single instance of the directory—no data is replicated by Active Directory outside the boundaries of the forest. Therefore, the forest defines a security boundary. Chapter 12 explores the concept of the forest further.

- **Tree** The DNS namespace of domains in a forest creates *trees* within the forest. If a domain is a subdomain of another domain, the two domains are considered a tree. For example, if the *treyresearch.net* forest contains two domains, *treyresearch.net* and *antarctica.treyresearch.net*, those domains constitute a contiguous portion of the DNS namespace, so they are a single tree. If, conversely, the two domains are *treyresearch.net* and *proseware.com*, which are not contiguous in the DNS namespace, the forest is considered to have two trees. Trees are the direct result of the DNS names chosen for domains in the forest.

Figure 1-2 illustrates an Active Directory forest for Trey Research, which maintains a small operation at a field station in Antarctica. Because the link from Antarctica to the headquarters is expensive, slow, and unreliable, Antarctica is configured as a separate domain. The DNS name of the forest is *treyresearch.net*. The Antarctica domain is a child domain in the DNS namespace, *antarctica.treyresearch.net*, so it is considered a child domain in the domain tree.

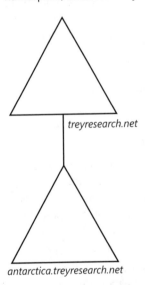

treyresearch.net

antarctica.treyresearch.net

FIGURE 1-2 An Active Directory forest with two domains

- **Functional level** The functionality available in an Active Directory domain or forest depends on its *functional level*. The functional level is an AD DS setting that enables advanced domain-wide or forest-wide AD DS features. There are six domain functional levels (Windows 2000 native, Windows 2000 mixed, Windows Server 2003, Windows Server 2003 interim, Windows Server 2008, and Windows Server 2008 R2) and five forest functional levels (Windows Server 2000, Windows Server 2003, Windows Server 2003 interim, Windows Server 2008, and Windows Server 2008 R2). As you raise the functional level of a domain or forest, features provided by that version of Windows become available to AD DS. For example, when the forest functional level is raised to Windows Server 2008 R2, the ability to enable the Active Directory Recycle Bin becomes available. With the Active Directory Recycle Bin, objects deleted within Active Directory are preserved in the state they were in prior to deletion. This allows easy restoration of previously deleted objects, if required. The important thing to know about functional levels is that they determine the versions of Windows permitted on domain controllers. Before you raise the domain functional level to Windows Server 2008, all domain controllers must be running Windows Server 2008. Chapter 12 discusses domain and forest functional levels.

- **Organizational units**   Active Directory is a hierarchical database. Objects in the data store can be collected in containers. One type of container is the object class called *container*. You see the default containers, including Users, Computers, and Builtin, when you open the Active Directory Users And Computers snap-in. Another type of container is the *organizational unit* (OU). OUs provide not only a container for objects but also a scope with which to manage the objects. That is because OUs can have objects called *Group Policy objects* (GPOs) linked to them. GPOs can contain configuration settings that will be applied automatically by users or computers in an OU. In Chapter 2, "Administering Active Directory Domain Services," you will learn more about OUs, and in Chapter 6, you will explore GPOs.

- **Sites**   When you consider the network topology of a distributed enterprise, you will certainly discuss the network's physical locations or sites. Sites in Active Directory, however, have a very specific meaning. An Active Directory site is an object that represents a portion of the enterprise within which consistent, high-bandwidth network connectivity is expected. A site creates a boundary of replication and service usage. Domain controllers within a site replicate changes within seconds. Between different sites, however, changes are replicated on a controlled basis with the assumption that intersite connections are slow, expensive, or unreliable compared to the connections within a site. Additionally, clients prefer to use distributed services provided by servers in their site or in the closest site. For example, when a user logs on to the domain, the Windows client first attempts to authenticate with a domain controller in its site. Only if no domain controller is available in the site will the client attempt to authenticate with a DC in another site. Chapter 11 describes the configuration and functionality of Active Directory sites.

Each of these components is discussed in detail later in this training kit. At this point, if you are less familiar with Active Directory, it is important only that you have a basic understanding of the terminology, the components, and their relationships.

Preparing to Create a New Windows Server 2008 Forest

Before you install the AD DS role on a server and promote it to act as a domain controller, plan your Active Directory infrastructure. Some of the information you will need to create a domain controller includes the following:

- The domain's name and DNS name. A domain must have a unique DNS name, such as contoso.com, as well as a short name, such as CONTOSO, called a *NetBIOS name*. NetBIOS is a network protocol that has been used since the first versions of Microsoft Windows NT and is still specified and used for backward compatibility.

- Whether the domain will need to support domain controllers running previous versions of Windows. When you create a new Active Directory forest, you will configure the functional level. If the domain will include only Windows Server 2008 R2 domain controllers, you can set the functional level accordingly to benefit from the enhanced features introduced by this version of Windows.

- Details for how DNS will be implemented to support Active Directory. It is a best practice to implement DNS for your Windows domain zones by using Windows DNS Service, as you will learn in Chapter 9, "Integrating Domain Name System with AD DS"; however, it is possible to support a Windows domain on a third-party DNS service.

- IP configuration for the domain controller. Domain controllers require static IP addresses and subnet mask values. Additionally, the domain controller must be configured with a DNS server address to perform name resolution. If you are creating a new forest and will run Windows DNS Service on the domain controller, you can configure the DNS address to point to the server's own IP address. After DNS is installed, the server can look to itself to resolve DNS names.

- The user name and password of an account in the server's Administrators group. The account must have a password—the password cannot be blank.

- The location in which the data store (including *Ntds.dit*) and system volume (SYSVOL) should be installed. By default, these stores are created in %SystemRoot%; for example, C:\Windows, in the NTDS and SYSVOL folders, respectively. When creating a domain controller, you can redirect these stores to other drives.

> *MORE INFO*   **DEPLOYMENT OF AD DS**
>
> This list comprises the settings that you are prompted to configure when creating a domain controller. There are several additional considerations regarding the deployment of AD DS in an enterprise setting that you should review. See the AD DS Deployment Guide at *http://technet.microsoft.com/en-us/library/cc753963(WS.10).aspx* for more information.

Adding the AD DS Role Using the Windows Interface

After you have collected the prerequisite information listed earlier, you are ready to add the AD DS role. There are several ways to do so. In this lesson, you learn how to create a domain controller by using the Windows interface. In the next lesson, you learn to do so by using the command line.

Windows Server 2008 provides role-based configuration, installing only the components and services required for the roles a server plays. This role-based server management is reflected in the administrative console, Server Manager, as shown in Figure 1-3. Server Manager consolidates the information, tools, and resources needed to support a server's roles.

You can add roles to a server by using the Add Roles link on the home page of Server Manager or by right-clicking the Roles node in the console tree and choosing Add Roles. The Add Roles Wizard presents a list of roles available for installation and guides you through the installation of selected roles.

FIGURE 1-3 Server Manager

Creating a Domain Controller

After you add the AD DS role, the files required to perform the role are installed on the server; however, the server is not yet acting as a domain controller. You must subsequently run the Active Directory Domain Services Installation Wizard, which can be launched by using the *Dcpromo.exe* command, to configure, initialize, and start Active Directory.

PRACTICE IT

Exercise 4, "Install a New Windows Server 2008 R2 Forest," at the end of this lesson guides you through configuration of AD DS, using the Active Directory Domain Services Installation Wizard.

Quick Check

- You want to use a new server running Windows Server 2008 R2 as a domain controller in your Active Directory domain. Which command do you use to launch configuration of the domain controller?

Quick Check Answer

- *Dcpromo.exe*

PRACTICE   Creating a Windows Server 2008 R2 Forest

In this practice, you create the AD DS forest for Contoso, Ltd. This forest will be used for exercises throughout this training kit. You begin by installing Windows Server 2008 R2 and performing post-installation configuration tasks. You then add the AD DS role and promote the server to a domain controller in the contoso.com forest, using the Active Directory Domain Services Installation Wizard.

EXERCISE 1   Install Windows Server 2008 R2

In this exercise, you install Windows Server 2008 R2 on a computer or virtual machine.

1. Power on the system and insert the Windows Server 2008 R2 installation DVD.

    If you are using a virtual machine (VM), you might have the option to mount an ISO image of the installation DVD. Consult the VM Help documentation for guidance.

    If the system's hard disk is empty, the system should boot to the DVD. If there is data on the disk, you might be prompted to press a key to boot to the DVD.

    If the system does not boot to the DVD or offer you a boot menu, go to the BIOS settings of the computer and configure the boot order to ensure that the system boots to the DVD.

    The Install Windows Wizard appears, as shown in Figure 1-4.

2. Select the language, regional setting, and keyboard layout that are correct for your system, and then click Next.

3. Click Install Now.

    Setup starts, and a list of versions to install appears, as shown in Figure 1-5.

4. Select Windows Server 2008 R2 Standard (Full Installation) and click Next.

5. Select the I Accept The License Terms check box and click Next.

6. Click Custom (Advanced).

7. On the Where Do You Want To Install Windows page, select the partition on which you want to install Windows Server 2008.

    If you need to create, delete, extend, or format partitions, or if you need to load a custom mass storage driver to access the disk subsystem, click Driver Options (Advanced).

FIGURE 1-4 The Install Windows Wizard

FIGURE 1-5 The Select The Operating System You Want To Install page

8. Click Next.

The Installing Windows page appears, as shown in Figure 1-6. The window keeps you apprised of the progress of Windows installation.

Note: If you are installing over an existing version of Windows, the installer warns you at this point and prompts you to continue.

Installation of Windows Server 2008 R2 is image based. Therefore, installation is significantly faster than previous versions of Windows, even though the operating systems themselves are much larger than earlier versions. The computer will restart one or more times during installation.

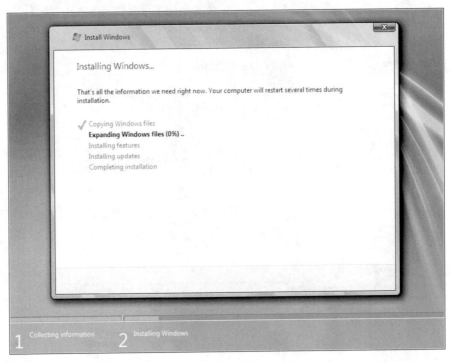

FIGURE 1-6 The Installing Windows page

When the installation is complete, you are informed that the user's password must be changed before logging on the first time.

9. Click OK.

10. Type a password for the Administrator account in both the New Password and Confirm Password boxes and press Enter.

The password must be at least seven characters long and must have at least three of four character types:

- Uppercase: A–Z
- Lowercase: a–z

- Numeric: 0–9
- Nonalphanumeric: symbols such as $, #, @, and !

> **NOTE DO NOT FORGET THIS PASSWORD**
>
> Without it, you will not be able to log on to the server to perform other exercises in this training kit. Alternately, you can select the Create A Password Reset Disk option to start a wizard that creates a disk that you can use to recover the password, should it be misplaced or forgotten.

11. Click OK.

    The desktop for the Administrator account appears.

EXERCISE 2 Perform Post-Installation Configuration

In this exercise, you perform post-installation configuration of the server to prepare the server with the name and TCP/IP settings required for exercises in this training kit.

1. Wait for the desktop for the Administrator account to appear.

   The Initial Configuration Tasks window appears, as shown in Figure 1-7. This tool is designed to make it easy for you to perform best practice, post-installation configuration tasks.

FIGURE 1-7 The Initial Configuration Tasks window

2. In the Initial Configuration Tasks window, click Provide Computer Name And Domain.

3. In the System Properties window on the Computer Name tab, click Change.

4. Change the text in the Computer Name box to SERVER01, and then click OK.

5. In the Computer Name/Domain Changes dialog box, click OK.

6. In the System Properties dialog box, click Close.

   You are prompted to restart the computer to apply these changes. Do not restart this computer until instructed to do so later in this exercise.

7. Click Restart Later.

8. Click Configure Networking in the Initial Configuration Tasks window.

   The remaining exercises in this lesson create a domain using IP addresses in the 10.0.0.11–10.0.0.20 range, with a subnet mask of 255.255.255.0. If these addresses are used in your production environment, and if the server is connected to your production environment, you must change the IP addresses used in this book accordingly so that the contoso.com domain you create in these practices does not conflict with your production network.

9. Right-click Local Area Connection, and then click Properties.

10. Click Internet Protocol Version 4 (TCP/IPv4), and then click Properties.

    Windows Server 2008 R2 also provides native support for Internet Protocol Version 6 (TCP/IPv6).

11. Click Use The Following IP Address. Enter the following configuration:
    - IP address: **10.0.0.11**
    - Subnet mask: **255.255.255.0**
    - Default gateway: **10.0.0.1**
    - Preferred DNS server: **10.0.0.11**

12. Click OK, and then click Close.

13. Close the Network Connections window.

14. Click Set Time Zone, and then configure the time zone as appropriate for your environment.

15. If the server is connected to the Internet, it is recommended that you click Download And Install Updates so that you can update the server with the latest security updates from Microsoft.

    Note the Add Roles and Add Features links in the Initial Configuration Tasks window.

    In the next exercise, you use Server Manager to add roles and features to SERVER01. These links are another way to perform the same tasks.

    The default behavior for the Initial Configuration Tasks window is to appear each time you log on to the server.

16. Select the Do Not Show This Window At Logon check box to prevent the Initial Configuration Tasks window from appearing the next time you log on.

If you need to open the Initial Configuration Tasks window in the future, run the *Oobe.exe* command.

17. Click Close.

18. When prompted to restart, click Yes.

> **NOTE   CREATE A SNAPSHOT OF YOUR VIRTUAL MACHINE AFTER RESTART**
>
> If you are using a virtual machine to perform this exercise, and the virtual machine enables you to create point-in-time snapshots of the machine's state, create a snapshot at this time. This baseline installation of Windows Server 2008 R2 can be used to perform the exercises in this chapter, which allow you to experiment with the variety of methods of adding the AD DS role.

EXERCISE 3   Install a New Windows Server 2008 R2 Forest with the Windows Interface

In this exercise, you add the AD DS role to the server you installed and configured in Exercise 1, "Install Windows Server 2008 R2," and Exercise 2, "Perform Post-Installation Configuration."

1. Log on to the server with the Administrator account and password used in Exercise 1.

   If Server Manager does not open automatically, open it from the Administrative Tools program group.

2. In the Roles Summary section of the home page, click Add Roles. You might need to scroll down to see the Roles Summary portion of the window.

3. In the first page of the Add Roles Wizard, click Next.

4. On the Select Server Roles page, select the check box next to Active Directory Domain Services.

5. When prompted to add required features for Active Directory Domain Services, click Add Required Features to proceed.

6. On the Select Server Roles page, click Next.

7. On the Active Directory Domain Services page, click Next.

8. On the Confirm Installation Selections page, click Install.

   The Installation Progress page reports the status of installation tasks.

9. On the Installation Results page, confirm that the installation succeeded, and then click Close.

   In the Roles Summary section of the Server Manager home page, you'll notice an error message indicated by a red circle with a white x. You'll also notice a message in the Active Directory Domain Services section of the page. Both of these links take you to the Active Directory Domain Services roles page of Server Manager, shown in Figure 1-8. The message shown reminds you that it is necessary to run *Dcpromo.exe*, which you will do in the next exercise.

FIGURE 1-8 The Active Directory Domain Services roles page in Server Manager

EXERCISE 4 Install a New Windows Server 2008 R2 Forest

In this exercise, you use the Active Directory Domain Services Installation Wizard
(Dcpromo.exe) to create a new Windows Server 2008 forest.

  1. Click Start, click Run, type **Dcpromo.exe**, and then click OK.

> **NOTE** *DCPROMO* **WILL ADD THE AD DS ROLE IF NECESSARY**
>
> In the previous exercise you added the AD DS role by using Server Manager. However,
> if you run *Dcpromo.exe* on a server that does not yet have the AD DS role installed,
> *Dcpromo.exe* will install the role automatically.

The Active Directory Domain Services Installation Wizard appears. In Chapter 10, you
will learn about advanced modes of the wizard.

  2. Click Next.

  3. On the Operating System Compatibility page, review the warning about the default
      security settings for Windows Server 2008 R2 domain controllers, and then click Next.

  4. On the Choose A Deployment Configuration page, select Create A New Domain In
      A New Forest, and then click Next.

  5. On the Name The Forest Root Domain page, type **contoso.com**, and then click Next.

The system performs a check to ensure that the DNS and NetBIOS names for the forest are not already in use on the network.

6. On the Set Forest Functional Level page, choose a forest functional level of Windows Server 2008 R2, and then click Next.

   Each of the functional levels is described in the Details box on the page. Choosing Windows Server 2008 R2 forest functional level ensures that all domains in the forest operate at the Windows Server 2008 R2 domain functional level, which enables several new features provided by Windows Server 2008 R2. You will learn more about functional levels in Chapter 12.

   The Additional Domain Controller Options page appears. DNS Server is selected by default. The Active Directory Domain Services Installation Wizard creates a DNS infrastructure during AD DS installation. The first domain controller in a forest must be a global catalog (GC) server and cannot be a read-only domain controller (RODC).

7. Click Next.

   A warning appears that informs you that a delegation for the DNS server cannot be created. In the context of this exercise, you can ignore this error. Delegations of DNS domains will be discussed in Chapter 9. Click Yes to dismiss the message.

8. On the Location For Database, Log Files, And SYSVOL page, accept the default locations for the database file, the directory service log files, and the SYSVOL files, and click Next.

   The best practice in a production environment is to store these files on three separate volumes that do not contain applications or other files not related to AD DS. This best practices design improves performance and increases the efficiency of backup and restore.

9. On the Directory Services Restore Mode Administrator Password page, type a strong password in both the Password and Confirmed Password boxes. Click Next.

   Do not forget the password you assigned to the Directory Services Restore Mode Administrator.

10. On the Summary page, review your selections.

    If any settings are incorrect, click Back to make modifications.

11. Click Next, and then click Finish.

    Configuration of AD DS begins. The server will require a reboot when the process is completed.

Lesson Summary

- Active Directory services comprise an integrated solution for identity and access in enterprise networks.

- Active Directory Domain Services (AD DS) provides the directory service and authentication components of IDA. Additionally, AD DS facilitates management of even large, complex, distributed networks.

- Windows Server 2008 systems are configured based on the roles they play. You can add the AD DS role by using Server Manager.
- Use *Dcpromo.exe* to configure AD DS and create a domain controller.

Lesson Review

You can use the following questions to test your knowledge of the information in Lesson 1, "Installing Active Directory Domain Services." The questions are also available on the companion CD if you prefer to review them in electronic form.

NOTE ANSWERS

Answers to these questions and explanations of why each answer choice is right or wrong are located in the "Answers" section at the end of the book.

1. Which of the following are required to create a domain controller successfully? (Each correct answer presents part of the solution. Choose all that apply.)

   A. A valid DNS domain name

   B. A valid NetBIOS name

   C. A DHCP server to assign an IP address to the domain controller

   D. A DNS server

2. Trey Research has recently acquired Litware, Inc. Because of regulatory issues related to data replication, it is decided to configure a child domain in the forest for Litware users and computers. The Trey Research forest currently contains only Windows Server 2008 R2 domain controllers. The new domain will be created by promoting a Windows Server 2008 R2 domain controller, but you might need to use existing Windows Server 2003 systems as domain controllers in the Litware domain. Which functional levels will be appropriate to configure?

   A. Windows Server 2008 R2 forest functional level and Windows Server 2008 R2 domain functional level for the Litware domain

   B. Windows Server 2008 R2 forest functional level and Windows Server 2003 domain functional level for the Litware domain

   C. Windows Server 2003 forest functional level and Windows Server 2008 R2 domain functional level for the Litware domain

   D. Windows Server 2003 forest functional level and Windows Server 2003 domain functional level for the Litware domain

Lesson 2: Active Directory Domain Services on Server Core

Security is an important consideration when deploying servers with the Active Directory Domain Services (AD DS) role installed. Many organizations store sensitive data within the directory, such as personal information and user passwords, which must be protected accordingly. Although the role-based configuration of Windows Server 2008 R2 reduces the attack surface of a server by installing only the components and services required by its roles, it is possible to further reduce the attack surface of the server by installing Windows Server 2008 R2 with the Server Core installation option. A Server Core installation is a minimal installation of Windows Server that installs only the most critical core operating system components required to run Windows Server 2008 R2. Most Windows graphical user interface (GUI) elements are not installed as part of a Server Core installation, limiting the ability of malicious users to gain access to the server using the familiar Windows Explorer interface.

A Server Core installation can be administered from another server using remote GUI tools such as Server Manager for most common tasks. However, to manage a Server Core installation locally, you must be familiar with the command-line tools necessary to administer a Windows Server 2008 R2 server and its installed roles. In this lesson, you learn more about the Server Core installation option. You also learn how to configure a domain controller from the command line within a Server Core installation and how to remove domain controllers from a domain.

> **After this lesson, you will be able to:**
> - Identify the benefits and functionality of installing Server Core.
> - Install and configure Server Core.
> - Add and remove AD DS by using command-line tools.
>
> **Estimated lesson time: 60 minutes**

Understanding Server Core

A Windows Server 2008 R2 Server Core installation is a minimal installation of Windows that consumes about 3 GB of disk space and less than 256 MB of memory. A Server Core installation limits the server roles and features that can be added but can improve the security and manageability of the server by reducing its attack surface. The number of services and components running at any one time are limited, so there are fewer opportunities for a user with malicious intent to compromise the security of the server. Because of the decreased roles and features installed, a Server Core installation also reduces the administrative burden of the server, which requires fewer updates and less maintenance.

Server Core supports the following server roles:

- Active Directory Certificate Services
- Active Directory Domain Services
- Active Directory Lightweight Directory Services (AD LDS)
- BranchCache Hosted Cache
- DNS Server
- Dynamic Host Configuration Protocol (DHCP) Server
- File Services
- Hyper-V
- Print and Media Services
- Streaming Media Services
- Web Server (IIS) (including a subset of ASP.NET)

Server core also supports these optional features:

- Failover Clustering
- Multipath I/O
- Network Load Balancing
- Quality of Service (QoS)
- Removable Storage Management
- Simple Network Management Protocol (SNMP)
- Subsystem for UNIX-based applications
- Telnet client
- Windows Bitlocker Drive Encryption
- Windows Internet Name Service (WINS)
- Windows-on-Windows 64-bit (WoW64)
- Windows PowerShell
- Windows Server Backup

Installing Server Core

You can install Server Core by using the same steps presented in Exercise 1 of Lesson 1. The following points outline the key differences between a full installation of Windows Server 2008 R2 and a Server Core installation:

- You must select the Server Core installation option when running the Windows Server 2008 R2 installation wizard, as shown in Figure 1-9.

- At the conclusion of the installation process, you are presented with a command prompt window, rather than the full Windows Server 2008 R2 GUI.

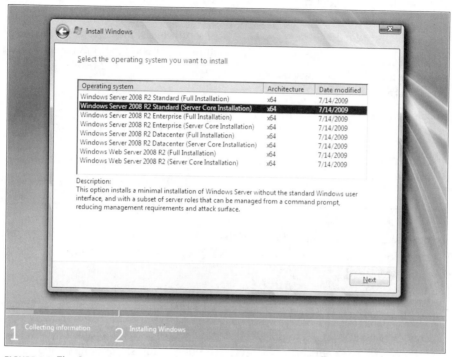

FIGURE 1-9 The Operating Systems selection page of the Install Windows Wizard

Performing Initial Configuration Tasks

On a server running a full installation of Windows Server 2008 R2, the Initial Configuration Tasks window guides you through post-installation configuration of the server. A Server Core installation provides no GUI, so you must complete the tasks by using command-line tools. Table 1-1 lists common configuration tasks and the commands you can use. To learn more about any command, open a command prompt and type the name of the command followed by **/?**.

TABLE 1-1 Server Core Configuration Commands

TASK	COMMAND
Change the Administrator password	Net user administrator *
Set a static IPv4 configuration	Netsh interface ipv4
Activate Windows Server	Cscript c:\windows\system32\slmgr.vbs -ato
Join a domain	Netdom

TASK	COMMAND
Install optional components (roles, role services, or features)	Ocsetup.exe <package or feature> Note that the package or feature names are case sensitive. List the valid packages and features by entering the command **Ocsetup /?**.
Display installed roles, components, and features	Oclist.exe
Enable Remote Desktop	Cscript c:\windows\system32\scregedit.wsf /AR 0
Promote a domain controller	Dcpromo.exe
Configure DNS	Dnscmd.exe
Configure DFS	Dfscmd.exe

The *Ocsetup.exe* command adds supported Server Core roles and features to the server. The exception to this rule is AD DS. Do not use *Ocsetup.exe* to add or remove AD DS. Use *Dcpromo.exe* instead.

Server Configuration

Windows Server 2008 R2 includes a menu-based command-line tool called *Server Configuration* for basic administrative tasks (see Figure 1-10). Server Configuration provides a simple set of administrative commands that can be run by entering context-based menu numbers mapped to standard command-line executables, rather than by typing the syntax of the command-line executables manually. Although Server Configuration can save time for simple administrative tasks, more complicated tasks, such as configuring Active Directory Domain Services, must still be performed from the command line.

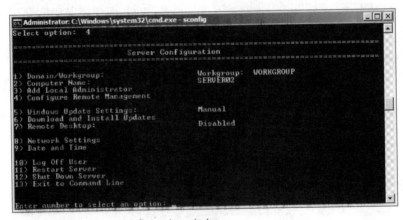

FIGURE 1-10 The Server Configuration window

Adding AD DS to a Server Core Installation

Because there is no Active Directory Domain Services Installation Wizard in Server Core, you must use the command line to run *Dcpromo.exe* with parameters that configure AD DS. To learn about the parameters of *Dcpromo.exe*, open a command line and type **dcpromo.exe /?**. Each configuration scenario has additional usage information. For example, type **dcpromo.exe /?:Promotion** for detailed usage instructions for promoting a domain controller.

Removing Domain Controllers

Occasionally, you might have a reason to take a domain controller offline for extended maintenance or to remove it permanently. It is important that you remove a domain controller correctly so that the information about the domain controller is cleaned up in Active Directory.

To remove a domain controller, use the *Dcpromo.exe* command. If you run the command on a domain controller by using the Windows interface, the Active Directory Domain Services Installation Wizard takes you through the process. If you want to use the command line or are removing AD DS from a Server Core installation, type **dcpromo.exe /?:Demotion** for usage information regarding parameters for the demotion operation.

When you demote a domain controller, you must provide a password that will be assigned to the local Administrator account of the server after demotion.

PRACTICE **Installing a Server Core Domain Controller**

In this exercise, you add a domain controller to the contoso.com forest you created in the Lesson 1 practice. To increase the security and reduce the management overhead of the new DC, you promote a server running Server Core to a domain controller. Before performing the exercises in this practice, you must have completed the practice in Lesson 1.

EXERCISE 1 **Install Server Core**

In this exercise, you install Server Core on a computer or virtual machine.

1. Insert the Windows Server 2008 R2 installation DVD.

   If you are using a VM, you might have the option to mount an ISO image of the installation DVD. Consult the VM Help documentation for guidance.

2. Power on the system.

   If the system's hard disk is empty, the system should boot to the DVD. If there is data on the disk, you might be prompted to press a key to boot to the DVD.

   If the system does not boot to the DVD or offer you a boot menu, go to the BIOS settings of the computer and configure the boot order to ensure that the system boots to the DVD.

3. Select the language, regional setting, and keyboard layout that are correct for your system, and then click Next.

4. Click Install Now.

5. Select Windows Server 2008 R2 Standard (Server Core Installation), and then click Next.

6. Select the I Accept The License Terms check box, and then click Next.

7. Click Custom (Advanced).

8. On the Where Do You Want To Install Windows page, select the partition on which you want to install Windows Server 2008 R2.

   If you need to create, delete, extend, or format partitions, or if you need to load a custom mass storage driver to access the disk subsystem, click Driver Options (Advanced).

9. Click Next.

10. When installation is complete, you are prompted to change the Administrator's password. Click OK.

11. Enter a password for the Administrator account in both the New Password and Confirm Password boxes, and then press Enter.

    The password must be at least seven characters long and must have at least three of four character types:

    A. Uppercase: A–Z

    B. Lowercase: a–z

    C. Numeric: 0–9

    D. Non-alphanumeric: symbols such as $, #, @, and !

    NOTE **DO NOT FORGET THIS PASSWORD**

    Without it, you will not be able to log on to the server to perform other exercises in this training kit.

12. Click OK.

    The command prompt for the Administrator account appears.

EXERCISE 2   Perform Post-Installation Configuration on Server Core

In this exercise, you perform post-installation configuration of the server to prepare it with the name and TCP/IP settings required for the remaining exercises in this lesson.

Note: Ensure that SERVER01 is running when performing these exercises. SERVER02 accesses SERVER01's AD DS database throughout the exercise.

1. Rename the server by typing **netdom renamecomputer %computername% /newname: SERVER02**. You are prompted to press Y to confirm the operation.

    Alternately, you can configure the computer's name by typing **sconfig** at the command line and using the menu-based Server Configuration tool. Either way, you are prompted to restart your computer after changing the computer name. Do not restart the computer until instructed to do so later in the practice.

    The Server Configuration tool can be used to perform steps 2 and 6 of this exercise as well.

2. Set the IPv4 address of the server by typing each of the following two netsh commands:

    ```
    netsh interface ipv4 set address name="Local Area Connection"
        source=static address=10.0.0.12 mask=255.255.255.0 gateway=10.0.0.1 1

    netsh interface ipv4 set dnsserver name="Local Area Connection"
        source=static address=10.0.0.11 primary
    ```

    If you receive an error, check that your network interface is called "Local Area Connection" by typing `netsh interface show interface`. Replace "Local Area Connection" in the commands shown above with the correct name of your network connection.

3. Confirm the IP configuration you entered previously with the command **ipconfig /all**.

4. Restart by typing **shutdown /r /t0**.

5. Log on as Administrator.

6. Join the domain by typing the command **netdom join %computername% / domain:contoso.com**.

7. Restart by typing **shutdown /r /t0**, and then log on again as Administrator.

8. Display installed server roles by typing **oclist | more**.

    Note the package identifier for the DNS server role: DNS-Server-Core-Role.

9. Type **ocsetup** and then press Enter.

    Surprise! There is a minor amount of GUI in Server Core.

10. Click OK to close the window.

11. Type **ocsetup DNS-Server-Core-Role**.

    Package identifiers are case sensitive.

12. Type **oclist** and confirm that the DNS server role is installed.

EXERCISE 3 Create a Domain Controller with Server Core

In this exercise, you add the AD DS role to the Server Core installation by using the *Dcpromo.exe* command.

1. Type **dcpromo.exe /?** and then press Enter.

    Review the usage information.

2. Type **dcpromo.exe /?:Promotion** and then press Enter.

    Review the usage information.

3. Type the following command to add and configure the AD DS role:

    ```
    dcpromo /unattend /replicaOrNewDomain:replica
    /replicaDomainDNSName:contoso.com /ConfirmGC:Yes
    /UserName:Administrator /userDomain:Contoso /Password:* /safeModeAdminPassword:
      P@ssword"
    is the password you used in Exercise 1.
    ```

4. When prompted to enter network credentials, type the password for the Administrator account in the contoso.com domain and then click OK.

    The AD DS role is installed and configured, and then the server reboots.

EXERCISE 4 Remove a Domain Controller

In this exercise, you remove AD DS from the Server Core installation.

1. Log on to the Server Core installation as Administrator.

2. Type **dcpromo /unattend /AdministratorPassword:*password*** where *password* is a strong password that will become the local Administrator password of the server after AD DS has been removed. Press Enter.

Lesson Summary

- Windows Server 2008 R2 Server Core Installation, better known simply as Server Core, is a minimal installation of Windows that supports a subset of server roles and features.
- Server Core can improve the security and manageability of Windows servers.
- The *Ocsetup.exe* command is used to add and remove Server Core roles except for AD DS, which is added by using *Dcpromo.exe*.
- You can fully configure an automated promotion or demotion operation by using the *Dcpromo.exe /unattend* command with parameters appropriate for the operation.

Lesson Review

Use the following questions to test your knowledge of the information in Lesson 2, "Active Directory Domain Services on Server Core." The questions are also available on the companion CD if you prefer to review them in electronic form.

1. You are logged on as Administrator to SERVER02, one of four domain controllers in the contoso.com domain that run Server Core. You want to demote the domain controller. Which of the following is required?

   A. The local Administrator password

   B. The credentials for a user in the Domain Admins group

   C. The credentials for a user in the Domain Controllers group

   D. The address of a DNS server

2. SERVER02 is running Server Core. It is already configured with the AD DS role. You want to add Active Directory Federated Services (AD FS) to the server. What must you do?

   A. Install the Active Directory Certificate Services role.

   B. Install the Active Directory Federated Services role.

   C. Install the AD Rights Management Services role.

   D. Reinstall the server as Windows Server 2008 R2 (Full Installation).

Chapter Review

To further practice and reinforce the skills you learned in this chapter, you can perform the following tasks:

- Review the chapter summary.
- Review the list of key terms introduced in this chapter.
- Complete the case scenario. This scenario sets up a real-world situation involving the topics of this chapter and asks you to create a solution.
- Take a practice test.

Chapter Summary

- Active Directory services perform identity access and management functions to protect and support an organization's network.
- A domain controller hosts the Active Directory data store and related services. Domain controllers are created by adding the AD DS role and then configuring AD DS by using *Dcpromo.exe*.
- Server Core helps to reduce the management costs and increase the security of your domain controllers.

Key Terms

The following terms were introduced in this chapter. Do you know what they mean?

- authentication
- domain
- forest
- forest root domain
- functional level
- global catalog (or partial attribute set)
- identity store
- Kerberos
- schema
- site

Case Scenario

In the following case scenario, you apply what you've learned about Server Core installation and related Active Directory Domain Services. You can find answers to these questions in the "Answers" section at the end of this book.

Case Scenario: Creating an Active Directory Forest

You have been asked to create a new Active Directory forest for a new research project at Trey Research. Because of the sensitive nature of the project, you must ensure that the directory is as secure as possible. You are considering the option of using a Server Core installation on the two servers that will act as domain controllers.

- Can you create an Active Directory forest by using only Server Core servers?
- Which command will you use to configure static IP addresses on the servers?
- Which command will you use to add the DNS server role?
- Which command will you use to add Active Directory Domain Services?

Take a Practice Test

The practice tests on this book's companion CD offer many options. For example, you can test yourself on just one exam objective, or you can test yourself on all 70-640 certification exam content. You can set up the test so that it closely simulates the experience of taking a certification exam, or you can set it up in study mode so that you can look at the correct answers and explanations after you answer each question.

> **MORE INFO** **PRACTICE TESTS**
>
> For details about all the practice test options available, see the "How to Use the Practice Tests" section in this book's introduction.

CHAPTER 2

Administering Active Directory Domain Services

Most administrators first experience Active Directory Domain Services (AD DS) by opening Active Directory Users And Computers and creating user, computer, or group objects within the organizational units (OUs) of a domain. Unfortunately, many administrators never take the time to elevate their skill sets with the Active Directory administrative tools. Whether you are a new administrator or a seasoned veteran, you need to work securely and efficiently. In this chapter, you will discover secrets of effective administration that are often learned only after months or years of experience.

Now that you have created a domain in Chapter 1, "Creating an Active Directory Domain," you can address the tools, tips, and best practices for creating and managing users, computers, groups, and OUs in an AD DS domain. Later chapters will explore each of these object classes in detail.

In this chapter, you will also look at two important, higher-level concerns within an enterprise: how to locate objects in the directory and how to ensure that Active Directory is secure while allowing support personnel to perform the tasks required of their roles.

Exam objective in this chapter:

- Maintain Active Directory accounts.

Lessons in this chapter:

Before You Begin

To complete the lessons in this chapter, you must have installed Windows Server 2008 R2 on a physical computer or virtual machine. The machine should be named SERVER01 and should be a domain controller in the contoso.com domain. The details for this setup are presented in Chapter 1.

REAL WORLD

Dan Holme

Y ou are certainly familiar with administrative tools, such as the Active Directory Users And Computers snap-in, and the basic skills required to create organizational units, users, computers, and groups. This chapter reviews those tools and skills so that you can fill in any gaps in your knowledge. More important, however, this chapter introduces ways in which you can elevate your productivity and effectiveness as an administrator. I find that many administrators continue to use the default consoles and, therefore, have to open multiple tools to do their jobs, instead of creating a single, customized Microsoft Management Console (MMC) that contains all the snap-ins they need. I also see administrators diving deep into their OU structure to locate and manage objects, rather than taking advantage of the power of Saved Queries to virtualize the view of their domains. Although this chapter covers only one exam objective, "Maintain Active Directory accounts," the tips and guidance provided here are some of the most valuable in the book because they will help you work more efficiently and more securely every day in the real world of your enterprise.

Lesson 1: Working with Active Directory Snap-ins

Active Directory's administrative tools, or *snap-ins*, expose the functionality you require to support the directory service. In this lesson, you identify and locate the most important Active Directory snap-ins. You also learn how to work effectively with them, using alternate credentials, and how to build custom consoles that can be distributed to administrators in your organization.

After this lesson, you will be able to:

- Identify the snap-ins within Server Manager and the native consoles used to administer AD DS.
- Install the Remote Server Administration Tools (RSAT).
- Perform basic administrative tasks with the Active Directory Users And Computers snap-in.
- Work with Microsoft Management Console.
- Launch administrative tools with alternate credentials, using Run As Administrator.
- Create, manage, and distribute a custom MMC.

Estimated lesson time: 35 minutes

Understanding the Microsoft Management Console

Windows administrative tools share a common framework called the Microsoft Management Console (MMC). The MMC displays administrative tools, called *snap-ins*, in a customizable window, with a left pane that displays the console tree (similar to the Windows Explorer tree) and a center pane that displays details. An Action pane on the right exposes commands, called *actions* by MMC. Figure 2-1 labels the components of the MMC.

In Figure 2-1, you can see the major components of the MMC, including the following:

- **The console tree**   The left pane that displays the console tree; also called the scope pane
- **The Show/Hide Console Tree toolbar button**   Turns the console tree pane on and off
- **Snap-ins**   Tools that provide administrative functionality
- **The details pane**   Displays the details of the scope selected in the console tree
- **The Action pane**   Displays commands that can be performed on the scope selected in the console tree, or on the item or items selected in the details pane
- **The Action menu**   Also displays commands that can be performed on the selected scope or items
- **The context menu (not shown)**   Appears when you right-click an item in the scope or details pane; a third location from which actions can be initiated
- **The Show/Hide Action Pane toolbar button**   Turns the Action pane on and off

Show/Hide console tree

Show/Hide action pane

Snap-in

Console tree   Details pane   Action pane

FIGURE 2-1 An MMC and snap-in

To control the visibility of the left and right panes, use the Show/Hide Console Tree and Show/Hide Action Pane buttons or the Customize command on the View menu.

Administrative tools—snap-ins—appear in the console tree. The details pane exposes the administrative functionality of the selected snap-in. You can think of an MMC as a tool belt to which you can attach one or more tools (snap-ins). Snap-ins cannot be launched directly; they can function within the context of an MMC only. Most of the tools in the Administrative Tools folder constitute a single console with a single snap-in. These tools include Event Viewer, Services, and Task Scheduler. Other tools, such as Computer Management, are consoles that contain multiple snap-ins, including some that exist as stand-alone consoles. For example, the Computer Management console contains Event Viewer, Services, and Task Scheduler.

As you are administering Windows with snap-ins, you are performing commands, called *actions* by the MMC, that you can find in the console's Action menu, on the short-cut menu that appears when you right-click an item, and in the Action pane on the right side of the console. Most experienced administrators find the context menu the most productive way to perform actions in an MMC snap-in. If you use the context menu exclusively, you can turn off the Action pane so that you have a larger area to display information in the details pane.

There are two types of MMC: preconfigured and custom. Preconfigured consoles are installed automatically when you add a role or feature, to support administration of that role or feature. They function in user mode, so you cannot modify them or save them. The user, however, can create custom consoles to provide exactly the tools and functionality required. The following sections examine both preconfigured and custom consoles.

Active Directory Administration Tools

Most Active Directory administration is performed with the following snap-ins and consoles:

- **Active Directory Users And Computers**   Manage most common day-to-day resources, including users, groups, computers, printers, and shared folders. This is likely the most heavily used snap-in for an Active Directory administrator.

- **Active Directory Sites And Services**   Manage replication, network topology, and related services. You will use this snap-in heavily in Chapter 11, "Managing Sites and Active Directory Replication."

- **Active Directory Domains And Trusts**   Configure and maintain trust relationships and the domain and forest functional levels. This tool is discussed in Chapter 12, "Managing Multiple Domains and Forests."

- **Active Directory Schema**   Examine and modify the definition of Active Directory attributes and object classes. This schema is the "blueprint" for Active Directory. It is rarely viewed and even more rarely changed. Therefore, the Active Directory Schema snap-in is not installed by default.

Finding the Active Directory Administrative Tools

Active Directory snap-ins and consoles are installed when you add the AD DS role to a server. Two commonly used Active Directory administrative tools are added to Server Manager when you install the AD DS role: the Active Directory Users And Computers snap-in and the Active Directory Sites And Services snap-in.

To administer Active Directory from a system that is not a domain controller, you must install the Remote Server Administration Tools (RSAT). The RSAT is a feature that can be installed from the Features node of Server Manager on Windows Server 2008 or Windows Server 2008 R2.

The RSAT can also be installed on Windows clients including Windows Vista Service Pack 1 (or later) and Windows 7. Simply download the RSAT installation files from *http://www .microsoft.com/downloads* and follow the Setup Wizard. After installation, you must also turn on the tool or tools you want to have visible. Use the Turn Windows Features On Or Off command in the Programs And Features application in Control Panel to do this.

Once installed and turned on, all Active Directory administrative consoles can be found in the Administrative Tools folder, which itself is found in Control Panel. In the classic view of Control Panel, you see the Administrative Tools folder displayed. In the Control Panel Home view, administrative tools are found in System And Maintenance.

The Active Directory Schema snap-in must be registered before you can add it to a console. The procedure for registering the snap-in is covered later in this lesson.

Adding the Administrative Tools to Your Start Menu

By default, administrative tools are not added to the Start menu on Windows Vista or Windows 7 clients. You can make the administrative tools easier to access by adding them to your Start menu.

1. Right-click the Start button and click Properties.
2. Click Customize.
3. If you are using the default Start menu, scroll to System Administrative Tools and select Display On The All Programs Menu And The Start Menu or Display On The All Programs Menu. If you are using the Classic Start menu, select Display Administrative Tools.
4. Click OK twice.

Creating a Custom Console with Active Directory Snap-ins

It's easier to administer Windows when the tools you need are in one place and can be customized to meet your needs. This is achieved by creating a customized MMC administrative console that contains the snap-ins you need to perform your administrative tasks. When you create a customized MMC console, you can:

- Add multiple snap-ins so that you do not have to switch between consoles to perform your job tasks, and so that you must launch only one console to perform any of your administrative tasks.
- Save the console so it can be used regularly.
- Distribute the console to other administrators.
- Save the console, and other consoles, to a shared location for unified, customized administration.

To create a customized MMC console:

1. Click Start. Then, in the Start Search box, type **mmc.exe** and press ENTER.
2. Click the File menu, then click Add/Remove Snap-ins.

The Add/Remove Snap-ins dialog box allows you to add, remove, reorder, and manage the console's snap-ins.

After you have installed the RSAT, all four Active Directory management snap-ins are installed; however, the Active Directory Schema snap-in does not appear in the Add/Remove Snap-ins dialog box until after you have registered the snap-in.

To register Active Directory Schema:

1. Open Command Prompt with the Run As Administrator option.
2. Type **regsvr32.exe schmmgmt.dll** and press ENTER.

Running Administrative Tools with Alternate Credentials

Many administrators log on to their computer by using their administrative accounts. This practice is dangerous, because an administrative account has more privileges and access to more of the network than a standard user account does. Therefore, malware that is launched with administrative credentials can cause significant damage. To avoid this problem, do not log on as an administrator. Instead, log on as a standard user and use the Run As Administrator feature to launch administrative tools in the security context of an administrative account:

1. Right-click the shortcut for an executable, Control Panel applet, or MMC console that you want to launch, and then click Run As Administrator. If you do not see the command, try holding down the Shift key and right-clicking.

   The User Account Control dialog box appears.

2. Click Use Another Account.

3. Enter the user name and password of your administrative account, as shown in Figure 2-2.

FIGURE 2-2 The User Account Control dialog box, prompting for administrative credentials

4. Click OK.

Windows 7 and Windows Server 2008 R2 have an additional method with which to run administrative tools. Press and hold the Shift key and right-click the shortcut to an administrative tool on the Start menu, and then click Run As Different User.

Saving and Distributing a Custom Console

If you plan to distribute a console, it is recommended that you save the console in user mode. To change a console's mode, choose Options on the File menu. By default, new consoles are saved in author mode, which enables adding and removing snap-ins, viewing all portions of the console tree, and saving customizations. User mode, by contrast, restricts the functionality of the console so that it cannot be changed. Three types of user modes are described in Table 2-1. User Mode – Full Access is commonly selected for a console provided to skilled administrators with diverse job tasks requiring broad use of the console snap-ins. User Mode – Limited Access (multiple window and single window) is a locked-down mode and is, therefore, selected for a console provided to administrators with a more narrow set of job tasks.

TABLE 2-1 MMC Console Modes

MODE	USE WHEN
Author	You want to continue customizing the console.
User Mode – Full Access	You want users of the console to be able to navigate between and use all snap-ins. Users cannot add or remove snap-ins or change the properties of snap-ins or the console.
User Mode – Limited Access, multiple window	You want users to navigate to and use only the snap-ins that you have made visible in the console tree, and you want to preconfigure multiple windows that focus on specific snap-ins. Users cannot open new windows.
User Mode – Limited Access, single window	You want users to navigate to and use only the snap-ins that you have made visible in the console tree within a single window.

After a console is no longer saved in author mode, you—the original author—can make changes to the console by right-clicking the saved console and clicking Author.

Consoles are saved with the .msc file extension. The default location to which consoles are saved is the Administrative Tools folder, but not the folder in Control Panel. Rather, they are saved in the Start menu folder of your user profile: *%userprofile%*\AppData\Roaming\Microsoft\Windows\StartMenu.

This location is problematic, because it is secured with permissions so that only your user account has access to the console. The best practice is to log on to your computer with an account that is not privileged and then run administrative tools, such as your custom console with alternate credentials that have sufficient privileges to perform administrative tasks. Because two accounts will be involved, saving the console to the Start menu subfolder of one account's user profile means additional navigation, at a minimum, and access-denied errors in a worst-case scenario.

Save your consoles to a location that can be accessed by both your user and your administrative credentials. It is recommended that you save consoles to a shared folder on the network so that you can access your tools when you are logged on to other computers. Optionally, the folder can be made accessible by other administrators to create a centralized store of customized consoles. You can also save consoles to a portable device such as a USB drive, or you can even send a console as an email attachment.

It is important to remember that consoles are basically a set of instructions that are interpreted by Mmc.exe—instructions that specify which snap-ins to add and which computers to manage with those snap-ins. Consoles do not contain the snap-ins themselves. Therefore, a console will not function properly if the snap-ins it contains have not been installed; be sure you have installed appropriate snap-ins from the RSAT on systems on which you will use the console.

 Quick Check

- Describe the difference between a console saved in user mode and a console saved in author mode.

Quick Check Answer

- Author mode allows users to add and remove snap-ins and thoroughly customize the console. User mode prevents users from making changes to the console.

Creating and Managing a Custom MMC

In this practice, you create a custom MMC. You add, remove, and reorder snap-ins, and then prepare the console for distribution to other administrators.

EXERCISE 1 Create a Custom MMC

In this exercise, you create a custom MMC with the Active Directory Users And Computers, Active Directory Schema, and Computer Management snap-ins. These tools are useful for administering Active Directory and domain controllers.

1. Log on to SERVER01 as Administrator.

2. Click the Start button and, in the Start Search box, type **mmc.exe** and press Enter.

   An empty MMC appears. By default, the new console window is not maximized within the MMC. Maximize it to take advantage of the application's full size.

3. On the File menu, click Add/Remove Snap-in.

   The Add Or Remove Snap-ins dialog box, shown in Figure 2-3, appears.

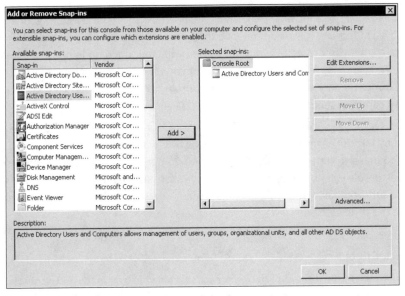

FIGURE 2-3 The Add Or Remove Snap-ins dialog box

If you do not see the snap-ins listed that you want, be sure you've installed the RSAT.

4. In the Add Or Remove Snap-ins dialog box, select Active Directory Users And Computers from the Available Snap-ins list.

5. Click Add to add the snap-in to the Selected Snap-ins list.

   Notice that the Active Directory Schema snap-in is not available to add. The Active Directory Schema snap-in is installed with the Active Directory Domain Services role with the RSAT, but it is not registered, so it does not appear.

6. Click OK to close the Add Or Remove Snap-ins dialog box.

7. Click the Start button. In the Start Search box, type **cmd.exe**.

8. Open Command Prompt using the Run As Administrator option, and then type **regsvr32.exe schmmgmt.dll**.

   This command registers the dynamic link library (DLL) for the Active Directory Schema snap-in. This is necessary to do one time on a system before you can add the snap-in to a console.

9. A prompt appears that indicates successful registration. Click OK.

10. Return to your custom MMC and repeat steps 2–6 to add the Active Directory Schema snap-in.

11. On the File menu, click Add/Remove Snap-in.

12. In the Add Or Remove Snap-ins dialog box, select Computer Management from the Available Snap-ins list.

13. Click Add to add the snap-in to the Selected Snap-ins list.

   When a snap-in supports remote administration, you are prompted to select the computer you wish to manage, as shown in Figure 2-4.

FIGURE 2-4 Selecting the computer to be managed by a snap-in

- To manage the computer on which the console is running, select Local Computer. This does not refer solely to the computer on which you are creating the console. If you launch the console from another computer, the console will manage that computer.

- To specify a single computer that the snap-in should manage, select Another Computer. Then enter the computer's name or click Browse to select the computer.

14. Click Another Computer and type **SERVER01** as the computer name.

15. Click Finish.

16. Click OK to close the Add Or Remove Snap-ins dialog box.

17. On the File menu, click Save. Save the console to your desktop with the name **MyConsole.msc**.

18. Close the console.

EXERCISE 2   Add a Snap-in to an MMC

In this exercise, you add Event Viewer to the console you created in Exercise 1. Event Viewer is useful for monitoring activity on domain controllers.

1. Open MyConsole.msc.

   If you did not save the console to your desktop in Exercise 1, and instead saved the console to the default location, you will find it in the Start\All Programs\Administrative Tools folder.

2. On the File menu, click Add/Remove Snap-in.

3. In the Add Or Remove Snap-ins dialog box, select Event Viewer from the Available Snap-ins list.

4. Click Add to add the snap-in to the Selected Snap-ins list.

   You are prompted to select a computer to manage.

5. Click Another Computer and type **SERVER01** as the computer name.

6. Click OK.

7. Click OK to close the Add Or Remove Snap-ins dialog box.

8. Save and close the console.

EXERCISE 3   Manage the Snap-ins of an MMC

In this exercise, you change the order of snap-ins and delete a snap-in. You also learn about extension snap-ins.

1. Open MyConsole.msc.

2. On the File menu, click Add/Remove Snap-in.

3. In the list of Selected snap-ins, select Event Viewer.

4. Click Move Up.

5. Select Active Directory Schema.

6. Click Remove.

7. In the list of Selected snap-ins, select Computer Management.

8. Click Edit Extensions.

   Extensions are snap-ins that exist within another snap-in to provide additional functionality. The Computer Management snap-in has many familiar snap-ins as extensions, each of which you can enable or disable.

9. Click Enable Only Selected Extensions.

10. Deselect Event Viewer. You have already added Event Viewer as a stand-alone snap-in for the console.

11. Click OK to close the Extensions For Computer Management dialog box.

12. Click OK to close the Add Or Remove Snap-in dialog box.

13. Save and close the console.

EXERCISE 4   Prepare a Console for Distribution to Users

In this exercise, you save your console in user mode so that users cannot add, remove, or modify snap-ins. Keep in mind that MMC users are typically administrators themselves.

1. Open MyConsole.msc.

2. On the File menu, click Options.

3. In the Console Mode drop-down list, select User Mode – Full Access.

4. Click OK.

5. Save and close the console.

6. Open the console by double-clicking it.

7. Click the File menu. Note that there is no Add/Remove Snap-in command.

8. Close the console.

9. Right-click the console and click Author.

10. Click the File menu. In author mode, the Add/Remove Snap-in command appears.

11. Close the console.

Lesson Summary

- Windows administrative tools are snap-ins that can be added to an MMC. Active Directory Users And Computers and other Active Directory management snap-ins are also added to Server Manager and are contained in preconfigured consoles in the Administrative Tools folder.

- Administrators should not log on to their computers with administrative credentials. Instead, they should use a standard user account for logon and launch administrative tools by using the Run As Administrator command.

- Create a custom MMC that contains all the snap-ins you require to perform your job tasks. Such a console can be saved to a location where you, and possibly other administrators, can access it and launch it with administrative credentials. Ideally, this should be the only tool you need to run as administrator if it is fully customized to your needs.

- It is recommended that you save a console in user mode so that changes cannot be made to the console or its snap-ins.

- Consoles require that the appropriate administrative tools be installed. Otherwise, console snap-ins will not function properly.

Lesson Review

You can use the following question to test your knowledge of the information in Lesson 1, "Working with Active Directory Snap-ins." The question is also available on the companion CD if you prefer to review it in electronic form.

> **NOTE ANSWERS**
>
> Answers to these questions and explanations of why each answer choice is right or wrong are located in the "Answers" section at the end of the book.

1. You are a support professional for Contoso, Ltd. The domain's administrators have distributed a custom console with the Active Directory Users And Computers snap-in. When you open the console and attempt to reset a user's password, you receive Access Denied errors. You are certain that you have been delegated permission to reset passwords for users. What is the best solution?

   A. Close the custom console and open Server Manager. Use the Active Directory Users And Computers snap-in in Server Manager.

   B. Close the custom console and open Command Prompt. Type **dsa.msc**.

   C. Close the custom console, and right-click the console, and then click Run As Administrator. Type the credentials for your secondary administrative account.

   D. Close the custom console, and then open Command Prompt. Use the *DSMOD USER* command with the *-p* switch to change the user's password.

Lesson 2: Creating Objects in Active Directory

Active Directory is a directory service, and it is the role of a directory service to maintain information about enterprise resources, including users, groups, and computers. Resources are divided into OUs to facilitate manageability and visibility—that is, they can make it easier to find objects. In this lesson, you learn how to create OUs, users, groups, and computers. You also learn important skills to help you locate and find objects when you need them.

If you are experienced with Active Directory, you can review the first few sections in this lesson quickly, but you might want to pay particular attention to the later sections, beginning with "Finding Objects in Active Directory," because they will help you make better use of Active Directory tools.

The practice exercises at the end of this lesson are important for you to complete, because they create some of the objects that will be used in future practices.

> **After this lesson, you will be able to:**
> - Create users, groups, computers, and organizational units.
> - Disable protection to delete an organizational unit.
> - Customize and take advantage of views and features of the Active Directory Users And Computers snap-in to work effectively with objects in the directory.
> - Create saved queries to provide rule-based views of objects in the directory.
>
> **Estimated lesson time: 45 minutes**

Creating an Organizational Unit

Organizational units (OUs) are administrative containers within Active Directory that are used to collect objects that share common requirements for administration, configuration, or visibility. What this means will become more clear as you learn more about OU design and management. For now, just understand that OUs provide an administrative hierarchy similar to the folder hierarchy of a disk drive: OUs create *collections* of objects that belong together for *administration*. The term *administration* is emphasized here because OUs are not used to assign permissions to resources—that is what groups are for. Users are placed into groups that are given permission to resources. OUs are administrative containers within which those users and groups can be managed by administrators.

To create an organizational unit:

1. Open the Active Directory Users And Computers snap-in.
2. Right-click the Domain node or the OU node in which you want to add the new OU, point to New, and then click Organizational Unit.
3. Type the name of the organizational unit.

   Be sure to follow the naming conventions of your organization.

4. Select Protect Container From Accidental Deletion.

   You'll learn more about this option later in this section.

5. Click OK.

   OUs have other properties that can be useful to configure. These properties can be set after the object has been created.

6. Right-click the OU and click Properties.

   Follow the naming conventions and other standards and processes of your organization.

   You can use the *Description* field to explain the purpose of an OU.

   If an OU represents a physical location, such as an office, the OU's address properties can be useful.

   You can use the Managed By tab to link to the user or group that is responsible for the OU. Click the Change button under the Name box. You'll learn about the Select Users, Contacts, Or Groups dialog box later in this lesson. The remaining contact information on the Managed By tab is populated from the account specified in the Name box. The Managed By tab is used solely for contact information—the specified user or group does not gain any permissions or access to the OU.

7. Click OK.

Windows Server 2008 introduced a new option when creating an OU: Protect Container From Accidental Deletion. This option adds a safety switch to the OU so that it cannot be accidentally deleted. Two permissions are added to the OU: Everyone::Deny::Delete and Everyone::Deny::Delete Subtree. No user, not even an administrator, will be able to delete the OU and its contents accidentally. It is highly recommended that you enable this protection for all new OUs.

If you want to delete the OU, you must first turn off the safety switch. To delete a protected OU, follow these steps:

1. In the Active Directory Users And Computers snap-in, click the View menu and select Advanced Features.

2. Right-click the OU and click Properties.

3. Click the Object tab.

   If you do not see the Object tab, you did not enable Advanced Features in step 1.

4. Clear the check box labeled Protect Object From Accidental Deletion.

5. Click OK.

6. Right-click the OU and click Delete.

7. You are prompted to confirm that you want to delete the OU. Click Yes.

8. If the OU contains any other objects, you are prompted by the Confirm Subtree Deletion dialog box to confirm that you want to delete the OU and all the objects it contains. Click Yes.

Creating a User Object

To create a new user in Active Directory, perform the following steps. Be certain to follow the naming conventions and processes specified by your organization.

1. Open the Active Directory Users And Computers snap-in.

2. In the console tree, expand the node that represents your domain (for instance, contoso.com) and navigate to the OU or container (for example, Users) in which you want to create the user account.

3. Right-click the OU or container, point to New, and then click User.

   The New Object – User dialog box appears, as shown in Figure 2-5.

4. In First Name, type the user's first name.

5. In Initials, type the user's middle initial(s).

   Note that this property is, in fact, meant for the initials of a user's middle name, not the initials of the user's first and last name.

6. In Last Name, type the user's last name.

7. The Full Name field is populated automatically. Make modifications to it if necessary.

   The Full Name field is used to create several attributes of a user object, most notably the common name (CN), and to display name properties. The CN of a user is the name displayed in the details pane of the snap-in. It must be unique within the container or OU. Therefore, if you are creating a user object for a person with the same name as an existing user in the same OU or container, you must enter a unique name in the Full Name field.

8. In User Logon Name, type the name that the user will log on with and, from the drop-down list, select the user principle name (UPN) suffix that will be appended to the user logon name following the @ symbol.

FIGURE 2-5 The New Object – User dialog box

User names in Active Directory can contain some special characters (including periods, hyphens, and apostrophes), which allows you to generate accurate user names such as O'Hara and Smith-Bates. However, certain applications can have other restrictions, so it is recommended that you use only standard letters and numerals until you have fully tested the applications in your enterprise for compatibility with special characters in logon names.

You can manage the list of available UPN suffixes by using the Active Directory Domains And Trusts snap-in. Right-click the root of the snap-in, Active Directory Domains And Trusts, choose Properties, and then use the UPN Suffixes tab to add or remove suffixes. The DNS name of your Active Directory domain will always be available as a UPN suffix and cannot be removed.

9. In the User logon name (Pre–Windows 2000) box of the Active Directory Users And Computers snap-in, enter the pre–Windows 2000 logon name, often called the downlevel logon name.

   In Chapter 3, "Administering User Accounts," you will learn about the two different logon names.

10. Click Next.

11. Enter an initial password for the user in the Password and Confirm Password boxes.

12. Select the User Must Change Password At Next Logon check box.

    It is recommended that you always select this option so that the user can create a new password unknown to the IT staff. Appropriate support staff members can always reset the user's password at a future date if they need to log on as the user or access the user's resources. However, only users should know their passwords on a day-to-day basis.

13. Click Next.

14. Review the summary and click Finish.

The New Object – User interface allows you to configure a limited number of account-related properties such as name and password settings. However, a user object in Active Directory supports dozens of additional properties. These can be configured after the object has been created.

15. Right-click the user object that you created and click Properties.

16. Configure user properties.

Be certain to follow the naming conventions and other standards of your organization.

You will learn more about many of the user properties in Chapters 3 and 8, "Improving the Security of Authentication in an AD DS Domain."

17. Click OK.

Creating a Group Object

Groups are an important class of object because they are used to collect users, computers, and other groups to create a single point of management. The most straightforward and common use of a group is to grant permissions to a shared folder. If a group has read access to a folder, for example, any of the group's members can read the folder. You do not have to grant read access directly to each individual member; you can manage access to the folder simply by adding and removing members of the group.

To create a group:

1. Open the Active Directory Users And Computers snap-in.

2. In the console tree, expand the node that represents your domain (for instance, contoso.com) and navigate to the OU or container (such as Users) in which you want to create the group.

3. Right-click the OU or container, point to New, and then click Group.

The New Object – Group dialog box appears, as shown in Figure 2-6.

4. Type the name of the new group in the Group Name box.

Most organizations have naming conventions that specify how group names should be created. Be sure to follow the guidelines of your organization.

By default, the name you type is also entered as the pre–Windows 2000 name of the new group. It is very highly recommended that you keep the two names the same.

5. Do not change the name in the Group Name (Pre–Windows 2000) box.

6. Choose the Group type.

   - A Security group can be given permissions to resources. It can also be configured as an email distribution list.

   - A Distribution group is an email-enabled group that cannot be given permissions to resources and is, therefore, used only when a group is an email distribution list that has no possible requirement for access to resources.

FIGURE 2-6 The New Object – Group dialog box

7. Select the Group Scope.

   ■ A Global group is used to identify users based on criteria such as job function, location, and so on.

   ■ A Domain Local group is used to collect users and groups who share similar resource access needs, such as all users who need to be able to modify a project report.

   ■ A Universal group is used to collect users and groups from multiple domains.

   Group scope is discussed in more detail in Chapter 4, "Managing Groups."

   Note that if the domain in which you are creating the group object is at a mixed or interim domain functional level, you can select only Domain Local or Global scopes for security groups. Domain functional levels will be discussed in Chapter 12.

8. Click OK.

   Group objects have several properties that are useful to configure. These can be specified after the object has been created.

9. Right-click the group and click Properties.

10. Configure the properties of the group.

    Be sure to follow the naming conventions and other standards of your organization.

    The group's Members and Member Of tabs specify who belongs to the group and what groups the group itself belongs to. Group membership is discussed in Chapter 4.

    The group's Description field, because it is easily visible in the details pane of the Active Directory Users And Computers snap-in, is a good place to summarize the purpose of the group and the contact information for individuals responsible for deciding who is and is not a member of the group.

    The group's Notes field can be used to provide more detail about the group.

The Managed By tab can be used to link to the user or group that is responsible for the group. Click Change under the Name box. To search for a group, you must first click Object Types and select Groups. The Select User, Contact, Or Group dialog box is discussed later in this lesson.

The remaining contact information on the Managed By tab is populated from the account specified in the Name box. The Managed By tab is typically used for contact information so that if a user wants to join the group, you can decide who in the business should be contacted to authorize the new member. However, if you select the Manager Can Update Membership List option, the account specified in the Name box is given permission to add and remove members of the group. This is one method for delegating administrative control over the group. Other delegation options are discussed in Lesson 3.

11. Click OK.

Creating a Computer Object

Computers are represented as accounts and objects in Active Directory, just as users are. In fact, behind the scenes, a computer logs on to the domain just as a user does. The computer has a user name—the computer's name with a dollar sign appended (for instance, DESKTOP101$)—and a password that is established when you join the computer to the domain. The password is changed automatically every 30 days or so thereafter. To create a computer object in Active Directory:

1. Open the Active Directory Users And Computers snap-in.

2. In the console tree, expand the node that represents your domain (such as contoso. com) and navigate to the OU or container (for instance, Users) in which you want to create the computer.

3. Right-click the OU or container, point to New, and then click Computer.

   The New Object – Computer dialog box appears, as shown in Figure 2-7.

4. In the Computer Name box, type the computer's name.

   Your entry automatically populates the Computer Name (Pre–Windows 2000) box.

5. Do not change the name in the Computer Name (Pre–Windows 2000) box.

6. The account specified in the User Or Group field will be able to join the computer to the domain. The default value is Domain Admins. Click Change to select another group or user.

   Generally, you will select a group that represents your deployment, desktop support, or help desk team. You can also select the user to whom the computer is assigned. You will explore the issues related to joining the computer to the domain in Chapter 5, "Configuring Computer Accounts."

7. Do not select the check box labeled Assign This Computer Account As A Pre-Windows 2000 Computer unless the account is for a computer running Microsoft Windows NT 4.0.

FIGURE 2-7 The New Object – Computer dialog box

8. Click OK.

   Computer objects have several properties that are useful to configure. These can be specified after the object has been created.

9. Right-click the computer and click Properties.

10. Enter the properties for the computer.

   Be sure to follow the naming conventions and other standards of your organization.

   The computer's Description field can be used to indicate who the computer is assigned to, its role (for instance, a training-room computer), or other descriptive information. Because Description is visible in the details pane of the Active Directory Users And Computers snap-in, it is a good place to store the information you find most useful to know about a computer.

   Several properties describe the computer, including DNS Name, DC Type, Site, Operating System Name, Version, and Service Pack. These properties are populated automatically when the computer joins the domain.

   The Managed By tab can be used to link to the user or group responsible for the computer. Click Change under the Name box. The Select Users, Contacts, Or Groups dialog box is discussed later in this lesson. The remaining contact information on the Managed By tab is populated from the account specified in the Name box. The Managed By tab is typically used for contact information. Some organizations use the tab to indicate the support team (group) responsible for the computer. Others use the information to track the user to whom the computer is assigned.

11. Click OK.

Finding Objects in Active Directory

You have learned how to create objects in Active Directory, but as your Active Directory becomes populated with user, group, computer, and other objects, it may become difficult to find a specific object or objects that you want to modify. You will need to locate objects in Active Directory on many occasions:

- **Granting permissions** When you configure permissions for a file or folder, you must select the group (or user) to which permissions should be assigned.

- **Adding members to groups** A group's membership can consist of users, computers, groups, or any combination of the three. When you add an object as a member of a group, you must select the object.

- **Creating links** Linked properties are properties of one object that refer to another object. Group membership is, in fact, a linked property. Other linked properties, such as the Managed By setting discussed earlier, are also links. When you specify the Managed By name, you must select the appropriate user or group.

- **Looking up an object** You can search for any object in your Active Directory domain.

Many other situations involve searching Active Directory, and you will encounter several user interfaces. In this section, you learn some techniques for working with each.

Using the Select Users, Contacts, Computers, Or Groups Dialog Box

When you add a member to a group, assign a permission, or create a linked property, you are presented with the Select Users, Contacts, Computers, Or Groups dialog box shown in Figure 2-8. This dialog box is referred to as the *Select dialog box* throughout this training kit. To see an example, open the properties of a group object, click the Members tab, and then click the Add button.

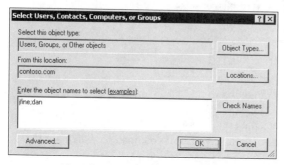

FIGURE 2-8 The Select Users, Contacts, Computers, Or Groups dialog box

If you know the names of the objects you need, you can type them directly into the Enter The Object Names To Select text box. Multiple names can be entered, separated by semicolons, as shown in Figure 2-8. When you click OK, Windows looks up each item in the list, converts it into a link to the object, and then closes the dialog box. The Check Names button also converts each name to a link but leaves the dialog box open, as shown in Figure 2-9.

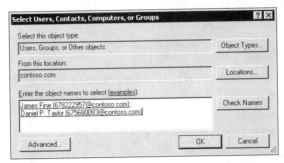

FIGURE 2-9 Names resolved to links using the Check Names button

You do not need to enter the full name; you can enter either the user's first or last name, or even just part of the first or last name. For example, Figure 2-8 shows the names jfine and dan. When you click OK or Check Names, Windows attempts to convert your partial name to the correct object. If there is only one matching object, such as the logon name jfine, the name is resolved as shown in Figure 2-9. If there are multiple matches, such as the name Dan, the Multiple Names Found box, shown in Figure 2-10, appears. Select the correct name or names and click OK. The selected name appears as shown in Figure 2-9.

FIGURE 2-10 The Multiple Names Found dialog box

By default, the Select dialog box searches the entire domain. If you are getting too many results and want to narrow down the scope of your search, or if you need to search another domain or the local users and groups on a domain member, click Locations.

Additionally, the Select dialog box, despite its full name—Select Users, Contacts, Computers, Or Groups—rarely searches all four object types. When you add members to a group, for example, computers are not searched by default. If you enter a computer name, it will not be resolved correctly. Click Object Types, use the Object Types dialog box shown in Figure 2-11 to select the correct types, and then click OK.

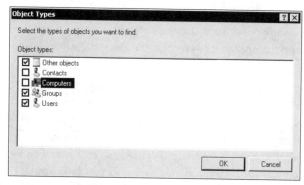

FIGURE 2-11 The Object Types dialog box

If you are having trouble locating the objects you want, click Advanced in the Select dialog box. The advanced view, shown in Figure 2-12, allows you to search both name and description fields as well as disabled accounts, non-expiring passwords, and stale accounts that have not logged on for a specific period of time.

FIGURE 2-12 The advanced view of the Select dialog box

Some of the fields on the Common Queries tab might be disabled, depending on the object type you are searching. Click Object Types to specify exactly the type of object you want.

Controlling the View of Objects in the Active Directory Users And Computers Snap-in

The details pane of the Active Directory Users And Computers snap-in can be customized to help you work effectively with the objects in your directory. Use the Add/Remove Columns command on the View menu to add columns to the details pane. Not every attribute is available to display as a column, but you are certain to find columns that are useful to display, such as User Logon Name. You might also find that some columns are unnecessary. If your OUs have only one type of object (user or computer, for example), the Type column may not be helpful.

When a column is visible, you can change the order of columns by dragging the column headings to the left or right. You can also sort the view in the details pane by clicking the column: the first click sorts in ascending order, the second in descending order, just like Windows Explorer. A common customization is to add the Last Name column to a view of users so that they can be sorted by last name. It is generally easier to find users by last name than by the Name column, which is the common name (CN) and is generally first name - last name.

To add the Last Name column to the details pane:

1. On the View menu, click Add/Remove Columns.

2. In the Available Columns list, click Last Name.

3. Click Add.

4. In the Displayed Columns list, click Last Name and click Move Up twice.

5. In the Displayed Columns list, click Type and click Remove.

6. Click OK.

7. In the details pane, click the Last Name column header to sort alphabetically by last name.

Using the Find Commands

Windows systems also provide the Active Directory query tool, called the Find box by many administrators. One way to launch the Find box is to click the Find Objects In Active Directory Domain Services button on the toolbar in the Active Directory Users And Computers snap-in. The button and the resulting Find box are shown in Figure 2-13.

FIGURE 2-13 The Find box

Use the Find drop-down list to specify the types of objects you want to query, or select Common Queries or Custom Search. The In drop-down list specifies the scope of the search.

It is recommended that, whenever possible, you narrow the scope of the search to avoid the performance impacts of a large, domain-wide search. Together, the Find and the In lists define the scope of the search.

Next, configure the search criteria. Commonly used fields are available as criteria based on the type of query you are performing. When you have specified your search scope and criteria, click Find Now. In the results list, you can right-click any item and choose administrative commands such as Move, Delete, and Properties.

For the most complete, advanced control over the query, choose Custom Search in the Find drop-down list. If you choose Custom Search and then click the Advanced tab, you can build powerful LDAP queries. For example, the query **OU=*main*** searches for any OU with a name that contains *main* and would return the Domain Controllers OU. Without the custom search, you can search based on the text at the *beginning* of the name only; the custom search with wildcards enables you to build a "contains" search.

The Find box also appears in other Windows locations, including the Add Printer Wizard when locating a network printer. The Network folder also has a Search Active Directory button. You can add a custom shortcut, perhaps to your Start menu or desktop, to make searches even more accessible. The target of the shortcut should be *rundll32 dsquery,OpenQueryWindow.*

Determining Where an Object Is Located

Sometimes you want to find an object by using the Find command, because you don't actually know where the object is.

To determine where an object is located:

1. On the View menu, click Advanced Features.
2. Click the Find Objects In Active Directory Domain Services toolbar button, and then perform a search for the object.
3. Right-click the object, click Properties, and then click the Object tab.
4. The Canonical Name Of Object shows you the path to the object, starting at the domain.

Alternately, in the Find dialog box, you can display the Published At column:

1. In the Find dialog box, click View, and then click Choose Columns.
2. In the Columns Available list, click Published At, and then click Add.
3. Click OK.

Using Saved Queries

Windows Server 2003 introduced the Saved Queries node of the Active Directory Users And Computers snap-in. This powerful function helps you create rule-driven views of your domain, displaying objects across one or more OUs.

To create a saved query:

1. Open the Active Directory Users And Computers snap-in.

   Saved Queries is not available in the Active Directory Users And Computers snap-in that is part of Server Manager. You must use the Active Directory Users And Computers console or a custom console with the snap-in.

2. Right-click Saved Queries, point to New, and then click Query.

3. Enter a name for the query.

4. Optionally, enter a description.

5. Click Browse to locate the root for the query.

   The search is limited to the domain or OU that you select. It is recommended that you narrow your search as much as possible to improve search performance.

6. Click Define Query to define your query.

7. In the Find dialog box, click the tab for the type of object you want to query.

   The tabs in the dialog box and the input controls on each tab change to provide options that are appropriate for the selected query.

8. Configure the criteria for your query.

9. Click OK.

After your query is created, it is saved within the instance of the Active Directory Users And Computers snap-in. So if you open the Active Directory Users And Computers console (dsa.msc), your query will be available the next time you open the console. If you created the saved query in a custom console, it will be available in that custom console. To transfer saved queries to other consoles or users, you can export the saved query as an XML file and then import it to the target snap-in.

The view of the saved query in the details pane can be customized, as described earlier, with specific columns and sorting. A very important benefit of saved queries is that the customized view is specific to each saved query. When you add the Last Name column to the normal view of an OU, the Last Name column is actually added to the view of *every* OU, so you see an empty Last Name column even for an OU of computers or groups. With saved queries, you can add the Last Name column to a query for user objects and other columns for other saved queries.

Saved queries are a powerful way to virtualize the view of your directory and monitor for issues such as disabled or locked accounts. Learning to create and manage saved queries is a worthwhile use of your time.

> **MORE INFO** **SAVED QUERIES**
>
> The following article is highly recommended for details and examples of saved queries:
> http://www.petri.co.il/saved_queries_in_windows_2003_dsa.htm.

Understanding DNs, RDNs, and CNs

Distinguished names (DNs) are a kind of path to an object in Active Directory. Each object in Active Directory has a completely unique DN. The user James Fine has the DN CN=James Fine,OU=User Accounts,DC=contoso,DC=com.

You can see what is happening: the DN is a path, starting at the object and working up to the top level domain in the contoso.com DNS namespace. CN means *common name*. You learned about this property earlier: When you create a user, the Full Name box is used to create the CN of the user object. As you know, OU means *organizational unit*. And DC means *domain component*.

The portion of the DN prior to the first OU or container is called the *relative distinguished name*, or RDN. In the case of James Fine, the RDN of the object is CN=James Fine. Not every RDN is a CN. The DN of the User Accounts OU is OU=User Accounts,DC=contoso,DC=com. The RDN of the User Accounts OU is, therefore, OU=User Accounts.

Because the DN of an object must be unique within the directory service, the RDN of an object must be unique within its container. That's why if you hire a second James Fine, and if both user objects need to be in the same OU, you will have to give that user a different CN. The same logic applies to files in a folder: you cannot have two files with identical names in a single folder.

You will encounter DNs regularly as you work with Active Directory, just as you encounter file paths regularly if you work with files and folders. It's very important to be able to read them and interpret them.

Finding Objects by Using Dsquery

Windows provides command-line utilities that perform functionality similar to that of user interface tools, such as the Active Directory Users And Computers snap-in. Many of those commands begin with the letters *DS*, so they are often referred to as *the DS commands*. DSQuery can locate objects in Active Directory.

DSQuery, like other DS commands, is well documented. Type **dsquery.exe /?** to learn its syntax and usage.

You use most DS commands by specifying the object type you want the command to work against. For example, you would type **dsquery user** to look for a user, whereas *DSQuery computer*, *DSQuery group*, and *DSQuery ou* would query for their respective object types.

If you use the *DSQuery objectType* command by itself, it returns the distinguished names of all the objects of the type specified by *objectType* in the domain. To prevent a runaway query, DSQuery limits itself to 100 results. You can use the *-limit* switch to specify how many results you want returned. Use *-limit 0* to return all objects.

Following the *objectType* specifier, you can use switches to indicate the criteria for the query. For example, each object can be located by its name, with the *-name* switch. Most objects can be queried based on the description (*-desc*). Security principals can be located based on their pre–Windows 2000 logon name (-*samid*). To learn which properties may be queried, use dsquery *objecttype* /?. For example, type **dsquery user /?**.

For example, if you want to locate the user named Tony Krijnen, you would enter this command: **dsquery user -name "Tony Krijnen"**. After the property switch, -*name* in this case, you can enter the criteria. Criteria are not case sensitive.

DSQuery can perform searches using wildcards, such as the asterisk (*), which represents zero or more characters. The following command retrieves all users whose names start with *Jam*:

```
dsquery user -name "Jam*"
```

The DSQuery command returns matching objects with their DNs by default, as you can see in Figure 2-14.

```
c:\>dsquery user -name jam*
"CN=James D. Kramer,OU=Employees,OU=People,DC=contoso,DC=com"
"CN=James Fine,OU=People,DC=contoso,DC=com"
"CN=James Hendergart,OU=Employees,OU=People,DC=contoso,DC=com"
"CN=James R. Hamilton,OU=Employees,OU=People,DC=contoso,DC=com"
"CN=James van Eaton,OU=Employees,OU=People,DC=contoso,DC=com"
"CN=Jamie Reding,OU=Employees,OU=People,DC=contoso,DC=com"
```

FIGURE 2-14 The Dsquery command

If DNs are not the results you would like to see, add the -*o* switch to the DSQuery command. You can add -*o samid*, for example, to return the results as pre–Windows 2000 logon names, or -*o upn* to return the list as user logon names, also called *user principal names* or *UPNs*.

Finally, you can limit the scope of the search performed by DSQuery by adding the DN of an OU or container after the *objectType* element of the command. For example, the following command searches for users whose names begin with *Dan*, but only in the Admins OU:

```
dsquery user "ou=Admins,dc=contoso,dc=com" -name "Dan*"
```

By default, the search includes all sub-OUs of the base. You can use the -*base* parameter to limit the search further—for example, to only the specified OU without its sub-OUs.

PRACTICE Creating and Locating Objects in Active Directory

In this practice, you create and then locate objects in Active Directory. You create OUs, users, groups, and computers, and then you create a saved query and customize the view of that saved query. The objects you create in this practice will be used in other practices in this training kit.

EXERCISE 1 Create Organizational Units

The default Users and Computers containers are provided to facilitate the setup of and migration to an Active Directory domain. It is recommended that you create OUs that reflect your administrative model and that you use these OUs to create and manage objects in your directory service. In this exercise, you create OUs for the example domain, contoso.com. These OUs will be used in practices and exercises later in this training kit.

1. Log on to SERVER01 as Administrator.
2. Open the Active Directory Users And Computers snap-in.
3. Expand the domain node, contoso.com.
4. Right-click the domain node, point to New, and then click Organizational Unit.
5. Type the name of the organizational unit: **User Accounts**.
6. Confirm that the Protect Container From Accidental Deletion check box is selected.
7. Click OK.
8. Right-click the OU and choose Properties.
9. In the *Description* box, type **Non-administrative user identities**.
10. Click OK.
11. Repeat steps 2–10 to create the following OUs.

OU NAME	OU DESCRIPTION
Clients	Client computers
Groups	Non-administrative groups
Admins	Administrative identities and groups
Servers	Servers

EXERCISE 2   Create Users

Now that you have created OUs in the contoso.com domain, you are ready to populate the directory service with objects. In this exercise, you create several users in two of the OUs you created in Exercise 1, "Create Organizational Units." You use a procedure similar to the procedure listed in the "Creating a User Object" section. For each user, create a complex, secure password. Remember the passwords you assign—you will be logging on as these user accounts in other exercises and practices in this training kit.

1. Log on to SERVER01 as Administrator and open the Active Directory Users And Computers snap-in.
2. In the console tree, expand the domain node, contoso.com, and click the User Accounts OU.
3. Right-click the User Accounts OU, point to New, and then click User.
   The New Object – User dialog box appears.
4. In First Name, type the user's first name: **Dan**.
5. In Last Name, type the user's last name: **Holme**.
6. In User Logon Name, type the user's logon name: **dholme**.
7. In the User Logon Name (Pre–Windows 2000) text box, type the pre–Windows 2000 logon name: **dholme**.
8. Click Next.

9. Enter an initial password for the user in the Password and Confirm Password boxes.

The default password policy for an Active Directory domain requires a password of seven or more characters. Additionally, the password must contain three of four character types: uppercase (A–Z), lowercase (a–z), numeric (0–9), and nonalphanumeric (for example, ! @ # $ %). The password cannot contain any of the user's name or logon name attributes.

Many training resources suggest using a generic password such as P@ssw0rd. You may use a generic password for the practices in this training kit; however, it is recommended that you create unique passwords, even in a practice, so that you are using best practices even in a lab environment.

10. Select the User Must Change Password At Next Logon check box.

11. Click Next.

12. Review the summary and click Finish.

13. Right-click the user object you created and choose Properties.

14. Examine the attributes that can be configured in the Properties dialog box. Do not change any of the user's properties at this time.

15. Click OK.

16. Repeat steps 3–12 and create the following users in the User Accounts OU.

- James Fine
  - First name: James
  - Last name: Fine
  - Full name: James Fine
  - User logon name: jfine
  - Pre–Windows 2000 logon name: jfine
- Barbara Mayer
  - First name: Barbara
  - Last name: Mayer
  - Full name: Barbara Mayer
  - User logon name: bmayer
  - Pre–Windows 2000 logon name: bmayer
- Barbara Moreland
  - First name: Barbara
  - Last name: Moreland
  - Full name: Barbara Moreland

- User logon name: bmoreland
- Pre–Windows 2000 logon name: bmoreland

Remember the password you assign to these users; you will be logging on as these user accounts in other exercises and practices in this training kit.

17. Repeat steps 3–12 and create a user account for yourself in the User Accounts OU. For the user logon name, use your first initial and last name—for example, dholme for Dan Holme. Create a complex, secure password.

18. Repeat steps 3–12 and create an administrative account for yourself in the Admins OU. This account will be given administrative privileges in Exercise 5 of this lesson. Create the user object in the Admins OU rather than in the User Accounts OU. For the user logon name, use your first initial and last name, followed by _admin—for instance, dholme_admin for Dan Holme's administrative account. Create a complex, secure password.

EXERCISE 3   Create Computers

Computer accounts should be created before joining machines to the domain. In this exercise, you create several computers in two of the OUs you created in Exercise 1. These computer objects will be used in practices and exercises later in this training kit.

1. Log on to SERVER01 as Administrator and open the Active Directory Users And Computers snap-in.

2. In the console tree, expand the domain node, contoso.com, and then click the Servers OU.

3. Right-click the Servers OU, point to New, and then click Computer.

   The New Object – Computer dialog box appears.

4. In the Computer Name box, type the computer's name: **FILESERVER01**.

   Your entry automatically populates the Computer Name (Pre–Windows 2000) box.

5. Do not change the name in the Computer Name (Pre–Windows 2000) box.

6. Take note of the account specified in the User Or Group Field text box. Do not change the value at this time.

7. Do not select the check box labeled Assign This Computer Account As A Pre-Windows 2000 Computer.

8. Click OK.

9. Right-click the computer and choose Properties.

10. Examine the properties that are available for a computer. Do not change any attributes at this time.

11. Click OK.

12. Repeat steps 3–8 to create computer objects for the following computers:

- SHAREPOINT02
- EXCHANGE03

13. Repeat steps 3–8 and create the following computers in the Clients OU rather than in the Servers OU.

- DESKTOP101
- DESKTOP102
- LAPTOP103

EXERCISE 4   Create Groups

It is a best practice to manage objects in groups rather than to manage each object individually. In this exercise, you create several groups in two of the OUs you created in Exercise 1. These groups will be used in practices and exercises later in this training kit.

1. Log on to SERVER01 as Administrator and open the Active Directory Users And Computers snap-in.

2. In the console tree, expand the domain node, contoso.com, and then click the Groups OU.

3. Right-click the Groups OU, point to New, and then click Group.

The New Object – Group dialog box appears.

4. Type the name of the new group in the Group Name text box: **Finance**.

5. Do not change the name in the Group Name (Pre–Windows 2000) box.

6. Select the Group Type: Security.

7. Select the Group Scope: Global.

8. Click OK.

Group objects have several properties that are useful to configure. These can be specified after the object has been created.

9. Right-click the group and choose Properties.

10. Examine the properties available for the group. Do not change any attributes at this time.

11. Click OK.

12. Repeat steps 3–8 to create the following global security groups in the Groups OU:

- Finance Managers
- Sales
- APP_Office 2010

13. Repeat steps 3–8 to create the following global security groups in the Admins OU rather than in the Groups OU.

- Help Desk
- Windows Administrators

EXERCISE 5   Add Users and Computers to Groups

Now that you have created groups, you can add objects as members of the groups. In this exercise, you add users and computers to groups. Along the way, you gain experience with the Select dialog box that is used in some procedures to locate objects in Active Directory.

1. Log on to SERVER01 as Administrator and open the Active Directory Users And Computers snap-in.
2. Open the properties of your administrative account in the Admins OU.
3. On the Member Of tab, click Add.
4. In the Select Groups dialog box, type the name **Domain Admins**.
5. Click OK, and then click OK again to close the account properties dialog box.
6. Open the properties of the Help Desk group in the Admins OU.
7. On the Members tab, click Add.
8. In the Select dialog box, type **Barb**.
9. Click Check Names.

   The Multiple Names Found box appears.
10. Select Barbara Mayer and click OK.
11. Click OK to close the Select dialog box.
12. Click OK again to close the group properties.
13. Open the properties of the APP_Office 2010 group in the Groups OU.
14. On the Members tab, click Add.
15. In the Select dialog box, type **DESKTOP101**.
16. Click Check Names.

    A Name Not Found dialog box appears, indicating that the object you specified could not be resolved.
17. Click Cancel to close the Name Not Found box.
18. In the Select box, click Object Types.
19. Select Computers as an object type and click OK.
20. Click Check Names. The name resolves now that the Select box is including computers in its resolution.
21. Click OK.

EXERCISE 6   Find Objects in Active Directory

When you need to find an object in your domain's directory service, it is sometimes more efficient to use search functionality than to click through your OU structure to browse for the object. In this exercise, you use three interfaces for locating objects in Active Directory.

1. Log on to SERVER01 and open the Active Directory Users And Computers snap-in.

   Open the Active Directory Users And Computers console, or a custom console with the snap-in. Do not use Server Manager, because the Active Directory Users And Computers snap-in in Server Manager does not support Saved Queries.

2. Click the Find Objects In Active Directory Domain Services toolbar button.

3. Make sure the In drop-down list is set to contoso.com (the domain name).

4. In the Name box, type **Barb**.

5. Click Find Now.

6. The two users named Barbara appear in the Search results.

7. Close the Find box.

8. In the Active Directory Users And Computers snap-in, right-click the Saved Queries node, point to New, and then then click Query.

9. In the Name box, type **All Users**.

10. In the Description box, type **Users for the entire domain**.

11. Click Define Query.

12. On the Users tab, in the Name box, choose Has A Value.

13. Click OK twice to close the dialog boxes.

    The results of the saved query appear. Note that it shows the users from both the User Accounts OU and the Admins OU, as well as built-in accounts from the Users container.

14. On the View menu, click Add/Remove Columns.

15. In the Available columns list, select Last Name and click Add.

16. In the Displayed columns list, select Type and click Remove.

17. Click OK.

18. Drag the Last Name column heading so that it is between Name and Description.

19. Click the Last Name column heading so that users are sorted alphabetically by last name.

Lesson Summary

- Organizational units (OUs) are administrative containers that collect objects sharing similar requirements for administration, configuration, or visibility. They provide a way to access and manage a collection of users, groups, computers, or other objects easily. An OU cannot be given permission to a resource such as a shared folder.

- When you create an object such as a user, computer, or group, you can configure only a limited number of its properties while creating it. After creating the object, you can open its properties and configure the attributes that were not visible during creation.

- Object properties such as Description, Managed By, and Notes can be used to document important information about an object.
- By default, OUs are created with protection, which prevents the accidental deletion of the OU. To disable protection, you must turn on Advanced Features from the View menu. Then, in the properties of the OU, click the Object tab to deselect protection.

Lesson Review

You can use the following question to test your knowledge of the information in Lesson 2, "Creating Objects in Active Directory." The question is also available on the companion CD if you prefer to review it in electronic form.

> **NOTE   ANSWERS**
>
> Answers to these questions and explanations of why each answer choice is right or wrong are located in the "Answers" section at the end of the book.

1. You have opened Command Prompt, using Run As Administrator, with credentials in the Domain Admins group. You use the DSRm command to remove an OU that had been created accidentally by James, a member of the Administrators group of the domain. You receive the response: Dsrm Failed: Access Is Denied. What is the cause of the error?

   A. You must launch Command Prompt as a member of Administrators to perform Active Directory tasks.

   B. Only administrators can delete OUs.

   C. Only the owner of the OU can delete an OU.

   D. The OU is protected from deletion.

Lesson 3: Delegation and Security of Active Directory Objects

In previous lessons of this chapter, you learned how to create users, groups, computers, and OUs and how to access the properties of those objects. Your ability to perform those actions was dependent on your membership in the Administrators group of the domain. You would not want every user on your help desk team to be a member of the domain's Administrators group just to reset user passwords and unlock user accounts. Instead, you should enable the help desk and each role in your organization to perform the tasks that are required of the role and no more. In this lesson, you learn how to delegate specific administrative tasks within Active Directory. This is achieved by changing the access control lists (ACLs) on Active Directory objects.

> **After this lesson, you will be able to:**
> - Describe the business purpose of delegation.
> - Assign permissions to Active Directory objects by using the security editor user interfaces and the Delegation Of Control Wizard.
> - View and report permissions on Active Directory objects by using user interface and command-line tools.
> - Evaluate effective permissions for a user or group.
> - Reset the permissions on an object to its default.
> - Describe the relationship between delegation and OU design.
>
> **Estimated lesson time: 35 minutes**

Understanding Delegation

In most organizations, there is more than one administrator, and as organizations grow, administrative tasks are often distributed to various administrators or support organizations. For example, in many organizations, the help desk can reset user passwords and unlock the accounts of users who are locked out. This capability of the help desk is a delegated administrative task.

The help desk cannot usually create new user accounts, but it can make specific changes to existing user accounts. The capability that is delegated is specific, or granular.

Continuing the example, in most organizations, the help desk's ability to reset passwords would apply to normal user accounts, but not to accounts used for administration or to service accounts. The delegation is thus said to be *scoped* to standard user accounts.

All Active Directory objects, such as the users, computers, and groups that you created in the previous lesson, can be secured by using a list of permissions. So you could give your help desk permission to reset passwords on user objects. The permissions on an object are called *access control entries* (ACEs), and they are assigned to users, groups, or computers (called *security principals*). ACEs are saved in the object's discretionary access control list (DACL). The DACL is a part of the object's ACL, which also contains the system access control list (SACL) that includes auditing settings. This may sound familiar to you if you have studied the permissions on files and folders—the terms and concepts are identical.

The delegation of administrative control, also called the delegation of control, or just delegation, simply means assigning permissions that manage access to objects and properties in Active Directory. Just as you can give a group the ability to change files in a folder, you can give a group the ability to reset passwords on user objects.

Viewing the ACL of an Active Directory Object

At the lowest level is the ACL on an individual user object in Active Directory.

To view the ACL on an object:

1. Open the Active Directory Users And Computers snap-in.
2. On the View menu, select the Advanced Features option.
3. Right-click an object and choose Properties.
4. Click the Security tab.

   If Advanced Features is not enabled, you will not see the Security tab in an object's Properties dialog box.

   The Security tab of the object's Properties dialog box is shown in Figure 2-15.

FIGURE 2-15 The Security tab of an Active Directory object's Properties dialog box

5. Click Advanced.

   The Security tab shows a very high-level overview of the security principals that have been given permissions to the object, but in the case of Active Directory ACLs, the Security tab is rarely detailed enough to provide the information you need to interpret or manage the ACL. You should always click Advanced to open the Advanced Security Settings dialog box.

   The Advanced Security Settings dialog box appears, shown in Figure 2-16.

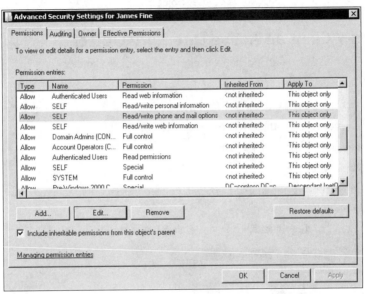

FIGURE 2-16 The Advanced Security Settings dialog box for an Active Directory object

   The Permissions page of the Advanced Security Settings dialog box shows the DACL of the object. You can see in Figure 2-16 that ACEs are summarized on a line of the Permission Entries list. In this dialog box, you are not seeing the granular ACEs of the DACL. For example, the permission entry that is selected in Figure 2-16 is actually comprised of two ACEs.

6. To see the granular ACEs of a permission entry, select the entry and click Edit.

   The Permission Entry dialog box appears, detailing the specific ACEs that make up the entry, as shown in Figure 2-17.

✔ **Quick Check**

   ■ You want to view the permissions assigned to an OU. You open the OU's Properties dialog box and the Security tab is not visible. What must you do?

Quick Check Answer

   ■ In the Active Directory Users And Computers snap-in, click the View menu and select Advanced Features.

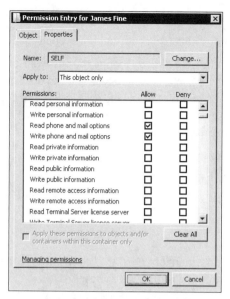

FIGURE 2-17 The Permission Entry dialog box

Property Permissions, Control Access Rights, and Object Permissions

The DACL of an object allows you to assign permissions to specific properties of an object. As you saw in Figure 2-17, you can allow (or deny) permission to change phone and email options. This is, in fact, not just one property, but a property set that includes multiple specific properties. Property sets make it easier to manage permissions to commonly used collections of properties. But you could get even more granular and allow or deny permission to change just the mobile telephone number or just the home street address.

Permissions can also be assigned to manage control access rights, which are actions such as changing or resetting a password. The difference between those two control access rights is important to understand. If you have the right to *change* a password, you must know and enter the current password before making the change. If you have the right to *reset* a password, you are not required to know the previous password.

Finally, permissions can be assigned to objects. For example, the ability to change permissions on an object is controlled by the Allow::Modify Permissions ACE. Object permissions also control whether you are able to create child objects. For example, you might give your desktop support team permissions to create computer objects in the Client Computers OU. The Allow::Create Computer Objects ACE would be assigned to the desktop support team at the Client Computers OU.

The type and scope of permissions are managed using the Object tab and Properties tab, and the Apply To drop-down lists on each tab.

Assigning a Permission Using the Advanced Security Settings Dialog Box

Imagine a scenario in which you want to allow the help desk to change the password on James Fine's account, and *only* James Fine's account. In this section, you learn to do it the most complicated way first: by assigning the ACE on the DACL of the user object. Later, you'll learn how to perform the delegation by using the Delegation Of Control Wizard for the entire OU of users, and you'll see why this latter practice is recommended.

1. Open the Active Directory Users And Computers snap-in.

2. On the View menu, select the Advanced Features option.

3. Right-click an object and click Properties.

4. On the the Security tab, click Advanced.

5. Click Add.

   If you have User Account Control enabled, you might need to click Edit and, perhaps, enter administrative credentials before the Add button will appear.

6. In the Select dialog box, select the security principal to which permissions will be assigned.

   It is an important best practice to assign permissions to groups, not to individual users.

   In this example, you would select your Help Desk group.

7. Click OK.

   The Permission Entry dialog box appears.

8. Configure the permissions you want to assign.

   For our example, on the Object tab, scroll down the list of Permissions and select Allow::Reset Password.

9. Click OK to close each dialog box.

Understanding and Managing Permissions with Inheritance

You can imagine that giving the help desk permission to reset passwords for each individual user object would be a nightmare. Luckily, you don't have to, and, in fact, it's a terrible practice to give permissions to individual objects in Active Directory. Instead, you give permissions to organizational units. The permissions you give to an OU are inherited by all objects in the OU. So, if you give the help desk permission to reset passwords for user objects, and you attach that permission to the OU that contains your users, all user objects within that OU inherit that permission. With one step, you delegate that administrative task.

Inheritance is an easy concept to understand. Child objects inherit the permissions of the parent container or OU. That container or OU in turn inherits its permissions from its parent container, OU, or, if it is a first-level container or OU, from the domain itself. The reason child objects inherit permissions from their parents is that, by default, each new object is created with the Include Inheritable Permissions From This Object's Parent option enabled. You can see the option in Figure 2-16.

However, note that as the option indicates, only *inheritable* permissions are inherited by the child object. Not every permission is inheritable. For example, the permission to reset passwords, when assigned to an OU, would not be inherited by group objects because group objects do not have a password attribute. So inheritance can be scoped to specific object classes; passwords are applicable to user objects, not to groups. Additionally, you can use the Apply To box of the Permission Entry dialog box to scope the inheritance of a permission. The conversation can start to get very complicated. What you should know is that, by default, new objects inherit inheritable permissions from their parent object—usually an OU or container.

What if the permission that is being inherited is not appropriate? You can do three things to modify the permissions that a child object is inheriting.

First, you can disable inheritance by clearing the Include Inheritable Permissions From This Object's Parent option in the Advanced Security Settings dialog box. When you do, the object no longer inherits any permissions from its parent—all permissions are explicitly defined for the child object. This is generally not a good practice, as it creates an exception to all the rules that are being created by permissions of parent containers.

The second option is to allow inheritance but override the inherited permission with a permission assigned specifically to the child object—an explicit permission. Explicit permissions always override permissions that are inherited from parent objects. This has an important implication: an explicit permission that *allows* access will actually override an inherited permission that *denies* the same access. If that sounds counterintuitive to you, it is not: the rule (Deny) is being defined by a parent, but the child object has been configured to be an exception (Allow).

Third, you can change the scope of inheritance on the parent permission itself by changing the option in the Apply To drop-down list in the Permission Entry dialog box. In most cases, this is the best practice. What you are doing, in effect, is defining the security policy in the form of the ACL more accurately at its source, rather than trying to override it further down the tree.

EXAM TIP

Look out for scenarios in which access or delegation are not performing as expected, either because inheritance has been broken—the child is no longer inheriting permissions from its parent—or because the child object has an explicit permission that overrides the permissions of the parent.

Delegating Administrative Tasks with the Delegation Of Control Wizard

You've seen the complexity of the DACL, and you've probably gleaned that managing permissions by using the Permission Entry dialog box is not a simple task. Luckily, the best practice is not to manage permissions by using the security interfaces but, rather, to use the Delegation Of Control Wizard. The following procedure explains the use of the wizard.

1. Open the Active Directory Users And Computers snap-in.

2. Right-click the node (Domain or OU) for which you want to delegate administrative tasks or control, and then click Delegate Control.

   In this example, select the OU that contains your users.

   The Delegation Of Control Wizard appears and guides you through the required steps.

3. Click Next.

   The first step is to select the administrative group to which you are granting privileges.

4. On the Users Or Groups page, click Add.

5. Use the Select dialog box to select the group and click OK.

6. Click Next.

   The next step is to specify the specific task you wish to assign that group.

7. On the Tasks To Delegate page, select the task.

   In this example, you select the Reset User Passwords And Force Password Change At Next Logon task.

8. Click Next.

9. Review the summary of the actions that have been performed and click Finish.

   The Delegation Of Control Wizard applies the ACEs that are required to enable the selected group to perform the specified task.

Reporting and Viewing Permissions

You can view and report permissions several ways when you need to know who can do what. You've already seen that you can view permissions on the DACL by using the Advanced Security Settings and Permission Entry dialog boxes.

DSACLs (Dsacls.exe) is also available as a command-line tool that reports on directory service objects. If you type the command followed by the distinguished name of an object, you see a report of the object's permissions. For example, this command produces a report of the permissions associated with the User Accounts OU:

```
dsacls.exe "ou=User Accounts,dc=contoso,dc=com"
```

DSACLs can also be used to set permissions—to delegate. Type **dsacls.exe /?** for help regarding the syntax and usage of DSACLs.

Removing or Resetting Permissions on an Object

How do you remove or reset permissions that have been delegated? Unfortunately, there is no "undelegate" command. You must do one of the following:

- Open the Advanced Security Settings and Permission Entry dialog boxes to remove permissions.

- If you want to reset the permissions on the object back to the defaults, open the Advanced Security Settings dialog box and click Restore Defaults. The default permissions are defined by the Active Directory schema for the class of object. After you've restored the defaults, you can reconfigure the explicit permissions you want to add to the DACL.

- DSACLs also provides the /s switch to reset permissions to the schema-defined defaults, and the /t switch to make the change for the entire "tree"—the object and all of its child objects. For example, to reset permissions on the User Accounts OU and all of its child OUs and objects, you would enter:

```
dsacls "ou=User Accounts,dc=contoso,dc=com" /s /t
```

Understanding Effective Permissions

Effective permissions are the resulting permissions for a security principal, such as a user or group, based on the cumulative effect of each inherited and explicit ACE. Your ability to reset a user's password, for example, may be a result of your membership in a group that was given Reset Password permission on an OU several levels above the user object. The inherited permission assigned to a group to which you belong resulted in an effective permission of Allow::Reset Password. Your effective permissions can be complicated when you consider Allow and Deny permissions, explicit and inherited ACEs, and the fact that you may belong to multiple groups, each of which may be assigned different permissions.

Permissions, whether assigned to your user account or to a group to which you belong, are equivalent. In the end, an ACE applies to you, the user. The best practice is to manage permissions by assigning them to groups, but it is also possible to assign ACEs to individual users or computers. A permission that has been assigned directly to you is neither more important nor less important than a permission assigned to a group to which you belong.

Permissions that allow access (Allow permissions) are cumulative. When you belong to several groups, and those groups have been granted permissions that allow a variety of tasks, you can perform all of the tasks assigned to all of those groups as well as tasks assigned directly to your user account.

Permissions that deny access (Deny permissions) override equivalent Allow permissions. If you are in one group that has been allowed the permission to reset passwords, and another group that has been denied permission to reset passwords, the Deny permission prevents you from resetting passwords.

> **NOTE   USE DENY PERMISSIONS SPARINGLY**
>
> It is generally unnecessary to assign Deny permissions. If you simply do not assign an allow permission, users cannot perform the task. Before assigning a Deny permission, check to see if you could achieve your goal by removing an Allow permission instead. Use Deny permissions rarely and thoughtfully.

Each permission is granular. For example, if you have been denied the ability to reset passwords, you might still have the ability, through other Allow permissions, to change the user's logon name or email address.

Finally, you learned earlier in this lesson that child objects inherit the inheritable permissions of parent objects by default, and that explicit permissions can override inheritable Permissions. This means that an explicit Allow permission actually overrides an inherited deny permission.

Unfortunately, the complex interaction of user, group, explicit, inherited, Allow, and Deny permissions can make evaluating effective permissions a bit of a chore. There is an Effective Permissions tab in the Advanced Security Settings dialog box of an Active Directory object, but the tab is practically useless: It does not expose enough permissions to provide the kind of detailed information you require. You can use the permissions reported by the DSACLs command or those reported on the Permissions tab of the Advanced Security Settings dialog box to begin evaluating effective permissions, but it will be a manual task.

> **MORE INFO   ROLE-BASED ACCESS CONTROL**
>
> The best way to manage delegation in Active Directory is through role-based access control. Although this approach will not be covered on the certification exam, it is well worth understanding for real-world implementation of delegation. See *Windows Administration Resource Kit: Productivity Solutions for IT Professionals,* by Dan Holme (Microsoft Press, 2008) for more information.

Designing an OU Structure to Support Delegation

OUs are, as you now know, administrative containers. They contain objects that share similar requirements for administration, configuration, and visibility. You now understand the first of those requirements: administration. Objects that will be administered the same way, by the same administrators, should be contained within a single OU. By placing your users in a single OU, perhaps called *User Accounts*, you could delegate the help desk permission to change all users' passwords by assigning one permission to one OU. Any other permissions that affect what an administrator can do to a user object would be assigned at the User Accounts OU. For example, you might allow your Human Resources managers to disable user accounts in the event of an employee's termination. You would delegate that permission, again, to the User Accounts OU.

Remember that administrators should be logging on to their systems with user credentials and launching administrative tools with the credentials of a secondary account that has appropriate permissions to perform administrative tasks. Those secondary accounts are the administrative accounts of the enterprise. It is not appropriate for the front-line help desk to be able to reset passwords on such privileged accounts, and you probably would not want human resources managers to disable administrative accounts. Therefore, administrative accounts should be administered differently than "normal" (non-administrative) user accounts. That's why you would have a separate OU, such as *Admins*, for administrative user objects. That OU would be delegated quite differently than the User Accounts OU.

Similarly, you might delegate to the desktop support team the ability to add computer objects to an OU called *Client Computers*, which contains your desktops and laptops, but not to the Servers OU, where only your Server Administration group has permissions to create and manage computer objects.

The primary role of OUs is to efficiently scope delegation—to apply permissions to objects and sub-OUs. When you design an Active Directory environment, you always *begin by designing an OU structure that will make delegation efficient*—a structure that reflects the administrative model of your organization. Rarely does object administration in Active Directory look like your organizational chart. Typically, all normal user accounts are supported the same way, by the same team—so user objects are often found in a single OU or a single OU branch. Quite often an organization that has a centralized help desk function to support users also has a centralized desktop support function, in which case all client computer objects are within a single OU or single OU branch. But if desktop support is decentralized, it would be likely that the Client Computers OU would be divided into sub-OUs representing geographic locations, where each location was delegated to allow the local support team to add computer objects to the domain in that location.

Design OUs first to enable the efficient permissioning (delegation) of objects in the directory. After you have achieved that design, you can refine the design to facilitate the configuration of computers and users through Group Policy, which is discussed in Chapter 6, "Implementing a Group Policy Infrastructure." Active Directory design is an art and a science.

PRACTICE   Delegating Administrative Tasks

In this practice, you manage the delegation of administrative tasks within the contoso.com domain and view the resulting changes to ACLs on Active Directory objects. Before performing the exercises in this practice, you must perform the practice in Lesson 2, "Creating Objects in Active Directory." The OUs created in that practice are required for these exercises.

EXERCISE 1   Delegate Control for Support of User Accounts

In this exercise, you enable the help desk to support users by resetting passwords and unlocking user accounts in the User Accounts OU.

1. Log on to SERVER01 as Administrator and open the Active Directory Users And Computers snap-in.

2. Expand the domain node, contoso.com, right-click the User Accounts OU, and click Delegate Control to launch the Delegation Of Control Wizard.

3. Click Next.

4. On the Users Or Groups page, click Add.

5. In the Select dialog box, type **Help Desk**, and then click OK.

6. Click Next.

7. On the Tasks To Delegate page, select the Reset User Passwords And Force Password Change At Next Logon task.

8. Click Next.

9. Review the summary of the actions that have been performed and click Finish.

EXERCISE 2   View Delegated Permissions

In this exercise, you view the permissions you assigned to the Help Desk group.

1. Log on to SERVER01 as Administrator and open the Active Directory Users And Computers snap-in.

2. Right-click the User Accounts OU and choose Properties.

   Note that the Security tab is not visible. If Advanced Features is not enabled, you cannot see the Security tab in an object's Properties dialog box.

3. Click OK to close the Properties dialog box.

4. On the View menu, select the Advanced Features option.

5. Right-click the User Accounts OU and choose Properties.

6. On the Security tab, click Advanced.

7. In the Permission Entries list, select the first permission assigned to the Help Desk group.

8. Click Edit.

9. In the Permission Entry dialog box, locate the permission that is assigned, and then click OK to close the dialog box.

10. Repeat steps 7–9 for the second permission entry assigned to the Help Desk group.

11. Right-click a user object in the User Accounts OU and choose Properties. Repeat steps 6–10 to examine the inherited permissions assigned to the Help Desk group.

12. Open Command Prompt, type **dsacls "ou=User Accounts,dc=contoso,dc=com"**, and press Enter.

13. Locate the permissions assigned to the Help Desk group.

Lesson Summary

- Delegation of control in Active Directory allows an organization to assign specific administrative tasks to appropriate teams and individuals.

- Delegation is the result of permissions, or ACEs, on the DACL of Active Directory objects.

- The DACL can be viewed and modified using the Advanced Security Settings of the object's Properties dialog box.

- The Delegation Of Control Wizard simplifies the underlying complexity of object ACLs by allowing you to assign tasks to groups.

- Permissions on an object can be reset to their defaults by using the Advanced Security Settings dialog box or DSACLs with the */resetDefaultDACL* switch.

- It is a best practice to delegate control by using organizational units. Objects within the OUs inherit the permissions of their parent OUs.

- Inheritance can be modified by disabling inheritance on a child object or by applying an explicit permission to the child object that overrides the inherited permission.

- Effective permissions are the result of user, group, allow, deny, inherited, and explicit permissions. Deny permissions override allow permissions, but explicit permissions override inherited permissions. Therefore, an explicit allow permission overrides an inherited deny permission.

Lesson Review

You can use the following question to test your knowledge of the information in Lesson 3, "Delegation and Security of Active Directory Objects." The question is also available on the companion CD if you prefer to review it in electronic form.

NOTE ANSWERS

Answers to these questions and explanations of why each answer choice is right or wrong are located in the "Answers" section at the end of the book.

1. You want to allow your help desk to reset user passwords and unlock user accounts. Which of the following tools can be used? (Choose all that apply.)

   A. The Delegation Of Control Wizard

   B. DSACLs

   C. DSUTIL

   D. The Advanced Security Settings dialog box

Chapter Review

To further practice and reinforce the skills you learned in this chapter, you can perform the following tasks:

- Review the chapter summary.
- Review the list of key terms introduced in this chapter.
- Complete the case scenario. This scenario sets up a real-world situation involving the topics of this chapter and asks you to create a solution.
- Complete the suggested practices.
- Take a practice test.

Chapter Summary

- The Active Directory Users And Computers snap-in, which is part of Server Manager and of the Active Directory Users And Computers console, can also be added to custom consoles and distributed to administrators.
- As you create objects with the Active Directory Users And Computers snap-in, you can configure a limited number of initial properties. After an object is created, you can populate a much larger set of properties. These properties can be used in saved queries to provide customizable views of your enterprise objects.
- Organizational units should be used to delegate administrative control so that teams in your enterprise can perform the tasks required of their role. With inheritance enabled, objects inherit the permissions of their parent OUs.

Key Terms

The following terms were introduced in this chapter. Do you know what they mean?

- delegation
- saved query

Case Scenario

In the following case scenario, you apply what you've learned about Active Directory snap-ins and object creation, delegation, and security. You can find answers to these questions in the "Answers" section at the end of this book.

Case Scenario: Managing Organizational Units and Delegation

You are an administrator at Contoso, Ltd. Contoso's Active Directory was created when the organization was very small. One OU was created for users and one for computers. Now the organization spans five geographic sites around the world, with over 1,000 employees. At each site, one or two members of desktop support personnel provide help to users with desktop applications and are responsible for installing systems and joining them to the domain. In addition, a small team at headquarters occasionally installs systems, joins them to the domain, and ships them to the site. If a user has forgotten his or her password, a centralized help desk telephone number is directed to one of the support personnel members, regardless of which site the user is in. Answer the following questions for your manager, who is concerned about manageability and least privilege, and explain how delegation would be managed.

1. Should computer objects remain in a single OU, or should the objects be divided by site? If divided, should the site OUs be under a single parent OU?

2. Should the ability to manage computer objects in sites be delegated directly to the user accounts of the desktop support personnel, or should groups be created, even though those groups might have only one or two members?

3. Should users be divided by site or remain within a single OU?

Suggested Practices

To help you successfully master the exam objectives presented in this chapter, complete the following tasks.

Maintain Active Directory Accounts

In this practice, you validate that delegation has been successful, and you experience what happens when an administrator attempts to perform a task that has not been delegated. You also experience the results of inheritance and OU protection.

To perform this practice, you must have performed the practices in Lessons 2 and 3. Specifically, ensure that:

- There is a user account in the Admins OU.
- There is a Help Desk group in the Admins OU.
- There is a user account for Barbara Mayer and at least one other user account in the User Accounts OU.
- The user Barbara Mayer is a member of the Help Desk group.
- The Help Desk group has been delegated the Reset User Passwords And Force Password Change At Next Logon permissions for the User Accounts OU.

In this and other practices in this training kit, you will log on to the domain controller with user accounts that are not a member of Domain Administrators or the domain's Administrators group. Therefore, you must give all user accounts the right to log on locally to the domain controllers in your practice environment. Follow the steps in the article, "Grant a Member the Right to Logon Locally," at *http://technet.microsoft.com/en-us/library/ee957044(WS.10).aspx* to grant the Allow Logon Locally right to the Administrators and Domain Users groups. If you will use Remote Desktop Services to connect to the domain controller—rather than logging on locally—grant the

Allow Logon Through Remote Desktop Services right. This is for the practice environment only. In a production environment, you should not grant users the right to log on to domain controllers.

- **Practice 1** Log on to SERVER01 as Barbara Mayer. She is a member of the Help Desk group. Validate that she can reset the password of users other than her own in the User Accounts OU. Then attempt to change the password of a user account in the Admins OU. Investigate the results.

- **Practice 2** Log on to SERVER01 as Administrator. Create a new OU within the User Accounts OU, called Branch. When you create the Branch OU, ensure that the Protect Container From Accidental Deletion option is selected, because you will attempt to delete this OU after this practice. Create a user account in the OU. Open the DACL of the user object in the Advanced Security Settings dialog box. Note the permissions assigned to the Help Desk group. Are they explicit or inherited? If inherited, where are they inherited from? Open the DACL of the Branch OU in the Advanced Security Settings dialog box. Clear the Include Inheritable Permissions From This Object's Parent option.

  Log off and log on as Barbara Mayer. Verify that she can reset the password of a user in the User Accounts OU. Now attempt to reset the password of the user in the Branch OU. Access is denied.

  Log off and log on as Administrator. Troubleshoot Barbara's lack of access by restoring inheritance to the Branch OU. Log off and log on as Barbara to validate the results. Can she successfully reset the password of a user in the Branch OU?

- **Practice 3** Log on to SERVER01 as Barbara Mayer. Attempt to delete the Branch OU. Access is denied. Log off and log on as Administrator. Attempt to delete the Branch OU. Access is denied. Open the properties of the Branch OU. Look for the Object tab. If it is not visible, turn on the Advanced Features view of the Active Directory Users And Computers snap-in. On the Object tab, unprotect the Branch OU. Finally, delete the Branch OU and the user account within it.

Take a Practice Test

The practice tests on this book's companion CD offer many options. For example, you can test yourself on just one exam objective, or you can test yourself on all the 70-640 certification exam content. You can set up the test so that it closely simulates the experience of taking a certification exam, or you can set it up in study mode so that you can look at the correct answers and explanations after you answer each question.

> **MORE INFO** **PRACTICE TESTS**
>
> For details about all the practice test options available, see the "How to Use the Practice Tests" section in this book's Introduction.

CHAPTER 3

Administering User Accounts

Chapter 1, "Creating an Active Directory Domain," introduced Active Directory Domain Services (AD DS) as an identity and access solution. User accounts stored in the directory are the fundamental component of identity. Because of their importance, knowledge of user accounts and the tasks related to supporting them is critical to the success of an administrator in a Microsoft Windows enterprise.

Your ability to work effectively with user accounts can make a big difference in your overall productivity. Effective techniques for creating or modifying a single user account, such as the procedures described in Chapter 2, "Administering Active Directory Domain Services," can be clumsy and inefficient when working with large numbers of accounts, such as when creating the accounts of newly hired employees.

In this chapter, you will learn how to apply tools and techniques to automate the creation and management of users and to locate and manipulate user objects and their attributes. Along the way, you will be introduced to Microsoft Windows PowerShell, which represents the future of command-line-based and automated administration for Windows technologies. You will learn a variety of options for performing each of the most common administrative tasks.

The certification exam will expect you to have a very basic understanding of the purpose and syntax of command-line utilities and Windows PowerShell. However, this chapter goes beyond the expectations of the exam to provide a solid introduction to scripting and automation. Practice what you learn in this chapter, not because you'll need to be a scripting guru to pass the exam, but because the more you can automate those tedious administrative tasks, the more you can elevate your productivity and your success.

Exam objectives in this chapter:

- Maintain Active Directory accounts.
- Automate creation of Active Directory accounts.

Lessons in this chapter:

Before You Begin

To complete the practices in this chapter, you must have created a domain controller named SERVER01 in a domain named contoso.com. See Chapter 1 for detailed steps for this task.

 REAL WORLD

Dan Holme

It's really amazing to stop and consider how much of our time as Windows administrators is spent performing basic tasks related to user objects. Each day in an enterprise network brings with it a unique set of challenges related to user management. Employees are hired, moved, married, and divorced, and most eventually leave the organization. As human beings, they make mistakes like forgetting passwords or locking out their accounts by logging on incorrectly.

Administrators must respond to all these changes, and user accounts are so complicated, with so many properties, that even the most well-intentioned administrators often stray from the procedures and conventions they've established. I believe that the key to efficient, effective, consistent, and secure user environments begins with raising the skill set of administrators.

Lesson 1: Automating the Creation of User Accounts

In Chapter 2, you learned how to create a user account by using the Active Directory Users And Computers snap-in. Although the procedures discussed in Chapter 2 can be applied to create a small number of users, you will need more advanced techniques to automate the creation of user accounts when a large number of users must be added to the domain. In this lesson, you will learn several of these techniques.

> **After this lesson, you will be able to:**
> - Create users from user account templates.
> - Import users with CSVDE.
> - Import users with LDIFDE.
>
> **Estimated lesson time: 30 minutes**

Creating Users with Templates

Users in a domain often share many similar properties. For example, all sales representatives can belong to the same security groups, log on to the network during similar hours, and have home folders and roaming profiles stored on the same server. When you create a new user, you can simply copy an existing user account rather than create a blank account and populate each property.

Since the days of Microsoft Windows NT 4.0, Windows has supported the concept of user account templates. A user account template is a generic user account prepopulated with common properties. For example, you can create a template account for sales representatives that is preconfigured with group memberships, logon hours, a home folder, and a roaming profile path.

To create a user account template, simply create a user account and prepopulate appropriate attributes. We recommend that you use a naming standard that makes templates easy to find. For example, configure the full name of the user with an underscore (_) as the first character, such as _Sales User. The underscore prefix will cause all templates to appear at the top of the list of users in an organizational unit (OU).

> **NOTE DISABLE TEMPLATE USER ACCOUNTS**
>
> The template account should not be used to log on to the network, so be sure to disable the account.

To create a user based on the template, perform the following steps:

1. Right-click the template user account, and then click Copy.

   The Copy Object – User Wizard appears.

2. In the First Name box, type the user's first name.

3. In the Last Name box, type the user's last name.

4. Modify the Full Name value if necessary.

5. In the User Logon Name box, type the user logon name, and then select the appropriate user principal name (UPN) suffix in the drop-down list.

6. In the User Logon Name (Pre-Windows 2000) box, type the user's pre–Windows 2000 user name, and then click Next.

7. In Password and Confirm Password, type the user's password.

8. Select the appropriate password options.

9. If the user account from which the new user account was copied was disabled, clear the Account Is Disabled check box to enable the new account.

10. Click Next, and then click Finish.

After a user is created by copying the template, you can view and modify its attributes in the Properties dialog box of the new account. It's important to realize that not all attributes are copied from the template. The list below summarizes the attributes that are copied from the template, grouped by the tabs in the Properties dialog box.

- **General tab**   No properties are copied from the General tab.

- **Address tab**   P.O. box, city, state or province, ZIP or postal code, and country or region are copied. Note that the street address itself is not copied.

- **Account tab**   Logon hours, logon workstations, account options, and account expiration are copied.

- **Profile tab**   Profile path, logon script, home drive, and home folder path are copied.

- **Organization tab**   Department, company, and manager are copied.

- **Member Of tab**   Group membership and primary group are copied.

EXAM TIP

Memorize the list of attributes that are copied from a template.

It is not useful to configure any other attributes in the template, as they will not be copied to new accounts.

NOTE   WHAT YOU SEE ISN'T ALL YOU GET

User accounts have additional properties that are not visible on the standard tabs in the Active Directory Users And Computers snap-in. These hidden attributes include useful properties such as assistant, division, employee type, and employee ID. To view these properties, click the View menu in the Active Directory Users And Computers snap-in and select the Advanced Features option. Then open the properties of a user account and click the Attribute Editor tab. Several of these attributes, including assistant, division, and employee type, are also copied from a template to a new account.

What Is Copied Is Not Enough

M any administrators consider the list of copied attributes to be somewhat limited. For example, you might want the job title and street address attributes to be copied. You can actually modify the Active Directory schema to include additional attributes when duplicating a user. See Knowledge Base article 827832 at *http://support.microsoft.com/kb/827832* for instructions.

However, you will be well served to use more advanced methods for automating the creation of user accounts. Later in this chapter, you will learn to use directory service (DS) commands, Comma-Separated Values Data Exchange (CSVDE), LDAP Data Interchange Format Data Exchange (LDIFDE), and Windows PowerShell to automate administrative tasks. With these tools, you will have full control over the process used to provision a new account.

Using Active Directory Command-Line Tools

In Chapter 2, you were introduced to DSQuery, one of a suite of Active Directory command-line tools collectively called *DS commands*. The following DS commands are supported in Windows Server 2008 R2:

- **DSAdd**   Creates an object in the directory.
- **DSGet**   Returns specified attributes of an object.
- **DSMod**   Modifies specified attributes of an object.
- **DSMove**   Moves an object to a new container or OU or rename and object.
- **DSRm**   Removes an object, all objects in the subtree beneath a container object, or both.
- **DSQuery**   Performs a query based on parameters provided at the command line and returns a list of matching objects. By default, the result set is presented as the distinguished names (DNs) of each object, but you can use the *–o* parameter with modifiers such as *dn, rdn, upn,* or *samid* to receive the results as DNs, relative DNs, user principal names (UPNs), or pre–Windows 2000 logon names (security accounts manager [SAM] IDs).

Most of the DS commands take two modifiers after the command itself: the object type and the object's DN. For example, the following command adds a user account for Mike Fitzmaurice:

```
dsadd user "cn=Mike Fitzmaurice,ou=User Accounts,dc=contoso,dc=com"
```

The object type, *user*, immediately follows the command. After the object type is the object's DN. When the object's DN includes a space, surround the DN with quotes. The following command removes the same user:

```
dsrm "cn=Mike Fitzmaurice,ou=User Accounts,dc=contoso,dc=com"
```

DS commands that read or manipulate attributes of objects include Dsquery.exe, Dsget.exe, and Dsmod.exe. To specify an attribute, include it as a parameter after the object's DN. For example, the following command retrieves the home folder path for Mike Fitzmaurice:

```
dsget user "cn=Mike Fitzmaurice,ou=User Accounts,dc=contoso,dc=com" -hmdir
```

The parameter of a DS command that represents an attribute, for example, *hmdir*, is not always the same as the name of the attribute in the Active Directory Users And Computers snap-in or in the schema.

Creating Users with DSAdd

Use the DSAdd command to create objects in Active Directory. The DSAdd User command creates a user object and accepts parameters that specify properties of the user. The following command shows the basic parameters required to create a user account:

```
dsadd user "User DN" -samid "pre-Windows 2000 logon name" -pwd {Password | *}
    -mustchpwd yes
```

The *-pwd* parameter specifies the password. If it is set to an asterisk (*), you are prompted for a user password. The *-mustchpwd* parameter specifies that the user must change the password at next logon.

DSAdd User accepts several parameters that specify properties of the user object. The following command creates a user with some of the more important fields populated:

```
dsadd user "cn=Amy Strande,ou=User Accounts,dc=contoso,dc=com" -samid Amy.Strande
    -fn Amy -ln Strande -display "Strande, Amy" -pwd Pa$$w0rd -desc "Vice President, IT"
```

Most parameter names are self-explanatory: *-email*, *-profile*, and *-company*, for example. Type **dsadd user /?** or search the Windows Server 2008 R2 Help and Support Center for thorough documentation of the DSAdd User parameters.

Exporting Users with CSVDE

CSVDE is a command-line tool that imports or exports Active Directory objects from or to a comma-delimited text file (also known as a *comma-separated value text file*, or .csv file). Comma-delimited files can be created, modified, and opened with tools as familiar as Notepad and Microsoft Office Excel. If you have user information in existing Excel or Microsoft Office Access databases, you will find that CSVDE is a powerful way to take advantage of that information to automate user account creation.

The basic syntax of the CSVDE command for export is:

```
csvde -f filename
```

However, that command will export all objects in your Active Directory domain. You will want to limit the scope of the export, which you can do with the following four parameters:

- **-d RootDN** Specifies the distinguished name of the container from which the export will begin. The default is the domain itself.

- **-p SearchScope** Specifies the scope of the search relative to the container specified by -d. SearchScope can be either *base* (this object only), *onelevel* (objects within this container), or *subtree* (this container and all subcontainers). The default is *subtree*.

- **-r Filter** Filters the objects returned within the scope configured by -d and -p. Filter is a Lightweight Directory Access Protocol (LDAP) query syntax. You will work with a filter in the practice for this lesson. LDAP query syntax is beyond the scope of this course. See *http://technet.microsoft.com/en-us/library/aa996205(EXCHG.65).aspx* for more information.

- **-l ListOfAttributes** Specifies the attributes that will be exported. Use the LDAP name for each attribute, separated by a comma, as in *-l DN,objectClass,sAMAccountName,sn, givenName,userPrincipalName*.

The output of a CSVDE export lists the selected, exported LDAP attribute names on the first line. Each object follows, one per line. Here's a sample file:

```
DN,objectClass,sn,givenName,sAMAccountName,userPrincipalName
"CN=David Jones,OU=User Accounts,DC=contoso,DC=com",user,Jones,David,david.jones,
    david.jones@contoso.com
"CN=Lisa Andrews,OU=User Accounts,DC=contoso,DC=com",user,Andrews,Lisa,lisa.andrews,
    lisa.andrews@contoso.com
```

Importing Users with CSVDE

CSVDE can also create user accounts by importing a .csv file. If you have user information in existing Excel or Access databases, you will find that CSVDE is a powerful way to take advantage of that information to automate user account creation.

The basic syntax of the CSVDE command for import is:

```
csvde -i -f Filename [-k]
```

The -i parameter specifies import mode; without it, the default mode of CSVDE is export. The -f parameter identifies the file name to import from or export to. The -k parameter is useful during import operations because it instructs CSVDE to ignore errors, including Object Already Exists errors.

The import file itself is a comma-delimited text file (.csv or .txt) in which the first line defines the imported attributes by their LDAP attribute names. Each object follows, one per line, and must contain exactly the attributes listed on the first line. Here's a sample file:

```
DN,objectClass,sn,givenName,sAMAccountName,userPrincipalName
"CN=David Jones,OU=User Accounts,DC=contoso,DC=com",user,Jones,David,david.jones,
    david.jones@contoso.com
"CN=Lisa Andrews,OU=User Accounts,DC=contoso,DC=com",user,Andrews,Lisa,lisa.andrews,
    lisa.andrews@contoso.com
```

This file, when imported by the CSVDE command, will create user objects for David Jones and Lisa Andrews in the User Accounts OU. The user logon names, last name and first name, are configured by the file. You cannot use CSVDE to import passwords, and without a password, the user account will be disabled initially. After you have reset the password, you can enable the object.

In Chapter 4, "Managing Groups," and Chapter 5, "Configuring Computer Accounts," you will use CSVDE to import computers and groups. For more information about CSVDE, including details regarding its parameters and usage to export directory objects, type **csvde /?** or search the Windows Server 2008 R2 Help And Support Center.

Importing Users with LDIFDE

You can also use Ldifde.exe to import or export Active Directory objects, including users. The LDAP Data Interchange Format (LDIF) is a draft Internet standard for a file format that can be used to perform batch operations against directories that conform to the LDAP standards. LDIF supports both import and export operations, as well as batch operations that modify objects in the directory. The LDIFDE command implements these batch operations by using LDIF files.

The LDIF file format consists of a block of lines that, together, constitute a single operation. Each line consists of an attribute name followed by a colon and the value of the attribute. For example, suppose you wanted to import user objects for two sales representatives named Bonnie Kearney and Bobby Moore. The contents of the LDIF file would look similar to the following example:

```
dn: CN=Bonnie Kearney,OU=User Accounts,DC=contoso,DC=com
changetype: add
objectClass: top
objectClass: person
objectClass: organizationalPerson
objectClass: user
cn: Bonnie Kearney
sn: Kearney
title: Operations
description: Operations (London)
givenName: Bonnie
displayName: Kearney, Bonnie
company: Contoso, Ltd.
sAMAccountName: bonnie.kearney
userPrincipalName: bonnie.kearney@contoso.com
mail: bonnie.kearney@contoso.com

dn: CN=Bobby Moore,OU=User Accounts,DC=contoso,DC=com
changetype: add
objectClass: top
objectClass: person
objectClass: organizationalPerson
objectClass: user
cn: Bobby Moore
sn: Moore
```

```
title: Legal
description: Legal (New York)
givenName: Bobby
displayName: Moore, Bobby
company: Contoso, Ltd.
sAMAccountName: bobby.moore
userPrincipalName: bobby.moore@contoso.com
mail: bobby.moore@contoso.com
```

Each operation begins with the *DN* attribute of the object that is the target of the operation. The next line, *changeType*, specifies the type of operation: *add*, *modify*, or *delete*. Multiple operations in a single file are separated by a blank line. Modify or delete operations end with a line containing only a dash (-), then the blank line.

As you can see, the LDIF file format is not as intuitive or familiar as the comma-separated text format. However, because the LDIF format is also a standard, many directory services and databases can export LDIF files.

After creating or obtaining an LDIF file, you can perform the operations specified by the file by using the LDIFDE command. From a command prompt, type **ldifde /?** for usage information. The two most important switches for the LDIFDE command are:

- *-i*   Turn on Import mode. Without this parameter, LDIFDE exports information.
- *-f filename*   The file from which to import, or to which to export.

For example, the following command imports objects from the file named Newusers.ldf:

```
ldifde -i -f newusers.ldf
```

The command accepts a variety of modifications using parameters. The most useful parameters are summarized in Table 3-1.

TABLE 3-1 LDIFDE Parameters

COMMAND	USAGE
GENERAL PARAMETERS	
-i	Import mode. (The default is Export mode.)
-f filename	Import or export file name.
-s servername	The domain controller to bind to for the query.
-c FromDN ToDN	Convert occurrences of *FromDN* to *ToDN*. This is useful when importing objects from another domain, for example.
-v	Turn on verbose mode.
-j path	Log file location.
-h	Enable Simple Authentication And Security Layer (SASL) encryption.
-?	Help.

COMMAND	USAGE
EXPORT-SPECIFIC PARAMETERS	
-d RootDN	The root of the LDAP search. The default is the root of the domain.
-r Filter	LDAP search filter. The default is (objectClass=*), meaning all objects.
-p SearchScope	The scope, or depth, of the search. Can be *subtree* (the container and all child containers), *base* (the immediate child objects of the container only), or *onelevel* (the container and its immediate child containers).
l list	Comma-separated list of attributes to include in export for resulting objects. Useful if you want to export a limited number of attributes.
-o list	List of attributes (comma-separated) to omit from export for resulting objects. Useful if you want to export all but a few attributes.
IMPORT-SPECIFIC PARAMETER	
-k	Ignore errors and continue processing if Constraint Violation or Object Already Exists errors appear.

EXAM TIP

For the 70-640 certification exam, you should understand that both CSVDE and LDIFDE are able to import and export objects by using their respective file formats. Both commands are in the export mode by default and require the *-i* parameter to specify import mode. Only LDIFDE is capable of modifying existing objects or removing objects. You can specify a user's password with DSAdd, and you can import a user's password with LDIFDE, but not with CSVDE. If you create users within a domain with a policy requiring passwords, the accounts will be disabled until you reset their passwords and enable the accounts.

NOTE   USER PASSWORDS

You can specify a user's password in an LDIFDE add or modify operation. To do so, you must configure the *unicodePwd* attribute. The value of the password is the user's password, surrounded by double quotes, converted to Base64. Because the attribute is Base64, the name of the attribute is followed by two, rather than one colon. Finally, you must perform the operation using SASL by including the *-h* parameter of the LDIFDE command. To learn more about the *unicodePwd* attribute, see *http://technet.microsoft.com/en-us/magazine/ff848710.aspx*. To learn about Base64 encoding, and to obtain a script to convert a password to Base64, see *http://www.rlmueller.net/Base64.htm*. The practice at the end of this lesson includes an exercise in which you will use LDIFDE to import users with passwords and enable the user accounts.

In this practice, you create several user accounts with automated methods discussed in this lesson. To perform the exercises in this practice, you will need the following objects in the contoso.com domain:

- A first-level OU named User Accounts
- A first-level OU named Groups
- A global security group in the Groups OU named Sales

EXERCISE 1   **Create Users with a User Account Template**

In this exercise, you create a user account template that is prepopulated with properties for sales representatives. You will then create a user account for a new sales representative by copying the user account template.

1. Log on to SERVER01 as Administrator.

2. Open the Active Directory Users And Computers snap-in and expand the domain.

3. Right-click the User Accounts OU, choose New, and then select User.

4. In the First Name box, type **_Sales**, including the underscore character.

5. In the Last Name box, type **Template**.

6. In the User Logon Name box, type **_salestemplate**, including the underscore character. Click Next.

7. Type a complex password in the Password and Confirm Password boxes.

8. Select the Account Is Disabled check box. Click Next. Click Finish.

   Notice that the underscore character at the beginning of the account's name ensures that the template appears at the top of the list of users in the User Accounts OU. Notice also that the icon of the user object includes a down arrow, indicating that the account is disabled.

9. Double-click the template account to open its Properties dialog box.

10. Click the Organization tab.

11. In the Department box, type **Sales**.

12. In the Company box, type **Contoso, Ltd**.

13. Click the Member Of tab, and then click Add.

14. Type **Sales**, and then click OK.

15. Click the Profile tab.

16. In the Profile Path box, type **\\server01\profiles\%username%** and then click OK.

    You have now created a template account that can be copied to generate new user accounts for sales representatives. Next, you will create an account based on the user account template.

17. Right-click _Sales Template and choose Copy.

18. In the First Name box, type **Jeff**.

19. In the Last Name box, type **Ford**.

20. In the User Logon Name box, type **jeff.ford**. Click Next.

21. Type a complex password in the Password and Confirm Password boxes.

22. Clear the Account Is Disabled check box.

23. Click Next, and then click Finish.

24. Open the properties of the Jeff Ford account and confirm that the attributes you configured in the template were copied to the new account.

EXERCISE 2   Create a User with the DSAdd Command

In this exercise, you use the DSAdd command to create a user account for Mike Fitzmaurice in the User Accounts OU.

1. Open Command Prompt, type the following command on one line, and then press Enter:

   ```
   dsadd user "cn=Mike Fitzmaurice,ou=User Accounts,dc=contoso,dc=com"
   -samid mike.fitz -pwd * -mustchpwd yes -company "Contoso, Ltd." -email
   mike.fitz@contoso.com
   ```

2. You are prompted to enter a password for the user twice. Type a password that is complex and at least seven characters long, the press Enter. You will not see the characters of the password as you type.

3. Switch to Active Directory Users And Computers, refresh the view of the User Accounts OU, and then open the properties of Mike's user account. Confirm that the properties you entered on the command line appear in the account.

EXERCISE 3   Import Users with CSVDE

In the previous two exercises, you created users one at a time. In this exercise, you use a comma-delimited text file to import two users.

1. Open Notepad and enter the following three lines:

   ```
   DN,objectClass,sn,givenName,sAMAccountName,userPrincipalName

   "CN=David Jones,OU=User Accounts,DC=contoso,DC=com",user,
       Jones,David,david.jones,david.jones@contoso.com

   "CN=Lisa Andrews,OU=User Accounts,DC=contoso,DC=com",user,
       Andrews,Lisa,lisa.andrews,lisa.andrews@contoso.com
   ```

2. Save the file to your Documents folder with the name **NewUsers.txt**, and then close Notepad.

3. Switch to Command Prompt.

4. Type **cd %userprofile%\Documents** and press Enter.

5. Type **csvde -i -f NewUsers.txt -k** and press Enter.

   The two users are imported. If you encounter any errors, examine the text file for typographical problems.

6. Switch to Active Directory Users And Computers, refresh the view of the User Accounts OU, and then confirm that the users were created successfully.

7. Examine the accounts to confirm that first name, last name, user principal name, and pre–Windows 2000 logon name are populated according to the instructions in NewUsers.txt.

EXERCISE 4   Import Users with LDIFDE

Like CSVDE, LDIFDE can be used to import users. The LDIF file format, however, is not a typical delimited text file. In this exercise, you use LDIFDE to import two users.

1. Open Notepad and type the following lines. Be sure to include the blank line between the two operations. Also note that there are two colons after *unicodePwd*.

```
DN: CN=April Stewart,OU=User Accounts,DC=contoso,DC=com
changeType: add
CN: April Stewart
objectClass: user
sAMAccountName: april.stewart
userPrincipalName: april.stewart@contoso.com
givenName: April
sn: Stewart
displayName: Stewart, April
mail: april.stewart@contoso.com
description: Sales Representative in the USA
title: Sales Representative
department: Sales
company: Contoso, Ltd.
unicodePwd::IgBQAGEAJAAkAHcAMAByAGQAIgA=
userAccountControl:512

DN: CN=Tony Krijnen,OU= User Accounts,DC=contoso,DC=com
changeType: add
CN: Tony Krijnen
objectClass: user
sAMAccountName: tony.krijnen
userPrincipalName: tony.krijnen@contoso.com
givenName: Tony
sn: Krijnen
displayName: Krijnen, Tony
mail: tony.krijnen@contoso.com
description: Sales Representative in The Netherlands
title: Sales Representative
department: Sales
company: Contoso, Ltd.
unicodePwd::IgBQAGEAJAAkAHcAMAByAGQAIgA=
userAccountControl:512
```

The value of the *unicodePwd* attribute, IgBQAGEAJAAkAHcAMAByAGQAIgA=, is the Base64 enconding of the password, *Pa$$w0rd*, surrounded by quotes.

The value of the *userAccountControl* attribute, 512 (Hex 200), specifies an enabled, normal user account.

2. Save the file to your Documents folder with the name **"NewUsers.ldf."** Surround the file name with quotes; otherwise, Notepad will add a .txt extension. Then close Notepad.

   Although you can import LDIF files with any extension, it is conventional to use the .ldf extension.

3. Switch to Command Prompt.

4. Type **cd %userprofile%\Documents** and press Enter.

5. Type **ldifde -i -f NewUsers.ldf -k -h** and press Enter.

   The two users are imported. If you encounter any errors, examine the text file for typographical problems.

6. Switch to Active Directory Users And Computers, refresh the view of the User Accounts OU, and then confirm that the users were created successfully and that the accounts are enabled.

7. Examine the accounts to confirm that user properties are populated according to the instructions in NewUsers.ldf.

Lesson Summary

- You can copy a user account in Active Directory to create a new account. A small subset of account properties is copied. To create a user account template, create a user and prepopulate the appropriate attributes. Then disable the template account so that it cannot be used for authentication. Copy the template as a basis for new user accounts.

- The DSAdd command enables you to create user objects from the command line, with parameters that specify properties of the user.

- You can import a comma-delimited text file of users and their properties with the CSVDE command.

- Use LDIFDE to perform operations in Active Directory, including adding, changing, and removing users. The LDIF file that specifies such operations is a standard format that enables the interchange of data between directories. LDIFDE supports importing user passwords.

Lesson Review

You can use the following questions to test your knowledge of the information in Lesson 1, "Automating the Creation of User Accounts." The questions are also available on the companion CD if you prefer to review them in electronic form.

1. You are an administrator at a large university, and you have just been sent an Excel file containing information about 2,000 students who will enter the school in two weeks. You want to create user accounts for the new students with as little effort as possible. Which of the following tasks should you perform?

    A. Create a user account template and copy it for each student.

    B. Run LDIFDE -i.

    C. Use CSVDE -i.

    D. Run the DSADD USER command.

2. You are an administrator at a large university. Which command can be used to delete user accounts for students who graduated?

    A. LDIFDE

    B. DSMod

    C. DEL

    D. CSVDE

Lesson 2: Administering with Windows PowerShell and Active Directory Administrative Center

In Lesson 1, you learned how to use command-line tools to add or import user accounts. In this lesson, you are introduced to Windows PowerShell, which is the recommended tool for administering and automating Active Directory from the command line. Windows PowerShell certainly deserves its *Power* moniker. As you will discover, Windows PowerShell enables you to perform tasks with a single command line that would require multiple clicks in Active Directory Users And Computers. Better yet, Windows PowerShell enables you to create scripts that can automate administrative tasks—for example, the creation of user accounts—more easily than with legacy tools like the DS commands. At the end of this lesson, you will explore Active Directory Administrative Center, a new graphical administrative tool that is based on Windows PowerShell.

> **After this lesson, you will be able to:**
> - Identify the requirements for administering AD DS with Windows PowerShell.
> - Understand Windows PowerShell concepts and syntax, including cmdlets, variables, aliases, namespaces, and providers.
> - Create a user by using Windows PowerShell.
> - Import users from a comma-separated values (CSV) file.
> - Use the Active Directory Administrative Center to navigate, search, and administer Active Directory.
>
> **Estimated lesson time: 90 minutes**

Introducing Windows PowerShell

Windows PowerShell is a task-based command-line shell and scripting language designed especially for system administration, and it is the recommended tool for performing and automating administrative tasks in Windows Server 2008 R2. Built on the Microsoft .NET Framework, Windows PowerShell helps IT professionals control and automate the administration of several Microsoft technologies, including the Windows operating system, AD DS, SharePoint 2010, and Microsoft Exchange Server 2007 and later.

With Windows PowerShell commands, called *cmdlets*, you can perform management tasks from the command line. With Windows PowerShell *providers*, you can access data stores, such as the registry and Active Directory, as easily as you access the file system. In addition, Windows PowerShell has a rich expression parser and a fully developed scripting language.

Windows PowerShell includes the following features:

- Cmdlets for performing common system administration tasks.

- A task-based scripting language.

- Support for existing scripts and command-line tools. For example, you can perform most Command Prompt (Cmd.exe) commands with Windows PowerShell.

- Consistent design. Because cmdlets and system data stores use common syntax and naming conventions, data can be shared easily and the output from one cmdlet can be used as the input to another cmdlet without reformatting or manipulation.

- Providers that expose system resources such as the registry, certificate store, and directory service for simplified navigation by using the same techniques that users employ to navigate the file system.

- Powerful object manipulation capabilities. You can manipulate objects directly or send them to other tools or databases.

- Extensible interface. Independent software vendors and enterprise developers can build custom tools and utilities to administer their software.

Preparing to Administer Active Directory Using Windows PowerShell

Windows PowerShell 2.0 is installed by default in Windows Server 2008 R2 and Windows 7. You can open a Windows PowerShell console from the Accessories, Windows PowerShell program group in the Start menu, or by running *Powershell.exe*.

Windows PowerShell provides native support for hundreds of commands called *cmdlets* (pronounced, "command-lets"), and you can add functionality to a session by importing *modules* or *snapins*. A module or snap-in is a package of cmdlets and other items. Windows Server 2008 R2 introduces the Active Directory module for Windows PowerShell. The module must be added to the system on which you will use Windows PowerShell to administer Active Directory—to your administrative workstation, for example. When you use Server Manager to add the Active Directory Domain Services (AD DS) role to a server running Windows Server 2008 R2, the Active Directory module for Windows PowerShell features is added by default.

You can install the Active Directory module on a server running Windows Server 2008 R2 by using Server Manager to add the feature. To install the module on your Windows 7 workstation, perform the following steps:

1. Download the Remote Server Administration Tools (RSAT) from *http://www.microsoft.com/downloads/en/details.aspx?FamilyID=7D2F6AD7-656B-4313-A005-4E344E43997D&displaylang=en*.

2. Install RSAT.

3. Open Control Panel, click the Programs category, and then, under Programs And Features, click Turn Windows Features On Or Off.

4. Expand Remote Server Administration Tools, and then expand AD DS And AD LDS Tools.

5. Select the Active Directory Module For Windows PowerShell checkbox.

6. Click OK.

The Active Directory module for Windows PowerShell is the client side of the administrative module. The module communicates with Active Directory by using a set of web services provided by the Active Directory Web Services (ADWS). ADWS—the server side of the administrative module—must be installed on at least one domain controller in the domain that can be accessed from your administrative workstation. ADWS is installed automatically when you promote a domain controller running Windows Server 2008 R2. If you want to add ADWS to a domain controller running an earlier version of Windows Server, you must download Active Directory Management Gateway Service (Active Directory Web Service for Windows Server 2003 and Windows Server 2008) from *http://www.microsoft .com/downloads/en/details.aspx?displaylang=en&FamilyID=008940c6-0296-4597-be3e-1d24c1cf0dda*. The service can be added to a domain controller running Windows Server 2003 or Windows Server 2008, as long as the .NET Framework version 3.5 with Service Pack 1 (SP1) is installed, along with the hotfixes listed on the download page.

> **NOTE** **WEB SERVICES FOR ACTIVE DIRECTORY**
> ADWS provides XML Web Services–based protocols to interact with Active Directory. The Active Directory module for Windows PowerShell communicates with these services to perform administrative tasks. This model is a departure from other interfaces including Lightweight Directory Access Protocol (LDAP) and Active Directory Services Interface (ADSI), which continue to be supported and used by legacy tools including Active Directory Users And Computers.

When ADWS is running on at least one domain controller (and remember, it is installed automatically on a Windows Server 2008 R2 domain controller), and the Active Directory Module For Windows PowerShell is available (which is also added automatically to a Windows Server 2008 R2 domain controller), you are ready to administer Active Directory with Windows PowerShell. You can open the Active Directory Module For Windows PowerShell from the Administrative Tools program group, or you can import the module into a PowerShell session by typing the following command:

```
Import-Module ActiveDirectory
```

The Windows PowerShell console looks very similar to the command prompt of Cmd. exe except that the prompt includes *PS*. Figure 3-1 shows two instances of the Windows PowerShell console. One instance was launched by opening the Active Directory Module For Windows PowerShell from the Administrative Tools program group. The second was launched by running Powershell.exe and then importing the Active Directory module. You could use either instance to administer the domain.

FIGURE 3-1 Windows PowerShell consoles with the Active Directory module

> **NOTE ONE WINDOWS, ONE SHELL**
>
> Windows PowerShell enables you to launch programs and execute commands that are identical to those in Command Prompt. For example, you can type **dir**, **cls**, **ipconfig /all**, and **robocopy** in Windows PowerShell, just as you can in Command Prompt. Therefore, Windows PowerShell is backward compatible for administrators. If you use Windows PowerShell, you can perform administrative tasks either with familiar *Cmd.exe* commands or with Windows PowerShell cmdlets.

cmdlets

In traditional shells such as Command Prompt (Cmd.exe), you issue commands such as *dir* or *copy* that access utilities built into the shell, or you call executable programs, such as Attrib.exe or Xcopy.exe, many of which accept parameters from the command line and return feedback in the form of output, errors, and error codes.

In Windows PowerShell, you issue directives by using cmdlets. A cmdlet is a single-feature command that manipulates an object. The Active Directory module ships with 76 cmdlets for Windows PowerShell, so it is not recommended that you try to memorize them all. Instead, you should know how to discover and get help about a cmdlet when you need it. Over time, you will memorize the cmdlets that you use regularly.

Luckily, Windows PowerShell is a modern command-line and automation interface, and it benefits from lessons learned from past command-line environments, such as Command Prompt. One of the most immediately useful sets of features are those that help you discover cmdlets and learn syntax easily.

The *Get-Command* cmdlet lists cmdlets. Simply type the following command to list all cmdlets available within the Windows PowerShell session:

```
Get-Command
```

Cmdlets are not case-sensitive. Therefore, the following cmdlets are equivalent:

- Get-Command
- get-command
- GET-COMMAND

Cmdlets always follow the *Verb-Noun* format, also called the *Action-Object* format. The *Noun* is always singular. For example, the cmdlet to list all services running on a computer is *Get-Service*. To list all processes running on a computer, type the following command:

```
Get-Service
```

Windows PowerShell standardizes cmdlets and supports a managed number of verbs. You can display a list of supported verbs with the *Get-Verb* cmdlet. Nouns follow naming standards managed by the Windows PowerShell team. For example, all Active Directory nouns begin with *AD*.

You can use these standards to list all Active Directory cmdlets. Type the following command:

```
Get-Command -Noun AD* | More
```

> **NOTE | MORE**
>
> Windows PowerShell supports much of the same syntax as Command Prompt, which eases the transition to Windows PowerShell. As in Command Prompt, adding | *more* to a command pages the output of the command.

The command shown in the preceding paragraph is a shortcut based on the fact that all Active Directory nouns begin with *AD*. A more technically accurate approach is to list all of the commands in the Active Directory for Windows PowerShell. To list the commands in the module, type the following command:

```
Get-Command -Module ActiveDirectory
```

You will instantly recognize the purpose of some cmdlets based on their names. For example, the *Get-ADGroupMember* cmdlet lists—or *enumerates*—members of a group.

Parameters

Most cmdlets accept parameters. Parameters have names preceded by a dash and are not case sensitive. For example, the *-Identity* parameter of the *Get-ADGroupMember* cmdlet specifies the group that you want to enumerate. The *-Identity* parameter is used by most Active Directory cmdlets to reference a specific object. The value of the parameter can be a distinguished name or a *sAMAccountName* (Pre-Windows 2000 Logon Name), as in the following examples:

```
Get-ADGroupMember -Identity "cn=Sales,ou=Groups,dc=contoso,dc=com"
Get-ADGroupMember -Identity Sales
```

You can also use an object name, a Globally Unique Identifier (GUID), or a Security Identifier (SID) to reference an object. Some parameters accept values without specifying the parameter name. The *-Identity* parameter of the *Get-ADGroupMember* cmdlet is one such parameter. The parameter name is optional. Therefore, the following command is also valid:

```
Get-ADGroupMember Sales
```

Get-Help

When you find a cmdlet that appears to support a task you want to perform, you can expose the documentation for the cmdlet using the *Get-Help* cmdlet. The simplest form of help is provided by typing the *Get-Help* cmdlet followed by the cmdlet name you want help with. For example:

```
Get-Help Get-ADGroupMember
```

Without a parameter, the *Get-Help* cmdlet shows a synopsis, a more detailed description, and the syntax of the cmdlet. The following optional parameters of *Get-Help* produce various types and levels of detail:

- **-Examples**   Shows usage examples of the cmdlet.
- **-Detailed**   Shows detailed information about the cmdlet and each of its parameters, as well as examples.
- **-Full**   Shows all documentation of the cmdlet.

For example, to get help, including examples, about the *Get-ADGroupMember* cmdlet, which lists—or *enumerates*—the members of a group, type the following:

```
Get-Help Get-ADGroupMember -detailed
```

The Windows PowerShell *Get-Help* cmdlet is the best place to start looking for information about cmdlets, especially when you are just getting started with Windows PowerShell. Windows PowerShell cmdlets are well documented with a standard documentation format, and the *Get-Help* cmdlet, with the *-Examples*, *-Detailed*, and *-Full* parameters, exposes that documentation.

> **MORE INFO**   **EXPLORE WINDOWS POWERSHELL CMDLETS**
>
> The following article, and its related articles, provide additional details regarding the fundamentals of Windows PowerShell cmdlets: "Windows PowerShell Basics," *http://technet.microsoft.com/en-us/library/dd347730.aspx.*

Objects

Unlike Command Prompt, in which commands return text that then must be parsed and processed as text, Windows PowerShell returns *objects*—representations of the resource itself.

An object is a programming construct. From a technical perspective, a .NET object is an instance of a .NET class that consists of data and the operations associated with that data. Think of an object as a virtual representation of a resource of some kind. For example, the *Get-ADUser* cmdlet returns an object representing a user. The following command returns an object representing the user with the *sAMAccountName* mike.fitz:

```
Get-ADUser -Identity mike.fitz
```

When you run this command, the console displays several properties of the user. But it is important to note that the cmdlet itself returns more than text: It returns an object representing the user. You can then manipulate the user by examining or setting its attributes or performing actions such as disabling the account.

Objects can have *properties*—also called *attributes*—that represent data maintained by the resource. An object representing a user, for example, has properties for the user's first and last name. When you get a property, you are retrieving the data of the resource. When you set a property, you are writing that data to the resource.

Objects also have *methods*, which are actions that you can perform on the object. When you perform a method on the object that represents the resource, you perform the action on the resource itself.

Variables

In the examples thus far, you have not yet done anything with the objects other than showing default properties. However, objects returned by a cmdlet can be stored in variables for later use. A *variable* is a named memory location that stores a value or object, and returns the value when needed. In Windows PowerShell, variable names are preceded by a dollar sign ($). The variable name itself is not case sensitive.

To assign a variable—that is, to create and define a variable—simply use the following syntax:

```
$variable = value
```

For example, the following command assigns the object retrieved by the *Get-ADUser* cmdlet to a variable named *$user*:

```
$user = Get-ADUser mike.fitz
```

A variable created from the Command Prompt persists during the Windows PowerShell session—that is, until you close the Windows PowerShell console. You can then use the variable as a parameter for another cmdlet. For example, the *Set-ADUser* cmdlet sets the value of a subset of the most common user attributes. You can use *Set-ADUser* to disable the user account represented by the variable *$user* by typing the following command:

```
Set-ADUser -Identity $user -Enabled $false
```

The *-identity* parameter name is optional. The value of the parameter, as mentioned earlier, can be a distinguished name, a SAM account name, an object name, a GUID, or a SID. The identity can also be provided as a user object—in this example, the user object stored in the variable *$user*.

Windows PowerShell has built-in variables, including the following:

- **$true**   Boolean true
- **$false**   Boolean false
- **$error**   Contains the error object of the most recent error

In the example earlier, the value of the *-Enabled* parameter is set to the Boolean value false by using the built-in variable *$false*.

> **MORE INFO**   **VARIABLES**
>
> The following article provides additional details regarding variables: "Using Variables to Store Objects" at *http://go.microsoft.com/fwlink/?LinkID=192734*.

Pipeline

You can also pipe the object or objects returned by one cmdlet as input to a subsequent cmdlet. Windows PowerShell features a *pipeline*: a channel through which the output of a cmdlet can be passed to the following cmdlet on the same command line. The pipeline is represented by the pipe character (|).

For example, type the following to disable the account for Mike Fitzmaurice:

```
Get-ADUser mike.fitz | Set-ADUser -Enabled $false
```

The *Get-ADUser* cmdlet gets an object representing the user and passes the object down the pipeline to the *Set-ADUser* cmdlet, which sets the value of the *enabled* flag to the logical value false.

The concept illustrated in this simple example is an important one. When working in Windows PowerShell, you will often get one or more objects, pass the objects down the pipeline, and do something to them. In this example, we created an object reference to one user, then passed that object to a cmdlet that disabled the user account. The next command in the pipeline could just as easily be the *Add-ADGroupMember* cmdlet to add the user to a group, or the *Remove-ADUser* cmdlet to delete the user account.

In addition, when a cmdlet returns more than one object (known as a *collection* of objects) and passes the collection down the pipeline, a subsequent cmdlet can operate on each of the objects it receives. For example, the *Get-ADGroupMember* cmdlet returns a collection of objects representing group members. To disable the accounts of all users in the Sales group, type the following command:

```
Get-ADGroupMember -Identity Sales | Set-ADUser -Enabled $false
```

The collection of users returned by the *Get-ADGroupMember* cmdlet is piped to the *Set-ADUser* cmdlet. The *Set-ADUser* cmdlet operates on each object that is passed to it, disabling each user.

> **NOTE SHORTCUT TAKEN**
>
> In the previous example, it is assumed that every member of the Sales group is a user. If the Sales group contained another group as a nested member, the command shown in the previous example would fail because the *Set-ADUser* cmdlet cannot operate on a group object piped to it. You could address this scenario by piping the output of *Get-ADGroupMember* to the *Where-Object* cmdlet, which can filter the pipeline to pipe only user objects to the *Set-ADUser* cmdlet.

Extend the Pipeline to More than One Line

A Windows PowerShell task may involve multiple cmdlets, parameters, and expressions. More complicated tasks may create a long pipeline with structures including functions, iterative loops, and conditional statements. Often, the pipeline is extended to more than one line to improve readability. There are several ways to enter one line of a pipeline and then continue the pipeline on a subsequent line:

- **The tick mark (`)**   When a tick mark is the last character of a line, it serves as a line break and line continuation marker. Windows PowerShell assumes that the subsequent line is a continuation of the current line. The following two-line command uses a tick mark to break the line for readability:

```
Get-ADGroupMember -Identity Sales | `
Set-ADUser -Enabled $false
```

- **The pipe symbol (|)**   When the pipe symbol is the last character of a line, it, too, serves to indicate that the command is not complete, so Windows PowerShell continues the command with the subsequent line, as in the following example:

```
Get-ADGroupMember -Identity Sales |
Set-ADUser -Enabled $false
```

- **Curly braces ({})**   Curly braces enclose a structure such as an expression or a proce-dure—a script block, for example. A left curly brace marks the beginning of a struc-ture. The pipeline continues on one or more lines until the right curly brace is found, marking the end of the structure.

When you type a line in the Windows PowerShell console and the line ends with a tick mark or a pipe symbol, or the line contains a left curly brace that is not closed with a right curly brace, the console prompt becomes a double right chevron, shown in Figure 3-2. This prompt is a visual indication that the command is being continued. To indicate that the command is complete, you must enter a blank line at the prompt, as shown in Figure 3-2. When Windows PowerShell receives the blank line, it executes the multi-line command.

FIGURE 3-2 A multi-line command

> **MORE INFO   THE WINDOWS POWERSHELL PIPELINE**
>
> The following article provides additional details regarding the Windows PowerShell Pipeline: "Understanding the Windows PowerShell Pipeline" at *http://go.microsoft.com/fwlink/?LinkID=192732*.

Aliases

Windows PowerShell allows a cmdlet to have *aliases*, which are alternate names for the cmdlet. For example, *gsv* is an alias for *Get-Service*, a cmdlet that returns a collection of services on a system. The *Get-Alias* cmdlet lists aliases. Without a parameter, *Get-Alias* lists all aliases in the current Windows PowerShell session. To list aliases for a specific cmdlet, type the following command:

```
Get-Alias -Definition cmdlet
```

where *cmdlet* is the cmdlet for which you want to list aliases.

If you see a cmdlet that does not follow the *Verb-Noun* syntax, the cmdlet is using an alias. Sometimes it can be difficult to interpret what a command is doing when an alias is used. To list the cmdlet associated with a specific alias, type the following command:

```
Get-Alias Alias
```

where *Alias* is the alias you want to define.

Windows PowerShell aliases enable you to use common Command Prompt (Cmd.exe) and UNIX commands. For example, *dir* and *ls* list the objects in a directory; they are aliases for the *Get-ChildItem* cmdlet. You can clear the Windows PowerShell console screen with the *Clear-Host* cmdlet, or you can use the alias *cls*. Windows PowerShell provides aliases for command-shell commands, however Windows PowerShell cmdlets do not take the same parameters as *Cmd.exe* commands. For example, to retrieve a directory of folders and all subfolders in Command Prompt, type **dir /s**. In Windows PowerShell, type **dir -recurse**.

> **MORE INFO**   **USING FAMILIAR COMMAND NAMES**
>
> The following article provides additional details regarding Windows PowerShell aliases: "Using Familiar Command Names" at *http://go.microsoft.com/fwlink/?LinkID=192733*.

Namespaces, Providers, and PSDrives

Cmdlets operate against objects in a namespace. A folder on a disk is an example of a namespace—a hierarchy that can be navigated. Namespaces are created by providers, which you can think of as drivers. For example, the file system has a Windows PowerShell provider, as does the registry, so Windows PowerShell can directly access and manipulate objects in the namespaces of those providers.

You are certainly familiar with the concept of representing the namespace of a disk volume with a letter or representing a shared network folder's namespace as a mapped drive letter. In Windows PowerShell, namespaces from any provider can be represented as *PSDrives*. Windows PowerShell automatically creates a PSDrive for each drive letter already defined by Windows.

Windows PowerShell takes this concept to the next level by creating additional PSDrives for commonly required resources. For example, it creates two drives, *HKCU* and *HKLM*, for the HKEY_CURRENT_USER and HKEY_LOCAL_MACHINE registry hives. Now you can navigate and manipulate the registry as easily as you can a file system. Type the following in the Windows PowerShell:

```
cd hklm:\software
dir
```

Drives are also created for aliases, the environment, certificates, functions, and variables. To list the PSDrives that have been created, type **Get-PSDrive.**

The Active Directory PowerShell Provider

Windows Server 2008 R2 adds a provider for Active Directory, so you can navigate Active Directory as easily as you navigate the folders on a disk volume. To use the Active Directory provider, type the following command:

```
cd AD:
```

The prompt changes to *PS AD:\>* to reflect the current directory, which is the top-level node in the Active Directory namespace, the root directory service entry or *RootDSE*. Type **dir** to list the partitions of Active Directory.

You can navigate to a partition by typing **cd** followed by the distinguished name of the partition. For example, to navigate to the domain partition for the contoso.com domain, type the following command:

```
cd "dc=contoso,dc=com"
```

To navigate to an OU, type **cd** followed by either the distinguished name or the relative distinguished name of the OU. For example, to navigate to the User Accounts OU, type the following command:

```
cd "ou=User Accounts"
```

> **TIP TAB EXPANSION**
>
> Windows PowerShell supports *tab expansion*, also called *tab completion*, so that you can type a few letters and then press Tab to complete your typing. This applies not only to paths, such as "OU=User Accounts," but also to cmdlets, parameter names, object attributes, and methods.

To create a new OU for Contractors in the User Accounts OU, type the following command:

```
md "ou=Contractors"
```

Md is an alias for the *New-Item* cmdlet. In the example, a number of defaults were used to create the result: a new OU named Contractors in the User Accounts OU. The *New-Item* cmdlet has several forms. Here, the value of the *-Name* parameter is "ou=Contractors." The parameter name itself is optional. The *-ItemType* parameter is not specified, so the default object class *organizationalUnit* is assumed.

Creating a User with Windows PowerShell

You are now ready to create a user in Active Directory by using the *New-ADUser* cmdlet. To create a user account for Mary North, type the following command:

```
New-ADUser -Name "Mary North"
```

When you create a new user account, you must specify the *-Name* parameter, which is the *ldapDisplayName* attribute and is also used for *CN* and several other object name attributes.

The user will be created in the default container for users in the domain—by default, the container named *Users*. You can create a user in a specific location by doing one of the following:

- Using the *-Path* parameter to specify the distinguished name of the OU in which to create the user. For example, to create a user account for Mary North in the User Accounts OU, type the following command:

```
New-ADUser -Path "ou=User Accounts,dc=contoso,dc=com" -Name "Mary North"
    -SAMAccountName "mary.north"
```

- Setting the current directory to an OU by using the Active Directory provider as described earlier in this lesson.

Other attributes can be configured with the many parameters of the *New-ADUser* cmdlet. Type **Get-Help New-ADUser -Detailed** for detailed information about the cmdlet and its parameters. In the practice for this lesson, you create a user and populate attributes by using the *New-ADUser* cmdlet.

You can also create a new account based on a template with the *New-ADUser* cmdlet. First you must create an object reference to the template user account and to the specific properties you want to copy. You can do this by using the *Get-ADUser* cmdlet to load attributes from a template account in Active Directory or the *New-ADUser* cmdlet to create a template in memory only. For example, to create a reference to the _Sales Template account created in Lesson 1, type the following command on one line:

```
$user = Get-ADUser "CN=_Sales Template,OU=User Accounts,DC=contoso,DC=com"
    -Properties MemberOf,Title,Department,Company,PhysicalDeliveryOfficeName
```

Note that the *-Properties* parameter specifies a comma-delimited list of properties that you want to copy to the new account. Provide the reference as the value of the *-Instance* parameter of the *New-ADUser* cmdlet. To create a new user account for Mary North based on the template, type the following command:

```
New-ADUser -path "ou=User Accounts,dc=contoso,dc=com" -Instance $user -Name "Mary North"
    -SAMAccountName "mary.north"
```

Note that you can override properties from the template by using parameters of the *New-ADUser* cmdlet.

Populating User Attributes

You've learned to configure attributes of a new account by using parameters of the *New-ADUser* cmdlet. You can also use the *Set-ADUser* cmdlet to configure user attributes. The *Set-ADUser* cmdlet provides parameters for the most commonly used attributes. For less commonly used attributes, the *–Add*, *-Replace*, *-Clear*, and *-Remove* parameters provide direct access to all attributes. There are three methods with which you can specify the user to be modified.

First, you can use the *-Identity* parameter of the cmdlet. For example, to change the email address of Mary North, type the following command:

```
Set-ADUser -Identity mary.north -EmailAddress "mary.north@contoso.com"
```

The name of the parameter is optional.

Second, you can pipe a user object to *Set-ADUser*, as in the following example:

```
Get-ADUser -Identity mary.north | Set-ADUser -EmailAddress "mary.north@contoso.com"
```

When you use either of these two methods, you are changing the properties of both the in-memory object reference and the object itself in the directory service. If you plan to change multiple properties, you can improve performance by making changes in memory, then committing the changes, all at once, to the directory. This third method requires that you create a variable representing the user, then make changes to the variable, and then use the *-Instance* parameter of the *Set-ADUser* cmdlet to commit the changes. For example, type the following commands:

```
$user = Get-ADUser -Identity mary.north
$user.mail = "mary.north@contoso.com"
Set-ADUser -Instance $user
```

In the second command, the property is set by using a syntax called the *dot notation*. A dot (.) separates the object from the LDAP name of the property. Notice that the LDAP name, *mail* in this example, is sometimes different than the name of the attribute in the user interface or as referenced by a parameter name. If you're not sure of the LDAP name for an attribute, click the Attribute Editor tab of a user account in the Active Directory Users And Computers snap-in. The tab is visible when you select Advanced Features from the View menu. The Attribute Editor shows all attributes of an object, including their LDAP names and values.

You do not use the same method to set a user's password. Instead, you use the *Set-ADAccountPassword* cmdlet to change or reset a password. When you change a password, you provide values for both the old and new passwords. When you reset a password, you specify the *-Reset* parameter and provide the value of only the new password. For example, to reset the password for Mary North, type the following command:

```
Set-ADAccountPassword -Identity "mary.north" -Reset
```

You are prompted to enter the new password.

Windows PowerShell does not allow a cmdlet to receive a secret, such as a password, in a plain text parameter. It must be passed securely. Therefore, if you want to include the password in the command line, it must be converted to a secure string before it can be used as a password parameter. For example, type the following command on one line:

```
Set-ADAccountPassword -Identity "mary.north" -Reset
    -NewPassword (ConvertTo-SecureString -AsPlainText "Pa$$w0rd" -Force)
```

You can also specify the password for a new account by using the -*AccountPassword* parameter of the *New-ADUser* cmdlet. You would use the same *ConvertTo-SecureString* cmdlet, in parentheses as shown in the example, as the value of the parameter. For example, the following command (typed on one line) will create an account for Mary North:

```
New-ADUser -Path "ou=User Accounts,dc=contoso,dc=com" -Name "Mary North"
    -SAMAccountName "mary.north"
    -AccountPassword (ConvertTo-SecureString -AsPlainText "Pa$$w0rd" -Force)
    -ChangePasswordAtLogon $true -Enabled $true
```

The account can be enabled by using the -*Enabled* parameter because a password is specified, and the -*ChangePasswordAtLogon* parameter ensures that the user will be prompted to change her password the first time she logs on.

Importing Users from a Database with Windows PowerShell

Although you will not be expected to understand database imports with Windows PowerShell for the 70-640 examination, learning how to do so can be a tremendous benefit to your efforts to automate the creation of users. As you'll see, it takes only a few lines of additional code with the powerful cmdlets of Windows PowerShell.

Assume that you receive an Excel worksheet from the human resources department with information about newly hired employees. Excel can save the file as a comma-delimited text file (.csv), which can be imported by Windows PowerShell. The first line of the .csv file must have field names that match parameter names of the *New-ADUser* cmdlet. Additional lines contain the values for each user. As a simple example, consider the following .csv file saved as Newusers.csv:

Newusers.csv

```
name,sAMAccountName,GivenName,Surname
John Woods,john.woods,Johnathan,Woods
Kim Akers,kim.akers,Kimberly,Akers
```

Windows PowerShell can import these users with one command:

```
import-csv "C:\Users\Administrator\Desktop\newusers.csv" | New-ADUser
```

You can even add parameters, as in the following example:

```
import-csv "C:\Users\Administrator\Desktop\newusers.csv" | New-ADUser -organization Contoso
```

Such parameters will override any values in the .csv file and will apply to all imported users.

If this doesn't convince you that Windows PowerShell deserves its *Power* moniker, then … well, you're a tough customer!

> **MORE INFO   WINDOWS POWERSHELL**
>
> The following resources provide detailed information about Windows PowerShell and using Windows PowerShell to manage Active Directory:
>
> - Windows PowerShell at *http://go.microsoft.com/fwlink/?LinkID=192735*
> - The Microsoft Script Center at *http://technet.microsoft.com/scriptcenter*
> - "Windows PowerShell 2.0 Brings Scripting to Active Directory—and Not Just for Windows Server 2008 R2" at *http://technet.microsoft.com/en-us/magazine/ee914610.aspx*
> - "Cool Pipeline Tricks, Redux" at *http://technet.microsoft.com/en-us/magazine/ff394367.aspx*
> - "PowerShell and Active Directory" at *http://www.windowsitpro.com/article/active-directory/powershell-and-active-directory.aspx*
> - "Managing AD in Bulk Using PowerShell" at *http://www.windowsitpro.com/article/active-directory/Managing-AD-in-Bulk-Using-PowerShell.aspx*

The Active Directory Administrative Center

The Active Directory Administrative Center (ADAC) is a new tool with which you can administer Active Directory. Unlike the legacy Active Directory Users And Computers snap-in, which continues to be supported, ADAC was built as a graphical interface on top of Windows PowerShell. When you perform a task with ADAC, you are running one or more Windows PowerShell cmdlets or scripts behind the scenes.

ADAC is available only on Windows Server 2008 R2 and on Windows 7. You cannot add ADAC to computers running earlier versions of Windows. ADAC is added by default when you promote a Windows Server 2008 R2 domain controller. You can add ADAC as a feature by using Server Manager, and you can add ADAC to a computer running Enterprise, Professional, or Ultimate editions of Windows 7 after installing RSAT.

ADAC appears in the Administrative Tools program group. When you open ADAC, shown in Figure 3-3, you will notice that ADAC is task focused. You can immediately reset a user's password or search for an object. This is in contrast to Active Directory Users And Computers, which is data focused and therefore requires you to locate an object in the hierarchy of the directory service before you can perform a task.

FIGURE 3-3 Active Directory Administrative Center

You can remove a content panel by clicking the X icon in the upper-right corner of the panel. For example, you can remove the Getting Started panel after you have acclimated to ADAC. To add a content panel, click Add Content.

ADAC provides a view of the domain hierarchy, similar to the view shown in Active Directory Users And Computers. Click the second tab (Tree View) in the navigation panel. The default view in the navigation panel, shown in Figure 3-3, is the List View tab.

Typically, an administrator focuses on objects in a subset of OUs in the domain—for example, the User Accounts and Client Computers OUs. You can add shortcuts to the OUs that you regularly access to the navigation panel by clicking Add Navigation Nodes. A navigation node is simply a shortcut. It appears on both the List View and Tree View tabs. You can rename, reorder, or remove navigation nodes in ADAC, but the underlying OU is not changed.

In the list view, click one of the navigation nodes to navigate the hierarchy of OUs beneath that node. Child nodes expand in a manner similar to the Windows Start menu. The list view shows the last three nodes to which you have navigated at the bottom of the list, as a most-recently used (MRU) list. Finally, at the top of ADAC is a breadcrumb bar that behaves similarly to the Windows Explorer breadcrumb bar. You can navigate the hierarchy of your domains by clicking breadcrumb elements, or you can specify a container to which to navigate by using an LDAP path, a distinguished name, or a hierarchical path.

When you select an object, a summary of object properties appears in the Summary panel, and common tasks appear in the Tasks panel. In Figure 3-4, the user account for April Stewart is selected.

FIGURE 3-4 The Summary and Tasks panels

To open an object in ADAC, double-click the object or click the Properties link in the Tasks panel. The properties page of an object is completely different than in Active Directory Users And Computers. An example is shown in Figure 3-5.

FIGURE 3-5 Properties of a user in ADAC

Click Tasks to perform common administrative tasks. Properties are shown in a single, long page. Shortcuts to sections that contain related properties appear on the left panel of the page. Click Add Sections to add or remove sections. The last section on the page, Extensions, shows the familiar tabbed interface of Active Directory Users And Computers through which you can access properties that are not shown elsewhere on the page.

When you need to find one or more objects, click Global Search in the left navigation panel. You can search based on preset examples, including Users With Enabled But Locked Accounts and Users With A Password Expiring In A Given Number Of Days, or you can build a search based on custom criteria. Click Convert To LDAP to fine-tune the query using LDAP syntax.

In the Normal view of the query, click Save to save your query for later reuse. Click Queries to open a previously saved query.

ADAC provides innovative ways to navigate, search, and administer your domain. Spend some time experimenting with this effective new interface.

PRACTICE   Creating Users with Windows PowerShell

In this practice, you explore Windows PowerShell and use it to create user accounts.
To perform the exercises in this practice, you must have performed the Practice in Lesson 1.

EXERCISE 1   Use Commands and cmdlets in Windows PowerShell

In this exercise, you start Windows PowerShell and use commands with which you are already familiar.

1. Log on to SERVER01 as **CONTOSO\Administrator**.
2. Click Start, type **powershell.exe**, and then press Enter.
3. In the Windows PowerShell console, type **dir**, and then press Enter.
4. Identify the cmdlet for which *dir* is an alias. Type **Get-Alias dir**, and then press Enter.

    Question: For which cmdlet is *dir* an alias?

    Answer: *Get-ChildItem*.
5. Type **ipconfig /all**, and then press Enter.
6. Type **cls**, and then press Enter.
7. Type **Get-Help New-ADUser**, and then press Enter.

    An error message appears. The *New-ADUser* cmdlet is not available because the Active Directory Module For PowerShell is not loaded.
8. Type **Import-Module ActiveDirectory**, and then press Enter.
9. Type **Get-Help New-ADUser**, and then press Enter.

    The Active Directory cmdlets and provider are now available.
10. Close Windows PowerShell.
11. Open Active Directory Module For Windows PowerShell from the Administrative Tools program group.

12. Type **Get-Help New-ADUser**, and then press Enter.

The Active Directory cmdlets and provider are immediately available because the Active Directory module is loaded by default.

EXERCISE 2 Identify and Explore a Windows PowerShell Cmdlet

In this exercise, you identify the command needed to create a new user and explore its built-in documentation.

1. List the Windows PowerShell cmdlets for Active Directory.

Type the following command, and then press Enter:

```
Get-Command -Module ActiveDirectory
```

Alternately, type the following command, and then press Enter:

```
Get-Command -Noun AD*
```

2. List the cmdlets that perform tasks related to users in Active Directory.

Type the following command, and then press Enter:

```
Get-Command -Noun AD*User*
```

Question: Which cmdlet deletes a user?

Answer: *Remove-ADUser.*

3. Display the summary Help documentation for the cmdlet.

Type the following command, and then press Enter:

```
Get-Help New-ADUser
```

4. Display usage examples for the cmdlet.

Type the following command, and then press Enter:

```
Get-Help New-ADUser -examples
```

Tip: You can press the Up Arrow key to select the previously entered command, and then type the additional parameter.

5. Display detailed Help for the cmdlet.

Type the following command, and then press Enter:

```
Get-Help New-ADUser -detailed
```

EXERCISE 3 Create an Organizational Unit Using *New-ADOrganizationalUnit*

In this exercise, you create a new OU called Employees in the User Accounts OU.

- Type the following command on one line, and then press Enter:

```
New-ADOrganizationalUnit -Name Employees
    -Path "ou=User Accounts,dc=contoso,dc=com"
    -ProtectedFromAccidentalDeletion $true
```

EXERCISE 4   Navigate Active Directory Using the Active Directory PSDrive

In this exercise, you navigate Active Directory using commands that are familiar to you from your experience navigating file systems in Command Prompt.

1.   Type **cd AD:**, and then press Enter.

2.   Type **cd "dc=contoso,dc=com"**, and then press Enter.

3.   Type **cd "ou=User Accounts"**, and then press Enter.

4.   Type **md "ou=Contractors"**, and then press Enter.

5.   Type the following command to create an OU called Employees in the User Accounts OU:

```
New-Item -Name "ou=New Hires" -ItemType organizationalUnit
```

6.   Type **dir**, and then press Enter.

7.   Type **cd c:**, and then press Enter.

8.   Open Active Directory Users And Computers. Navigate to the User Accounts OU and confirm that the Employees, Contractors and New Hires OUs were created.

EXERCISE 5   Create Users with Windows PowerShell

In this exercise, you use Windows PowerShell to create users in Active Directory. You then modify attributes of one of the users.

1.   In Active Directory Module For Windows PowerShell, type the following command on one line, and then press Enter:

```
New-ADUser -Path "ou=User Accounts,dc=contoso,dc=com" -Name "Mike Danseglio"
    -SAMAccountName "mike.danseglio" -UserPrincipalName "mike.danseglio@contoso.com"
```

2.   Type the following two commands, on one line each, and then press Enter:

```
New-ADUser -Path "ou=User Accounts,dc=contoso,dc=com" -Name "Linda Mitchell"
    -SAMAccountName "linda.mitchell" -UserPrincipalName "linda.mitchell@contoso.com"
New-ADUser -Path "ou=User Accounts,dc=contoso,dc=com" -Name "Scott Mitchell"
    -SAMAccountName "scott.mitchell" -UserPrincipalName "scott.mitchell@contoso.com"
```

3.   Create a user with additional attributes. Type the following command on one line, and then press Enter.

```
New-ADUser -Path "ou=User Accounts,dc=contoso,dc=com" -Name "Mary North"
    -SAMAccountName "mary.north" -UserPrincipalName "mary.north@contoso.com"
    -EmailAddress "mary.north@contoso.com" -GivenName "Mary" -Surname "North"
    -Description "Sales Representative in Australia"
    -Company "Contoso, Ltd." -Department "Sales"
    -Office "Sydney" -AccountPassword (ConvertTo-SecureString
    -AsPlainText "Pa$$w0rd" -Force)
    -ChangePasswordAtLogon $true -Enabled $true
```

4. Switch to Active Directory Users And Computers. Refresh the view of the User Accounts OU. Open the properties of the user accounts you just created, and confirm that the attributes you specified were configured as expected.

   Notice that the user accounts for Linda Mitchell and Scott Mitchell are disabled. They cannot be enabled until a password has been specified. Reset the password of each account, but do not enable the accounts at this time. You will enable the accounts in the practice in Lesson 3.

5. Switch to Active Directory Module For Windows PowerShell.

6. Type the following commands:

```
$user = Get-ADUser "mary.north"
Set-ADUser $user -EmployeeNumber 12345
```

7. Type the following command, and then press Enter:

```
Get-ADUser "mary.north" | Set-ADUser -DisplayName "North, Mary"
```

8. Type the following command, and then press Enter:

```
Get-ADUser "mary.north" -Properties *
```

By default, the *Get-ADUser* cmdlet returns only a few of the most commonly used attributes. You can specify the properties to return by using the *-Properties* parameter. An asterisk (*) returns all properties.

Lesson Summary

- Windows PowerShell is the preferred command-line administration and automation interface for SharePoint 2010. Windows PowerShell provides support for performing administrative tasks from a command line and from scripts.
- The Active Directory module for Windows PowerShell enables you to administer Active Directory by using Windows PowerShell. You can add the Active Directory module feature to a computer running Windows Server 2008 R2. It is added automatically when you promote a Windows Server 2008 R2 domain controller. You can add the Active Directory module feature to a computer running Windows 7 after you have installed RSAT.
- The Active Directory module communicates with Active Directory Web Services (ADWS) on a domain controller. ADWS is available by default on Windows Server 2008 R2 and is installed automatically when you promote a Windows Server 2008 R2 domain controller.
- ADWS can be added to computers running Windows 2003 SP2, Windows 2003 R2 SP2, Windows Server 2008, and Windows Server 2008 SP2. This package is called the *Active Directory Management Gateway Service*.
- Windows PowerShell cmdlets follow strict standards, including *Verb-Noun* syntax with singular nouns and Help documentation.
- The *Get-Command* and *Get-Help* cmdlets expose commands and syntax.

- Windows PowerShell works with .NET objects. A cmdlet returns objects and can send them to subsequent cmdlets or into variables for later use.
- The Active Directory module includes a provider that helps you navigate Active Directory as a PSDrive.
- You can create a user with the *New-ADUser* cmdlet. The *Set-ADUser* cmdlet can configure attributes of an existing user object.
- The Active Directory Administrative Center (ADAC) is a graphical tool that supports task-based administration of Active Directory, efficient navigation, and powerful search. Behind the scenes, tasks are performed by using Windows PowerShell cmdlets.

Lesson Review

You can use the following questions to test your knowledge of the information in Lesson 2, "Administering with Windows PowerShell and Active Directory Administrative Center." The questions are also available on the companion CD if you prefer to review them in electronic form.

> **NOTE ANSWERS**
>
> Answers to these questions and explanations of why each answer choice is right or wrong are located in the "Answers" section at the end of the book.

1. You have just opened the Active Directory Module For Windows PowerShell. You want to create a user account for Mary North. Which of the following should you do?

    A Use the *New-Item* cmdlet.

    B. Use the *New-SPUser* cmdlet.

    C. Use the *New-ADUser* cmdlet.

    D. Use the *Set-ADUser* cmdlet.

2. You want to import users from a file maintained by Human Resources in Microsoft Office Excel. What can you do? (Choose all that apply.)

    A Use LDIFDE.

    B. Use the *Import-CSV* cmdlet.

    C. Use the *DSAdd* command.

    D. Use CSVDE.

3. You want to specify a password for a new user account. What do you do? (Choose all that apply. Each correct answer is a part of the solution.)

    A Use the *New-ADUser* cmdlet.

    B. Use the *ConvertTo-SecureString* cmdlet.

    C. Use the *Reset-ADPassword* cmdlet.

    D. Pipe the user to the *Remove-ADUser* cmdlet.

Lesson 3: Supporting User Objects and Accounts

The first two lessons of this chapter explained the methods with which to create user accounts. That is only the first step in the life cycle of a user in a domain. After creating the user, you must configure attributes that define both the properties of the security principal (the account) and the properties that manage the user. A user object in Active Directory is far more than just a handful of properties related to the user's security identity or account. A user object includes attributes that describe the individual and his or her relationship with the organization, as well as contact information and configuration of the user's experience on his or her computer. In this lesson, you will explore many of the more useful attributes of user objects, and you will learn how to administer these attributes for one or more users.

You must also know how and when to administer the account, to perform password resets and unlock the account. Finally, you must be able to move the user between OUs and, eventually, de-provision the account by disabling or deleting it. This lesson covers the procedures used to support a user object through its life cycle—procedures you can perform using the Windows interface, Command Prompt, and Windows PowerShell.

After this lesson, you will be able to:

- Identify the purpose and requirements of user account attributes and user name properties.
- View and modify hidden attributes of user objects.
- Modify attributes of multiple users simultaneously.
- Manage users with the Active Directory Users And Computers snap-in, DS commands, and Windows PowerShell.
- Perform common administrative tasks to support user accounts.

Estimated lesson time: 90 minutes

Managing User Attributes with Active Directory Users And Computers

When you use the New Object–User Wizard in the Active Directory Users And Computers snap-in to create a user, you are prompted for some common properties, including logon names, password, and user first and last names. A user object in Active Directory, however, supports dozens of additional properties that you can configure at any time with the Active Directory Users And Computers snap-in.

To read and modify the attributes of a user object, right-click the user and then click Properties. The user's Properties dialog box appears, as shown in Figure 3-6.

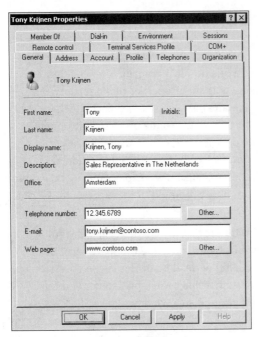

FIGURE 3-6 The Properties dialog box for a user

Attributes of a user object fall into several broad categories that appear on tabs of the dialog box:

- **Account attributes: the Account tab** These properties include logon names, the password, and account flags. Many of these attributes can be configured when you create a new user with the Active Directory Users And Computers snap-in. The Account Properties section details account attributes.

- **Personal information: the General, Address, Telephones, and Organization tabs** The General tab exposes the name properties that are configured when you create a user object, as well as basic description and contact information. The Address and Telephones tabs provide detailed contact information. The Telephones tab also contains the Notes field, which maps to the info attribute and is a very useful general-purpose text field that is underused by many enterprises. The Organization tab shows job title, department, company, and organizational relationships.

- **User configuration management: the Profile tab** Here you can configure the user's profile path, logon script, and home folder.

- **Group membership: the Member Of tab** You can add the user to and remove the user from groups and change the user's primary group. Group memberships and the primary group will be discussed in Chapter 4, "Managing Groups."

- **Terminal services: the Terminal Services Profile, Environment, Remote Control, and Sessions tabs** These four tabs enable you to configure and manage the user's experience when the user is connected to a Terminal Services session.

MORE INFO   TERMINAL SERVICES SETTINGS

For more information about configuring Terminal Services settings, see *MCTS Self-Paced Training Kit (Exam 70-643): Configuring Windows Server 2008 Applications Infrastructure*, (2nd Edition), by J. C. Mackin (Microsoft Press, 2011).

- **Remote access: the Dial-in tab**   You can enable and configure remote access permission for a user on the Dial-in tab.

- **Applications: the COM+ tab**   This tab enables you to assign users to an Active Directory COM+ partition set. This feature facilitates the management of distributed applications and is beyond the scope of the 70-640 exam.

Viewing All Attributes

A user object has even more properties than are visible in its Properties dialog box. Some of the so-called *hidden properties* can be quite useful to your enterprise. The Attribute Editor allows you to view and edit all attributes of a user object. The Attribute Editor tab is not visible until you enable Advanced Features from the View menu of the Microsoft Management Console (MMC). Click the View menu and select the Advanced Features option. Then open the Properties dialog box of the user to view the Attribute Editor tab, as shown in Figure 3-7.

FIGURE 3-7 The Attribute Editor tab

The Attribute Editor displays all the system attributes of the selected object. The Filter button lets you choose to see even more attributes, including backlinks and constructed attributes.

Backlinks are attributes that result from references to the object from other objects. The easiest way to understand backlinks is to look at an example: the *memberOf* attribute. When a user is added to a group, it is the group's *member* attribute that is changed: The distinguished name of the user is added to this multivalued attribute. Therefore, the *member* attribute of a group is called a *forward link attribute*. A user's *memberOf* attribute is updated automatically by Active Directory when the user is referred to by a group's *member* attribute. You do not ever write directly to the user's *memberOf* attribute; it is dynamically maintained by Active Directory.

A *constructed* attribute is one of the results from a calculation performed by Active Directory. An example is the *tokenGroups* attribute. This attribute is a list of the security identifiers (SIDs) of all the groups to which the user belongs, including nested groups. To determine the value of *tokenGroups*, Active Directory must calculate the effective membership of the user, which takes a few processor cycles. Therefore, the attribute is not stored as part of the user object or dynamically maintained. Instead, it is calculated when needed. Because of the processing required to produce constructed attributes, the Attribute Editor does not display them by default. They also cannot be used in LDAP queries.

As you can see in Figure 3-7, some attributes of a user object could be quite useful, including *division*, *employeeID*, *employeeNumber*, and *employeeType*. Although the attributes are not shown on the standard tabs of a user object, they are now available through the Attribute Editor, and they can be accessed programmatically with Windows PowerShell.

> **MORE INFO** **HIDDEN ATTRIBUTES OF OBJECTS**
>
> For more information on using hidden attributes of objects and extending the schema with custom attributes, see *Windows Administration Resource Kit: Productivity Solutions for IT Professionals* by Dan Holme (Microsoft Press, 2008).

Managing Attributes of Multiple Users

The Active Directory Users And Computers snap-in enables you to modify the properties of multiple user objects simultaneously.

To modify attributes of multiple users in the Active Directory Users And Computers snap-in:

1. Select several user objects by holding the Ctrl key as you click each user, or by using any other multiselection technique.

   Be certain that you select only objects of one class, such as users.

2. After you have multiselected the objects, right-click any one of them and then click Properties.

When you have multiselected the user objects, a subset of properties is available for modification:

- **General** Description, Office, Telephone Number, Fax, Web Page, E-mail
- **Account** UPN Suffix, Logon Hours, Computer Restrictions (logon workstations), all Account Options, Account Expires

- **Address**   Street, P.O. Box, City, State/Province, ZIP/Postal Code, Country/Region
- **Profile**   Profile Path, Logon Script, and Home Folder
- **Organization**   Title, Department, Company, Manager

EXAM TIP

Be sure to know which properties can be modified for multiple users simultaneously. Exam scenarios and simulations that suggest a *need* to change many user object properties as quickly as possible are often testing your understanding of multiselecting. In the real world, remember that you can and should use automation tools such as DSMod, Windows PowerShell, and VBScript.

Managing User Attributes with DSMod and DSGet

The DSMod and DSGet commands are two Active Directory command-line tools, called *DS commands*. You encountered DSQuery in Chapter 2 and DSAdd in Lesson 1 of this chapter.

DSMod

DSMod modifies the attributes of one or more existing objects. DS commands were introduced in Lesson 1. Like other DS commands, the basic syntax of DSMod is the following:

```
dsmod user UserDN ... parameters
```

UserDN specifies the distinguished name of the user to modify. The remaining parameters indicate the attribute to change and the new value. For example, the following command changes the *office* attribute of Tony Krijnen:

```
dsmod user "cn=Tony Krijnen,ou=User Accounts,dc=contoso,dc=com" -office "Amsterdam"
```

The attribute parameters do not map directly to the names of LDAP attributes of a user object. For example, the *dept* parameter of the DSMod User command modifies the *department* attribute of a user object. Additionally, DSMod User can modify only a subset of user attributes. Type **dsmod user /?** for usage information and a list of supported parameters.

Piping Multiple DNs to DSMod

The *UserDN* parameter of the DSMod command does not have to be entered directly into the command line. There are two ways to pipe DNs to it. The first is to enter the DNs into the console. Let's assume you need to change the *office* attribute of two users, Linda Mitchell and Scott Mitchell, to reflect their relocation to the Sydney office. At the command prompt, type the following command:

```
dsmod user -office "Sydney"
```

The *UserDN* parameter is missing. The console waits for you to enter DNs of users. Enter one per line, surrounded with quotes, pressing Enter at the end of each DN. After entering the last DN and pressing Enter, press Ctrl+Z at the beginning of the next line and press Enter to indicate that you are finished. The command will then execute against each of the DNs you have entered.

A more sophisticated way to send DNs to the DSMod command is by piping the results of a DSQuery command. DSQuery was covered in Chapter 2; it searches Active Directory for specified criteria and returns the DNs of matching objects. For example, to change the *office* attribute of Linda Mitchell and Scott Mitchell's accounts to Sydney, use the following command:

```
dsquery user -name "* Mitchell" | dsmod user -office "Sydney"
```

The DSQuery User command searches Active Directory for users whose names end with *Mitchell*. The resulting objects' DNs are then piped to DSMod User, which changes the *office* attribute to *Sydney*.

As another example, assume you want to assign all users a home folder on SERVER01. The following command (typed on one line) changes the *homeDirectory* and *homeDrive* attributes of user objects in the User Accounts OU:

```
dsquery user "ou=User Accounts,dc=contoso,dc=com" |
    dsmod user  -hmdir "\\server01\users\$username$\documents" -hmdrv "U:"
```

The special token *$username$* represents the user logon name (pre–Windows 2000)— the *sAMAccountName* attribute—in the value of the *-email*, *-hmdir*, *-profile*, and *-webpg* parameters. For example, to configure a home folder for a user, add the following parameter:

```
-hmdir \\server01\users\$username$\documents
```

EXAM TIP

The username token for the DS commands is *$username$*, not *%username%*.

NOTE $USERNAME$ BUG ALERT

Microsoft documentation suggests that the token *$username$* can be used with the DSAdd command, so you should remember this fact for the exam. However, testing shows that, in fact, you cannot use the *$username$* token successfully until *after* an account has been created. Therefore, in practice you can use *$username$* only with the DSMod command, to change the value of one of the four attributes listed earlier for an existing account. Documentation that suggests you can use *$username$* with DSAdd is incorrect.

DSGet

The DSGet command gets and outputs selected attributes of one or more objects. Its syntax, like that of DSMod, is:

```
dsget user UserDN... parameters
```

You can supply the DNs of one or more user objects by specifying them on the command line, separated by spaces; by entering them in the console; or by piping the results of a DSQuery User command. Unlike DSMod, DSGet takes only a parameter and not an associated value. For example, DSGet takes the *-samid* parameter like DSMod does, but you do not specify a value. Instead, DSGet reports the current value of the attribute. For example, to display the pre–Windows 2000 logon name of Jeff Ford in the User Accounts OU, use the following command:

```
dsget user "cn=Jeff Ford,ou=User Accounts,dc=contoso,dc=com" -samid
```

To display the email addresses of all users whose *description* attribute indicates that they are in the Sydney office, use this command:

```
dsquery user -desc "*Sydney*" | dsget user -email
```

Managing User Attributes with Windows PowerShell

To read an attribute of a user object with Windows PowerShell, use the *Get-ADUser* cmdlet and its *-Properties* parameter. As you learned in Lesson 2, the *Get-ADUser* cmdlet returns one or more user objects and a subset of commonly used properties. You can specify a comma-separated list of attributes to retrieve as the value for the *-Properties* attribute, or you can use an asterisk (*) as the value of the attribute, which instructs the cmdlet to return all attributes of the user object.

The *Get-ADUser* cmdlet was presented in Lesson 2 with examples that retrieved a single user object. However, you can use the cmdlet's parameters to return a collection of users that match specified criteria, within a scope of your Active Directory forest. You can pipe the resulting collection of users to the *Set-ADUser* cmdlet.

The *Set-ADUser* cmdlet, also presented in Lesson 2, enables you to modify attributes of a user. It has several parameters for common attributes, and you can use the *-Add*, *-Replace*, *-Clear*, and *-Remove* parameters to manipulate all attributes. See Lesson 2 for more information about the *Set-ADUser* cmdlet.

Understanding Name and Account Attributes

Two sets of attributes tend to appear on the certification exams and to present challenges to Windows administrators: name attributes and account attributes.

User Object Names

Several attributes are related to the name of a user object and an account. It is important to understand the distinctions between them.

- A user's *User Logon Name (Pre–Windows 2000)* is, behind the scenes, the *sAMAccountName* attribute. It's also sometimes called the *samid*. It must be unique for the entire domain. Many organizations use initials or some combination of first and last name to generate the *sAMAccountName*. This approach can be problematic because an organization of any size is likely to have users with names similar enough that the rules for generating the *sAMAccountName* would generate a duplicate name, so exceptions have to be built into the system; eventually, the rules are riddled with exceptions. This problem is solved if the employee number or some other unique attribute of the users is used for the *sAMAccountName*. If you have the ability to direct the naming conventions at your organization, a unique, name-independent logon name is recommended.

- The *User Logon Name* is the *userPrincipalName* attribute, abbreviated as UPN. The UPN consists of a logon name and a UPN suffix which is, by default, the DNS name of the domain in which you create the object. The UPN must be unique for the entire forest. Email addresses, which must be unique for the whole world, certainly meet that requirement. Consider using email addresses as UPNs. If your Active Directory domain name is not the same as your email domain name, you must add the email domain name as an available UPN suffix. To do this, open the Active Directory Domains And Trusts snap-in, right-click the root of the snap-in, and then click Properties.

- The *Name* of a user is shown in the first column in the details pane of the Active Directory Users And Computers snap-in; it is also presented as Full Name in some interfaces, including the New Object–User dialog box. It must be unique in the OU. The Name field is actually the common name (CN), stored as the *cn* attribute. The *cn* must be unique in the OU because it is the first element of the distinguished name (DN), the *distinguishedName* attribute, which must be unique within the forest.

- The RDN must be unique within an OU. For users, this means the *cn* attribute must be unique within the OU. This can be a tricky one. If you have a single, flat OU for users that already contains a user named Scott Miller, and you hire a second Scott Miller, his user object cannot have the same common name as the first. Unfortunately, there's no perfect answer to this problem for all organizations. Design a naming standard that applies a single rule for all CNs. Perhaps the CN should include an employee's number—for example, *Scott Miller (645928)*. If your OU structure for user accounts is flat, be prepared to address this challenge.

  Additionally, many organizations choose to configure the *cn* attribute as *LastName, FirstName* because by doing so, you can sort users by last name in the Active Directory Users And Computers snap-in. This is not a recommended method to achieve the goal. Instead of using a last-name-first format for *cn*, add the Last Name column to your view in the Active Directory Users And Computers snap-in by clicking the View menu and choosing Add/Remove Columns. Then click the Last Name column header to sort by last name.

- The *Display Name* is the *displayName* attribute that appears in the Microsoft Exchange global address list (GAL). It can be easier to locate users in the GAL if they are sorted by last name, so you can create a naming convention for your organization that specifies that the *displayName* attribute take the *LastName, FirstName* syntax. There is no requirement for uniqueness of the *displayName* attribute, although it is certainly easier to locate users in the GAL if each has a unique display name.

Rename a User Account

When you need to rename a user account, you must change one or more attributes.

To rename a user in the Active Directory Users And Computers snap-in:

1. Right-click the user, and then click Rename.
2. Type the new common name (CN) for the user, and then press Enter.

   The Rename User dialog box prompts you to enter additional name attributes.
3. Type the Full Name (which maps to the *cn* and *name* attributes).
4. Type the First Name and Last Name, Display Name, User Logon Name, and User Logon Name (Pre–Windows 2000).

   From a command prompt, you can use the DSMod command with the following syntax:

```
dsmod user UserDN [-upn UPN][-fn FirstName][-mi Initial][-ln LastName][-display
DisplayName][-email EmailAddress]
```

where *UserDN* is the distinguished name (DN) of the user object. Each parameter, *-display*, for example, is preceded by a dash and followed by the value to which the corresponding attribute will be configured.

You cannot change the *sAMAccountName* attribute by using DSMod, and you cannot change the CN of the object using DSMod.

You can use the DSMove command with the *-newname* parameter to change the CN of the object.

Use the *Set-ADUser* Windows PowerShell cmdlet to change name attributes of a user.

Account Properties

On the Account tab of a user's Properties dialog box, shown in Figure 3-8, you can find the attributes that are directly related to the fact that a user is a security principal, meaning that it is an identity to which permissions and rights can be assigned. Other security principals include computers, groups, and the *inetOrgPerson* object class.

Several of the account properties are worth highlighting because they are potentially quite useful and not self-explanatory. Table 3-2 describes these properties.

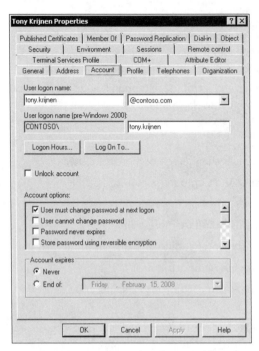

FIGURE 3-8 Account properties of a user object

TABLE 3-2 User Account Properties

PROPERTY	DESCRIPTION
Logon Hours	Click Logon Hours to configure the hours during which a user is allowed to log on to the network.
Log On To	Click Log On To if you want to limit the workstations to which the user can log on. This is called *Computer Restrictions* in other parts of the user interface and maps to the *userWorkstations* attribute. You must have NetBIOS over TCP/IP enabled for this feature to have any effect, because it uses the computer name rather than the Media Access Control (MAC) address of a computer's network card to restrict logon.
User Must Change Password At Next Logon	Select this check box if you want the user to change the password you have entered the first time he or she logs on. You cannot select this option if you have selected Password Never Expires. Selecting this option automatically clears the mutually exclusive option User Cannot Change Password.
User Cannot Change Password	Select this check box if you have more than one person using the same domain user account (such as Guest) or to maintain control over user account passwords. This option is commonly used to manage service account passwords. You cannot select this option if you have selected User Must Change Password At Next Logon.

PROPERTY	DESCRIPTION
Password Never Expires	Select this check box if you never want the password to expire. This option will automatically clear the User Must Change Password At Next Logon setting because they are mutually exclusive.
Account Is Disabled	Select this check box to disable the user account—for example, when creating an object for a newly hired employee who does not yet need access to the network.
Store Password Using Reversible Encryption	This option, which stores the password in Active Directory without using Active Directory's powerful, nonreversible encryption hashing algorithm, exists to support applications that require knowledge of the user password. If it is not absolutely required, do not enable this option because it weakens password security significantly. Passwords stored using reversible encryption are similar to those stored as plaintext.
Smart Card Is Required For Interactive Logon	Smart cards are portable, tamper-resistant hardware devices that store unique identification information for a user. They are attached to, or inserted into, a system and provide an additional, physical identification component to the authentication process.
Account Is Trusted For Delegation	This option enables a service account to impersonate a user to access network resources on behalf of a user. This option is not typically selected, certainly not for a user object representing a human being. It is used more often for service accounts in three-tier (or multitier) application infrastructures.
Account Expires	Use the Account Expires controls to specify when an account expires.

NOTE LOCK DOWN ACCOUNTS THAT HAVE PASSWORDS THAT DO NOT EXPIRE

It is not best practice to configure an account with a password that does not expire. In situations that require such an approach, be sure you use a long, complex password for the account. If the account needs access to a limited number of systems, you can increase the security of the account by configuring the Log On To property with the list of computers to which the account requires access. In the past, nonexpiring passwords were often configured for service accounts. A new feature in Windows Server 2008 R2, Active Directory Managed Service Accounts, addresses this problem. Managed Service Accounts are discussed in Chapter 8, "Improving the Security of Authentication in an AD DS Domain."

Administering User Accounts

The primary purpose of user objects in Active Directory is to support authentication of a human being or a service. Accounts are provisioned, administered, and, eventually, deprovisioned. The most common administrative tasks related to existing user accounts are resetting a password; unlocking an account; and disabling, enabling, deleting, moving, and renaming user objects.

The following sections examine each of these tasks and how they can be performed using the Windows interface, Windows PowerShell, or Command Prompt. Each of these tasks requires you to have appropriate permissions to the user objects. Delegating administrative permissions was discussed in Chapter 2.

Resetting a User's Password

If the user forgets his or her password and attempts to log on, he or she will receive a logon message, as shown in Figure 3-9.

FIGURE 3-9 A logon message notifying a user that the user name or password is invalid

Before the user can log on successfully, you will have to reset that password. You do not need to know the user's old password to do so.

To reset a user's password in the Active Directory Users And Computers snap-in:

1. Right-click the user object, and then click Reset Password.

2. In the Reset Password dialog box, shown in Figure 3-10, enter the new password in both the New Password and Confirm Password boxes.

   It is a best practice to assign a temporary, unique, strong password for the user.

FIGURE 3-10 The Reset Password dialog box

3. Select the User Must Change Password At Next Logon check box.

   It is a best practice to force the user to change the password at the next logon, so that the user ends up with a password known only by the user.

4. Click OK.

5. Communicate the temporary password to the user in a secure manner.

You can also use the DSMod command to reset a user's password and, optionally, force the user to change that password at the next logon. Type the following command:

```
dsmod user UserDN -pwd NewPassword -mustchpwd yes
```

where *UserDN* is the distinguished name (DN) of the user object and *NewPassword* is the new password. The *-mustchpwd yes* parameter forces the user to change the password at the next logon.

To reset a user's password by using Windows PowerShell, use the *Set-AccountPassword* cmdlet, as explained in Lesson 2.

You may also change passwords using LDIFDE, a command introduced in Lesson 1. Use a *change* operation and specify the password with the same Base64 encoding of the password, surrounded by double quotes, for the *unicodePwd* attribute.

Unlocking an Account

An Active Directory domain supports account lockout policies. A lockout policy is designed to prevent an intruder from attempting to penetrate the enterprise network by logging on repeatedly with various passwords until he or she finds a correct password. When a user attempts to log on with an incorrect password, a logon failure is generated. When too many logon failures occur within a specified period of time, defined by the lockout policy, the account is locked out. The next time the user attempts to log on, a notification clearly states the account lockout. You will learn to configure account lockout policies in Chapter 8, "Improving the Security of Authentication in an AD DS Domain."

> **NOTE** **WATCH FOR DRIVES MAPPED WITH ALTERNATE CREDENTIALS**
>
> A common cause of account lockout is a drive mapped with alternate credentials. If the alternate credentials' password is changed, and the Windows client attempts repeatedly to connect to the drive, the account whose credentials were used to map the drive will be locked out.

Your lockout policy can define a period of time after which a lockout account is automatically unlocked. But when a user is trying to log on and discovers that he or she is locked out, it is likely he or she will contact the help desk for support.

To unlock a user account in the Active Directory Users And Computers snap-in:

1. Right-click the user object, and then click Properties.
2. Click the Account tab.
3. Select the Unlock Account check box.

Windows Server 2008 R2 also includes the option to unlock a user's account when you choose the Reset Password command.

To unlock a user account while resetting the user's password:

- In the Reset Password dialog box, select the Unlock The User's Account check box, shown in Figure 3-10.

This method is particularly handy when a user's account has become locked out because the user did, in fact, forget the password. You can now assign a new password, specify that the user must change the password at next logon, and unlock the user's account in one dialog box.

Use the *Unlock-ADAccount* cmdlet to unlock an account by using Windows PowerShell. The DS commands do not provide a method to unlock an account.

Disabling and Enabling a User Account

User accounts are security principals—identities that can be given access to network resources. Because each user is a member of Domain Users and of the Authenticated Users special identity, each user account has at least read access to a vast amount of information in Active Directory and on your file systems unless you have been severe and unusually successful at locking down access control lists (ACLs).

Therefore, it is important not to leave user accounts open. You should configure password policies and auditing—both discussed in Chapter 8—and procedures to ensure that accounts are being used appropriately. If a user account is provisioned before it is needed, or if an employee will be absent for an extended period of time, disable the account.

To disable an account in the Active Directory Users And Computers snap-in, right-click a user and choose Disable. If an account is already disabled, the Enable Account command will appear when you right-click the user.

From the command line, you can use the DSMod command, as in the following example:

```
dsmod user UserDN -disabled yes
```

Enabling an account is just a matter of changing *yes* to *no* for the DSMod command:

```
dsmod user UserDN -disabled no
```

In each command, UserDN is the distinguished name (DN) of the user object, and the *-disabled {yes|no}* parameter disables or enables the account.

As you learned in Lesson 2, the *-Enabled* parameter of the *Set-ADUser* cmdlet allows you to enable the account with the Boolean value *true* or disable the account with the Boolean value *false*.

Deleting a User Account

When an account is no longer necessary, you can delete it from your directory.

To delete a user account in Active Directory Users And Computers, perform the following steps:

1. Select the user and press Delete, or right-click the user and then choose Delete.

   You are prompted to confirm your choice because of the significant implications of deleting a security principal.

2. Confirm the prompt.

You can delete objects from Active Directory by using the DSRm command, another of the DS commands. DSRm uses a simple syntax:

```
dsrm UserDN
```

where *UserDN* is the distinguished name (DN) of the user object. Notice that, unlike other DS commands, DSRm is not followed by the *User* object class keyword.

Use the *Remove-ADUser* cmdlet to delete a user in Windows PowerShell.

It is critical to consider that once the account has been deleted, it is eventually purged entirely from the directory. You cannot simply re-create a new account with the same name as a deleted account and hope it has the same group memberships and access to resources; it will not. The loss of the user's SID and group memberships can cause significant problems if you later realize you need the account.

Therefore, many organizations choose to decommission a user account in stages. First, the account is disabled. After a period of time, it is deleted. Active Directory actually maintains a subset of the account's properties—most notably its SID—for a period of time called the *tombstone lifetime*, which is 180 days by default. After that time, the account's record is removed from the directory. Windows Server 2008 R2 introduces the ability to recover an account from the Active Directory Recycle Bin, a feature discussed in Chapter 13.

You can also consider recycling a user account. If a user leaves your organization, you may eventually hire a replacement who will need very similar resource access, group memberships, and user rights as the previous user. You can disable the account until a replacement is found, then rename the account to match the new user's name. The previous user's SID, group memberships, and resource access are thereby transferred to the replacement. Alternately, you can use the previous user's account as a template and create a copy of the account for the new user. Lesson 1 explained the procedure for copying an account in Active Directory Users And Computers and indicated the limited number of properties that are copied. Lesson 2 explained how to copy a user account by using Windows PowerShell.

Moving a User Account

To move a user object in the Active Directory Users And Computers snap-in:

1. Right-click the user, and then click Move.
2. Click the folder to which you want to move the user account, and then click OK.

Alternately, you can:

- Drag the user object and drop it onto the destination OU.

To move a user with a command-line tool, use DSMove. DSMove uses the following syntax:

```
dsmove UserDN -newparent TargetOUDN
```

DSMove does not specify the *User* object class keyword. Instead, it simply indicates the DN of the user to move and, in the *TargetOUDN* placeholder, the distinguished name of the OU to which the user will be moved.

Consider that when you move a user, you might change the Group Policy objects (GPOs) that apply to that user. GPOs are discussed in a Chapter 6, "Implementing a Group Policy Infrastructure."

You can use the DSMove command with the -*newname* parameter to change the common name (CN) of the object.

In Windows PowerShell, you can use the *Move-ADObject* or *Move-Item* cmdlets to move a user to another OU.

PRACTICE Supporting User Objects and Accounts

In this practice, you perform procedures that reflect common tasks required to support users in an enterprise environment. To perform the exercises in this practice, you should have performed the practices in Lessons 1 and 2 so that the following user objects exist in the User Accounts OU:

- April Stewart
- Jeff Ford
- Mike Fitzmaurice
- Tony Krijnen

EXERCISE 1 View All Attributes of a User

In this exercise, you explore the Attribute Editor and use it to reveal and modify user attributes that are not visible in the Active Directory Users And Computers snap-in.

1. Log on to SERVER01 as Administrator and open the Active Directory Users And Computers snap-in.
2. In the User Accounts OU, right-click Tony Krijnen and choose Properties.
3. Examine the tabs of the Properties dialog box.

   What attributes are visible? Do you see any that you have not seen before? Do you see any attributes that, if configured, can provide useful information to your enterprise?
4. Click the Telephones tab and enter information into the Notes field. Click OK.
5. Click the View menu and select Advanced Features.
6. Open the properties of Tony Krijnen again and click the Attribute Editor tab.
7. Scroll to locate the *info* attribute.

   What do you see there?
8. Locate the *division* attribute, double-click it, type **Subsidiary,** and then click OK.
9. Locate the *employeeID* attribute, double-click it, type **104839,** and then click OK.
10. Examine other attributes that are visible in the Attribute Editor.

What attributes do you see that are not visible in the Active Directory Users And Computers snap-in? Can any of the hidden attributes, if configured, provide useful information to your enterprise?

11. Click OK to close the Properties dialog box.

EXERCISE 2   Manage Attributes of Multiple Objects

In this exercise, you select multiple objects and configure properties of the objects.

1. In the User Accounts OU, select April Stewart.

2. Hold the Ctrl key and select Jeff Ford and Mike Fitzmaurice.

   You should have three users selected now.

3. Right-click any of the selected users and choose Properties.

   A Properties dialog box appears with a subset of user properties that can be applied to multiple users simultaneously.

4. On the General tab, select the Office check box and type **Miami** in the Office text box.

5. Select the Description check box and type **Salesperson in Miami** in the Description text box.

6. Click the Account tab.

   In this scenario, these three users work on weekdays. They are not allowed to log on during the weekend.

7. Select the Logon Hours check box, and then click the Logon Hours button.

8. Click Sunday and click the Logon Denied button.

9. Click Saturday and click the Logon Denied button. Then click OK.

10. On the Address tab, select the Street, City, State/Province, and ZIP/Postal Code check boxes. Enter fictitious address information in these boxes.

11. Click the Organization tab and configure the company name, Contoso, Ltd.

12. Click OK.

13. Open the user objects to confirm that the changes were applied.

EXERCISE 3   Manage User Attributes with DS Commands

In this scenario, three users are relocating from Miami to Sydney. They will be taking several weeks to perform the relocation. You will manage their accounts through the process.

1. Open Active Directory Module For Windows PowerShell from the Administrative Tools program group.

   Windows PowerShell can launch executables just like Command Prompt.

2. Spend some time considering how you could, with a single command, change the *office* attribute of the three users to *Sydney* and disable the accounts so that they cannot be used while the employees are away. In addition, you want to change

the *description* attribute of the users to *Salesperson in Sydney.* What DS commands would you use?

3. Type the following command as one line, and then press Enter:

```
dsquery user -desc "*Miami*" | dsmod user -office "Sydney"
    -desc "Salesperson in Sydney" -disabled yes
```

You might think that it would be more efficient to query for users in the Miami office, and then change the office to Sydney. Unfortunately, the DSQuery command does not support the *office* attribute. Therefore, you must use another attribute as a criteria for the query. In this scenario, the *description* attribute of a user includes an indication of the office in which the user works.

4. In the Active Directory Users And Computers snap-in, open the user accounts to confirm that the changes were made.

5. You need to make a record of the pre–Windows 2000 logon names and user principal names of the salespeople in Sydney. What DS commands could you enter to show you that information?

6. Type the following command and press Enter:

```
dsquery user -desc "*Sydney*" | dsget user -samid -upn
```

The salespeople have arrived in Sydney. It is now time to enable their accounts.

7. You want to use Windows PowerShell cmdlets to enable the accounts of users in the Sydney office. Use the *Get-Help* cmdlet to learn about the *-Filter* parameter of the *Get-ADUser* cmdlet. Review the material in Lesson 2 about how to use *Set-ADUser* to enable a user account. Try to identify the command needed to achieve the task. Then continue to the next step, which presents the solution.

8. Type the following command and press Enter:

```
Get-ADUser -Filter {office -eq "Sydney"} | Set-ADUser -enabled $true
```

9. In the Active Directory Users And Computers snap-in, confirm that the three users' accounts are once again enabled.

EXERCISE 4   Reset a Password and Unlock a User Account

While he was relocating from Miami to Sydney, David Jones forgot his password. After you enabled his account, he attempted to log on several times with an incorrect password, and then his account was locked. In this exercise, you reset David's password and unlock his account.

1. In the Active Directory Users And Computers snap-in, select the User Accounts OU.

2. In the details pane, right-click David Jones' account and choose Reset Password.

3. Enter a new password for David in the New Password and Confirm Password boxes.

4. Ensure that the User Must Change Password At Next Logon check box is selected.

5. Select the Unlock The User's Account check box, and then click OK.

Lesson Summary

- Use the Attribute Editor to view and modify all attributes of a user object.
- User account properties can restrict the workstations to which a user logs on, the hours during which logon is allowed, and the date on which the account will expire.
- You can modify the attributes of multiple objects simultaneously by multi-selecting objects in the Active Directory Users And Computers snap-in, or by using DSMod. However, the properties you can change with these methods are limited. You can use the *Set-ADUser* cmdlet to modify all attributes of user objects as well.
- After you delete a user account, you can re-create an account with the same name, but the new account will not belong to the same groups or have the same resource access. You will have to rebuild those memberships and permissions for the new account.

Lesson Review

You can use the following questions to test your knowledge of the information in Lesson 3, "Supporting User Objects and Accounts." The questions are also available on the companion CD if you prefer to review them in electronic form.

> **NOTE ANSWERS**
>
> Answers to these questions and explanations of why each answer choice is right or wrong are located in the "Answers" section at the end of the book.

1. You want to set the Description property of 10 users in two different OUs. The users currently have the *Description* property configured as *Salesperson in Miammi*. You recently discovered the typographic error and want to change it to *Salesperson in Miami*. What can you do to make the change? (Choose all that apply.)

   A. Select all 10 users by holding the Ctrl key and opening the Properties dialog box.

   B. Use DSGet and DSMod.

   C. Use DSQuery and DSMod.

   D. Use Get-ADUser and Set-ADUser.

2. You want to move a user from the Paris OU to the Moscow OU. Which tools can you use? (Choose all that apply.)

   A. Move-Item

   B. Move-ADObject

   C. DSMove

   D. Redirusr.exe

   E. Active Directory Migration Tool

3. A user reports that she is receiving a logon message that states, "Your account is configured to prevent you from using the computer. Please try another computer." What should you do to enable her to log on to the computer?

   A. Click the Log On To button on the Account tab of her user account.

   B. Click the Allowed To Join Domain button in the New Computer dialog box.

   C. Use the DSMove command.

   D. Give her the right to log on locally, using the local security policy of the computer.

Chapter Review

To further practice and reinforce the skills you learned in this chapter, you can perform the following tasks:

- Review the chapter summary.
- Review the list of key terms introduced in this chapter.
- Complete the case scenarios. These scenarios set up real-word situations involving the topics of this chapter and ask you to create a solution.
- Complete the suggested practices.
- Take a practice test.

Chapter Summary

- A variety of tools are at your disposal for managing user objects throughout the life cycle of the account.
- Windows PowerShell is a powerful tool with which to automate administrative tasks.
- Because users are security principals, it is particularly important to manage accounts carefully and to be comfortable with the tasks, including resetting passwords; unlocking, enabling, and disabling accounts; moving and renaming accounts; and, eventually, deleting accounts.
- If you have a data source of user information, it is likely that you will be able to import it into Active Directory with CSVDE, LDIFDE, or Windows PowerShell.

Key Terms

The following terms were introduced in this chapter. Do you know what they mean?

- Object
- Method
- Property
- cmdlet
- pipeline

Case Scenario

In the following case scenario, you apply what you have learned about creating and maintaining user accounts. You can find answers to these questions in the "Answers" section at the end of this book.

Case Scenario: Import User Accounts

You are an administrator at a large university. Each term you receive a file containing information about incoming students. Your job is to create a user account for each of the new students. The file you receive is created in Microsoft Excel, and it contains name and contact information for each student. Your manager has asked you to have all accounts created four weeks before the beginning of the new term. In the past, you have created the accounts manually. This year, you want to automate the creation of the user accounts.

1. Which tool discussed in this chapter should you use to import the user accounts from the database? Why do you believe that tool is better than the other available user import tools?

2. What can you do to increase the security of the accounts you are creating, considering that they will be created four weeks before they are used for the first time?

3. After creating the accounts, you realize that you forgot to populate the *company* attribute with the name of your university. All the new student accounts are in an OU dedicated to new students. What can you do quickly to populate that attribute, using the Active Directory Users And Computers snap-in, Command Prompt, or Windows PowerShell?

Suggested Practices

To help you successfully master the exam objectives presented in this chapter, complete the following tasks.

Automate the Creation of User Accounts

In this practice, you apply the method presented in Lesson 2 to import users from a data source by using Windows PowerShell.

- **Practice 1** Create an Excel worksheet that will serve as a database of user accounts. In the first row of the worksheet, type the following attribute names, one attribute per column: *name,sAMAccountName,GivenName,Surname*. Populate the file with sample data. Remember that *GivenName* is the user's first name, and *Surname* is the user's last name. Save the file as a comma-separated text file. Use Windows PowerShell to create users from the data source. Refer to the section "Importing Users from a Database with Windows PowerShell" of Lesson 2 if you need assistance.

Maintain Active Directory Accounts

In this practice, you apply the methods presented in Chapter 3, "Administering User Accounts," for managing user accounts.

- **Practice 2** Lesson 3 illustrated several options for performing administrative tasks to support user accounts. It is an extremely valuable learning experience to step through the examples provided in the chapter and apply them, hands on. Treat each of the commands and scripts illustrated in this chapter as a practice. Be aware that the commands and scripts create and manipulate Active Directory objects that you might have created during practices in this lesson. You might have to delete or rename some of the objects you created during practices to avoid errors.

Use the Active Directory Administrative Console

In this practice, you explore the Active Directory Administrative Console (ADAC).

- **Practice 3** The section entitled "The Active Directory Administrative Center" in Lesson 2 discussed the ADAC. Perform the skills described in the section as a practice. Learn to switch between the list view and the tree view. Add and remove content from the Overview page. Add navigation nodes and navigate to containers beneath a navigation node. Explore the Tasks and Summary panels of a selected user object. Open a user object and examine the properties page. Experiment with the functionality of the Global Search feature.

Take a Practice Test

The practice tests on this book's companion CD offer many options. For example, you can test yourself on just one exam objective, or you can test yourself on all the 70-640 certification exam content. You can set up the test so that it closely simulates the experience of taking a certification exam, or you can set it up in study mode so that you can look at the correct answers and explanations after you answer each question.

> **MORE INFO** **PRACTICE TESTS**
>
> For details about all the practice test options available, see the "How to Use the Practice Tests" section in this book's Introduction.

CHAPTER 4

Managing Groups

A lthough users and computers, and even services, change over time, business roles and rules tend to remain more stable. Your business probably has a finance role, which requires certain capabilities in the enterprise. The user or users who perform that role will change, but the role will remain. For that reason, it is not practical to manage an enterprise by assigning rights and permissions to individual user, computer, or service identities. Management tasks should be associated with groups. In this training kit, you will learn to use groups to identify administrative and user roles, to filter Group Policy, to assign unique password policies, to assign rights and permissions, and more. To prepare you for those tasks, this lesson demonstrates how to create, modify, delete, and support group objects in an Active Directory Domain Services (AD DS) domain.

Exam objectives in this chapter:

- Automate creation of Active Directory accounts.
- Maintain Active Directory accounts.

Lessons in this chapter:

Before You Begin

This chapter applies Windows PowerShell, Csvde.exe, and Ldifde.exe to the task of automating computer account creation. Read Lesson 1, "Automating the Creation of User Accounts," and Lesson 2, "Administering with Windows PowerShell and Active Directory Administrative Center," of Chapter 3, "Administering User Accounts," prior to reading this chapter.

In addition, to perform exercises in this chapter, you must have created a domain controller named SERVER01 in a domain named contoso.com. See Chapter 1, "Creating an Active Directory Domain," for detailed steps of this task.

REAL WORLD

Dan Holme

Efficient and effective group management is a tremendous enabler for security, consistency, and productivity in an IT environment. As a consultant, I spend a lot of time with clients, aligning technology with their business needs. In the case of Microsoft Windows technologies, this entails defining and implementing business roles and rules so that administration can be defined, documented, and automated. And that process often requires improving clients' group management knowledge, technologies, and processes. Many IT professionals have come into Windows Server 2008 R2 Active Directory with practices developed in previous versions of Windows that do not take advantage of groups as fully as possible. In fact, I've seen so much wasted productivity and decreased security due to poor group management that I dedicated two chapters of my book, *Windows Administration Resource Kit: Productivity Solutions for IT Professionals* (Microsoft Press, 2008), to improving and automating group management. In this lesson, you learn what you need to know for the certification exam, and I share with you a few of the tips and best practices that you'll need to make the most of groups in a production environment. I highly recommend reading the resource kit for more information, guidance, and fantastic tools related to group management.

Lesson 1: Managing an Enterprise with Groups

You are certainly familiar with the purpose of groups: to collect items and manage them as a single entity. The implementation of group management in Active Directory is not intuitive; Active Directory is designed to support large, distributed environments, so it includes seven types of groups: two types of domain groups with three scopes each, plus local security groups. In this lesson, you learn the purpose of each of these groups, as well as how to align your business requirements with the potentially complex options that Active Directory provides.

After this lesson, you will be able to:
- Understand the role of groups in managing an enterprise.
- Define group naming conventions.
- Create groups by using the Active Directory Users And Computers snap-in.
- Understand, manage, and convert group type and scope.
- Identify group membership and nesting possibilities.
- Manage group membership.
- Develop a group management strategy.

Estimated lesson time: 45 minutes

Understanding the Importance of Groups

Groups are an important class of object because they collect users, computers, and other groups to create a single point of management.

The most straightforward and common use of a group is to grant permissions to a shared folder. A security group is a security principal with a security identifier (SID) and a *member* attribute that identifies members—users, computers, and other groups. If a group has Read access to a folder, for example, any of the group's members can read the folder. You do not have to grant Read access to each individual member—you can manage access to the folder simply by adding and removing members of the group.

Challenges of Managing Without Groups

- Imagine that all of the 100 users in the sales department require Read-level access to a shared folder called Sales on a server. Assigning permissions to each user individually is not a manageable solution. When new salespeople are hired, you must add the new accounts to the access control list (ACL) of the folder. When accounts are deleted, you must remove the permissions from the ACL to avoid an Account Unknown entry on the

ACL (as shown in Figure 4-1), which results from a SID on the ACL that refers to an account that cannot be resolved.

FIGURE 4-1 Access management without groups

- Imagine now that all of the 100 users in the sales department require Read access to three shared folders on three different servers; the management difficulty just increased significantly. How many permissions would you have to apply just to configure access to three folders on three different servers for 100 users? 300!

When you manage permissions by adding and removing identities to and from an ACL, it becomes difficult to answer the question, "Who can read the Sales folder?" To answer the question, you must reverse engineer the ACL. And, in the broader example, if the Sales folders are distributed across three servers, you would have to evaluate three separate ACLs to answer the question.

Groups Add Manageability

The example presented in the previous section may seem extreme, because you have no doubt learned that although assigning permissions to a resource for an individual identity—user or computer—is possible, the best practice is to assign a single permission to a group and then manage access to the resource simply by changing the membership of the group.

So, to continue the example, you could create a group called Sales and assign the group Allow Read permission on the Sales folder. This implementation is shown in Figure 4-2.

FIGURE 4-2 Assigning Allow Read permission to a group; groups add manageability

You now have a single point of management. The Sales group effectively manages access to the shared folder. You can add new sales users to the group, and they will gain access to the shared folder. When you delete an account, it is automatically deleted from the group, so you will not have irresolvable SIDs on your ACL. It is also easier to answer the question, "Who can read the Sales folder?" You can simply enumerate the membership of the Sales group. The Sales group has become the focus of access management tasks.

There's an extra benefit: Your ACL remains stable because the Sales group has Allow Read permission, so your backups will be easier. When you change the ACL of a folder, the ACL propagates to all child files and folders, setting the Archive flag and thereby requiring a backup of all files, even if the contents of the files have not changed.

Groups Add Scalability

If the sales users require Read access to three folders on three separate servers, you could assign the Sales group Allow Read permission on each of the three folders. After you assign the three permissions, the Sales group provides a single point of management for resource access, as shown in Figure 4-3.

The Sales group effectively manages access to all three shared folders. You can add new sales users to the group, and they will gain access to the three shared folders on the three servers. When you delete an account, it is automatically deleted from the group, so you will not have irresolvable SIDs on your ACLs.

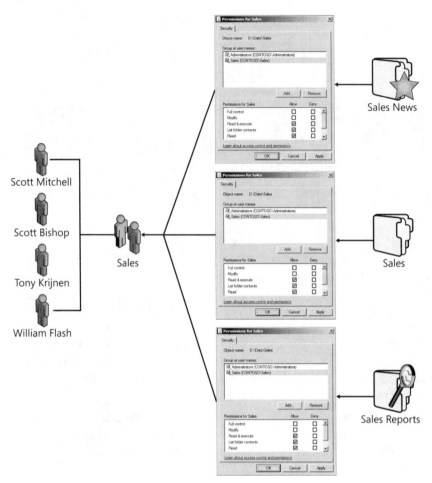

FIGURE 4-3 Assigning Allow Read permission on three folders; groups add scalability

One Type of Group Is Not Enough

Imagine now that it is not only salespeople who require Read access to the folders. The executives, the marketing department employees, and the sales consultant hired by your organization also require Read permission to the same folders.

You could add those groups to the ACL of the folders, granting each of them Allow Read permission, but soon you would have an ACL with multiple permissions, this time assigning the Allow Read permission to multiple groups instead of multiple users. This is shown in Figure 4-4.

FIGURE 4-4 One kind of group is not enough to efficiently manage permissions

To give the three groups and one user permission to the three folders on the three servers, you would have to add 12 permissions! The next group that required access would require three more changes to grant permissions to the ACLs of the three shared folders.

What if eight users who are not salespeople, marketing employees, or executives have a business need for Read access to the three folders? Do you add their individual user accounts to the ACLs? If so, that's 24 more permissions to add and manage!

You can see that using only one type of group—a role group that defines the business roles of users—quickly becomes an ineffective way of enabling management of access to the three folders. If the management rule suggests that three roles and nine additional users require access to the resource, you are assigning a total of 36 permissions on ACLs. It becomes very difficult to maintain compliance and to audit. Even simple questions such as, "Can you tell me every user who can read the Sales folders?" become difficult to answer.

Role-Based Management: Role Groups and Rule Groups

The solution is to recognize that you must address two management tasks to effectively manage this scenario: You must manage the users as collections, based on their business roles, and, separately, you must manage access to the three folders.

The three folders are also a collection of items: They are a single resource—a collection of Sales folders—that just happens to be distributed across three folders on three servers. And you are trying to manage Read access to that resource. You need a single point of management with which to manage access to the resource.

This requires another group—a group that represents Read access to the three folders on the three servers. Imagine that you create a group called ACL_Sales Folders_Read. This group will be assigned the Allow Read permission on the three folders. The Sales, Marketing, and Executives groups, along with the individual users, will all be members of the ACL_Sales Folders_Read group. You assign only three permissions: one on each folder, granting Read access to the ACL_Sales Folders_Read group. This is shown in Figure 4-5.

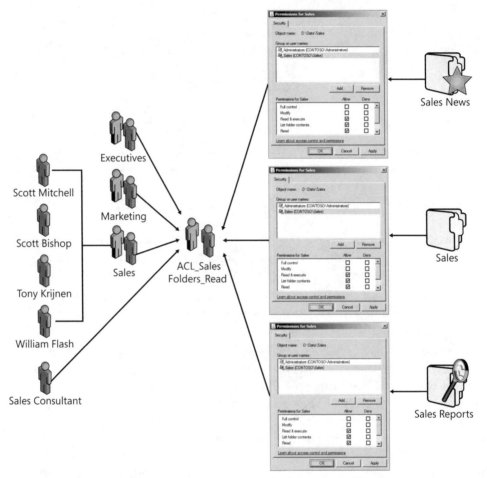

FIGURE 4-5 Role-based management uses role groups and rule groups to efficiently manage access to folders

The ACL_Sales Folders_Read group becomes the focus of access management. As additional groups or users require access to the folders, you add them to that group. It also becomes much easier to report who has access to the folders. Instead of having to examine the ACLs on each of the three folders, you simply examine the membership of the ACL_Sales Folders_Read group.

To effectively manage even a slightly complex enterprise, you need groups that perform two distinct purposes:

- **Groups that define roles**   These groups, referred to as *role groups*, contain users, computers, and other role groups based on common business characteristics such as location and job type.

- **Groups that define management rules**   These groups, referred to as *rule groups*, define how an enterprise resource is managed.

This approach to managing the enterprise with groups is called *role-based management*. You define roles of users based on business characteristics (for example, department or division affiliation such as sales, marketing, and executives), and you define management rules (for example, the rule that manages which roles and individuals can access the three folders).

You can achieve both management tasks by using groups in a directory. Roles are represented by groups that contain users, computers, and other roles. That's right, roles can include other roles—for example, a Managers role might include the Sales Managers, Finance Managers, and Production Managers roles. Management rules, such as the rule that defines and manages Read access to the three folders, are represented by groups as well. Rule groups contain roles and, occasionally, individual users or computers such as the sales consultant and eight other users in the example.

The key takeaway is that groups serve two distinct purposes: one group defines the role, and another defines how a resource is managed.

To achieve manageability of an enterprise of any size or complexity, you must manage groups effectively and have an infrastructure of groups that provide single points of management for roles and rules. That means, technically, that you will need groups that can include as members users, computers, other groups, and, possibly, security principals from other domains.

For more information about role-based management, see *Windows Administration Resource Kit: Productivity Solutions for IT Professionals*.

Defining Group Naming Conventions

To create a group by using the Active Directory Users And Computers snap-in, simply right-click the organizational unit (OU) in which you want to create a group, point to New, and then click Group. The New Object – Group dialog box, shown in Figure 4-6, lets you specify fundamental properties of the new group.

The following name properties can be configured here:

- **Group name**   *cn* attribute of group object; must be unique only within OU

- **Group name (Pre–Windows 2000)**   *sAMAccountName* attribute of group; unique in domain

FIGURE 4-6 The New Object – Group dialog box

The first properties you must configure are the group's names. A group, like a user or computer, has several names. The first, shown in the Group Name box in Figure 4-6, is used by Windows 2000 and later systems to identify the object—it becomes the *cn* and *name* attributes of the object. The second, the pre–Windows 2000 name, is the *sAMAccountName* attribute, used to identify the group to some applications and devices such as network attached storage (NAS) devices running non-Microsoft operating systems. The *cn* and *name* attributes must be unique only within the container—the OU—in which the group exists. The *sAMAccountName* must be unique in the entire domain. Technically, the *sAMAccountName* could be a different value than the *cn* and *name*, but this is highly discouraged. Choose a name that is unique in the domain, and use it in both name boxes in the New Object – Group dialog box.

> **BEST PRACTICE** **GROUP NAMES**
>
> Use the same name (unique in the domain) for both group name properties.

The following naming conventions are recommended:

- **Role groups.** Simple, unique name, such as Sales or Consultants
- **Management groups.** For example, ACL_Sales Folders_Read
  - **Prefix** This identifies the management purpose of group, such as ACL for groups managing access permissions to shared resources.
  - **Resource identifier** This is a unique identifier for what is being managed.
  - **Suffix** For resource access groups, this is the type of access the group manages.
  - **Delimiter** This should be a consistently used marker separating prefix, identifier, and suffix, such as an underscore (_). Do not use the delimiter elsewhere in the name—use it only as a delimiter.

The name you choose should help you manage the group and your enterprise on a day-to-day basis. It is recommended to follow a naming convention that identifies the type of group and the purpose of the group.

The example in the previous section used a group name, ACL_Sales Folders_Read. Let's examine how the recommendations listed earlier apply to the group name.

- **Prefix**   The prefix identifies the management purpose of the group. In this case, it is a group used to manage access permissions to a folder. It is used on access control lists, so the prefix ACL is used.

- **Resource identifier**   The main part of the name uniquely identifies the resource that is being managed with the group—in this example, Sales Folders.

- **Suffix**   The suffix further defines what is being managed by the group. In the case of resource access management groups, the suffix defines the level of access provided to members of the group. In our example, that is Read.

- **Delimiter**   A delimiter—in this case, an underscore—is used to separate parts of the name. Note that the delimiter is not used between the words *Sales* and *Folder*. Spaces are acceptable in group names—you just need to enclose such group names in quotes when you refer to them in commands or scripts. You can create scripts that use the delimiter to deconstruct group names to facilitate auditing and reporting.

Remember that role groups that define user roles are often used by non-technical users. For example, you might email-enable the Sales group so that it can be used as an email distribution list. Therefore, your naming convention for role groups should be simple and straightforward. In other words, do not use prefixes, suffixes, or delimiters when naming role groups—just use a descriptive user-friendly name.

For more information about managing groups effectively, see *Windows Administration Resource Kit: Productivity Solutions for IT Professionals*.

Understanding Group Types

There are two types of groups: security and distribution. When you create a group, you select the group type in the New Object – Group dialog box.

Distribution groups are used primarily by email applications. These groups are not security enabled so they cannot be given permission to resources. Sending a message to a distribution group sends the message to all members of the group.

Security groups are security principals with SIDs. These groups can therefore be used in permission entries in ACLs to control security for resource access. Security groups can also be used as distribution groups by email applications. If a group will be used to manage security, it must be a security group.

Because security groups can be used for both resource access and email distribution, many organizations use only security groups. However, if a group will be used only for email distribution, you should create the group as a distribution group. Otherwise, the group is assigned a SID and the SID is added to the user's security access token, which can lead to unnecessary bloat of the security token.

Understanding Group Scope

Groups have members: users, computers, and other groups; groups can be members of other groups, and groups can be referred to by ACLs, Group Policy object (GPO) filters, and other management components. *Group scope* affects each of these characteristics of a group: what it can contain, what it can belong to, and where it can be used. There are four group scopes: local, domain local, global, and universal.

The characteristics that define each scope fall into these categories:

- **Replication**   Where is the group defined and to what systems is the group replicated?

- **Membership**   What types of security principals can the group contain as members? Can the group include security principals from trusted domains? In Chapter 12, "Managing Multiple Domains and Forests," you learn about trust relationships, or *trusts*. A trust allows a domain to refer to another domain for user authentication, to include security principals from the other domain as group members, and to assign permissions to security principals in the other domain. The terminology used can be confusing. If Domain A trusts Domain B, then Domain A is the *trusting* domain and Domain B is the *trusted* domain. Domain A accepts the credentials of users in Domain B. It forwards requests by Domain B users to authenticate to a domain controller in Domain B because it *trusts* the identity store and authentication service of Domain B. Domain A can add Domain B's security principals to groups and ACLs in Domain A. See Chapter 12 for more detail.

- **Availability**   Where can the group be used? Is the group available to add to another group? Is the group available to add to an ACL?

Keep these broad characteristics in mind as you explore the details of each group scope.

EXAM TIP

In the context of group membership, remember that if Domain A trusts Domain B, Domain B is *trusted*, and its users and global groups can be members of domain local groups in Domain A. Additionally, Domain B's users and global groups can be assigned permissions to resources in Domain A.

Local Groups

Local groups are truly local—defined on and available to a single computer. Local groups are created in the security accounts manager (SAM) database of a domain member computer—both workstations and servers have local groups.

Local groups have the following characteristics:

- **Replication**   A local group is defined only in the local SAM database of a domain member server. The group and its membership are not replicated to any other system.
- **Membership**   A local group can include as members:
  - Any security principals from the domain: users, computers, global groups, or domain local groups
  - Users, computers, and global groups from any domain in the forest
  - Users, computers, and global groups from any trusted domain
  - Universal groups defined in any domain in the forest
- **Availability**   A local group has only computer-wide scope. It can be used in ACLs on the local computer only. A local group cannot be a member of any other group.

> **BEST PRACTICE   DO NOT MANAGE WITH LOCAL GROUPS**
>
> In a workgroup, you use local groups to manage security of resources on a system. In a domain, however, managing the local groups of individual computers becomes unwieldy and is, for the most part, unnecessary. It is not recommended to create custom local groups on domain members. In fact, the Users and Administrators local groups are the only local groups that you should be concerned with managing in a domain environment.

Domain Local Groups

Domain local groups are used primarily to manage permissions to resources. For example, the ACL_Sales Folder_Read group discussed earlier in the lesson would be created as a domain local group. Domain local groups have the following characteristics:

- **Replication**   A domain local group is defined in the domain naming context. The group object and its membership (the *member* attribute) are replicated to every domain controller in the domain.
- **Membership**   A domain local group can include as members:
  - Any security principals from the domain: users, computers, global groups, or other domain local groups
  - Users, computers, and global groups from any domain in the forest
  - Users, computers, and global groups from any trusted domain
  - Universal groups defined in any domain in the forest
- **Availability**   A domain local group can be added to ACLs on any resource on any domain member. Additionally, a domain local group can be a member of other domain local groups or even computer local groups.

The membership capabilities of a domain local group are identical to those of local groups, but the replication and availability of the domain local group make it useful across the entire domain.

> **BEST PRACTICE** **MANAGE ACCESS TO RESOURCES WITH DOMAIN LOCAL GROUPS**
>
> Domain local groups are well suited for defining business management rules, such as resource access rules, because the group can be applied anywhere in the domain, and it can include members of any type within the domain as well as members from trusted domains. For example, a domain local security group named ACL_Sales Folders_Read might be used to manage Read access to a collection of folders that contain sales information on one or more servers.

Global Groups

Global groups are used primarily to define collections of domain objects based on business roles. Role groups, such as the Sales and Marketing groups mentioned earlier, as well as roles of computers such as a Sales Laptops group, would be created as global groups. Global groups have the following characteristics:

- **Replication** A global group is defined in the domain naming context. The group object, including the *member* attribute, is replicated to all domain controllers in the domain.

- **Membership** A global group can include as members users, computers, and other global groups in the same domain only.

- **Availability** A global group is available for use by all domain members as well as by all other domains in the forest and all trusting external domains. A global group can be a member of any domain local or universal group in the domain or in the forest. It can also be a member of any domain local group in a trusting domain. Finally, a global group can be added to ACLs in the domain, in the forest, or in trusting domains.

As you can see, global groups have the most limited membership (only users, computers, and global groups from the same domain) but the broadest availability across the domain, the forest, and trusting domains.

> **BEST PRACTICE** **DEFINE ROLES WITH GLOBAL GROUPS**
>
> Global groups are well suited to defining roles, because roles are generally collections of objects from the same directory. For example, global security groups named Consultants and Sales might be used to define users who are consultants and salespeople, respectively.

Universal Groups

Universal groups have the following characteristics:

- **Replication** A universal group is defined in a single domain in the forest but is replicated to the global catalog. You will learn more about the global catalog in Chapter 12. Objects in the global catalog are readily accessible across the forest.

- **Membership** A universal group can include as members users, global groups, and other universal groups from any domain in the forest.

- **Availability** A universal group can be a member of a universal group or domain local group anywhere in the forest. Additionally, a universal group can be used to manage resources—for example, to assign permissions—anywhere in the forest and in trusting forests.

Universal groups are useful in multidomain forests. They let you define roles, or manage resources, that span more than one domain.

The best way to understand universal groups is through an example. Trey Research has a forest with three domains: Americas, Asia, and Europe. Each domain has user accounts and a global group called Regional Managers that includes the managers of that domain's region. Remember that global groups can contain only users from the same domain. A universal group called Trey Research Regional Managers is created, and the three Regional Managers groups are added as members. The Trey Research Regional Managers group therefore defines a role for the entire forest. As users are added to any one of the Regional Managers groups, they will, through group nesting, be members of the Trey Research Regional Managers group.

Trey Research is planning to release a new product that requires collaboration across its regions. Resources related to the project are stored on file servers in each domain. To define who has the ability to modify files related to the new product, a universal group is created called *ACL_New Product_Modify*. That group is assigned the Allow Modify permission to the shared folders on each of the file servers in each of the domains. The Trey Research Regional Managers group is made a member of the *ACL_New Product_Modify* group, as are various global groups and a handful of users from each of the regions.

> **BEST PRACTICE** **MANAGE ROLES AND RULES ACROSS DOMAINS IN A FOREST WITH UNIVERSAL GROUPS**
>
> As you can see from the example in this section, universal groups can help you represent and consolidate roles that span domains in a forest and define rules that can be applied across the forest.

Summarizing Group Membership Possibilities

For both the certification examinations and day-to-day administration, it is important that you are completely familiar with the membership characteristics of each group scope.

Table 4-1 summarizes the objects that can be members of each group scope.

TABLE 4-1 Group Scope and Members

GROUP SCOPE	MEMBERS FROM THE SAME DOMAIN	MEMBERS FROM ANOTHER DOMAIN IN THE SAME FOREST	MEMBERS FROM A TRUSTED EXTERNAL DOMAIN
Local	Users Computers Global groups Universal groups Domain local groups Local users defined on the same computer as the local group	Users Computers Global groups Universal groups	Users Computers Global groups
Domain Local	Users Computers Global groups Universal groups Domain local groups	Users Computers Global groups Universal groups	Users Computers Global groups
Universal	Users Computers Global groups Universal groups	Users Computers Global groups Universal groups	N/A
Global	Users Computers Global groups	N/A	N/A

✔ **Quick Check**

- Which types of objects can be members of a global group in a domain?

Quick Check Answer

- Global groups can contain only users, computers, and other global groups from the same domain.

Converting Group Scope and Type

If, after creating a group, you determine that you need to modify the group's scope or type, you can do so. Open the Properties dialog box of an existing group and, on the General tab, shown in Figure 4-7, you see the existing scope and type. At least one more scope and type are available for selection.

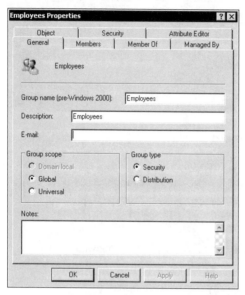

FIGURE 4-7 The General tab of a group's Properties dialog box

You can convert the group type at any time by changing the selection in the Group Type section of the General tab. Be cautious, however. When you convert a group from security to distribution, any resources to which the group had been assigned permission will no longer be accessible in the same way. After the group becomes a distribution group, users who log on to the domain will no longer include the group's SID in their security access tokens.

You can change the group scope in the following ways:

- Global to universal
- Domain local to universal
- Universal to global
- Universal to domain local

The only scope changes that you cannot make directly are from global to domain local or domain local to global. However, you can make these changes indirectly by first converting to universal scope, then converting to the desired scope. So all scope changes are possible.

Remember, however, that a group's scope determines the types of objects that can be members of the group. If a group already contains members or is a member of another group that would violate the new scope, you would be prevented from changing scope. For example, if a global group is a member of another global group, you cannot change the first group to universal scope, because a universal group cannot be a member of a global group. An explanatory error message, such as that shown in Figure 4-8, appears. You must correct the group's membership conflicts before you can change the group's scope.

FIGURE 4-8 The error produced when a group's membership will not allow a change of scope

The DSMod command, introduced in Chapter 3, can be used to change group type and scope by using the following syntax:

```
dsmod group GroupDN –secgrp { yes | no } –scope { l | g | u }
```

The *GroupDN* is the distinguished name of the group to modify. The following two parameters affect group scope and type:

- *-secgrp { yes | no }* specifies group type: security (*yes*) or distribution (*no*).
- *-scope { l | g | u }* determines the group scope: domain local (*l*), global (*g*), or universal (*u*).

Managing Group Membership

You can add or remove members of a group by using one of several methods.

The Members Tab

You can open the group's Properties dialog box and click the Members tab. To manage group membership using the group's Members tab:

1. Open the group's Properties dialog box.
2. Click the Members tab.
3. To remove a member, simply select the member and click Remove.
4. To add a member, click Add. The Select Users, Contacts, Computers, Or Groups dialog box appears, as shown in Figure 4-9.

FIGURE 4-9 Adding a member to a group

There are several tips worth mentioning about this process:

- In the Select dialog box, in the Enter The Object Names box, you can type multiple accounts separated by semicolons. For example, in Figure 4-9, both *sales* and *finance* are
entered, separated by a semicolon.

- You can type partial names of accounts—you do not need to type the full name.
Windows searches Active Directory for accounts that begin with the name you entered.
If there is only one match, Windows selects it automatically. If multiple accounts match,
the Multiple Names Found dialog box appears, in which you can select the object you
want. This shortcut—typing partial names—can save time when adding members to
groups and can help when you don't remember the exact name of a member.

- By default, Windows searches only for users and groups that match the names you
enter in the Select dialog box. If you want to add computers to a group, you must click
Object Types and select Computers.

- By default, Windows searches only domain accounts. If you want to search local
accounts, click Locations in the Select dialog box.

- If you cannot find the member you want to add, click Advanced in the Select dialog
box. A more powerful query window appears, giving you more options for searching
Active Directory.

The Member Of Tab

To manage group membership using the member object's Member Of tab:

1. Open the properties of the member object, and then click its Member Of tab.

2. To remove the object from a group, select the group and then click Remove.

3. To add the object to a group, click Add and select the group.

The Add To A Group Command

To manage group membership using the Add To A Group command:

1. Right-click one or more selected objects in the Active Directory Users And Computers details pane.

2. Click Add To A Group.

3. Use the Select dialog box to specify the group.

The *Member* and *MemberOf* Attributes

When you add a member to a group, you change the group's *member* attribute. The *member* attribute is a multivalued attribute. Each member is a value represented by the distinguished name (DN) of the member. If the member is moved or renamed, Active Directory automatically updates the *member* attributes of groups that include the member.

When you add a member to a group, the member's *memberOf* attribute is also updated, indirectly. The *memberOf* attribute is a special type of attribute called a *backlink*. It is updated by Active Directory when a forward link attribute, such as *member*, refers to the object. When you add a member to a group, you are always changing the group's *member* attribute. Therefore, when you use the Member Of tab of an object to add to a group, you are actually changing the group's *member* attribute, and Active Directory updates the member's *memberOf* attribute automatically.

Helping Membership Changes Take Effect Quickly

When you add a user to a group, the membership does not take effect immediately. Group membership is evaluated at logon for a user (at startup for a computer). Therefore, a user must log off and log on before the membership change becomes a part of the user's token.

Additionally, there can be a delay while the group membership change replicates. Replication is discussed in Chapter 11, "Managing Sites and Active Directory Replication." This is particularly true if your enterprise has more than one Active Directory site. You can facilitate the speed with which a change affects a user by making the change on a domain controller in the user's site. Right-click the domain in the Active Directory Users And Computers snap-in and choose Change Domain Controller.

Developing a Group Management Strategy

Adding groups to other groups—a process called *nesting*—can create a hierarchy of groups that support your business roles and management rules. Now that you have learned the business purposes and technical characteristics of groups, it is time to align the two in a strategy for group management.

Earlier in this lesson, you learned which types of objects *can* be members of each group scope. Now it is time to identify which types of objects *should* be members of each group scope. This leads to the best practice for group nesting, known as *IGDLA:*

- **I**dentities (user and computer accounts) are members of
- **G**lobal groups that represent business roles. Those role groups (global groups) are members of
- **D**omain **L**ocal groups that represent management rules—for example, managing who has Read permission to a specific collection of folders. These rule groups (domain local groups) are granted
- **A**ccess to resources. In the case of a shared folder, for example, access is granted by adding the domain local group to the folder's ACL, with a permission that provides the appropriate level of access.

A multidomain forest also contains universal groups that fit in between global and domain local groups. Global groups from multiple domains are members of a single universal group. That universal group is a member of domain local groups in multiple domains. You can remember the nesting as *IGUDLA*.

> **NOTE IGDLA VS. UGDLA**
>
> Some texts abbreviate the group nesting strategy as *UGDLA*: *U*sers go into *G*lobal groups, which go into *D*omain *L*ocal groups, which are given *A*ccess to resources. This text, and others, changes the abbreviation to *IGDLA*. Although users are members of groups, so are computers. For example, to deploy software to a collection of computers, you can make them members of a group that is used as a deployment target by your software distribution tools. Therefore, *identities* is more accurate than *users*. In addition, the change allows *U* to be used for *U*niversal groups in multidomain forest group nesting.

This best practice for implementing group nesting translates well even in multidomain scenarios. Consider Figure 4-10.

Figure 4-10 represents a group implementation that reflects not only the technical view of group management best practices (IGDLA) but also the business view of role-based, rule-based management.

FIGURE 4-10 A group management implementation

Consider the following scenario. The sales force at Contoso, Ltd., has just completed their fiscal year. Sales files from the previous year are in a folder called Sales. The sales force needs Read access to the Sales folder. Additionally, a team of auditors from Woodgrove Bank, a potential investor, requires Read access to the Sales folder to perform an audit. The steps to implement the security required by this scenario are as follows:

1. Assign users with common job responsibilities or other business characteristics to role groups implemented as global security groups.

   This happens separately in each domain. Salespeople at Contoso are added to a Sales role group. Auditors at Woodgrove Bank are added to an Auditors role group.

2. Create a group to represent the business rule regarding who can access the Sales folder with Read permission.

   This is implemented in the domain that is managing the business rule. In this case, the business rule is Read-level access to the Sales folder, and the Contoso domain (in which the Sales folder resides) manages the access. The resource access management rule group is created as a domain local group, ACL_Sales Folders_Read.

3. Add the role groups to the resource access management rule group ACL_Sales Folders_Read to represent the management rule.

   The role groups you add can come from any domain in the forest or from a trusted domain such as Woodgrove Bank. Global groups from trusted external domains, or from any domain in the same forest, can be members of a domain local group.

4. Assign to the rule group the permission that implements the required level of access.

   In this case, grant the Allow Read permission to the domain local group ACL_Sales Folders_Read.

This strategy results in single points of management, reducing the management burden. One point of management defines who is in Sales, and one defines who is an Auditor. Those roles, of course, are likely to have a variety of permissions to resources beyond simply the Contoso domain's Sales folder. Another single point of management determines who has Read access to the Sales folder. And, of course, the Sales folder might not just be a single folder on a single server: It could be a collection of folders across multiple servers, each of which assigns Allow Read permission to the single domain local group.

> **NOTE ROLE-BASED MANAGEMENT**
>
> Role-based management is a concept used throughout information technology and information protection, and it can be attained with out-of-the-box capabilities of Active Directory. IGDLA is the implementation of role-based management using Active Directory groups.

PRACTICE Creating and Managing Groups

In this practice, you create groups, experiment with group membership, and convert group type and scope. Before performing the exercises in this practice, you must create the following objects in the contoso.com domain:

- A first-level OU named Groups
- A first-level OU named User Accounts
- User objects in the User Accounts OU for David Jones, Jeff Ford, and Tony Krijnen

EXERCISE 1 Create Groups

In this exercise, you create groups of different scopes and types.

1. Log on to SERVER01 as Administrator. Open the Active Directory Users And Computers snap-in and click the Groups OU in the tree pane.

   If the Sales group already exists, delete the group.

2. Right-click the Groups OU, point to New, and then click Group.

3. In the Group Name box, type **Sales**.

4. Select the Global group scope and Security group type. Click OK.

5. Right-click the Sales group and choose Properties.

6. On the Members tab, click Add. Type **Jeff; Tony** and click OK. Click OK to close the Properties dialog box.

7. Repeat steps 2–4 to create two global security groups named Marketing and Consultants.

8. Repeat steps 2–4 to create a domain local security group named ACL_Sales Folder_Read.

9. Open the properties of the ACL_Sales Folder_Read group.

10. On the Members tab, click Add. Type **Sales;Marketing;Consultants** and click OK.

11. Click Add. Type **David** and click OK. Click OK to close the Properties dialog box.

12. Open the Properties dialog box of the Marketing group.

13. On the Members tab, click Add.

14. Type **ACL_Sales Folder_Read** and click OK.

   You are unable to add a domain local group to a global group.

15. Close all open dialog boxes.

16. Create a folder named Sales on the C drive.

17. Right-click the Sales folder, click Properties, and then click the Security tab.

18. Click Edit, and then click Add.

19 Click Advanced, and then click Find Now.

   Notice that by using a prefix for group names, such as the *ACL_* prefix for resource access groups, you can find them quickly, grouped together at the top of the list.

20. Close all open dialog boxes.

21. Switch to Active Directory Users And Computers, right-click the Groups OU, click New, and then click Group.

22. In the Group Name box, type **Employees**.

23. Select the Domain Local group scope and the Distribution group type. Click OK.

EXERCISE 2   Convert Group Type and Scope

In this exercise, you learn how to convert group type and scope.

1. Right-click the Employees group and choose Properties.

2. Change the group type to Security. Click Apply.

   Consider: Can you change the group scope from Domain Local to Global? How?

3. Change the group scope to Universal. Click Apply.

4. Change the group scope to Global. Click Apply.

5. Click OK to close the Properties dialog box.

Lesson Summary

- There are two types of groups: security and distribution. Security groups can be assigned permissions and can be mail-enabled. Distribution groups are used primarily as email distribution lists—they cannot be assigned permissions to resources.

- In addition to local groups, which are maintained only in the local SAM database of a domain member server, there are three domain group scopes: global, domain local, and universal.

- The group scope affects the group's replication, the types of objects that can be members of the group, and the group's availability to be a member of another group or to be used for management tasks such as assigning permissions.

- You can convert group type and scope after creating the group.

- An enterprise group management strategy involves defining user roles as global security groups, and then creating groups that enable you to manage rules. For example, to manage access to a resource at a particular level, such as Read, you create a domain local security group, and then assign that group Read permission to the resource. The result is that user and computer identities become members of global groups, which are then nested into domain local groups, which are given access to resources. This group nesting strategy is abbreviated as *IGDLA*.

Lesson Review

You can use the following questions to test your knowledge of the information in Lesson 1, "Managing an Enterprise with Groups." The questions are also available on the companion CD if you prefer to review them in electronic form.

> **NOTE   ANSWERS**
>
> Answers to these questions and explanations of why each answer choice is right or wrong are located in the "Answers" section at the end of the book.

1. A new project requires that users in your domain and in the domain of a partner organization have access to a shared folder on your file server. Which type of group should you create to manage the access to the shared folder?

   A. Universal security group

   B. Domain local security group

   C. Global security group

   D. Domain local distribution group

2. Your domain includes a global distribution group named Company Update. It has been used to send company news by email to its members. You have decided to allow all members to contribute to the newsletter by creating a shared folder on a file server. What must you do to allow group members access to the shared folder?

    A. Change the group scope to domain local

    B. Change the group scope to universal

    C. Add the group to the Domain Users group

    D. Use DSMod with the *-secgrp yes* parameter

3. You have created a global security group in the contoso.com domain named Corporate Managers. Which members can be added to the group? (Choose all that apply.)

    A. Sales Managers, a global group in the fabrikam.com domain, a trusted domain of a partner company

    B. Sales Managers, a global group in the tailspintoys.com domain, a domain in the contoso.com forest

    C. Linda Mitchell, a user in the tailspintoys.com domain, a domain in the contoso.com forest

    D. Jeff Ford, a user in the fabrikam.com domain, a trusted domain of a partner company

    E. Mike Danseglio, a user in the contoso.com domain

    F. Sales Executives, a global group in the contoso.com domain

    G. Sales Directors, a domain local group in the contoso.com domain

    H. European Sales Managers, a universal group in the contoso.com forest

Lesson 2: Automating the Creation and Management of Groups

In Lesson 1 you learned the steps for creating groups, choosing group scope and type, and configuring group membership, using the Active Directory Users And Computers snap-in. When you need to create more than one group at a time, or when you want to automate group creation, you must use other tools. Chapter 3 introduced you to command-line and automation tools, including CSVDE, LDIFDE, DSAdd, and Windows PowerShell. These tools can also be used to automate the creation and management of group objects. In this lesson, you'll learn how to manage the life cycle of group objects, from beginning to end, by using command-line and automation tools.

> **After this lesson, you will be able to:**
> - Create groups with DSAdd, CSVDE, and LDIFDE.
> - Manage group membership with DSMod, LDIFDE, and Windows PowerShell.
> - Enumerate group membership with DSGet.
> - Move and delete groups with DSMove and DSRm.
> - Copy group membership.
>
> **Estimated lesson time: 45 minutes**

Creating Groups with DSAdd

The DSAdd command, introduced in Chapter 3, lets you add objects to Active Directory. To add a group, type the following command:

```
dsadd group GroupDN
```

where *GroupDN* is the distinguished name (DN) of the group, such as "CN=Finance Managers, OU=Groups,DC=contoso,DC=com." Be certain to surround the DN with quotes if the DN includes spaces.

For example, to create a new global security group named Marketing in the Groups OU of the contoso.com domain, the command would be:

```
dsadd group "CN=Marketing,OU=Groups,DC=contoso,DC=com" -samid Marketing -secgrp
yes -scope g
```

You can also provide the *GroupDN* parameter in one of the following ways:

- By piping a list of DNs from another command such as DSQuery.
- By typing each DN on the command line, separated by spaces.

- By leaving the DN parameter empty, at which point you can type the DNs one at a time at the keyboard console of the command prompt. Press Enter after each DN. After the last DN, press Ctrl+Z, and then press Enter.

Each of these three options allows you to generate multiple groups simultaneously with DSAdd. You can also use the DSAdd command with more than one *GroupDN* on the command line, each separated by a space, to generate multiple groups.

The DSAdd command can also configure attributes of the groups you create with the following optional parameters:

- **-secgrp { yes | no }**   Specifies group type: security (*yes*) or distribution (*no*).

- **-scope { l | g | u }**   Determines the group scope: domain local (*l*), global (*g*), or universal (*u*).

- **-samid *Name***   Specifies the *sAMAccountName* of the group. If not specified, the name of the group from its DN is used. It is recommended that the *sAMAccountName* and the group name be the same, so you do not need to include this parameter when using DSAdd.

- **-desc *Description***   Configures the group's description.

- **-members *MemberDN***   Adds members to the group. Members are specified by their DNs in a space-separated list.

- **-member of *GroupDN ...***   Makes the new group a member of one or more existing groups. The groups are specified by their DNs in a space-separated list.

Importing Groups with CSVDE

Chapter 3 also introduced you to Comma-Separated Values Data Exchange (CSVDE), which imports data from comma-separated values (.csv) files. It also exports data to a .csv file. The following example shows a .csv file that will create a group, Marketing, and populate the group with two initial members, Linda Mitchell and Scott Mitchell.

```
objectClass,sAMAccountName,DN,member
group,Marketing,"CN=Marketing,OU=Groups,DC=contoso,DC=com",
    "CN=Linda Mitchell,OU=User Accounts,DC=contoso,DC=com;
    CN=Scott Mitchell,OU=User Accounts,DC=contoso,DC=com"
```

The .csv file is two lines. The first line contains the attribute names, and the second line contains the values for the new group, *Marketing*. The second line is wrapped for presentation in this text.

Take note of the use of quotation marks in the preceding example. Quotation marks are required when an attribute includes a comma; without quotation marks, the comma would be interpreted as a delimiter. The DN of the group includes commas, so it must be surrounded by quotation marks. In the case of a multivalued attribute such as *member*, each value is separated by a semicolon—there are two values in *member* in the example. The entire *member* attribute is surrounded by quotation marks, not each individual value of the *member* attribute.

You can import this file into Active Directory by using the command:

```
csvde -i -f "filename" [-k]
```

The -i parameter specifies import mode. Without it, CSVDE uses export mode. The -f parameter precedes the filename, and the -k parameter ensures that processing continues even if errors are encountered, such as if the object already exists or the member cannot be found.

EXAM TIP

CSVDE can be used to create objects, but not to modify existing objects. You cannot use CSVDE to import members to existing groups.

Importing Groups with LDIFDE

LDAP Data Interchange Format Data Exchange (LDIFDE), as you learned in Chapter 3, is a tool that imports and exports files in the Lightweight Directory Access Protocol Data Interchange Format (LDIF) format. LDIF files are text files within which operations are specified by a block of lines separated by a blank line. Each operation begins with the DN of the object that is the target of the operation. The next line, *changeType*, specifies the type of operation: *add*, *modify*, or *delete*.

The following LDIF file creates two groups, Finance and Research, in the Groups OU of the contoso.com domain:

```
DN: CN=Finance,OU=Groups,DC=contoso,DC=com
changeType: add
CN: Finance
description: Finance Users
objectClass: group
sAMAccountName: Finance

DN: CN=Research,OU=Groups,DC=contoso,DC=com
changeType: add
CN: Research
description: Research Users
objectClass: group
sAMAccountName: Research
```

Convention would suggest saving the file with an .ldf extension—for example, Groups.ldf. To import the groups into the directory, issue the Ldifde.exe command, as shown here:

```
ldifde -i -f groups.ldf -k
```

The -i parameter specifies import mode. Without it, LDIFDE uses export mode. The -f parameter precedes the filename, and the -k parameter ensures that processing continues even if errors are encountered, such as if the object already exists.

Modifying Group Membership with LDIFDE

LDIFDE can also be used to modify existing objects in Active Directory, using LDIF operations with a *changeType* of *modify*. To add two members to the Finance group, the LDIF file would be:

```
dn: CN=Finance,OU=Groups,DC=contoso,DC=com
changeType: modify
add: member
member: CN=April Stewart,OU=User Accounts,dc=contoso,dc=com
member: CN=Mike Fitzmaurice,OU=User Accounts,dc=contoso,dc=com
-
```

The *changeType* is set to *modify*, and then the change operation is specified: *add* objects to the *member* attribute. Each new member is then listed on a separate line that begins with the *member* attribute name. The change operation is terminated with a line containing a single dash. Changing the third line to the following would remove the two specified members from the group:

```
delete: member
```

Retrieving Group Membership with DSGet

The DSMod and DSGet commands discussed in Chapter 3 are particularly helpful for managing the membership of groups. There is no option in the Active Directory Users And Computers snap-in to list all the members of a group including nested members. You can see only direct members of a group on the group's Members tab. Similarly, there is no way to list all the groups to which a user or computer belongs, including nested groups. You can see only direct membership on the user's or computer's Member Of tab.

The DSGet command lets you retrieve a complete list of a group's membership, including nested members, with the following syntax:

```
dsget group "GroupDN" -members [-expand]
```

The *-expand* parameter performs the magic of expanding nested groups' members.

Similarly, the DSGet command can be used to retrieve a complete list of groups to which a user or computer belongs, again by using the *-expand* parameter in the following commands:

```
dsget user "UserDN" -memberof [-expand]
dsget computer "ComputerDN" -memberof [-expand]
```

The *-memberof* parameter returns the value of the user's or computer's *memberOf* attribute, showing the groups to which the object directly belongs. When you add the *-expand* parameter, those groups are searched recursively, producing an exhaustive list of all groups to which the object belongs in the domain.

Changing Group Membership with DSMod

The DSMod command was applied in Lesson 1 to modify the scope and type of a group. The command's basic syntax is:

```
dsmod group "GroupDN" [options]
```

You can use options such as *-samid* and *-desc* to modify the *sAMAccountName* and *description* attributes of the group. Most useful, however, are the options that allow you to modify a group's membership:

- **-addmbr** *"Member DN"*   Adds members to the group
- **-rmmbr** *"Member DN"*   Removes members from the group

As with all DS commands, *Member DN* is the distinguished name of another Active Directory object, surrounded by quotes if the DN includes spaces. Multiple *Member DN* entries can be included, separated by spaces. For example, to add Mike Danseglio to the Research group, the DSMod command would be:

```
dsmod group "CN=Research,OU=Groups,DC=contoso,DC=com"
   -addmbr "CN=Mike Danseglio,OU=User Accounts,DC=contoso,DC=com"
```

Copying Group Membership

You can use DSGet in combination with DSMod to copy group membership. In the following example, the DSGet command is used to get information about all the members of the Sales group, and then, by piping that list to DSMod, add those users to the Marketing group:

```
dsget group "CN=Sales,OU=Groups,DC=contoso,DC=com" -members |
   dsmod group "CN=Marketing,OU=Groups,DC=contoso,DC=com" -addmbr
```

Notice the use of piping. The "output" of DSGet (distinguished names of members of the first group) is piped, using the pipe symbol ("|"), to act as the input for the DNs that are omitted after the *-addmbr* parameter.

Similarly, the DSGet and DSMod commands can work together to copy the group membership of one object, such as a user, to another object:

```
dsget user "Source User DN" -memberof | dsmod group -addmbr "Target User DN"
```

Moving and Renaming Groups with DSMove

You can move and rename groups in Active Directory Users And Computers by right-clicking the group and then clicking the Move or the Rename command.

The DSMove command, also discussed in Chapter 3, enables you to move or rename an object within a domain. You cannot use it to move objects between domains. Its basic syntax is:

```
dsmove ObjectDN [-newname NewName] [-newparent TargetOUDN]
```

The object is specified by using its distinguished name in the *ObjectDN* parameter. To rename the object, specify its new common name as the value of the *-newname* parameter. To move an object to a new location, specify the distinguished name of the target container as the value of the *-newparent* parameter.

For example, to change the name of the Marketing group to Public Relations, type:

```
dsmove "CN=Marketing,OU=Groups,DC=contoso,DC=com" -newname "Public Relations"
```

To then move that renamed group to the Marketing OU, type:

```
dsmove "CN=Public Relations,OU=Groups,DC=contoso,DC=com" -newparent
"OU=Marketing,DC=contoso,DC=com"
```

> **NOTE YOU'RE NOT LIMITED TO THE COMMAND LINE**
>
> You can also move or rename a group in the Active Directory Users And Computers snap-in by right-clicking the group and choosing Move or Rename from the context menu.

Deleting Groups with DSRm

DSRm can be used to delete a group or any other Active Directory object. The basic syntax of DSRm is:

```
dsrm ObjectDN ... [-subtree [-exclude]] [-noprompt] [-c]
```

The object is specified by its distinguished name in the *ObjectDN* parameter. You are prompted to confirm the deletion of each object unless you specify the *-noprompt* parameter. The *-c* parameter puts DSRm into continuous operation mode, in which errors are reported, but the command keeps processing additional objects. Without the *-c* switch, processing halts on the first error.

The *-subtree* parameter causes DSRm to delete the object and all child objects. The *-subtree -exclude* option deletes all child objects, but not the object itself.

To delete the Public Relations group, type:

```
dsrm "CN=Public Relations,OU=Marketing,DC=contoso,DC=com"
```

You can also delete a group in the Active Directory Users And Computers snap-in by right-clicking the group and choosing the Delete command.

> **NOTE KNOW THE IMPACT BEFORE DELETING A GROUP**
>
> When you delete a group, you are removing a point of management in your organization. Be certain that you have evaluated the environment to verify that no permissions or other resources rely on the group. Deleting a group is a serious action with potentially significant consequences. When you delete a group, you remove its SID. Re-creating the group with the same name does not restore permissions, because the new group's SID is different from that of the original group.

It is recommended that, before you delete a group, you record its membership and remove all members for a period of time to determine whether the members lose access to any resources. If anything goes wrong, simply re-add the members. If the test succeeds, delete the group.

Managing Groups with Windows PowerShell

Windows PowerShell makes it easy to manage groups. The following cmdlets work with Active Directory group objects:

- **New-ADGroup**   Creates a group.
- **Remove-ADGroup**   Deletes a group.
- **Get-ADGroup**   Retrieves an object reference to a group.
- **Set-ADGroup**   Configures properties of a group.
- **Add-ADGroupMember**   Adds a member to a group.
- **Remove-ADGroupMember**   Removes a member from a group.
- **Get-ADGroupMember**   Enumerates the members of a group. The *-recursive* parameter enumerates members of nested groups.

As you learned in Chapter 3, you can use the *Get-Help* cmdlet to learn more about these cmdlets. You use Windows PowerShell to create groups in the Practice for this lesson.

PRACTICE   **Automating the Creation and Management of Groups**

In this practice, you use DS commands, CSVDE, LDIFDE, and Windows PowerShell to perform group management tasks. Before performing the exercises in this practice, you need to create the following objects in the contoso.com domain:

- A first-level OU named Groups
- A first-level OU named User Accounts
- User objects in the User Accounts OU for Linda Mitchell, Scott Mitchell, Jeff Ford, Mike Fitzmaurice, Mike Danseglio, April Stewart, and Tony Krijnen

In addition, *delete* any groups with the following names: Finance, Accounting.

EXERCISE 1   **Manage Groups with Windows PowerShell**

In this exercise, you use Windows PowerShell to create a group.

1. Log on to SERVER01 as Administrator.
2. Open Active Directory Module For Windows PowerShell. Type the following command on one line:

```
New-ADGroup -Path "OU=Groups,DC=contoso,DC=com" -Name "PowerShell Experts"
   -sAMAccountName "PowerShell Experts" -GroupCategory Security -GroupScope Global
```

3. Open the Active Directory Users And Computers snap-in. Select the Groups OU and confirm that the PowerShell Experts group was created.

4. Switch to Windows PowerShell. Type the following command on one line:

```
Add-ADGroupMember -Identity "PowerShell Experts"
   -Members "CN=Mike Danseglio,OU=User Accounts,DC=contoso,DC=com"
```

5. Type the following command:

```
Get-ADGroupMember -Identity "PowerShell Experts"
```

6. Type the following command:

```
Get-Command *ADGroup*
```

EXERCISE 2 Create a Group with DSAdd

In this exercise, you use DSAdd to create a group. DSAdd can create a group, and even populate its membership, with a single command.

1. Type the following command on one line. Then press Enter.

```
dsadd group "CN=Finance,OU=Groups,DC=contoso,DC=com" -samid Finance -secgrp
yes -scope g
```

2. Open the Active Directory Users And Computers snap-in and confirm that the group was created successfully. If the Active Directory Users And Computers snap-in was open prior to performing step 2, refresh the view.

EXERCISE 3 Import Groups with CSVDE

1. Open Notepad and type the following two lines. Note that the second line is wrapped for readability in this text.

```
objectClass,sAMAccountName,DN,member

group,Accounting,"CN=Accounting,OU=Groups,DC=contoso,DC=com",
    "CN=Linda Mitchell,OU=User Accounts,DC=contoso,DC=com;
    CN=Scott Mitchell,OU=User Accounts,DC=contoso,DC=com"
```

2. Save the file to your Documents folder with the name **"Importgroups.csv"** (including the quotes so that Notepad doesn't add a .txt extension).

3. Open Command Prompt, and type the following command:

```
csvde -i -f "%userprofile%\documents\importgroups.csv"
```

4. Switch to the Active Directory Users And Computers snap-in, refresh the view of the Groups OU, and check to confirm that the group was created successfully.

EXERCISE 4　Modify Group Membership with LDIFDE

CSVDE cannot modify the membership of existing groups, but LDIFDE can. In this exercise, you use LDIFDE to modify the group membership of the Accounting group you imported in Exercise 3, "Import Groups with CSVDE."

1. Open Notepad and type the following lines:

```
dn: CN=Accounting,OU=Groups,DC=contoso,DC=com
changetype: modify
add: member
member: CN=April Stewart,OU=User Accounts,dc=contoso,dc=com
member: CN=Mike Fitzmaurice,OU=User Accounts,dc=contoso,dc=com
-

dn: CN= Accounting,OU=Groups,DC=contoso,DC=com
changetype: modify
delete: member
member: CN=Linda Mitchell,OU=User Accounts,dc=contoso,dc=com
-
```

   Be sure to include the dashes after each block and the blank line between the two blocks.

2. Save the file to your Documents folder as "**MembershipChange.ldf**" (including the quotes so that Notepad doesn't add a .txt extension).

3. Switch to Command Prompt.

4. Type the following command and press Enter:

```
ldifde -i -f "%userprofile%\documents\membershipchange.ldf"
```

5. Using the Active Directory Users And Computers snap-in, confirm that the membership of the Accounting group changed according to the instructions of the LDIF file. It should now include April Stewart, Mike Fitzmaurice, and Scott Mitchell.

EXERCISE 5　Modify Group Membership with DSMod

In this exercise, you add a user and a group to the Finance group, using the DSMod command.

1. Switch to Command Prompt.

2. Type the following command on one line to change the membership of the Finance group:

```
dsmod group "CN=Finance,OU=Groups,DC=contoso,DC=com"
    -addmbr "CN=Tony Krijnen,OU=User Accounts,DC=contoso,DC=com"
    "CN=Accounting,OU=Groups,DC=contoso,DC=com"
```

3. In the Active Directory Users And Computers snap-in, confirm that the membership of the Finance group consists of Tony Krijnen and the Accounting group.

EXERCISE 6 Confirm Group Membership with DSGet and Windows PowerShell

Evaluating effective group membership is difficult with the Active Directory Users And Computers snap-in but easy with the DSGet command in Windows PowerShell. In this exercise, you look at both the full membership of a group and the group memberships of a user.

1. Switch to Command Prompt.

2. List the direct members of the Accounting group by typing the following command and then pressing Enter:

   ```
   dsget group "CN=Accounting,OU=Groups,DC=contoso,DC=com" -members
   ```

3. List the direct members of the Finance group by typing the following command and then pressing Enter:

   ```
   dsget group "CN=Finance,OU=Groups,DC=contoso,DC=com" -members
   ```

4. List the full list of members of the Finance group by typing the following command and then pressing Enter:

   ```
   dsget group "CN=Finance,OU=Groups,DC=contoso,DC=com" -members -expand
   ```

5. List the direct group membership of Scott Mitchell by typing the following command and then pressing Enter:

   ```
   dsget user "CN=Scott Mitchell,OU=User Accounts,DC=contoso,DC=com" -memberof
   ```

6. List the full group membership of Scott Mitchell by typing the following command and then pressing Enter:

   ```
   dsget user "CN=Scott Mitchell,OU=User Accounts,DC=contoso,DC=com" -memberof
   -expand
   ```

7. Switch to Active Directory Module For Windows PowerShell, type the following command, and then press Enter:

   ```
   Get-ADGroupMember "Finance" -recursive | Select sAMAccountName
   ```

   Select is an alias for the *Select-Object* cmdlet, which takes the objects in the pipeline and selects one or more properties of the objects. Used here, it makes the output of the *Get-ADGroupMember* cmdlet more readable. Try it without the pipe and the *Select* cmdlet to see the difference.

Lesson Summary

- You can create groups with DSAdd, CSVDE, LDIFDE, and Windows PowerShell.
- LDIFDE, DSMod, and Windows PowerShell can modify the membership of existing groups.
- The DSGet command and Windows PowerShell can list the full membership of a group, including nested groups.

Lesson Review

You can use the following questions to test your knowledge of the information in Lesson 2, "Automating the Creation and Management of Groups." The questions are also available on the companion CD if you prefer to review them in electronic form.

> **NOTE ANSWERS**
>
> Answers to these questions and explanations of why each answer choice is right or wrong are located in the "Answers" section at the end of the book.

1. Which of the following can be used to remove members from a group? (Choose all that apply.)

   A. Remove-Item

   B. DSRm

   C. DSMod

   D. LDIFDE

   E. CSVDE

2. You are using DSMod to add a domain local group named GroupA to a global group named GroupB. You are receiving errors. Which command will solve the problem so that you can add GroupA to GroupB? (Choose all that apply.)

   A. Dsrm.exe

   B. Dsmod.exe

   C. Dsquery.exe

   D. Dsget.exe

3. Your management has asked you to produce a list of all users who belong to the Special Project group, including those users belonging to groups nested into Special Project. Which of the following can you use? (Choose all that apply.)

   A. *Get-ADGroupMember*

   B. Dsquery.exe

   C. LDIFDE

   D. Dsget.exe

Lesson 3: Administering Groups in an Enterprise

Lessons 1 and 2 prepared you to perform daily administrative tasks related to groups in Active Directory. You learned to create, modify, and delete groups, using a variety of tools and procedures. This lesson rounds out your exploration of groups by preparing you to take advantage of useful group attributes for documenting groups, delegate the management of group membership to specific administrative teams or individuals, and break away from reliance on some of the Active Directory and Windows default groups.

> **After this lesson, you will be able to:**
> - Document the purpose of a group by using the group's attributes.
> - Protect a group from accidental deletion.
> - Delegate group membership management using the Managed By tab.
> - Create a shadow group.
> - Understand default (Builtin) groups.
> - Assign permissions to special identities.
>
> **Estimated lesson time: 45 minutes**

Best Practices for Group Attributes

Creating a group in Active Directory is easy. It is not so easy to make sure that the group is used correctly over time. You can facilitate the correct management and use of a group by documenting its purpose to help administrators understand how and when to use the group. The following best practices which, although unlikely to be addressed by the certification exam, will prove immensely useful to your enterprise group administration:

- **Establish and adhere to a strict naming convention** Lesson 1 addressed a suggested naming convention. In the context of ongoing group administration, establishing and following group naming standards increases administrative productivity. Using prefixes to indicate the purpose of a group, and using a consistent delimiter between the prefix and the descriptive part of the group names, can help locate the correct group for a particular purpose. For example, the prefix APP can be used to designate groups that are used to manage applications, and the prefix ACL can be used for groups that are assigned permissions on ACLs. With such prefixes, it becomes easier to locate and interpret the purpose of groups named APP_Accounting versus ACL_Accounting_Read. The former is used to manage the deployment of the accounting software, and the latter provides read access to the accounting folder. Prefixes also help group the names of groups in the user interface. Figure 4-11 shows an example. When attempting to locate a group to use when assigning permissions to a folder, you can type the prefix ACL_ in the Select dialog box and click OK. A Multiple Names Found dialog box appears, showing only the *ACL_* groups in the directory, thereby ensuring that permissions will be assigned to a group that is designed to manage resource access.

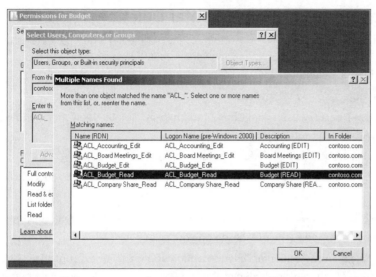

FIGURE 4-11 Selecting a group by using a group prefix to filter the correct type of group

- **Summarize a group's purpose with its description attribute** Use the *description* attribute of a group to summarize the group's purpose. Because the Description column is enabled by default in the details pane of the Active Directory Users And Computers snap-in, the group's purpose can be highly visible to administrators.

- **Detail a group's purpose in its Notes** When you open a group's Properties dialog box, the Notes text box is visible at the bottom of the General tab. This text box can be used to document the group's purpose. For example, you can list the folders to which a group has been given permission, as shown in Figure 4-12.

FIGURE 4-12 A group's Properties dialog box, showing the Notes box used to provide details of the group's purpose

Protecting Groups from Accidental Deletion

Protect yourself from the potentially devastating results of deleting a group by protecting each group you create from deletion. Windows Server 2008 R2 makes it easy to protect any object from accidental deletion.

To protect an object, follow these steps:

1. In the Active Directory Users And Computers snap-in, click the View menu and make sure that Advanced Features is selected.

2. Open the Properties dialog box for a group.

3. On the Object tab, select the Protect Object From Accidental Deletion check box.

4. Click OK.

This is one of the few places in Windows in which you must click OK instead of Apply. Clicking Apply does not modify the ACL based on your selection.

The Protect Object From Accidental Deletion option applies an access control entry (ACE) to the ACL of the object that explicitly denies the Everyone group both the Delete permission and the Delete Subtree permission. If you really do want to delete the group, you can return to the Object tab of the Properties dialog box and clear the Protect Object From Accidental Deletion check box.

Deleting a group has a significant impact on administrators and, potentially, on security. Consider a group used to manage access to resources. If the group is deleted, access to that resource is changed. Either users who should have access to the resource are suddenly prevented access, creating a denial-of-service scenario, or inappropriate access to the resource becomes possible if you had used the group to deny access to a resource with a Deny permission.

Additionally, if you re-create the group, the new group object will have a new security identifier (SID), which will not match the SIDs on ACLs of resources. So you must instead perform object recovery to reanimate the deleted group before the tombstone interval is reached. When a group has been deleted for the tombstone interval—180 days by default—the group and its SID are permanently deleted from Active Directory.

When you reanimate a tombstoned object, you must re-create most of its attributes, including, importantly, the *member* attribute of group objects. This means you must rebuild the group membership after restoring the deleted object. Alternately, you can perform an authoritative restore or turn to your Active Directory snapshots to recover both the group and its membership.

Finally, Windows Server 2008 R2 introduces the Active Directory Recycle Bin, which lets you recover a deleted object in its entirety, reducing or eliminating the impact of accidentally deleting an object. Authoritative restore, snapshots, and the Active Directory Recycle Bin are discussed in Chapter 13, "Directory Business Continuity."

Recovering a deleted group is a skill you should hope to use only in worst-case scenarios, not in day-to-day operations of a production environment. Protect yourself from the potentially devastating results of group object deletion by protecting each group you create.

Delegating the Management of Group Membership

After creating a group, you might want to delegate the management of the group's membership to a team or an individual who has the business responsibility for the resource that the group manages.

For example, let's assume that your finance manager is responsible for creating next year's budget. You create a shared folder for the budget and assign Write permission to a group named ACL_Budget_Edit. If someone needs access to the budget folder, he or she contacts the help desk to enter a request, the help desk contacts the finance manager for business approval, and then the help desk adds the user to the ACL_Budget_Edit group. You can improve the responsiveness and accountability of the process by allowing the finance manager to change the group's membership. Then users needing access can request it directly from the finance manager, removing the intermediate step of contacting the help desk.

To delegate the management of a group's membership, you must assign to the finance manager the Allow Write Member permission for the group. The *member* attribute is the multivalued attribute that is the group's membership.

Delegating Membership Management with the Managed By Tab

The easiest way to delegate membership management of a single group is to use the Managed By tab of a group object's Properties dialog box, shown in Figure 4-13.

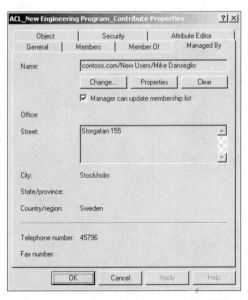

FIGURE 4-13 The Managed By tab of a group's Properties dialog box

The Managed By tab serves two purposes. First, it provides contact information related to the manager of a group. You can use this information to contact the business owner of a group to obtain approval prior to adding a user to the group.

The second purpose served by the Managed By tab is to manage the delegation of the *member* attribute. Note the Manager Can Update Membership List check box shown in Figure 4-13. When this check box is selected, the user or group shown in the Name box is given the Allow Write Member permission. If you change or clear the manager, the appropriate change is made to the group's ACL.

> **NOTE   CLICK OK**
>
> This is another of the strange and rare places in which you must actually click OK to implement the change. Clicking Apply does not change the ACL on the group.

It is not quite so easy to insert a group onto the Managed By tab of another group. When you click Change, the Select User, Contact, Or Group dialog box appears. If you enter the name of a group and click OK, an error occurs. That's because this dialog box is not configured to accept groups as valid object types, even though *Group* is in the name of the dialog box itself. To work around this odd limitation, click Object Types, and then select the check box next to Groups, as shown in Figure 4-14. Click OK to close both the Object Types and Select dialog boxes. Be sure to select the Manager Can Update Membership List check box if you want to assign the Write Member permission to the group. When a group is used on the Managed By tab, no contact information is visible because groups do not maintain contact-related attributes.

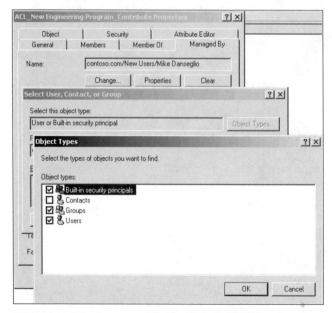

FIGURE 4-14 Selecting a group for the Managed By tab

After you have delegated group membership management, users do not require Active Directory Users And Computers to modify the membership of the group. A user can simply use the Search Active Directory capability of Windows clients to find the group, and then change its membership.

To find a group:

1. Click Start, and then click Network.
2. Click the Search Active Directory button on the toolbar.
3. Type the name of the group and click Find Now.

Delegating Membership Management Using Advanced Security Settings

You can use the Advanced Security Settings dialog box to assign the Allow Write Member permission directly. You can assign the permission for an individual group or for all the groups in an OU.

To delegate the management of membership for an individual group, perform the following steps:

1. In the Active Directory Users And Computers snap-in, click the View menu and make sure Advanced Features is selected.
2. Right-click the group's name and choose Properties.
3. On the Security tab, click Advanced.
4. In the Advanced Security Settings dialog box, click Add.

    If the Add button is not visible, click Edit, and then click Add.

5. In the Select Users, Contacts, Service Account, Or Group dialog box, enter the name for the group to which you want to grant permission, or click Browse to search for the group. When you are finished, click OK.

    The Permission Entry dialog box appears.

6. On the Properties tab, in the Apply To list, choose This Object And All Descendant Objects.

7. In the Permissions list, select the Allow check boxes for the Read Members and Write Members permissions.

    By default, all users have the Read Members permission, so that permission is not required. However, role-based access control is best implemented by assigning all the permissions required to achieve the desired capability, rather than relying on permissions assigned indirectly.

    Figure 4-15 shows the resulting Permission Entry dialog box.

FIGURE 4-15 The Permission Entry dialog box showing the delegation of group membership management for a group

8. Click OK to close each of the security dialog boxes.

To delegate the ability to manage membership for all groups in an OU, perform the following steps:

1. In the Active Directory Users And Computers snap-in, click the View menu and make sure Advanced Features is selected.

2. Right-click the OU and then choose Properties.

3. On the Security tab, click Advanced.

4. In the Advanced Security Settings dialog box, click Add.

   If the Add button is not visible, click Edit, and then click Add.

5. In the Select dialog box, enter the name for the group to which you want to grant permission, or click Browse to search for the group. When you are finished browsing, click OK.

   The Permission Entry dialog box appears.

6. On the Properties tab, in the Apply To list, choose Descendant Group Objects.

7. In the Permissions list, select the Allow check boxes for the Read Members and Write Members permissions.

   By default, all users have the Read Members permission, so that permission is not required. However, role-based access control is best implemented by assigning all the permissions required to achieve the desired capability, rather than relying on permissions assigned indirectly.

Figure 4-16 shows the resulting Permission Entry dialog box.

FIGURE 4-16 The Permission Entry dialog box showing the delegation of group membership management for all groups in the Groups OU

8. Click OK to close each of the security dialog boxes.

Understanding Shadow Groups

Most management of an enterprise is implemented with groups. Groups are assigned permission to resources. Groups can be used to filter the scope of Group Policy objects. Groups are assigned fine-grained password policies. Groups can be used as collections for configuration management tools such as Microsoft System Center Configuration Manager. The list goes on. OUs, however, are not used as frequently to manage the enterprise, and in some cases, they cannot be used. For instance, OUs cannot be assigned permissions to resources, nor can they be assigned fine-grained password policies (discussed in Chapter 8, "Improving the Security of Authentication in an AD DS Domain"). Instead, the primary purpose of an OU is to provide a scope of management for the delegation of administrative permissions for the objects in that OU. In other words, an OU of users enables you to delegate to your help desk the ability to reset passwords for all users in the OU. OUs are administrative containers.

The reason for this separation of purpose between OUs and groups is that OUs do not provide the same flexibility as groups. A user or computer (or other object) can exist only within the context of a single OU, whereas a security principal can belong to many groups. Therefore, groups are used for aligning identities with the capabilities required by those identities.

Sometimes, you might want to manage using an OU when it is not possible. For example, you might want to give all users in an OU access to a folder. Or you might want to assign a unique password policy to users in an OU. You cannot do so directly, but you can achieve your goal by creating what is called a *shadow group*. A shadow group is a group that contains the same users as an OU. More accurately, a shadow group contains users that meet a certain criterion.

The easiest way to create a shadow group is to create the group, and then, in the OU containing the users, press Ctrl+A to select all users. Right-click any selected user and choose Add To Group. Type the name of the group and click OK.

EXAM TIP

On the 70-640 exam, be prepared to see the term *shadow group* in use. Know that it means a group that contains, as members, the users in an OU.

Unfortunately, Windows does not yet provide a way to maintain the membership of a shadow group dynamically. When you add or remove a user in an OU, you must also add or remove the user in the shadow group.

> **MORE INFO**   **MAINTAINING SHADOW GROUPS DYNAMICALLY**
>
> See *Windows Administration Resource Kit: Productivity Solutions for IT Professionals* for scripts that help maintain shadow groups dynamically.

Default Groups

Several groups are created automatically on a server running Windows Server 2008 R2. These are called *default local groups*, and they include well-known groups such as Administrators, Backup Operators, and Remote Desktop Users. Additional groups are created in a domain, in both the Builtin and Users containers, including Domain Admins, Enterprise Admins, and Schema Admins. The following list provides a summary of capabilities of the subset of default groups that have significant permissions and user rights related to the management of Active Directory:

- **Enterprise Admins (Users container of the forest root domain)**   This group is a member of the Administrators group in every domain in the forest, giving it complete access to the configuration of all domain controllers. It also owns the Configuration partition of the directory and has full control of the domain naming context in all forest domains.

- **Schema Admins (Users container of the forest root domain)**   This group owns and has full control of the Active Directory schema.

- **Administrators (Builtin container of each domain)**   This group has complete control over all domain controllers and data in the domain naming context. It can change the membership of all other administrative groups in the domain, and the Administrators group in the forest root domain can change the membership of Enterprise Admins, Schema Admins, and Domain Admins. The Administrators group in the forest root domain is arguably the most powerful service administration group in the forest.

- **Domain Admins (Users container of each domain)** This group is added to the Administrators group of its domain. Therefore, it inherits all the capabilities of the Administrators group. It is also, by default, added to the local Administrators group of each domain member computer, giving Domain Admins ownership of all domain computers.

- **Server Operators (Builtin container of each domain)** This group can perform maintenance tasks on domain controllers. It has the right to log on locally, start and stop services, perform backup and restore operations, format disks, create or delete shares, and shut down domain controllers. By default, this group has no members.

- **Account Operators (Builtin container of each domain)** This group can create, modify, and delete accounts for users, groups, and computers located in any organizational unit in the domain (except the Domain Controllers OU), as well as in the Users and Computers containers. Account Operators cannot modify accounts that are members of the Administrators or Domain Admins groups, nor can they modify those groups. Account Operators can also log on locally to domain controllers. By default, this group has no members.

- **Backup Operators (Builtin container of each domain)** This group can perform backup and restore operations on domain controllers as well as log on locally and shut down domain controllers. By default, this group has no members.

- **Print Operators (Builtin container of each domain)** This group can maintain print queues on domain controllers. It can also log on locally and shut down domain controllers.

The default groups that provide administrative privileges should be managed carefully because they typically have broader privileges than are necessary for most delegated environments and because they often apply protection to their members.

The Account Operators group is a perfect example. If you examine its capabilities in the preceding list, you see that its rights are very broad, indeed. It can even log on locally to a domain controller. In very small enterprises, such rights are probably appropriate for one or two individuals who might be domain administrators anyway. In enterprises of any size, the rights and permissions granted to Account Operators are usually far too broad.

Additionally, the Account Operators group is, like the other administrative groups listed previously, a *protected group*. Protected groups are defined by the operating system and cannot be unprotected. Members of a protected group become protected. The result of protection is that the permissions (ACLs) of members are modified so that they no longer inherit permissions from their OU but, rather, receive a copy of an ACL that is quite restrictive. For example, if Jeff Ford is added to the Account Operators group, his account becomes protected and the help desk, which can reset all other user passwords in the User Accounts OU, cannot reset Jeff Ford's password.

For these reasons—overdelegation and protection—strive to avoid adding users to the groups listed previously that do not have members by default: Account Operators, Backup Operators, Server Operators, and Print Operators. Instead, create custom groups to which you assign permissions and user rights that achieve your business and administrative requirements.

For example, if Scott Mitchell needs to perform backup operations on a domain controller, but he should not be able to perform restore operations that could lead to database rollback or corruption and he should not be able to shut down a domain controller, don't put Scott in the Backup Operators group. Instead, create a group, assign it only the Backup Files And Directories user right, and then add Scott as a member.

Special Identities

Windows and Active Directory also support *special identities*, groups for which membership is controlled by the operating system. You cannot view the groups in any list (in the Active Directory Users And Computers snap-in, for example), you cannot view or modify the membership of these special identities, and you cannot add them to other groups. You can, however, use these groups to assign rights and permissions. The most important special identities, often referred to as *groups* for convenience, are described in the following list:

- **Anonymous Logon** Represents connections to a computer and its resources that are made without supplying a user name and password. In versions of Windows earlier than Windows Server 2003, this group was a member of the Everyone group. In Windows Server 2003 and later versions, this group is no longer a default member of the Everyone group.

- **Authenticated Users**   Represents identities that have been authenticated. This group does not include Guest, even if the Guest account has a password.

- **Everyone**   Includes Authenticated Users and Guest. On computers running versions of Windows earlier than Windows Server 2003, this group includes Anonymous Logon.

- **Interactive**   Represents users accessing a resource while logged on locally to the computer hosting the resource, as opposed to accessing the resource over the network. When a user accesses any given resource on a computer to which the user is logged on locally, the user is automatically added to the Interactive group for that resource. Interactive also includes users logged on through a remote desktop connection.

- **Network**   Represents users accessing a resource over the network, as opposed to users who are logged on locally at the computer hosting the resource. When a user accesses any given resource over the network, the user is automatically added to the Network group for that resource.

The importance of these special identities is that they enable you to provide access to resources based on the type of authentication or connection rather than on the user account. For example, you could create a folder on a system that allows users to view its contents when logged on locally to the system but does not allow the same users to view the contents from a mapped drive over the network. This is achieved by assigning permissions to the Interactive special identity.

PRACTICE   Administering Groups in an Enterprise

In this practice, you perform best-practices group management tasks to improve the administration of groups in the contoso.com domain. To perform the exercises in this practice, you need to have the following objects in the contoso.com domain:

- A first-level OU named Groups.

- A global security group named Finance in the Groups OU.

- A first-level OU named User Accounts.

- A user account named Mike Danseglio in the User Accounts OU. Populate the user account with sample contact information: address, phone, and email. Reset the password of the account so that you know it. Make sure the account is enabled and that the user is *not* required to change the password at the next logon.

In this and other practices in this training kit, you will log on to the domain controller with user accounts that are not a member of Domain Administrators or the domain's Administrators group. Therefore, you must give all user accounts the right to log on locally to the domain controllers in your practice environment. Follow the steps in the article, "Grant a Member the Right to Logon Locally," at *http://technet.microsoft.com/en-us/library/ee957044(WS.10).aspx* to grant the Allow Logon Locally right to the Administrators and Domain Users groups. If you will use Remote Desktop Services to connect to the domain controller—rather than logging on locally—grant the Allow Logon Through Remote Desktop Services right. This is for the practice environment only. In a production environment, you should not grant users the right to log on to domain controllers.

EXERCISE 1   Create a Well-Documented Group

In this exercise, you create a group to manage access to the Budget folder, and you follow the best-practices guidelines presented in this lesson.

1. Log on to SERVER01 as Administrator and open the Active Directory Users And Computers snap-in.

2. Select the Groups OU in the console tree.

3. Right-click the Groups OU, point to New, and click Group.

4. In the Group Name box, type **ACL_Budget_Edit**.

5. Select Domain Local in the Group Scope section and Security in the Group Type section, and then click OK.

6. Click the View menu and ensure that Advanced Features is selected.

7. Right-click the ACL_Budget_Edit group and choose Properties.

8. On the Object tab, select the Protect Object From Accidental Deletion check box and click OK.

9. Open the group's Properties again.

10. In the Description box, type **BUDGET (EDIT)**.

11. In the Notes box, type the following paths to represent the folders that have permissions assigned to this group:

    \\server23\data$\finance\budget
    \\server32\data$\finance\revenue projections

12. Click OK.

EXERCISE 2   Delegate Management of Group Membership

In this exercise, you give Mike Danseglio the ability to manage the membership of the ACL_Budget_Edit group.

1. Open the Properties dialog box of the ACL_Budget_Edit group.

2. On the Managed By tab, click Change.

3. Type the user name for Mike Danseglio, **mike.danseglio**, and then click OK.

4. Select the Manager Can Update Membership List check box. Click OK.

EXERCISE 3   Validate the Delegation of Membership Management

In this exercise, you test the delegation you performed in Exercise 2, "Delegate Management of Group Membership," by modifying the membership of the group as Mike Danseglio.

1. Open Command Prompt and type the following command: **runas/user:mike .danseglio cmd.exe**.

2. When prompted, enter the password for Mike Danseglio.

   A new command prompt window appears, running as Mike Danseglio.

3. Type the following command on one line, and then press Enter:

```
dsmod group "CN=ACL_Budget_Edit,OU=Groups,DC=contoso,DC=com"
    -addmbr "CN=Finance,OU=Groups,DC=contoso,DC=com"
```

4. Close both Command Prompt windows.

5. In the Active Directory Users And Computers snap-in, examine the membership of the ACL_Budget_Edit group and confirm that the Finance group was added successfully.

Lesson Summary

- Use the Description and Notes text boxes in a group's Properties dialog box to document the purpose of the group.

- The Managed By tab lets you specify a user or group that is responsible for a group. You can also select the Manager Can Update Membership List check box to delegate membership management to the user or group indicated on the Managed By tab.

- To delegate the management of group membership, grant the Allow Write Members permission.

- Use the Protect Object From Accidental Deletion check box to prevent the potential security and management problems created when a group is accidentally deleted.

- Windows Server 2008 R2 and Active Directory contain default groups with significant permissions and user rights. You should not add users to the default domain groups that do not already have members (Account Operators, Backup Operators, Print Operators, and Server Operators), and you should seriously restrict membership in other service administration groups (Enterprise Admins, Domain Admins, Schema Admins, and Administrators).

- Special identities such as Authenticated Users, Everyone, Interactive, and Network can be used to assign rights and permissions. Their membership is determined dynamically by the operating system and cannot be viewed or modified.

Lesson Review

You can use the following questions to test your knowledge of the information in Lesson 3, "Administering Groups in an Enterprise." The questions are also available on the companion CD if you prefer to review them in electronic form.

> **NOTE ANSWERS**
>
> Answers to these questions and explanations of why each answer choice is right or wrong are located in the "Answers" section at the end of the book.

1. Your company is conducting a meeting for a special project. The data is particularly confidential. The team is meeting in a conference room, and you have configured a folder on the conference room computer that grants permission to the team members. The folder is a subfolder of a shared folder to which all employees have access. You want to ensure that team members access the data only while logged on to the computer in the conference room, not from other computers in the enterprise. What must you do?

   A. Assign the Allow Read permission to the Interactive group.

   B. Assign the Allow Read permission to the team group.

   C. Assign the Deny Traverse Folders permission to the team group.

   D. Assign the Deny Full Control permission to the Network group.

2. You want to allow a user named Mike Danseglio to add and remove users in a group called Special Project. Where can you configure this permission?

   A. The Members tab of the group

   B. The Security tab of Mike Danseglio's user object

   C. The Member Of tab of Mike Danseglio's user object

   D. The Managed By tab of the group

3. Which of the following groups can shut down a domain controller? (Choose all that apply.)

   A. Account Operators

   B. Print Operators

   C. Backup Operators

   D. Server Operators

   E. Interactive

Chapter Review

To further practice and reinforce the skills you learned in this chapter, you can perform the following tasks:

- Review the chapter summary.
- Review the list of key terms introduced in this chapter.
- Complete the case scenario. This scenario sets up a real-world situation involving the topics of this chapter and asks you to create a solution.
- Complete the suggested practices.
- Take a practice test.

Chapter Summary

- Group scopes (global, universal, domain local, and local) define group characteristics related to membership, replication, and availability of the group.
- In an enterprise, role-based management suggests that groups should be viewed as either defining a role or defining a business rule. Role groups are generally implemented as global groups, and rules are defined by using domain local groups.
- A group's *member* attribute is a multivalued attribute containing the DNs of the group's members. Each member's *memberOf* attribute is automatically updated to reflect changes in membership. When you add a user to a group, you are always changing the group's *member* attribute. The *memberOf* attribute, which is read-only, is called a backlink.
- You can delegate the management of group membership by assigning the Allow Write Members permission, which grants write permission to the *member* attribute.
- You can use Directory Services tools such as DSQuery, DSGet, and DSMod to list, create, and modify groups and their membership.
- CSVDE and LDIFDE can import and export groups. Additionally, LDIFDE can modify the membership of existing groups.
- The DSAdd, DSMove, and DSRm commands can add, move, and delete groups, respectively.

Key Terms

The following terms were introduced in this chapter. Do you know what they mean?

- backlink
- shadow group
- special identities

Case Scenario

In the following case scenario, you apply what you've learned about administering groups in an enterprise. You can find answers to these questions in the "Answers" section at the end of this book.

Case Scenario: Implementing a Group Strategy

You are an administrator at Trey Research. A new product development initiative called Sliced Bread is underway, and there is confidential information about the project in shared folders on three servers in three different sites. Users in Research, Marketing, and Finance need access to the project data. Additionally, the CEO and her assistant need access. Of these, only Marketing and Research require Write access. Several interns are currently working in the Marketing department, and you want to prevent them from gaining access. Finally, a team of auditors from Woodgrove Bank, an investor in Trey Research, need Read access as well. You have a trust relationship configured so that the Trey Research domain trusts the Woodgrove Bank domain.

1. What types and scopes of groups do you create to represent the user roles in Trey Research? What type and scope of group do you ask administrators at Woodgrove Bank to create to represent the auditors' role?

2. What types and scopes of groups do you create to manage Read and Write access to the Sliced Bread folders?

3. Describe the nesting of users and groups you implement to achieve the security required by this project.

Suggested Practices

To help you successfully master the exam objectives presented in this chapter, complete the following tasks.

Automate Group Membership and Shadow Groups

In this practice, you create a shadow group to reflect the user accounts in the User Accounts OU. You apply the DSQuery and DSMod commands to keep the membership up to date.

To perform this practice, you must have the following objects in the contoso.com domain:

- A first-level OU named Groups
- An OU named User Accounts
- Several sample user accounts in the User Accounts OU

Also, perform the following practices.

- **Practice 1** In the Groups OU, create a global security group named All Users. Then click the User Accounts OU in the tree pane of the Active Directory Users And

Computers snap-in. Click any user in the details pane and press Ctrl+A to select all. Right-click any selected user and choose Add To Group. Add the users to the All Users group. Examine the Members tab of the All Users group to confirm that all users were added successfully.

- **Practice 2** Open Command Prompt. Delete the All Users group you created in Practice 1. Type the following two commands to create the All Users shadow group:

```
dsadd group "CN=All Users,OU=Groups,DC=contoso,DC=com" -secgrp yes -scope g
dsquery user "OU=User Accounts,DC=contoso,DC=com" |
    dsmod group "CN=Users,OU=Groups,DC=contoso,DC=com" -addmbr
```

- **Practice 3** In a command prompt, type the following two commands to remove all members of the group and repopulate it with the current users in the User Accounts OU:

```
dsget group "CN=All Users,OU=Groups,DC=contoso,DC=com" -members |
    dsmod group "CN=All Users,OU=Groups,DC=contoso,DC=com" -rmmbr
dsquery user "OU=User Accounts,DC=contoso,DC=com" |
    dsmod group "CN=All Users,OU=Groups,DC=contoso,DC=com" -addmbr
```

Take a Practice Test

The practice tests on this book's companion CD offer many options. For example, you can test yourself on just one exam objective, or you can test yourself on all the 70-640 certification exam content. You can set up the test so that it closely simulates the experience of taking a certification exam, or you can set it up in study mode so that you can look at the correct answers and explanations after you answer each question.

> **MORE INFO** **PRACTICE TESTS**
>
> For details about all the practice test options available, see the "How to Use the Practice Tests" section in this book's Introduction.

CHAPTER 5

Configuring Computer Accounts

omputers in a domain are security principals, as are users. Computers have an account with a logon name and password that Microsoft Windows changes automatically every 30 days or so. They authenticate with the domain. They can belong to groups, have access to resources, and can be configured by Group Policy. And, like users, computers sometimes lose track of their passwords (requiring a reset) or have accounts that must be disabled or enabled.

Managing computers—both the objects in Active Directory Domain Services (AD DS) and the physical devices—is part of the day-to-day work of most IT professionals. New systems are added to the organization, computers are taken offline for repairs, computers are exchanged between users or roles, and older equipment is retired or upgraded, leading to the acquisition of replacement systems. Each of these activities requires managing the identity of the computer represented by its object, or account, and Active Directory.

Unfortunately, most enterprises do not invest the same kind of care and process in the creation and management of computer accounts as they do for user accounts, even though both are security principals. In this chapter, you will learn how to create computer objects, which include attributes required for the object to be an account. You will learn how to support computer accounts through their life cycle, including configuration, troubleshooting, repairing, and deprovisioning computer objects. You will also deepen your understanding of the process through which a computer joins a domain so that you can identify and avoid potential points of failure.

Exam objectives in this chapter:

- Automate creation of Active Directory accounts.
- Maintain Active Directory accounts.

Lessons in this chapter:

Before You Begin

This chapter applies Microsoft Windows PowerShell, Comma-Separated Values Data Exchange (CSVDE), and LDAP Data Interchange Format Data Exchange (LDIFDE) to the task of automating computer account creation. These tools are introduced in Chapter 3, "Administering User Accounts." Familiarize yourself with these tools by reading Chapter 3 prior to reading this chapter.

REAL WORLD

Dan Holme

"Computers are people, too," or at least in Active Directory they are. In fact, computers have the *objectClass* attribute of *user*. They have accounts, just as users do. They can even forget their passwords, like users do. Because computers are security principals and can be used to scope Group Policy (as you'll learn in the next chapter), it is important to treat computer accounts with the same care as you would with user accounts.

I'm sure you've run into a situation when you had to remove a computer from a domain and then had it rejoin the domain. As you will see in Lesson 3, "Supporting Computer Objects and Accounts," that's a bad practice, equivalent to deleting and re-creating a user's account just because the user forgot his or her password. That's just one example of scenarios I see regularly, in which administrators are a bit less careful with computer accounts than they probably should be.

In this lesson, you'll learn the best practices for supporting computer accounts with the same level of respect as with other security principals (including users and groups) in the domain. You'll also learn how to use command-line tools and Windows PowerShell scripts to automate the creation and management of computer objects. You'll see a lot of similarities with the procedures discussed in Chapter 3. Why? Because computers are people, too!

Lesson 1: Creating Computers and Joining the Domain

The default configuration of Windows Server 2008 R2—as well as all other versions of Windows server and client operating systems—is that the computer belongs to a workgroup. Before you can log on to a computer with a domain account, that computer must belong to the domain. To join the domain, the computer must have an account in the domain which, like a user account, includes a logon name (*sAMAccountName*), a password, and a security identifier (SID) that uniquely represents the computer as a security principal in the domain. Those credentials enable the computer to authenticate against the domain and create a secure relationship that then allows users to log on to the system with domain accounts. In this lesson, you learn the steps to prepare the domain for a new computer account, and you explore the process through which a computer joins the domain.

After this lesson, you will be able to:
- Design an OU structure for computers.
- Create computer objects in the domain.
- Delegate the creation of computer objects.
- Join computers to the domain.
- Redirect the default computer container.
- Prevent nonadministrative users from creating computers and joining the domain.

Estimated lesson time: 45 minutes

Understanding Workgroups, Domains, and Trusts

In a workgroup, each system maintains an identity store of user and group accounts against which users can be authenticated and access can begin. The local identity store on each computer is called the *Security Accounts Manager* (SAM) database. If a user logs on to a workgroup computer, the system authenticates the user against its local SAM database. If a user connects to another system, to access a file, for example, the user is re-authenticated against the identity store of the remote system. From a security perspective, a workgroup computer is, for all intents and purposes, a stand-alone system.

When a computer joins a domain, it delegates the task of authenticating users to the domain. Although the computer continues to maintain its SAM database to support local user and group accounts, user accounts are typically created in the central domain directory. When a user logs on to the computer with a domain account, the user is now authenticated by a domain controller rather than by the SAM. Said another way, the computer now *trusts* another authority to validate a user's identity. Trust relationships are generally discussed in the context of two domains, as you will learn in Chapter 12, "Managing Multiple Domains and Forests," but there is also a trust between each domain member computer and its domain that is established when the computer joins the domain.

Identifying Requirements for Joining a Computer to the Domain

To join a computer to an Active Directory domain, the following three requirements must be met:

- A computer object must be created in the directory service.

- You must have appropriate permissions to the computer object. The permissions allow you to join a computer with the same name as the object to the domain.

- You must be a member of the local Administrators group on the computer to change its domain or workgroup membership.

The next sections examine each of these requirements.

The Computers Container and OUs

Before you create a computer object in the directory service—the first of the three requirements for joining a computer to the domain—you must have a place to put it.

The Default Computers Container

When you create a domain, the Computers container is created by default (CN=Computers, dc=*company*,dc=*com*). This container is not an organizational unit (OU); it is an object of class *container*. There are subtle but important differences between a container and an OU: You cannot create an OU within a container, so you cannot subdivide the Computers OU; and you cannot link a Group Policy object to a container. Therefore, it is highly recommended that you create custom OUs to host computer objects instead of using the Computers container.

OUs for Computers

Most organizations create at least two OUs for computer objects: one to host computer accounts for client computers—desktops, laptops, and other user systems—and another for servers. These two OUs are in addition to the Domain Controllers OU created by default during the installation of Active Directory. In each of these OUs, computer objects are created. There is no technical difference between a computer object in a clients OU and a computer object in a servers or domain controllers OU; computer objects are computer objects. But separate OUs are typically created to provide unique scopes of management so that you can delegate management of client objects to one team and management of server objects to another.

Your administrative model might necessitate further dividing your client and server OUs. Many organizations create sub-OUs beneath a server OU to collect and manage specific types of servers—for example, an OU for file and print servers and an OU for database servers. By doing so, the team of administrators for each type of server can be delegated permissions to manage computer objects in the appropriate OU. Similarly, geographically distributed organizations with local desktop support teams often divide a parent OU for clients into sub-OUs for each site. This approach allows each site's support team to create computer objects in the site for client computers and join computers to the domain using those computer objects. This is an example only: What is most important is that your OU structure reflect your administrative model so that your OUs provide single points of management for the delegation of administration.

Figure 5-1 illustrates a typical OU design for an organization whose server administration teams are focused on specific types of servers and whose desktop support teams are focused on clients in specific geographical areas.

FIGURE 5-1 A common OU design illustrating site-based administration of clients and role-based administration of servers

Additionally, separate OUs allow you to create different baseline configurations, using different Group Policy objects (GPOs) linked to the client and the server OUs. Group Policy, discussed in detail in Chapter 6, "Implementing a Group Policy Infrastructure," lets you specify configuration for collections of computers by linking GPOs that contain configuration instructions to OUs. Organizations commonly separate clients into desktop and laptop OUs. GPOs specifying desktop or laptop configuration can then be linked to appropriate OUs.

If your organization has decentralized, site-based administration and wants to manage unique configurations for desktops and laptops, you face a design dilemma. Should you divide your clients OU based on administration and then subdivide desktops and laptops, or should you divide your clients OU into desktop and laptop OUs and then subdivide based on administration? The options are illustrated in Figure 5-2.

FIGURE 5-2 OU design options

Because the primary design driver for Active Directory OUs is the efficient delegation of administration through the inheritance of access control lists (ACLs) on OUs, the design on the left is recommended.

Delegating Permission to Create Computers

By default, the Enterprise Admins, Domain Admins, Administrators, and Account Operators groups have permission to create computer objects in any new OU. However, as discussed in Chapter 4, "Managing Groups," it is recommended that you tightly restrict membership in the first three groups and that you do not add administrators to the Account Operators group.

Instead, you should delegate the permission to create computer objects to appropriate administrators or support personnel. The permission required to create a computer object is Create Computer Objects. This permission, assigned to a group for an OU, allows members of the group to create computer objects in that OU. For example, you might allow your desktop support team to create computer objects in the clients OU and allow your file server administrators to create computer objects in the file servers OU.

> **NOTE PRACTICE IT**
>
> At the end of this lesson, Exercise 3, "Delegate the Ability to Create Computer Objects," steps you through the procedure required to delegate the creation of computer objects.

Prestaging a Computer Account

You can and should create a computer account in the correct OU before joining the computer to the domain. This process of pre-creating a computer account is called *prestaging* a computer.

After you have been given permission to create computer objects, you can do so by right-clicking the OU and choosing Computer from the New menu. The New Object – Computer dialog box, shown in Figure 5-3, appears.

FIGURE 5-3 The New Object – Computer dialog box

Enter the computer name, following the naming convention of your enterprise, and select the user or group that will be allowed to join the computer to the domain with this account. The two computer names—Computer Name and Computer Name (Pre–Windows 2000)—should be the same: There is rarely, if ever, a justification for configuring them separately.

> **NOTE   THE NEW OBJECT – COMPUTER WIZARD OVER-DELEGATES**
>
> The permissions applied to the user or group you select in the New Object – Computer Wizard are more than are necessary simply to join a computer to the domain. The selected user or group is also given the ability to modify the computer object in other ways. For guidance regarding a least-privilege approach to delegating permission to join a computer to the domain, see *Windows Administration Resource Kit: Productivity Solutions for IT Professionals* by Dan Holme (Microsoft Press, 2008).

Prestaging a computer offers two major advantages:

- The account is in the correct OU and is therefore delegated according to the security policy defined by the ACL of the OU.
- The computer is within the scope of GPOs linked to the OU, before the computer joins the domain.

Prestaging is highly recommended for reasons discussed in the "Prestaging Computer Objects" section.

Joining a Computer to the Domain

By prestaging the computer object, you fulfill the first two requirements for joining a computer to a domain: the computer object exists, and you have specified who has permissions to join a computer with the given name to the domain. Now, a local administrator of the computer can change the computer's domain membership and enter the specified domain credentials to successfully complete the process.

To join a computer to the domain, follow these steps:

1. Log on to the computer with credentials that belong to the local Administrators group on the computer.

   Only local administrators can alter the domain or workgroup membership of a computer.

2. Open the System Properties dialog box using one of the following methods:

   On earlier versions of Windows (Windows XP or Windows Server 2003), open the System properties dialog box by doing one of the following:

   - Right-click My Computer and click Properties.
   - Press Windows Logo+Pause.

   On newer versions of Windows (Windows Vista, Windows 7, Windows Server 2008, or Windows Server 2008 R2), perform the following steps:

   a. Open the System properties dialog box. You can right-click Computer, and then click Properties, or press Windows Logo+Pause.

   b. In the Computer Name, Domain, And Workgroup Settings section, click Change Settings.

   c. If prompted by User Account Control, click Continue or enter administrative credentials as appropriate.

3. On the Computer Name tab, click Change.

4. Under Member Of, select Domain.

5. Type the name of the domain you want to join and click OK.

> **NOTE   USE THE FULL DNS NAME OF THE DOMAIN**
>
> Use the full DNS name of the Active Directory domain. Not only is this more accurate and more likely to succeed, but if it does not succeed, it indicates that there could be a problem with DNS name resolution that should be rectified before joining the computer to the domain.

6. Windows prompts for the credentials of your user account in the domain.

   The domain checks to see whether a computer object already exists with the name of the computer. One of the following three things happens:

   - If the object exists and a computer with that name has already joined the domain, an error is returned, and you cannot join the computer to the domain.
   - If the object exists and it is prestaged—a computer with the same name has not joined the domain—the domain confirms that the domain credentials you entered have permission to join the domain using that account. These permissions were discussed in the "Prestaging a Computer Account" section.

- If the computer account is not prestaged, Windows verifies whether you have permissions to create a new computer object in the default computer container. If you do have permissions, the object is created with the name of the computer. This method of joining a domain is supported for backward compatibility but is not recommended. It is recommended that you prestage the account as indicated earlier and as detailed in the section entitled, "Prestaging Computer Objects."

The computer then joins the domain by assuming the identity of its Active Directory object. It configures its SID to match the domain computer account's SID and sets an initial password with the domain. The computer then performs other tasks related to joining the domain. It adds the Domain Admins group to the local Administrators group and the Domain Users group to the local Users group.

7. You are prompted to restart the computer. Click OK to close this message.

8. Click Close (in newer versions of Windows) or OK (in earlier versions of Windows) to close the System Properties dialog box.

9. You are prompted, again, to restart the computer, after which the system is fully a member of the domain and you can log on using domain credentials.

The Netdom.exe command allows you to join a computer to the domain in Command Prompt. The basic syntax of the command is:

```
netdom join MachineName /Domain:DomainName [/OU:"DN of OU"]
    [/UserO:LocalUsername] [/PasswordO:{LocalPassword|*} ]
    [/UserD:DomainUsername] [/PasswordD:{DomainPassword|*} ]
    [/SecurePasswordPrompt] [/REBoot[:TimeInSeconds]]
```

It can be useful to join a computer to a domain from the Command Prompt. The first reason this is useful is because the join can be included in a script that performs other actions. For example, you could create a batch file that creates the computer account using NetDom or DSAdd—the latter of which allows you to specify other attributes, including description—and then joins the machine to that account using NetDom. Second, NetDom can be used to remotely join a computer to the domain. Third, NetDom lets you specify the OU for the computer object. The command's parameters are, for the most part, self-explanatory. *UserO* and *PasswordO* are credentials that are members of the workgroup computer's local Administrators group. Specifying * for the password causes NetDom to prompt for the password at the command prompt. *UserD* and *PasswordD* are domain credentials with permission to create a computer object, if the account is not prestaged, or with permission to join a computer to a prestaged account. The *REBoot* parameter causes the system to reboot after joining the domain. The default timeout is 30 seconds. The *SecurePasswordPrompt* parameter displays a popup for credentials when * is specified for either *PasswordO* or *PasswordD*.

> **NOTE USING NETDOM REMOTELY REQUIRES FIREWALL CONFIGURATION**
>
> If you want to use NetDom remotely, the Windows Firewall configuration on the computer that will be joined to the domain must allow Network Discovery and Remote Administration.

Secure Computer Creation and Joins

It is important to secure your enterprise so that only appropriate users can create computer accounts and join computers to the domain. The following sections outline best practices for managing computer account creation and domain joins.

Prestaging Computer Objects

The best practice is to prestage a computer account prior to joining the computer to the domain. Unfortunately, Windows allows you to join a computer to a domain without following best practices. You can log on to a workgroup computer as a local administrator and change the computer's membership to the domain. Then, on demand, Windows creates a computer object in the default computer container, gives you permission to join a computer to that object, and then proceeds to join the system to the domain.

There are three problems with this behavior of Windows:

- First, the computer account created automatically by Windows is placed in the default computer container, which is not where the computer object belongs in most enterprises.

- Second, you must move the computer from the default computer container into the correct OU, which is an extra step that is often forgotten.

- Third, any user can do this—no domain-level administrative permissions are required. Any user can join any computer to the domain if you don't manage and secure the process. Because a computer object is a security principal, and because the creator of a computer object owns the object and can change its attributes, this exposes a potential security vulnerability. The next sections detail these disadvantages.

Configuring the Default Computer Container

When you join a computer to the domain and the computer object does not already exist in Active Directory, Windows automatically creates a computer account in the default computer container, which is called *Computers* (CN=Computers,DC=*domain*, by default). The problem with this relates to the discussion of OU design earlier in the lesson. If you have implemented the best practices described there, you have delegated permissions to administer computer objects in specific OUs for clients and servers. Additionally, you might have linked GPOs to those OUs to manage the configuration of these computer objects. If a new computer object is created outside of those OUs, in the default computer container, the permissions and configuration it inherits from its parent container will be different than what it should have received. You will then need to remember to move the computer from the default container to the correct OU after joining the domain.

Two recommended steps reduce the likelihood of this problem. First, you should endeavor to always prestage computer accounts. If an account is prestaged for a computer in the correct OU, the computer will use the existing account when it joins the domain and will be subject to the correct delegation and configuration.

Second, to reduce the impact of systems being joined to the domain without a prestaged account, you should change the default computer container so that it is not the Computers container itself but, instead, an OU that is subject to appropriate delegation and configuration. For example, if you have an OU called Clients, you can instruct Windows to use that OU as the default computer container, so that if computers are joined to the domain without prestaged accounts, the objects are created in the Clients OU.

The Redircmp.exe command, available on domain controllers, is used to redirect the default computer container with the following syntax:

```
redircmp "DN of OU for new computer objects"
```

Now, if a computer joins the domain without a prestaged computer account, Windows creates the computer object in the specified organizational unit.

Redirecting the Default User Container

The same concepts apply to the creation of user accounts. By default, if a user account is created using a legacy practice that does not specify the OU for the account, the object is created in the default user container (CN=Users,DC=*domain*, by default). The Redirusr.exe command, available on domain controllers, can redirect the default container to an actual OU that is delegated and configured appropriately. RedirUsr, like RedirCmp, takes a single parameter: the distinguished name (DN) of the OU that will become the default user container.

EXAM TIP

The Redircmp.exe command redirects the default computer container to a specified OU. Redirusr.exe does the same for the default user container. You might see these two commands used as *distracters*—presented as potential (but incorrect) answers to questions that have nothing to do with the default computer or user containers. As you look at any exam question, evaluate the possible answers to determine whether the answers are proposing to use real commands but in the wrong application of those commands.

Restricting the Ability of Users to Create Computers

When a computer account is prestaged, the permissions on the account determine who is allowed to join that computer to the domain. When an account is not prestaged, Windows will, by default, allow any authenticated user to create a computer object in the default computer container. In fact, Windows will allow any authenticated user to create 10 computer objects in the default computer container. The creator of a computer object, by default, has permission to join that computer to the domain. It is through this mechanism that any authenticated user can join 10 computers to the domain without any explicit permissions to do so.

The 10-computer quota is configured by the *ms-DS-MachineAccountQuota* attribute of the domain. It allows any authenticated user to join a computer to the domain, no questions asked. This is problematic from a security perspective because computers are security principals. And the creator of a security principal has permission to manage that computer's properties. In a way, the quota is like allowing any domain user to create 10 user accounts, without any controls.

It is highly recommended that you close this loophole so that non-administrative users cannot join computers to the domain. To change the *ms-DS-MachineAccountQuota* attribute, follow these steps:

1. Open ADSI Edit from the Administrative Tools folder.

2. Right-click ADSI Edit and click Connect To.

3. In the Connection Point section, click Select A Well Known Naming Context, and then select Default Naming Context from the drop-down list.

4. Click OK.

5. In the console tree, expand Default Naming Context.

6. Right-click the domain folder—"dc=contoso,dc=com", for example—and then choose Properties.

7. Select ms-DS-MachineAccountQuota and click Edit.

8. Type **0** and click OK.

The Authenticated Users group also is assigned the user right to add workstations to the domain, but you do not have to modify this right if you have changed the default value of the *ms-DS-MachineAccountQuota* attribute.

After you have changed the *ms-DS-MachineAccountQuota* attribute to 0, you can be assured that the only users who can join computers to the domain are those who have been specifically delegated permission to join prestaged computer objects or create new computer objects.

 Quick Check

- What two things determine whether you can join a computer account to the domain?

Quick Check Answer

- To join a computer to a prestaged account, you must be given permission on the account to join it to the domain. If the account is not prestaged, the ms-DS-MachineAccountQuota attribute determines the number of computers you can join to the domain in the default computer container without explicit permission.

After you've eliminated this loophole, you must make sure you have given appropriate administrators explicit permission to create computer objects in the correct OUs, as described in the "Delegating Permission to Create Computers" section; otherwise, the error message shown in Figure 5-4 will appear.

FIGURE 5-4 The message that appears when a user exceeds the default computer account quota specified by the *ms-DS-MachineAccountQuota* attribute

Offline Domain Join

Windows Server 2008 R2 and Windows 7 introduce a new option for joining computers to a domain, called *offline domain join*. As the name of the feature suggests, offline domain join allows you to join a server or client to the domain even if the computer does not have network connectivity or cannot currently contact a domain controller. You use a new command, *Djoin.exe*, in a process that is detailed later in this section, to inject the Windows directory of a workgroup computer with the information it requires to join the domain at startup.

Offline domain join is an important feature for datacenters, virtual desktop infrastructures, and other wide-scale machine deployments. In such environments, physical or virtual machines are often provisioned on demand, in large numbers, and using automated methods.

If a machine runs an earlier version of Windows, the machine must be started in workgroup configuration, joined to the domain, and then restarted. If a machine runs Windows 7 or Windows Server 2008 R2, its disk can be injected with the domain join information, and it will be a member of the domain at startup. By eliminating a restart, the total cost of ownership of these environments is reduced.

Offline domain join is also useful when a computer is deployed in a lab or other disconnected environment. When the computer is connected to the domain network and started for the first time, it will already be a member of the domain. This also helps to ensure that Group Policy settings are applied at the first startup.

Four major steps are required to join a computer to the domain by using offline domain join:

1. Log on to a computer in the domain that is running Windows Server 2008 R2 or Windows 7 with an account that has permissions to join computers to the domain.

2. Use the DJoin command to provision a computer for offline domain join. This step prepopulates Active Directory with the information that Active Directory needs to join the computer to the domain, and exports the information called a *blob* to a text file.

3. At the offline computer that you want to join the domain use DJoin to import the blob into the Windows directory.

4. When you start or restart the computer, it will be a member of the domain.

Each of these steps is examined in detail in the sections that follow.

Prepare for Offline Domain Join

To perform an offline domain join, you must have the right to join computers to the domain. The Domain Admins group has this right by default. If you are not a member of the Domain Admins group, a member of the Domain Admins group must complete one of the following actions to allow you to join workstations to the domain:

- **Use Group Policy to grant you the required user rights** After you have been granted the right to join computers to the domain through Group Policy, you can create a computer account anywhere in the domain, and join a computer to the domain.

- **Edit the access control list (ACL) of the default computers container for the domain** After you have been assigned the Create Child - Allow permission for computer objects on the default Computers container, you can perform offline domain join and computers will be created in the default Computers container. You learned in an earlier topic that, by default, the Computers container is CN=Computers,dc=*domain*, and that you can use the RedirCmp command to change the default to any OU in the domain.

- **Edit the ACL of any OU and use the */machineOU* parameter** After you have been assigned the Create Child – Allow permission for computer objects in an OU, you can provision computers for offline domain join by using the */machineOU* parameter of the DJoin command.

Before you can proceed to provision a computer for offline domain join, you must log on as an account that has the right to join computers to the domain. The computer to which you log on must be running either Windows Server 2008 R2 or Windows 7. DJoin is not available in earlier versions of Windows.

Provision a Computer in Active Directory for Offline Domain Join

Run Djoin.exe from an elevated Command Prompt to provision the computer account in Active Directory. The basic syntax of DJoin is as follows:

```
djoin.exe /provision /domain DomainDNSName /machine ComputerName /savefile Filename
```

where:

- The */provision* parameter creates a new computer account in Active Directory. If the computer account already exists, add the */reuse* parameter to provision the existing computer account for offline domain join.

- *DomainDNSName* is the DNS name of the domain—for example, contoso.com.

- *ComputerName* is the name of the computer to create or reuse.

- *Filename* is the path and name of a text file that will be created. The file will contain the blob of metadata that can be used by the computer to join the domain.

For example, to create a new computer account for COMPUTER007 in the contoso.com domain, and to export its offline domain join blob to a file named COMPUTER007_Join.txt on the desktop, run the following command:

```
djoin.exe /provision /domain contoso.com /machine COMPUTER007 /savefile COMPUTER007_Join.txt
```

DJoin accepts several parameters, the most commonly used of which are the following:

- /machineOU *OU* specifies the OU in which to create the computer account, where *OU* is the distinguished name of the OU—for example, OU=Client Computers,DC=contoso,DC=com.

- /dcname *domainControllerName* specifies the DC on which to create the computer account. By default, the domain controller location process selects a domain controller automatically. With this switch, you can select a particular DC.

- /downlevel specifies that the domain controller runs a version of Windows earlier than Windows Server 2008 R2.

The computer account is provisioned in Active Directory, and account metadata is exported as a base64-encoded blob to the file specified by the */savefile* parameter. Although the information is encrypted, it is highly sensitive. It contains the machine account password and information about the domain including the domain name, the name of a domain controller, and the SID of the domain. Therefore, the blob and the file that contains it should be treated just as securely as a plaintext password. Care must be taken when transferring the information.

Perform an Offline Domain Join

The account metadata that was exported in a blob to a text file by using Djoin.exe /provision can be imported to a computer, after which the computer will become a domain member at the next startup.

On a computer that is already running Windows, you can import the account metadata by using the DJoin command, which uses the following syntax:

```
djoin.exe /requestODJ /loadfile Filename /windowspath %SystemRoot% /localos
```

where:

- /requestODJ specifies that you want to perform an offline domain join operation.

- *Filename* is the path and file name of the text file that contains the account metadata blob. This is the file that you created by using Djoin.exe /provision.

- %SystemRoot% is the built-in Windows variable that represents the directory in which Windows is installed. Alternately, you can use the variable %WinDir%.

- /localos specifies that you are injecting the domain join information into the local computer.

For example, on COMPUTER007, run the following command:

```
djoin.exe /requestODJ /loadfile COMPUTER007_Join.txt /windowspath %SystemRoot% /localos
```

On a computer that is installed but not started, you can inject the account metadata into the Windows folder of the system. Consider a scenario in which you have deployed a new physical or virtual machine by applying a standardized, corporate image. The new computer has not yet been started.

In this scenario, you must mount the disk drive of the new computer to an existing computer by using one of several procedures, described later. When you mount the disk drive, it appears as an additional volume on the existing computer. You can then run DJoin with the following syntax:

```
djoin.exe /requestODJ /loadfile Filename /windowspath PathToWindowsFolder
```

where:

- /requestODJ specifies that you want to perform an offline domain join operation.
- *Filename* is the path and file name of the text file that contains the account metadata blob. This is the file that you created by using Djoin.exe /provision.
- *PathToWindowsFolder* is the path to the Windows folder of the offline computer. The path you enter must be the path as it is seen on the computer that you are using to run DJoin.

For example, let's assume that you are logged on to a computer named DESKTOP101 that is running Windows 7. You have just applied an image to a new computer that is named COMPUTER007. You mount COMPUTER007's hard disk, and it appears as the D:\ drive. You open an elevated Command Prompt and run the following command:

```
djoin.exe /requestODJ /loadfile COMPUTER007_Join.txt /windowspath PathToWindowsFolder
```

If the computer you want to join the domain is a physical computer, you can mount the hard disk drive of the computer as an additional disk for a computer that is already running Windows. For example, you could put the new computer's disk into an external disk enclosure and attach it to a computer with a USB cable.

If the computer you want to join the domain is a virtual machine, you can mount its virtual disk to a virtual machine that is already running Windows. The steps for mounting a virtual disk to an existing virtual machine vary depending on the virtualization software that you are using.

If the computer you want to join the domain is a Hyper-V virtual machine, you can mount its virtual disk to a physical computer that is already installed. In the Computer Management console, first select Disk Management, then right-click Disk Management, and then choose Attach VHD.

In each of these scenarios, the computer you use to mount the disk of the new computer must be running Windows 7 or Windows Server 2008 R2 so that you can use the DJoin command.

MORE INFO   **OFFLINE DOMAIN JOIN**

The following articles provide additional details regarding offline domain join: "What's New in AD DS: Offline Domain Join" at *http://technet.microsoft.com/en-us/library/ dd391977(WS.10).aspx*, and "Offline Domain Join (Djoin.exe) Step-by-Step Guide" at *http://technet.microsoft.com/en-us/library/offline-domain-join-djoin-step-by-step(WS.10).aspx*. The DJoin command and its syntax are defined at *http://technet.microsoft.com/en-us/library/ff793312(WS.10).aspx*.

PRACTICE   Creating Computers and Joining the Domain

In this practice, you implement best practices for creating computers and joining systems to the domain. You begin by creating an OU structure to host new computer objects. You then create prestaged computer objects and delegate permission to join the computers to the domain. You delegate permission to create computer objects, and you redirect the default computer container. Finally, you provision a computer account for offline domain join.

Before performing the exercises, you must have certain objects in the contoso.com domain. Some of these objects were created in practices in earlier chapters. If the objects already exist, move them to the locations indicated.

- A first-level OU named Admins with a sub-OU named Groups.

- A global security group in the Admins\Groups OU named Server Admins.

- A global security group in the Admins\Groups OU named Help Desk.

- A first-level OU named User Accounts.

- A user in the User Accounts OU named Jeff Ford. The user is a member of Domain Users and Server Admins. Ensure that the account has a password and is enabled.

- A user in the User Accounts OU named Linda Mitchell. The user is a member of Domain Users and Help Desk. Ensure that the account has a password and is enabled.

In addition, if a computer object for DESKTOP101 already exists, delete it. Finally, in this and other practices in this training kit, you will log on to the domain controller with user accounts that are not a member of Domain Administrators or the domain's Administrators group. Therefore, you must give all user accounts the right to log on locally to the domain controllers in your practice environment. Follow the steps in the article, "Grant a Member the Right to Logon Locally," at *http://technet.microsoft.com/en-us/library/ee957044(WS.10).aspx* to grant the Allow Logon Locally right to the Administrators and Domain Users groups. If you will use Remote Desktop Services to connect to the domain controller—rather than logging on locally—grant the Allow Logon Through Remote Desktop Services right. Reboot the server or otherwise refresh Group Policy. This is for the practice environment only. In a production environment, you should not grant users the right to log on to domain controllers.

EXERCISE 1   Create OUs for Client and Server Computer Objects

Before you can create computer accounts, you must create OUs for the objects. In this exercise, you create OUs for server and computer objects. If the Clients and Servers OUs already exist, you can skip this exercise.

1. Log on to SERVER01 as Administrator.
2. Open the Active Directory Users And Computers snap-in and expand the domain.
3. Right-click the contoso.com domain, point to New, and then click Organizational Unit.
4. Type **Clients** and click OK.
5. Right-click the contoso.com domain, point to New, and then click Organizational Unit.
6. Type **Servers** and click OK.

EXERCISE 2   Create Computer Objects

After creating an OU for computer objects, you can prestage accounts for computers that will join the domain. In this exercise, you prestage an account for a client and an account for a server and delegate the ability to join the computers to the domain.

1. Right-click the Clients OU, point to New, and then click Computer.
2. The New Object – Computer dialog box appears, as shown in Figure 5-3.
3. Type the computer's name in the Computer Name box: **DESKTOP101**.
4. Click Change next to the User Or Group box.
5. In the Select User Or Group dialog box that appears, type the name of the user or group that will be allowed to join the computer to the domain: **Help Desk**. Click OK.
6. Click OK to close the New Object – Computer dialog box.
7. Right-click the Servers OU, point to New, and then click Computer.
8. The New Object – Computer dialog box appears, as shown in Figure 5-3.
9. Type the computer's name in the Computer Name box: **SERVER15**.
10. Click Change next to the User Or Group box.
11. In the Select User Or Group dialog box that appears, enter the name of the user or group that will be allowed to join the computer to the domain: **Server Admins**. Click OK.
12. Click OK to close the New Object – Computer dialog box.

EXERCISE 3   Delegate the Ability to Create Computer Objects

You must have permission to create computer objects to create accounts as you did in Exercise 2, "Create Computer Objects." The Administrator account has such permissions, but you might want to delegate the ability to create computer accounts to other groups. In this exercise, you delegate least-privilege permissions to create computer objects.

1. On SERVER01, open the Active Directory Users And Computers snap-in.
2. Click the View menu and ensure that Advanced Features is selected.
3. Right-click Clients and choose Properties.

4. On the Security tab, click Advanced.

5. Click Add.

6. Type **Help Desk** and click OK.

7. On the Object tab, in the Apply To drop-down list, choose This Object And All Descendant Objects.

8. In the Permissions list, select the Allow check box next to the Create Computer Objects permission.

9. Click OK three times to close all dialog boxes.

10. Optionally, you can test your delegation by running Command Prompt as Linda Mitchell and performing Exercise 1, "Create a Computer with DSAdd," in Lesson 2, "Automating the Creation of Computer Objects."

   To run Command Prompt as another user, hold the Shift key and right-click Command Prompt in the Start menu, and then click Run As Different User. In the credentials dialog box, enter the user name and password for Linda Mitchell.

EXERCISE 4   Redirect the Default Computer Container

It is recommended that you redirect the default computer container so that any new computer objects generated by joining a computer to the domain without a prestaged account will be created in a managed OU rather than in the Computers container. In this exercise, you use Redircmp.exe to redirect the default computer container.

1. On SERVER01, open Command Prompt.

2. Type the following command and press Enter:

   ```
   redircmp "OU=Clients,DC=contoso,DC=com"
   ```

EXERCISE 5   Provision a Computer for Offline Domain Join

In this exercise, you use the DJoin command to provision a computer account for offline domain join.

1. On SERVER01, open Command Prompt.

2. Type the following command and press Enter:

   ```
   djoin.exe /provision /domain contoso.com /machine LAPTOP101
       /machineOU "OU=Clients,DC=contoso,DC=com"
       /savefile "C:\Users\Administrator\Desktop\LAPTOP101_Join.txt"
   ```

3. Open the LAPTOP101_Join.txt file on the desktop.

   The account metadata is base64 encoded.

Lesson Summary

- The Computers container does not support linking Group Policy objects or creating child OUs. Create an OU structure to reflect the administrative model of your organization.

- Always prestage computer accounts: Create a computer object in Active Directory prior to joining the system to the domain.

- To join the domain successfully, you must be a local Administrator of the computer, a computer account must be created, and you must provide domain credentials that have permission on the computer object to join the domain.

- You use Redircmp.exe to redirect the default computer container to an OU that has been delegated and configured to meet your business requirements.

- By default, the *ms-DS-MachineAccountQuota* attribute allows all authenticated users to join up to 10 systems to the domain. Windows will create computer objects for the joined systems in the default computer container. Reduce this quota to zero to prevent nonadministrative users from creating security principals.

Lesson Review

You can use the following questions to test your knowledge of the information in Lesson 1, "Creating Computers and Joining the Domain." The questions are also available on the companion CD if you prefer to review them in electronic form.

> **NOTE ANSWERS**
>
> Answers to these questions and explanations of why each answer choice is right or wrong are located in the "Answers" section at the end of the book.

1. You want to require all new computer accounts created when computers join the domain to be placed in the Clients OU. Which command should you use?

   A. DSMove

   B. Move-Item

   C. NetDom

   D. RedirCmp

2. You want to prevent nonadministrative users from joining computers to the domain. What should you do?

   A. Set *ms-DS-MachineAccountQuota* to zero.

   B. Set *ms-DS-DefaultQuota* to zero.

   C. Remove the Add Workstations To Domain user right from Authenticated Users.

   D. On the domain, deny the Authenticated Users group the Create Computer Objects permission.

3. You want to join a remote computer to the domain. Which command should you use?

   A. Dsadd.exe

   B. Netdom.exe

   C. Dctest.exe

   D. System.cpl

Lesson 2: Automating the Creation of Computer Objects

The steps you learned in Lesson 1 for creating a computer account become burdensome if you are tasked with creating dozens or even hundreds of computer accounts at the same time. Commands such as CSVDE, LDIFDE, DSAdd, and Windows PowerShell can import and automate the creation of computer objects. In this lesson, you learn to import, automate, and provision computer objects. You build upon the knowledge of these commands that you gained from reading Lessons 1 and 2 of Chapter 3, which are a prerequisite for this lesson.

> **After this lesson, you will be able to:**
> - Use CSVDE and LDIFDE to import computers.
> - Create computers with DSAdd.
> - Create computers with NetDom.
> - Create computers with Windows PowerShell.
>
> **Estimated lesson time: 30 minutes**

Importing Computers with CSVDE

You were introduced to the Comma-Separated Values Data Exchange (CSVDE) command in Lesson 1 of Chapter 3. CSVDE is a command-line tool that imports or exports Active Directory objects from or to a comma-delimited text file (also known as a comma-separated value text file, or .csv file). The basic syntax of the CSVDE command is:

```
csvde [-i] [-f "Filename"] [-k]
```

The -*i* parameter specifies import mode; without it, the default mode of CSVDE is export. The -*f* parameter identifies the file name to import from or export to. The -*k* parameter is useful during import operations because it instructs CSVDE to ignore errors, including Object Already Exists, Constraint Violation, and Attribute Or Value Already Exists errors.

Comma-delimited files can be created, modified, and opened with tools as familiar as Notepad and Microsoft Office Excel. The first line of the file defines the attributes by their Lightweight Directory Access Protocol (LDAP) attribute names. Each object follows, one per line, and must contain exactly the attributes listed on the first line. A sample file is shown in Excel in Figure 5-5.

When importing computers, be sure to include the *userAccountControl* attribute and set it to 4096. This attribute ensures that the computer can join the domain by using the account. Also include the pre-Windows 2000 logon name of the computer, the *sAMAccountName* attribute, which is the name of the computer followed by a dollar sign ($), as shown in Figure 5-5.

	A	B	C	D	E
1	DN	objectClass	name	userAccountControl	sAMAccountName
2	CN=DESKTOP103,OU=Clients,DC=contoso,DC=con	computer	DESKTOP103	4096	DESKTOP103$
3	CN=DESKTOP104,OU=Clients,DC=contoso,DC=con	computer	DESKTOP104	4096	DESKTOP104$
4	CN=SERVER02,OU=Servers,DC=contoso,DC=com	computer	SERVER02	4096	SERVER02$

FIGURE 5-5 A .csv file, opened in Excel, that creates three computer accounts

---

MORE INFO   CSVDE

In Chapters 3 and 4, you used the CSVDE command to import users and groups. For more information about CSVDE, including details regarding its parameters and usage to export directory objects, type **csvde /?** or search the Windows Server 2008 R2 Help and Support Center.

Importing Computers with LDIFDE

Chapter 3 also introduced you to Ldifde.exe, which imports data from files in the LDAP Data Interchange Format (LDIF) format. LDIF files are text files within which operations are specified by a block of lines separated by a blank line. Each operation begins with the *DN* attribute of the object that is the target of the operation. The next line, *changeType*, specifies the type of operation: *add*, *modify*, or *delete*.

The following listing is an LDIF file that creates two server accounts:

```
dn: CN=SERVER10,OU=Servers,DC=contoso,DC=com
changetype: add
objectClass: top
objectClass: person
objectClass: organizationalPerson
objectClass: user
objectClass: computer
cn: SERVER10
userAccountControl: 4096
sAMAccountName: SERVER10$

dn: CN=SERVER11,OU=Servers,DC=contoso,DC=com
changetype: add
objectClass: top
objectClass: person
objectClass: organizationalPerson
objectClass: user
objectClass: computer
cn: SERVER11
userAccountControl: 4096
sAMAccountName: SERVER11$
```

The basic syntax of the LDIFDE command is similar to that of the CSVDE command:

```
ldifde [-i] [-f "Filename"] [-k]
```

By default, LDIFDE is in export mode. The *-i* parameter specifies import mode. You must specify the *-f* mode to identify the file you are using for import or export. LDIFDE will stop when it encounters errors unless you specify the *-k* parameter, in which case, LDIFDE continues processing.

Creating Computers with DSAdd

The DSAdd command was used in previous chapters to create objects in Active Directory. To create computer objects, simply type **dsadd computer *ComputerDN*** where *ComputerDN* is the distinguished name (DN) of the computer, such as "CN=Desktop123,OU=Desktops, DC=contoso,DC=com".

If the computer's DN includes a space, surround the entire DN with quotation marks. The *ComputerDN* parameter can include more than one distinguished name for new computer objects, making DSAdd Computer a handy way to generate multiple objects at the same time. The parameter can be entered in one of the following ways:

- By typing each DN on the command line, separated by spaces.
- By leaving the *DN* parameter empty, at which point you can type the DNs, one at a time, at the keyboard console of the command prompt. Press Enter after each DN. Press Ctrl+Z and Enter after the last DN.
- By piping a list of DNs from another command such as DSQuery.

The DSAdd Computer command can take the following optional parameters after the DN parameter:

- -samid *ComputerName*
- -desc *Description*
- -loc *Location*

Creating Computers with NetDom

The DSAdd command was used in previous chapters to create objects in Active Directory.

To create computer objects, simply type dsadd computer ComputerDN where *ComputerDN* is the distinguished name (DN) of the computer, such as "CN=Desktop123,OU=Desktops, DC=contoso,DC=com". If the computer's DN includes a space, surround the entire DN with quotation marks.

The DSAdd Computer command can take the following optional parameters after the DN parameter:

- -samid ComputerName

* -desc Description
* -loc Location

If you type DSAdd Computer /?, the help text for the command states the following:

> If you enter multiple values, the values must be separated by spaces (for example, a list of computer distinguished names).

This is not accurate. You cannot use the DSAdd Computer command to add multiple computers with a single command.

Creating Computers with Windows PowerShell

Chapter 3 introduced you to Windows PowerShell, the new administrative and automation shell for Active Directory. You learned how to create users in that chapter. As with user objects, you can use Windows PowerShell to manage computer objects.

The following cmdlets work with Active Directory group objects:

- **New-ADComputer** Creates a computer.

  As with the *New-ADUser* cmdlet, you can use a template to create a new computer with specific properties preconfigured.

  Windows PowerShell provides cmdlets that you can use to consume a data source. For example, the *Import-CSV* cmdlet can consume a CSV file of computer names and pipe each name to *New-ADComputer* to create more than one computer.

- **Remove-ADComputer** Deletes a computer.

- **Get-ADComputer** Retrieves an object reference to a computer.

- **Set-ADComputer** Configures properties of a computer.

As you learned in Chapter 3, you can use the *Get-Help* cmdlet to learn more about these cmdlets. You will use Windows PowerShell to create groups in the Practice for this lesson.

PRACTICE **Automating the Creation of Computer Objects**

In this practice, you implement automation to import and create computers in the contoso.com domain. Before performing the exercises in this practice, be sure that you have the following objects in the contoso.com domain.

- A first-level OU called Clients
- A first-level OU called Servers

EXERCISE 1 **Create a Computer with DSAdd**

The DSAdd command adds a computer in Command Prompt. An advantage of the DSAdd command is that it requires only the computer's DN. It creates the *sAMAccountName* and *userAccountControl* attributes automatically. In this exercise, you create a computer with *Dsadd.exe*. (If you have already performed this exercise as part of the last step of Exercise 3 in

Lesson 1, you do not need to perform it a second time. If you try to add the computer twice, you will receive an error.)

1. Log on to SERVER01 as Administrator.

2. Open Command Prompt.

3. Type the following command and press Enter:

```
dsadd computer "CN=DESKTOP152,OU=Clients,DC=contoso,DC=com"
```

4. Using the Active Directory Users And Computers snap-in, verify that the computer was created successfully.

EXERCISE 2 Import Computers by Using CSVDE

When you want to create more than a few computers, you might find it easier to import the computer objects from a data source such as a .csv file. In this exercise, you use CSVDE to import computer accounts from a .csv file.

1. In Notepad, type the following lines.

```
DN,objectClass,name,userAccountControl,sAMAccountName
"CN=DESKTOP103,OU=Clients,DC=contoso,DC=com",computer,DESKTOP103,4096,DESKTOP103$
"CN=DESKTOP104,OU=Clients,DC=contoso,DC=com",computer,DESKTOP104,4096,DESKTOP104$
"CN=SERVER03,OU=Servers,DC=contoso,DC=com",computer,SERVER03,4096,SERVER03$
```

2. Save the file to your Documents folder with the name "Computers.csv", including the quotes so that Notepad does not add a .txt extension.

3. Open Command Prompt, type the following command, and then press Enter:

```
csvde -i -f "%userprofile%\documents\computers.csv"
```

4. Open the Active Directory Users And Computers snap-in and verify that the computer objects were created successfully.

EXERCISE 3 Import Computers from an LDIF File

LDIF files are not as familiar to most administrators as .csv files, but they are powerful and relatively easy to master. In this exercise, you create an LDIF file and import it by using Ldifde.exe.

1. In Notepad, enter the following, making certain to include a blank line between the two operations (before the *dn* line for *SERVER11*):

```
dn: CN=SERVER10,OU=Servers,DC=contoso,DC=com
changetype: add
objectClass: top
objectClass: person
objectClass: organizationalPerson
objectClass: user
objectClass: computer
cn: SERVER10
userAccountControl: 4096
sAMAccountName: SERVER10$
```

```
dn: CN=SERVER11,OU=Servers,DC=contoso,DC=com
changetype: add
objectClass: top
objectClass: person
objectClass: organizationalPerson
objectClass: user
objectClass: computer
cn: SERVER11
userAccountControl: 4096
sAMAccountName: SERVER11$
```

2. Save the file to your Documents folder with the name "Computers.ldf", including the quotation marks so Notepad doesn't add a .txt extension.

3. Open Command Prompt, type the following command, and then press Enter:

```
ldifde -i -f "%userprofile%\documents\computers.ldf"
```

4. Open the Active Directory Users And Computers snap-in and verify that the computers were created successfully.

EXERCISE 4 Create a Computer with Windows PowerShell

Windows PowerShell lets you use ADSI to create and manipulate Active Directory objects. In this exercise, you create a computer with Windows PowerShell.

1. Open Windows PowerShell, type the following command on one line, and press Enter:

```
New-ADComputer -Name "DESKTOP154" -sAMAccountName "DESKTOP154" -Path
    "OU=Clients,DC=contoso,DC=com"
```

2. Open the Active Directory Users And Computers snap-in and confirm that DESKTOP154 was created in the Clients OU.

Lesson Summary

- Use CSVDE to import computers from comma-delimited text files, which can be edited with tools as simple as Notepad or Excel.
- Use LDIFDE to import LDIF files containing computer add operations.
- DSAdd can add a computer to the domain with a single command.
- You can use Windows PowerShell to manage computers.

Lesson Review

You can use the following questions to test your knowledge of the information in Lesson 2, "Automating the Creation of Computer Objects." The questions are also available on the companion CD if you prefer to review them in electronic form.

1. Your manager has asked you to create an account for DESKTOP234. Which of the following lets you do that in one step? (Choose all that apply.)

   A. CSVDE

   B. LDIFDE

   C. DSAdd

   D. Windows PowerShell

2. Your hardware vendor has given you an Excel worksheet containing the asset tags of computers that will be delivered next week. You want to create computer objects for the computers in advance. Your naming convention specifies that computers' names are their asset tags. Which of the following tools can you use to import the computers? (Choose all that apply.)

   A. CSVDE

   B. LDIFDE

   C. DSAdd

   D. Windows PowerShell

Lesson 3: Supporting Computer Objects and Accounts

A computer account begins its lifecycle when it is created and when the computer joins the domain. Day-to-day administrative tasks include configuring computer properties; moving the computer between OUs; managing the computer itself; and renaming, resetting, disabling, enabling, and eventually deleting the computer object. This lesson looks closely at the computer properties and procedures involved with these tasks and equips you to administer computers in a domain.

After this lesson, you will be able to:

- Configure the properties of a computer object in Active Directory.
- Move a computer between OUs.
- Rename a computer.
- Disable and enable computer accounts.
- Reset the secure channel of a domain member computer.
- Perform administrative tasks with the Active Directory Users And Computers snap-in, command-line commands, and Windows PowerShell.

Estimated lesson time: 45 minutes

Configuring Computer Properties

When you create a computer object using Active Directory Users And Computers, you are prompted to configure only the most fundamental attributes, including the computer name and the delegation to join the computer to the domain. Computers have several properties that are not visible when you are creating the computer object; you should configure these properties as part of the process of staging the computer account.

Open a computer object's Properties dialog box to set its location and description, configure its group memberships and dial-in permissions, and link it to the user object of the user to whom the computer is assigned. The Operating System tab is read-only. The information is blank until a computer joins the domain using that account, at which time the client publishes the information to its account.

Several object classes in Active Directory support the *managedBy* attribute that is shown on the Managed By tab. This linked attribute creates a cross-reference to a user object. All other properties—the addresses and telephone numbers—are displayed directly from the user object. They are not stored as part of the computer object itself. Some organizations use the Managed By tab to link the computer to the primary user of the computer. Alternately, you might choose to link the computer to a group that is responsible for the support of a computer—an option that might be attractive for computer accounts that represent servers, for example.

On the Member Of tab of a computer's Properties dialog box, you can add the computer to groups. The ability to manage computers in groups is an important and often underutilized feature of Active Directory. A group to which computers belong can be used to assign resource access permissions to the computer, to filter the application of a GPO, or as a collection for a software management tool, such as Microsoft System Center Configuration Manager 2007.

As with users and groups, you can select more than one computer object and subsequently manage or modify properties of all selected computers simultaneously.

Configuring Computer Attributes with DSMod and Windows PowerShell

The DSMod command, which you learned about in Chapter 3 and Chapter 4, is able to modify only the *description* and the *location* attributes. It uses the following syntax:

```
dsmod computer "DN of Computer" [-desc Description] [-loc Location]
```

In Windows PowerShell, you can use the *Set-ADComputer* cmdlet to configure computer object attributes.

Moving a Computer

Many organizations have multiple OUs for computer objects. Some domains, for example, have computer OUs based on geographic sites, as shown in Figure 5-1. If you have more than one OU for computers, it is likely that someday you will need to move a computer between OUs.

To move a computer using the Active Directory Users And Computers snap-in:

- Drag and drop or
- Right-click the computer, and then click Move.

You must have appropriate permissions to move an object in Active Directory. Default permissions allow Account Operators to move computer objects between containers, including the Computers container and any OUs *except* into or out of the Domain Controllers OU. Administrators, which include Domain Admins and Enterprise Admins, can move computer objects between any containers, including the Computers container, the Domain Controllers OU, and any other OUs. There is no way to delegate the specific task of moving an object in Active Directory. Instead, your ability to move a computer is derived from your ability to delete an object in the source container and create an object in the destination container. When you move the object, you are not actually deleting and re-creating it; those are just the permissions that are evaluated to allow you to perform a move.

The DSMove command allows you to move a computer object or any other object. The syntax of DSMove is:

```
dsmove ObjectDN [-newname NewName] [-newparent ParentDN]
```

The -*newname* parameter lets you rename an object. The -*newparent* parameter lets you move an object. To move a computer named DESKTOP153 from the Computers container to the Clients OU, you would type the following:

```
dsmove "CN=DESKTOP153,CN=Computers,DC=contoso,DC=com" -newparent
  "OU=Clients,DC=contoso,DC=com"
```

In Windows PowerShell, you can use the *Move-ADObject* or *Move-Item* cmdlets to move a user to another OU.

Before you move a computer, consider the implications to delegation and configuration. The target OU might have different permissions than the originating OU, in which case the object inherits new permissions affecting who is able to manage the object further. The target OU might also be within the scope of different GPOs, which would change the configuration of settings on the system itself.

Managing a Computer from the Active Directory Users And Computers Snap-In

One of the beneficial but lesser-used features of the Active Directory Users And Computers snap-in is the *Manage* command. Select a computer in the Active Directory Users And Computers snap-in, right-click it, and choose Manage. The Computer Management console opens, focused on the selected computer, giving you instant access to the computer's event logs, local users and groups, shared folder configuration, and other management extensions. The tool launches with the credentials used to run the Active Directory Users And Computers snap-in, so you must be running the Active Directory Users And Computers snap-in as a member of the remote computer's Administrators group to gain the maximum functionality from the Computer Management console.

Understanding the Computer's Logon and Secure Channel

Every member computer in an Active Directory domain maintains a computer account with a user name (*sAMAccountName*) and password, just like a user account does. The computer stores its password in the form of a local security authority (LSA) secret and changes its password with the domain every 30 days or so. The NetLogon service uses the credentials to log on to the domain, which establishes the secure channel with a domain controller.

Recognizing Computer Account Problems

Computer accounts and the secure relationships between computers and their domain are robust. However, certain scenarios might arise in which a computer is no longer able to authenticate with the domain. Examples of such scenarios include the following:

- After reinstalling the operating system on a workstation, the workstation cannot authenticate even though the technician used the same computer name. Because the new installation generated a new SID the new computer does not belong to the domain, and because the new computer does not know the computer account password in the domain, it cannot authenticate to the domain.

- A computer is completely restored from backup and cannot authenticate. It is likely that the computer changed its password with the domain after the backup operation. Computers change their passwords every 30 days, and Active Directory remembers the current and previous passwords. If the restore operation restored the computer with a significantly outdated password, the computer will not be able to authenticate.

- A computer's LSA secret gets out of sync with the password known by the domain. You can think of this as the computer forgetting its password, although it did not forget its password; it just disagrees with the domain over what the password is. When this happens, the computer cannot authenticate and the secure channel cannot be created.

The most common signs of computer account problems are:

- Messages at logon indicate that a domain controller cannot be contacted, that the computer account might be missing, that the password on the computer account is incorrect, or that the trust relationship (another way of saying "the secure relationship") between the computer and the domain has been lost. An example of an error indicating a lost trust relationship is shown in Figure 5-6.

FIGURE 5-6 An error message indicating a failed secure channel

- Error messages or events in the event log indicate similar problems or suggest that passwords, trusts, secure channels, or relationships with the domain or a domain controller have failed. One such error is NETLOGON Event ID 3210: Failed To Authenticate, which appears in the computer's event log.

- A computer account is missing in Active Directory.

Resetting a Computer Account

When the secure channel fails, you must reset it. Many administrators do so by removing the computer from the domain, putting it in a workgroup, and then rejoining the domain. This is not a good practice because it has the potential to delete the computer account altogether, which loses the computer's SID and, more importantly, its group memberships. When you rejoin the domain, even though the computer has the same name, the account has a new SID, and all the group memberships of the previous computer object must be re-created.

To reset the secure channel between a domain member and the domain, use the Active Directory Users And Computers snap-in, Dsmod.exe, Netdom.exe, or Nltest.exe. If you reset the account, the computer's SID remains the same and it maintains its group memberships.

To reset the secure channel using the Active Directory Users And Computers snap-in:

1. Right-click a computer, and then click Reset Account.

2. Click Yes to confirm your choice.

3. Re-join the computer to the domain, and then restart the computer.

To reset the secure channel using DSMod:

1. Type the following command:

   dsmod computer "*Computer DN*" -reset.

2. Re-join the computer to the domain, and then restart the computer.

To reset the secure channel using NetDom, type the following command:

netdom reset *MachineName* /domain *DomainName* /User0 *UserName* /Password0 {*Password* | *}

where the account with the credentials provided as *UserName* and *Password* is a member of the local Administrators group of the computer.

This command resets the secure channel by attempting to reset the password on both the computer and the domain, so it does not require rejoining or restarting.

To reset the secure channel using NLTest, on the computer that has lost its trust type the command:

nltest /Server:*ServerName* /SC_Reset:*DOMAIN\DomainController*

For example:

nltest /server:SERVER02 /sc_reset:CONTOSO\SERVER01

This command, like NetDom, attempts to reset the secure channel by resetting the password on both the computer and in the domain, so it does not require rejoining or rebooting.

Because NLTest and NetDom reset the secure channel without requiring a reboot, you should try those commands first. Only if those are not successful should you use the Reset Account command or DSMod to reset the computer account.

Renaming a Computer

When you rename a computer, you must be careful to do it correctly. Remember that the computer uses its name to authenticate with the domain, so if you rename only the domain object, or only the computer itself, they will be out of sync. You must rename the computer in such a way that both the computer and the domain object are changed.

You can rename a computer correctly by logging on to the computer itself, either locally or with a remote desktop session.

1. Open System Properties from Control Panel.

2. In the Computer Name, Domain, And Workgroup Settings section, click Change Settings.

3. If you are prompted by User Account Control, click Continue.

4. On the Computer Name tab, click Change.

5. Type the new name and click OK twice to close the dialog boxes.

6. Restart the computer to allow the change to take effect.

In Command Prompt, you can use the NetDom command with the following syntax:

```
netdom renamecomputer MachineName /NewName:NewName
    [/UserO:LocalUsername] [/PasswordO:{LocalPassword|*} ]
    [/UserD:DomainUsername] [/PasswordD:{DomainPassword|*} ]
    [/SecurePasswordPrompt] [/REBoot[:TimeInSeconds]]
```

In addition to specifying the computer to rename (*MachineName*) and the desired new name (*NewName*), you must have credentials that are a member of the local Administrators group on the computer and credentials that have permission to rename the domain computer object. By default, *Netdom.exe* uses the credentials with which the command is executed. You can specify credentials, using *UserO* and *PasswordO* for the credentials in the computer's local Administrators group, and *UserD* and *PasswordD* for the domain credentials with permission to rename the computer object. Specifying * for the password causes *Netdom.exe* to prompt for the password on the command line. The *SecurePasswordPrompt* parameter displays a popup for credentials when * is specified for either *PasswordO* or *PasswordD*. After you rename a computer, you must restart it. The *REBoot* parameter causes the system to reboot after 30 seconds unless otherwise specified by *TimeInSeconds*.

When you rename a computer, you can adversely affect services running on it. For example, Active Directory Certificate Services (AD CS) relies on the server's name. Be certain to consider the impact of renaming a computer before doing so. Do not use these methods to rename a domain controller.

 Quick Check

- A user complains that when she attempts to log on, she receives an error message indicating the trust with the domain has been lost. You want to attempt to reset the secure channel without rebooting her system. Which two commands can you use?

Quick Check Answer

- The Netdom.exe and Nltest.exe commands reset the secure channel without requiring you to rejoin the computer to the domain; therefore, they don't require restarting the computer.

Disabling and Enabling Computer Accounts

If a computer is taken offline or is not to be used for an extended period of time, you should consider disabling the account. This recommendation reflects the security principle that an identity store should allow authentication only of the minimum number of accounts required to achieve the goals of an organization. Disabling the account does not modify the computer's SID or group membership, so when the computer is brought back online, the account can be enabled.

To disable a computer in the Active Directory Users And Computers snap-in, right-click the computer, and then click Disable Account. A disabled account appears with a down-arrow icon in the Active Directory Users And Computers snap-in, as shown in Figure 5-7.

FIGURE 5-7 A disabled computer account

While an account is disabled, the computer cannot create a secure channel with the domain. The result is that users who have not previously logged on to the computer, and who, therefore, do not have cached credentials on the computer, will be unable to log on until the secure channel is reestablished by enabling the account.

To enable a computer account, right-click the computer, and then click Enable Account.

To disable or enable a computer in Command Prompt, use the DSMod command. The syntax used to disable or enable computers is:

```
dsmod computer ComputerDN -disabled yes
dsmod computer ComputerDN -disabled no
```

Deleting Computer Accounts

You have learned that each computer account, like each user account, maintains a unique SID, which allows an administrator to grant permissions to computers. Also like user accounts, computers can belong to groups. Therefore, like user accounts, it is important to understand the effect of deleting a computer account. When a computer account is deleted, its group memberships and SID are lost. If the deletion is accidental, and another computer account is created with the same name, it is nonetheless a new account with a new SID. Group memberships must be reestablished, and any permissions assigned to the deleted computer must be reassigned to the new account. Delete computer objects only when you are certain that you no longer require those security-related attributes of the object.

To delete a computer account using Active Directory Users And Computers:

1. Right-click the computer object, and then click Delete.

   You are prompted to confirm the deletion and, because deletion is not reversible, the default response to the prompt is No.

2. Click Yes to delete the object.

The DSRm command, introduced in Chapter 3, deletes a computer object in Command Prompt. To delete a computer with DSRm, type:

```
dsrm ObjectDN
```

where *ObjectDN* is the distinguished name of the computer, such as "CN=Desktop153, OU=Clients,DC=contoso,DC=com." Again, you will be prompted to confirm the deletion.

Recycling Computer Accounts

If a computer account's group memberships and SID, and the permissions assigned to that SID, are important to the operations of a domain, you do not want to delete that account. So what would you do if a computer was replaced with a new system with upgraded hardware? This is another scenario in which you would reset a computer account.

Resetting a computer account resets its password but maintains all of the computer object's properties. With a reset password, the account becomes, in effect, available for use. Any computer can then join the domain using that account, including the upgraded system. In effect, you've recycled the computer account, assigning it to a new piece of hardware. You can even rename the account. The SID and group memberships remain the same.

As you learned earlier in this lesson, the *Reset Account* command is available in the context menu when you right-click a computer object. The DSMod command can also be used to reset a computer account. For example, type:

```
dsmod computer "ComputerDN" -reset.
```

PRACTICE   **Supporting Computer Objects and Accounts**

In this practice, you support and troubleshoot computer accounts with the skills you learned in this chapter. To perform the exercises in this practice, you must have the following objects in the contoso.com domain.

- A first-level OU named Clients.
- Two computer objects, DESKTOP154 and DESKTOP155, in the Clients OU.
- An OU named Desktops and an OU named Laptops in the Clients OU.
- A first-level OU named User Accounts.
- User accounts in the User Accounts OU for Linda Mitchell and Scott Mitchell. Populate sample contact information for the accounts: address, telephone, and e-mail.
- A first-level OU named Groups.
- A global security group in the Groups OU named Sales Desktops.

EXERCISE 1   Manage Computer Objects

In this exercise, you perform several common administrative tasks related to computers as you support the computers assigned to Linda Mitchell and Scott Mitchell, two salespeople at Contoso, Ltd.

1. Log on to SERVER01 as Administrator.

2. Open the Active Directory Users And Computers snap-in.

3. Select the Clients OU.

4. In the details pane, right-click DESKTOP154 and choose Properties.

5. On the Managed By tab, click Change.

6. Type the user name for Scott Mitchell and click OK.

   The Managed By tab reflects the contact information you populated in Scott Mitchell's user object.

7. Click Properties.

   The Properties button on the Managed By tab takes you to the object referred to by the *managedBy* attribute.

8. Click OK to close each dialog box.

9. Repeat steps 4–8 to associate DESKTOP155 with Linda Mitchell.

10. In the console details pane of the Clients OU, select both DESKTOP154 and DESKTOP155.

11. Drag both objects into the Desktops OU. Click Yes to confirm your action.

12. In the console tree, select the Desktops OU.

13. In the details pane, select both DESKTOP154 and DESKTOP155.

14. Right-click one of the two selected computers and choose Properties.

   The Properties For Multiple Items dialog box appears.

15. Select the Change The Description Text For All Selected Objects check box and type **Sales Desktop**. Click OK.

16. With both computers selected, right-click one of the selected computers and choose Add To A Group.

17. Type **Sales Desktops** and click OK.

   A success message appears. Click OK.

18. In the console tree, select the Domain Controllers OU.

19. In the details pane, right-click SERVER01 and choose Manage.

   The Computer Management console appears.

20. Close the Computer Management console.

EXERCISE 2   Troubleshoot Computer Accounts

In this exercise, you simulate resetting the secure channel on a domain member. If you have a second computer joined to the contoso.com domain, you can use its name in step 4 of this exercise to actually perform a secure channel reset.

1.   Open Command Prompt.

2.   The NLTest command can test the secure channel and perform several useful domain-related tests. Type **nltest /?** and review the options supported by Nltest.exe.

3.   The NetDom command performs several tasks related to computers and the domain. Type **netdom /?** and review the options supported by Netdom.exe.

4.   Simulate resetting a computer's secure channel by typing **netdom reset desktop154**. You will receive an error, The RPC Server Is Not Available, because the system is not online.

Lesson Summary

- You can configure computer properties by using the Active Directory Users And Computers snap-in, DSMod, or Windows PowerShell.

- Computers maintain accounts that, like users, include a SID and group memberships. Be careful about deleting computer objects. Disabling computer objects allows you to enable the objects again when the computer needs to participate in the domain.

- When a computer's secure channel is broken, you can use the Reset Account context menu command in the Active Directory Users And Computers snap-in, the DSMod command, Netdom.exe, or Nltest.exe to reset the secure channel.

Lesson Review

You can use the following questions to test your knowledge of the information in Lesson 3, "Supporting Computer Objects and Accounts." The questions are also available on the companion CD if you prefer to review them in electronic form.

> **NOTE ANSWERS**
>
> Answers to these questions and explanations of why each answer choice is right or wrong are located in the "Answers" section at the end of the book.

1.   A server administrator reports Failed To Authenticate events in the event log of a file server. What should you do?

    A.   Reset the server account.

    B.   Reset the password of the server administrator.

    C.   Disable and enable the server account.

    D.   Delete the account of the server administrator.

2.   A computer has permissions assigned to its account to support a system service. It also belongs to 15 groups. The computer is being replaced with new hardware. The new hardware has a new asset tag, and your naming convention uses the asset tag as

the computer name. What should you do? (Choose all that apply. Each correct answer is a part of the solution.)

A. Delete the computer account for the existing system.

B. Create a computer account for the new system.

C. Reset the computer account for the existing system.

D. Rename the computer account for the existing system.

E. Join the new system to the domain.

3. Your enterprise recently created a child domain to support a research project in a remote location. Computer accounts for researchers were moved to the new domain. When you open Active Directory Users And Computers, the objects for those computers are displayed with a down-arrow icon. What is the most appropriate course of action?

A. Reset the accounts.

B. Disable the accounts.

C. Enable the accounts.

D. Delete the accounts.

Chapter Review

To further practice and reinforce the skills you learned in this chapter, you can perform the following tasks:

- Review the chapter summary.
- Review the key term introduced in this chapter.
- Complete the case scenarios. These scenarios set up real-world situations involving the topics of this chapter and ask you to create a solution.
- Complete the suggested practices.
- Take a practice test.

Chapter Summary

- Computers maintain accounts which, like users, include a logon name, SID, and password. Computer accounts must, therefore, be created, managed, and supported with the same level of care as user accounts.
- You can create computer accounts by using the Active Directory Users And Computers snap-in, DSAdd, Netdom.exe, and Windows PowerShell.
- You should prestage computer accounts before joining computers to the domain.
- You must have permissions on the Active Directory OU to create a computer object, and you must have permissions on the computer object to join a computer to the domain.
- If a computer's secure channel is broken and it loses its trust with the domain, you should reset the account, using Netdom.exe, Nltest.exe, DSMod, or the Active Directory Users And Computers snap-in.

Key Term

The following term was introduced in this chapter. Do you know what it means?

- secure channel

Case Scenarios

In the following case scenarios, you apply what you've learned about creating and supporting computer objects, automating their creation, and joining domains. You can find answers to these questions in the "Answers" section at the end of this book.

Case Scenario 1: Creating Computer Objects and Joining the Domain

During your security audit, you discover several computers in the Computers container. This is against your procedures, which dictate that a computer account should be prestaged in the Clients OU. You are concerned about this fact because the Computers container is not within the scope of Group Policy objects that apply your corporate security baseline settings. You want to restrict administrators and users from adding computers to the Computers container.

1. Under what circumstances are computers added to the Computers container?
2. How can you ensure that computers are added to the Clients OU by default?
3. What can you do to prevent nonadministrative users from joining computers to the domain?

Case Scenario 2: Automating the Creation of Computer Objects

You recently ordered 100 laptops to support expansion of your remote sales force. The vendor sent you a list of asset tags as an Excel file. You want to create computer accounts for the systems, using the asset tags as the computer names.

1. Which tool will you use to import the computers?
2. You import the computers into a single, new OU. You want to disable all the accounts with a single command line. What command can you use?
3. You open one of the imported objects in the Active Directory Users And Computers snap-in and realize you forgot to configure the *Description* attribute to be *Sales Laptop*. How can you configure the description for all 100 systems within the Active Directory Users And Computers snap-in?

Suggested Practices

To help you successfully master the exam objectives presented in this chapter, complete the following task.

Create and Maintain Computer Accounts

In this practice, you perform key administrative tasks that support the life cycle of a computer in a domain.

To perform this practice, you must have the following objects in the contoso.com domain:

- A first-level OU named Clients
- A first-level OU named Servers
- A first-level OU named Admins with a child OU named Groups
- A group named Help Desk in the Admins OU
- A first-level OU named User Accounts

- A user account for Linda Mitchell and April Stewart in the User Accounts OU
- Linda Mitchell as a member of the Help Desk group

Finally, you need a second computer that can be used to join the domain. The computer can be a system running either Windows Server 2008 R2 or Windows Vista, and it must be in a workgroup. Name the computer DESKTOP555.

- **Practice 1** Log on to SERVER01 as Administrator and, in the Clients OU, create a computer account for DESKTOP555. In the User Or Group section, click Change and select the Help Desk group so that the Help Desk group can join the computer to the domain.

- **Practice 2** Log on to DESKTOP555 as Administrator. Join the domain. When prompted for domain credentials, enter the user name and password for Linda Mitchell. Restart the system and log on as the domain user April Stewart.

- **Practice 3** Open the Active Directory Users And Computers snap-in, right-click DESKTOP555, and choose Reset Account. This completely breaks the secure channel between DESKTOP555 and the domain. Attempt to log on to DESKTOP555 as Linda Mitchell. You receive an error message explaining that the trust with the domain has been broken. Because you used the *Reset Account* command to break the secure channel, you will not be successful using Netdom.exe or Nltest.exe to repair the secure channel. Under normal troubleshooting scenarios, you should try those tools first. In this case, rejoin the computer to the domain, as in Practice 4 that follows.

- **Practice 4** Remove DESKTOP555 from the domain, putting it back in a workgroup. Be certain its account has been deleted from Active Directory. Use the Redircmp.exe command to redirect the default computer container to the Clients OU. Log on to DESKTOP555 as Administrator and join the domain. When prompted for credentials, enter those of April Stewart as standard user. The computer joins the domain with a new object in the Clients OU. Remove the computer from the domain again. Follow the procedures in Lesson 1 in the "Restricting the Ability of Users to Create Computers" section to reduce *ms-DS-MachineAccountQuota* to zero. Then try to join DESKTOP555 to the domain again with April Stewart's standard user credentials. Your attempt should be prevented with the message shown in Figure 5-4.

Take a Practice Test

The practice tests on this book's companion CD offer many options. For example, you can test yourself on just one exam objective, or you can test yourself on all the 70-640 certification exam content. You can set up the test so that it closely simulates the experience of taking a certification exam, or you can set it up in study mode so that you can look at the correct answers and explanations after you answer each question.

> **MORE INFO** **PRACTICE TESTS**
>
> For details about all the practice test options available, see the "How to Use the Practice Tests" section in this book's Introduction.

CHAPTER 6

Implementing a Group Policy Infrastructure

In Chapter 1, "Creating an Active Directory Domain," you learned that Active Directory Domain Services (AD DS) provides the foundational services of an identity and access solution for enterprise networks running Microsoft Windows, and that AD DS goes further to support the management and configuration of even the largest, most complex networks. Chapter 2 "Administering Active Directory Domain Services"; Chapter 3, "Administering User Accounts"; Chapter 4, "Managing Groups"; and Chapter 5, "Configuring Computer Accounts," focused on the administration of Active Directory directory service security principals: users, groups, and computers. Now you begin an examination of the management and configuration of users and computers by using Group Policy. Group Policy provides an infrastructure within which settings can be defined centrally and deployed to users and computers in the enterprise.

In an environment managed by a well-implemented Group Policy infrastructure, little or no configuration needs to be made by directly touching a desktop. All configuration is defined, enforced, and updated using settings in Group Policy objects (GPOs) that affect a portion of the enterprise as broad as an entire site or domain or as narrow as a single organizational unit (OU) or group. In this chapter, you will learn what Group Policy is, how it works, and how best to implement Group Policy in your organization. Later chapters in this training kit apply Group Policy to specific management tasks such as security configuration, software deployment, password policy, and auditing.

Exam objectives in this chapter:
- Create and apply Group Policy objects (GPOs).
- Configure GPO templates.
- Monitor Active Directory.

Lessons in this chapter:

Before You Begin

To complete the practices in this chapter, you must have created a domain controller named SERVER01 in a domain named contoso.com. See Chapter 1 for detailed steps for this task.

REAL WORLD

Dan Holme

Many of my clients are attempting to do more with less: to increase security, decrease costs, and increase user productivity. All these goals are easier to achieve when you are able to manage change and configuration in your organization. When a new security concern arises, you want to be able to respond quickly to plug any holes. When help desk logs indicate a high number of calls from users requiring help to configure something on their systems, you want to be able to deploy a change centrally that proactively helps users work more effectively. If a new piece of software is required to win new business, you want to deploy it quickly. These are just a few examples of the types of change and configuration management I see tackled every day in enterprises large and small. Group Policy is a phenomenal technology that can deliver a great amount of value to an organization. Too often, I see businesses that underuse Group Policy or implement Group Policy in a poorly designed strategy. In this chapter, you will learn the workings of Group Policy. Not only will your knowledge help you answer a variety of Group Policy questions on the certification exam, but your expertise in Group Policy will be a great asset to your IT organization.

Lesson 1: Implementing Group Policy

A Group Policy infrastructure has a lot of moving parts. It is important that you understand not only what each part does but also how the parts work together and why you might want to assemble them in various configurations. This lesson provides a comprehensive overview of Group Policy: its components, its functions, and its inner workings.

> **After this lesson, you will be able to:**
> - Identify the business drivers for configuration management.
> - Understand the core components and terminology of Group Policy.
> - Explain the fundamentals of Group Policy processing.
> - Create, edit, and link Group Policy objects.
> - Create the central store for administrative templates.
> - Search for specific policy settings in a GPO.
> - Create a GPO from a Starter GPO.
>
> **Estimated lesson time: 90 minutes**

What Is Configuration Management?

If you have only one computer in your environment (at home, for example) and you need to make a change (modify the desktop background, for example), you have several choices. Most people would probably open Personalization from Control Panel and make the change using the Windows interface. That works well for one user, but it becomes tedious if you want to make the change across multiple users. Say, for example, that you want the same background for yourself and your family. You have to make the change multiple times, and then if you ever change your mind and want to change the background yet again, you have to return to each user's profile and make the change. Implementing the change, and maintaining a consistent environment, becomes even more difficult across multiple computers.

Configuration management is a centralized approach to applying one or more changes to one or more users or computers. If you keep that in mind, everything else will be easier to understand. The key elements of configuration management are:

- A centralized definition of a change, also called a *setting*. The setting brings a user or a computer to a desired state of configuration.

- A definition of the users or computers to whom the change applies, called the *scope* of the change.

- A mechanism that ensures that the setting is applied to users and computers within the scope. This process is called the *application*.

An Overview and Review of Group Policy

Group Policy is a framework within Windows—with components that reside in Active Directory, on domain controllers, and on each Windows server and client—that allows you to centrally manage configuration in an AD DS domain. As we turn our attention to Group Policy, which can become very complex, always remember that everything boils down to these few basic elements of configuration management.

Policy Settings

The most granular component of Group Policy is an individual *policy setting*, also known simply as a *policy*, that defines a specific configuration change to apply. For example, a policy setting exists that prevents a user from accessing registry editing tools. If you define that policy setting and apply it to the user, the user will be unable to run tools such as Regedit.exe. Another policy setting is available that allows you to rename the local Administrator account. You can use this policy setting to rename the Administrator account on all user desktops and laptops, for example.

Thousands of policy settings can be managed by Group Policy, and the framework is extensible, so you can manage just about anything with Group Policy. You configure policy settings by using the Group Policy Management Editor (GPME), shown in Figure 6-1, or by using Windows PowerShell.

FIGURE 6-1 Group Policy Management Editor

Policy settings such as the setting that prevents access to registry editing tools affect a user, regardless of the computer to which the user logs on. Such policy settings are often referred to as *user configuration settings* or *user settings*. Other policy settings—such as the one that renames the Administrator account—affect a computer, regardless of which user logs on to that computer. Such policy settings are referred to as *computer configuration settings* or *computer settings*. You will also hear policy settings categorized as either "user policies" or "computer policies." The terminology used in the industry is not exact. You can see in Figure 6-1 that policy settings are grouped into Computer Configuration and User Configuration collections in the left navigation pane.

Configuring Policy Settings

To define a policy setting, double-click the policy setting in the GPME. The policy setting's Properties dialog box appears. An example is shown in Figure 6-2.

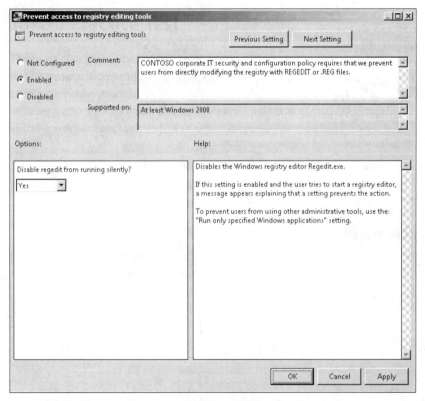

FIGURE 6-2 The Properties dialog box of a policy setting

A policy setting can have one of three states: Not Configured, Enabled, and Disabled. In a new GPO, every policy setting is Not Configured, as you can see in Figure 6-1. This means that the GPO will not modify the existing configuration of that particular setting for a user or computer. If you enable or disable a policy setting, a change is made to the configuration of users and computers to which the GPO is applied. The effect of the change depends on the policy setting itself. For example, if you enable the Prevent Access To Registry Editing Tools policy setting, users will be unable to launch Regedit.exe—the Registry Editor. If you disable the policy setting, you ensure that users can launch the Registry Editor. Notice the double negative in this policy setting: You disable a policy that prevents an action, so you allow the action.

Some policy settings bundle several configurations into one policy and might require additional parameters. In Figure 6-2, you can see that by enabling the policy to restrict registry editing tools, you can also define whether registry files can be merged into the system silently, using Regedit /s.

> **NOTE UNDERSTAND AND TEST ALL POLICY SETTINGS**
>
> Many policy settings are complex, and the effect of enabling or disabling them might not be immediately clear. Also, some policy settings affect only certain versions of Windows. Be sure to review a policy setting's explanatory text in the Group Policy Management Editor details pane, shown in Figure 6-1, or in the Help box of the policy setting's Properties dialog box seen in Figure 6-2. Additionally, always test the effects of a policy setting, and its interactions with other policy settings, before deploying a change in the production environment.

Group Policy Objects

Policy settings are defined and exist within a *Group Policy object* (GPO). A GPO is an object that contains one or more policy settings and thereby applies one or more configuration settings for a user or computer.

Creating and Managing GPOs

You can manage GPOs in Active Directory by using the Group Policy Management console (GPMC), shown in Figure 6-3. GPOs are displayed in a container named Group Policy Objects.

To create a new GPO in a domain, right-click the Group Policy Objects container, and then click New.

Editing a GPO

To modify the configuration settings in a GPO, right-click the GPO and choose Edit. The GPO opens in the Group Policy Management Editor (GPME) snap-in, formerly known as the Group Policy Object Editor (GPO Editor), in Figure 6-1.

The GPME displays the thousands of policy settings available in a GPO in an organized hierarchy that begins with the division between computer settings and user settings: the Computer Configuration node and the User Configuration node. The next levels of the hierarchy are two nodes called Policies and Preferences. You will learn about the difference between these two nodes as this lesson progresses. Deeper in the hierarchy, the GPME displays folders, also called *nodes* or *policy setting groups*. Within the folders are the policy settings themselves. The Prevent Access To Registry Editing Tools policy setting is selected in Figure 6-1.

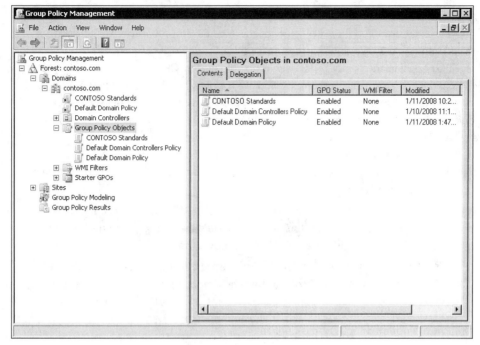

FIGURE 6-3 The Group Policy Management console

GPO Scope

Configuration is defined by policy settings in Group Policy objects. However, the configuration changes in a GPO do not affect computers or users in your enterprise until you have specified the computers or users to which the GPO applies. This is called *scoping* a GPO. The *scope* of a GPO is the collection of users and computers that will apply the settings in the GPO.

You can use several methods to manage the scope of GPOs. The first is the *GPO link*. GPOs can be linked to sites, domains, and OUs in Active Directory. The site, domain, or OU then becomes the maximum scope of the GPO. All computers and users within the site, domain, or OU, including those in child OUs, are affected by the configurations specified by policy settings in the GPO. A single GPO can be linked to more than one site or OU.

You can further narrow the scope of the GPO with one of two types of filters: *security filters* that specify global security groups to which the GPO should or should not apply, and *Windows Management Instrumentation (WMI) filters* that specify a scope, by using characteristics of a system such as operating system version or free disk space. Use security filters and WMI filters to narrow or specify the scope within the initial scope created by the GPO link. Scoping GPOs is discussed in Lesson 2, "Managing Group Policy Scope."

Windows Server 2008 introduced a new component of Group Policy: Group Policy Preferences. Settings that are configured by Group Policy Preferences within a GPO can be filtered, or *targeted*, based on several criteria. *Targeted preferences* allow you to further refine the scope of Preferences within a single GPO. Targeting preferences is covered in Lesson 2.

Group Policy Client and Client-Side Extensions

And how, exactly, are the policy settings applied? When a Group Policy refresh begins, a service running on all Windows systems (called the *Group Policy Client*) determines which GPOs apply to the computer or user. It downloads any GPOs that it does not already have cached. Then a series of processes called *client-side extensions* (CSEs) do the work of interpreting the settings in a GPO and making appropriate changes to the local computer or the currently logged-on user. Each major category of policy setting has CSEs, such as a Security CSE that applies security changes, a CSE that executes startup and logon scripts, a CSE that installs software, and a CSE that makes changes to registry keys and values. Each version of Windows has added CSEs to extend the functional reach of Group Policy. Several dozen CSEs are now in Windows.

One of the more important concepts to remember about Group Policy is that it is client driven. The Group Policy Client pulls the GPOs from the domain, triggering the CSEs to apply settings locally. Group Policy is not a "push" technology.

You can configure the behavior of CSEs by using Group Policy. Most CSEs apply settings in a GPO only if that GPO has changed. This behavior improves overall policy processing by eliminating redundant applications of the same settings. Most policies are applied in such a way that standard users cannot change the setting on their system—they are always subject to the configuration enforced by Group Policy. However, some settings can be changed by standard users, and many can be changed if a user is an administrator on that system. If users in your environment are administrators on their computers, consider configuring CSEs to reapply policy settings even if the GPO has not changed. That way, if an administrative user changes a configuration so that it is no longer compliant with policy, the configuration will be reset to its compliant state at the next Group Policy refresh.

> *NOTE* **CONFIGURE CSES TO REAPPLY POLICY SETTINGS EVEN IF THE GPO HAS NOT CHANGED**
>
> You can configure CSEs to reapply policy settings, even if the GPO has not changed, at a background refresh. To do so, configure a GPO scoped to computers and define the settings in the Computer Configuration\Policies\Administrative Templates\System\ Group Policy node. For each CSE you want to configure, open its policy processing setting—for example, Registry Policy Processing for the Registry CSE. Click Enabled and select the check box labeled Process Even If The Group Policy Objects Have Not Changed.

Settings managed by the Security CSE are an important exception to the default policy processing settings. Security settings are reapplied every 16 hours even if a GPO has not changed.

Group Policy Refresh

When are policies applied? Policy settings in the Computer Configuration node are applied
at system startup and every 90 to 120 minutes thereafter. User Configuration policy settings
are applied at logon and every 90 to 120 minutes thereafter. The application of policies is
called *Group Policy refresh*.

You can also force a policy refresh by using the GPUpdate command.

Manually Refreshing Group Policy with GPUpdate

When you are experimenting with Group Policy or trying to troubleshoot
Group Policy processing, you might need to initiate a Group Policy refresh
manually so that you do not have to wait for the next background refresh.
The Gpupdate.exe command can be used to initiate a Group Policy refresh. Used on
its own, Gpupdate.exe triggers processing identical to a background Group Policy
refresh. Both computer policy and user policy is refreshed. Use the
/target:computer or */target:user* parameter to limit the refresh to computer or user
settings, respectively. During background refresh, by default, settings are applied
only if the GPO has been updated. The */force* switch causes the system to reapply
all settings in all GPOs scoped to the user or computer. Some policy settings require
a logoff or reboot before they actually take effect. The */logoff* and */boot* switches
of Gpupdate.exe cause a logoff or reboot, respectively, if settings are applied that
require one.

Resultant Set of Policy

Computers and users within the scope of a GPO apply the policy settings specified in the
GPO. An individual user or computer is likely to be within the scope of multiple GPOs linked
to the sites, domain, or OUs in which the user or computer exists. This leads to the possibility

that policy settings might be configured differently in multiple GPOs. You must be able to understand and evaluate the Resultant Set Of Policy (RSOP), which determines the settings that are applied by a client when the settings are configured divergently in more than one GPO. RSOP is examined in Lesson 3, "Supporting Group Policy."

Slow Links and Disconnected Systems

One of the tasks that can be automated and managed with Group Policy is software installation. Group Policy Software Installation (GPSI) is supported by the software installation CSE. You can configure a GPO to install one or more software packages. Imagine, however, if a user were to connect to your network over a slow connection. You would not want large software packages to be transferred over the slow link because performance would be problematic.

The Group Policy Client addresses this concern by detecting the speed of the connection to the domain and determining whether the connection should be considered a slow link. That determination is then used by each CSE to decide whether to apply settings. The software extension, for example, is configured to forgo policy processing so that software is not installed if a slow link is detected. By default, a link is considered slow if it is less than 500 kilobits per second (kbps).

If a user is working while disconnected from the network, the settings previously applied by Group Policy continue to take effect, so a user's experience is identical whether he or she is on the network or working away from the network. This rule has exceptions, most notably that startup, logon, logoff, and shutdown scripts will not run if the user is disconnected.

If a remote user connects to the network, the Group Policy Client wakes up and determines whether a Group Policy refresh window has been missed. If so, it performs a Group Policy refresh to obtain the latest GPOs from the domain. Again, the CSEs determine, based on their policy processing settings, whether settings in those GPOs are applied. This does not apply to Windows XP or Windows Server 2003 systems—only to Windows Vista, Windows Server 2008, and later operating systems.

Group Policy Objects

Now that you have a broad understanding of Group Policy and its components, you can look more closely at each component. This section examines GPOs in detail. To manage configuration for users and computers, you create GPOs that contain the policy settings you require. Each computer has several GPOs stored locally on the system—the *local GPOs*—and can be within the scope of any number of domain-based GPOs.

Local GPOs

Computers running Windows 2000, Windows XP, and Windows Server 2003 each have one local GPO, which can manage configuration of that system. The local GPO exists whether or not the computer is part of a domain, workgroup, or non-networked environment. It is stored in %SystemRoot%\System32\GroupPolicy. The policies in the local GPO affect only the computer on which the GPO is stored. By default, only the Security Settings policies are configured on a system's local GPO. All other policies are set at Not Configured.

When a computer does not belong to an Active Directory domain, the local policy is useful to configure and enforce configuration on that computer. However, in an Active Directory domain, settings in GPOs that are linked to the site, domain, or OUs override local GPO settings and are easier to manage than GPOs on individual computers.

Windows Vista and Windows Server 2008 and later systems have multiple local GPOs. The Local Computer GPO is the same as the GPO in previous versions of Windows. In the Computer Configuration node, configure all computer-related settings. In the User Configuration node, configure settings you want to apply to all users on the computer. The user settings in the Local Computer GPO can be modified by the user settings in two new local GPOs: Administrators and Non-Administrators. These two GPOs apply user settings to logged-on users according to whether they are members of the local Administrators group, which determines whether they use the Administrators GPO or the Non-Administrators GPO. You can further refine user settings with a local GPO that applies to a specific user account. User-specific local GPOs are associated with local, not domain, user accounts.

RSOP is easy to determine for computer settings: the Local Computer GPO is the only local GPO that can apply computer settings. User settings in a user-specific GPO override conflicting settings in the Administrators and Non-Administrators GPOs, which themselves override settings in the Local Computer GPO. The concept is simple: the more specific the local GPO, the higher the precedence of its settings.

To create and edit local GPOs:

1. Click the Start button and then, in the Start Search box, type **mmc.exe** and press Enter.

    An empty Microsoft Management Console (MMC) opens.

2. Click File, and then click Add/Remove Snap-in.

3. Select the Group Policy Object Editor and click Add.

    A dialog box appears, prompting you to select the GPO to edit.

4. The Local Computer GPO is selected by default. If you want to edit another local GPO, click Browse. On the Users tab, you can see the Non-Administrators and Administrators GPOs and one GPO for each local user. Select the GPO and click OK.

5. Click Finish, and then click OK to close each of the dialog boxes.

    The Group Policy Object editor snap-in is added, focused on the selected GPO.

Remember that local GPOs are designed for nondomain environments. Configure them for your computer at home, for example, to manage the settings for your spouse or children. In a domain environment, settings in domain-based GPOs override conflicting settings in local GPOs, and it is a best practice to manage configuration by using domain-based GPOs.

Domain-Based GPOs

Domain-based GPOs are created in Active Directory and stored on domain controllers. They are used to manage configuration centrally for users and computers in the domain. The remainder of this training kit refers to domain-based GPOs rather than local GPOs, unless otherwise specified.

When AD DS is installed, two default GPOs are created:

- **Default Domain Policy**   This GPO is linked to the domain and has no security group or WMI filters. Therefore, it affects all users and computers in the domain (including computers that are domain controllers). This GPO contains policy settings that specify password, account lockout, and Kerberos policies. As discussed in Chapter 8, "Improving the Security of Authentication in an AD DS Domain," you modify the default settings in this GPO only to align with your enterprise password and account lockout policies. You should not add unrelated policy settings to this GPO. If you need to configure other settings to apply broadly in your domain, create additional GPOs linked to the domain.

- **Default Domain Controllers Policy**   This GPO is linked to the Domain Controllers OU. Because computer accounts for domain controllers are kept exclusively in the Domain Controllers OU, and other computer accounts should be kept in other OUs, this GPO affects only domain controllers. The Default Domain Controllers GPO should be modified to implement your auditing policies, as discussed in Chapter 7, "Managing Enterprise Security and Configuration with Group Policy Settings," and Chapter 8. It should also be modified to assign user rights required on domain controllers.

Creating, Linking, and Editing GPOs

To create a GPO, right-click the Group Policy Objects container and choose New.

You must have permission to the Group Policy Objects container to create a GPO. By default, the Domain Admins group and the Group Policy Creator Owners group are delegated the ability to create GPOs. To delegate permission to other groups, select the Group Policy Objects container in the Group Policy Management console tree and then click the Delegation tab in the console details pane.

After you have created a GPO, you can create the initial scope of the GPO by linking it to a site, domain, or OU.

To link a GPO, right-click the site, domain, or OU and then choose Link An Existing GPO. You can also create and link a GPO with a single step: right-click a site, domain, or OU, and then click Create A GPO In This Domain And Link It Here.

Note that you will not see your sites in the Sites node of the GPMC until you right-click Sites, choose Show Sites, and select the sites you want to manage.

You must have permission to link GPOs to a site, domain, or OU. In the GPMC, select the container in the console tree and then click the Delegation tab in the console details pane. In the Permission drop-down list, select Link GPOs. The users and groups displayed hold the permission for the selected OU. Click the Add or Remove buttons to modify the delegation.

To edit a GPO, right-click the GPO in the Group Policy Objects container and choose Edit.

The GPO is opened in the GPME. You must have at least Read permission to open the GPO in this way. To make changes to a GPO, you must have Write permission to the GPO. You can set permissions for the GPO by selecting the GPO in the Group Policy Objects container and then clicking the Delegation tab in the details pane.

The GPME displays the name of the GPO as the root node. The GPME also displays the domain in which the GPO is defined and the server from which the GPO was opened and to which changes are saved. The root node is in the *GPOName* [*ServerName*] format. In Figure 6-1, the root node is CONTOSO Standards [SERVER01.contoso.com] Policy. The GPO name is CONTOSO Standards, and it was opened from SERVER01.contoso.com, meaning that the GPO is defined in the contoso.com domain.

> **NOTE EDITING GPOS IN A MULTI-SITE DOMAIN**
>
> By default, both the GPMC and the GPME connect to a specific domain controller in your environment: the domain controller acting as the PDC emulator. In Lesson 2 of Chapter 10, "Administering Domain Controllers," you will learn to identify and manage which domain controller has this role.
>
> Connecting to the PDC emulator reduces the possibility that a GPO might be changed on two different domain controllers, at which point during replication there would be no way to reconcile the changes, and only one version of the entire GPO would "win" and be replicated. Focusing the administrative tools on one domain controller helps ensure that changes are made in one place.
>
> However, in a large, distributed environment, the PDC emulator may be in a distant site, resulting in slow performance for the GPMCs. You can right-click the root node of each console and connect to a specific domain controller closer to you. Just be cognizant of the replication issue: If you are the only one who is editing a GPO, it is perfectly acceptable for you to do so on a local, higher-performing domain controller.

Manage GPOs and Their Settings

When you right-click a GPO in the GPMC, you are presented with a menu of useful management commands:

- **Copy** This command copies the GPO. You can then right-click the Group Policy Objects container and click Paste to create a new GPO that contains the settings and configuration of the copied GPO. This is useful when you want to create a new GPO in the same domain and start with the same settings as an existing GPO. It is also useful to copy a GPO into another domain—for example, between a test domain and a production domain. To copy a GPO between domains, add the target trusted domain to the GPMC. You must have permission to create GPOs in the target domain. When you paste a GPO, you have the option to copy the access control list (ACL) from the original GPO, which preserves the security filtering, or to use the default ACL for new GPOs in the target domain.

- **Back Up**   As with any critical data, it's important to back up GPOs. Because a GPO consists of several files, objects, permissions, and links, managing the backup and restore of GPOs could be quite difficult. Luckily, the Back Up command pulls all of those pieces into a single place and makes restore easy.

- **Restore From Backup**   This command restores an entire GPO, including its files, objects, permissions, and links, into the same domain in which the GPO originally existed.

- **Import Settings**   This command imports only the settings from a backed up GPO. This operation does not import permissions or links; it can be useful for transferring GPOs between non-trusted domains that cannot use copy and paste. If a GPO includes potentially domain-specific settings, including the UNC paths or names of security groups, you are asked whether you want to import those settings exactly as they were backed up, or use a migration table that maps source to destination names.

- **Save Report**   Use this to save an HTML report of the GPO settings.

- **Delete**   This command deletes the GPO. All links to the GPO are also deleted.

- **Rename**   This command changes the name of the GPO. Because a GPO is referred to by its globally unique identifier (GUID), all links to the GPO are preserved.

GPO Storage

Group Policy settings are presented as GPOs in Active Directory user interface tools, but a GPO is actually two components: a Group Policy Container (GPC) and Group Policy Template (GPT). The GPC is an Active Directory object stored in the Group Policy Objects container within the domain naming context of the directory. Like all Active Directory objects, each GPC includes a GUID attribute that uniquely identifies the object within Active Directory. The GPC defines basic attributes of the GPO, but it does not contain any of the settings. The settings are contained in the GPT, a collection of files stored in the SYSVOL of each domain controller in the %SystemRoot%\SYSVOL\Domain\Policies*GPOGUID* path, where *GPOGUID* is the GUID of the GPC. When you make changes to the settings of a GPO, the changes are saved to the GPT of the server from which the GPO was opened.

By default, when Group Policy refresh occurs, the CSEs apply settings in a GPO only if the GPO has been updated. The Group Policy Client can identify an updated GPO by its version number. Each GPO has a version number that is incremented each time a change is made. The version number is stored as an attribute of the GPC and in a text file, GPT.ini, in the GPT folder. The Group Policy Client knows the version number of each GPO it has previously applied. If, during Group Policy refresh, it discovers that the version number of the GPC has been changed, the CSEs are informed that the GPO is updated.

Quick Check

- Describe the default Group Policy processing behavior, including refresh intervals and CSE application of policy settings.

Quick Check Answer

- Every 90 to 120 minutes, the Group Policy Client service determines which GPOs are scoped to the user or computer and downloads any GPOs that have been updated, based on the GPOs' version numbers. CSEs process the policies in the GPOs according to their policy processing configuration. By default, most CSEs apply policy settings only if a GPO has been updated. Some CSEs also do not apply settings if a slow link is detected.

GPO Replication

The two parts of a GPO are replicated between domain controllers by using distinct mechanisms. The GPC in Active Directory is replicated by the Directory Replication Agent (DRA), using a topology generated by the Knowledge Consistency Checker (KCC) that can be refined or defined manually. You will learn more about these services in Chapter 11, "Managing Sites and Active Directory Replication." The result is that the GPC is replicated within seconds to all domain controllers in a site, and between sites based on your intersite replication configuration, which will also be discussed in Chapter 11.

The GPT in the SYSVOL is replicated by using one of two technologies. The File Replication Service (FRS) is used to replicate SYSVOL. If all domain controllers are running Windows Server 2008 or later, you can configure SYSVOL replication to use Distributed File System Replication (DFS-R), a much more efficient and robust mechanism.

Because the GPC and GPT are replicated separately, it is possible for them to become out of sync for a short time. Typically, when this happens, the GPC replicates to a domain controller first. Systems that obtained their ordered list of GPOs from that domain controller identify the new GPC, attempt to download the GPT, and notice that the version numbers are not the same. A policy processing error is recorded in the event logs. If the reverse happens, and the GPO replicates to a domain controller before the GPC, clients obtaining their ordered list of GPOs from that domain controller are not notified of the new GPO until the GPC has replicated.

On the Microsoft Download Center, you can download the Group Policy Verification Tool, Gpotool.exe, which is part of Windows Resource Kits. This tool reports the status of GPOs in the domain and can identify instances in which, on a domain controller, the GPC and the GPT do not have the same version. For more information about Gpotool.exe, type **gpotool /?** in Command Prompt.

EXAM TIP

Gpotool.exe is used to troubleshoot GPO status, including problems caused by the replication of GPOs that lead to inconsistent versions of a GPC and GPT.

Policy Settings

Group Policy settings, also known simply as policies, are contained in a GPO and are viewed and modified by using the GPME. This section examines the categories of settings available in a GPO.

Computer Configuration and User Configuration

There are two major divisions of policy settings: computer settings, contained in the Computer Configuration node, and user settings, contained in the User Configuration node.

The Computer Configuration node contains settings applied to computers, regardless of who logs on to them. Computer settings are applied when the operating system starts up and during background refresh every 90 to 120 minutes thereafter. The User Configuration node contains settings that are applied when a user logs on to the computer and during background refresh every 90 to 120 minutes thereafter.

Within the Computer Configuration and User Configuration nodes are the Policies and Preferences nodes. Policies are settings that are configured and behave similarly to the policy settings in earlier versions of Windows. Preferences were introduced in Windows Server 2008. The following sections examine these nodes.

Software Settings Node

Within the Policies nodes under Computer Configuration and User Configuration are a hierarchy of folders containing policy settings. Because there are thousands of settings, it is beyond the scope of the exam and of this training kit to examine individual settings. It is worthwhile, however, to define the broad categories of settings in the folders. The first of these nodes is the Software Settings node, which contains only the Software Installation extension. The Software Installation extension helps you specify how applications are installed and maintained within your organization. It also provides a place for independent software vendors to add settings. Software deployment with Group Policy is discussed in Chapter 7.

Windows Settings Node

In both the Computer Configuration and User Configuration nodes, the Policies node contains a Windows Settings node that includes the Scripts, Security Settings, and Policy-Based QoS nodes.

The Scripts extension allows you to specify two types of scripts: startup/shutdown (in the Computer Configuration node) and logon/logoff (in the User Configuration node). Startup/shutdown scripts run at computer startup or shutdown. Logon/logoff scripts run when a user logs on or off the computer. When you assign multiple logon/logoff or startup/shutdown scripts to a user or computer, the Scripts CSE executes the scripts from top to bottom. You can determine the order of execution for multiple scripts in the Properties dialog box. When a computer is shut down, the CSE first processes logoff scripts, followed by shutdown scripts. By default, the timeout value for processing scripts is 10 minutes. If the logoff and shutdown scripts require more than 10 minutes to process, you must adjust the timeout value with a policy setting. You can use any ActiveX scripting language to write scripts. Some possibilities include Microsoft Visual Basic Scripting Edition (VBScript), Microsoft JScript, Perl, and Microsoft MS DOS style batch files (.bat and .cmd). Logon scripts on a shared network directory in another forest are supported for network logon across forests.

The Security Settings node allows a security administrator to configure security by using GPOs. This can be done after, or instead of, using a security template to set system security. For a detailed discussion of system security and the Security Settings node, refer to Chapter 7.

The Policy-Based QoS node defines policies that manage network traffic. For example, you might want to ensure that users in the Finance department have priority for running a critical network application during the end-of-year financial reporting period. Policy-Based QoS enables you to do that.

In the User Configuration node only, the Windows Settings folder contains the additional Remote Installation Services, Folder Redirection, and Internet Explorer Maintenance nodes. Remote Installation Services (RIS) policies control the behavior of a remote operating system installation, using RIS. Folder Redirection allows you to redirect user data and settings folders (AppData, Desktop, Documents, Pictures, Music, and Favorites, for example) from their default user profile location to an alternate location on the network, where they can be centrally managed and accessed. Internet Explorer Maintenance lets you administer and customize Microsoft Internet Explorer.

Administrative Templates Node

In both the Computer Configuration and User Configuration nodes, the Administrative Templates node contains registry-based Group Policy settings. Thousands of such settings are available for configuring the user and computer environment. As an administrator, you might spend a significant amount of time manipulating these settings. To assist you with the settings, a description of each policy setting is available in two locations:

- In the Help section of the Properties dialog box for the setting. In addition, the Supported On section lists the required operating system or software for the setting.

- On the Extended tab of the GPME. The Extended tab appears at the bottom of the right details pane and provides a description of each selected setting in a column between the console tree and the settings pane. The required operating system or software for each setting is also listed.

The Administrative Templates node is discussed in detail in the "Registry Policies in the Administrative Templates Node" section.

Preferences Node

Underneath both Computer Configuration and User Configuration is a Preferences node. Introduced in Windows Server 2008 and Windows Vista, preferences provide more than 20 CSEs to help you manage an incredible number of additional settings, including:

- Environment variables
- Applications such as Microsoft Office
- Mapped drives
- Registry settings
- Power options
- Folder options
- Regional options
- Start menu options

Preferences also helps you deploy the following:

- Files and folders
- Shortcuts
- Printers
- Scheduled tasks
- Network connections

Many enterprises also benefit from Preferences because the options can be used to enable or disable hardware devices or classes of devices. For example, you can use Preferences to prevent USB hard drives, including personal media players, from being connected to computers.

You must use the correct version of the GPME to configure preferences. The correct version is part of the Remote Server Administration Tools (RSAT) that can be installed on Windows Server 2008, Windows Vista, and later operating systems. You can download RSAT from the Microsoft Download Center at *http://www.microsoft.com/downloads*.

To apply preferences, systems require the preferences CSEs, which are included with Windows Server 2008, Windows Server 2008 R2, and Windows 7. CSEs for Windows XP, Windows Server 2003, and Windows Vista can be downloaded from the Microsoft Download Center.

The interface you use to configure many preferences looks identical to the Windows user interface in which you would make the change manually. Figure 6-4 shows a Folder Options (Windows Vista and later) preference *item*—a collection of settings that are processed by the preferences CSE. You can see the similarity to the Folder Options application in Control Panel.

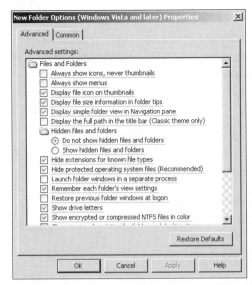

FIGURE 6-4 A Folder Options preference item

Registry Policies in the Administrative Templates Node

The Administrative Templates node contains thousands of settings that allow you to control many aspects of Windows.

In Figure 6-2, you can see the Properties dialog box for the Prevent Access To Registry Editing Tools policy setting. If this setting is enabled and the user tries to start a registry editor, a message appears, explaining that a setting prevents the action.

> **TIP RESTRICTING APPLICATIONS**
>
> **To prevent users from using other administrative tools, use either the Run Only Specified Windows Applications setting or AppLocker, which is discussed in Chapter 7.**

Policies in the Administrative Templates node make changes to the registry. Settings in the Computer Configuration node modify registry values in the HKEY_LOCAL_MACHINE (HKLM) key. Settings in the Administrative Templates node in the User Configuration node modify registry values in the HKEY_CURRENT_USER (HKCU) key.

In the case of the registry editing policy setting, the following registry value is modified:

HKCU\Software\Microsoft\Windows\CurrentVersion\Policies\System\DisableRegeditMode

If you choose to restrict Regedit from running silently, that value is set to 2. If you choose to restrict only the Registry Editor UI tool, the value is set to 1. This section explores the features and workings of the policy settings in the Administrative Templates node.

Filtering Administrative Template Policy Settings

With thousands of policies to choose from, it can be difficult to locate exactly the setting you want to configure. The GPME introduced in Windows Server 2008 solves this problem for Administrative Template settings: You can now create filters to locate specific policy settings.

To create a filter:

1. Right-click Administrative Templates and choose Filter Options.

2. To locate a specific policy, select Enable Keyword Filters, enter the words with which to filter, and select the fields within which to search. Figure 6-5 shows an example of a search for policy settings related to the screen saver.

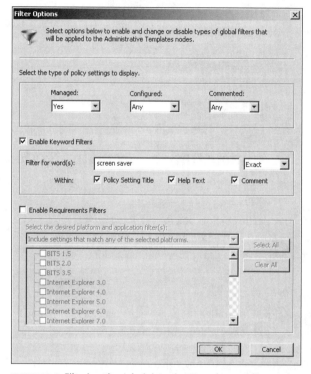

FIGURE 6-5 Filtering the Administrative Templates policy settings

In the top section of the Filter Options dialog box shown in Figure 6-5, you can filter the view to show only policy settings that are configured. This can help you locate and modify settings that are already specified in the GPO.

You can also filter for Group Policy settings that apply to specific versions of Windows, Internet Explorer, and other Windows components.

Unfortunately, the filter applies only to settings in the Administrative Templates nodes.

Managed and Unmanaged Policy Settings

There is a nuance to the registry policy settings configured by the Administrative Templates node that is important to understand: the difference between managed and unmanaged policy settings.

A *managed policy setting* has the following characteristics:

- The user interface (UI) is locked so a user cannot change the setting. Managed policy settings result in the appropriate UI element being disabled. For example, if you configure the Screensaver Timeout policy setting, a user cannot change the timeout delay in the UI.

- Changes are made in one of four keys in the registry reserved for managed policy settings:
  - HKLM\Software\Policies (computer settings)
  - HKCU\Software\Policies (user settings)
  - HKLM\Software\Microsoft\Windows\Current Version\Policies (computer settings)
  - HKCU\Software\Microsoft\Windows\Current Version\Policies (user settings)

  These keys are secured so that only administrators can make a change. Together with UI lockout, this means that non-administrative users receive the change specified by the policy setting and cannot modify the setting on their computer.

- **Changes made by a Group Policy setting, and the UI lockout, are "released" if the user or computer falls out of scope of the GPO.** For example, if you delete a GPO, managed policy settings that had applied to a user are released. This means that the setting reverts back to its previous state. Additionally, the UI interface for the setting is enabled.

The registry policy settings that have been discussed so far and that are encountered in the practices of this chapter are examples of managed policy settings. A managed policy setting causes a configuration change of some kind when the setting is applied by a GPO. When the user or computer is no longer within the scope of the GPO, the configuration is released automatically.

For example, if a GPO prevents access to registry editing tools, and then the GPO is deleted, disabled, or scoped so that it no longer applies to users, those users regain access to registry editing tools at the next policy refresh (which is Windows' default behavior) unless you have implemented a restriction at some other level.

In contrast, an *unmanaged policy setting* makes a change that is persistent in the registry. If the GPO no longer applies, the setting remains. This is often called *tattooing* the registry—making a permanent change. To reverse the effect of the policy setting, you must deploy a change that reverts the configuration to the desired state. Additionally, an unmanaged policy setting does not lock the UI for that setting.

By default, the GPME hides unmanaged policy settings to discourage you from implementing a configuration that is difficult to revert. However, you can make many useful changes with unmanaged policy settings, particularly for custom administrative templates to manage configuration for applications.

To control which policy settings are visible, right-click Administrative Templates and choose Filter Options. Make a selection from the Managed drop-down list, shown in Figure 6-5.

Later in this chapter, you will work with Group Policy preferences. When a change is made by a preference, the change tattoos the system. However, some preferences include an option to remove the preference when it no longer applies to the user or computer. This is not the same as a managed policy setting, which is released and often returned to its original value. Instead, when a preference is removed, the setting is actually deleted entirely.

Templates

Why are these nodes of the GPME labeled as "Administrative Templates"? An *administrative template* is a text file that specifies the registry change to be made and that generates the user interface to configure the Administrative Templates policy settings in the GPME. Figure 6-2 shows the properties dialog box for the Prevent Access To Registry Editing Tools policy setting. The fact that the setting exists, and that it provides a drop-down list with which to disable Regedit.exe from running silently, is determined in an administrative template. The registry setting that is made based on how you configure the policy is also defined in the administrative template.

You can add administrative templates to the GPME by right-clicking the Administrative Templates node and choosing Add/Remove Templates. Some software vendors provide administrative templates as a mechanism to manage the configuration of their application centrally. For example, you can obtain administrative templates for all recent versions of Microsoft Office from the Microsoft Download Center. You can also create your own custom administrative templates. A tutorial on creating custom administrative templates is beyond the scope of this training kit.

In versions of Windows prior to Windows Vista, an administrative template had an .adm extension. ADM files have several drawbacks. First, all localization must be performed within the ADM file. That is, if you want to create an ADM file to help deploy configuration in a multilingual organization, you need separate ADM files for each language to provide a user interface for administrators who speak that language. If you were to decide later to make a modification related to the registry settings managed by the templates, you would need to make the change to each ADM file.

The second problem with ADM files is the way they are stored. An ADM file is stored as part of the GPT in the SYSVOL. If an ADM file is used in multiple GPOs, it is stored multiple times, contributing to SYSVOL bloat. Maintaining version control over ADM files also presented challenges.

To add classic administrative templates to the GPME, right-click the Administrative Templates node and then click Add/Remove Templates.

In Windows Vista, Windows Server 2008, and later versions of Windows, an administrative template is a pair of XML files, one with an .admx extension that specifies changes to be made to the registry, and the other with an .adml extension that provides a language-specific user interface in the GPME. When changes must be made to settings managed by the administrative template, they can be made to the single ADMX file. Any administrator who modifies a GPO that uses the template accesses the same ADMX file and calls the appropriate ADML file to populate the user interface.

To add ADMX/ADML administrative templates to the GPME, copy the ADMX file into the %SystemRoot%\PolicyDefinitions folder on your client, or in the central store. Copy the ADML file into the language-and-region-specific subfolder, such as *en-us*, of %SystemRoot%\PolicyDefinitions on your client, or in the central store. The central store is discussed in the next section.

> **NOTE NO NEED TO TAKE SIDES**
>
> ADM and ADMX/ADML administrative templates can coexist. Settings generated by ADM files appear under the Administrative Templates node in a node labeled Classic Administrative Templates (ADM).

Central Store

As previously stated, ADM files are stored as part of the GPO itself, in the GPT. When you edit a GPO that uses administrative templates in the ADM format, the GPME loads the ADM from the GPT to produce the user interface. When ADMX/ADML files are used as administrative templates, the GPO contains only the data that the client needs for processing Group Policy, and when you edit the GPO, the GPME pulls the ADMX and ADML files from the local workstation.

This works well for smaller organizations, but for complex environments that include custom administrative templates or require more centralized control, Windows Server 2008 and Windows Vista introduced Central Store. Central Store is a single folder in SYSVOL that holds all the ADMX and ADML files that are required. After you have set up Central Store, the GPME recognizes it and loads all administrative templates from Central Store instead of from the local computer.

To create a central store:

1. Create a folder called PolicyDefinitions in the *fqdn*\SYSVOL*fqdn*\Policies path, where *fqdn* is the fully qualified domain name of the AD DS domain.

    For example, the central store for the contoso.com domain would be

    ```
    \\contoso.com\SYSVOL\contoso.com\Policies\PolicyDefinitions
    ```

    If you log on to a domain controller, locally or by using Remote Desktop, the local path to the PolicyDefinitions folder is:

    ```
    %SystemRoot%\SYSVOL\domain\Policies\PolicyDefinitions
    ```

2. Copy all ADMX files from the %SystemRoot%\PolicyDefinitions folder of a computer running Windows Server 2008 or later to the new SYSVOL PolicyDefinitions folder.

3. Copy the ADML files from the appropriate language-specific subfolder of %SystemRoot%\PolicyDefinitions into the language-specific subfolder of the new SYSVOL PolicyDefinitions folder.

   For example, English (United States) ADML files are located in %SystemRoot%\PolicyDefinitions\en-us. Copy them into *fqdn*\SYSVOL*fqdn* \Policies\PolicyDefinitions\en-us.

4. If additional languages are required, copy the folder that contains the ADML files to Central Store.

After you have copied all ADMX and ADML files, the PolicyDefinitions folder on the domain controller should contain the ADMX files and one or more folders containing language-specific ADML files.

EXAM TIP

If you are logging on to a domain controller, locally or by using Remote Desktop, the local path to the PolicyDefinitions folder is %SystemRoot%\SYSVOL\domain\Policies\PolicyDefinitions.

NOTE CENTRAL STORE IN A MIXED ENVIRONMENT

You can use the Central Store in a mixed environment, with clients and servers running operating systems earlier than Windows Vista and Windows Server 2008. However, you must use a Windows Vista, Windows Server 2008, or later operating system to *manage* Group Policy. That is, your administrative workstation must be running a version of Windows that can work with the Central Store. The GPOs you create can be applied to previous versions of Windows.

Commenting

Windows Server 2008 and later versions allow you to add comments to policy settings in the Administrative Templates node. To do so, double-click a policy setting and add a comment in the Comment box.

It is a best practice to add comments to configured policy settings to document the justification for a setting and its intended effect. You should also add comments to the GPO itself. Windows Server 2008 and later versions allow you to attach comments to a GPO. In the GPME, right-click the root node in the console tree and choose Properties, and then click the Comment tab.

You can also search and filter based on policy-setting comments.

Starter GPOs

Another Group Policy feature introduced in Windows Server 2008 is starter GPOs. A starter GPO contains Administrative Template settings. You can create a new GPO from a starter GPO, in which case the new GPO is prepopulated with a copy of the settings in the starter GPO. A starter GPO is, in effect, a template. (Unfortunately, Microsoft was already using the term *template* in the context of administrative templates, so another name had to be found.) When you create a new GPO, you can choose to begin with a blank GPO or select one of the preexisting starter GPOs or a custom starter GPO.

After you create a GPO from a starter GPO, there is no "link" to the starter GPO. Changes to the starter GPO do not affect the GPOs that were previously created from the starter GPO.

Starter GPOs can contain only Administrative Templates policy settings. There are two other ways to copy settings from one GPO into another, new GPO:

- You can copy and paste entire GPOs in the Group Policy Objects container of the GPMC so that you have a new GPO with all the settings of the source GPO.

- To transfer settings between GPOs in different domains or forests, right-click a GPO and choose Back Up. In the target domain, create a new GPO, right-click it, and choose Import Settings to import the settings of the backed-up GPO.

PRACTICE Implementing Group Policy

In this practice, you implement configuration in the contoso.com domain by using Group Policy. You create, configure, and scope GPOs, and you also gain hands-on experience with the features of Group Policy in Windows Server 2008 R2.

EXERCISE 1 Create, Edit, and Scope a Group Policy Object

In this exercise, you create a GPO that implements a setting mandated by the corporate security policy of Contoso, Ltd., and you scope the setting to all users and computers in the domain.

1. Log on to SERVER01 as Administrator.

2. Open the Group Policy Management console from the Administrative Tools folder.

3. Expand Forest, Domains, the contoso.com domain, and the Group Policy Objects container.

4. Right-click the Group Policy Objects Container in the console tree and choose New.

5. In the Name box, type **CONTOSO Standards**. Click OK.

6. Right-click the CONTOSO Standards GPO and choose Edit.

   Group Policy Management Editor appears.

7. Right-click the root node of the console, CONTOSO Standard, and choose Properties.

8. Click the Comment tab and type **Contoso corporate standard policies. Settings are scoped to all users and computers in the domain. Person responsible for this GPO:** *your name*. Then click OK.

   In this scenario, the Contoso corporate IT security policy specifies that computers cannot be left unattended and logged on for more than 10 minutes. To meet this requirement, you configure the screen saver timeout and password-protected screen saver policy settings. You use the search functionality of Group Policy to locate the policy settings.

9. Expand User Configuration\Policies\Administrative Templates.

10. Spend a few moments browsing the settings beneath this node. Review the explanatory text of policy settings that sound interesting to you. Do not make any configuration changes.

11. Right-click Administrative Templates in the User Configuration node and choose Filter Options.

12. Select the Enable Keyword Filters check box.

13. In the Filter For Word(s) text box, type **screen saver**.

14. In the drop-down list next to the text box, choose Exact.

15. Click OK.

    Administrative Templates policy settings are filtered to show only those that contain the words *screen saver*.

16. Browse to examine the screen saver policies that you have found.

17. In the Control Panel\Personalization node, click the policy setting Screen Saver Timeout. Note the explanatory text in the left margin of the console's details pane.

18. Double-click the policy setting Screen Saver Timeout.

19. Review the explanatory text in the Help box.

20. Click Enabled.

21. In the Seconds box, type **600**.

22. In the Comment box, type **Corporate IT Security Policy implemented with this policy in combination with Password Protect The Screen Saver**.

23. Click OK.

24. Double-click the Password Protect The Screen Saver policy setting.

25. Click Enabled.

26. In the Comment box, type **Corporate IT Security Policy implemented with this policy in combination with Screen Saver Timeout**.

27. Click OK.

28. Close the GPME.

    Changes you make in the GPME are saved in real time. There is no Save command.

29. In the Group Policy Management console, right-click the contoso.com domain and choose Link An Existing GPO.

30. Select the CONTOSO Standards GPO and click OK.

EXERCISE 2   View the Effects of Group Policy Application

In this exercise, you experience the effect of the Group Policy setting you configured in Exercise 1, "Create, Edit, and Scope a Group Policy Object," and you practice triggering a manual policy refresh, using Gpupdate.exe.

1. On SERVER01, start Control Panel, and then click Appearance.

2. Click Change Screen Saver.

3. Note that you can change the screen saver timeout and the option to display the logon screen on resume. Close the Screen Saver Settings dialog box.

4. Open Command Prompt and type **gpupdate.exe /force /boot /logoff**.

   These options of the Gpupdate.exe command invoke the most complete Group Policy refresh. Wait until the command has completed.

5. Return to the Screen Saver Settings dialog box. Note that you can no longer change the screen saver timeout or resume option.

EXERCISE 3   Explore a GPO

Now that you've seen a GPO in action, you explore the GPO itself to learn about the inner workings of Group Policy.

1. In the Group Policy Management console, in the console tree under the Group Policy Objects container, select the CONTOSO Standards GPO.

2. On the Scope tab, notice that the GPO reports its links in the Links section.

3. Click the Settings tab to see a report of the policy settings in the GPO.

   If you have Internet Explorer Enhanced Security Configuration (IE ESC) enabled, you are prompted to confirm that you want to add about:security_mmc.exe to your Trusted Sites zone. Click Add. In the Trusted Sites dialog box, click Add, and then click Close.

4. Click the Show All link at the top of this settings report to expand all sections of the report. Notice that the policy setting comments you added are part of the settings report.

5. Point to the text for the policy Screen Saver Timeout. Notice that the policy title is actually a hyperlink. Click the link to open a new window that shows the explanatory text for the policy setting.

   If you have IE ESC enabled, you are prompted to confirm that you want to add about:security_mmc.exe to your Trusted Sites zone. Click Add. In the Trusted Sites dialog box, click Add, and then click Close. If a Script Error dialog box appears, click Yes. If you continue to have problems clicking the Screen Saver Timeout link, open Server Manager and disable IE ESC.

6. In the Group Policy Management console, click the Details tab. Notice that your GPO comments appear on this tab along with GPO version information.

7. Write down the Unique ID shown on the Details tab.

8. In Windows Explorer, open the following folder: \\contoso.com\SYSVOL\contoso.com\ Policies.

9. Double-click the folder with the same name as the GPO's Unique ID.

   This is the GPT of the GPO.

EXERCISE 4   Explore Administrative Templates

Administrative templates provide the instructions with which the GPME creates a user interface to configure Administrative Templates policy settings and specify the registry changes that must be made based on those policy settings. In this exercise, you examine an administrative template.

1. In Windows Explorer, open the %SystemRoot%\PolicyDefinitions folder.

2. Open the en-us folder or the folder for your region and language.

3. Double-click ControlPanelDisplay.adml. Choose the Select A Program From A List Of Installed Programs option and click OK. Choose to open the file with Notepad and click OK.

4. Turn on Word Wrap from the Format menu.

5. Search for the ScreenSaverIsSecure text.

6. Note the label for the setting and, on the next line, the explanatory text.

7. Close the file and navigate up to the PolicyDefinitions folder.

8. Double-click ControlPanelDisplay.admx. Choose the Select A Program From A List Of Installed Programs option and click OK. Choose to open the file with Notepad and click OK.

9. Search for the text shown here:

```
<policy name="CPL_Personalization_ScreenSaverIsSecure" class="User"
            displayName="$(string.CPL_Personalization_ScreenSaverIsSecure)"
            explainText="$(string.CPL_Personalization_ScreenSaverIsSecure_Help)"
            key="Software\Policies\Microsoft\Windows\Control Panel\Desktop"
            valueName="ScreenSaverIsSecure">
    <parentCategory ref="Personalization" />
    <supportedOn ref="windows:SUPPORTED_Win2kSP1" />
    <enabledValue>
        <string>1</string>
    </enabledValue>
    <disabledValue>
        <string>0</string>
    </disabledValue>
</policy>
```

10. Identify the parts of the template that define the following:

   • The name of the policy setting that appears in the GPME

   • The explanatory text for the policy setting

- The registry key and value affected by the policy setting
- The data put into the registry if the policy is enabled
- The data put into the registry if the policy is disabled

EXERCISE 5   Create a Central Store

In this exercise, you create a central store of administrative templates to centralize the management of templates.

1. In the Group Policy Management console, right-click CONTOSO Standards and choose Edit.

2. Expand User Configuration\Policies\Administrative Templates, and then click Administrative Templates.

3. Note that the node reports Policy Definitions (ADMX Files) Retrieved From The Local Machine.

4. Close the GPME.

5. In Windows Explorer, open the following folder: \\contoso.com\SYSVOL\contoso.com\ Policies.

6. Create a folder named PolicyDefinitions.

7. Copy the contents of the %SystemRoot%\PolicyDefinitions folder to the \\contoso.com\ SYSVOL\contoso.com\Policies\PolicyDefinitions folder you created in the previous step.

8. In the Group Policy Management console, right-click CONTOSO Standards and choose Edit.

9. Expand User Configuration\Policies\Administrative Templates, and then click Administrative Templates.

10. Note that the node reports Policy Definitions (ADMX Files) Retrieved From The Central Store.

Lesson Summary

- GPOs contain policy settings that define configuration. When GPOs are scoped to a site, domain, or OU, users and computers within the scope of the GPO apply its policy settings.

- Processes on Windows clients determine the GPOs that must be downloaded and applied. Group Policy processing occurs at startup and every 90 to 120 minutes thereafter for computer settings and at logon and every 90 to 120 minutes thereafter for user settings.

- By default, CSEs apply settings only if the GPO has changed, except for Security settings, which are applied every 16 hours, whether or not the GPO is changed. CSEs can be configured to reapply settings at each policy refresh and to apply or skip policy application if a slow link is detected.

- Windows Server 2008 introduced Group Policy Preferences, which adds more than 20 CSEs to manage a wide variety of user and computer settings.

- Administrative templates (ADM or ADMX/ADML files) define the user interface and registry changes for policy settings in the Administrative Templates node of the GPO.

- You can centralize the management of administrative templates by creating a central store.

- Windows Server 2008 also added the ability to attach comments to GPOs and policy settings and to create new GPOs based on starter GPOs that contain a baseline of Administrative Templates policy settings.

Lesson Review

You can use the following questions to test your knowledge of the information in Lesson 1, "Implementing Group Policy." The questions are also available on the companion CD if you prefer to review them in electronic form.

NOTE ANSWERS

Answers to these questions and explanations of why each answer choice is right or wrong are located in the "Answers" section at the end of the book.

1. Litware, Inc., has three business units, each represented by an OU in the litwareinc.com domain. The business unit administrators want the ability to manage Group Policy for the users and computers in their OUs. Which actions should you perform to give the administrators the ability to manage Group Policy fully for their business units? (Choose all that apply. Each correct answer is a part of the solution.)

   A. Copy administrative templates from the central store to the PolicyDefinitions folder on the administrators' Windows Vista workstations.

   B. Add business unit administrators to the Group Policy Creator Owners group.

   C. Delegate Link GPOs permission to the administrators in the litwareinc.com domain.

   D. Delegate Link GPOs permission to the each business unit's administrators in the business unit's OU.

2. You are an administrator at Contoso, Ltd. The contoso.com domain has a child domain, es.contoso.com, for the branch in Spain. Administrators of that domain have asked you to provide a Spanish-language interface for Group Policy Management Editor. How can you provide Spanish-language versions of administrative templates?

   A. Log on to a domain controller in the es.contoso.com domain, open %SystemRoot% \SYSVOL\domain\Policies\PolicyDefinitions, and copy the ADM files to the ES folder.

   B. Copy ADML files to the \\es.contoso.com\SYSVOL\es.contoso.com\policies\ PolicyDefinitions\es folder.

C. Log on to a domain controller in the es.contoso.com domain, open %SystemRoot%\SYSVOL\domain\Policies\PolicyDefinitions, and copy the ADMX files to the ES folder.

D. Install the Boot.wim file from the Windows Server 2008 R2 DVD on a domain controller in the child domain.

3. You are an administrator at Contoso, Ltd. At a recent conference, you had a conversation with administrators at Fabrikam, Inc. You discussed a particularly successful set of configurations you have deployed using a GPO. The Fabrikam administrators have asked you to copy the GPO to their domain. Which steps can you and the Fabrikam administrators perform?

A. Right-click the Contoso GPO and choose Save Report. Create a GPO in the Fabrikam domain, right-click it, and choose Import.

B. Right-click the Contoso GPO and choose Back Up. Right-click the Group Policy Objects container in the Fabrikam domain and choose Restore From Backup.

C. Right-click the Contoso GPO and choose Back Up. Create a GPO in the Fabrikam domain, right-click it, and choose Paste.

D. Right-click the Contoso GPO and choose Back Up. Create a GPO in the Fabrikam domain, right-click it, and choose Import Settings.

Lesson 2: Managing Group Policy Scope

A GPO is, by itself, just a collection of configuration instructions that are processed by the CSEs of computers. Until the GPO is scoped, it does not apply to any users or computers. The GPO's scope determines which computers' CSEs will receive and process the GPO, and only the computers or users within the scope of a GPO apply the settings in that GPO. Several mechanisms are used to scope a GPO:

- The GPO link to a site, domain, or OU and whether that link is enabled
- The Enforce option of a GPO
- The Block Inheritance option on an OU
- Security group filtering
- WMI filtering
- Policy node enabling or disabling
- Preferences targeting
- Loopback policy processing

You must be able to define the users or computers to which configuration is deployed, and therefore you must master the art of scoping GPOs. In this lesson, you learn each of the mechanisms with which you can scope a GPO and, in the process, master the concepts of Group Policy application, inheritance, and precedence.

***

After this lesson, you will be able to:
- Manage GPO links.
- Identify the relationship between OU structure and GPO application.
- Evaluate GPO inheritance and precedence.
- Understand the Block Inheritance and Enforced link options.
- Use security filtering to narrow the scope of a GPO.
- Apply a WMI filter to a GPO.
- Implement loopback policy.
- Target Group Policy Preferences.
- Identify best practices for scoping Group Policy.

Estimated lesson time: 90 minutes

***

GPO Links

A GPO can be linked to one or more Active Directory sites, domains, or OUs. After a policy is linked to a site, domain, or OU, the users or computers and users in that container are within the scope of the GPO, including computers and users in child OUs.

As you learned in Lesson 1, you can link a GPO to the domain or to an OU. To link a GPO, right-click the domain or OU in the GPMC console tree, and then click Link An Existing GPO. If you have not yet created a GPO, click Create A GPO In This {Domain | OU | Site} And Link It Here.

You can choose the same commands to link a GPO to a site, but by default, your Active Directory sites are not visible in the GPME. To show sites in the GPMC, right-click Sites in the GPMC console tree and choose Show Sites.

Site-Linked GPOs and Domain Controller Placement

A GPO linked to a site affects all computers in the site without regard to the domain to which the computers belong (as long as all computers belong to the same Active Directory forest). Therefore, when you link a GPO to a site, that GPO can be applied to multiple domains within a forest. Site-linked GPOs are stored on domain controllers in the domain in which the GPO was created. Therefore, domain controllers for that domain must be accessible for site-linked GPOs to be applied correctly. If you implement site-linked policies, you must consider policy application when planning your network infrastructure. Either place a domain controller from the GPO's domain in the site to which the policy is linked or ensure that wide area network (WAN) connectivity provides accessibility to a domain controller in the GPO's domain.

When you link a GPO to a site, domain, or OU, you define the initial scope of the GPO. Select a GPO and click the Scope tab to identify the containers to which the GPO is linked. In the details pane of the GPMC, the GPO links are displayed in the first section of the Scope tab, as shown in Figure 6-6.

FIGURE 6-6 A GPO's links displayed on the Scope tab of the GPMC

The impact of the GPO's links is that the Group Policy Client downloads the GPO if either the computer or the user objects fall within the scope of the link. The GPO is downloaded only if it is new or updated. The Group Policy Client caches the GPO to make policy refresh more efficient.

Linking a GPO to Multiple OUs

You can link a GPO to more than one site, domain, or OU. It is common, for example, to apply configuration to computers in several OUs. You can define the configuration in a single GPO and link that GPO to each OU. If you later change settings in the GPO, your changes apply to all OUs to which the GPO is linked.

Deleting or Disabling a GPO Link

After you have linked a GPO, the GPO link appears in the GPMC under the site, domain, or OU. The icon for the GPO link has a small shortcut arrow. When you right-click the GPO link, a context menu appears, as shown in Figure 6-7.

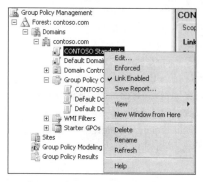

FIGURE 6-7 The context menu of a GPO link

To delete a GPO link, right-click the GPO link in the GPMC console tree and then click Delete. Deleting a GPO link does not delete the GPO itself, which remains in the Group Policy Objects container. Deleting the link does change the scope of the GPO so that it no longer applies to computers and users within a site, domain, or OU to which it was previously linked.

You can also modify a GPO link by disabling it. To disable a GPO link, right-click the GPO link in the GPMC console tree and clear the Link Enabled option. Disabling the link also changes the scope of the GPO so that it no longer applies to computers and users within that container. However, the link remains so that it can be easily re-enabled.

GPO Inheritance and Precedence

A policy setting can be configured in more than one GPO, and GPOs can be in conflict with one another. For example, a policy setting can be enabled in one GPO, disabled in another GPO, and not configured in a third GPO. In this case, the *precedence* of the GPOs determines which policy setting the client applies. A GPO with higher precedence prevails over a GPO with lower precedence. Precedence is shown as a number in the GPMC. The smaller the number—that is, the closer to 1—the higher the precedence, so a GPO with a precedence of 1 prevails over other GPOs. Select the domain or OU, and then click the Group Policy Inheritance tab to view the precedence of each GPO.

When a policy setting is enabled or disabled in a GPO with higher precedence, the configured setting takes effect. However, remember that policy settings are set to Not Configured by default. If a policy setting is not configured in a GPO with higher precedence, the policy setting (either enabled or disabled) in a GPO with lower precedence will take effect.

A site, domain, or OU can have more than one GPO linked to it. The link order of GPOs determines the precedence of GPOs in such a scenario. GPOs with higher-link order take precedence over GPOs with lower-link order. When you select an OU in the GPMC, the Linked Group Policy Objects tab shows the link order of GPOs linked to that OU.

The default behavior of Group Policy is that GPOs linked to a higher-level container are inherited by lower-level containers. When a computer starts up or a user logs on, the Group Policy Client examines the location of the computer or user object in Active Directory and evaluates the GPOs with scopes that include the computer or user. Then the client-side extensions apply policy settings from these GPOs. Policies are applied sequentially, beginning with the policies linked to the site, followed by those linked to the domain, followed by those linked to OUs—from the top-level OU down to the OU in which the user or computer object exists. It is a layered application of settings: A GPO that is applied later in the process, because it has higher precedence, overrides settings applied earlier in the process. This default order of applying GPOs is illustrated in Figure 6-8.

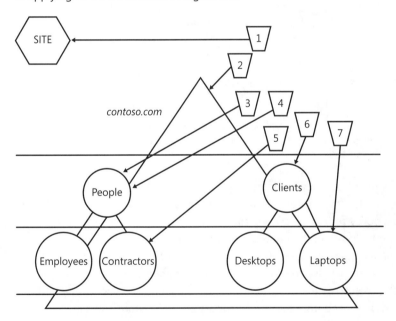

GPO processing order for the Contractors OU = 1, 2, 3, 4, 5
GPO processing order for the Laptops OU = 1, 2, 6, 7

FIGURE 6-8 Default processing of site, domain, and OU GPOs

This sequential application of GPOs creates an effect called *policy inheritance*. Policies are inherited, so the resultant set of group policies for a user or computer is the cumulative effect of site, domain, and OU policies.

By default, inherited GPOs have lower precedence than GPOs linked directly to the container. For example, you might configure a policy setting to disable the use of registry-editing tools for all users in the domain by configuring the policy setting in a GPO linked to the domain. That GPO and its policy setting are inherited by all users within the domain. However, you probably want administrators to be able to use registry-editing tools, so in this example you should link a GPO to the OU that contains administrators' accounts and configure the policy setting to allow the use of registry-editing tools. Because the GPO linked to the administrators' OU takes higher precedence than the inherited GPO, administrators can use registry-editing tools. Figure 6-9 shows this example.

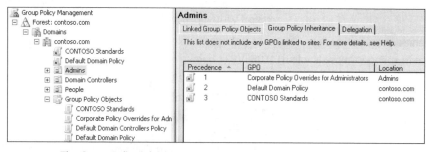

FIGURE 6-9 The Group Policy inheritance tab

A policy setting that restricts registry-editing tools is defined in the CONTOSO Standards GPO, linked to the contoso.com domain. In the Corporate Policy Overrides For Administrators GPO, a policy setting specifically allows the use of registry-editing tools. The administrator's GPO is linked to the Admins OU. When you select an OU such as the Admins OU, the details pane of the GPMC displays a Group Policy Inheritance tab that reveals GPO precedence for that OU. You can see that the Corporate Policy Overrides For Administrators GPO has precedence. Any setting in that GPO that is in conflict with a setting in CONTOSO Standards is applied from the administrators GPO. Therefore, users in the Admins OU can use registry-editing tools, although users elsewhere in the domain cannot. As you can see from this simple example, the default order of precedence ensures that the policy that is closest to the user or computer prevails.

Precedence of Multiple Linked GPOs

An OU, domain, or site can have more than one GPO linked to it. In the event of multiple GPOs, the GPOs' *link order* determines their precedence. In Figure 6-10, two GPOs are linked to the People OU.

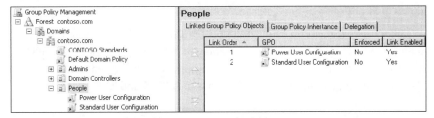

FIGURE 6-10 GPO link order

The object higher on the list, with a link order of 1, has the highest precedence. Therefore, settings that are enabled or disabled in the Power User Configuration GPO have precedence over these same settings in the Standard User Configuration GPO.

To change the precedence of a GPO link:

1. Select the OU, site, or domain in the GPMC console tree.

2. Click the Linked Group Policy Objects tab in the details pane.

3. Select the GPO.

4. Use the Up, Down, Move To Top, and Move To Bottom arrow icons to change the link order of the selected GPO.

Blocking Inheritance

A domain or OU can be configured to prevent the inheritance of policy settings. To block inheritance, right-click the domain or OU in the GPME and choose Block Inheritance.

The Block Inheritance option is a property of a domain or OU, so it blocks *all* Group Policy settings from GPOs linked to parents in the Group Policy hierarchy. When you block inheritance on an OU, for example, GPO application begins with any GPOs linked directly to that OU—GPOs linked to higher-level OUs, the domain, or the site do not apply.

The Block Inheritance option should be used sparingly, if ever. Blocking inheritance makes it more difficult to evaluate Group Policy precedence and inheritance. In the section entitled, "Using Security Filtering to Modify GPO Scope," you learn how to scope a GPO so that it applies to only a subset of objects or so that it is prevented from applying to a subset of objects. With security group filtering, you can carefully scope a GPO so that it applies to only the correct users and computers, making it unnecessary to use the Block Inheritance option.

Enforcing a GPO Link

A GPO link can be set to Enforced. To enforce a GPO link, right-click the GPO link in the console tree, and then select the Enforced option on the context menu shown in Figure 6-7.

When a GPO link is set to Enforced, the GPO takes the highest level of precedence; policy settings in that GPO prevail over any conflicting policy settings in other GPOs. In addition, a link that is enforced applies to child containers even when those containers are set to Block Inheritance. The Enforced option causes the policy to apply to all objects within its scope. Enforced causes policies to override any conflicting policies and applies regardless of whether a Block Inheritance option is set.

In Figure 6-11, Block Inheritance has been applied to the Clients OU. As a result, GPO 1, which is applied to the site, is blocked and does not apply to the Clients OU. However, GPO 2, linked to the domain with the Enforced option, does apply. In fact, it is applied last in the processing order, meaning that its settings override those of GPOs 6 and 7.

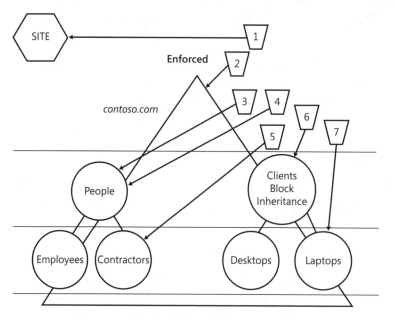

GPO processing order for the Contractors OU = 1, 3, 4, 5, 2
GPO processing order for the Laptops OU = 6, 7, 2

FIGURE 6-11 Policy processing with Block Inheritance and Enforced options

When you configure a GPO that defines configuration mandated by your corporate IT security and usage policies, you want to ensure that those settings are not overridden by other GPOs. You can do this by enforcing the link of the GPO. Figure 6-12 shows just this scenario. Configuration mandated by corporate policies is deployed in the CONTOSO Corporate IT Security & Usage GPO, which is linked with an enforced link to the contoso.com domain. The icon for the GPO link has a padlock—the visual indicator of an enforced link. On the People OU, the Group Policy Inheritance tab shows that the GPO takes precedence even over the GPOs linked to the People OU itself.

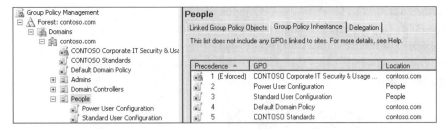

FIGURE 6-12 The precedence of the GPO with an enforced link

To facilitate evaluation of GPO precedence, you can simply select an OU (or domain) and click the Group Policy Inheritance tab. This tab displays the resulting precedence of GPOs, accounting for GPO link, link order, inheritance blocking, and link enforcement. This tab does not account for policies that are linked to a site, nor does it account for GPO security or WMI filtering.

EXAM TIP

Although it is recommended that you use the Block Inheritance and Enforced options sparingly in your Group Policy infrastructure, the 70-640 exam will expect you to understand the effect of both options.

Using Security Filtering to Modify GPO Scope

By now, you've learned that you can link a GPO to a site, domain, or OU. However, you might need to apply GPOs only to certain groups of users or computers rather than to all users or computers within the scope of the GPO. Although you cannot directly link a GPO to a security group, there is a way to apply GPOs to specific security groups. The policies in a GPO apply only to users who have Allow Read and Allow Apply Group Policy permissions to the GPO.

Each GPO has an access control list (ACL) that defines permissions to the GPO. Two permissions, Allow Read and Allow Apply Group Policy, are required for a GPO to apply to a user or computer. If a GPO is scoped to a computer (for example, by its link to the computer's OU), but the computer does not have Read and Apply Group Policy permissions, it will not download and apply the GPO. Therefore, by setting the appropriate permissions for security groups, you can filter a GPO so that its settings apply only to the computers and users you specify.

By default, Authenticated Users are given the Allow Apply Group Policy permission on each new GPO. This means that by default, *all* users and computers are affected by the GPOs set for their domain, site, or OU, regardless of the other groups in which they might be members. Therefore, there are two ways of filtering GPO scope:

- Remove the Apply Group Policy permission (currently set to Allow) for the Authenticated Users group, but do not set this permission to Deny. Then determine the groups to which the GPO should be applied and set the Read and Apply Group Policy permissions for these groups to Allow.

- Determine the groups to which the GPO should not be applied and set the Apply Group Policy permission for these groups to Deny. If you deny the Apply Group Policy permission to a GPO, the user or computer will not apply settings in the GPO, even if the user or computer is a member of another group that is allowed the Apply Group Policy Permission.

Filtering a GPO to Apply to Specific Groups

To apply a GPO to a specific security group, perform the following steps:

1. Select the GPO in the Group Policy Objects container in the console tree.

2. In the Security Filtering section, select the Authenticated Users group and click Remove.

3. Click OK to confirm the change.

4. Click Add.

5. Select the group to which you want the policy to apply and click OK.

> **NOTE USE GLOBAL SECURITY GROUPS TO FILTER GPOs**
>
> GPOs can be filtered only with global security groups—not with domain local security groups.

The result will look similar to Figure 6-13—the Authenticated Users group is not listed, and the specific group to which the policy should apply is listed.

FIGURE 6-13 Security filtering of a GPO

Filtering a GPO to Exclude Specific Groups

Unfortunately, the Scope tab of a GPO does not allow you to exclude specific groups. To exclude a group—that is, to deny the Apply Group Policy permission—you must click the Delegation tab.

To deny a group the Apply Group Policy permission:

1. Select the GPO in the Group Policy Objects container in the console tree.
2. Click the Delegation tab.
3. Click Advanced.

   The Security Settings dialog box appears.
4. Click Add.
5. Select the group you want to exclude from the GPO. Remember, it must be a global group. GPO scope cannot be filtered by domain local groups.
6. Click OK.

   The group you selected is given the Allow Read permission by default.
7. Clear the Allow check box next to Read.
8. Select the Deny check box next to Apply Group Policy.

   Figure 6-14 shows an example that denies the Help Desk group the Apply Group Policy permission and, therefore, excludes the group from the scope of the GPO.

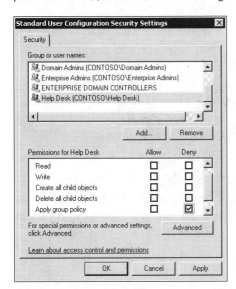

FIGURE 6-14 Excluding a group from the scope of a GPO with the Deny Apply Group Policy permission

9. Click OK.

   You are warned that Deny permissions override other permissions.

Because Deny permissions override Allow permissions, it is recommended that you use Deny permissions sparingly. Microsoft Windows reminds you of this best practice with the warning message. Excluding groups with the Deny Apply Group Policy permission is more difficult to manage than including groups in the Security Filtering section of the Scope tab.

10. Confirm that you want to continue.

> **NOTE DENY PERMISSIONS ARE NOT EXPOSED ON THE SCOPE TAB**
>
> Unfortunately, when you exclude a group, the exclusion is not shown in the Security Filtering section of the Scope tab. This is yet one more reason to use Deny permissions sparingly.

WMI Filters

Windows Management Instrumentation (WMI) is a management infrastructure technology that allows administrators to monitor and control managed objects in the network. A WMI query is capable of filtering systems based on characteristics, including RAM, processor speed, disk capacity, IP address, operating system version and service pack level, installed applications, and printer properties. Because WMI exposes almost every property of every object within a computer, the list of attributes that can be used in a WMI query is virtually unlimited. WMI queries are written using WMI Query Language (WQL).

You can use a WMI query to create a WMI filter, with which a GPO can be filtered. A good way to understand the purpose of a WMI filter, both for the certification exams and for real-world implementation, is through examples. Group Policy can be used to deploy software applications and service packs—a capability that is discussed in Chapter 7. You might create a GPO to deploy an application and then use a WMI filter to specify that the policy should apply only to computers with a certain operating system and service pack— Windows XP SP3, for example. The WMI query to identify such systems is:

```
Select * FROM Win32_OperatingSystem WHERE Caption="Microsoft
    Windows XP Professional" AND CSDVersion="Service Pack 3"
```

When the Group Policy Client evaluates GPOs that it has downloaded to determine which should be handed off to the CSEs for processing, it performs the query against the local system. If the system meets the criteria of the query, the query result is a logical *True*, and the CSEs will process the GPO.

WMI exposes *namespaces*, within which are classes that can be queried. Many useful classes, including *Win32_Operating System*, are found in a namespace called *root\CIMv2*.

To create a WMI filter:

1. Right-click the WMI Filters node in the Group Policy Management console tree and choose New.

   Type a name and description for the filter, and then click Add.

2. In the Namespace box, type the namespace for your query.

3. In the Query box, enter the query.

4. Click OK, and then click Save.

To filter a GPO with a WMI filter:

1. Select the GPO or GPO link in the console tree.

2. Click the Scope tab.

3. Click the WMI drop-down list, and select the WMI filter.

A GPO can be filtered by only one WMI filter, but that WMI filter can be a complex query, using multiple criteria. A single WMI filter can be linked to, and thereby used to filter, one or more GPOs. The General tab of a WMI filter, shown in Figure 6-15, displays the GPOs that use the WMI filter.

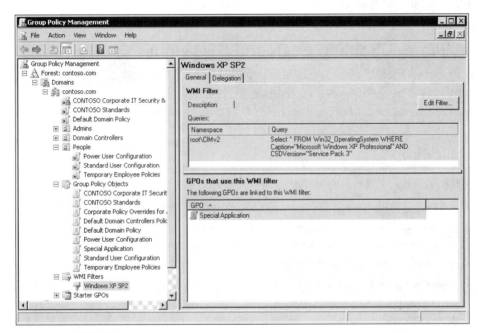

FIGURE 6-15 A WMI filter

There are two significant caveats regarding WMI filters. First, the WQL syntax of WMI queries can be challenging to master. You can often find examples on the Internet if you search using the keywords *WMI filter* and *WMI query* along with a description of the query you want to create.

> **MORE INFO** **WMI FILTER EXAMPLES**
>
> You can find examples of WMI filters at *http://technet.microsoft.com/en-us/library/cc779036(WS.10).aspx*. You can also refer to the Windows Management Instrumentation (WMI) software development kit (SDK), which can be found at *http://msdn2.microsoft.com/en-us/library/aa394582.aspx*.

Second, WMI filters are expensive in terms of Group Policy processing performance. Because the Group Policy Client must perform the WMI query at each policy processing interval, there is a slight impact on system performance every 90 to 120 minutes. With the performance of today's computers, the impact might not be noticeable, but you should certainly test the effects of a WMI filter prior to deploying it widely in your production environment. The WMI query is only processed *one* time, even if it is used to filter the scope of multiple GPOs.

EXAM TIP

Although it is unlikely that you will be asked to recognize WQL queries on the 70-640 exam, you should be familiar with the basic functionality of WMI queries as discussed in this section. Be certain to remember that Windows 2000 systems apply settings in GPOs with WMI filters because Windows 2000 ignores WMI filters during policy processing.

Enabling or Disabling GPOs and GPO Nodes

You can prevent the settings in the Computer Configuration or User Configuration nodes from being processed during policy refresh by changing GPO Status.

To enable or disable a GPO's nodes, select the GPO or GPO link in the console tree; click the Details tab, shown in Figure 6-16; and then choose one of the following from the GPO Status drop-down list:

- **Enabled**   Both computer configuration settings and user configuration settings will be processed by CSEs during policy refresh.

- **All Settings Disabled**   CSEs will not process the GPO during policy refresh.

- **Computer Configuration Settings Disabled**   During computer policy refresh, computer configuration settings in the GPO will not be applied. The GPO will not be processed during user policy refresh.

- **User Configuration Settings Disabled**   During user policy refresh, user configuration settings in the GPO will not be applied. The GPO will not be processed during computer policy refresh.

You can configure GPO status to optimize policy processing. If a GPO contains only user settings, for example, setting the GPO Status option to disable computer settings prevents the Group Policy client from attempting to process the GPO during computer policy refresh. Because the GPO contains no computer settings, there is no need to process the GPO, and you can save a few cycles of the processor.

NOTE   **USE DISABLED GPOS FOR DISASTER PREPAREDNESS**

You can define a configuration that should take effect in case of an emergency, security incident, or other disaster in a GPO, and link the GPO so that it is scoped to appropriate users and computers. Then, disable the GPO. In the event that you require the configuration to be deployed, simply enable the GPO.

FIGURE 6-16 The Details tab of a GPO

Targeting Preferences

Preferences, which were introduced in Windows Server 2008 and Windows Vista, have a built-in scoping mechanism called *item-level targeting*. You can have multiple preference items in a single GPO, and each preference item can be targeted or filtered. So, for example, you could have a single GPO with a preference that specifies folder options for engineers and another item that specifies folder options for salespeople. You can target the items by using a security group or OU. Over a dozen other criteria can be used, including hardware and network characteristics, date and time, LDAP queries, and more.

> **NOTE** **PREFERENCES CAN TARGET WITHIN A GPO**
>
> What's new about preferences is that you can target multiple preference items within a single GPO instead of requiring multiple GPOs. With traditional policies, you often need multiple GPOs filtered to individual groups to apply variations of settings.

Like WMI filters, item-level targeting of preferences requires the CSE to perform a query to determine whether to apply the settings in a preferences item. You must be aware of the potential performance impact of item-level targeting, particularly if you use options such as Lightweight Directory Access Protocol (LDAP) queries, which require processing time and a response from a domain controller to process. As you design your Group Policy infrastructure, balance the configuration management benefits of item-level targeting against the performance impact you discover during testing in a lab.

Group Policy Processing

Now that you have learned more about the concepts, components, and scoping of Group Policy, you are ready to examine Group Policy processing closely. As you read this section, keep in mind that Group Policy is all about applying configurations defined by GPOs, that GPOs are applied in an order (site, domain, and OU), and that GPOs applied later in the order have higher precedence; their settings, when applied, override settings applied earlier. The following sequence describes the process through which settings in a domain-based GPO are applied to affect a computer or user:

1. The computer starts, and the network starts. Remote Procedure Call System Service (RPCSS) and Multiple Universal Naming Convention Provider (MUP) are started. The Group Policy Client is started.

2. The Group Policy Client obtains an ordered list of GPOs scoped to the computer.

   The order of the list determines the order of GPO processing, which is, by default, local, site, domain, and OU:

   - Local GPOs. Each computer running Windows Server 2003, Windows XP, and Windows 2000 has exactly one GPO stored locally. Computers running Windows Vista, Windows Server 2008, and later versions of Windows have multiple local GPOs. The precedence of local GPOs is discussed in the "Local GPOs" section in Lesson 1.

   - Site GPOs. Any GPOs that have been linked to the site are added to the ordered list next. When multiple GPOs are linked to a site (or domain or OU), the *link order*, configured on the Scope tab, determines the order in which they are added to the list. The GPO that is highest on the list, with the number closest to 1, has the highest precedence and is added to the list last. It is, therefore, applied last, and its settings override those of GPOs applied earlier.

   - Domain GPOs. Multiple domain-linked GPOs are added as specified by the link order.

   > **NOTE DOMAIN-LINKED POLICIES ARE NOT INHERITED BY CHILD DOMAINS**
   > Policies from a parent domain are not inherited by a child domain. Each domain maintains distinct policy links. However, computers in several domains might be within the scope of a GPO linked to a site.

   - OU GPOs. GPOs linked to the OU highest in the Active Directory hierarchy are added to the ordered list, followed by GPOs linked to its child OU, and so on. Finally, the GPOs linked to the OU that contains the computer are added. If several group policies are linked to an OU, they are added in the order specified by the link order.

   - Enforced GPOs. These are added at the end of the ordered list, so their settings are applied at the end of the process and therefore override settings of GPOs earlier in the list and in the process. As a point of trivia, enforced GPOs are added to the list in reverse order: OU, domain, and then site. This is relevant when you apply corporate security policies in a domain-linked, enforced GPO. That GPO will be at the end of the ordered list and applied last, so its settings will take precedence.

3. The GPOs are processed synchronously in the order specified by the ordered list. This means that settings in the local GPOs are processed first, followed by GPOs linked to the site, the domain, and the OUs containing the user or computer. GPOs linked to the OU of which the computer or user is a direct member are processed last, followed by enforced GPOs.

   As each GPO is processed, the system determines whether its settings should be applied based on the GPO status for the computer node (enabled or disabled) and whether the computer has the Allow Group Policy permission. If a WMI filter is applied to the GPO, and if the computer is running Windows XP or later, it performs the WQL query specified in the filter.

4. If the GPO should be applied to the system, CSEs trigger to process the GPO settings. Policy settings in GPOs overwrite policies of previously applied GPOs in the following ways:

   - If a policy setting is configured (set to Enabled or Disabled) in a GPO linked to a parent container (OU, domain, or site), and the same policy setting is Not Configured in GPOs linked to its child container, the resultant set of policies for users and computers in the child container will include the parent's policy setting. If the child container is configured with the Block Inheritance option, the parent setting is not inherited unless the GPO link is configured with the Enforced option.

   - If a policy setting is configured (set to Enabled or Disabled) for a parent container, and the same policy setting *is* configured for a child, the child container's setting overrides the setting inherited from the parent. If the parent GPO link is configured with the Enforced option, the parent setting has precedence.

   - If a policy setting of GPOs linked to parent containers is Not Configured, and the child OU setting is also Not Configured, the resultant policy setting is the setting that results from the processing of local GPOs. If the resultant setting of local GPOs is also Not Configured, the resultant configuration is the Windows default setting.

5. When the user logs on, steps 2, 3, and 4 are repeated for user settings. The client obtains an ordered list of GPOs scoped to the user, examines each GPO synchronously, and hands over GPOs that should be applied to the appropriate CSEs for processing. This step is modified if User Loopback Group Policy Processing is enabled. Loopback policy processing is discussed in the next section.

> **NOTE POLICY SETTINGS IN BOTH THE COMPUTER CONFIGURATION AND USER CONFIGURATION NODES**
>
> Most policy settings are specific to either the User Configuration or Computer Configuration node. A small handful of settings appear in both nodes. Although in most situations the setting in the Computer Configuration node overrides the setting in the User Configuration node, it is important to read the explanatory text accompanying the policy setting to understand the setting's effect and its application.

6. Every 90 to 120 minutes after computer startup, computer policy refresh occurs, and steps 2, 3, and 4 are repeated for computer settings.

7. Every 90 to 120 minutes after user logon, user policy refresh occurs, and steps 2, 3, and 4 are repeated for user settings.

> **NOTE   SETTINGS MIGHT NOT TAKE EFFECT IMMEDIATELY**
>
> Although most settings are applied during a background policy refresh, some CSEs do not apply the setting until the next startup or logon event. Newly added startup and logon script policies, for example, will not run until the next computer startup or logon. Software installation, discussed in Chapter 7, will occur at the next startup if the software is assigned in computer settings. Changes to folder redirection policies will not take effect until the next logon.

Loopback Policy Processing

By default, a user's settings come from GPOs scoped to the user object in Active Directory. Regardless of which computer the user logs on to, the resultant set of policies that determine the user's environment is the same. There are situations, however, in which you might want to configure a user differently, depending on the computer in use. For example, you might want to lock down and standardize user desktops when users log on to computers in closely managed environments such as conference rooms, reception areas, laboratories, classrooms, and kiosks. It is also important for virtual desktop infrastructure (VDI) scenarios, including remote virtual machines and Remote Desktop Services (Terminal Services).

Imagine a scenario in which you want to enforce a standard corporate appearance for the Windows desktop on all computers in conference rooms and other public areas of your office. How could you centrally manage this configuration, using Group Policy? Policy settings that configure desktop appearance are located in the User Configuration node of a GPO. Therefore, by default, the settings apply to users regardless of which computer they log on to. The default policy processing does not give you a way to scope user settings to apply to computers, regardless of which user logs on. That's where loopback policy processing comes in.

Loopback policy processing alters the default algorithm used by the Group Policy client to obtain the ordered list of GPOs that should be applied to a user's configuration. Instead of user configuration being determined by the User Configuration node of GPOs that are scoped to the user object, user configuration can be determined by the User Configuration node policies of GPOs that are scoped to the *computer* object.

The User Group Policy Loopback Processing Mode policy, located in the Computer Configuration\Policies\Administrative Templates\System\Group Policy folder in GPME, can be, like all policy settings, set to Not Configured, Enabled, or Disabled.

When enabled, the policy can specify Replace or Merge mode:

- **Replace**   In this case, the GPO list for the user (obtained in step 5 in the "Group Policy Processing" section) is replaced in its entirety by the GPO list already obtained for the computer at computer startup (during step 2). The settings in the User Configuration policies of the computer's GPOs are applied to the user. Replace mode is useful in a situation such as a classroom, where users should receive a standard configuration rather than the configuration applied to those users in a less managed environment.

- **Merge**   In this case, the GPO list obtained for the computer at computer startup (step 2 in the "Group Policy Processing" section) is appended to the GPO list obtained for the user when logging on (step 5). Because the GPO list obtained for the computer is applied later, settings in GPOs on the computer's list have precedence if they conflict with settings in the user's list. This mode would be useful for applying additional settings to users' typical configurations. For example, you might allow a user to receive his or her typical configuration when logging on to a computer in a conference room or reception area but replace the wallpaper with a standard bitmap and disable the use of certain applications or devices.

EXAM TIP

The 70-640 exam is likely to include several questions that test your knowledge of Group Policy scope. Sometimes, questions that seem to be addressing the technical details of a policy setting are, in fact, testing your ability to scope the setting to appropriate systems. When you encounter Group Policy questions, ask yourself, "Is this really about a specific policy setting, or is it about the scope of that setting?"

NOTE   LOOPBACK AND FILTERING

It is an underdocumented fact that when you combine loopback processing with security group filtering, the application of user settings during policy refresh uses the credentials of the computer to determine which GPOs to apply as part of the loopback processing, but the logged-on user must also have the Apply Group Policy permission for the GPO to be successfully applied.

PRACTICE   Configuring Group Policy Scope

In this practice, you follow a scenario that builds upon the GPO you created and configured in Lesson 1. In each vignette, you refine your application of Group Policy scoping. Before performing these exercises, complete the exercises in Lesson 1.

EXERCISE 1   Create a GPO with a Policy Setting That Takes Precedence
over a Conflicting Setting

Imagine you are an administrator of the contoso.com domain. The CONTOSO Standards
GPO, linked to the domain, configures a policy setting that requires a 10-minute screen saver
timeout. An engineer reports that a critical application that performs lengthy calculations
crashes when the screens saver starts, and the engineer has asked you to prevent the setting
from applying to the team of engineers that use the application every day.

1. Log on to SERVER01 as Administrator.

2. Open the Active Directory Users And Computers snap-in and create a first-level OU
   called User Accounts (if one does not already exist) and a child OU called Engineers.

3. Open Group Policy Management.

4. Expand the console tree so that you can see the Engineers OU. Right-click
   the Engineers OU and choose Create A GPO In This Domain, And Link It Here.

5. Enter the name **Engineering Application Override** and click OK.

6. Expand the Engineers OU, right-click the GPO, and choose Edit.

7. Expand User Configuration\Policies\Administrative Templates\Control Panel
   and then click the Personalization folder.

8. Double-click the Screen Saver Timeout policy setting.

9. Click Disabled, and then click OK.

10. Close the GPME.

11. In Group Policy Management, click the Engineers OU, and then click the Group Policy
    Inheritance tab.

12. Notice that the Engineering Application Override GPO has precedence over
    the CONTOSO Standards GPO.

    The setting you configured, which explicitly disables the screen saver, overrides
    the setting in the CONTOSO Standards GPO.

EXERCISE 2   Configure the Enforced Option

You want to ensure that all systems receive changes to Group Policy as quickly as possible.
To do this, you want to enable the Always Wait For The Network Group Policy setting
described in Lesson 1. You do not want any administrators to override the policy; it must be
enforced for all systems.

1. In the GPMC, right-click the contoso.com domain and choose Create A GPO In This
   Domain, And Link It Here.

2. Enter the name **Enforced Domain Policies** and click OK.

3. Right-click the GPO and choose Edit.

4. Expand Computer Configuration\Policies\Administrative Templates\System
   and then click the Logon folder.

5. Double-click the Always Wait For The Network At Computer Startup And Logon policy setting.

6. Select Enabled and click OK.

7. Close the GPME.

8. Right-click the Enforced Domain Policies GPO and choose Enforced.

9. Select the Engineers OU, and then click the Group Policy Inheritance tab.

   Note that your enforced domain GPO has precedence even over GPOs linked to the Engineers OU. Settings in a GPO such as Engineering Application Override cannot successfully override settings in an enforced GPO.

EXERCISE 3 Configure Security Filtering

As time passes, you discover that a small number of users must be exempted from the screen saver timeout policy configured by the CONTOSO Standards GPO. You decide that it is no longer practical to use overriding settings. Instead, you will use security filtering to manage the scope of the GPO.

1. Open the Active Directory Users And Computers snap-in and create an OU called Groups, if it does not already exist. In the Groups OU, create a global security group named GPO_CONTOSO Standards_Exceptions.

2. In the GPMC, expand the Group Policy Objects container.

3. Right-click the Engineering Application Override GPO and choose Delete. Click Yes to confirm your choice.

4. In the console tree, select the CONTOSO Standards GPO in the Group Policy Objects container.

5. On the Delegation tab, click Advanced.

6. In the Security Settings dialog box, click Add.

7. Type the name of the group, **GPO_CONTOSO Standards_Exceptions**, and click OK.

8. In the permissions list, scroll down and select the Deny permission for Apply Group Policy. Then click OK.

9. Click Yes to confirm your choice.

10. Note the entry shown on the Delegation tab in the Allowed Permissions column for the GPO_CONTOSO Standards_Exceptions group.

11. Click the Scope tab and examine the Security Filtering section.

    The default security filtering of the new GPO is that the Authenticated Users group has the Allow Apply Group Policy permission, so all users and computers within the scope of the GPO link will apply the settings in the GPO. Now you have configured a group with the Deny Apply Group Policy permission, which overrides the Allow permission. If any user requires exemption from the policies in the CONTOSO Standards GPO, you can simply add the user to the GPO_CONTOSO Standards_Exceptions group.

EXERCISE 4   Implement Loopback Policy Processing

Recently, a salesperson at Contoso, Ltd., turned on his computer to give a presentation to an important customer, and the desktop wallpaper was a picture that exhibited questionable taste on the part of the salesperson. The management of Contoso, Ltd., has asked you to ensure that the laptops used by salespeople will have no wallpaper. It is not necessary to manage the wallpaper of salespeople when they are logged on to desktop computers at the office. Because policy settings that manage wallpaper are user configuration settings, but you need to apply the settings to sales laptops, you must use loopback policy processing. In addition, the computer objects for sales laptops are scattered across several OUs, so you will use security filtering to apply the GPO to a group rather than to an OU of sales laptops.

1. Open the Active Directory Users And Computers snap-in and create a global security group called Sales Laptops in the Groups OU. Also create an OU called Clients for client computer objects, if the Clients OU does not already exist.

2. In the GPMC, right-click the Group Policy Objects container and choose New.

3. In the Name box, type **Sales Laptop Configuration** and click OK.

4. Right-click the GPO and choose Edit.

5. Expand User Configuration\Policies\Administrative Templates\Desktop and then click the Desktop subfolder.

6. Double-click the Desktop Wallpaper policy setting.

7. Review the explanatory text in the Help box.

8. In the Comment box, type **Corporate standard wallpaper for sales laptops**.

9. In the Supported On box, review the supported versions of Windows.

10. Select Enabled.

11. In the Wallpaper Name box, type **c:\windows\web\Wallpaper\server.jpg**.

12. Click OK.

13. Expand Computer Configuration\Policies\Administrative Templates\System, and then click the Group Policy folder.

14. Double-click the User Group Policy Loopback Processing Mode policy setting.

15. Click Enabled and, in the Mode drop-down list, select Merge.

16. Click OK and close the GPME.

17. In the GPMC, select the Sales Laptop Configuration GPO in the Group Policy Objects container.

18. On the Scope tab, in the Security Filtering section, select the Authenticated Users group and click Remove. Click OK to confirm your choice.

19. Click Add in the Security Filtering section.

20. Type the group name, **Sales Laptops**, and click OK.

21. Click Add in the Security Filtering section.

22. Type the group name, **Domain Users**, and click OK.

It is an underdocumented fact that when you combine the loopback processing with security group filtering, the application of user settings during policy refresh uses the credentials of the computer to determine which GPOs to apply as part of the loopback processing, but the logged-on user must also have the Apply Group Policy permission for the GPO to be successfully applied.

23. Right-click the Clients OU and choose Link An Existing GPO.

24. Select Sales Laptop Configuration and click OK.

You have now filtered a GPO so that it applies only to objects in the Sales Laptops group. You can add computer objects for sales laptops as members of the group, and those laptops will be within the scope of the GPO. The GPO configures the laptops to perform loopback policy processing in Merge mode. When any user in the domain logs on to one of the sales laptops, user configuration settings scoped to the user are applied and then user configuration settings in GPOs scoped to the computer are applied, including the Sales Laptop Configuration GPO.

Lesson Summary

- The initial scope of the GPO is established by GPO links. A GPO can be linked to one or more sites, domains, or OUs. The scope of the GPO can be further refined by using security filtering or WMI filters.

- CSEs apply GPOs in the following order: local GPOs, GPOs linked to the site in which a user or computer logs on, GPOs linked to the user or computer domain, and then GPOs linked to OUs. The layered application of policy settings creates the effect of policy inheritance.

- Policy inheritance can be blocked by configuring the Block Inheritance option on a domain or OU.

- A GPO link can be set to Enforced. The settings in an enforced GPO are applied to computers and users within the scope of the GPO, even if the Block Inheritance option is set. Additionally, settings in an enforced GPO take precedence, so they override conflicting settings.

- You can use security filtering to specify the groups to which a GPO applies or the groups that are exempted from the GPO. Only global security groups can be used to filter GPOs.

- Under normal policy processing, during user policy refresh (at logon and every 90 to 120 minutes thereafter), the system applies user configuration policy settings from GPOs scoped to the logged-on user.

- Loopback policy processing causes the system to change the way it applies GPOs during user policy refresh. In Merge mode, after applying settings from GPOs scoped to the logged-on user, the system applies policy settings from GPOs scoped to the computer. These settings take precedence over conflicting settings from user GPOs. In loopback processing Replace mode, user configuration settings from GPOs scoped to the logged-on user are not applied. Instead, only user configuration settings from GPOs scoped to the computer are applied.

Lesson Review

You can use the following questions to test your knowledge of the information in Lesson 2, "Managing Group Policy Scope." The questions are also available on the companion CD if you prefer to review them in electronic form.

> **NOTE ANSWERS**
>
> Answers to these questions and explanations of why each answer choice is right or wrong are located in the "Answers" section at the end of the book.

1. You want to deploy a GPO named Northwind Lockdown that applies configuration to all users at Northwind Traders. However, you want to ensure that the settings do not apply to members of the Domain Admins group. How can you achieve this goal? (Choose all that apply.)

    A. Link the Northwind Lockdown GPO to the domain, and then right-click the domain and choose Block Inheritance.

    B. Link the Northwind Lockdown GPO to the domain, right-click the OU that contains the user accounts of all users in the Domain Admins group, and choose Block Inheritance.

    C. Link the Northwind Lockdown GPO to the domain, and then assign the Domain Admins group the Deny Apply Group Policy permission.

    D. Link the Northwind Lockdown GPO to the domain, and then configure security filtering so that the GPO applies to Domain Users.

2. You want to create a standard lockdown desktop experience for users when they log on to computers in your company's conference and training rooms. You have created a GPO called Public Computers Configuration with desktop restrictions defined in the User Configuration node. What additional steps must you take? (Choose all that apply. Each correct answer is a part of the solution.)

    A. Enable the User Group Policy Loopback Processing Mode policy setting.

    B. Link the GPO to the OU containing user accounts.

    C. Select the Block Inheritance option on the OU containing conference and training room computers.

    D. Link the GPO to the OU containing conference and training room computers.

Lesson 3: Supporting Group Policy

Group Policy application can be complex to analyze and understand, with the interaction of multiple settings in multiple GPOs scoped using a variety of methods. You must be equipped to effectively evaluate and troubleshoot your Group Policy implementation, identify potential problems before they arise, and solve unforeseen challenges. Microsoft Windows provides two indispensible tools for supporting Group Policy: Resultant Set Of Policy (RSOP) and the Group Policy Operational Logs. In this lesson, you explore the use of these tools in both proactive and reactive troubleshooting and support scenarios.

> **After this lesson, you will be able to:**
> - Analyze the set of GPOs and policy settings that have been applied to a user or computer.
> - Proactively model the impact of Group Policy or Active Directory changes on resultant set of policy.
> - Locate the event logs containing Group Policy–related events.
>
> **Estimated lesson time: 30 minutes**

Understanding When Settings Take Effect

If you understand the way in which policy settings are created, stored, and applied to clients, you can troubleshoot Group Policy more effectively. In this section, you review the components, processes, and dependencies of the Group Policy framework. For policies to take effect:

- **GPO replication must occur.** Before a GPO can take effect, the GPC in Active Directory must be replicated to the domain controller from which the Group Policy Client obtains its ordered list of GPOs. Additionally, the GPT in SYSVOL must replicate to the same domain controller.

- **Group changes must be incorporated.** If you have added a new group, or changed the membership of a group that is used to filter the GPO, that change must also have replicated, and the change must be in the security token of the computer and the user, which requires a restart (for the computer to update its group membership) or a logoff and logon (for the user to update its group membership).

- **The user or computer Group Policy refresh must occur.** As you know, refresh happens at startup (for computer settings) and logon (for user settings) and every 90 to 120 minutes thereafter, by default.

> **NOTE AN AVERAGE OF 45–60 MINUTES**
>
> Keep in mind that the practical impact of the Group Policy refresh interval is that when you make a change in your environment, it will be *on average* one-half that time, or 45 to 60 minutes, before the change *starts* to take effect.

Even if all of the preceding conditions are true, a setting might not apply correctly. When this happens, consider the following:

- **Startup behavior of Windows clients might not apply the latest policies.** By default, Windows XP, Windows Vista, and Windows 7 clients perform only background refreshes at startup and logon, meaning that a client might start up and a user might log on *without receiving the latest policies from the domain*. It is highly recommended that you change this default behavior so that policy changes are implemented in a managed, predictable way. Enable the Always Wait For The Network At Computer Startup And Logon policy setting for all Windows clients. See Lesson 1 for more information about this policy setting.

- **Settings might not take effect immediately.** Although most settings are applied during a background policy refresh, some CSEs do not apply the setting until the next startup or logon event. Newly added startup and logon script policies, for example, do not run until the next computer startup or logon. Software installation, discussed in Chapter 7, occurs at the next startup if the software is assigned in computer settings. Changes to folder redirection policies do not take effect until the next logon.

- **Most CSEs do not re-apply settings if the GPO has not changed.** Remember that most CSEs apply settings in a GPO only if the GPO version has changed. That means that if a user can change a setting that was originally specified by Group Policy, the setting will not be brought back into compliance with the settings specified by the GPO until the GPO changes. Luckily, most policy settings cannot be changed by a nonprivileged user. However, if a user is an administrator of his or her computer, or if the policy setting affects a part of the registry or system that the user has permissions to change, this could be a real problem.

  You have the option of instructing each CSE to reapply the settings of GPOs even if the GPOs have not been changed. Processing behavior of each CSE can be configured in policy settings found in Computer Configuration\Policies\Administrative Templates\System\Group Policy.

When settings do not apply as expected, you can do the following:

- **Manually refresh Group Policy with GPUpdate.** When you are experimenting with Group Policy or trying to troubleshoot Group Policy processing, you might need to initiate a Group Policy refresh manually so that you do not have to wait for the next background refresh. The GPUpdate command can be used to initiate a Group Policy refresh. Used without parameters, GPUpdate triggers processing identical to a background Group Policy refresh. Both computer policy and user policy are refreshed. Use the */target:computer* or */target:user* parameter to limit the refresh to computer or user settings, respectively. During background refresh, by default, settings are applied only if the GPO has been updated. The */force* switch causes the system to reapply all settings in all GPOs scoped to the user or computer. Some policy settings require a logoff or reboot before they actually take effect. The */logoff* and /boot switches of GPUpdate cause a logoff or reboot, respectively, if settings are applied that require one.

So the command that causes a total refresh, application of updated policy settings, and (if necessary) reboot and logon is:

```
gpupdate /force /logoff /boot
```

EXAM TIP

In Windows 2000, the Secedit.exe command was used to refresh policy, so you might encounter a mention of the Secedit.exe command on the exam.

Resultant Set Of Policy

In Lesson 2, you learned that a user or computer can be within the scope of multiple GPOs. Group Policy inheritance, filters, and exceptions are complex, and it's often difficult to determine just which policy settings will apply.

Resultant Set Of Policy (RSOP) is the net effect of GPOs applied to a user or computer, taking into account GPO links, exceptions such as Enforced and Block Inheritance, and the application of security and WMI filters.

RSOP is also a collection of tools that help you evaluate, model, and troubleshoot the application of Group Policy settings. RSOP can query a local or remote computer and report back the exact settings that were applied to the computer and to any user who has logged on to the computer. RSOP can also model the policy settings that are anticipated to be applied to a user or computer under a variety of scenarios, including moving the object between OUs or sites or changing the object's group membership. With these capabilities, RSOP can help you manage and troubleshoot conflicting policies.

Windows Server 2008 R2 provides the following tools for performing RSOP analysis:

- The Group Policy Results Wizard
- The Group Policy Modeling Wizard
- Gpresult.exe

Generating RSOP Reports with the Group Policy Results Wizard

To help you analyze the cumulative effect of GPOs and policy settings on a user or computer in your organization, Group Policy Management includes the Group Policy Results Wizard. If you want to understand exactly which policy settings have applied to a user or computer, and why, the Group Policy Results Wizard is the tool to use.

The Group Policy Results Wizard reaches into the WMI provider on a local or remote computer. The WMI provider can report everything there is to know about the way Group Policy was applied to the system. It knows when processing occurred, which GPOs were applied, which GPOs were not applied and why, errors that were encountered, and the exact policy settings that took precedence and their source GPOs.

There are several requirements for running the Group Policy Results Wizard:

- You must have administrative credentials on the target computer.

- The target computer must be running Windows XP or later. The Group Policy Results Wizard cannot access Windows 2000 systems.

- You must be able to access WMI on the target computer. That means that it must be powered on, connected to the network, and accessible through ports 135 and 445.

> **NOTE ENABLE REMOTE ADMINISTRATION OF CLIENT COMPUTERS**
>
> Performing RSOP analysis by using the Group Policy Results Wizard is just one example of remote administration. Windows includes a firewall that prevents unsolicited inbound connections, even from members of the Administrators group. To perform remote administration, you might need to configure inbound rules for the firewall used by your clients and servers.
>
> Group Policy provides a simple way to enable remote administration. In the Computer Configuration\Policies\Administrative Templates\Network\Network Connections\Windows Firewall\Domain Profile folder, there is a policy setting named Windows Firewall: Allow Inbound Remote Administration Exception. When you enable this policy setting, you can specify the IP addresses or subnets from which inbound remote administration packets will be accepted. As with all policy settings, review the explanatory text in the Help box and test the effect of the policy in a lab environment before deploying it in production.

- The WMI service must be started on the target computer.

- If you want to analyze RSOP for a user, that user must have logged on at least once to the computer. It is not necessary for the user to be currently logged on.

After you have ensured that the requirements are met, you are ready to run an RSOP analysis. To run an RSOP report, right-click Group Policy Results in the GPMC console tree, and then click Group Policy Results Wizard.

The wizard prompts you to select a computer. It then connects to the WMI provider on that computer and provides a list of users who have logged on to it. You can then select one of the users or opt to skip RSOP analysis for user configuration policies.

The wizard produces a detailed RSOP report in a dynamic HTML format. If Internet Explorer Enhanced Security Configuration (IE ESC) is enabled, you are prompted to allow the console to display the dynamic content. You can expand or collapse each section of the report by clicking the Show or Hide link or by double-clicking the heading of the section. The report is displayed on three tabs:

- **Summary** The Summary tab displays the status of Group Policy processing at the last refresh. You can identify information that was collected about the system, the GPOs that were applied and denied, security group membership that might have affected GPOs filtered with security groups, WMI filters that were analyzed, and the status of CSEs.

- **Settings**   The Settings tab displays the resultant set of policy settings applied to the computer or user. This tab shows you exactly what has happened to the user through the effects of your Group Policy implementation. A tremendous amount of information can be gleaned from the Settings tab, but some data isn't reported, such as IPSec, wireless, and disk quota policy settings.

- **Policy Events**   The Policy Events tab displays Group Policy events from the event logs of the target computer.

After you have generated an RSOP report with the Group Policy Results Wizard, you can right-click the report to rerun the query, print the report, or save the report as either an XML file or an HTML file that maintains the dynamic expanding and collapsing sections. Either file type can be opened with Internet Explorer, so the RSOP report is portable outside the GPMC. If you right-click the node of the report itself underneath the Group Policy Results folder in the console tree, you can switch to Advanced View. In Advanced View, RSOP is displayed using the RSOP snap-in, which exposes all applied settings, including IPSec, wireless, and disk quota policies.

Generating RSOP Reports with Gpresult.exe

The Gpresult.exe command is the command-line version of the Group Policy Results Wizard. GPResult accesses the same WMI provider as the wizard, produces the same information, and, in fact, enables you to create the same graphical reports. GPResult is available on computers running Windows XP or later versions of Windows. Windows 2000 includes a Gpresult.exe command, which produces a limited report of Group Policy processing but is not as sophisticated as the command included in later versions of Windows.

When you run the GPResult command, you are likely to use the following options:

- **/s computername**   Specifies the name or IP address of a remote system. If you use a dot (.) as the computer name, or do not include the /s option, the RSOP analysis is performed on the local computer.

- **/scope [user | computer]**   Displays RSOP analysis for user or computer settings. If you omit the /scope option, RSOP analysis includes both user and computer settings.

- **/user username**   Specifies the name of the user for which RSOP data is displayed.

- **/r**   Displays a summary of RSOP data.

- **/v**   Displays verbose RSOP data, which presents the most meaningful information.

- **/z**   Displays super-verbose data, including the details of all policy settings applied to the system. Often, this is more information than you require for typical Group Policy troubleshooting.

- **/u domain\user /p password**   Provides credentials that are in the Administrators group of a remote system. Without these credentials, GPResult runs using the credentials with which you are logged on.
- **[/x | /h] filename**   Saves the reports in XML or HTML format, respectively.

✔ **Quick Check**

- You want to perform RSOP analysis on a remote system. Which two tools can you use?

Quick Check Answer

- You can use the Group Policy Results Wizard and Gpresult.exe to perform RSOP analysis on a remote system.

Troubleshooting Group Policy with the Group Policy Results Wizard and Gpresult.exe

As an administrator, you are likely to encounter scenarios that require Group Policy troubleshooting. You might need to diagnose and solve problems, including the following:

- GPOs are not being applied at all.
- The resultant set of policies for a computer or user is not what was expected.

The Group Policy Results Wizard and Gpresult.exe often provide the most valuable insight into Group Policy processing and application problems. Remember that these tools examine the WMI RSOP provider to report exactly what happened on a system. Examining the RSOP report often points you to a GPO that is scoped incorrectly or policy processing errors that prevented the application of settings in a GPO.

Performing What-If Analyses with the Group Policy Modeling Wizard

If you move a computer or user between sites, domains, or OUs, or change its security group membership, the GPOs scoped to that user or computer change and, therefore, the RSOP for the computer or user is different. RSOP also changes if slow link or loopback processing occurs or if there is a change to a system characteristic that is targeted by a WMI filter.

Before you make any of these changes, you should evaluate the potential impact to the RSOP of the user or computer. The Group Policy Results Wizard can perform RSOP analysis only on what has actually happened. To predict the future and to perform what-if analyses, you can use the Group Policy Modeling Wizard.

To perform Group Policy modeling, right-click the Group Policy Modeling node in the Group Policy Management console tree, click Group Policy Modeling Wizard, and then perform the steps in the wizard.

Modeling is performed by conducting a simulation on a domain controller, so you are first asked to select a domain controller that is running Windows Server 2003 or later. You do not need to be logged on locally to the domain controller, but the modeling request will be performed on the domain controller. You are then asked to specify the settings for the simulation:

- Select a user or computer object to evaluate, or specify the OU, site, or domain to evaluate.
- Choose whether slow link processing should be simulated.
- Specify whether to simulate loopback processing and, if so, choose Replace or Merge mode.
- Select a site to simulate.
- Select security groups for the user and the computer.
- Choose which WMI filters to apply in the simulation of user and computer policy processing.

When you have specified the settings for the simulation, you receive a report that is very similar to the Group Policy Results report discussed earlier. The Summary tab shows which GPOs will be processed, and the Settings tab displays the policy settings that will be applied to the user or computer. You can save this report by right-clicking it and choosing Save Report.

Examining Policy Event Logs

Windows Vista, Windows Server 2008, and later versions of Windows improve your ability to troubleshoot Group Policy not only with RSOP tools but also with improved logging of Group Policy events.

The System log provides high-level information about Group Policy, including errors created by the Group Policy Client when it cannot connect to a domain controller or locate GPOs. The Application log captures events recorded by CSEs. The Group Policy Operational Log provides detailed information about Group Policy processing.

To find these Group Policy logs, open the Event Viewer snap-in or console. The System and Application logs are in the Windows Logs node. The Group Policy Operational Log is found in Applications And Services Logs\Microsoft\Windows\GroupPolicy\Operational.

PRACTICE   **Configuring Group Policy Scope**

In this practice, you follow a scenario that builds upon the GPOs you created and configured in Lessons 1 and 2. You perform RSOP results and modeling analysis and examine policy-related events in the event logs. To perform these exercises, you must have completed the practices in Lessons 1 and 2.

EXERCISE 1   Use the Group Policy Results Wizard

In this exercise, you use the Group Policy Results Wizard to examine RSOP on SERVER01. You confirm that the policies you created in Lessons 1 and 2 have applied.

1. Log on to SERVER01 as Administrator.

2. Open Command Prompt and type **gpupdate.exe /force /boot** to initiate a Group Policy refresh.

   If the system reboots, log on as Administrator. If the system does not reboot, close Command Prompt.

   Make a note of the current system time; you will need to know the time of the refresh for Exercise 3, "View Policy Events."

3. Open the Group Policy Management console.

4. Expand Forest.

5. Right-click Group Policy Results and click Group Policy Results Wizard.

6. Click Next.

7. On the Computer Selection page, select This Computer and click Next.

8. On the User Selection page, select Display Policy Settings For, select Select A Specific User, and select CONTOSO\Administrator. Then click Next.

9. On the Summary Of Selections page, review your settings and click Next.

10. Click Finish.

    The RSOP report appears in the details pane of the console.

11. On the Summary tab, click the Show All link at the top of the report.

12. Review the Group Policy Summary results. For both user and computer configuration, identify the time of the last policy refresh and the list of allowed and denied GPOs. Identify the components that were used to process policy settings.

13. Click the Settings tab and click the Show All link at the top of the page. Review the settings that were applied during user and computer policy application and identify the GPO from which the settings were obtained.

14. Click the Policy Events tab and locate the event that logs the policy refresh you triggered with the Gpupdate.exe command in step 2.

15. Click the Summary tab, right-click the page, and choose Save Report. Save the report as an HTML file to your Documents folder with a name of your choice.

16. Open the saved RSOP report from your Documents folder.

EXERCISE 2   Use the Gpresult.exe Command

In this exercise, you perform RSOP analysis in Command Prompt, using Gpresult.exe.

1. Open Command Prompt.

2. Type **gpresult /r** and press Enter.

   RSOP summary results are displayed. The information is very similar to the Summary tab of the RSOP report produced by the Group Policy Results Wizard.

3. Type **gpresult /v** and press Enter.

   A more detailed RSOP report is produced. Notice many of the Group Policy settings applied by the client are listed in this report.

4. Type **gpresult /z** and press Enter.

   The most detailed RSOP report is produced.

5. Type **gpresult /h:"%userprofile%\Documents\RSOP.html"** and press Enter.

   An RSOP report is saved as an HTML file to your Documents folder.

6. Open the saved RSOP report from your documents folder. Compare the report, its information, and its formatting to the RSOP report you saved in the previous exercise.

EXERCISE 3   View Policy Events

As a client performs a policy refresh, Group Policy components log entries to the Windows event logs. In this exercise, you locate and examine Group Policy–related events.

1. Open the Event Viewer console from the Administrative Tools folder.

2. Expand Windows Logs and click System.

3. Locate events with GroupPolicy as the Source. You can even click the Filter Current Log link in the Actions pane and then select GroupPolicy in the Event Sources drop-down list.

4. Review the information associated with GroupPolicy events.

5. Click the Application node in the console tree under Windows Logs.

6. Sort the Application log by the Source column.

7. Review the logs by Source and identify the Group Policy events that have been entered in this log.

   Which events are related to Group Policy application, and which are related to the activities you have been performing to manage Group Policy?

8. In the console tree, expand Applications And Services Logs\Microsoft\Windows \GroupPolicy and click Operational.

9. Locate the first event related to the Group Policy refresh that you initiated in Exercise 1, "Use the Group Policy Results Wizard," with the Gpupdate.exe command. Review that event and the events that followed it.

EXERCISE 4   Perform Group Policy Modeling

In this exercise, you use Group Policy modeling to evaluate the potential effect of your policy settings on users who log on to sales laptops.

1. Open the Active Directory Users And Computers snap-in.

2. Create a user account for Mike Danseglio in the User Accounts OU. If the account already exists from a previous chapter's practice, ensure that the account is moved to the User Accounts OU.

3. Create a computer account in the Clients OU called LAPTOP101.

   If the account already exists from a previous chapter's practice, ensure that the account is moved to the Clients OU.

4. Add LAPTOP101 to the Sales Laptops group.

5. In the Group Policy Management console, expand Forest.

6. Right-click Group Policy Modeling and choose Group Policy Modeling Wizard.

7. Click Next.

8. On the Domain Controller Selection page, click Next.

9. On the User And Computer Selection page, in the User Information section, click User, click Browse, and then select Mike Danseglio.

10. In the Computer Information section, click Computer, click Browse, and select LAPTOP101 as the computer.

11. Click Next.

12. On the Advanced Simulation Options page, select the Loopback Processing check box and select Merge.

    Even though the Sales Laptop Configuration GPO specifies the loopback processing, you must instruct the Group Policy Modeling Wizard to consider loopback processing in its simulation.

13. Click Next.

14. On the Alternate Active Directory Paths page, click Next.

15. On the User Security Groups page, click Next.

16. On the Computer Security Groups page, click Next.

17. On the WMI Filters For Users page, click Next.

18. On the WMI Filters For Computers page, click. Next.

19. Review your settings on the Summary Of Selections page. Click Next, and then click Finish.

20. Review the information in the Group Policy Modeling report. Confirm that the following policy settings will be applied to Mike when he logs on to LAPTOP101:

- The laptop will wait for the network at startup, so that any changes to policy settings are applied before a user is allowed to log on.
- A password-protected screensaver will launch after 10 minutes.
- The standard wallpaper will be used.

Lesson Summary

- RSOP reports can be generated in the Windows interface by using the Group Policy Results Wizard, a component of the GPMC. RSOP reports reveal the actual results of policy processing at the last policy refresh.
- RSOP reports can be generated in Command Prompt, using Gpresult.exe. The */scope* option can be used to generate a report containing only user or computer settings. The */s* switch can be used to run GPResult against a remote system.
- The Group Policy Modeling Wizard allows you to simulate the application of Group Policy to evaluate the possible effect of changes to your Group Policy infrastructure or of moving users and computers between OUs and groups.
- Group Policy components create entries in the Windows event logs.

Lesson Review

You can use the following questions to test your knowledge of the information in Lesson 3, "Supporting Group Policy." The questions are also available on the companion CD if you prefer to review them in electronic form.

> **NOTE ANSWERS**
>
> Answers to these questions and explanations of why each answer choice is right or wrong are located in the "Answers" section at the end of the book.

1. A user calls the help desk at your organization and reports problems that you suspect might be related to changes that were recently made to Group Policy. You want to examine information regarding Group Policy processing on her system. Which tools can you use to gather this information remotely? (Choose all that apply.)

    A. Group Policy Modeling Wizard

    B. Group Policy Results Wizard

    C. Gpupdate.exe

D. Gpresult.exe

E. Msconfig.exe

2. You are the administrator at Contoso, Ltd. The contoso.com domain has five GPOs linked to the domain, one of which configures the password-protected screen saver and screen saver timeout required by corporate policy. Some users report that the screen saver is not launching after 10 minutes as expected. How do you find out when the GPO was applied?

A. Run Gpresult.exe for the users.

B. Run Gpresult.exe -*computer*.

C. Run Gpresult -*scope computer*.

D. Run Gpupdate.exe /*Target:User*.

Chapter Review

To further practice and reinforce the skills you learned in this chapter, you can perform the following tasks:

- Review the chapter summary.
- Review the list of key terms introduced in this chapter.
- Complete the case scenario. This scenario sets up a real-world situation involving the topics of this chapter and asks you to create a solution.
- Complete the suggested practices.
- Take a practice test.

Chapter Summary

- Group Policy helps you manage and change configuration centrally in an enterprise environment.
- Thousands of policy settings can be configured within a GPO. By default, these policy settings are set to Not Configured. When a setting is enabled or disabled, it causes a change.
- GPOs can be scoped to apply to users and computers with a variety of mechanisms, including links to sites, domains, and OUs. You can also filter GPOs with security groups and WMI filters.
- You can support and troubleshoot Group Policy with tools, including RSOP tools and event logs.

Key Terms

The following terms were introduced in this chapter. Do you know what they mean?

- Group Policy object (GPO)
- policy setting or policy
- Resultant Set of Policies (RSOP)
- scope

Case Scenario

In the following case scenario, you apply what you've learned about implementing GPOs, managing Group Policy scope, and supporting Group Policy. You can find answers to these questions in the "Answers" section at the end of this book.

Case Scenario: Implementing Group Policy

You are an administrator at Northwind Traders. Your company is converting to a new enterprise resource planning (ERP) application and, in the process, will be conducting a large number of training sessions. You are responsible for configuring the computers in the training rooms, and you want to provide a single, consistent user experience for any student who logs on to the systems. For example, you want to implement a specific desktop wallpaper, prevent users from accessing registry editing tools, and disable the password-protected screen saver policy that is implemented by a GPO linked to the domain.

1. Are the policy settings that will configure the desired desktop environment found in the Computer Configuration or the User Configuration node of a GPO?

2. After you configure the settings, should you link the GPO to the OU containing user accounts or to the OU containing the training computers?

3. What must you do to ensure that the settings are applied when users log on to computers in the training rooms and not when they log on to their normal computers?

4. What setting must be configured to prevent policy settings that normally apply to users from being applied when the users log on to training computers?

5. What must you do to prevent the domain's screen saver policies from applying to training room computers?

Suggested Practices

To help you successfully master the exam objectives presented in this chapter, complete the following tasks.

Create and Apply GPOs

In this practice, you configure the environment proposed in the case scenario. You create an OU for training room computers and configure a standard user desktop experience for those computers, using loopback Group Policy processing. You also prevent a domain policy from applying to training room computers. You confirm your work by performing RSOP analysis.

- **Practice 1**   Create an OU called **Training Room**. Create several sample computer objects within the OU. Then create a global security group called **Training Room Computers** and add the computer objects as members of the group.

- **Practice 2**   Create a GPO called **Training Room Configuration**. In the GPO, enable a policy that prevents access to registry editing tools and configure a standard desktop wallpaper. Both of these settings are user configuration settings in the Administrative Templates node. If you need assistance finding them, filter the settings with keywords. In the Computer Configuration node, locate the administrative templates setting that enables loopback policy processing. Enable this setting and choose to implement loopback processing in Replace mode.

- **Practice 3**   Link the Training Room Configuration GPO to the Training Room OU.
- **Practice 4**   In Lesson 1, you created the CONTOSO Standards GPO and configured it to implement screen saver policy settings. If you no longer have this GPO, perform Exercise 1 of Lesson 1. Using the Delegation tab of the GPO, add a permission that denies the Training Room Computers group the Apply Group Policy permission.
- **Practice 5**   Use the Group Policy Modeling Wizard to evaluate RSOP for a user logging on to one of the sample computers. Be sure in the wizard to select the option to simulate loopback processing and Replace mode.

Take a Practice Test

The practice tests on this book's companion CD offer many options. For example, you can test yourself on just one exam objective, or you can test yourself on all the 70-640 certification exam content. You can set up the test so that it closely simulates the experience of taking a certification exam, or you can set it up in study mode so that you can look at the correct answers and explanations after you answer each question.

> **MORE INFO**   **PRACTICE TESTS**
>
> For details about all the practice test options available, see the "How to Use the Practice Tests" section in this book's Introduction.

Managing Enterprise Security and Configuration with Group Policy Settings

You can use Group Policy to manage the configuration of an enormous variety of components and features of Microsoft Windows. In the previous chapter, you learned how to configure a Group Policy infrastructure. In this chapter, you learn to apply that infrastructure to manage several types of configuration related to security and software installation. You also discover tools, such as the Security Configuration Wizard, that make it easier to determine which settings should be configured based on a server's roles. Finally, you learn how to configure auditing of files and folders and of Active Directory Domain Services (AD DS) changes.

Exam objectives in this chapter:
- Create and apply Group Policy objects.
- Configure GPO templates.
- Configure audit policy by using GPOs.

Lessons in this chapter:

Before You Begin

To complete the practices in this chapter, you must have created a domain controller named SERVER01 in a domain named contoso.com. See Chapter 1, "Creating an Active Directory Domain," for detailed steps to perform this task.

REAL WORLD

Dan Holme

I am often brought in by clients to perform "sanity checks" on their Active Directory implementations. These sanity checks involve an examination of Group Policy settings and a discussion of how to take better advantage of Group Policy to manage change and configuration. It amazes me that a full eight years after the introduction of Group Policy, many organizations do not yet use its full capability, particularly in the area of security. Three of the four lessons in this chapter focus on the interaction between security configuration and Group Policy. Configuration such as the membership of the Administrators group and assignment of user rights, service startup modes, and audit policies can be effectively managed with Group Policy. What you learn in this chapter will not only help you pass the 70-640 exam, it will also help you increase the manageability and security of your entire enterprise. This includes Active Directory itself. For the past 11 years, I've constantly been asked, "How can I know what changes have been made by administrators in Active Directory?" Now, thanks to Directory Service Changes auditing, introduced in Windows Server 2008, you can simply check your security log. Even if you are already using policy to manage your security configuration, this new feature, along with the vastly improved Security Configuration Wizard, will surely take your security management capabilities to a higher level.

Lesson 1: Delegating the Support of Computers

Many enterprises have one or more personnel dedicated to supporting end users, a role often referred to as the *help desk*, *desktop support*, or just *support*. Help desk personnel are often asked to perform troubleshooting, configuration, or other support tasks on client computers, and these tasks often require administrative privileges. Therefore, the credentials used by support personnel must be at the level of a member of the local Administrators group on client computers, but desktop support personnel do not need the high level of privilege given to the Domain Admins group, so it is not recommended that you place them in that group. Instead, you should configure client systems so that a group representing support personnel is added to the local Administrators group. Restricted groups policies allow you to do just that, and in this lesson, you learn how to use restricted groups policies to add the help desk personnel to the local Administrators group of clients, thereby delegating support of those computers to the help desk. The same approach can be used to delegate the administration of any scope of computers to the team responsible for those systems.

> **After this lesson, you will be able to:**
> - Delegate the administration of computers.
> - Use Restricted Groups policies to modify or enforce the membership of groups.
> - Use Group Policy Preferences to modify or enforce the membership of groups.
>
> **Estimated lesson time: 30 minutes**

Understanding Restricted Groups Policies

When you edit a Group Policy object (GPO) and expand the Computer Configuration node, the Policies node, the Windows Settings node, and the Security Settings node, you find the Restricted Groups policy node, shown in Figure 7-1.

FIGURE 7-1 The Restricted Groups policy node of a Group Policy object

Restricted groups policy settings allow you to manage the membership of groups. There are two types of settings: This Group Is A Member Of (the Member Of setting) and Members Of This Group (the Members setting). Figure 7-2 shows examples.

FIGURE 7-2 Member Of and Members restricted groups policies

It's very important to understand the difference between these two settings. A Member Of setting indicates that the group specified by the policy is a member of another group. On the left side of Figure 7-2, you can see a typical example: The CONTOSO\Help Desk group is a member of the Administrators group. When a computer applies this policy setting, it ensures that the Help Desk group from the domain becomes a member of its local Administrators group. If there is more than one GPO with restricted groups policies, each Member Of policy is applied. For example, if a GPO linked to the Clients organizational unit (OU) specifies CONTOSO\Help Desk as a member of Administrators, and a second GPO linked to the NYC OU (a sub-OU of the Clients OU) specifies CONTOSO\NYC Support as a member of Administrators, a computer in the NYC OU adds both the Help Desk and NYC Support groups to its Administrators group in addition to any existing members of the group such as Domain Admins. This example is illustrated in Figure 7-3. As you can see, restricted groups policies that use the Member Of setting are cumulative.

The second type of restricted groups policy setting is the Members setting, which specifies the entire membership of the group specified by the policy. The right side of Figure 7-2 shows a typical example: the Administrators group's Members list is specified as CONTOSO\Help Desk. When a computer applies this policy setting, it ensures that the local Administrators group's membership consists *only* of CONTOSO\Help Desk. Any members not specified in the policy are removed, including Domain Admins. The Members setting is the authoritative policy—it defines the final list of members. If there is more than one GPO with restricted

FIGURE 7-3 Results of restricted groups policies using the Member Of setting

group policies, the GPO with the highest priority prevails. For example, if a GPO linked to the Clients OU specifies the Administrators group membership as CONTOSO\Help Desk, and another GPO linked to the NYC OU specifies the Administrators group membership as CONTOSO\NYC Support, computers in the NYC OU will have only the NYC Support group in their Administrators group. This example is illustrated in Figure 7-4.

FIGURE 7-4 Restricted groups policies using the Members setting

EXAM TIP

Before taking the 70-640 exam, you should be able to identify the differences between restricted groups policies that use the Member Of setting and those that use the Members setting. Remember that Member Of settings are cumulative and that if GPOs use the Members setting, only the Members setting with the highest GPO processing priority is applied and its list of members prevails.

Delegating Administration Using Restricted Groups Policies with the Member Of Setting

You can use restricted groups policies with the Member Of setting to manage the delegation of administrative privileges for computers by following these steps:

1. In Group Policy Management Editor, navigate to Computer Configuration\Policies\ Windows Settings\Security Settings\Restricted Groups.

2. Right-click Restricted Groups and click Add Group.

3. Click Browse and, in the Select Groups dialog box, type the name of the group you want to add to the Administrators group (for example, **CONTOSO\Help Desk**) and click OK.

4. Click OK to close the Add Group dialog box.

    A Properties dialog box appears.

5. Click Add next to the This Group Is A Member Of section.

6. Type **Administrators** and click OK.

    The Properties group policy setting should look something like the left side of Figure 7-2.

7. Click OK again to close the Properties dialog box.

Delegating the membership of the local Administrators group in this manner adds the group specified in step 3 to that group. It does not remove any existing members of the Administrators group. The group policy simply tells the client, "Make sure this group is a member of the local Administrators group." This allows for the possibility that individual systems could have other users or groups in their local Administrators group. This Group Policy setting is also cumulative. If multiple GPOs configure different security principals as members of the local Administrators group, all will be added to the group.

Delegating Administration Using Restricted Groups Policies with the Members Of This Group Setting

To take complete control of the local Administrators group, follow these steps:

1. In Group Policy Management Editor, navigate to Computer Configuration\Policies\ Windows Settings\Security Settings\Restricted Groups.

2. Right-click Restricted Groups and click Add Group.

3. Type **Administrators** and click OK.

 A Properties dialog box appears.

4. Click Add next to the Members Of This Group section.

5. Click Browse, type the name of the group you want to make the sole member of the Administrators group (for example, **CONTOSO\Help Desk**), and click OK.

6. Click OK again to close the Add Member dialog box.

 The group policy setting Properties should look something like the right side of Figure 7-2.

7. Click OK again to close the Properties dialog box.

When you use the Members setting of a restricted groups policy, the Members list defines the final membership of the specified group. The steps just listed result in a GPO that authoritatively manages the Administrators group. When a computer applies this GPO, it adds all members specified by the GPO and removes all members not specified by the GPO, including Domain Admins. Only the local Administrator account is not removed from the Administrators group, because Administrator is a permanent and nonremovable member of Administrators.

 Quick Check

- You want to add a group to the local Administrators group on computers without removing accounts that already exist in the group. Describe the restricted groups policy you should create.

Quick Check Answer

- Create a restricted groups policy for the group you want to add. Use the Member Of policy setting (This Group Is A Member Of) and specify Administrators.

If you use both Members and Member Of restricted groups policies, the highest-priority Members policy setting sets the authoritative baseline membership for the group, and then the cumulative memberships of Member Of policies augment that baseline. This complex interaction of the two policy settings is not something that you are likely to encounter on an exam, but you might see it in a production environment. Therefore, in your enterprise, be careful to design and test your restricted groups policies to ensure that they achieve the desired result.

Defining Group Membership with Group Policy Preferences

You can also use Group Policy Preferences to define the membership of groups. Local Group preferences are available in both Computer Configuration and User Configuration. The settings for a Local Group preference are shown in Figure 7-5.

FIGURE 7-5 Configuring a Local Group preference

The three options related to "current user" are available only in the Local Group preference in User Configuration, not in Computer Configuration.

You can create, delete, replace, or modify (update) a local group. As you can see in the previous screen shot, you can rename the group, change its description, or make modifications to the group's membership.

Local Group preferences cannot remove members from a group if those members were added to a group by using a restricted groups policy setting. Additionally, if a restricted groups policy setting uses the Members method to define the authoritative membership of a group, preferences can neither add nor remove members.

The interactions between Members restricted groups policy settings, Member Of restricted groups policy settings, Local Group preferences scoped as computer settings, and Local Group preferences scoped as user settings can be complex and difficult to understand. Be sure to thoroughly test the results if you choose to implement multiple methods of managing group membership with Group Policy.

PRACTICE Delegating the Support of Computers

In this practice, you use Group Policy to delegate the membership of the Administrators group. You first create a GPO with a restricted groups policy setting that ensures that the Help Desk group is a member of the Administrators group on all client systems. You then create a GPO that adds the NYC Support group to Administrators on clients in the NYC OU. Finally, you confirm that in the NYC OU, both the Help Desk and NYC Support groups are administrators.

To perform this practice, you need the following objects in the contoso.com domain:

- A first-level OU named Admins
- A global security group named Help Desk in the Admins OU
- A global security group named NYC Support in the Admins OU
- A first-level OU named Clients
- An OU named NYC in the Clients OU
- A computer object named DESKTOP101 in the NYC OU

If you have performed practices in earlier lessons, some of these objects might already exist in other OUs, in which case you can move the object to the OU specified above.

EXERCISE 1 Delegate the Administration of All Clients in the Domain

In this exercise, you create a GPO with a restricted groups policy setting that ensures that the Help Desk group is a member of the Administrators group on all client systems.

1. Open Group Policy Management, and then expand Forest\Domains\contoso.com. Click the Group Policy Objects container in the console tree.
2. Right-click the Group Policy Objects container and click New.
3. In the Name box, type **Corporate Help Desk** and click OK.
4. Right-click the GPO and click Edit.
5. In Group Policy Management Editor, navigate to Computer Configuration\Policies \Windows Settings\Security Settings\Restricted Groups.
6. Right-click Restricted Groups and click Add Group.
7. Click Browse and, in the Select Groups dialog box, type **CONTOSO\Help Desk** and click OK.
8. Click OK to close the Add Group dialog box.
9. Click Add next to the This Group Is A Member Of section.
10. Type **Administrators** and click OK.

    The group policy setting properties should look like the left side of Figure 7-2.
11. Click OK again to close the Properties dialog box.
12. Close Group Policy Management Editor.
13. In the Group Policy Management console, right-click the Clients OU and click Link An Existing GPO.
14. Select the Corporate Help Desk GPO and click OK.

EXERCISE 2 Delegate the Administration of a Subset of Clients in the Domain

In this exercise, you create a GPO with a restricted groups policy setting that adds the NYC Support group to the Administrators group on all client systems in the NYC OU.

1. In the Group Policy Management console, expand Forest\Domains\Contoso.com. Click the Group Policy Objects container in the console tree.

2. Right-click the Group Policy Objects container and click New.

3. In the Name box, type **New York Support** and click OK.

4. Right-click the GPO and click Edit.

5. Repeat steps 5–12 of Exercise 1, "Delegate the Administration of All Clients in the Domain," but type **CONTOSO\NYC Support** as the group name in step 7.

6. In the Group Policy Management console, expand the Clients OU, right-click the NYC OU, and then click Link An Existing GPO.

7. Select the New York Support GPO and click OK.

EXERCISE 3   Confirm the Cumulative Application of Member Of Policies

You can use Group Policy Modeling to produce a report of the effective policies applied to a computer or user. In this exercise, you use Group Policy Modeling to confirm that a computer in the NYC OU includes both the Help Desk and NYC Support groups in its Administrators group.

1. In the Group Policy Management console, expand Forest and click the Group Policy Modeling node.

2. Right-click the Group Policy Modeling node and click Group Policy Modeling Wizard.

3. Click Next.

4. On the Domain Controller Selection page, click Next.

5. On the User And Computer Selection page, in the Computer Information section, click Browse.

6. Expand the domain and the Clients OU, and then click the NYC OU.

7. Click OK.

8. Select the Skip To The Final Page Of This Wizard Without Collecting Additional Data check box.

9. Click Next.

10. On the Summary Of Selections page, click Next.

11. Click Finish.

    The Group Policy Modeling report appears.

    If an Internet Explorer warning appears, it is because Internet Explorer Enhanced Security Configuration (IE ESC) is enabled. Open Server Manager. In the Security Information section, click the Configure IE ESC link. In the Administrators section, click Off. In the Users section, click Off. Click OK. Close Server Manager. In the GPME, click Close to close the Internet Explorer warning. If you continue to receive warnings, close and re-open Group Policy Management, and then repeat steps 1–11.

12. On the Settings tab, click Security Settings.

13. Click Restricted Groups.

You should see both the Help Desk and NYC Support groups listed. Restricted groups policies using the This Group Is A Member Of setting are cumulative. Notice that the report does not specify that the listed groups are members of the Administrators group. The omission of the Member Of column is a limitation of the report.

OPTIONAL EXERCISE 4   **Confirm the Membership of the Administrators Group**

If your test environment includes a client computer that is a member of the contoso.com domain, move the computer object in Active Directory to the NYC OU. Restart the computer, log on as the domain's Administrator, and then open the Computer Management console. In Computer Management, expand the Local Users And Groups node and, in the Groups folder, open the Administrators group. You should see the following members listed:

- CONTOSO\Help Desk, applied by the Corporate Help Desk GPO
- CONTOSO\NYC Support, applied by the New York Support GPO
- Domain Admins, made a member of Administrators when the computer joined the domain
- The local Administrator account, a default member that cannot be removed

Lesson Summary

- To delegate support of computers in your domain, you must manage the membership of the Administrators groups on those systems.
- GPOs using the Member Of setting of restricted groups policies can add domain groups to the Administrators group. Member Of settings are cumulative, so multiple GPOs can add groups to Administrators.
- A GPO using the Members setting of restricted groups policies can define the membership of the Administrators group. The Members setting is final and authoritative. If more than one GPO applies a Members setting to a computer, the GPO with the highest precedence determines the membership of the Administrators group.

Lesson Review

You can use the following questions to test your knowledge of the information in Lesson 1, "Delegating the Support of Computers." The questions are also available on the companion CD if you prefer to review them in electronic form.

> **NOTE   ANSWERS**
>
> Answers to these questions and explanations of why each answer choice is right or wrong are located in the "Answers" section at the end of the book.

1. The contoso.com domain contains a GPO named Corporate Help Desk, linked to the Clients OU, and a GPO named Sydney Support, linked to the Sydney OU within the Clients OU. The Corporate Help Desk GPO includes a restricted groups policy for the CONTOSO\Help Desk group that specifies This Group Is A Member Of Administrators. The Sydney Support GPO includes a restricted groups policy for the CONTOSO\Sydney Support group that specifies This Group Is A Member Of Administrators. A computer named DESKTOP234 joins the domain in the Sydney OU. Which of the following accounts will be a member of the Administrators group on DESKTOP234? (Choose all that apply.)

   A. Administrator

   B. Domain Admins

   C. Sydney Support

   D. Help Desk

   E. Remote Desktop Users

2. The contoso.com domain contains a GPO named Corporate Help Desk, linked to the Clients OU, and a GPO named Sydney Support, linked to the Sydney OU within the Clients OU. The Corporate Help Desk GPO includes a restricted groups policy for the Administrators group that specifies the Members Of This Group setting to be CONTOSO\Help Desk. The Sydney Support GPO includes a restricted groups policy for the Administrators group that specifies the Members Of This Group setting to be CONTOSO\Sydney Support. A computer named DESKTOP234 joins the domain in the Sydney OU. Which of the following accounts will be a member of the Administrators group on DESKTOP234? (Choose all that apply.)

   A. Administrator

   B. Domain Admins

   C. Sydney Support

   D. Help Desk

   E. Remote Desktop Users

3. The contoso.com domain contains a GPO named Corporate Help Desk, linked to the Clients OU, and a GPO named Sydney Support, linked to the Sydney OU within the Clients OU. The Corporate Help Desk GPO includes a restricted groups policy for the Administrators group that specifies the Members Of This Group setting to be CONTOSO\Help Desk. The Sydney Support GPO includes a restricted groups policy for the CONTOSO\Sydney Support group that specifies This Group Is A Member Of Administrators. A computer named DESKTOP234 joins the domain in the Sydney OU.

Which of the following accounts will be a member of the Administrators group on DESKTOP234? (Choose all that apply.)

A. Administrator

B. Domain Admins

C. Sydney Support

D. Help Desk

E. Remote Desktop Users

Lesson 2: Managing Security Settings

Security is a primary concern for all Windows administrators. Windows Server 2008 R2 includes numerous settings that affect the services that are running, the ports that are open, the network packets that are allowed into or out of the system, the rights and permissions of users, and the activities that are audited. You can manage an enormous number of settings, and, unfortunately, there is no magic formula that applies the perfect security configuration to a server. The appropriate security configuration for a server depends on the roles that server plays, the mix of operating systems in the environment, and the security policies of the organization, which themselves depend on compliance regulations enforced from outside the organization.

Therefore, you must work to determine and configure the security settings that are required for servers in your organization, and you must be prepared to manage those settings in a way that centralizes and optimizes security configuration. Windows Server 2008 R2 provides several mechanisms with which to configure security settings on one or more systems. In this lesson, you discover these mechanisms and their interactions.

> **After this lesson, you will be able to:**
> - Configure security settings on a computer by using the Local Security Policy.
> - Create and apply security templates to manage security configuration.
> - Analyze security configuration based on security templates.
> - Create, edit, and apply security policies using the Security Configuration Wizard.
> - Deploy security configuration with Group Policy.
>
> **Estimated lesson time: 60 minutes**

What Is Security Policy Management?

Security policy management involves designing, deploying, managing, analyzing, and revising security settings for one or more configurations of Windows systems. There are likely to be several system configurations in a typical enterprise: desktops and laptops, servers, and domain controllers. Most enterprises define even more configurations—for example, by delineating various types or roles of servers.

The first words are important: *Security Policy*. Before you even touch the technology, you need to understand what your enterprise security policy requires; if you do not yet have a written security policy, begin by creating one. After you know where you are heading, you are ready to start the journey.

Your security policy, and the requirements it contains, probably require multiple customizations to the default, out-of-box security configuration of Windows client and server operating systems. To manage security configuration, you need to:

- Create a security policy for a new application or server role not included in Server Manager.

- Use security policy management tools to apply security policy settings that are unique to your environment.

- Analyze server security settings to ensure that the security policy applied to a server is appropriate for the server role.

- Update a server security policy when the server configuration is modified.

This lesson covers the tools, concepts, and processes required to perform these tasks. The tools used in this lesson include:

- Local Group Policy

- Security Configuration Wizard

- Security Templates snap-in

- Security Configuration And Analysis snap-in

- Domain Group Policy

Configuring the Local Security Policy

Each server running Windows Server 2008 R2 maintains a collection of security settings that can be managed by using the local GPO. You can configure the local GPO by using the Group Policy Object Editor snap-in or the Local Security Policy console. The available policy setting categories are shown in Figure 7-6.

FIGURE 7-6 The security settings available in the local GPO

This lesson focuses on the mechanisms with which to configure and manage security settings, rather than on the details of the settings themselves. Many of the settings—including account policies, audit policy, and user rights assignment—are discussed elsewhere in this training kit.

Because domain controllers (DCs) do not have local user accounts (only domain accounts), the policies in the Account Policies container of the local GPO on DCs cannot be configured. Instead, account policies for the domain should be configured as part of a domain-linked GPO such as the Default Domain Policy GPO. Account policies are discussed in the first lesson of Chapter 8, "Improving the Security of Authentication in an AD DS Domain."

The settings found in the local Security Settings policies are a subset of the policies that can be configured using domain-based Group Policy, shown in Figure 7-7. As you learned in Chapter 6, "Implementing a Group Policy Infrastructure," it is a best practice to manage configuration by using domain-based Group Policy rather than on a machine-by-machine basis using local Group Policy. This is particularly true for domain controllers. The Default Domain Controllers Policy GPO is created when the first domain controller is promoted for a new domain. It is linked to the Domain Controllers OU and should be used to manage baseline security settings for all DCs in the domain so that DCs are consistently configured.

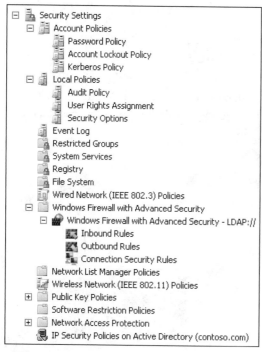

FIGURE 7-7 Security settings in a domain-based GPO

Managing Security Configuration with Security Templates

The second mechanism for managing security configuration is the security template. A security template is a collection of configuration settings stored as a text file with the .inf extension. As you can see in Figure 7-8, a security template contains settings that are a subset of the settings available in a domain-based GPO but a somewhat different subset than those managed by the local GPO. The tools used to manage security templates present settings in an interface that allows you to save your security configurations as files and deploy them when and where they are needed. You can also use a security template to analyze the compliance of a computer's current configuration against the desired configuration.

FIGURE 7-8 Security settings in a security template

Storing security configuration in security templates offers several advantages. For example, because the templates are plaintext files, you can work with them manually as with any text file, cutting and pasting sections as needed. Further, templates make it easy to store security configurations of various types so that you can easily apply different levels of security to computers performing different roles.

Security templates allow you to configure any of the following types of policies and settings:

- **Account Policies** Specify password restrictions, account lockout policies, and Kerberos policies.
- **Local Policies** Configure audit policies, user rights assignments, and security options policies.
- **Event Log Policies** Configure maximum event log sizes and rollover policies.
- **Restricted Groups** Specify the users permitted to be members of specific groups.
- **System Services** Specify the startup types and permissions for system services.
- **Registry Permissions** Set access control permissions for specific registry keys.
- **File System Permissions** Specify access control permissions for NTFS files and folders.

You can deploy security templates in a variety of ways: by using Active Directory Group Policy Objects, the Security Configuration And Analysis snap-in, or Secedit.exe. When you associate a security template with an Active Directory Group Policy object, the settings in the template become part of the GPO. You can also apply a security template directly to a computer, in which case the settings in the template become part of the computer's local policies. This lesson discusses each of these options. Remember to test security changes before deploying them in a production environment.

Using the Security Templates Snap-in

To work with security templates, you use the Security Templates snap-in. Windows Server 2008 R2 does not include a console with the Security Templates snap-in, so you have to create one yourself using the MMC Add/Remove Snap-in menu command. The snap-in creates a folder called Security and a subfolder called Templates in your Documents folder, and the resulting Documents\Security\Templates folder becomes the template search path, where you can store one or more security templates.

To create a new security template, right-click the node that represents your template search path—C:\Users\Administrator\Documents\Security\Templates, for example—and then click New Template. You can also create a template that reflects the current configuration of a server; you learn how to do that in the "Creating a Security Template" section.

Settings are configured in the template in the same way that settings are configured in a GPO. The Security Templates snap-in configures settings in a security template. It is just an editor—it does not play any role in actually applying those settings to a system. Configure security settings in a template by using the Security Templates snap-in. Although the template itself is a text file, the syntax can be confusing. Using the snap-in ensures that settings are changed using the proper syntax.

The exception to this rule is adding registry settings that are not already listed in the Local Policies\Security Option portion of the template. As new security settings become known, if they can be configured using a registry key, you can add them to a security template. To do so, you add them to the Registry Values section of the template.

> **NOTE** SAVE YOUR SETTINGS
>
> Be sure to save your changes to a security template by right-clicking the template and clicking Save.

When you install a server or promote it to a domain controller, a default security template is applied by Windows. You can find that template in the %SystemRoot%\Security\Templates folder. On a domain controller, the template is called DC security.inf. You should not modify this template directly, but you can copy it to your template search path and modify the copy.

Deploying Security Templates by Using Group Policy Objects

Creating and modifying security templates does not improve security until you apply those templates. To configure several computers in a single operation, you can import a security template into the Group Policy Object for a domain, site, or organizational unit object in Active Directory.

To import a security template into a GPO, right-click the Security Settings node and click Import Policy. In the Import Policy From dialog box, if you select the Clear This Database Before Importing check box, all security settings in the GPO will be erased prior to importing the template settings, so the GPO's security settings will match the template's settings.

If you leave the Clear This Database Before Importing check box cleared, the GPO's security policy settings will remain and the template's settings will be imported. Any settings defined in the GPO that are also defined in the template will be replaced with the template's setting.

Security Configuration And Analysis Tool

You can use the Security Configuration And Analysis snap-in to apply a security template to a computer interactively. The snap-in also provides the ability to analyze the current system security configuration and compare it to a baseline saved as a security template. This helps you quickly determine whether someone has changed a computer's security settings and whether the system conforms to your organization's security policies.

As with the Security Templates snap-in, Windows Server 2008 R2 does not include a console with the Security Configuration And Analysis snap-in, so you must add the snap-in to a console yourself.

To use the Security Configuration And Analysis snap-in, you must first create a database that will contain a collection of security settings. The database is the interface between the actual security settings on the computer and the settings stored in your security templates.

To create a database (or open an existing one), right-click the Security Configuration And Analysis node in the console tree. You can then import one or more security templates. If you import more than one template, you must decide whether to clear the database. If the database is cleared, only the settings in the new template will be part of the database. If the database is not cleared, additional template settings that are defined will override settings from previously imported templates. If settings in newly imported templates are not defined, the settings in the database from previously imported templates will remain.

To summarize, the Security Configuration And Analysis snap-in creates a database of security settings composed of imported security template settings. The settings in the database can be applied to the computer or used to analyze the computer's compliance and discrepancies with the desired state.

> **IMPORTANT DATABASE SETTINGS VS. THE COMPUTER'S SETTINGS**
>
> Settings in a database do not modify the computer's settings or the settings in a template until that database is either used to configure the computer or exported to a template.

Applying Database Settings to a Computer

After you have imported one or more templates to create the database, you can apply the database settings to the computer.

To apply a database, right-click Security Configuration And Analysis and click Configure Computer Now. You are prompted for a path to an error log that will be generated during the application of settings. After applying the settings, examine the error log for any problems.

 Quick Check

- Describe the procedure used to apply a security template to a single computer.

Quick Check Answer

- Use the Security Configuration And Analysis snap-in to create a database. Import the template into the database. Configure the computer by using the database.

Analyzing the Security Configuration of a Computer

Before applying the database settings to a computer, you might want to analyze the computer's current configuration to identify discrepancies.

To analyze the security configuration of a computer, right-click Security Configuration And Analysis and click Analyze Computer Now. The system prompts you for the location of its error log file and then proceeds to compare the computer's current settings to the settings in the database. After the analysis is complete, the console produces a report such as the one shown in Figure 7-9.

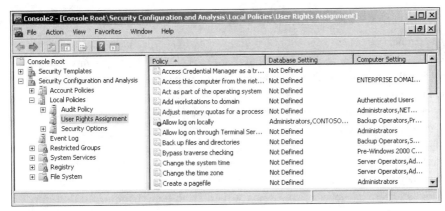

FIGURE 7-9 The Security Configuration And Analysis snap-in displays an analysis of the computer's configuration.

Unlike the display of policy settings in the Group Policy Management Editor, Group Policy Object Editor, Local Security Policy, or Security Templates snap-ins, the report shows for each policy the setting defined in the database (which was derived from the templates you imported) and the computer's current setting. The two settings are compared, and the comparison result is displayed as a flag on the policy name. For example, in Figure 7-9, the Allow Log On Locally policy setting shows a discrepancy between the database setting and the computer setting. The meanings of the flags are as follows:

- **X in a red circle**   Indicates that the policy is defined both in the database and on the computer but that the configured values do not match

- **Green check mark in a white circle**   Indicates that the policy is defined both in the database and on the computer and that the configured values do match

- **Question mark in a white circle**   Indicates that the policy is not defined in the database and, therefore, was not analyzed, or that the user running the analysis did not have the permissions needed to access the policy on the computer

- **Exclamation point in a white circle**   Indicates that the policy is defined in the database but does not exist on the computer

- **No flag**   Indicates that the policy is not defined in the database or on the computer

Correcting Security Setting Discrepancies

As you examine the elements of the database and compare its settings with those of the computer, you might find discrepancies and want to make changes to the computer's configuration or to the database to bring the two settings into alignment. You can double-click any policy setting to display its Properties dialog box and modify its value in the database. After you've made changes to the database, you can apply the database settings to the computer by performing the steps described earlier, in the section called "Applying Database Settings to a Computer."

Alternately, you can modify the computer's security settings directly by using the Local Security Policy console, by modifying the appropriate Group Policy object, or by manually manipulating file system or registry permissions. After making such changes, return to the Security Configuration And Analysis snap-in and click the Analyze Computer Now command to refresh the comparison of the database and computer's settings.

Creating a Security Template

You can create a new security template from the database. To do so, right-click Security Configuration And Analysis and click Export Template. The template contains the settings in the database that have been imported from one or more security templates and that you have modified to reflect the current settings of the analyzed computer.

Secedit.exe

Secedit.exe is a command-line utility that can perform the same functions as the Security Configuration And Analysis snap-in. The advantage of Secedit.exe is that you can call it from scripts and batch files, which allows you to automate your security template deployments. Another big advantage of Secedit.exe is that you can use it to apply only part of a security template to a computer, something you cannot do with the Security Configuration And Analysis snap-in or Group Policy Objects. For example, if you want to apply the file system's permissions from a template but leave all the other settings alone, Secedit.exe is the only way to do so.

To use Secedit.exe, you run the program from Command Prompt with one of the following six main parameters, plus additional parameters for each function:

- **/Configure** Applies all or part of a security database to the local computer. You can also configure the program to import a security template into the specified database before applying the database settings to the computer.

- **/Analyze** Compares the computer's current security settings with those in a security database. You can configure the program to import a security template into the database before performing the analysis. The program stores the results of the analysis in the database itself, which you can view later, using the Security Configuration And Analysis snap-in.

- **/Import** Imports all or part of a security template into a specific security database.
- **/Export** Exports all or part of the settings from a security database to a new security template.
- **/Validate** Verifies that a security template is using the correct internal syntax.
- **/Generaterollback** Creates a security template that you can use to restore a system to its original configuration after applying another template.

For example, to configure the machine by using a template called BaselineSecurity, use the following command:

```
secedit /configure /db BaselineSecurity.sdb
/cfg BaselineSecurity.inf /log BaselineSecurity.log
```

To create a rollback template for the BaselineSecurity template, use the following command:

```
secedit /generaterollback /cfg BaselineSecurity.inf
/rbk BaselineSecurityRollback.inf
/log BaselineSecurityRollback.log
```

> **MORE INFO** **SECEDIT.EXE**
>
> For full details regarding Secedit.exe and its switches, see *http://technet.microsoft.com/ en-us/library/bb490997.aspx.*

The Security Configuration Wizard

You can use the Security Configuration Wizard to enhance the security of a server by closing ports and disabling services not required for the server's roles.

The Security Configuration Wizard can be launched from the home page of Server Manager (in the Security Information section) or from the Administrative Tools folder.

There is also a command-line version of the tool, scwcmd.exe. Type **scwcmd.exe /?** at Command Prompt for help on the command, or see *http://go.microsoft.com/ fwlink/?LinkId=168678.*

The Security Configuration Wizard is a next-generation security management tool, more advanced than the Security Configuration And Analysis snap-in. The Security Configuration Wizard is role based in accordance with the role-based configuration of Windows Server 2008 R2. The Security Configuration Wizard creates a security policy— an .xml file—that configures the following:

- Services
- Network security including firewall rules

- Registry values
- Audit policy
- Other settings based on the roles of a server

That security policy can then be modified, applied to another server, or transformed into a GPO for deployment to multiple systems.

Creating a Security Policy

To create a security policy:

1. Launch the Security Configuration Wizard from the Administrative Tools folder or the Security Information section on the home page of Server Manager.

   You can open the Security Configuration Wizard Help file by clicking the Security Configuration Wizard link on the first page of the wizard.

2. Click Next.

3. On the Configuration Action page, click Create A New Security Policy, and then click Next.

4. Enter the name of the server to scan and analyze, and then click Next.

The security policy is based on the roles being performed by the specified server. You must be an administrator on the server for the analysis of its roles to proceed. Ensure also that all applications using inbound IP ports are running before you run the Security Configuration Wizard.

The Security Configuration Wizard begins the analysis of the selected server's roles. It uses a security configuration database that defines services and ports required for each server role supported by the Security Configuration Wizard. The security configuration database is a set of .xml files installed in %SystemRoot%\Security\Msscw\Kbs.

> **NOTE** **CENTRALIZING THE SECURITY CONFIGURATION DATABASE**
>
> In an enterprise environment, centralize the security configuration database so that administrators use the same database when running the Security Configuration Wizard. Copy the files in the %SystemRoot%\Security\Msscw\Kbs folder to a network folder. Then launch the Security Configuration Wizard with the Scw.exe command, using the syntax scw.exe /kb *DatabaseLocation*. For example, the command scw.exe /kb \\server01\ scwkb launches the Security Configuration Wizard, using the security configuration database in the shared folder scwkb on SERVER01.

The Security Configuration Wizard uses the security configuration database to scan the selected server and identifies the following:

- Roles that are installed on the server
- Roles that the server is likely to be performing
- Services installed on the server but not defined in the security configuration database
- IP addresses and subnets configured for the server

The information discovered about the server is saved in a file named Main.xml. This server-specific file is called the *configuration database,* not to be confused with the security configuration database used by the Security Configuration Wizard to perform the analysis. To display the configuration database, click View Configuration Database on the Processing Security Configuration page.

The initial settings in the configuration database are called the *baseline settings.* After the server has been scanned and the configuration database has been created, you have the opportunity to modify the database, which will be used to generate the security policy to configure services, firewall rules, registry settings, and audit policies. The security policy can then be applied to the server or to other servers playing similar roles. The Security Configuration Wizard presents each of these four categories of the security policy in a section—a series of wizard pages:

- **Role-Based Service Configuration** The outcome of this section is a set of policies that configure the startup state of services on the server. You want to ensure that only the services required by the server's roles start and that other services do not start. To achieve this outcome, the Security Configuration Wizard presents pages that display the server roles, client features, and administration and other options detected on the scanned server. You can add or remove roles, features, and options to reflect the de-sired role configuration. The last page of the section, titled "Confirm Service Changes" and shown in Figure 7-10, shows the changes that will be made to services based on the roles you specify.

The server shown in Figure 7-10 is a domain controller, and you can see that the AD DS service is currently configured to start automatically; the policy will also set the service to start automatically to support the AD DS role. However, audio is not required for a DC, so the service named Audiosrv used by the Windows Audio option will be configured by the policy as disabled.

FIGURE 7-10 The Confirm Service Changes page of the Security Configuration Wizard

You cannot change the startup states on the Confirm Service Changes page of the Security Configuration Wizard. Instead, you must click the Back button to locate the role, service, or option indicated in the Used By column and either select or deselect that item. The service startup policies on the Confirm Service Changes page are determined by the selected roles, services, and options. The wizard disables services for roles that you did not select by configuring the service startup policy as disabled. It is conceivable that the server on which you run the Security Configuration Wizard has services that are not defined by the Security Configuration Wizard security configuration database. The Select Additional Services page of the wizard allows you to include those services in the security policy so that, if the services exist on a system to which you apply the policy, those services will be started according to the startup setting in the baseline configuration database.

It is also conceivable that a server to which you apply the security policy might have services not found on the server from which you created the security policy. On the Handling Unspecified Services page, you can specify whether such services should be disabled or allowed to remain in their current startup mode.

- **Network Security** The Network Security section produces the firewall settings of the security policy. Those settings are applied by Windows Firewall With Advanced Security. Like the Role-Based Service Configuration section, the Network Security section displays a page of settings derived from the baseline settings in the configuration database. The settings in the Network Security section, however, are firewall rules rather than service startup modes. Figure 7-11 shows the rule that allows incoming ping requests to a domain controller. You can edit existing rules or add and remove custom rules.

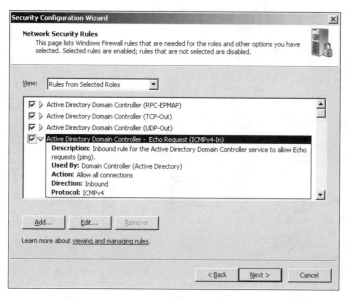

FIGURE 7-11 The Network Security Rules page of the Security Configuration Wizard

Windows Firewall with Advanced Security combines Internet Protocol Security (IPSec) and a stateful firewall that inspects and filters all IP version 4 (IPv4) and IP version 6 (IPv6) packets, discarding unsolicited packets unless a firewall rule has been created to allow traffic explicitly to a port number, application name, or service name. The security policy generated by the Security Configuration Wizard manages firewall rules, but IPSec configuration is not provided by the Security Configuration Wizard.

- **Registry Settings** The Registry Settings section configures protocols used to communicate with other computers. These wizard pages determine server message block (SMB) packet signing, Lightweight Directory Access Protocol (LDAP) signing, LAN Manager (LM) authentication levels, and storage of password LM hash values. Each of these settings is described on the appropriate page, and a link on each page takes you to a Security Configuration Wizard Help page that explains the setting.

- **Audit Policy** The Audit Policy section generates settings that manage the auditing of success and failure events and the file system objects that are audited. Additionally, the section allows you to incorporate a security template called SCWAudit.inf into the security policy. Use the Security Templates snap-in, described earlier in this lesson, to examine the settings in the template, which is located in %SystemRoot%\Security\Msscw\Kbs.

You can skip any of the last three sections if you you do not want to include those configurations in your security policy. When all the configuration sections have been completed or skipped, the Security Configuration Wizard presents the Security Policy section. On the Security Policy File Name page, shown in Figure 7-12, you can specify a path, a name, and a description for the security policy.

FIGURE 7-12 The Security Policy File Name page of the Security Configuration Wizard

To examine the settings of the security policy, click View Security Policy. The settings are very well documented by the Security Configuration Wizard. You can also import a security template into the security policy by clicking Include Security Templates.

Security templates, discussed earlier in this lesson, contain settings that are not provided by the Security Configuration Wizard, including restricted groups, event log policies, and file system and registry security policies. By including a security template, you can incorporate a richer collection of configuration settings in the security policy. If any settings in the security template conflict with the Security Configuration Wizard, the settings in the Security Configuration Wizard take precedence. When you click Next, you have the option to apply the security template to the server immediately or to apply the policy later.

Editing a Security Policy

To edit a saved security policy:

1. Open the Security Configuration Wizard.
2. On the Configuration Action page, click Edit An Existing Security Policy.
3. Click Browse to locate the policy .xml file. When prompted to select a server, select the server that was used to create the security policy.

Applying a Security Policy

To apply a security policy to a server:

1. Open the Security Configuration Wizard.
2. On the Configuration Action page, click Apply An Existing Security Policy.
3. Click Browse to locate the policy .xml file.
4. On the Select Server page, select a server to which you want to apply the policy.

Many of the changes specified in a security policy, including the addition of firewall rules for applications already running and the disabling of services, require that you restart the server. Therefore, as a best practice, it is recommended that you restart a server anytime you apply a security policy.

Rolling Back an Applied Security Policy

If a security policy is applied and causes undesirable results, you can roll back the changes. To roll back an applied security policy:

1. Open the Security Configuration Wizard.
2. On the Configuration Action page, click Rollback The Last Applied Security Policy.

When a security policy is applied by the Security Configuration Wizard, a rollback file is generated that stores the original settings of the system. The rollback process applies the rollback file.

Modifying Settings of an Applied Security Policy

Alternately, if an applied security template does not produce an ideal configuration, you can manually change settings by using the Local Security Policy console discussed at the beginning of this lesson in the "Configuring the Local Security Policy" section. Thus, you can see the whole picture of security configuration, from manual settings to the generation of security templates to the creation of security policies with the Security Configuration Wizard (which can incorporate security templates), to the application of security policies and back to the manual configuration of settings.

Deploying a Security Policy Using Group Policy

You can apply a security policy created by the Security Configuration Wizard to a server by using the Security Configuration Wizard itself, by using the Scwcmd.exe command, or by transforming the security policy into a GPO.

To transform a security policy into a GPO, log on as a domain administrator and run Scwcmd.exe with the transform command. For example:

```
scwcmd transform /p:"Contoso DC Security.xml" /g:"Contoso DC Security GPO"
```

This command creates a GPO called Contoso DC Security GPO with settings imported from the Contoso DC Security.xml security policy file. The resulting GPO can be linked to an appropriate scope—site, domain, or OU—by using the Group Policy Management console. Be sure to type **scwcmd.exe transform /?** for help and guidance about this process.

Settings, Templates, Policies, and GPOs

As suggested in the introduction to this lesson, you can manage security settings by using several mechanisms. You can use tools such as the Local Security Policy console to modify settings on an individual system. You can use security templates, which have existed since Windows 2000, to manage settings on one or more systems and to compare the current state of a system's configuration against the desired configuration defined by the template. Security policies generated by the Security Configuration Wizard are the most recent addition to the security configuration management toolset. They are role-based .xml files that define service startup modes, firewall rules, audit policies, and some registry settings. Security policies can incorporate security templates. Both security templates and security policies can be deployed using Group Policy.

The plethora of tools available can make it difficult to identify the best practice for managing security on one or more systems. Plan to use Group Policy whenever possible to deploy security configuration. You can generate a GPO from a role-based security policy produced by the Security Configuration Wizard, which itself incorporates additional settings from a security template. After the GPO has been generated, you can make additional changes to the GPO by using the Group Policy Management Editor snap-in. Settings not managed by Group Policy can be configured on a server-by-server basis, using the local GPO security settings.

In this practice, you manage security settings, using each of the tools discussed in this lesson. To perform the exercises in this practice, you must have the following objects in the directory service for the contoso.com domain:

- A first-level OU named Admins.

- An OU named Admin Groups in the Admins OU.

  If you have an OU named Groups in the Admins OU from an earlier practice, you can rename that OU Admin Groups.

- A global security group named SYS_DC Remote Desktop in the Admins OU. The group must be a member of the Remote Desktop Users group. This membership gives the SYS_DC Remote Desktop group the permissions required to connect to the RDP-Tcp connection.

Alternately, you can add the SYS_DC Remote Desktop group to the access control list (ACL) of the RDP-Tcp connection, using the Remote Desktop Session Host Configuration console. Right-click RDP-Tcp and click Properties; then click the Security tab, click Add, and type **SYS_DC Remote Desktop**. Click OK twice to close the dialog boxes.

EXERCISE 1   Configure the Local Security Policy

In this exercise, you use the local security policy to enable a group to log on using Remote Desktop to the domain controller named SERVER01. The local security policy of a domain controller affects only that individual DC—it is not replicated between DCs.

1. Log on to SERVER01 as Administrator.
2. Open the Local Security Policy console from the Administrative Tools folder.
3. Expand Security Settings\Local Policies and then click User Rights Assignment.
4. In the details pane, double-click Allow Log On Through Remote Desktop Services.
5. Click Add User Or Group.
6. Type **CONTOSO\SYS_DC Remote Desktop** and then click OK.
7. Click OK again.

   You will now remove the setting because you will manage the setting by using other tools in later exercises.

8. Double-click Allow Log On Through Remote Desktop Services.
9. Select CONTOSO\SYS_DC Remote Desktop.
10. Click Remove.
11. Click OK.

EXERCISE 2   Create a Security Template

In this exercise, you create a security template that gives the SYS_DC Remote Desktop group the right to log on using Remote Desktop.

1. Log on to SERVER01 as Administrator.

2. Click Start, and then click Run.

3. Type **mmc** and press Enter.

4. Click File, and then click Add/Remove Snap-in.

5. Select Security Templates from the Available Snap-ins list and click Add. Click OK.

6. Choose Save from the File menu, and save the console to your desktop with the name Security Management.

7. In the console tree, expand the Security Templates node. Right-click C:\Users\ Administrator\Documents\Security\Templates and click New Template.

8. Type **DC Remote Desktop** and click OK.

9. Expand the console tree so that you can select DC Remote Desktop\Local Policies\ User Rights Assignment.

10. In the details pane, double-click Allow Log On Through Remote Desktop Services.

11. Select Define These Policy Settings In The Template.

12. Click Add User Or Group.

13. Type **CONTOSO\SYS_DC Remote Desktop** and click OK.

14. Click OK.

15. Right-click DC Remote Desktop and click Save.

EXERCISE 3   Use the Security Configuration And Analysis Snap-in

In this exercise, you analyze the configuration of SERVER01, using the DC Remote Desktop security template to identify discrepancies between the server's current configuration and the desired configuration defined in the template. You then create a new security template.

1. Log on to SERVER01 as Administrator. Open the Security Management console you created and saved in Exercise 2, "Create a Security Template."

2. Click File, and then click Add/Remove Snap-in.

3. Select Security Configuration And Analysis from the Available Snap-ins list and click Add. Click OK.

4. Choose Save from the File menu to save the modified console.

5. Select the Security Configuration And Analysis console tree node.

6. Right-click the same node and click Open Database.

   The Open Database menu command allows you to create a new security database.

7. Type **SERVER01Test** and click Open.

   The Import Template dialog box appears.

8. Select the DC Remote Desktop template you created in Exercise 2 and click Open.

9. Right-click Security Configuration And Analysis and click Analyze Computer Now.

10. Click OK to confirm the default path for the error log.

11. Expand the console tree so that you can select Security Configuration And Analysis\ Local Policies\User Rights Assignment.

12. Notice that the Allow Log On Through Remote Desktop Services policy is flagged with a red circle and an X. This indicates a discrepancy between the database setting and the computer setting.

13. Double-click Allow Log On Through Remote Desktop Services.

14. Notice the discrepancies. The computer is not configured to allow the SYS_DC Remote Desktop Users group to log on through Remote Desktop Services.

15. Notice also that the Computer Setting currently allows Administrators to log on through Remote Desktop Services. This is an important setting that should be incorporated into the database.

16. Select the check box next to Administrators under Database Setting, and then click OK. This adds the right for Administrators to log on through Remote Desktop Services to the database. It does not change the template, and it does not affect the current configuration of the computer.

17. Right-click Security Configuration And Analysis and click Save.

This saves the security database, which includes the settings imported from the template plus the change you made to allow Administrators to log on through Remote Desktop Services. The hint displayed in the status bar when you click Save suggests that you are saving the template. That is incorrect. You are saving the database.

18. Right-click Security Configuration And Analysis and click Export Template.

19. Select DC Remote Desktop and click Save.

You have now replaced the template created in Exercise 2 with the settings defined in the database of the Security Configuration And Analysis snap-in.

20. Close and reopen your Security Management console.

This is necessary to refresh fully the settings shown in the Security Templates snap-in.

21. Expand Security Templates\C:\Users\Administrator\Documents\Security\Templates\ DC Remote Desktop\Local Policies, and then click User Rights Assignment.

22. In the details pane, double-click Allow Log On Through Remote Desktop Services.

23. Notice that both the Administrators and SYS_DC Remote Desktop groups are allowed to log on through Remote Desktop Services in the security template. Click OK.

24. Right-click Security Configuration And Analysis and click Configure Computer Now.

25. Click OK to confirm the error log path.

The settings in the database are applied to the server. You will now confirm that the change to the user right was applied.

26. Open the Local Security Policy console from the Administrative Tools folder.

If the console was already open during this exercise, right-click Security Settings and click Reload.

27. Expand Security Settings\Local Policies\User Rights Assignment. Double-click Allow Log On Through Remote Desktop Services.

28. Confirm that both Administrators and SYS_DC Remote Desktop are listed.

The Local Security Policy console displays the actual, current settings of the server.

EXERCISE 4 **Use the Security Configuration Wizard**

In this exercise, you use the Security Configuration Wizard to create a security policy for domain controllers in the contoso.com domain based on the configuration of SERVER01.

1. Log on to SERVER01 as Administrator.

2. Open the Security Configuration Wizard from the Administrative Tools folder.

3. Click Next.

4. Select Create A New Security Policy and click Next.

5. Accept the default server name, SERVER01, and click Next.

6. On the Processing Security Configuration Database page, you can optionally click View Configuration Database and explore the configuration that was discovered on SERVER01.

7. Click Next and, on the Role Based Service Configuration section introduction page, click Next.

8. Explore the settings that were discovered on SERVER01, but do not change any settings, on the following pages of the wizard: Select Server Roles, Select Client Features, Select Administration And Other Options; Select Additional Services; and Handling Unspecified Services.

9. On the Confirm Service Changes page, click the View drop-down list and choose All Services. Examine the settings in the Current Startup Mode column, which reflect service startup modes on SERVER01, and compare them to the settings in the Policy Startup Mode column. Click the View drop-down list and choose Changed Services. Click Next.

10. On the Network Security section introduction page, click Next.

11. On the Network Security Rules page, you can optionally examine the firewall rules derived from the configuration of SERVER01. Do not change any settings. Click Next.

12. On the Registry Settings section introduction page, click Next.

13. Click through each page of the Registry Settings section. Examine the settings, but do not change any of them. When the Registry Settings Summary page appears, examine the settings and click Next.

14. On the Audit Policy section introduction page, click Next.

15. On the System Audit Policy page, examine but do not change the settings. Click Next.

16. On the Audit Policy Summary page, examine the settings in the Current Setting and Policy Setting columns. Click Next.

17 On the Save Security Policy section introduction page, click Next.

18. In the Security Policy File Name text box, click after the end of the default path, and then type **DC Security Policy**.

19. Click Include Security Templates.

20. Click Add.

21. Browse to locate the DC Remote Desktop template created in Exercise 3, "Use the Security Configuration And Analysis Snap-in," located in your Documents\Security\ Templates folder. When you have located and selected the template, click Open.

22. Click OK to close the Include Security Templates dialog box.

23. Click View Security Policy to examine the settings in the security policy. You are prompted to confirm the use of the ActiveX control; click Yes. Close the window after you have examined the policy, and then click Next in the Security Configuration Wizard window.

24. If you are prompted to confirm that you are replacing the default DC Security Policy, click Yes.

24. Accept the Apply Later default setting and click Next.

25. Click Finish.

EXERCISE 5   Transform a Security Configuration Wizard Security Policy to a Group Policy

In this exercise, you convert the security policy generated in Exercise 4, "Use the Security Configuration Wizard," to a GPO, which can then be deployed to computers by using Group Policy.

1. Log on to SERVER01 as Administrator.

2. Open Command Prompt.

3. Type **cd c:\windows\security\msscw\policies** and press Enter.

4. Type **scwcmd transform /?** and press Enter.

5. Type **scwcmd transform /p:"DC Security Policy.xml" /g:"DC Security Policy"** and press Enter.

6. Open the Group Policy Management console from the Administrative Tools folder.

7. Expand the console tree nodes Forest, Domains, contoso.com, and Group Policy Objects.

8. Select DC Security Policy.

   This is the GPO created by the Scwcmd.exe command.

9. Click the Settings tab to examine the settings of the GPO.

10. Click the Show link next to Security Settings.

11. Click the Show link next to Local Policies/User Rights Assignment.

12. Confirm that the BUILTIN\Administrators and CONTOSO\SYS_DC Remote Desktop groups are given the Allow Log On Through Remote Desktop Services user right.

    The GPO is not applied to DCs because it is not linked to the Domain Controllers OU. In this practice, do not link the GPO to the domain, site, or any OU. In a production environment, you would spend more time examining, configuring, and testing security settings in the security policy before deploying it as a GPO to production domain controllers.

13. In the tree pane, under Group Policy Objects, right-click DC Security Policy and click Delete. Click Yes to confirm the deletion. This ensures the policy can't inappropriately be linked in your test environment.

Lesson Summary

- Security settings can be configured by editing the local GPO on an individual computer. The local GPO can be edited by using the Group Policy Object Editor snap-in or the Local Security Policy console.

- Security settings can be defined in a security template with the Security Templates snap-in. Security templates can define a large number of security-related settings.

- Security templates can be used by the Security Configuration And Analysis snap-in to create a database. The snap-in can then analyze the configuration of a system for discrepancies between the computer's current settings and those specified in the database. The snap-in can also apply the database settings to the computer or export the database settings to a security template.

- Secedit.exe is the command-line tool that performs and extends the functionality of the Security Configuration And Analysis snap-in.

- Security policies are collections of settings created by the Security Configuration Wizard that define service startup modes, firewall rules, certain registry settings, and audit policies. The Security Configuration Wizard creates security policies based on the roles of a server.

- A security policy can incorporate the settings in a security template. In the event of conflicting settings, the settings in the security policy take precedence.

- Scwcmd.exe is the command-line tool that performs and extends the functionality of the Security Configuration Wizard.

- You can import a security template into a GPO.

- You can use Scwcmd.exe Transform to convert a security policy into a GPO.

Lesson Review

You can use the following questions to test your knowledge of the information in Lesson 2, "Managing Security Settings." The questions are also available on the companion CD if you prefer to review them in electronic form.

> **NOTE ANSWERS**
>
> Answers to these questions and explanations of why each answer choice is right or wrong are located in the "Answers" section at the end of the book.

1. You want to deploy security settings to multiple servers by using Group Policy. The settings need to apply the user rights that you have configured and validated on a server in your test environment. Which tool should you use?

   A. Local Security Policy

   B. Security Configuration And Analysis

   C. Security Configuration Wizard

   D. Security Templates

2. You want to deploy security settings to multiple servers by using Group Policy. The settings need to configure services, firewall rules, and audit policies appropriate for servers in your enterprise that act as file and print servers. Which tool would be the best choice for you to use?

   A. Local Security Policy

   B. Security Configuration And Analysis

   C. Security Configuration Wizard

   D. Security Templates

3. You created a security policy by using the Security Configuration Wizard. Now you want to deploy the settings in that security policy to the servers in your Servers OU. Which of the following steps are required? (Choose two. Each correct answer is a part of the solution.)

   A. Use Scwcmd.exe Transform.

   B. Create a Group Policy object in the Group Policy Objects container.

   C. Right-click the Security Settings node of a GPO and click Import.

   D. Link the GPO to the Servers OU.

Lesson 3: Managing Software with Group Policy

You might be aware of several tools that can be used to deploy software within an organization, including Microsoft System Center Configuration Manager (SCCM or, simply, Configuration Manager) and its predecessor, Microsoft Systems Management Server (SMS). Although these tools provide great benefits, including features to meter software use and inventory systems, you can effectively deploy most software without these tools, using only Group Policy software installation (GPSI). Another feature of Windows, AppLocker, lets you use Group Policy to control which applications are allowed to run or are prevented from running.

After this lesson, you will be able to:

- Deploy software to computers and users by using GPSI.
- Remove software installed originally with GPSI.

Estimated lesson time: 45 minutes

Understanding Group Policy Software Installation

Group Policy software installation (GPSI) is used to create a managed software environment that has the following characteristics:

- Users have access to the applications they need to do their jobs, no matter which computer they log on to.
- Computers have the required applications, without intervention from a technical support representative.
- Applications can be updated, maintained, or removed to meet the needs of the organization.

The software installation extension is one of the many client-side extensions (CSEs) that support change and configuration management using Group Policy. CSEs were discussed in Chapter 6. The extension allows you to centrally manage the initial deployment, the upgrades, and the removal of software. All configuration of the software deployment is managed within a GPO, using procedures described later in this lesson.

Windows Installer Packages

GPSI uses the Windows Installer service to install, maintain, and remove software. The Windows Installer service manages software, using information contained in the application's Windows Installer package. The Windows Installer package is in a file with an .msi extension that describes the installed state of the application. The package contains explicit instructions regarding the installation and removal of an application. You can customize Windows Installer packages by using one of the following types of files:

- **Transform (.mst)**   These files provide a means for customizing the installation of an application. Some applications provide wizards or templates that permit a user to create transforms. For example, Adobe provides an enterprise deployment tool for Adobe Acrobat Reader that generates a transform. Many enterprises use the transform to configure agreement with the end user license agreement and to disable certain features of the application such as automatic updates that involve access to the Internet.

- **Patch (.msp)**   These files are used to update an existing .msi file for security updates, bug fixes, and service packs. An .msp file provides instructions about applying the updated files and registry keys in the software patch, service pack, or software update. For example, updates to Microsoft Office 2003 and later are provided as .msp files.

> **NOTE   INSTALLATION OF .MSP AND .MST FILES**
>
> You cannot deploy .mst or .msp files alone. They must be applied to an existing Windows Installer package.

GPSI can make limited use of non-MSI application files (.zap files), also known as down-level application packages, that specify the location of the software distribution point (SDP) and the setup command. See Knowledge Base Article 231747 at *http://support .microsoft.com/kb/231747* for details. Most organizations do not use .zap files, however, because the installation of the application requires the user to have administrative privileges on the system. When GPSI installs an application by using a Windows Installer package, the user does not require administrative privileges, allowing for a more secure enterprise.

> **NOTE   GPSI AND WINDOWS INSTALLER PACKAGES**
>
> GPSI can fully manage applications only if the applications are deployed using Windows Installer packages. Other tools, including Configuration Manager and SMS, can manage applications that use other deployment mechanisms.

The .msi file transforms, and other files required to install an application are stored in a shared SDP.

Software Deployment Options

You can deploy software by assigning applications to users or computers or by publishing applications for users. You *assign* required or mandatory software to users or computers. You *publish* software that users might find useful in performing their jobs.

EXAM TIP

Know the difference between assigning applications and publishing applications.

ASSIGNING APPLICATIONS

When you assign an application to a user, the application's local registry settings, including file name extensions, are updated and its shortcuts are created on the Start menu or desktop, thus advertising the availability of the application. The application advertisement follows the user regardless of which physical computer he or she logs on to. This application is installed the first time the user activates the application on the computer, either by selecting the application on the Start menu or by opening a document associated with the application. When you assign an application to the computer, the application is installed during the computer's startup process.

PUBLISHING APPLICATIONS

When you publish an application to users, the application does not appear as if it is installed on the users' computers. No shortcuts are visible on the desktop or Start menu. Instead, the application appears as an available application for the user to install by using Add Or Remove Programs in Control Panel on a Windows XP system or in Programs And Features on a Windows Server 2008, Windows Vista, or later system. Additionally, the application can be installed when a user opens a file type associated with the application. For example, if Acrobat Reader is published to users, it is installed if a user opens a file with a .pdf extension.

Given that applications can be either assigned or published and targeted to users or computers, you can establish a workable combination to meet your software management goals. Table 7-1 describes the different software deployment options.

TABLE 7-1 Software Deployment Options

	PUBLISH (USER ONLY)	ASSIGN (USER)	ASSIGN (COMPUTER)
After deployment of the GPO, the software is available for installation:	The next time a user logs on.	The next time a user logs on.	The next time the computer starts.
Typically, the user installs the software from:	Control Panel Add Or Remove Programs (Windows XP) or Programs And Features (Windows Server 2008, Windows Vista, and later).	The Start menu or a desktop shortcut. An application can also be configured to install automatically at logon.	The software is installed automatically when the computer starts.
If the software is not installed and the user opens a file associated with the software, does the software install?	Yes (if auto-install is enabled).	Yes.	Does not apply; the software is already installed.

	PUBLISH (USER ONLY)	ASSIGN (USER)	ASSIGN (COMPUTER)
Can the user remove the software by using Control Panel?	Yes, and the user can choose to install it again from Control Panel.	Yes, and the software is available for installation again from the Start menu, shortcuts, or file associations.	No. Only a local administrator can remove the software; a user can run a repair on the software.
Supported installation files:	Windows Installer packages (.msi files) and .zap files.	Windows Installer packages (.msi files).	Windows Installer packages (.msi files).

 Quick Check

- You want to use GPSI to deploy an administrative tool so that it is available for administrators on any system to which they log on. You do not want the tool to install automatically because administrators do not need the tool on each computer, but you want the tool to install easily. Should you publish or assign the application? Describe how an administrator would install the tool.

Quick Check Answer

- Publish the application. An administrator would use the Programs And Features Control Panel application to install the application. On a Windows XP or Windows Server 2003 system, use Add/Remove Programs to install the application.

Preparing an SDP

Now that you understand GPSI at a high level, you are ready to prepare the SDP. The SDP is simply a shared folder from which users and computers can install applications. Create a shared folder and create a separate folder for each application. Then copy the software package, modifications, and all other necessary files to the application folders. Set appropriate permissions on the folders that allow users or computers Read & Execute permission—the minimum permission required to successfully install an application from the SDP. The administrators of the SDP must be able to change and delete files to maintain the SDP over time.

Creating a Software Deployment GPO

To create a software deployment GPO:

1. Use the Group Policy Management console to create a new GPO or select an existing GPO.

2. Edit the GPO using the Group Policy Management Editor.

3. Expand the console nodes Computer Configuration\Policies\Software Settings\ Software Installation. Alternately, select the Software Installation node in the User Configuration branch.

4. Right-click Software Installation, point to New, and then click Package.

5. Browse to locate the .msi file for the application. Click Open.

   The Deploy Software dialog box appears, shown in Figure 7-13.

FIGURE 7-13 The Deploy Software dialog box

6. Select Published, Assigned, or Advanced.

   You cannot publish an application to computers, so the option will not be available if you are creating the package in the Software Installation node in Computer Configuration.

   The Advanced option lets you specify whether the application is published or assigned and gives you the opportunity to configure advanced properties of the software package. Therefore, it is recommended that you choose Advanced. The package properties dialog box appears. Among the more important properties that you can configure are the following choices:

   - **Deployment Type** On the Deployment tab, configure Published or Assigned.
   - **Deployment Options** Based on the selected deployment type, different choices appear in the Deployment Options section. These options, along with other settings on the Deployment tab, manage the behavior of the application installation.
   - **Uninstall This Application When It Falls Out Of The Scope Of Management** If this option is selected, the application will be automatically removed when the GPO no longer applies to the user or computer.

- **Upgrades** On the Upgrades tab, you can specify the software that this package will upgrade. Upgrades are discussed in the "Maintaining Applications Deployed with Group Policy" section later in this lesson.

- **Categories** The Categories tab allows you to associate the package with one or more categories. Categories are used when an application is published to a user. When the user goes to Control Panel to install a program, applications published using GPSI are presented in groups based on these categories.

    To create categories that are available to associate with packages, right-click Software Installation and click Properties; then click the Categories tab.

- **Modifications** If you have a transform (.mst file) that customizes the package, click Add to associate the transform with the package. Most tabs in the package Properties dialog box are available for you to change settings at any time. However, the Modifications tab is available only when you create the new package and choose the Advanced option shown in Figure 7-13.

Managing the Scope of a Software Deployment GPO

After you have created a software deployment GPO, you can scope the GPO to distribute the software to appropriate computers or users. In many software management scenarios, applications should be assigned to computers rather than to users. This is because most software licenses allow an application to be installed on one computer, and if the application is assigned to a user, the application is installed on each computer to which the user logs on.

As you learned in Chapter 6, you can scope a GPO by linking the GPO to an OU or by filtering the GPO so that it applies only to a selected global security group. Many organizations find that it is easiest to manage software by linking an application's GPO to the domain and filtering the GPO with a global security group that contains the users and computers to which the application should be deployed. For example, a GPO that deploys the XML Notepad tool (available from the Microsoft downloads site at *http://www.microsoft.com/ downloads*) would be linked to the domain and filtered with a group containing developers that require the tool. The group would have a descriptive name that indicates its purpose to manage the deployment of XML Notepad—*APP_XML Notepad*, for example.

EXAM TIP

On the 70-640 exam, you are likely to encounter questions that present software installation scenarios but are in fact testing your knowledge of how to scope a GPO effectively. As you read questions on the exam, try to identify what knowledge the question is really targeting.

Maintaining Applications Deployed with Group Policy

After a computer has installed an application by using the Windows Installer package specified by a GPO, the computer will not attempt to reinstall the application at each Group Policy refresh. There might be scenarios in which you want to force systems to reinstall the application. For example, small changes might have been made to the original Windows Installer package.

To redeploy an application deployed with Group Policy, right-click the package in the GPO, point to All Tasks, and then click Redeploy Application.

You can also upgrade an application that has been deployed with GPSI:

1. Create a package for the new version of the application in the Software Installation node of the GPO.

   The package can be in the same GPO as the package for the previous version or in any different GPO.

2. Right-click the package and click Properties.

3. On the Upgrades tab, click Add.

   The Add Upgrade Package dialog box appears, shown in Figure 7-14.

FIGURE 7-14 The Add Upgrade Package dialog box

4. Select whether the package for the previous version of the application is in the current GPO or in another GPO. If the previous package is in another GPO, click Browse to select that GPO.

5. Select the package from the Package To Upgrade list.

6. Based on your knowledge of the application's upgrade behavior, choose one of the following upgrade options at the bottom of the dialog box shown at the bottom of Figure 7-14:

   - Uninstall The Existing Package, Then Install The Upgrade Package
   - Package Can Upgrade Over The Existing Package

7. Click OK.

You can also remove an application that was deployed with GPSI:

1. Right-click the package, point to All Tasks, and then click Remove.

2. In the Remove Software dialog box, choose one of the following two options:

   - **Immediately Uninstall The Software From Users And Computers** This option, known as forced removal, causes computers to remove the application. The software installation extension removes an application when the computer restarts if the application was deployed with a package in the Computer Configuration portion of the GPO. If the package is in the User Configuration portion, the application will be uninstalled the next time the user logs on.

   - **Allows Users To Continue To Use The Software, But Prevents New Installations** This setting, known as optional removal, causes the software installation extension to avoid adding the package to systems that do not yet have the package installed. Computers that had previously installed the application do not forcibly uninstall the application, so users can continue using it.

If you use one of these two options to remove software using GPSI, it is important that you allow the settings in the GPO to propagate to all computers within the scope of the GPO before you delete, disable, or unlink the GPO. Clients need to receive this setting that specifies forced or optional removal. If the GPO is deleted or no longer applied before all clients have received this setting, the software is not removed according to your instructions. This is particularly important in environments with mobile users on laptop computers that might not connect to the network on a regular basis.

If, when creating the software package, you chose the Uninstall This Application When It Falls Out Of The Scope Of Management option, you can simply delete, disable, or unlink the GPO and the application will be forcibly removed by all clients that have installed the package with that setting.

GPSI and Slow Links

When a client performs a Group Policy refresh, it tests the performance of the network to determine whether it is connected using a slow link, defined by default as 500 kilobits per second (kbps). Each client-side extension is configured to process Group Policy or to skip the application of settings on a slow link. By default, GPSI does not process Group Policy settings over a slow link because the installation of software over a slow link could cause significant delays.

You can change the slow link policy processing behavior of each client-side extension by using policy settings located in Computer Configuration\Policies\Administrative Templates\System\Group Policy. For example, you could modify the behavior of the software installation extension so that it does process policies over a slow link.

You can also change the connection speed threshold that constitutes a slow link. By configuring a low threshold for the connection speed, you can convince the client-side extensions that a connection is not a slow link, even if it actually is. Group Policy Slow Link

Detection has separate policy settings for computer policy processing and user policy processing. The policies are in the Administrative Templates\System\Group Policy folders in Computer Configuration and User Configuration.

Understanding AppLocker

In a typical enterprise, computers are deployed with a highly managed configuration that is based on an image of the operating system and core applications. But, over time, the applications that are installed on a computer drift away from the managed, well-defined initial state. When a user logs on as a non-privileged user—when she is not a member of the local Administrators groups of her computer—her ability to install new applications is greatly restricted, but not entirely prevented. For example, a user can copy a self-contained application in a single executable (.exe file) to her desktop and launch it.

When a user installs unmanaged applications, the risk and cost of supporting that user increases. The new applications may cause instability or incompatibility with other applications, resulting in increased support calls, or may introduce malware into the environment. Additionally, a new application may not be licensed correctly for use in your enterprise.

For these and other manageability reasons, it is best practice to restrict program execution—to ensure that users can run only those applications that have been vetted by the enterprise for compatibility, security, and licensing. Windows XP and Windows Vista featured Software Restriction Policy (SRP), with which you could specify applications that were allowed or disallowed. But SRP was difficult to manage effectively, because—in its best practice configuration—an application policy was associated with the signature of a specific executable or component. If the application was patched or updated, the policy had to be revised to reflect the updated signature.

Windows 7 and Windows Server 2008 R2 feature AppLocker, a more powerful, robust, and manageable framework with which to restrict application execution. AppLocker uses Allow rules and Deny rules, which both support exceptions. For example, you can define a rule that allows users to run all components of the Windows operating system, except built-in games and Registry Editor. You could create a rule that denies users the ability to launch any executable that is in the C:\Users folder, except ZoomIt.exe. An enterprise typically applies a combination of Allow and Deny rules, and exceptions, to implement application lock-down with a minimal number of rules.

As with SRP, rules can be associated with the path or hash of an executable, but these rules can be circumvented and are difficult to manage. AppLocker rules can also be associated with the digital signature of a publisher, the name of a product, and the name and versions of a file. Such rules are more flexible, more manageable, and more secure. For example, you could define a rule that allows users to run Adobe Reader version 9.0 or greater. Rules can also be associated with a collection of files so that a user can launch an installer, which itself executes related components. And rules can be applied to users or groups so that, for example, you could allow the Finance group to run the approved accounting software, but other users would not be able to run the same application.

Rules can be created on a computer running Windows 7 Professional, Windows 7 Ultimate, Windows 7 Enterprise, or Windows Server 2008 R2. For Group Policy deployment of rules, you must use the Windows Server 2008 R2 version of Group Policy Management, which can be installed on Windows 7 by adding the Remote Server Administration Tools (RSAT). AppLocker rules can be enforced on most editions of Windows Server 2008 R2, Windows 7 Enterprise, or Windows 7 Ultimate. You cannot enforce AppLocker rules on Windows 7 Professional, Windows 7 Home Premium, or any other consumer-focused edition of Windows 7. You also cannot enforce AppLocker rules on Windows Web Server 2008 R2 or Windows Server 2008 R2 Foundation.

AppLocker is a powerful framework, and it requires careful planning, testing, deployment, and ongoing management. More information can be found at *http://technet.microsoft.com/ en-us/library/dd723678(WS.10).aspx* and *http://technet.microsoft.com/en-us/library/ dd759117.aspx*.

PRACTICE Managing Software with Group Policy

In this practice, you install, upgrade, and remove software, using GPSI. You practice software management by using XML Notepad, a simple XML editor available from the Microsoft Download Center. To perform this practice, you must complete the following preparatory steps:

- Create a first-level OU named Groups and, within that OU, create an OU called Applications.

- In the Applications OU, create a global security group named APP_XML Notepad to represent the users and computer to which XML Notepad is deployed.

- Create a folder named Software on the C drive of SERVER01. Within that folder, create a folder named XML Notepad. Grant the APP_XML Notepad group Read And Execute permission to the XML Notepad folder. Share the Software folder with the share name Software, and grant the Everyone group the Allow Full Control share permission.

- Download XML Notepad from the Microsoft Download Center at *http://www.microsoft .com/downloads/en/details.aspx?FamilyID=72d6aa49-787d-4118-ba5f-4f30fe913628*. Save it to the Software\XML Notepad folder. Make a note of the version you have downloaded. At the time of writing this chapter, the current version is XML Notepad 2007.

EXERCISE 1 Create a Software Deployment GPO

In this exercise, you create a GPO that deploys XML Notepad to developers who require the application.

1. Log on to SERVER01 as Administrator.

2. Open the Group Policy Management console.

3. Right-click the Group Policy Objects container and click New.

4. In the Name box, type the name of the application (for example, **XML Notepad**), and then click OK.

5. Right-click the XML Notepad GPO and click Edit.

6. Expand User Configuration\Policies\Software Settings.

7. Right-click Software Installation, point to New, and then click Package.

8. In the File Name text box, type the network path to the software distribution folder (for example, **\\server01\software\XML Notepad**), and then click Open. Select the Windows Installer package (for example, XmlNotepad.msi), and then click Open.

9. In the Deploy Software dialog box, select Advanced and click OK.

   There is a short pause while the package is created.

10. On the General tab, note that the name of the package includes the version—for example, XML Notepad 2007.

11. On the Deployment tab, click Assigned.

12. Select the Install This Application At Logon check box.

13. Select Uninstall This Application When It Falls Out Of The Scope Of Management.

14. Click OK.

15. Close Group Policy Management Editor.

16. In the Group Policy Management console, select the XML Notepad GPO in the Group Policy Objects container.

17. On the Scope tab, in the Security Filtering section, select Authenticated Users and click Remove. Click OK to confirm your action.

18. Click Add.

19. Type the name of the group that represents users and computers to which the application should be deployed—for example **APP_XML Notepad**.

20. Click OK.

    The GPO is now filtered to apply only to the APP_XML Notepad group. However, the GPO settings will not apply until it is linked to an OU, a site, or the domain.

21. Right-click the domain, contoso.com, and click Link An Existing GPO.

22. Select XML Notepad from the Group Policy Objects list and click OK.

    You can optionally test the GPO by adding the Administrator account to the APP_XML Notepad group. Log off and then log on. XML Notepad is installed when you log on.

EXERCISE 2 Upgrade an Application

In this exercise, you simulate deploying an upgraded version of XML Notepad.

1. Log on to SERVER01 as Administrator.

2. Open the Group Policy Management console.

3. Right-click the XML Notepad GPO in the Group Policy Objects container and click Edit.

4. Expand User Configuration\Policies\Software Settings.

5. Right-click Software Installation, point to New, and then click Package.

6. In the File Name text box, enter the network path to the software distribution folder (for example, **\\server01\software\XML Notepad**), and then click Open. Select the .msi file name, and then click Open.

   This exercise uses the existing XmlNotepad.msi file as if it is an updated version of XML Notepad.

7. In the Deploy Software dialog box, select Advanced and click OK.

8. On the General tab, change the name of the package to suggest that it is the next version of the application—for example, **XML Notepad 2008**.

9. On the Deployment tab, select Assigned.

10. Select the Install This Application At Logon check box.

11. On the Upgrades tab, click Add.

12. Select the Current Group Policy Object (GPO) option.

13. In the Package To Upgrade list, select the package for the simulated earlier version— XML Notepad 2007, for example.

14. Select Uninstall The Existing Package Then Install The Upgrade Package.

15. Click OK.

16. Click OK again.

    If this were an actual upgrade, the new package would upgrade the previous version of the application as clients applied the XML Notepad GPO. Because this is only a simulation of an upgrade, you can remove the simulated upgrade package.

17. Select Software Installation. Right-click the package that you just created to simulate an upgrade, point to All Tasks, and then click Remove.

18. In the Remove Software dialog box, select the Immediately Uninstall The Software From Users And Computers option.

19. Click OK.

Lesson Summary

- Group Policy software installation (GPSI) can be used to deploy, maintain, upgrade, and remove software.

- You can assign a software package in the Computer Configuration portion of a GPO. Client computers within the scope of the GPO will install the application at startup.

- You can assign a software package in the User Configuration portion of a GPO. The application will be installed when a user launches the application by using a shortcut in the Start menu or opens a file type associated with the application. You can optionally configure a user-assigned application to install at logon.

- You can publish a software package in the User Configuration portion of a GPO. The application is advertised in the Programs And Features Control Panel application. On Windows XP and Windows Server 2003 systems, the application is advertised in the Add/Remove Programs Control Panel application.

- Transforms (.mst files) can be used to modify the behavior of a Windows Installer package deployed using GPSI.

- Applications managed using GPSI can be redeployed or removed by the software installation extension.

- A software package can be configured to upgrade other applications deployed using GPSI.

- GPSI settings are not applied when a slow link is detected.

Lesson Review

You can use the following questions to test your knowledge of the information in Lesson 3, "Managing Software with Group Policy." The questions are also available on the companion CD if you prefer to review them in electronic form.

> **NOTE ANSWERS**
>
> Answers to these questions and explanations of why each answer choice is right or wrong are located in the "Answers" section at the end of the book.

1. You want to deploy an application by using Group Policy to client computers in the headquarters and a branch office. The branch office is connected to the headquarters with a wide area network connection that is 364 kbps. What steps must you take to deploy the software? (Choose two. Each correct answer is part of the solution.)

    A. Create a GPO that applies to all client computers in the headquarters and branch office. In the GPO, create a software package in the User Configuration node that assigns the application.

    B. Create a GPO that applies to all client computers in the headquarters and branch office. In the GPO, create a software package in the Computer Configuration node that assigns the application.

    C. In a GPO that applies to all computers, configure the slow link detection policy connection speed in the User Configuration node to 256 kbps.

    D. In a GPO that applies to computers in the branch office, configure the slow link detection policy connection speed in the Computer Configuration node to 256 kbps.

    E. In a GPO that applies to computers in the branch office, configure the slow link detection policy connection speed in the Computer Configuration node to 1,000 kbps.

2. In your domain, the Employees OU contains all user accounts. Each site has an OU within which a Sales OU contains accounts for the computers in the Sales department at that site. You want to deploy an application so that it is available to all users in the organization's Sales departments. Which methods can you use? (Choose all that apply.)

   A. Create a GPO linked to the domain. Create a group containing all Sales users. Filter the GPO so that it applies only to the group. In the GPO's User Configuration policies, create a software package that assigns the application.

   B. Create a GPO linked to each site's Sales OU. In the GPO's User Configuration policies, create a software package that assigns the application.

   C. Create a GPO linked to the domain. Create a group containing all Sales users. Filter the GPO so that it applies only to the group. In the GPO's Computer Configuration policies, create a software package that assigns the application.

   D. Create a GPO linked to each site's Sales OU. In the GPO User Configuration policies, create a software package that assigns the application. In the GPO's Computer Configuration, enable loopback policy processing in merge mode.

3. Your organization consists of 10 branch offices. Within your Active Directory, an Employees OU is divided into 10 child OUs containing user accounts at each branch office. You want to deploy an application to users at four branches. The application should be fully installed before users open the application for the first time. Which steps should you take? (Choose four. Each correct answer is a part of the solution.)

   A. Create a software deployment GPO linked to the Employees OU.

   B. Create a package in the User Configuration polices that publishes the application.

   C. Select the Install This Application At Logon deployment option.

   D. Create a shadow group that includes the users in the four branches. Filter the software deployment GPO so that it applies only to the shadow group.

   E. Create a package in the User Configuration policies that assigns the application.

   F. Select the Required Upgrade For Existing Packages option.

Lesson 4: Implementing an Audit Policy

Auditing is an important component of security. Auditing involves logging specified activities in your enterprise to the Windows Security log, which you can monitor to understand those activities and identify issues that warrant further investigation. Auditing can log successful activities to provide documentation of changes. It can also log failed and potentially malicious attempts to access enterprise resources. Auditing involves up to three management tools: audit policy, auditing settings on objects, and the Security log. In this lesson, you learn how to configure auditing to address several common scenarios.

> **After this lesson, you will be able to:**
> - Configure audit policy.
> - Configure auditing settings on file system and directory service objects.
> - View the Security log, using the Event Viewer snap-in.
> - Configure audit policy to enable Directory Service Changes auditing.
> - Specify auditing settings on Active Directory objects.
> - Identify event log entries created by Directory Access auditing and Directory Service Changes auditing.
>
> **Estimated lesson time: 45 minutes**

Audit Policy

Audit Policy configures a system to audit categories of activities. If Audit Policy is not enabled, a server does not audit those activities. Figure 7-15 shows the expanded Audit Policy node of a GPO.

FIGURE 7-15 The Audit Policy node of a GPO

To configure auditing, you must define the policy setting. Double-click any policy setting and select the Define These Policy Settings check box. Then select whether to enable auditing of Success events, Failure events, or both. Table 7-2 defines each audit policy and its default settings on a Windows Server 2008 R2 domain controller.

TABLE 7-2 Audit Policies

AUDIT POLICY SETTING	EXPLANATION	DEFAULT SETTING FOR WINDOWS SERVER 2008 R2 DOMAIN CONTROLLERS
Audit Account Logon Events	Creates an event when a user or computer attempts to authenticate using an Active Directory account. For example, when a user logs on to any computer in the domain, an account logon event is generated.	Successful account logons are audited.
Audit Logon Events	Creates an event when a user logs on interactively (locally) to a computer or over the network (remotely). For example, if a workstation and a server are configured to audit logon events, the workstation audits a user logging on directly to that workstation. When the user connects to a shared folder on the server, the server logs that remote logon. When a user logs on, the domain controller records a logon event because logon scripts and policies are retrieved from the DC.	Successful logons are audited.
Audit Account Management	Audits events, including the creation, deletion, or modification of user, group, or computer accounts and the resetting of user passwords.	Successful account management activities are audited.
Audit Directory Service Access	Audits events that are specified in the system ACL (SACL), which is seen in an Active Directory object's Properties Advanced Security Settings dialog box. In addition to defining the audit policy with this setting, you must also configure auditing for the specific object or objects using the SACL of the object or objects. This policy is similar to the Audit Object Access policy used to audit files and folders, but this policy applies to Active Directory objects.	Successful directory service access events are audited, but few objects' SACLs specify audit settings. See the discussion in the "Auditing Directory Service Changes" section for more information.
Audit Policy Change	Audits changes to user rights assignment policies, audit policies, or trust policies.	Successful policy changes are audited.

AUDIT POLICY SETTING	EXPLANATION	DEFAULT SETTING FOR WINDOWS SERVER 2008 R2 DOMAIN CONTROLLERS
Audit Privilege Use	Audits the use of a privilege or user right. See the explanatory text for this policy in Group Policy Management Editor (GPME).	No auditing is performed, by default.
Audit System Events	Audits system restart, shutdown, or changes that affect the system or security log.	Successful system events are audited.
Audit Process Tracking	Audits events such as program activation and process exit. See the explanatory text for this policy in GPME.	No events are audited.
Audit Object Access	Audits access to objects such as files, folders, registry keys, and printers that have their own SACLs. In addition to enabling this audit policy, you must configure the auditing entries in objects' SACLs.	No events are audited.

EXAM TIP

Microsoft certification exams often test your knowledge of audit policies at a high level. Commit the information in Table 7-2 to memory, and you are likely to be able to answer one or more exam items correctly.

NOTE DEFAULTS, NOT POLICY

The default settings listed in Table 7-2 are default settings applied to a Windows Server 2008 R2 server when it is promoted to a domain controller. They are *not* settings that are applied by default Group Policy objects. If you examine the Default Domain Policy and the Default Domain Controllers Policy, all audit policy settings are Not Configured, so these system-level defaults remain intact.

As you can see, most major Active Directory events are already audited by domain controllers, assuming that the events are successful. Therefore, the creation of a user, the resetting of a user's password, the logon to the domain, and the retrieval of a user's logon scripts are all logged.

However, not all failure events are audited by default. You might need to implement additional failure auditing based on your organization's IT security policies and requirements. Auditing failed account logon events, for example, exposes malicious attempts to access the domain by repeatedly trying to log on as a domain user account without yet knowing the account's password. Auditing failed account management events can reveal someone attempting to manipulate the membership of a security-sensitive group.

One of the most important tasks you must fulfill is to balance and align audit policy with your corporate policies and reality. Your corporate policy might state that all failed logons and successful changes to Active Directory users and groups must be audited. That's easy to achieve in Active Directory. But how, exactly, are you going to use that information? Verbose auditing logs are useless if you don't know how or don't have the tools to manage those logs effectively. To implement auditing, you must have the business requirement to audit, a well-configured audit policy, and the tools with which to manage audited events.

Auditing Access to Files and Folders

Many organizations elect to audit file system access to provide insight into resource usage and potential security issues. Windows Server 2008 R2 supports granular auditing based on user or group accounts and the specific actions performed by those accounts. To configure auditing, you must complete three steps: specify auditing settings, enable audit policy, and evaluate events in the security log.

Specifying Auditing Settings on a File or Folder

You can audit access to a file or folder by adding auditing entries to its system access control list (SACL).

1. Open the properties dialog box of the file or folder, and then click the Security tab.

2. Click Advanced.

3. Click the Auditing tab.

   The Advanced Security Settings dialog box of a folder named Confidential Data is shown Figure 7-16.

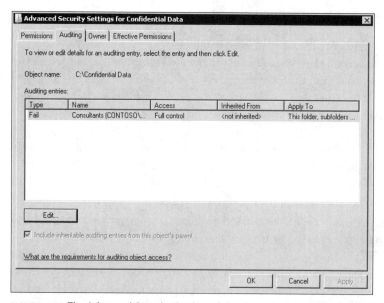

FIGURE 7-16 The Advanced Security Settings dialog box of a folder named Confidential Data

4. To add an entry, click Edit to open the Auditing tab in Edit mode.

5. Click Add to select the user, group, or computer to audit.

6. In the Auditing Entry dialog box shown in Figure 7-17, indicate the type of access to audit.

FIGURE 7-17 The Auditing Entry dialog box

You can audit for successes, failures, or both as the specified user, group, or computer attempts to access the resource by using one or more of the granular access levels.

You can audit successes to:

- Log resource access for reporting and billing.

- Monitor access that would suggest users are performing actions greater than what you had planned, indicating that permissions are too generous.

- Identify access that is out of character for a particular account, which might be a sign that a user account has been breached by a hacker.

Auditing failed events helps you to:

- Monitor for malicious attempts to access a resource to which access has been denied.

- Identify failed attempts to access a file or folder to which a user does require access, indicating that the permissions are not sufficient to achieve a business requirement.

Auditing entries instruct Windows to audit the successful or failed activities of a security principal (user, group, or computer) to use a specific permission. The example in Figure 7-16 audits for unsuccessful attempts by users in the Consultants group to access data in the Confidential Data folder at any level. It does that by configuring an auditing entry for Full Control access. Full Control includes all the individual access levels, so this entry covers any type of access. If a Consultant group member attempts access of any kind and fails, the activity is logged.

Typically, auditing entries reflect the permission entries for the object. In other words, you would configure the Confidential Data folder with permissions that prevent members of the Consultants group from accessing its contents. You would then use auditing to monitor members of the Consultants group who nonetheless attempt to access the folder. Keep in mind, of course, that a member of the Consultants group can also belong to another group that does have permission to access the folder. Because that access will be successful, the activity is not logged. Therefore, if you are concerned about keeping users out of a folder and making sure they do not access it in any way, monitor failed access attempts; however, also audit successful access to identify situations in which a user is accessing the folder through another group membership that is potentially incorrect.

> **NOTE DON'T OVER-AUDIT**
>
> Audit logs tend to get quite large quite rapidly, so a best practice for auditing is to configure the bare minimum required to achieve the business task. For example, specifying to audit the successes and failures on an active data folder for the Everyone group using Full Control (all permissions) would generate enormous audit logs that could affect the performance of the server and make locating a specific audited event all but impossible.

Enabling Audit Policy

Configuring auditing entries in the security descriptor of a file or folder does not, in itself, enable auditing. Auditing must be enabled by defining the Audit Object Access setting shown in Figure 7-18. After auditing is enabled, the security subsystem begins to pay attention to the audit settings and to log access as directed by those settings.

The policy setting must be applied to the server that contains the object being audited. You can configure the policy setting in the server's local GPO or use a GPO scoped to the server.

You can define the policy to audit Success events, Failure events, or both. The policy setting (shown in Figure 7-18) must specify auditing of Success or Failure attempts that match the type of auditing entry in the object's SACL (shown in Figure 7-17). For example, to log a failed attempt by a member of the Consultants group to access the Confidential Data folder, you must configure the Audit Object Access policy to audit failures, and you must configure the SACL of the Confidential Data folder to audit failures. If the resultant audit policy audits successes only, the failure entries in the folder's SACL will not trigger logging.

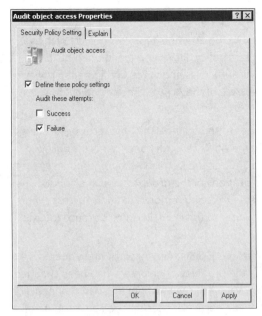

FIGURE 7-18 The Audit Object Access setting

> **NOTE** **MAKING SURE AUDIT POLICY MATCHES AUDITING ENTRIES**
>
> Remember that access that is audited and logged is the combination of the audit entries on specific files and folders and the settings in Audit Policy. If you've configured audit entries to log failures, but the policy enables only logging for successes, your audit logs will remain empty.

Evaluating Events in the Security Log

After you have enabled the Audit Object Access policy setting and specified the access you want to audit, using object SACLs, the system begins to log access according to the audit entries. You can view the resulting events in the Security log of the server. Open the Event Viewer console from Administrative Tools. Expand Windows Logs\Security.

EXAM TIP

Auditing access to objects such as files and folders requires three components. First, the Audit Object Access policy must be enabled and configured to audit Success or Failure events as appropriate for the scenario. Second, the SACL of the object must be configured to audit successful or failed access. Third, you must examine the Security log. Audit Policy is often managed by using a GPO, so the GPO must be scoped to apply to the server with the file or folder, which is usually a file server rather than a domain controller. Some exam questions that appear to be testing your knowledge of auditing are actually testing your ability to scope a GPO with Audit Policy to the correct servers.

Auditing Directory Service Changes

Just as the Audit Object Access policy allows you to log attempts to access objects such as files and folders, the Audit Directory Service Access policy allows you to log attempts to access objects in Active Directory. The same basic principles apply. You configure the policy to audit Success or Failure. You then configure the SACL of the Active Directory object to specify the types of access you want to audit.

As an example, if you want to monitor changes to the membership of a security-sensitive group such as Domain Admins, you can enable the Audit Directory Service Access policy to audit Success events. You can then open the SACL of the Domain Admins group and configure an auditing entry for successful modifications of the group's *member* attribute. In fact, in Windows Server 2008 and later, the default configuration is to audit Success events for Directory Service Access, and to audit all changes to the Domain Admins group. You will see this in an exercise in this lesson's practice.

In Microsoft Windows Server 2003 and Windows 2000 Server, you could audit directory service access and be notified that an object, or the property of an object, had been changed, but you could not identify the previous and new values of the attribute that had changed. For example, an event could be logged indicating that a particular user changed an attribute of Domain Admins, but you could not easily identify which attribute was changed, and there was no way to determine from the audit log exactly what change was made to that attribute.

Windows Server 2008 added an auditing category called Directory Service Changes. The important distinction between Directory Service Changes and Directory Service Access is that with Directory Service Changes auditing, you can identify the previous and current values of a changed attribute.

Enabling Directory Service Changes Auditing

Directory Service Changes is not enabled by default. Instead, Directory Service Access is enabled to mimic the auditing functionality of previous versions of Windows. To enable auditing of successful Directory Service Changes, open Command Prompt on a domain controller and type this command:

```
auditpol /set /subcategory:"directory service changes" /success:enable
```

EXAM TIP

The *auditpol* command enables auditing of directory service changes.

Although you can use the preceding command to enable Directory Service Changes auditing in a lab and explore the events that are generated, don't implement this in a domain until you've read the documentation on TechNet, starting with the step-by-step guide found at *http://go.microsoft.com/fwlink/?LinkId=168805*.

Specifying Auditing Settings for Directory Service Changes

You must still modify the SACL of objects to specify which attributes should be audited.

To access the SACL and its audit entries:

1. In Active Directory Users And Computers, open the Properties dialog box of the object you want to audit.

2. On the Security tab, click Advanced.

3. Click the Auditing tab.

To add an audit entry:

1. Click Add.

2. Select the user, group, or computer to audit. Often this will be the Everyone group.

3. In the Auditing Entry dialog box, indicate the type of access to audit.

   You can audit for successes, failures, or both as the specified user, group, or computer attempts to access the resource using one or more of the granular access levels.

Viewing Audited Events in the Security Log

After you have enabled the desired audit policy setting and specified the access you want to audit using object SACLs, the system begins to log access according to the audit entries. You can view the resulting events in the Security Log of the server. Open the Event Viewer console from Administrative Tools. Expand Windows Logs, and select Security Log.

When Directory Service Changes auditing is enabled and auditing entries are configured in the SACL of directory service objects, events are logged to the Security Log that clearly indicate the attribute that was changed and the change made. In most cases, event log entries show the previous and current value of the changed attribute.

 Quick Check

- You want to audit changes to properties of user accounts provided for temporary employees. When a change is made, you want to see the previous and new value of the changed attribute. What type of auditing do you perform?

Quick Check Answer

- Directory Service Changes auditing

PRACTICE **Implementing an Audit Policy**

In this practice, you configure auditing settings, enable audit policies for object access, and filter for specific events in the Security log. The business objective is to monitor a folder containing confidential data that should not be accessed by users in the Consultants group.

You also configure auditing to monitor changes to the membership of the Domain Admins group. To perform this practice, you must complete the following preparatory tasks:

- Create a folder called Confidential Data on the C drive.
- Create a global security group called Consultants.
- Create a user named James Fine, and add the user to the Consultants group.

If you have performed earlier practices, some of these objects may already exist. Finally, in this and other practices in this training kit, you will log on to the domain controller with user accounts that are not a member of Domain Administrators or the domain's Administrators group. Therefore, you must give all user accounts the right to log on locally to the domain controllers in your practice environment. Follow the steps in the article, "Grant a Member the Right to Logon Locally," at *http://technet.microsoft.com/en-us/library/ee957044(WS.10).aspx* to grant the Allow Logon Locally right to the Administrators and Domain Users groups. If you will use Remote Desktop Services to connect to the domain controller—rather than logging on locally—grant the Allow Logon Through Remote Desktop Services right. Reboot the server or otherwise refresh Group Policy. This is for the practice environment only. In a production environment, you should not grant users the right to log on to domain controllers.

EXERCISE 1 Configure Permissions and Audit Settings

In this exercise, you configure permissions on the Confidential Data folder to deny access to consultants. You then enable auditing of attempts by consultants to access the folder.

1. Log on to SERVER01 as Administrator.
2. Open the properties of the C:\Confidential Data folder and click the Security tab.
3. Click Edit.
4. Click Add.
5. Type **Consultants** and click OK.
6. Select the Deny check box for the Full Control permission.
7. Click Apply. Click Yes to confirm the use of a Deny permission.
8. Click OK to close the Permissions dialog box.
9. Click Advanced.
10. On the Auditing tab, click Edit.
11. Click Add.
12. Type **Consultants** and click OK.
13. In the Auditing Entry dialog box, select the check box under Failed next to Full Control.
14. Click OK to close all dialog boxes.

EXERCISE 2 Enable Audit Policy

Because SERVER01 is a domain controller, you use the existing Default Domain Controllers Policy GPO to enable auditing. On a stand-alone server, you would enable auditing by using Local Security Policy or a GPO scoped to the server.

1. Open Group Policy Management and select the Group Policy Objects container.

2. Right-click the Default Domain Controllers Policy and click Edit.

3. Expand Computer Configuration\Policies\Windows Settings\Security Settings\Local Policies and click Audit Policy.

4. Double-click Audit Object Access.

5. Select Define These Policy Settings.

6. Select the Failure check box.

7. Click OK, and then close the console.

8. To refresh the policy and ensure that all settings have been applied, open Command Prompt and type the command **gpupdate**.

EXERCISE 3   Generate Audit Events

You now attempt to access the Confidential Data folder as a member of the Consultants group.

1. Log on to SERVER01 as James Fine.

2. Open the C:\ folder. Attempt to open the C:\Confidential Data folder.

3. Create a text file on your desktop and attempt to cut and paste the file into the Confidential Data folder.

EXERCISE 4   Examine the Security Log

You can now view the attempts by a consultant to access the Confidential Data folder.

1. Log on to SERVER01 as Administrator.

2. Open Event Viewer from the Administrative Tools folder.

3. Expand Windows Logs and click Security.

4. Which types of events do you see in the Security log? Remember that policies can enable auditing for numerous security-related actions, including directory service access, account management, logon, and more. Notice that the source of events indicated in the Source column is Microsoft Windows security auditing.

5. To filter the log and narrow the scope of your search, click the Filter Current Log link in the Actions pane.

6. Configure the filter to be as narrow as possible.

   What do you know about the event you are trying to locate? You know it occurred within the last hour, that the source is Microsoft Windows security auditing, and that it is a File System event.

7. Check your work by referring to Figure 7-19.

8. Click OK.

   Can you more easily locate the events generated when James Fine attempted to access the Confidential Data folder?

You cannot filter for the C:\Confidential Data folder name in the Filter dialog box shown in Figure 7-19. But you can locate events for that folder by exporting the file to a log analysis tool or even to a text file.

9. Click the Save Filtered Log File As link in the Actions pane.

10. In the Save As dialog box, click the Desktop link in the Favorite Links pane.

FIGURE 7-19 Filtering the Security Log for recent File System events

11. In the Save As Type drop-down list, select Text.

12. In the File Name text box, type **Audit Log Export**.

13. Click Save.

14. Open the resulting text file in Notepad and search for instances of C:\Confidential Data.

EXERCISE 5   Use Directory Service Changes Auditing

In this exercise, you see the Directory Service Access auditing that is enabled by default in Windows Server 2008 R2. You then implement the Directory Service Changes auditing feature, introduced in Windows Server 2008, to monitor changes to the Domain Admins group.

1. Open the Active Directory Users And Computers snap-in.

2. On the View menu, ensure that Advanced Features is selected.

3. Select the Users container.

4. Right-click Domain Admins and click Properties.

5. On the Security tab, click Advanced.

6. On the Auditing tab, select the auditing entry with Special listed in the Access column.

7. Click Edit.

8. Confirm that auditing is already enabled for successful writes to all properties.

9. Click OK.

10. Click OK to close the Advanced Security Settings dialog box.

    By default, Windows Server 2008 R2 audits any changes to the *member* attribute of the Domain Admins group. You now make two changes to the group's membership.

11. In the properties dialog box of the Domain Admins group, click the Members tab.

12. Add the user James Fine and click Apply.

13. Select James Fine, click Remove, click Yes to confirm, and then click Apply.

14. Click OK to close the Domain Admins Properties dialog box.

15. Open the Security log and locate the events that were generated when you added and removed James Fine. The Event ID is 4662. Examine the information provided on the General tab.

    You can identify that a user (Administrator) accessed an object (Domain Admins) and used a Write Property access. The property itself is displayed as a globally unique identifier (GUID)—you cannot readily identify that the *member* attribute was changed. The event also does not describe the change that was made to the property.

    You now enable Directory Service Changes auditing, a feature introduced in Windows Server 2008.

16. Open Command Prompt and type the following command:

    ```
    auditpol /set /subcategory:"directory service changes" /success:enable
    ```

17. Open the properties of Domain Admins and add James Fine to the group.

18. Return to the Event Viewer snap-in and refresh the view of the Security log. You should see both a Directory Service Access event (Event ID 4662) and a Directory Service Changes event (Event ID 5136). If you do not see the Directory Service Changes event, wait a few moments, and then refresh the view. It can take a few seconds for the Directory Service Changes event to be logged.

19. Examine the information in the Directory Service Changes event.

    The information on the General tab clearly indicates that a user (Administrator) made a change to an object in the directory (Domain Admins) and that the specific change made was adding James Fine.

Lesson Summary

- Audit Policy defines whether success or failure events are audited. Several audit policies are related to specific types of activities such as account logon, object access, and directory service changes.

- To audit file system access, you must add auditing entries to the SACL of a file or folder, define the Audit Object Access policy setting, and evaluate resulting audit entries in the Security log.

- Windows Server 2008 R2 supports detailed auditing of changes to objects in Active Directory. You can use the Auditpol.exe command to enable this new category of auditing. Events display the attribute that was changed and clearly indicate the type of change that was made or the previous and current value of the attribute.

Lesson Review

You can use the following questions to test your knowledge of the information in Lesson 4, "Implementing an Audit Policy." The questions are also available on the companion CD if you prefer to review them in electronic form.

> **NOTE ANSWERS**
>
> Answers to these questions and explanations of why each answer choice is right or wrong are located in the "Answers" section at the end of the book.

1. You are concerned that an individual is trying to gain access to computers by logging on with valid domain user names and a variety of attempted passwords. Which audit policy should you configure and monitor for such activities?

   A. Logon Event failures

   B. Directory Service Access failures

   C. Privilege Use successes

   D. Account Logon Event failures

   E. Account Management failures

2. You want to audit changes to attributes of user accounts used by administrators in your organization. When a change is made, you want to see both the previous and changed values of the attribute. What must you do to achieve your goal?

   A. Define Account Management audit policy.

   B. Use the Auditpol.exe command.

   C. Enable Privilege Use auditing.

   D. Define Directory Service Access audit policy.

3. Your organization includes 10 file servers, which have computer accounts in the Servers OU of your domain. A GPO named Server Configuration is linked to the Servers OU.

On five of the servers, a folder called Confidential Data exists. You have hired a team of consultants to assist on a project, and you want to ensure that those consultants cannot access the Confidential Data folder. You configure permissions on the folder to prevent access by consultants, and you want to audit any attempt by consultants to open or manipulate the folder. Which steps must you take? (Choose three. Each correct answer is part of the solution.)

A. Add audit entries to the Confidential Data folder to audit successful Full Control access.

B. Evaluate entries in the Security logs on the domain controllers.

C. Define the Audit Directory Service Access policy in the Server Configuration GPO.

D. Define the Audit Object Access policy in the Default Domain Controllers GPO.

E Define the Audit Object Access policy in the Server Configuration GPO.

F. Evaluate entries in the Security logs on each file server.

G. Add audit entries to the Confidential Data folder to audit failed Full Control access.

Chapter Review

To further practice and reinforce the skills you learned in this chapter, you can perform the following tasks:

- Review the chapter summary.
- Review the list of key terms introduced in this chapter.
- Complete the case scenarios. These scenarios set up real-world situations involving the topics of this chapter and ask you to create a solution.
- Complete the suggested practices.
- Take a practice test.

Chapter Summary

- Group Policy can be used to configure the membership of groups, security settings, software management, and auditing.
- In addition to the Group Policy Management console and a Group Policy Management Editor, numerous tools affect Group Policy, including security templates, the Security Configuration Wizard, Scwcmd.exe, and Auditpol.exe.
- It is critical that you know how to scope GPOs effectively, both for the 70-640 exam and for the success of Group Policy in your enterprise.
- Restricted groups policies can add members to a group in a cumulative manner or can define the single, authoritative membership of a group.
- The new Security Configuration Wizard creates role-based security policies that can incorporate security templates managed by snap-ins that have existed in previous versions of Windows. The Scwcmd.exe command can transform a security policy into a GPO.
- You can assign software to users or computers, or you can publish it to users for installation by using Control Panel. Group Policy Software Installation can also manage the redeployment, upgrade, or removal of an application.
- Auditing file system access, directory service access, or directory service changes requires defining Audit Policy and auditing entries in the SACL of objects.

Key Terms

The following terms were introduced in this chapter. Do you know what they mean?

- audit policy
- delegation
- firewall

- security template
- Windows Installer package (.msi file)
- Windows Installer transform (.mst file)

Case Scenarios

In the following case scenarios, you apply what you've learned about managing security settings, Group Policy with software installation, and auditing. You can find answers to these questions in the "Answers" section at the end of this book.

Case Scenario 1: Installing Software with Group Policy Software Installation

You are an administrator at Contoso, Ltd. You will be deploying a new application to the users in your mobile sales force, and you would like to do so using Group Policy software installation (GPSI). In your Active Directory, all users are in the Employees OU, and all client computer accounts are in the Clients OU. The application is licensed per machine. When sales personnel are at the office, they log on to other systems such as computers in conference rooms. You want to ensure that the application is installed only on the sales force's desktops and laptops—not on other computers. You have created a transform that automates installation of the application's Windows Installer package.

1. Should the package for the application be created in the Computer Configuration node or User Configuration node of a GPO? Why?

2. When you create the package, should you choose Publish, Assign, or Advanced? Why?

3. How should you scope the GPO so that it applies only to the mobile sales force users?

Case Scenario 2: Configuring Security

You are an administrator at Contoso, Ltd. You maintain 20 servers for the Human Resources department—servers that are distributed across seven global sites. The Salaries folder is replicated to a server in each site. Because the folder contains highly sensitive information about employee compensation, you have been asked to secure it thoroughly and audit inappropriate attempts to access it. You have applied NTFS permissions that allow only appropriate HR personnel access to the Salaries folders; even the Administrators groups on the servers do not have access. Of course, members of a server's Administrators group can always take ownership of a resource and give themselves permissions, but that can be audited as well. To improve the security of these servers and their sensitive data further, you want to ensure that only your user account and that of the vice president of HR are administrators of the server—the vice president's account is to be used as a backup when you are not available. You want to deploy this configuration to all seven servers without having to reproduce each step manually. You are not delegated permissions to create or modify Group Policy objects in your organization.

1. You must audit inappropriate attempts to access the Salaries folder. You are also to audit any access to the folder by members of the Administrators group on the server, including attempts to take ownership of the folder. What auditing entries should you configure on the Salaries folder?

2. What policy setting should you configure to enforce the limited membership of the Administrators group? Can you remove the Administrator account with this policy?

3. Which audit policies should you configure?

4. How can you deploy this configuration to the seven servers without Group Policy?

5. Can policy settings in Active Directory–based GPOs override your settings? If so, how can you monitor the servers occasionally to ensure that your configuration is not being changed?

Suggested Practices

To help you successfully master the exam objectives presented in this chapter, complete the following tasks.

Configure Restricted Groups

In this practice, you create a best practices framework for the delegation of support for client computers. You configure the Administrators group on client computers so that it includes the corporate help desk and a support group specific to a geographical site. Administrators will not include Domain Admins.

To perform this practice, you must have the following objects in the Active Directory domain:

- A first-level OU named Admins.
- Two child OUs in the Admins OU: Identities and Groups.
- A global security group named Help Desk in the Admins\Admin Groups OU.
- A global security group named NYC Support in the Admins\Admin Groups OU.
- One or more user accounts representing corporate help desk personnel in the Admins\Identities OU. These users are members of the Help Desk group.
- One or more users representing members of the New York desktop support team in the Admins\Identities OU. These users are members of the NYC Support group.
- A first-level OU named Clients.
- An OU named NYC in the Clients OU.
- A computer object named DESKTOP101 in the Clients\NYC OU.

- **Practice 1**   In this practice, you create intermediate groups to manage the delegation of administration. Create two domain local security groups in the Admins\Groups OU: SYS_Clients_Admins and SYS_NYC_Admins. Add the Help Desk group as a member of SYS_Clients_Admins and add the NYC Support group as a member of SYS_NYC_Admins.

- **Practice 2**   Create a GPO that defines the membership of Administrators as *only* the SYS_Clients_Admins group. Refer to the steps in Exercise 2, "Delegate the Administration of a Subset of Clients in the Domain," of Lesson 1 if you need help. In this practice, however, you must create a restricted groups policy for Administrators that uses the Members Of This Group setting and specifies SYS_Clients_Admins. Scope the GPO to apply to all computers in the Clients OU.

- **Practice 3**   This practice is identical to Exercise 3, "Confirm the Cumulative Application of Member Of Policies," of Lesson 1. Create a GPO that ensures that the SYS_NYC_Admins group is a member of Administrators. Create a restricted group policy for SYS_NYC_Admins that uses the This Group Is A Member Of setting and specifies Administrators. Scope the GPO to apply to all computers in the NYC OU.

- **Practice 4**   Use RSoP Modeling to verify that the Administrators group contains SYS_Clients_Admins and SYS_NYC_Admins. Refer to Exercise 3 in Lesson 1 for the required steps if you need assistance. If you have a test computer named DESKTOP101 joined to the domain, refer to Optional Exercise 4, "Confirm the Membership of the Administrators Group," in Lesson 1 for the required steps to log on and validate the membership of the Administrators group. On DESKTOP101, you will see that the Administrators group no longer includes Domain Admins.

This set of suggested practices appears similar to the practice in Lesson 1, but it varies in two significant ways. First, Practice 2 uses the Members setting of a restricted groups policy, which has the effect of removing the Domain Admins group from the local Administrators group. This is a best practice, because the Domain Admins group should be used only for directory service and domain controller–related administration, not for universal system support. Second, in Lesson 1, you used Group Policy to add the Help Desk and NYC Support groups directly to the Administrators group of clients. In this practice, you added the intermediate groups—SYS_Clients_Admins and SYS_NYC_Admins—to the Administrators group on client systems, so the help desk and NYC support teams are still members, but indirectly. The advantage of the indirect structure is that if other groups need to be members of the Administrators group, you do not need to change your policies and configuration— you simply add them to the domain local group. If, for example, you deploy an application that requires local administrative credentials on all clients, you do not need to touch each system, and you do not need to change your GPOs. You simply add the application's account to the SYS_Clients_Admins group. Similarly, if a team of auditors is assigned to examine all computers in New York, you add the team to the SYS_NYC_Admins group. No change to security configuration or GPOs is required.

Manage Security Configuration

In this practice, you implement a security configuration similar to that proposed in Case Scenario 2, "Configuring Security." Review Case Scenario 2 before proceeding. You need the following objects in Active Directory to perform these practices:

- A first-level OU named Admins with a sub-OU named Admin Groups
- A group in the Admin Groups OU named HR Server Admins
- A first-level OU named Groups
- A group in the Groups OU named Human Resources

In addition, you need a folder named Salaries on the C drive of SERVER01.

- **Practice 1**   In the Security Templates snap-in, create a new security template called HR Server. In the Local Policies\Audit Policy node, configure Audit Object Access to audit success and failure events and configure Audit Privilege Use to audit successes. In the Restricted Groups node, add a new restricted group policy for Administrators that defines Members Of This Group as HR Server Admins. In Active Directory Users And Computers, make a note of the current membership of the Administrators group (in the BUILTIN OU) so that you can restore the membership to this state after the practice. Save the template by right-clicking HR Server and clicking Save.

- **Practice 2**   Case Scenario 2 suggested that you would manually configure permissions and auditing entries on the Salaries folder. Windows provides file system policies that allow you to configure permissions and auditing entries through policies so that you do not have to do so manually and so that security can be reapplied and enforced through policy. In the HR Server security template, right-click the File System node and click Add File. In the dialog box that appears, type C:\Salaries in the Folder text box and click OK. In the Database Security dialog box, remove all entries and add a permission for Human Resources that gives the group Full Control permission. That should be the only permission applied. Click Advanced, and then click the Auditing tab. Add an auditing entry for Everyone that audits failed full-control access. Add a second auditing entry for Administrators that audits successful full-control access. Click OK to close all dialog boxes, accepting all defaults. Save the template by right-clicking HR Server and clicking Save.

- **Practice 3**   In the Security Configuration And Analysis snap-in, open a new database named HR Server Configuration. Import the HR Server template you created in Practices 1 and 2. Right-click Security Configuration And Analysis and click Analyze Computer Now. Click OK. Examine the three nodes of security settings that you modified: Audit Policy, Restricted Groups, and File System. Locate the discrepancies between the computer's current settings and the settings in the template.

- **Practice 4**   Right-click Security Configuration And Analysis and click Configure Computer Now. Click OK. Confirm the changes that were made by examining the membership of the Administrators group in the BUILTIN OU and by examining the security and auditing settings on the C:\Salaries folder.

Be sure to reset the membership of the Administrators group to the original members you recorded in Practice 1. If you did not record the original membership of the group, make sure that Enterprise Admins and Domain Admins are members.

Take a Practice Test

The practice tests on this book's companion CD offer many options. For example, you can test yourself on just one exam objective, or you can test yourself on all the 70-640 certification exam content. You can set up the test so that it closely simulates the experience of taking a certification exam, or you can set it up in study mode so that you can look at the correct answers and explanations after you answer each question.

> **MORE INFO** **PRACTICE TESTS**
>
> For details about all the practice test options available, see the "How to Use the Practice Tests" section in this book's Introduction.

Improving the Security of Authentication in an AD DS Domain

When a user logs on to an Active Directory Domain Services (AD DS) domain, she enters her user name and password, and the client uses those credentials to *authenticate* the user—to validate the user's identity against her Active Directory account. In Chapter 3, "Administering User Accounts," you learned how to create and manage user accounts and their properties, including their passwords. In this chapter, you will explore the domain-side components of authentication, including the policies that specify password requirements and the auditing of authentication-related activities. You will also discover three new options to improve the security of accounts and authentication: managed service accounts' password settings objects (PSOs, better known as fine-grained password policy); and read-only domain controllers (RODCs).

Exam objectives in this chapter:

- Maintain Active Directory accounts.
- Configure account policies.
- Configure audit policy by using GPOs.
- Configure Active Directory replication.
- Configure the read-only domain controller (RODC).

Lessons in this chapter:

Before You Begin

To complete the lessons in this chapter, you must have installed a domain controller named SERVER01 in the contoso.com domain.

 REAL WORLD

Dan Holme

As I work with clients to implement AD DS, I must constantly balance the need to maintain high levels of security with the need to continue conducting the client's business. With versions of Microsoft Windows prior to Windows Server 2008, I constantly encountered three scenarios in which this balance was particularly difficult to reach.

The first relates to the security of user accounts with high levels of privilege within the enterprise. Such accounts are especially attractive to hackers, so they should be locked down with particularly lengthy and complex passwords. In earlier versions of Windows, only one password policy could be applied to all accounts in the domain. Therefore, I either had to apply the highly restrictive password policy to all users in the domain, which was never a palatable solution, or ask administrators to follow the more restrictive policy but with no way to require compliance. Windows Server 2008 introduced fine-grained password policies that can be used to apply more or less restrictive password policies beyond the requirements for groups or users in a domain.

Branch offices were also problematic because I had to balance the need for quick and reliable user authentication at the branch office against the desire to centralize control over the physical security of domain controllers. Placing a domain controller in a branch office would clearly improve performance for users in the office but would also typically expose the domain controller to lower levels of security than those maintained at the data center. Coming to the rescue once again, Windows Server 2008 and Windows Server 2008 R2 can act as a read-only domain controller, authenticating users and the branch office without storing all domain user credentials, thus reducing the risk to the enterprise in the event of a stolen branch office domain controller.

Another significant challenge is the management of service accounts. Services such as backup, antivirus, Microsoft SQL Server, and IIS application pools run in the context of a user account. When you change the password of a service account, you must configure the service with the new password as well. Managing service accounts was so problematic that many organizations simply configured service accounts with non-expiring passwords, which is a very poor practice from a security perspective. Windows Server 2008 R2 addresses this scenario with a new feature: managed service accounts.

If you have worked with Active Directory for any period of time, you already appreciate the value of fine-grained password policies, read-only domain controllers, and managed service accounts. If you are new to Active Directory, you are lucky to be able to work with these much-anticipated features.

Lesson 1: Configuring Password and Lockout Policies

By default in a Windows Server 2008 R2 domain, users are required to change their password every 42 days, and a password must be at least seven characters long and meet complexity requirements, including the use of three of four character types: uppercase, lowercase, numeric, and non-alphanumeric. Three password policies—maximum password age, password length, and password complexity—are among the first policies encountered by administrators and users alike in an Active Directory domain. Rarely do these default settings align precisely with the password security requirements of an organization. Your organization might require passwords to be changed more or less frequently or to be longer. In this lesson, you learn how to implement your enterprise's password and lockout policies by modifying the Default Domain Policy Group Policy object (GPO).

As you know, there are exceptions to every rule, and you likely have exceptions to your password policies. To enhance the security of your domain, you can enforce more restrictive password requirements for accounts assigned to administrators, for accounts used by services such as Microsoft SQL Server, or for a backup utility. In versions of Windows prior to Windows Server 2008, this was not possible; a single password policy applied to all accounts in the domain. In this lesson, you learn to configure fine-grained password policies, a feature of Windows Server 2008 and Windows Server 2008 R2 that lets you assign different password policies to users and groups in your domain.

> **After this lesson, you will be able to:**
> - Implement your domain password and account lockout policy.
> - Configure and assign fine-grained password policies.
>
> **Estimated lesson time: 45 minutes**

Understanding Password Policies

Your domain's password policy is configured by a GPO scoped to the domain. Within the GPO, in the Computer Configuration\Policies\Windows Settings\Security Settings\Account Policies\Password Policy node, you can configure the policy settings that determine password requirements. The Password Policy node is shown in Figure 8-1.

You can understand the effects of the policies by considering the life cycle of a user password. A user is required to change his or her password within the number of days specified by the Maximum Password Age policy setting. When the user enters a new password, the length of the new password is compared to the number of characters in the Minimum Password Length policy. If the Password Must Meet Complexity Requirements policy is enabled, the password must contain at least three of four character types:

- Uppercase—for example, A to Z
- Lowercase—for example, a to z

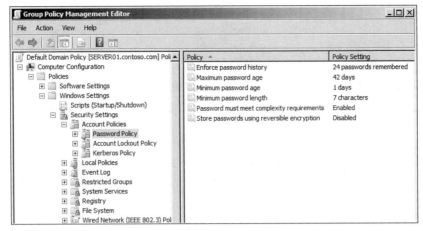

FIGURE 8-1 The Password Policy node of a GPO

- Numeric—0 to 9
- Nonalphanumeric—symbols such as !, #, %, or &

If the new password meets the requirements, Active Directory puts the password through a mathematical algorithm that produces a representation of the password called the *hash code*. The hash code is unique; no two passwords can create the same hash code. The algorithm used to create the hash code is called a *one-way function*. You cannot put the hash code through a reverse function to derive the password. The fact that it is a hash code, and not the password itself, that is stored in Active Directory helps to increase the security of the user account.

Occasionally, applications require the ability to read a user's password. This is not possible because, by default, only the hash code is stored in Active Directory. To support such applications, you can enable the Store Passwords Using Reversible Encryption policy. This policy is not enabled by default, but if you enable the policy, user passwords are stored in an encrypted form that can be decrypted by the application. Reversible encryption significantly reduces the security of your domain, so it is disabled by default, and you should strive to eliminate applications that require direct access to passwords.

Additionally, Active Directory can check a cache of the user's previous hash codes to make sure that the new password is not the same as the user's previous passwords. The number of previous passwords against which a new password is evaluated is determined by the Enforce Password History policy. By default, Windows maintains the previous 24 hash codes.

If a user is determined to reuse her password when the password expiration period occurs, she could simply change her password 25 times to work around the password history. To prevent that from happening, the Minimum Password Age policy specifies an amount of time that must pass between password changes. By default, it is one day. Therefore, the determined user would have to change her password once a day for 25 days to reuse a password. This type of deterrent is generally successful at discouraging such behavior.

These policy settings—history, minimum age, and maximum age—affect users changing their passwords. The settings do not affect administrators using the Reset Password command to change another user's password.

Understanding Account Lockout Policies

An intruder can gain access to the resources in your domain by determining a valid user name and password. User names are relatively easy to identify because most organizations create user names from an employee's email address, initials, combinations of first and last names, or employee IDs. After a user name is known, the intruder might determine the correct password by guessing or by repeatedly logging on with combinations of characters or words until the logon is successful.

This type of attack, called *brute force*, can be thwarted by limiting the number of incorrect logons allowed. That is exactly what account lockout policies achieve. Account lockout policies are located in the node of the GPO directly below Password Policy. The Account Lockout Policy node is shown in Figure 8-2.

FIGURE 8-2 The Account Lockout Policy node of a GPO

Three settings are related to account lockout. The first of these settings, Account Lockout Threshold, determines the number of invalid logon attempts permitted within a time specified by the second of these settings, Reset Account Lockout Counter After. If an attack results in more unsuccessful logons within that time frame, the user account is locked out. When an account is locked out, Active Directory denies logon to that account, even if the correct password is specified.

An administrator can unlock a locked user account by following the procedure you learned in Chapter 3. You can also configure Active Directory to automatically unlock the account after a delay specified by a third setting, the Account Lockout Duration policy setting.

Configuring the Domain Password and Lockout Policy

Active Directory supports one set of password and lockout policies for a domain. These policies are configured in a GPO that is scoped to the domain. A new domain contains a GPO called Default Domain Policy that is linked to the domain and includes the default policy settings for password, account lockout, and Kerberos policies, shown in Figures 8-1 and 8-2. You can change the settings by editing the Default Domain Policy.

> **PRACTICE IT**
>
> You can practice configuring a domain's password and lockout policies in Exercise 1, "Configure the Domain's Password and Lockout Policies," in the practice for this lesson.

> **BEST PRACTICE** **DO NOT OVERLOAD THE DEFAULT DOMAIN POLICY GPO**
>
> The best practice is to edit the Default Domain Policy GPO to specify the password policy settings for your organization. You should also use the Default Domain Policy GPO to specify account lockout policies and Kerberos policies. Do not use the Default Domain Policy GPO to deploy any other custom policy settings. In other words, use the Default Domain Policy GPO to define the password, account lockout, and Kerberos policies for the domain, and nothing else. Additionally, do not define password, account lockout, or Kerberos policies for the domain in any other GPO.

> **NOTE** **ACCOUNT SETTINGS OVERRIDE POLICIES**
>
> The password settings configured in the Default Domain Policy affect all user accounts in the domain. The settings can be overridden, however, by the password-related properties of the individual user accounts. On the Account tab of a user's Properties dialog box, shown in Figure 8-3, you can specify settings such as Password Never Expires or Store Password Using Reversible Encryption. For example, if five users have an application that requires direct access to their passwords, you can configure the accounts for those users to store their passwords using reversible encryption.

Fine-Grained Password and Lockout Policy

You can also override the domain password and lockout policy by using a feature introduced in Windows Server 2008 called *fine-grained password and lockout policy*, often shortened to simply *fine-grained password policy*. Fine-grained password policy enables you to configure a policy that applies to one or more groups or users in your domain.

FIGURE 8-3 Password-related properties of a user account

Fine-grained password policy is a highly anticipated addition to Active Directory. There are several scenarios for which fine-grained password policy can be used to increase the security of your domain. Accounts used by administrators are delegated privileges to modify objects in Active Directory; therefore, if an intruder compromises an administrator's account, more damage can be done to the domain than could be done with the account of a standard user. For that reason, you should consider implementing stricter password requirements for administrative accounts. For example, you might require greater password length and more frequent password changes.

To use fine-grained password policy, your domain must be at the Windows Server 2008 domain functional level or higher, which means that all of your domain controllers in the domain are running Windows Server 2008 or later and the domain functional level has been raised to Windows Server 2008 or higher. Domain functional level is described in Chapter 12, "Managing Multiple Domains and Forests."

To confirm and modify the domain functional level:

1. Open Active Directory Domains And Trusts.

2. In the console tree, expand Active Directory Domains And Trusts, and then expand the tree until you can see the domain.

3. Right-click the domain and choose Raise Domain Functional Level.

Other account types that require special treatment in a domain are those used by services and Internet Information Services (IIS) application pools. A service performs its tasks with credentials that must be authenticated with a user name and password just like those of a human user. However, most services are not capable of changing their own password, so administrators configure service accounts with the Password Never Expires option enabled. When an account's password will not be changed, you should make sure the password is difficult to compromise. You can use fine-grained password policies to specify an extremely long minimum password length and no password expiration. Better yet, you can use a new feature of Windows Server 2008 R2—managed service accounts—for which passwords are automatically changed. Managed service accounts are discussed in Lesson 4 of this chapter.

Understanding Password Settings Objects

The settings managed by fine-grained password policy are identical to those in the Password Policy and Accounts Policy nodes of a GPO. However, fine-grained password policies are not implemented as part of Group Policy, nor are they applied as part of a GPO. Instead, a separate class of object in Active Directory maintains the settings for fine-grained password policy: the *password settings object* (PSO).

EXAM TIP

There can be one, and only one, authoritative set of password and lockout policy settings that applies to all users in a domain. Those settings are configured in the Default Domain Policy GPO. Fine-grained password policies, which apply to individual groups or users in the domain, are implemented using PSOs.

You can manage most Active Directory objects with user-friendly graphical user interface (GUI) tools such as the Active Directory Users And Computers snap-in. You manage PSOs, however, with low-level tools, including Active Directory Service Interface Editor (ADSI Edit).

MORE INFO   PASSWORD POLICY BASIC

Although it will not be addressed on the 70-640 exam, it is highly recommended that you use Password Policy Basic by Specops Software to manage fine-grained password policy. You can download the free GUI tool from *http://www.specopssoft.com*.

You can create one or more PSOs in your domain. Each PSO contains a complete set of password and lockout policy settings. A PSO is applied by linking the PSO to one or more global security groups or users. For example, to configure a strict password policy for administrative accounts, create a global security group, add the service user accounts as members, and link a PSO to the group. Applying fine-grained password policies to a group in this manner is more manageable than applying the policies to each individual user account. If you create a new service account, you simply add it to the group and the account becomes managed by the PSO.

PSO Precedence and Resultant PSO

A PSO can be linked to more than one group or user, an individual group or user can have more than one PSO linked to it, and a user can belong to multiple groups. So which fine-grained password and lockout policy settings apply to a user? One and only one PSO determines the password and lockout settings for a user—this PSO is called the *resultant PSO*. Each PSO has an attribute that determines the precedence of the PSO. The precedence value is any number greater than 0, where the number 1 indicates the highest precedence. If multiple PSOs apply to a user, the PSO with the highest precedence (closest to 1) takes effect. Active Directory exposes the resultant PSO in a user object attribute, *msDS-ResultantPSO*, so you can readily identify the PSO that will affect a user. PSOs contain all password and lockout settings, so there is no inheritance or merging of settings. The resultant PSO is the authoritative PSO. The rules that determine precedence, and thus the resultant PSO, are as follows:

- If multiple PSOs apply to groups to which the user belongs, the PSO with the highest precedence wins.

- If one or more PSOs are linked directly to the user, PSOs linked to groups are ignored, regardless of their precedence. The user-linked PSO with highest precedence wins.

- If one or more PSOs have the same precedence value, Active Directory must make a choice. It picks the PSO with the lowest globally unique identifier (GUID). GUIDs are like serial numbers for Active Directory objects—no two objects have the same GUID. GUIDs have no particular meaning—they are just identifiers—so picking the PSO with the lowest GUID is, in effect, an arbitrary decision. You should configure PSOs with unique, specific precedence values so that you avoid this scenario.

To view the *msDS-ResultantPSO* attribute of a user:

1. Ensure that Advanced Features is enabled on the View menu.

2. Open the properties of the user account.

3. On the Attribute Editor tab, click Filter and ensure that Constructed is selected.

   The attribute you locate in the next step is a *constructed* attribute, meaning that the resultant PSO is not a hard-coded attribute of a user; rather, it is calculated by examining the PSOs linked to a user in real time.

4. Locate the *msDS-ResultantPSO* attribute.

> **PRACTICE IT**
>
> You will examine the *msDS-ResultantPSO* attribute in the practice at the end of this lesson.

PSOs and OUs

PSOs can be linked to global security groups or users. PSOs cannot be linked to organizational units (OUs). If you want to apply password and lockout policies to users in an OU, you must create a global security group that includes all of the users in the OU. This type of group is called a *shadow group*—its membership shadows, or mimics, the membership of an OU.

Shadow groups are conceptual, not technical objects. You simply create a group and add the users that belong to the OU. If you change the membership of the OU, you must also change the membership of the group.

> **MORE INFO   SHADOW GROUPS**
>
> Additional information about PSOs and shadow groups is available at *http://technet .microsoft.com/en-us/library/cc770842(WS.10).aspx*.

> **MORE INFO   MAINTAINING SHADOW GROUP MEMBERSHIP WITH SCRIPTS**
>
> You can use scripts to maintain the membership of shadow groups dynamically so that they always reflect the users in OUs. You can find example scripts in *Windows Administration Resource Kit: Productivity Solutions for IT Professionals* by Dan Holme (Microsoft Press, 2008).

PRACTICE   **Configuring Password and Lockout Policies**

In this practice, you use Group Policy to configure the domain-wide password and lockout policies for contoso.com. You then secure administrative accounts by configuring more restrictive, fine-grained password and lockout policies.

EXERCISE 1   Configure the Domain's Password and Lockout Policies

In this exercise, you modify the Default Domain Policy GPO to implement a password and lockout policy for users in the contoso.com domain.

1. Log on to SERVER01 as Administrator.
2. Open Group Policy Management from the Administrative Tools program group.
3. Expand Forest, Domains, and contoso.com.
4. Right-click Default Domain Policy underneath the contoso.com domain and choose Edit.

5. You might be prompted with a reminder that you are changing the settings of a GPO. If so, click OK.

The Group Policy Management Editor appears.

6. Expand Computer Configuration, Policies, Windows Settings, Security Settings, and Account Policies, and then click Password Policy.

7. Double-click the following policy settings in the console details pane and configure the settings indicated:

- Maximum Password Age: 90 Days
- Minimum Password Length: 10 characters

8. Select Account Lockout Policy in the console tree.

9. Double-click the Account Lockout Threshold policy setting and configure it for 5 Invalid Logon Attempts. Then click OK.

10. In the Suggested Value Changes dialog box, click OK.

The values for Account Lockout Duration and Reset Account Lockout Counter After are automatically set to 30 minutes.

11. Close the Group Policy Management Editor window.

EXERCISE 2 Create a Password Settings Object

In this exercise, you create a PSO that applies a restrictive, fine-grained password policy to users in the Domain Admins group.

Before you proceed with this exercise, open Active Directory Users And Computers and confirm that the Domain Admins group is in the Users container. If it is not, move it to the Users container.

1. Open ADSI Edit from the Administrative Tools program group.

2. Right-click ADSI Edit and choose Connect To.

3. In the Name box, type **contoso.com**. Click OK.

4. Click and then expand contoso.com, and then click DC=contoso,DC=com.

5. Expand DC=contoso,DC=com and click CN=System.

6. Expand CN=System and click CN=Password Settings Container.

All PSOs are created and stored in the Password Settings Container (PSC).

7. Right-click the PSC, point to New, and then choose Object.

The Create Object dialog box prompts you to select the type of object to create. There is only one choice: msDS-PasswordSettings—the technical name for the object class referred to as a PSO.

8. Click Next.

You are prompted for the value for each attribute of a PSO. The attributes are similar to those found in the GPO you examined in Exercise 1.

9. Configure each attribute as indicated in the following list. Click Next after each attribute.

- cn: **My Domain Admins PSO**. This is the friendly name of the PSO.
- msDS-PasswordSettingsPrecedence: **1**. This PSO has the highest possible precedence because its value is the closest to 1.
- msDS-PasswordReversibleEncryptionEnabled: **False**. The password is not stored using reversible encryption.
- msDS-PasswordHistoryLength: **30**. The user cannot reuse any of the last 30 passwords.
- msDS-PasswordComplexityEnabled: **True**. Password complexity rules are enforced.
- msDS-MinimumPasswordLength: **15**. Passwords must be at least 15 characters long.
- msDS-MinimumPasswordAge: **1:00:00:00**. A user cannot change his or her password within one day of a previous change. The format is d:hh:mm:ss (days, hours, minutes, seconds).
- MaximumPasswordAge: **45:00:00:00**. The password must be changed every 45 days.
- msDS-LockoutThreshold: **5**. Five invalid logons within the time frame specified by msDS-LockoutObservationWindow (the next attribute) will result in account lockout.
- msDS-LockoutObservationWindow: **0:01:00:00**. A given number of invalid logons (specified by the previous attribute) within one hour will result in account lockout.
- msDS-LockoutDuration: **1:00:00:00**. An account, if locked out, will remain locked for one day or until it is unlocked manually. A value of zero will result in the account remaining locked out until an administrator unlocks it.

The attributes listed are required. After clicking Next on the *msDS-LockoutDuration* attribute page, you can configure optional attributes.

10. Click More Attributes.

11. In the Select A Property To View list, select msDS-PSOAppliesTo.

12. In the Edit Attributes box, type the following:

    CN=Domain Admins,CN=Users,DC=contoso,DC=com

13. Click Add, click OK, and then click Finish.

EXERCISE 3   Identify the Resultant PSO for a User

In this exercise, you identify the PSO that controls the password and lockout policies for an individual user.

1. Open the Active Directory Users And Computers snap-in.

2. Click the View menu and make sure that Advanced Features is selected.

3. Expand the contoso.com domain and click the Users container in the console tree.

4. Right-click the Administrator account and choose Properties.

5. On the Attribute Editor tab, click Filter and make sure that Constructed is selected.

   The attribute you will locate in the next step is a *constructed* attribute, meaning that the resultant PSO is not a hard-coded attribute of a user; rather, it is calculated by examining the PSOs linked to a user in real time.

6. In the Attributes list, locate *msDS-ResultantPSO*.

7. Identify the PSO that affects the user.

   The My Domain Admins PSO that you created in Exercise 2, "Create a Password Settings Object," is the resultant PSO for the Administrator account.

EXERCISE 4   Delete a PSO

In this exercise, you delete the PSO you created in Exercise 2 so that its settings do not affect you in later exercises.

1. Repeat steps 1–6 of Exercise 2 to select the Password Settings Container in ADSI Edit.

2. In the console details pane, select CN=My Domain Admins PSO.

3. Press Delete.

4. Click Yes.

Lesson Summary

- Password policy settings determine when a password can or must be changed and what the requirements of the new password are.

- Account lockout settings cause Active Directory to lock out a user account if a specified number of invalid logons occurs within a specified period of time. Lockout helps prevent intruders from repeatedly attempting to log on to a user account in an effort to guess the user's password.

- A domain can have only one set of password and lockout policies that affect all users in the domain. These policies are defined using Group Policy. You can modify the default settings in the Default Domain Policy GPO to configure the policies for your organization.

- Windows Server 2008 R2 gives you the option to specify different password and lockout policies for global security groups and users in your domain. Fine-grained password policies are deployed not with Group Policy but with password settings objects.

- If more than one PSO applies to a user or to groups to which a user belongs, a single PSO, called the resultant PSO, determines the effective password and lockout policies for the user. The PSO with the highest precedence (precedence value closest to 1) prevails. If one or more PSOs are linked directly to the user rather than indirectly to groups, group-linked PSOs are not evaluated to determine the resultant PSO, and the user-linked PSO with the highest precedence prevails.

Lesson Review

You can use the following questions to test your knowledge of the information in Lesson 1, "Configuring Password and Lockout Policies." The questions are also available on the companion CD if you prefer to review them in electronic form.

> **NOTE ANSWERS**
>
> Answers to these questions and explanations of why each answer choice is right or wrong are located in the "Answers" section at the end of the book.

1. You are an administrator at Tailspin Toys. Your Active Directory domain includes an OU called Service Accounts that contains all user accounts. Because you have configured service accounts with passwords that never expire, you want to apply a password policy that requires passwords of at least 40 characters. Which of the following steps should you perform? (Choose all that apply. Each correct answer is part of the solution.)

   A. Set the Minimum Password Length policy in the Default Domain Policy GPO.

   B. Link a PSO to the Service Accounts OU.

   C. Create a group called Service Accounts.

   D. Link a PSO to the Service Accounts group.

   E. Add all service accounts as members of the Service Accounts group.

2. You want to configure account lockout policy so that a locked account will not be unlocked automatically. Rather, you want to require an administrator to unlock the account. Which configuration change should you make?

   A. Configure the Account Lockout Duration policy setting to 100.

   B. Configure the Account Lockout Duration policy setting to 1.

   C. Configure the Account Lockout Threshold to 0.

   D. Configure the Account Lockout Duration policy setting to 0.

3. As you evaluate the password settings objects in your domain, you discover a PSO named PSO1 with a precedence value of 1 that is linked to a group named Help Desk. Another PSO, named PSO2, with a precedence value of 99, is linked to a group named Support. Mike Danseglio is a member of both the Help Desk and Support groups. You discover that two other PSOs are linked directly to Mike. PSO3 has a precedence value of 50, and PSO4 has a precedence value of 200. Which PSO is the resultant PSO for Mike?

   A. PSO1

   B. PSO2

   C. PSO3

   D. PSO4

Lesson 2: Auditing Authentication

In Chapter 7, "Managing Enterprise Security and Configuration with Group Policy Settings," you learned to configure auditing for several types of activities, including access to folders and changes to directory service objects. Windows Server 2008 R2 also allows you to audit the logon activity of users in a domain. By auditing successful logons, you can look for instances in which an account is being used at unusual times or in unexpected locations, which might indicate that an intruder is logging on to the account. Auditing failed logons can reveal attempts by intruders to compromise an account. In this lesson, you learn to configure auditing of logon authentication.

> **After this lesson, you will be able to:**
> - Configure auditing of authentication-related activity.
> - Distinguish between account logon and logon events.
> - Identify authentication-related events in the Security log.
>
> **Estimated lesson time: 30 minutes**

Account Logon and Logon Events

This lesson examines two specific policy settings: Audit Account Logon Events and Audit Logon Events. It is important that you understand the difference between these two similarly named policy settings.

When a user logs on to any computer in the domain using a domain user account, a domain controller authenticates the attempt to log on to the domain account. This generates an account logon event on the domain controller.

The computer to which the user logs on—for example, the user's laptop—generates a logon event. The computer did not authenticate the user against his or her account—it passed the account to a domain controller for validation. The computer did, however, allow the user to log on interactively to the computer. Therefore, the event is a logon event.

When the user connects to a folder on a server in the domain, that server authorizes the user for a type of logon called a *network logon*. Again, the server does not authenticate the user—it relies on the ticket given to the user by the domain controller. However, the connection by the user generates a logon event on the server.

EXAM TIP

Be certain that you can distinguish between *account logon events* and *logon events*. The simplest way to remember the difference is that an account logon event occurs where the account lives: on the domain controller that authenticates the user. A logon event occurs on the computer to which the user logs on interactively. It also occurs on the file server to which the user connects using a network logon.

Configuring Authentication-Related Audit Policies

Account logon and logon events can be audited by Windows Server 2008 R2. The settings that manage auditing are located in a GPO in the Computer Configuration\Policies\Windows Settings\Security Settings\Local Policies\Audit Policy node. The Audit Policy node and the two settings detailed in the previous section are shown in Figure 8-4.

Policy ▲	Policy Setting
Audit account logon events	Success, Failure
Audit account management	Not Defined
Audit directory service access	Not Defined
Audit logon events	Success, Failure
Audit object access	Not Defined
Audit policy change	Not Defined
Audit privilege use	Not Defined
Audit process tracking	Not Defined
Audit system events	Not Defined

FIGURE 8-4 Authentication-related policy settings

To configure an audit policy, double-click the policy, and its properties dialog box appears. The Audit Account Logon Events Properties dialog box is shown in Figure 8-5.

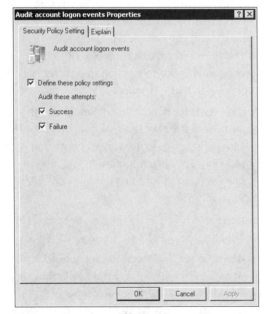

FIGURE 8-5 The Audit Account Logon Events Properties dialog box

The policy setting can be configured to one of the following four states:

- **Not defined**   If the Define These Policy Settings check box is cleared, the policy setting is not defined. In this case, the server audits events based on its default settings or on the settings specified in another GPO.

- **Defined for no auditing** If the Define These Policy Settings check box is selected, but the Success and Failure check boxes are cleared, the server will not audit these events.
- **Audit successful events** If the Define These Policy Settings check box is selected, and the Success check box is selected, the server will log successful events in its Security log.
- **Audit failed events** If the Define These Policy Settings check box is selected, and the Failure check box is selected, the server will log unsuccessful events in its Security log.

A server's audit behavior is determined by the settings that are applied as the resultant set of policy. In Windows Server 2008 R2, the default setting is to audit successful account logon events and successful logon events. So both types of events are, if successful, entered in the server's Security log. If you want to audit failures or turn off auditing, you must define the appropriate setting in the audit policy.

Scoping Audit Policies

As with all policy settings, you should scope settings so that they affect the correct systems. For example, if you want to audit attempts by users to connect to remote desktop servers in your enterprise, you can configure logon event auditing in a GPO linked to the OU that contains your remote desktop servers. If, on the other hand, you want to audit logons by users to desktops in your human resources department, you can configure logon event auditing in a GPO linked to the OU containing human resources computer objects. Remember that domain users logging on to a client computer or connecting to a server will generate a logon event—not an account logon event—on that system.

Only domain controllers generate account logon events for domain users. Remember that an account logon event occurs on the domain controller that authenticates a domain user, regardless of where that user logs on. If you want to audit logons to domain accounts, you should scope account logon event auditing to affect only domain controllers. In fact, the Default Domain Controllers GPO that is created when you install your first domain controller is an ideal GPO in which to configure account logon audit policies.

✔ **Quick Check**

- You are concerned that an intruder is attempting to gain access to your network by guessing a user's password. You want to identify the times at which the intruder is trying to log on. What type of event should you audit? Should you configure the policy setting in the Default Domain Policy or in the Default Domain Controllers Policy?

Quick Check Answer

- Enable auditing of failed account logon events (not logon events) in the Default Domain Controllers GPO. Only domain controllers generate account logon events related to the authentication of domain users. The Default Domain Controllers GPO is scoped correctly to apply only to domain controllers.

Viewing Logon Events

Account logon and logon events, if audited, appear in the Security log of the system that generated the event. Figure 8-6 shows an example. So if you are auditing logons to computers in the human resources department, the events are entered in each computer's Security log. Similarly, if you are auditing unsuccessful account logons to identify potential intrusion attempts, the events are entered in each domain controller's Security log. This means, by default, that you will need to examine the Security logs of all domain controllers to get a complete picture of account logon events in your domain.

FIGURE 8-6 Authentication events in the Security log

As you can imagine, in a complex environment with multiple domain controllers and many users, auditing account logons or logons can generate a tremendous number of events. If there are too many events, it can be difficult to identify problematic events worthy of closer investigation. You should balance the amount of logging you perform with the security requirements of your business and the resources you have available to analyze logged events.

PRACTICE **Auditing Authentication**

In this practice, you use Group Policy to enable auditing of logon activity by users in the contoso.com domain. You then generate logon events and view the resulting entries in the event logs.

EXERCISE 1 Configure Auditing of Account Logon Events

In this exercise, you modify the Default Domain Controllers Policy GPO to implement auditing of both successful and failed logons by users in the domain.

1. Open Group Policy Management from the Administrative Tools program group.
2. Expand Forest, Domains, Contoso.com, and Domain Controllers.
3. Right-click Default Domain Controllers Policy and choose Edit.

   Group Policy Management Editor appears.
4. Expand Computer Configuration, Policies, Windows Settings, Security Settings, and Local Policies, and then click Audit Policy.
5. Double-click Audit Account Logon Events.
6. Select the Define These Policy Settings check box.

7. Select both the Success and Failure check boxes. Click OK.

8. Double-click Audit Logon Events.

9. Select the Define These Policy Settings check box.

10. Select both the Success and Failure check boxes. Click OK.

11. Close Group Policy Management Editor.

12. Open Command Prompt and type **gpupdate.exe /force**.

   This command causes SERVER01 to update its policies, at which time the new auditing settings take effect.

EXERCISE 2   Generate Account Logon Events

In this exercise, you generate account logon events by logging on with both incorrect and correct passwords.

1. Log off of SERVER01.

2. Attempt to log on as Administrator with an incorrect password. Repeat this step once or twice.

3. Log on to SERVER01 with the correct password.

EXERCISE 3   Examine Account Logon Events

In this exercise, you view the events generated by the logon activities in Exercise 2.

1. Open Event Viewer from the Administrative Tools program group.

2. Expand Windows Logs, and then click Security.

3. Identify the failed and successful events.

Lesson Summary

- Account logon events occur on a domain controller as it authenticates users logging on anywhere in the domain.

- Logon events occur on systems to which users log on—for example, to their individual desktops and laptops. Logon events are also generated in response to a network logon—for example, when a user connects to a file server.

- By default, Windows Server 2008 R2 systems audit successful account logon and logon events.

- To examine account logon events in your domain, you must look at the individual event logs from each domain controller.

Lesson Review

You can use the following questions to test your knowledge of the information in Lesson 2, "Auditing Authentication." The questions are also available on the companion CD if you prefer to review them in electronic form.

1. You want to obtain a log that will help you isolate the times of day that failed logons are causing a user's account to be locked out. Which policy should you configure?

   A. Define the Audit Account Logon Events policy setting for Success events in the Default Domain Policy GPO.

   B. Define the Audit Account Logon Events policy setting for Failure events in the Default Domain Policy GPO.

   C. Define the Audit Logon Events policy setting for Success events in the Default Domain Policy GPO.

   D. Define the Audit Logon Events policy setting for Failure events in the Default Domain Policy GPO.

2. You want to keep track of when users log on to computers in the human resources department of Adventure Works. Which of the following methods will allow you to obtain this information?

   A. Configure the policy setting to audit successful account logon events in the Default Domain Controllers GPO. Examine the event log of the first domain controller you installed in the domain.

   B. Configure the policy setting to audit successful logon events in a GPO linked to the OU containing user accounts for employees in the human resources department. Examine the event logs of each computer in the human resources department.

   C. Configure the policy setting to audit successful logon events in a GPO linked to the OU containing computer accounts in the human resources department. Examine the event logs of each computer in the human resources department.

   D. Configure the policy setting to audit successful account logon events in a GPO linked to the OU containing computer accounts in the human resources department. Examine the event logs of each domain controller.

Lesson 3: Configuring Read-Only Domain Controllers

Branch offices present a unique challenge to an enterprise's IT staff: If a branch office is separated from the hub site by a wide area network (WAN) link, should you place a domain controller (DC) in the branch office? In previous versions of Windows, the answer to this question was not a simple one. Windows Server 2008, however, introduced a new type of domain controller—the read-only domain controller (RODC)—that made the question easier to answer. In this lesson, you explore the issues related to branch office authentication and domain controller placement, and you learn how to implement and support a branch-office RODC.

> **After this lesson, you will be able to:**
> - Identify the business requirements for RODCs.
> - Install an RODC.
> - Configure password replication policy.
> - Monitor the caching of credentials on an RODC.
>
> **Estimated lesson time: 60 minutes**

Authentication and Domain Controller Placement in a Branch Office

Consider a scenario in which an enterprise is characterized by a hub site and several branch offices. The branch offices connect to the hub site over WAN links that might be congested, expensive, slow, or unreliable. Users in the branch office must be authenticated by Active Directory to access resources in the domain. Should a DC be placed in the branch office?

In branch office scenarios, many of the services provided by IT are centralized in a hub site that is carefully maintained by the IT staff. In larger organizations, the hub site may include a robust datacenter. Branch offices, however, are often smaller sites at which no datacenter exists. In fact, many branch offices have no significant IT presence other than a small handful of servers. There may be no physically secure facility to house branch office servers. There may be few, if any, local IT staff to support the servers.

If a DC is not placed in the branch office, authentication and service ticket activities are directed to the hub site over the WAN link. Authentication occurs when a user first logs on to his computer in the morning. *Service tickets* are a component of the Kerberos authentication mechanism used by AD DS domains. You can think of a service ticket as a key issued by the domain controller to a user. The key allows the user to connect to a service such as the file and print services on a file server. When a user first tries to access a specific service, the user's client requests a service ticket from the domain controller. Because users typically connect to multiple services during a workday, service ticket activity happens regularly. Authentication and service ticket activity over the WAN link between a branch office and a hub site can result in slow or unreliable performance.

If a DC is placed in the branch office, authentication is much more efficient but there are several potentially significant risks. A DC maintains a copy of all attributes of all objects in its domain, including secrets such as information related to user passwords. If a DC is accessed or stolen, it becomes possible for a determined expert to identify valid user names and passwords, at which point the entire domain is compromised. At a minimum, you must reset the passwords of every user account in the domain. Because the security of servers at branch offices is often less than ideal, a branch office DC poses a considerable security risk.

A second concern is that changes to the Active Directory database on a branch office DC replicate to the hub site and to all other DCs in the environment. Therefore, corruption to the branch office DC poses a risk to the integrity of the enterprise directory service. For example, if a branch office administrator performs a restore of the DC from an outdated backup, there can be significant repercussions for the entire domain.

The third concern relates to administration. A branch office domain controller might require maintenance—for example, a new device driver. To perform maintenance on a standard domain controller, you must log on as a member of the Administrators group on the domain controller, which means you are effectively an administrator of the domain. It might not be appropriate to grant that level of capability to a support team at a branch office.

Read-Only Domain Controllers

These concerns—security, directory service integrity, and administration—left many enterprises with a difficult choice to make, and there was no best practice answer. Windows Server 2008 introduced the RODC, which is designed specifically to address the branch office scenario. An RODC is a domain controller, typically placed in the branch office, that maintains a copy of all objects in the domain and all attributes except for secrets such as password-related properties. When a user in the branch office logs on, the RODC receives the request and forwards it to a domain controller in the hub site for authentication.

You can configure a password replication policy (PRP) for the RODC that specifies user accounts the RODC is allowed to cache. If the user logging on is included in the PRP, the RODC caches that user's credentials, so the next time authentication is requested the RODC can perform the task locally. As users who are included in the PRP log on, the RODC builds its cache of credentials so that it can perform authentication locally for those users. These concepts are illustrated in Figure 8-7.

Because the RODC maintains only a subset of user credentials, if the RODC is compromised or stolen, the effect of the security exposure is limited. Only the user accounts that had been cached on the RODC must have their passwords changed. Writable domain controllers maintain a list of all cached credentials on individual RODCs. When you delete the account of the stolen or compromised RODC from Active Directory, you have the option to reset the passwords of all user accounts that were cached on the RODC. The RODC replicates changes to Active Directory from DCs in the hub site. Replication is one way, from a writable domain controller to the RODC. No changes to the RODC are replicated to any other domain controller. This eliminates the exposure of the directory service to corruption resulting from changes made to a compromised branch office DC. Finally, RODCs, unlike writable DCs, have some local groups, most notably a local Administrators group. You can give one or more local support personnel the ability to maintain an RODC fully, without granting them the equivalence of domain administrators.

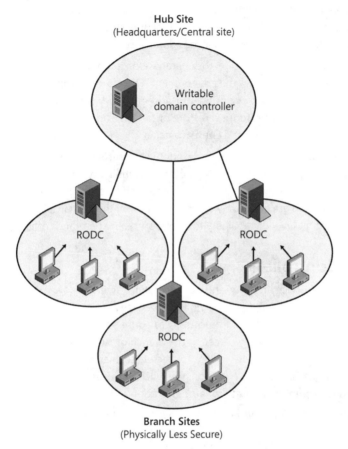

FIGURE 8-7 A branch office scenario supported by RODCs

Deploying an RODC

The high-level steps to install an RODC are as follows:

- Ensure that the forest functional level is Windows Server 2003 or higher.
- If the forest has any DCs running Microsoft Windows Server 2003, run ADPrep /RODCPrep.
- Ensure that at least one writable DC is running Windows Server 2008 or Windows Server 2008 R2.
- Install the RODC.

Each of these steps is detailed in the following sections.

Verifying and Configuring Forest Functional Level of Windows Server 2003 or Higher

Functional levels enable features unique to specific versions of Windows and are, therefore, dependent on the versions of Windows running on domain controllers. If all domain controllers are Windows Server 2003 or later, the domain functional level can be set to Windows Server 2003. If all domains are at Windows Server 2003 domain functional level, the forest functional level can be set to Windows Server 2003. Domain and forest functional levels are discussed in detail in Chapter 12.

RODCs require that the forest functional level is Windows Server 2003 or higher. That means that all domain controllers in the entire forest are running Windows Server 2003 or later.

To determine the functional level of your forest:

1. Open Active Directory Domains And Trusts.

2. In the console tree, right-click the root node, Active Directory Domains And Trusts [*Server Name*], and then click Properties..

3. Verify the forest functional level, as shown in Figure 8-8.

FIGURE 8-8 The forest Properties dialog box

Any user can verify the forest functional level in this way. No special administrative credentials are required to view the forest functional level.

If the forest functional level is not at least Windows Server 2003, examine the properties of each domain to identify any domains for which the domain functional level is not at least Windows Server 2003. If you find such a domain, you must ensure that all domain controllers in the domain are running Windows Server 2003. Then, in Active Directory Domains And Trusts, right-click the domain and choose Raise Domain Functional Level. After you have raised each domain functional level to at least Windows Server 2003, right-click the root node of the Active Directory Domains And Trusts snap-in and choose Raise Forest Functional Level. In the Select An Available Forest Functional Level drop-down list, choose Windows Server 2003 and click Raise. You must be an administrator of a domain to raise the domain's functional level. To raise the forest functional level, you must be either a member of the Domain Admins group in the forest root domain or a member of the Enterprise Admins group.

Running ADPrep /RODCPrep

If you are upgrading an existing forest to include domain controllers running Windows Server 2008 or Windows Server 2008 R2, you must run ADPrep /RODCPrep. This command configures permissions so that RODCs can replicate DNS application directory partitions. DNS application directory partitions are discussed in Chapter 9, "Integrating Domain Name System with AD DS." If you are creating a new Active Directory forest that will have only domain controllers running Windows Server 2008 or Windows Server 2008 R2, you do not need to run ADPrep /RODCPrep.

The command is found in the \support\adprep folder of the Windows Server 2008 or Windows Server 2008 R2 installation DVD. Copy the folder to the domain controller acting as the schema master. The schema master role is discussed in Chapter 10, "Administering Domain Controllers." Log on to the schema master as a member of the Enterprise Admins group, open Command Prompt, change directories to the ADPrep folder, and type **adprep /rodcprep**.

Before running ADPrep /RODCPrep, you must run ADPrep /ForestPrep and ADPrep /DomainPrep. See Chapter 10 for more information about preparing a Windows Server 2003 domain and forest for the first Windows Server 2008 or Windows Server 2008 R2 domain controller.

Placing a Writable Windows Server 2008 or Windows Server 2008 R2 Domain Controller

An RODC must replicate domain updates from a writable domain controller running Windows Server 2008 or Windows Server 2008 R2. It is critical that an RODC can establish a replication connection with a writable Windows Server 2008 or Windows Server 2008 R2 domain controller. Ideally, the writable domain controller should be in the closest site—the hub site. In Chapter 11, "Managing Sites and Active Directory Replication," you learn about Active Directory replication, sites, and site links. If you want the RODC to act as a DNS server, the writable Windows Server 2008 or Windows Server 2008 R2 domain controller must also host the DNS domain zone.

Quick Check

- Your domain consists of a central site and four branch offices. The central site has two domain controllers. Each branch office site has one domain controller. All domain controllers run Windows Server 2003. Your company decides to open a fifth branch office, and you want to configure it with a new Windows Server 2008 R2 RODC. What must you do before introducing the first RODC into your domain?

Quick Check Answer

- You must first ensure that the forest functional level is Windows Server 2003. Then you must upgrade one of the existing domain controllers to Windows Server 2008 or Windows Server 2008 R2 so that there is one writable Windows Server 2008 domain controller. You must run ADPrep /DomainPrep and ADPrep /ForestPrep to prepare the domain and forest for the first Windows 2008 or Windows Server 2008 R2 domain controller, as you will learn in Chapter 10. You must also run ADPrep /RODCPrep from the Windows Server 2008 R2 installation DVD.

Installing an RODC

After completing the preparatory steps, you can install an RODC. An RODC can be either a full or Server Core installation of Windows Server 2008 or Windows Server 2008 R2. With a full installation of Windows Server 2008 or Windows Server 2008 R2, you can use the Active Directory Domain Services Installation Wizard to create an RODC. Simply select Read-Only Domain Controller (RODC) on the Additional Domain Controller Options page of the wizard, as shown in Figure 8-9.

FIGURE 8-9 Creating an RODC with the Active Directory Domain Services Installation Wizard

Alternately, you can use the dcpromo.exe command with the */unattend* switch to create the RODC. On a Server Core installation of Windows Server 2008 or Windows Server 2008 R2, you must use the DCPromo /unattend command.

It is also possible to delegate the installation of the RODC, which allows a user who is not a domain administrator to create the RODC by adding a new server in the branch office and running Dcpromo.exe. To delegate the installation of an RODC, pre-create the computer account for the RODC in the Domain Controllers OU and specify the credentials that will be used to add the RODC to the domain. That user can then promote a server running Windows Server 2008 or Windows Server 2008 R2 as an RODC, using the prestaged RODC account. The server must be a member of a workgroup—not of the domain—when creating an RODC by using delegated installation.

Password Replication Policy

Password Replication Policy (PRP) determines which users' credentials can be cached on a specific RODC. If PRP allows an RODC to cache a user's credentials, authentication and service ticket activities of that user can be processed by the RODC. If a user's credentials cannot be cached on an RODC, authentication and service ticket activities are referred by the RODC to a writable domain controller.

An RODC's PRP is determined by two multivalued attributes of the RODC's computer account. These attributes are commonly known as the *Allowed List* and the *Denied List*. If a user's account is on the Allowed List, the user's credentials are cached. You can include groups on the Allowed List, in which case all users who belong to the group can have their credentials cached on the RODC. If the user is on both the Allowed List and the Denied List, the user's credentials will not be cached—the Denied List takes precedence.

Configuring Domain-Wide Password Replication Policy

To facilitate the management of PRP, Windows Server 2008 R2 creates two domain local security groups in the Users container of Active Directory. The first group, Allowed RODC Password Replication Group, is added to the Allowed List of each new RODC. By default, the group has no members. Therefore, by default, a new RODC will not cache any user's credentials. If you have users whose credentials you want to be cached by all domain RODCs, add those users to the Allowed RODC Password Replication Group.

The second group is named Denied RODC Password Replication Group. It is added to the Denied List of each new RODC. If you have users whose credentials you want to ensure are never cached by domain RODCs, add those users to the Denied RODC Password Replication Group. By default, this group contains groups for security-sensitive accounts including Domain Admins, Enterprise Admins, and Group Policy Creator Owners.

> **NOTE COMPUTERS ARE PEOPLE, TOO**
>
> Remember that it is not only users that generate authentication and service ticket activity. Computers in a branch office also require such activity. To improve performance of systems in a branch office, allow the branch RODC to cache appropriate computer credentials as well.

Configuring RODC-Specific Password Replication Policy

The two groups described in the previous section provide a method to manage PRP on all RODCs. However, to best support a branch office scenario, you must allow the RODC in each branch office to cache credentials of users and computers in that specific location. Therefore, you must configure the Allowed List and the Denied List of each RODC.

To configure an RODC's PRP, open the properties of the RODC's computer account in the Domain Controllers OU. On the Password Replication Policy tab, shown in Figure 8-10, you can view the current PRP settings and add or remove users or groups from the PRP.

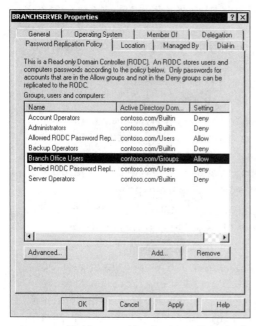

FIGURE 8-10 The Password Replication Policy tab of an RODC

Administering RODC Credentials Caching

When you click the Advanced button on the Password Replication Policy tab shown in Figure 8-10, an Advanced Password Replication Policy dialog box appears. An example is shown in Figure 8-11.

FIGURE 8-11 The Advanced Password Replication Policy dialog box

In the drop-down list at the top of the Policy Usage tab, you can select one of two reports for the RODC:

- **Accounts Whose Passwords Are Stored On This Read-Only Domain Controller** Displays the list of user and computer credentials that are currently cached on the RODC. Use this list to determine whether credentials are being cached that you do not want cached on the RODC. Then modify the PRP accordingly.

- **Accounts That Have Been Authenticated To This Read-Only Domain Controller** Displays the list of user and computer credentials that have been referred to a writable domain controller for authentication or service ticket processing. Use this list to identify users or computers that are attempting to authenticate with the RODC. If any of these accounts are not being cached, consider adding them to the PRP.

In the same dialog box, you can use the Resultant Policy tab to evaluate the effective caching policy for an individual user or computer. Click Add to select a user or computer account for evaluation.

Under normal circumstances, if a user or computer is on the Allowed List of an RODC, the account credentials can be cached on the RODC but will not be cached until the authentication or service ticket events cause the RODC to replicate the credentials from a writable domain controller. However, you can also use the Advanced Password Replication

Policy dialog box to prepopulate user and computer credentials in the RODC cache. This ensures that authentication and service ticket activity will be processed locally by the RODC even when the user or computer is authenticating for the first time. To prepopulate credentials, click Prepopulate Passwords and select the appropriate users and computers.

Administrative Role Separation

RODCs in branch offices can require maintenance such as an updated device driver. Additionally, small branch offices might combine the RODC role with the file server role on a single system, in which case it is important to be able to back up the system. RODCs support local administration through a feature called *administrative role separation*. Each RODC maintains a local database of groups for specific administrative purposes. You can add domain user accounts to these local roles to enable support of a specific RODC.

You can configure administrative role separation by using the Dsmgmt.exe command. To add a user to the Administrators role on an RODC, follow these steps:

1. Open Command Prompt on the RODC.

2. Type **dsmgmt** and press Enter.

3. Type **local roles** and press Enter.

   At the Local Roles prompt, you can type **?** and press Enter for a list of commands. You can also type **list roles** and press Enter for a list of local roles.

4. Type **add** *username* **administrators**, where *username* is the pre–Windows 2000 logon name of a domain user, and press Enter.

You can repeat this process to add other users to the various local roles on an RODC.

MORE INFO   IMPROVING AUTHENTICATION AND SECURITY

RODCs are a valuable new feature for improving authentication and security in branch offices. Be sure to read the detailed documentation at *http://technet2.microsoft.com/ windowsserver2008/en/library/ea8d253e-0646-490c-93d3-b78c5e1d9db71033.mspx*.

PRACTICE   **Configuring Read-Only Domain Controllers**

In this practice, you implement read-only domain controllers in a simulation of a branch office scenario. You install an RODC, configure password replication policy, monitor credential caching, and prepopulate credentials on the RODC. To perform this practice, you must complete the following preparatory tasks:

- Install a second server running a full installation of Windows Server 2008 R2. Name the server BRANCHSERVER. Do not join the computer to the domain. Set the server's IP configuration as follows:
  - IP Address: 10.0.0.12
  - Subnet Mask: 255.255.255.0

- Default Gateway: 10.0.0.1
- DNS Server: 10.0.0.11 (the address of SERVER01)

■ Create the following Active Directory objects:

- A global security group named Branch Office Users
- A user named James Fine, who is a member of Branch Office Users
- A user named Adam Carter, who is a member of Branch Office Users
- A user named Mike Danseglio, who is *not* a member of Branch Office Users

In this and other practices in this training kit, you will log on to the domain controller with user accounts that are not a member of Domain Administrators or the domain's Administrators group. Therefore, you must give all user accounts the right to log on locally to the domain controllers in your practice environment. Follow the steps in the article, "Grant a Member the Right to Logon Locally," at *http://technet.microsoft.com/en-us/library/ee957044(WS.10).aspx* to grant the Allow Logon Locally right to the Administrators and Domain Users groups. If you will use Remote Desktop Services to connect to the domain controller—rather than logging on locally—grant the Allow Logon Through Remote Desktop Services right. Reboot the server or otherwise refresh Group Policy. This is for the practice environment only. In a production environment, you should not grant users the right to log on to domain controllers.

EXERCISE 1   Install an RODC

In this exercise, you configure the BRANCHSERVER server as an RODC in the contoso.com domain.

1. Log on to BRANCHSERVER as Administrator.
2. Click Start, and then click Run.
3. Type **dcpromo** and click OK.

   A window appears, informing you that the Active Directory Domain Services binaries are being installed. When installation is complete, the Active Directory Domain Services Installation Wizard appears.

4. On the first page of the wizard, click Next.
5. On the Operating System Compatibility page, click Next.
6. On the Choose A Deployment Configuration page, click Existing Forest, and then click Add A Domain Controller To An Existing Domain. Click Next.
7. On the Network Credentials page, type **contoso.com**.
8. Click Set.
9. In the User Name box, type **CONTOSO\Administrator**.
10. In the Password box, type the password for the domain's Administrator account. Click OK, and then click Next.
11. On the Select A Domain page, select contoso.com and click Next.

12. On the Select A Site page, select Default-First-Site-Name and click Next.

    In a production environment, you would select the site for the branch office in which the RODC is being installed. Sites are discussed in Chapter 11.

13. On the Additional Domain Controller Options page, select Read-Only Domain Controller (RODC). Also ensure that DNS Server and Global Catalog are selected. Then click Next.

14. On the Delegation Of RODC Installation And Administration page, click Next.

15. On the Location For Database, Log Files, And SYSVOL page, click Next.

16. On the Directory Services Restore Mode Administrator Password page, type a password in the Password and Confirm Password boxes, and then click Next.

17. On the Summary page, click Next.

18. In the progress window, select the Reboot On Completion check box.

EXERCISE 2   Configure Password Replication Policy

In this exercise, you configure PRP at the domain level and for an individual RODC. PRP determines whether the credentials of a user or computer are cached on an RODC.

1. Log on to SERVER01 as Administrator.

2. Open the Active Directory Users And Computers snap-in, expand the domain, and select the Users container.

3. Examine the default membership of the Allowed RODC Password Replication Group.

4. Open the properties of the Denied RODC Password Replication Group.

5. Add the DNSAdmins group as a member of the Denied RODC Password Replication Group. Click OK to close the group Properties dialog box.

6. Select the Domain Controllers OU.

7. Open the properties of BRANCHSERVER.

8. On the Password Replication Policy tab, identify the PRP settings for the two groups: Allowed RODC Password Replication Group and Denied RODC Password Replication Group.

9. Click Add.

10. Select Allow Passwords For The Account To Replicate To This RODC and click OK.

11. In the Select Users, Computers, Or Groups dialog box, type **Branch Office Users** and click OK, and then click OK again.

EXERCISE 3   Monitor Credential Caching

In this exercise, you simulate the logon of several users to the branch office server and evaluate the credentials caching of the server.

1. Log on to BRANCHSERVER as James Fine, and then log off.

2. Log on to BRANCHSERVER as Mike Danseglio, and then log off.

3. Log on to SERVER01 as Administrator and open the Active Directory Users And Computers snap-in.

4. Open the properties of BRANCHSERVER in the Domain Controllers OU.

5. On the Password Replication Policy tab, click Advanced.

6. On the Policy Usage tab, in the Display Users And Computers That Meet The Following Criteria drop-down list, select Accounts Whose Passwords Are Stored On This Read-Only Domain Controller.

7. Locate the entry for James Fine.

   Because you had configured the PRP to allow caching of credentials for users in the Branch Office Users group, James Fine's credentials were cached when he logged on in step 1. Mike Danseglio's credentials are not cached.

8. In the drop-down list, select Accounts That Have Been Authenticated To This Read-Only Domain Controller.

9. Locate the entries for James Fine and Mike Danseglio.

10. Click Close, and then click OK.

EXERCISE 4   Prepopulate Credentials Caching

In this exercise, you prepopulate the cache of the RODC with the credentials of a user.

1. Log on to SERVER01 as Administrator and open the Active Directory Users And Computers snap-in.

2. Open the properties of BRANCHSERVER in the Domain Controllers OU.

3. On the Password Replication Policy tab, click Advanced.

4. Click Prepopulate Passwords.

5. Type **Adam Carter** and click OK.

6. Click Yes to confirm that you want to send the credentials to the RODC. A dialog box informs you that the action was successful. Click OK.

7. On the Policy Usage tab, select Accounts Whose Passwords Are Stored On This Read-Only Domain Controller.

8. Locate the entry for Adam Carter.

   Adam's credentials are now cached on the RODC.

9. Click Close, and then click OK.

Lesson Summary

- RODCs contain a read-only copy of the Active Directory database.
- An RODC replicates updates to the domain from a writable domain controller using inbound-only replication.

- Password replication policy defines whether the credentials of the user or computer are cached on an RODC. The Allowed RODC Password Replication Group and Denied RODC Password Replication Group are in the Allowed List and Denied List, respectively, in each new RODC. You can, therefore, use the two groups to manage a domain-wide password replication policy. You can further configure the individual PRP of each domain controller.

- An RODC can be supported by configuring administrator role separation to allow one or more users to perform administrative tasks without granting those users permissions to other domain controllers or to the domain. The DSMgmt command implements administrator role separation.

- An RODC requires a Windows Server 2008 or Windows Server 2008 R2 writable domain controller in the same domain. Additionally, the forest functional level must be at least Windows Server 2003, and the ADPrep /RODCPrep command must be run prior to installing the first RODC.

Lesson Review

You can use the following questions to test your knowledge of the information in Lesson 3, "Configuring Read-Only Domain Controllers." The questions are also available on the companion CD if you prefer to review them in electronic form.

> **NOTE ANSWERS**
>
> Answers to these questions and explanations of why each answer choice is right or wrong are located in the "Answers" section at the end of the book.

1. Your domain consists of five domain controllers, one of which is running Windows Server 2008 R2. All other DCs are running Windows Server 2003. What must you do before installing a read-only domain controller?

    A. Upgrade all domain controllers to Windows Server 2008.

    B. Run ADPrep /RODCPrep.

    C. Run DSMgmt.

    D. Run DCPromo /unattend.

2. During a recent burglary at a branch office of Tailspin Toys, the branch office RODC was stolen. Where can you find out which users' credentials were stored on the RODC?

    A. The Policy Usage tab

    B. The membership of the Allowed RODC Password Replication Group

    C. The membership of the Denied RODC Password Replication Group

    D. The Resultant Policy tab

3. Next week, five users are relocating to 1 of the 10 overseas branch offices of Litware, Inc. Each branch office contains an RODC. You want to ensure that when the users

log on for the first time in the branch office, they do not experience problems authenticating over the WAN link to the data center. Which steps should you perform? (Choose all that apply. Each correct answer is part of the solution.)

A. Add the five users to the Allowed RODC Password Replication Group.

B. Add the five users to the Password Replication Policy tab of the branch office RODC.

C. Add the five users to the Log On Locally security policy of the Default Domain Controllers Policy GPO.

D. Click Prepopulate Passwords.

Lesson 4: Managing Service Accounts

Services, like users, must log on. A service is configured with a user name and password of an account with which it logs on. The rights, permissions, and privileges assigned to the account allow the service to access the resources it requires. Because service account credentials are registered in the Service Control Manager (SCM) of a machine on which a service runs, managing and securing service accounts often requires that you make changes not only to Active Directory, but to the SCM of one or more machines as well.

In Lesson 1, you learned to use fine-grained password policies to configure password requirements for service accounts. Windows Server 2008 R2 introduces a new feature, *managed service accounts*, which reduces the burden of password management for service accounts.

> **After this lesson, you will be able to:**
> - Configure managed accounts.
>
> **Estimated lesson time: 30 minutes**

Understanding Managed Accounts

Services require access to resources, so they need rights, permissions, and privileges—at a minimum, the right to log on to a system. To be assigned access, a service must have an account—an identity with a user name and password—with which a system can authenticate the service when the service starts. The service is assigned the account in the SCM, which you manage by using the Services console in the Administrative Tools folder or one of several other tools, including the Sc.exe command and Windows PowerShell.

When a service runs on a single computer, an administrator can configure the service to run as Local Service, Network Service, or Local System. These three accounts are built in to Windows. They are simple to configure and use, but they are typically shared among multiple services and cannot be managed on a domain level.

You can centralize the management of service accounts by creating a domain account. After you create a domain account for a service, you can assign the account to the service on more than one system. For example, an enterprise backup service can be configured to run on multiple servers under a single domain account. You can create a unique account for each service to isolate the privileges for the services.

However, when you need to change the password of a domain service account, you must update the SCM on each computer on which the service is assigned the account. This management burden has led too many organizations to configure service accounts with non-expiring passwords, which is certainly not a security best practice. Other organizations have built or acquired custom scripts or tools to manage service account passwords in the enterprise.

Windows Server 2008 R2 reduces the management burden of service accounts with a new object class—the *managed service account*. The managed service account is a domain account that is associated with a service on a single computer, and one or more services on that computer can use the managed service account as a logon identity. The computer automatically changes the password of each managed service account on the computer, every 30 days by default.

Another burden associated with service accounts is the management of service principal names (SPNs). SPNs are a critical component of Kerberos authentication. Managed service accounts ensure that if the name of a computer is changed, SPNs associated with services running on the computer are changed in the domain. In addition, SPN management can be delegated to other administrators.

Requirements for Managed Service Accounts

Managed service accounts require minimal changes to your domain. You must prepare your schema for managed service accounts. Run **adprep /forestprep** at the forest level, and then run **adprep /domainprep** in each domain where you want to use managed service accounts. For more information about ADPrep, see Chapter 10 and visit *http://technet.microsoft.com/en-us/library/cc731728(WS.10).aspx*.

You use Windows PowerShell to administer managed service accounts. Therefore, at least one domain controller must support administration of Active Directory with Windows PowerShell by running one of the following:

- Windows Server 2008 R2
- Windows Server 2008 with the Active Directory Management Gateway Service
- Windows Server 2003 R2 with the Active Directory Management Gateway Service
- Windows Server 2003 with the Active Directory Management Gateway Service

Other domain controllers can be running Windows Server 2003 or later. If the domain functional level is Windows Server 2008 R2, you can take advantage of automatic password management of managed service accounts and simplified SPN management. If the domain functional level is lower than Windows Server 2008 R2, automatic password management of managed service accounts is available, but SPNs must be managed manually.

To create and configure managed accounts in Active Directory, you must use Windows PowerShell on a computer running Windows 7 or Windows Server 2008 R2. In other words, your administrative workstation must be running Windows 7 or Windows Server 2008 R2. You must ensure that the Active Directory Module For Windows PowerShell is installed on the computer. You can install the feature by using the Add Features link in Server Manager if the computer is running Windows Server 2008 R2, or the Turn Windows Features On Or Off link in Control Panel if the computer is running Windows 7. In Remote Server Administration Tools, Role Administration Tools, AD DS And AD LDS Tools group, you will find the Active Directory Module For Windows PowerShell feature.

Finally, each computer that uses a managed account—any computer on which services are associated with managed accounts—must be running Windows Server 2008 R2 or Windows 7 and must have the Active Directory Module For Windows PowerShell installed. Earlier versions of Windows cannot assign a managed account to a service.

Creating and Configuring a Managed Service Account

To create and configure managed service accounts in the domain, you use Windows PowerShell cmdlets. There is no UI support for correctly creating and configuring managed service accounts. The *New-ADServiceAccount* cmdlet creates a managed service account.

The following example creates a managed service account:

```
New-ADServiceAccount SRV_APP01 -Enabled $true -Path "CN=Managed Service Accounts,
    DC=contoso,DC=com"
```

The *-Path* parameter specifies the Managed Service Accounts container—a new container in Active Directory. You can specify a custom container or OU. You can also use the *-ServicePrincipalNames* parameter to specify SPNs for the account.

The *sAMAccountName* attribute of the managed service account is the name specified by the *New-ADServiceAccount* cmdlet, followed by a dollar sign ($). For example, the *sAMAccountName* of the managed service account created in the preceding example is *SRV_APP01$*.

NOTE **USE AN ACCOUNT NAME OF FEWER THAN 15 CHARACTERS**

When you create a managed service account, specify a short account name of fewer than 15 characters. The dollar sign suffix will lengthen the name; the resulting *sAMAccountName must be* 15 characters or less. Although you can create a managed service account with a longer name in Active Directory, you will be unable to install or use the managed account on a computer.

To configure properties of the account, you can use the *Set-ADServiceAccount* cmdlet or the Attribute Editor tab of the Active Directory Users And Computers snap-in. The *Get-ADServiceAccount* cmdlet returns an object reference to a managed service account. To delete a managed service account, use the *Remove-ADServiceAccount* cmdlet.

Installing and Using a Managed Service Account

The *Install-ADServiceAccount* cmdlet installs the managed service account on a computer so that you can assign the account to one or more services on the computer. For example, the following command installs the managed service account named *SRV_APP01* on the local computer:

```
Install-ADServiceAccount -Identity SRV_APP01
```

After you have installed the managed service account, you can configure a service to use the account as its logon identity. In the Services console, open the properties of a service and click the Log On tab. Select This Account, then click Browse. Type the name of the managed service account, and then click OK. On the Log On tab, confirm that the name appears with a dollar sign ($). The account will be given the Log On As Service right (*SeServiceLogonRight*).

If you move a service to another computer and you want to use the same managed service account on the target system, you must first use the *Uninstall-ADServiceAccount* cmdlet to remove the managed service account from the current computer. Then repeat the same procedures described in the previous example on the target computer: Use the *Install-ADServiceAccount* cmdlet and then configure the service to use the managed service account.

You must be a local administrator on the computer to install a managed service account and configure the logon identity of a service. You must also have rights to modify the managed service account in Active Directory to install or uninstall a managed service account on a computer.

Managing Delegation and Passwords

You can delegate permissions to configure a managed service account in Active Directory. There is no cmdlet in Windows PowerShell to do so. You must use the DSACLs command, which was introduced in Chapter 2, "Administering Active Directory Domain Services." The following command delegates to the user named *ServiceAdmin* the permissions needed to manage a service account named *SRV_APP01*.

```
dsacls "CN=SRV_APP01,CN=Managed Service Accounts,DC=contoso,DC=com"
   /G "CONTOSO\ServiceAdmin:SDRCLCRPLOCA" "CONTOSO\ServiceAdmin:WP;Logon Information"
   "CONTOSO\ServiceAdmin:WP;Description" "CONTOSO\ServiceAdmin:WP;DisplayName"
   "CONTOSO\ServiceAdmin:WP;Account Restrictions"
   "CONTOSO\ServiceAdmin:WS;Validated write to DNS host name"
   "CONTOSO\ServiceAdmin:WS;Validated write to service principal name"
```

A managed service account is a unique object class, *msDS-ManagedServiceAccount*, that inherits from the *computer* object class. Managed service accounts, like computers, do not observe domain or fine-grained password policies. Instead, like computers, a managed service account establishes a complex, cryptographically random, 240-character password and changes that password when the computer changes its password—every 30 days by default. A managed service account cannot be locked out and cannot perform interactive logons.

Under normal circumstances, you will not need to worry about changing the password of a managed service account; however, there may be scenarios in which you want to force a reset of the password. You can use the *Reset-ADServiceAccountPassword* cmdlet to do so.

Limitations of Managed Service Accounts

Managed service accounts are an important new feature of Windows Server 2008 R2, but here are some important restrictions and caveats related to their use:

- A component must support managed service accounts. Generally speaking, services that you add to a computer, and that are listed in the Services console, can be configured to use a managed service account, as can IIS application pools. You cannot use managed service accounts for identities of applications or non-Windows services. Furthermore, a component must support managed service accounts, and not all services do. For example, Microsoft SQL Server does not support managed service accounts, despite vague and contradictory information in some online resources including Microsoft TechNet. This notable exception is true for versions of SQL Server up to SQL Server 2008 R2. This limitation might be removed in future versions of SQL Server.

- Each managed service account can be used on only one computer. Services on multiple computers cannot use a single managed service account. Therefore, you cannot use managed service accounts for load balanced and clustered services. For example, you should not use managed service accounts as identities for Microsoft SharePoint Server, because a SharePoint farm can be more than one computer. Similarly, a managed service account cannot be used for a service in a cluster, because a cluster contains more than one computer.

- A computer can have more than one managed service account. For example, if you have five services running on a computer, those five services can share a single managed service account or can use five separate managed service accounts.

PRACTICE **Managing Service Accounts**

In this practice, you create a managed service account for an IIS application pool.

EXERCISE 1 **Add the Internet Information Services Role**

In this exercise, you add the Internet Information Services (IIS) role and verify that the default website is created.

1. Log on to SERVER01 as Administrator.
2. Open Server Manager.

3. In the Roles Summary section, click Add Roles.

   You might need to scroll down to see the Roles Summary section.

4. In the Add Roles Wizard, on the Before You Begin page, click Next.

5. On the Select Server Roles page, select the Web Server (IIS) check box, and then click Next.

6. On the Web Server (IIS) page, click Next.

7. On the Select Role Services page, click Next.

8. On the Confirm Installation Selections page, click Install.

   The Web Server (IIS) role and its default services are installed.

9. On the Installation Results page, click Close.

10. Open Internet Explorer.

    If the Set Up Windows Internet Explorer 8 dialog box opens, click Next. On the Turn On Suggested Sites page, click No, Don't Turn On, and then click Next. On the Choose Your Settings page, click Use Express Settings, and then click Finish.

11. Browse to http://server01.contoso.com.

    The IIS7 page opens. This is the default page of the default web application that is created when you install IIS. Leave Internet Explorer running.

EXERCISE 2   Create a Managed Service Account

In this exercise, you create a managed service account.

1. Open the Active Directory Users And Computers snap-in. Click the View menu and ensure that the Advanced Features option is selected.

2. Expand contoso.com and click the Managed Service Accounts OU. Note that the OU is currently empty.

3. Open Active Directory Module For Windows PowerShell from the Administrative Tools program group.

4. Type the following command:

   ```
   New-ADServiceAccount SRV_APP01 -Enabled $true -Path "CN=Managed Service Accounts,
       DC=contoso,DC=com"
   ```

5. Type the following command:

   ```
   Get-ADServiceAccount -Identity SRV_APP01
   ```

6. Type the following command:

   ```
   Set-ADServiceAccount -Identity SRV_APP01 -Description "Application Pool 01
       on SERVER01"
   ```

   Question: What is the value of the *sAMAccountName* attribute for this account?

   Answer: SRV_APP01$

7. Switch to Active Directory Users And Computers.

8. Click the Managed Service Accounts container and confirm that the SRV_APP01 account exists.

   You might have to refresh the view.

   Question: What is displayed in the Type column for the account?

   Answer: msDS-ManagedServiceAccount

9. Right-click SRV_APP01 and choose Properties.

10. Observe the limited number of tabs in the Properties dialog box, and then close it.

EXERCISE 3 Configure a Service to Use a Managed Service Account

In this exercise, you configure the default application pool of IIS to use the managed service account.

1. Switch to Active Directory Module For Windows PowerShell.

2. Type the following command:

   ```
   Install-ADServiceAccount -Identity SRV_APP01
   ```

3. Switch to Server Manager.

4. In the console tree, expand Roles, expand Web Server (IIS), and then click Internet Information Services (IIS) Manager.

5. In the Connections panel, expand SERVER01, and then click Application Pools.

6. In the Application Pools panel, right-click DefaultAppPool and choose Advanced Settings.

7. In the Advanced Settings dialog box, in the Process Model section, click Identity, and then click the browse button.

   The browse button is the button that appears next to the current identity. The button's label is an ellipsis (...).

8. In the Application Pool Identity dialog box, select Custom Account.

9. Click Set.

10. In the Set Credentials dialog box, type **CONTOSO\SRV_APP01$**.

11. Leave the Password and Confirm Password boxes blank.

12. Click OK to close each of the three open dialog boxes.

13. Right-click DefaultAppPool and choose Stop.

14. Switch to Internet Explorer and refresh the page, or browse back to *http://server01.contoso.com*.

   The Service Unavailable page appears. IIS cannot serve the page to the browser, because the application pool that hosts the web server process for the site is stopped.

15. Switch to Server Manager.

16. Right-click DefaultAppPool and choose Start.

17. Switch to Internet Explorer and refresh the page.

    The default IIS 7 page appears.

18. Open Task Manager.

19. On the Processes tab, click the User Name column to sort by the identity used by each process.

20. Locate the process that is running with the SRV_APP01$ identity.

    W3WP.exe is the worker process thread that is supporting the IIS site.

Lesson Summary

- You can create a managed service account in Active Directory, install the account on a computer, and then configure a service running on the computer to use the managed service account as the logon identity for the service.

- You use Windows PowerShell to create, install, and configure managed service accounts.

- A computer automatically changes the password of managed service accounts installed on the computer.

- If the domain functional level is Windows Server 2008 R2, SPNs associated with the managed service account are automatically changed if the name of the computer is changed.

Lesson Review

You can use the following questions to test your knowledge of the information in Lesson 4, "Managing Service Accounts." The questions are also available on the companion CD if you prefer to review them in electronic form.

NOTE ANSWERS

Answers to these questions and explanations of why each answer choice is right or wrong are located in the "Answers" section at the end of the book.

1. You have been asked to create a new managed account and configure a service on SERVER02 to use the account. What tools must you use? (Choose all that apply. Each correct answer is part of the solution.)

    A Active Directory Users And Computers

    B. Windows PowerShell

    C. Regedit

    D. Services.msc

2. You have been asked to create the first managed account in your domain and configure a service on SERVER02 to use the account. SERVER02 is a member server running Windows Server 2003. The domain has a mix of Windows Server 2003 and Windows Server 2008 domain controllers. Which of the following statements are true? (Choose all that apply.)

   A. You must upgrade SERVER02 to Windows Server 2008 R2.

   B. You must raise the domain functional level to Windows Server 2008 R2.

   C. You must upgrade the forest functional level to Windows Server 2008 R2.

   D. You must run adprep /forestprep.

   E. You must run adprep /domainprep.

Chapter Review

To further practice and reinforce the skills you learned in this chapter, you can perform the following tasks:

- Review the chapter summary.
- Review the list of key terms introduced in this chapter.
- Complete the case scenarios. These scenarios set up real-world situations involving the topics of this chapter and ask you to create a solution.
- Complete the suggested practices.
- Take a practice test.

Chapter Summary

- Windows Server 2008 R2 allows you to specify password and account lockout settings for the entire domain by modifying the Default Domain Policy GPO. You can then use fine-grained password and lockout policies contained in password settings objects (PSOs) to configure specific policies for groups or individual users.

- When a domain user logs on to a computer in a domain, the computer generates a logon event, and the domain generates an account logon event. These events can be audited to monitor authentication activity. By default, Windows Server 2008 R2 audits successful account logon and logon events.

- Read-only domain controllers (RODCs) provide valuable support for branch office scenarios by authenticating users in the branch office. RODCs reduce the security risk associated with placing a domain controller in a less secure site. You can configure which credentials an RODC will cache. You can also delegate administration of the RODC without granting permissions to other domain controllers or to the domain.

- A managed service account can be used as the logon identity for a service running on a computer. The computer automatically changes the password of the managed service account.

Key Terms

Use these key terms to understand better the concepts covered in this chapter.

- managed service account
- password replication policy (PRP)
- password settings object (PSO)
- read-only domain controller (RODC)
- resultant PSO

Case Scenarios

In the following case scenarios, you apply what you've learned about fine-grained password policies and RODCs. You can find answers to these questions in the "Answers" section at the end of this book.

Case Scenario 1: Increasing the Security of Administrative Accounts

You are an administrator at Contoso, Ltd., which recently won a contract to deliver an important and secret new product. The contract requires that you increase the security of your Active Directory domain. You must ensure that accounts used by domain administrators are at least 25 characters long and are changed every 30 days. You believe it would not be reasonable to enforce such strict requirements on all users, so you wish to limit the scope of the new password requirements to only domain administrators. Additionally, your contract requires that you monitor attempts by potential intruders to gain access to the network by using an administrative account.

1. Your domain currently contains four Windows Server 2003 domain controllers and eight Windows Server 2008 domain controllers. What must you do before you can implement fine-grained password policies that meet the requirements of the new contract?

2. Which tool do you use to configure fine-grained password and lockout policies?

3. You return from a vacation and discover that other administrators have created several new PSOs with precedence values ranging from 10 through 50. You want to ensure that the PSO you created for domain administrators has the highest precedence so that it always takes effect for those users. What value should you assign to the precedence of your PSO?

4. How should you configure the domain to monitor attempts by potential intruders to gain access to the network by using an administrative account? Which GPO should you modify? Which settings should you define?

Case Scenario 2: Increasing the Security and Reliability of Branch Office Authentication

You are an administrator at Contoso, Ltd. You maintain the domain's directory service on four domain controllers at a data center in your main site. The domain controllers run Windows Server 2003. Contoso has decided to open a new office overseas. Initially, the office will have 10 salespeople. You are concerned about the speed, expense, and reliability of the connection from the branch office to the data center, so you decide to place a read-only domain controller in the branch office.

1. What must you do to your existing domain controllers and to functional levels before you can install an RODC?

2. Because of customs regulations, you decide to ask one of the employees in the branch office to purchase a server locally. Can you allow the employee to create an RODC without giving the user domain administrative credentials?

3. You want the same user to be able to log on to the RODC to perform regular maintenance. Which command should you use to configure administrator role separation?

Suggested Practices

To help you successfully master the exam objectives presented in this chapter, complete the following tasks.

Configure Multiple Password Settings Objects

In this practice, you experience the effects of PSO precedence by creating several PSOs that apply to a single user and evaluating the resultant PSO for that user.

To perform this practice, create the following objects in the contoso.com domain:

- A global security group named **Human Resources**
- A global security group named **Secure Users**
- A user account named **James Fine** that is a member of both the Human Resources and Secure Users groups
- **Practice 1**   Create a PSO named **PSO1** that is linked to the Human Resources group. Give *PSO1* a precedence value of *10*. You can use any valid settings for the other attributes of the PSO. Create a second PSO named **PSO2** and give it a precedence value of *5*. You can use any valid settings for the other attributes of the PSO. Use the steps in Exercise 2, "Create a Password Settings Object," of Lesson 1 as a reference if necessary.
- **Practice 2**   Identify the PSO that affects James Fine. Use the steps in Exercise 3, "Identify the Resultant PSO for a User," of Lesson 1 as a guide to evaluating resultant PSOs. Which PSO applies to James Fine?
- **Practice 3**   Create a PSO named **PSO3** that is linked to James Fine's user account. Give *PSO3* a precedence value of *20*. You can use any valid settings for the other attributes of the PSO. Use the steps in Exercise 2 of Lesson 1 as a reference if needed. Use the steps in Exercise 3 of Lesson 1 as a guide to evaluating resultant PSO. Identify the PSO that affects James Fine.

Recover from a Stolen Read-Only Domain Controller

In this practice, you learn how to recover if an RODC is stolen or compromised, by simulating the loss of the server named BRANCHSERVER. To perform this practice, you must have completed the practice in Lesson 3, "Configuring Read-Only Domain Controllers."

When an RODC is stolen or compromised, any user credentials that had been cached on the RODC should be considered suspect and should be reset. Therefore, you must identify the credentials that had been cached on the RODC and reset the passwords of each account.

- **Practice 1** Determine the user and computer accounts that had been cached on BRANCHSERVER by examining the Policy Usage tab of the BRANCHSERVER Advanced Password Replication Policy dialog box. Use the steps in Exercise 3, "Monitor Credential Caching," of Lesson 3 if you require reminders for how to identify accounts whose passwords were stored on the RODC. Export the list to a file on your desktop.

- **Practice 2** Open the Active Directory Users And Computers snap-in and, in the Domain Controllers OU, select BRANCHSERVER. Press Delete and click Yes. Examine the options you have for automatically resetting user and computer passwords.

Take a Practice Test

The practice tests on this book's companion CD offer many options. For example, you can test yourself on just one exam objective, or you can test yourself on all the 70-640 certification exam content. You can set up the test so that it closely simulates the experience of taking a certification exam, or you can set it up in study mode so that you can look at the correct answers and explanations after you answer each question.

> **MORE INFO** **PRACTICE TESTS**
>
> For details about all the practice test options available, see the "How to Use the Practice Tests" section in this book's Introduction.

CHAPTER 9

Integrating Domain Name System with AD DS

Without the Domain Name System (DNS), using the Internet would not be easy. You could still use the Internet, because the underlying technology for the Internet is really TCP/IP, but going to *http://207.46.198.248* isn't quite like going to *http://technet .microsoft.com*, especially when you have to type the address in your browser. When you look up a new technology such as Windows Server 2008 R2 in Windows Live Search and receive a collection of IP addresses hosting information as the result of your query, it doesn't inspire confidence that these sites are safe to navigate to. IP addresses do not mean much to humans, whereas domain names do.

This is why users rely so much on DNS: it translates IP addresses into common terms or domain names that humans can relate to more easily. In fact, DNS is at the very core of the TCP/IP protocol, whether it is IPv4—the traditional, 32-bit addressing scheme—or IPv6— the new 128-bit addressing scheme built into Windows. Each time you set up a system in a network, it is identified by its IP address or addresses. In a Windows Server 2008 R2 network running Active Directory Domain Services (AD DS), each of the devices linked to the directory is also linked to the DNS name resolution system and relies on it to identify each of the services it interacts with.

For example, when you boot a computer that is part of a domain, a standard process takes place. This process begins with the identification of Service Location (SRV) records from a DNS server to identify the closest domain controller (DC). After DNS has done its work, the authentication process between the computer and the DC begins. However, without the name resolution for the SRV by DNS, it would be difficult for AD DS to authenticate a member computer.

Because it provides the translation of IP addresses to names, DNS enables programming standards through common names in applications. When programmers know they need a process that supports the discovery of a specific service, they use a common name for that service; then, when the customer implements the DNS service along with the new application, DNS renders the common name to the actual IP address assigned to the computer hosting the service.

In addition, because it is a technology designed to manage naming on the Internet, DNS is one of the technologies contained within Windows Server 2008 R2 that allows you to extend the authority of your network to the outside world. Like Active Directory Certificate Services (AD CS), Active Directory Rights Management Services (AD RMS), Active Directory Lightweight Directory Services (AD LDS), and Active Directory Federation Services (AD FS), DNS is integrated with AD DS, but it can also run independently in a perimeter network and beyond. (See Figure 9-1.) When it does so, it allows other organizations and individuals to locate you from anywhere in the world. When they find you, they can interact with you or the applications you might share with customers, partners, mobile users, and anyone else through some form of electronic communication.

FIGURE 9-1 DNS extends your organization's authority beyond the borders of your internal network

Whether it communicates on the Internet or in your internal network, DNS always relies on TCP/IP port 53. All clients and servers are tuned to this port to locate and identify information about the computer names they need to interact with.

The naming structure supported by DNS is hierarchical. Names begin with a root and extend from the root when additional tiers are added to the hierarchy. The actual root of the DNS hierarchy is the dot (.) itself. However, this dot is not used in Internet naming. Commonly, standard root names are registered on the Internet and include names such as .com, .biz., .net, .info, .name, .ms, .edu, .gov, .org, and so on. Organizations can link to the Internet through the binding of a common name with the root name. For example, Microsoft.com is two levels down from the root name but three levels down from the actual DNS root, as shown in Figure 9-2. Technet.microsoft.com is three levels down from the name but four from the DNS root, and so on. AD DS relies on this hierarchy to create the domain structure of a forest.

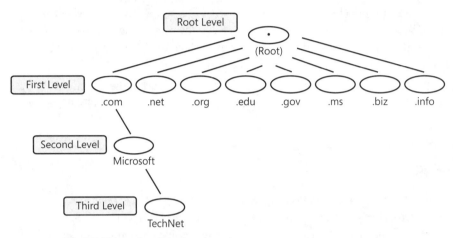

FIGURE 9-2 The DNS hierarchy of the Internet

Exam objectives in this chapter:

- Configure zones.
- Configure DNS server settings.
- Configure zone transfers and replication.

Lessons in this chapter:

Before You Begin

To complete the lessons in this chapter, you must have installed:

- Windows Server 2008 R2 on a physical or virtual computer that should be named SERVER10 and should be a stand-alone server. This computer hosts the DNS server and DC service that you install and create through the exercises in this chapter. Assign an IPv4 address from one of the private ranges, such as 192.168.x.x, and map its DNS server address to its own address.

- Windows Server 2008 R2 on a physical or virtual computer that should be named SERVER20 and should be a stand-alone server. This computer hosts the DNS server and DC service that you install and create through the exercises in this chapter. Assign an IPv4 address from one of the private ranges, such as 192.168.x.x, and map its DNS server address to the address you assigned to SERVER10.

- Windows Server 2008 R2 on a physical or virtual computer that should be named SERVER30 and should be a stand-alone server. This computer hosts the DNS server and DC service that you install and create through the exercises in this chapter. Assign an IPv4 address from one of the private ranges, such as 192.168.x.x, and map its DNS server address to the address you assigned to SERVER10.

We strongly recommend using virtual machines (VMs) in support of the exercises. The DC and DNS server roles are ideal for virtualization through Windows Server 2008 R2 Hyper-V.

 REAL WORLD

Danielle Ruest and Nelson Ruest

In late 2002, we were putting finishing touches to our second book: *Windows Server 2003, Best Practices for Enterprise Deployments* for McGraw-Hill Osborne. This book was based on our experiences with customers in designing and deploying Windows 2000–based Active Directory (AD) structures. One feature that intrigued us the most was the new application directory partition feature in Microsoft Windows Server 2003. According to the documentation provided with the beta versions, application directory partitions would be used to store DNS data within the directory and control their replication scope.

As our customers would create best-practices forests, using a forest root domain and a single, global child production domain, we discovered that when you created the forest root domain, DNS data was properly located within the forest root domain partition, but when you created a child domain, the data would not be stored automatically within the child domain partition. This caused a serious problem with DNS data. All our customers would use a two-DC forest root to keep it as secure as possible and tightly control access to forest root administration. Because of this design choice, the forest root DCs would always be located within central headquarter sites. The child production domain, however, would be highly distributed and include domain controllers within each remote site that had more than a certain number of users.

Because DNS data for the child domain was actually included in the forest root domain partition and not in the child partition, each client had to perform DNS lookups over the WAN to contact the forest root DCs. However, if DNS data was stored in the directory and made available to DCs, it should be in the local DC, not a remote DC.

We discovered that we could change the replication scope of the child domain DNS data after the directory service was deployed, but we have always been proponents of doing things right in the first place, not correcting them afterward. This meant we needed to find a way to make sure the DNS data would be stored in the proper location during installation, rather than later.

We contacted the Microsoft Active Directory development team and reported this DNS behavior as a bug, and they agreed that this should be corrected at installation, not afterward. Further research demonstrated that because a child domain namespace is an extension of the root domain's namespace, the child domain name would resolve properly during the verification checks that the Active Directory Installation Wizard performed. Because of this, the wizard would store the data within the forest root domain. In fact, the wizard was behaving properly; we just didn't give it enough information.

Further investigation revealed that if you created a manual DNS delegation before creating the child domain, the wizard would locate the data properly within the child domain partition—the manual delegation would point to a server that did not exist yet because the child domain was not created. For example, if you had a root domain named treyresearch.net and a child domain that would be named intranet.treyresearch.net, you would point the delegation to a server named *servername.intranet.treyresearch.net*. Because no server of that name existed until the child domain was actually created, the delegation would contain dummy data and would be called a dummy DNS delegation. When the wizard would run, it would find this server in DNS and try to use it to resolve the child domain's DNS name. The resolution would fail and force the wizard to install DNS during the creation of the domain and create the appropriate DNS data partition.

The Active Directory Domain Services Installation Wizard now properly creates delegations for child domains. Many AD implementations based on Windows Server 2003 did not locate DNS data in the proper partition during installation, and only IT administrators who knew how to use the dummy delegation before creating a child domain were aware of the issue. Windows Server 2008 has resolved this problem.

Lesson 1: Understanding and Installing Domain Name System

Domain name resolution is a complex process that relies on a naming hierarchy to match IP addresses, both IPv4 and IPv6, to system names. DNS name resolution also supports the identification of service locations. This is how the AD DS logon process works. In fact, DNS plays an essential role in this process and, because of this, services such as those provided by AD DS would simply not be possible without the DNS service.

To match names to IP addresses, the DNS service relies on name records. Records can be inscribed manually, such as in a primary DNS server that provides read-write services. However, writes are supported only from administrators, or they can be inscribed automatically such as with dynamic DNS servers that accept name records from devices. Smart devices such as computers running editions of Windows 2000, Windows XP, Windows 2003, Windows Vista, Windows 7, Windows Server 2008, or Windows Server 2008 R2 can register their own names within a DDNS, but devices running earlier operating systems such as Microsoft Windows NT cannot. Former devices rely on the Dynamic Host Configuration Protocol (DHCP) to perform the inscription for them; however, this is a less secure implementation of a DDNS infrastructure.

DNS contains a host of record types that can be used to provide name resolution for specific service types or specific computer types. In addition, these records are stored within DNS zones—special placeholders that provide a given name resolution functionality for a specific namespace.

Understanding the various components of the Windows Server 2008 R2 DNS service is critical to understanding how it works and how it should be used.

> **MORE INFO**   **DNS IN WINDOWS SERVER 2008 R2**
>
> For more information on DNS in Windows Server 2008 R2, go to *http://technet.microsoft* *.com/en-us/library/cc732997%28WS.10%29.aspx.*

After this lesson, you will be able to:
- Understand basic DNS concepts.
- Understand when to use DNS.
- Install DNS.
- Locate and view the DNS installation.

Estimated lesson time: 70 minutes

DNS and IPv6

In Windows Server 2008 R2, DNS has been updated to integrate with IPv6. Unlike IPv4, which is composed of four octets of binary digits to form the 32-bit IP address, IPv6 uses eight 16-bit pieces to form the 128-bit IP that is usually displayed in hexadecimal format. For example, FE80:: refers to the autogenerated link-local IPv6 address that Windows 7 or Windows Server 2008 R2 assigns to your computer if you rely on the DHCP and there is no available DHCP server to respond with an actual address. The FE80:: address is the same as the Automatic Private IP Addressing (APIPA) address that your system generates if the same thing happens with an IPv4 address allocation.

In IPv6, each time a 16-bit address piece is composed of all zeros, you can abbreviate the address and represent the all-zero pieces with two colons (::). The two colons represent any number of 16-bit sections that are composed of all zeros, as long as they are contiguous. This facilitates writing out IPv6 addresses; otherwise, IPv6 notation could become quite complex.

Like IPv4, IPv6 provides several types of addresses:

- **Link-local** Addresses that enable direct neighbors to communicate with each other. Any computer on the same network segment can communicate with any other by using this address type. This is the address type assigned by default when IPv6 is turned on but does not use a static address and cannot communicate with a dynamic address provider such as a DHCPv6 server. These addresses are similar to the 169.254.0.0/16 addresses used by the APIPA process.

- **Site-local** Addresses that support private address spaces and that you can use internally without having your own IPv6 address allocation. Site-local addresses can be routed, but should never have a routed connection to the Internet. They are similar to the 10.0.0.0/8, 172.16.0.0/12, and 192.168.0.0/16 addresses that organizations use internally with IPv4.

- **Global unicast** Addresses that are entirely unique and can be used on the Internet to identify an interface. These addresses are routable on the Internet and enable direct communication to any device. These are comparable to the public IPv4 addresses that organizations use on the Internet today.

The advantage of IPv6 is the sheer number of addresses it provides. With the world population growing rapidly, the number of services and devices requiring IP addresses increasing, and the number of IPv4 addresses dwindling, it is time for the IP infrastructure of the Internet to evolve to the next level. By providing 340 billion billion billion billion—or 2^{128} addresses—IPv6 should support the next stage of the Internet for a long time. All you have to do is compare it to the 4 billion IPv4 addresses to see the difference.

Table 9-1 lists the most common IPv6 address types.

TABLE 9-1 Common IPv6 Address Types

ADDRESS TYPE	FORMAT	DESCRIPTION
Unspecified	::	Indicates the absence of an address. Comparable to 0.0.0.0 in IPv4.
Loopback	::1	Indicates the loopback interface and enables a node to send packets to itself. Comparable to 127.0.0.1 in IPv4.
Link-local	FE80::	Local network browsing address only. Comparable to APIPA or addresses in the 169.254.0.0/16 range in IPv4. Not routable by IPv6 routers.
Site-local	FEC0::	Site-level internal address space. Routable but not to the Internet. Comparable to addresses in the 10.0.0.0/8, 172.16.0.0/12, and 192.168.0.0/16 ranges in IPv4.
Global unicast	All others	Unique addresses assigned to specific interfaces.

To comply with Internet standards and support the move to IPv6, DNS in Windows Server 2008 R2 is updated to support the longer address form of the IPv6 specification. IPv6 is installed and enabled by default in Windows 7 and Windows Server 2008 R2. This means that you can use this technology, at least internally, with little risk. It will be some time before all the elements that require an IPv6 connection to the Internet—intrusion detection systems, firewalls, anti-spam filtering, and so on—have been upgraded to support secure IPv6 transmissions.

> **MORE INFO**   **IPV6**
>
> For more information on IPv6, go to *http://www.microsoft.com/technet/network/ipv6/ ipv6rfc.mspx*.

The Peer Name Resolution Protocol

Because they fully support IPv6, Windows Server 2008 R2 and Windows 7 also include a secondary name resolution system called Peer Name Resolution Protocol (PNRP). Unlike DNS, which relies on a hierarchical naming structure, PNRP relies on peer systems to resolve the location of a computer system. Basically, PNRP is a referral system that performs lookups based on known data. For example, if you need to look up Computer A and you are near Computers B and C, your system asks Computer B if it knows Computer A. If Computer B says yes, it provides you with a link to Computer A. If not, your system asks Computer C if it knows Computer A and uses the same process as with Computer B. If neither Computer B nor Computer C knows Computer A, your system sends a request to other computers near it until it finds one that knows of Computer A.

PNRP is different from the DNS service in several ways:

- It is a distributed naming system that does not rely on a central server to locate objects. It is almost entirely serverless, but in some instances, servers are required to develop the name resolution process by themselves. Windows Server 2008 R2 includes PNRP server components as an add-on feature.

- PNRP can scale to billions of names, unlike the DNS service, which hosts only a small number of names and relies on another DNS server to locate the names over which it is not authoritative.

- Because it is distributed and relies on clients as much as servers, PNRP is fault tolerant. Several computers can host the same name, providing multiple paths to that name.

- Name publication is instantaneous, free, and does not require administrative intervention in the way DNS does.

- Names are updated in real time, unlike DNS, which relies heavily on caching to improve performance. Because of this, PNRP does not return stale addresses the way a DNS server—especially an earlier, nondynamic DNS server—can.

- PNRP supports the naming of services as well as of computers because the PNRP name includes an address, a port, and a potential payload such as a service's function.

- PNRP names can be protected through digital signatures. Protecting the names in this way ensures that they cannot be spoofed or replaced with counterfeit names by malicious users.

To provide resolution services, PNRP relies on the concept of a cloud. Two different clouds can exist. The first is the global cloud and includes the entire IPv6 global address scope, which encompasses the entire Internet. The second is a link-local cloud and is based on the link-local IPv6 address scope. Local links usually represent a single subnet. There can be several link-local clouds but only a single global cloud.

Just as the world has not fully moved to IPv6 yet, it also hasn't moved to PNRP and continues to rely on DNS to provide name resolution services. However, PNRP is an important new technology that will have a greater and greater impact on Internet operation as organizations move to IPv6.

MORE INFO **PNRP**

For more information on PNRP, go to *http://technet.microsoft.com/en-us/library/ bb726971.aspx.*

DNS Structures

DNS has been around since the Internet was first developed and has evolved with it. Because of this, the DNS service in Windows Server 2008 R2 can provide several roles. There are three possible types of DNS servers:

- **Dynamic DNS servers** Servers that are designed to accept name registrations from a wide variety of devices through dynamic updates are deemed to be dynamic DNS (DDNS) servers. DDNS is designed to enable devices—clients and servers—to self-register to the DNS server so that other devices can locate them. When the DNS service runs on a DC and is integrated with the directory service, it runs in DDNS mode, enabling computers that use DHCP to register their own names within it automatically. This enables AD DS to locate the client when it needs to send it management data such as Group Policy objects (GPOs). DDNS servers are read-write servers, but they accept registrations from known entities only.

EXAM TIP

Note that the exam refers to dynamic updates as well as Active Directory–integrated DNS zones and DDNS. Anytime a DNS server is updated automatically through authorized clients, it is a DDNS server. Keep this in mind when taking the exam.

- **Read-write DNS servers** Earlier DNS servers that are not running in dynamic mode but that will accept writes from known sources such as authorized operators are deemed read-write DNS servers. The most common type of read-write DNS server is the primary DNS server. Primary DNS servers are usually deployed in perimeter networks and are not integrated with AD DS.

- **Read-only DNS servers** DNS servers that hold a read-only copy of DNS data that originates from another location are deemed read-only DNS servers. In Windows Server 2008 R2, there are two types of read-only DNS servers. The first is the secondary DNS server. Secondary DNS servers are linked to primary DNS servers and accept and host DNS data provided by the primary parent server. They make data available locally but cannot be modified because they support only one-way replication from the primary. A second type of read-only DNS server in Windows Server 2008 R2 is the DNS server that runs on a read-only domain controller (RODC). These servers run primary read-only zones when integrated with RODCs.

By using these three types of DNS servers, you can construct a name resolution strategy that meets all your naming requirements. (See Figure 9-3.) For example, you could pair DDNS servers with every domain controller in your network because the DNS data is usually integrated with the directory store. Because it is contained in the directory store, the DNS data is replicated to every DC in a domain and sometimes in a forest through the same mechanism that replicates directory traffic. This means that each DC has a local copy of DNS data. Installing the DNS service on the DC automatically gives it access to this data and can provide local rather than remote name resolution services, avoiding wide area network (WAN) traffic. In addition, you can use the RODC DNS service in read-only mode in unsecured locations within your network, locations that warrant local services but do not have local administrative staff. You can also use the stand-alone primary DNS service in perimeter networks. These servers contain few records but support access to any application or service you host in your perimeter. Last, you could use read-only secondary DNS servers in unsecured locations facing the Internet.

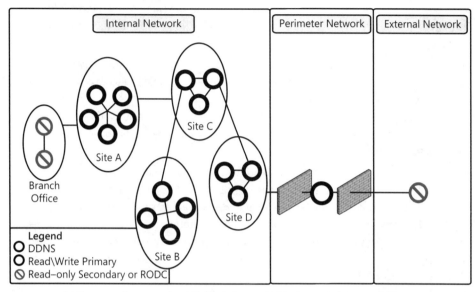

FIGURE 9-3 DNS server placement in a Windows Server 2008 R2 network: DDNS follows DCs, primaries are protected, and RODCs are internal, whereas secondaries are external

MORE INFO   DOMAIN NAME SYSTEM

For more information on DNS, go to *http://technet2.microsoft.com/windowsserver2008/en/ servermanager/dnsserver.mspx*.

The Split-Brain Syndrome

One of the most basic tenets of internetworking is the segregation of the internal network from the Internet. Small and large organizations alike endeavor to protect their internal network through a variety of systems and technology. The most common protection mechanism is the firewall, which protects your network by blocking entry of undesirable traffic through the control of TCP/IP ports. Accepted ports are open and all unacceptable ports are closed. It's as simple as that.

Similarly, when you work with Windows Server 2008 R2 and especially with AD DS, you need to work with two namespaces. Because AD DS directories are based on the DNS hierarchical naming system, you must use a properly formed DNS name, often called a fully qualified domain name (FQDN), to name your directory forests and the domains they contain. Frequently, organizations use the same name they use to represent themselves on the Internet.

For example, this book suggests names such as contoso.com or woodgrovebank.com as potential names for your internal networks. This is by no means a best practice. This book uses these names because they are legally acceptable names that Microsoft Press is allowed to use to represent fictitious organizations. However, using the same name internally for your AD DS directory structure that you use for your external exposure to the Internet means you must implement a split-brain DNS service.

That's because you need to maintain two namespaces for two purposes all across a firewall. Nothing could be more complex. Your users must be able to locate both internal and external resources that rely on the same name. If Contoso, Ltd., were a real company, and it used contoso.com for both its internal and its external namespaces, its DNS administrators would need to manage the separation manually between internal and external name resolution mechanisms.

However, if Contoso used contoso.com exclusively for its external presence and used a corresponding name with a different extension, such as .net, for its internal AD DS namespace, the DNS administrators would have to do nothing to segregate the two namespaces. The very fact that they use different roots automatically segregates the names and the two DNS services that would be used to support them. The only thing that needs to transit through the firewall is standard name references that you would normally use for any name that is not located within your network.

In addition, it is very easy for Contoso to buy and maintain all the possible combinations of its Internet name, including common roots such as .com, .net, .info, .ms, .ws, and more. This way, Contoso knows it can use any of the names it owns for any forest implementation, production, testing, development, or staging or for whichever purpose it needs it and never conflict with anyone else, even if it faces a merger or an acquisition.

Issues that commonly arise around this topic are often based on the ownership of the DNS service. Traditionally, network operators own previous DNS services and, very often, these DNS services are maintained in environments that are not Microsoft Windows–based. However, Windows and, especially, AD DS are designed to rely very tightly on the Windows DNS service. Although it is possible to use Windows with non-Windows DNS servers, it is not recommended because it requires so much more work. When you use the Windows DNS service and integrate it with your AD DS service, everything becomes automatic. When you don't, everything remains manual and, very often, you'll find that specific components don't work because the manual configuration was not completed or was misconfigured by non-Windows system administrators.

If you are in this situation and you must run two DNS technologies, the best and ideal network configuration is to use a whole-brain approach and rely on two different namespaces, integrate the internal namespace with Windows DNS servers running on DCs, and simply link the two namespaces through standard DNS resolution mechanisms. This will provide you with the implementation that requires the least amount of administrative effort and ensures that all services work at all times. (See Figure 9-4.)

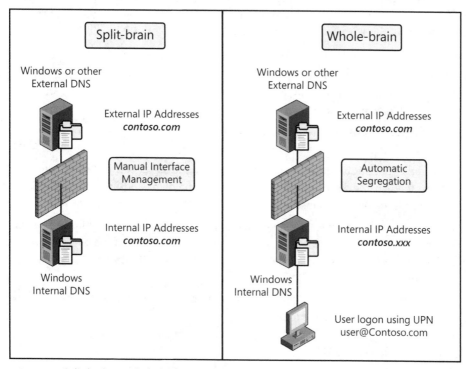

FIGURE 9-4 Split-brain vs. whole-brain DNS structures

Further, you needn't worry about users. If you are using a different namespace internally, but you want them to log on with the external network name (for example, contoso.com), just add it as the preferred user principal name (UPN) suffix in your directory. DNS will be simpler to manage, your internal network will be protected from external access, and your users won't know the difference!

MORE INFO **SPLIT-BRAIN DNS**

For more information on split-brain DNS setups, go to *http://technet.microsoft.com/en-us/library/ee382323(WS.10).aspx.*

Understanding DNS

The first thing to understand when working with DNS is how it works to resolve a name. You already know that DNS relies on a hierarchy of servers because a DNS server cannot hold all possible name records within itself. Because of this, the DNS service relies on name referrals to perform name resolution.

Here's how name resolution works. The process is illustrated in Figure 9-5:

- You try to look up a webpage on the Microsoft TechNet website. To do so, you type **http://technet.microsoft.com** in the address bar of your browser and press Enter. That's when name resolution begins.

- Your computer sends out a request to its local DNS server, or at least to one of the servers listed in its IP configuration settings for the name.

- If this server does not include the name in its own database or cache, it sends a referral request to the name server. Because the Microsoft site name ends in .com, the DNS server sends the referral to the .com name server.

- The .com name server is the authority for all names that end in the .com suffix. This server knows the location of all DNS servers that are the final authorities for a particular name ending with .com. In this case, it sends the request to the authoritative DNS server for the Microsoft.com name.

- The DNS server for Microsoft.com sends the corresponding IP address for the requested page to the client computer.

- The name resolver on the client uses the IP address to request the actual page from its Internet provider.

- If the page is not already in the local cache of the Internet provider, the provider requests the actual page and sends it to the client.

This name resolution procedure occurs within seconds, and the webpage appears almost as fast as you type it, depending on the speed of your connection and the current load of the requested server. This process is part of what is happening when the green progress bar at the bottom of your browser is advancing. The actual progress also includes downloading content such as text and graphics to your own computer.

DNS is a system that does not and cannot work alone. It must rely on other servers to operate. In addition, the DNS service includes a terminology of its own. Table 9-2 outlines the most common terms you will encounter when working with DNS.

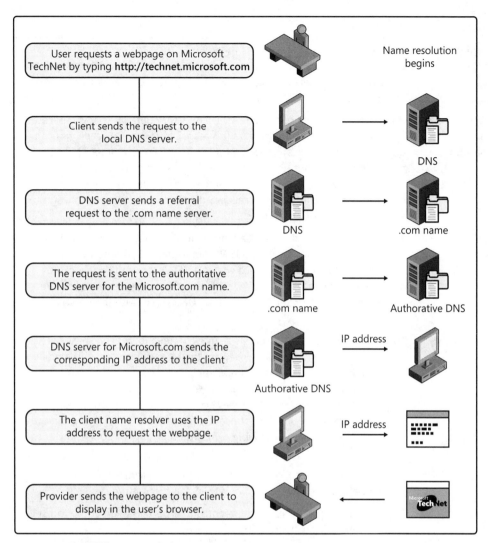

FIGURE 9-5 The DNS name resolution process

TABLE 9-2 DNS Terms and Concepts

TERM	DESCRIPTION
Active Directory Integrated (ADI) zone	When a DNS zone is integrated with Active Directory, it is hosted in the AD DS database, *NTDS.dit*, and is replicated throughout the directory with other directory data.

TERM	DESCRIPTION
Aging	DNS records are associated with an age or a Time-to-Live (TTL). When the record lasts beyond its age, it is no longer valid and can result in false positives, giving users the impression they are going to a specific location when the location is no longer valid.
Application directory partitions	When DNS data is stored within AD DS directory databases, it is replicated by default with the directory data it is associated with. However, you can define a custom replication scope for DNS data. For example, DNS data that belongs to a root domain for a forest must be made available to the entire forest, whereas DNS data for a specific domain is really required only for that domain. You control DNS data replication scopes through application directory partitions.
DDNS	This is a DNS service that can be automatically updated by the clients that rely on it. In Windows Server 2008 R2, you install DDNS whenever you choose to install the DNS service with AD DS. Because all the clients in a DDNS implementation have AD DS accounts, they are deemed secure clients and are authorized to update the DNS server with their record information.
DNS Notify	Traditional or former DNS servers manage data in local files. These files are located on the primary server. They are then transferred through a polling and zone transfer mechanism to read-only secondary servers. However, large zones often require frequent record updating. This could lead to incorrect records located within the secondary server. To correct this situation, DNS uses a special notification process that notifies dependent servers that an update is available, which then prompts a zone transfer to the read-only servers.
Domain DNS zone	This is the zone that contains the records for a particular domain, either a root or a child domain, within an AD DS forest structure.
Forest DNS zone	This is the zone that contains the records that pertain to an entire forest within an AD DS forest structure.
Forward lookup	DNS supports two types of lookups: forward and reverse. A forward lookup relies on a client providing an FQDN to the server. The server then matches this FQDN to the corresponding IP address.
Forward lookup zone	This comprises DNS containers—databases or text files—that include name resolutions for forward lookups.

TERM	DESCRIPTION
Forwarders	DNS servers have two mechanisms for name resolution: forwarders and root hints. DNS servers that provide name resolution services to the internal network often rely on forwarders to forward any request they cannot resolve on their own to a trusted external DNS server. Windows Server 2008 R2 also includes the ability to rely on conditional forwarders or forwarders that are used only when specific conditions are met in a request. For example, if the name is for an internal domain, but not one managed by this server, it can automatically forward the request to the internal name server for that domain.
Global Names Zone (GNZ)	NetBIOS names are single-label names that do not use the FQDN format. For example, down-level computer names are single-label names. Traditionally, these names are managed by Windows Internet Name Service (WINS). In an effort to remove this prior service from a Windows-based network, Microsoft has implemented the GlobalNames Zone in DNS in Windows Server 2008 R2. GNZs can contain single-label names and replace WINS in a Windows-based network.
Legacy DNS	Nondynamic DNS servers that rely on manual updating of zone records are deemed legacy DNS servers. Because it complies with the set of request for comments (RFC) that defines and standardizes the DNS protocol on the Internet, Windows Server 2008 R2 can support former DNS services as well as the dynamic DNS service required by AD DS. Legacy DNS servers host either primary or secondary zones.
Name recursion	Name resolutions can be either iterative or recursive. In an iterative request, each DNS server holds only part of the answer for a query and must rely on other DNS servers to complete the query. In a recursive query, the DNS server holds the complete answer and provides it to the requester. Because of record aging, it is possible for a recursive query to respond with an erroneous IP address.
Primary zones	These are zones that contain read-write information for a particular domain. Primary zones are stored on nondynamic or dynamic DNS servers. When stored on nondynamic DNS servers, primary zones are contained within text files and are edited manually by an administrator. When stored on DDNS servers, primary zones are contained within Active Directory and are updated either automatically by each record holder or manually by an administrator.
Resource records	These are the name records contained within DNS databases. Resource records usually link an IP address with an FQDN.
Reverse lookup	DNS supports two types of lookups: forward and reverse. A reverse lookup relies on a client providing an IP address and requesting the FQDN that corresponds to the address.

TERM	DESCRIPTION
Reverse lookup zone	This zone comprises DNS containers—databases or text files—that include name resolutions for reverse lookups for a particular domain.
Root hints	DNS servers have two mechanisms for name resolution: forwarders and root hints. DNS servers that provide name resolution services to the internal network but also have a direct connection to the Internet can rely on root hints to locate authoritative servers for root names such as .com, .org, .net, and so on on the Internet and provide resolution services to internal clients. By default, Windows Server 2008 R2 DNS servers rely on root hints for external name resolution. These hints are regularly updated through Microsoft Update. Root hints are contained within a special file named Cache.dns, which can also be used to reset root hints in the event of issues with the external name resolution process.
Round robin	DNS services can be used to provide some form of high availability. This is done by creating multiple records for the same resource, each with a different IP address. When queried, the DNS server provides the first address, then the second address, then the third, and so on, balancing the load between multiple servers that host the same service. For example, Microsoft Exchange Server 2007 Edge Transport Servers—servers that face the Internet to accept and send internal email—rely on the round robin process to provide email load balancing.
Secondary zone	A secondary zone is a read-only zone obtained from a primary DNS server. Secondary zones provide local DNS resolution in highly distributed networks.
Server scavenging	This is a feature that was introduced with the dynamic DNS service released with Windows 2000 Server. Because records have an age or time to live, they can become stale when they extend beyond their expected duration. Server scavenging scours the DNS database to locate records that have aged beyond their usefulness and automatically removes them.
Single-label names	These are NetBIOS names that do not use the FQDN format. For example, down-level computer names are single-label names. These names include 16 characters and do not support special characters such as dots. Only the first 15 characters of a single-label name can be used, because the sixteenth character is reserved by the system to complete the name. Traditionally, these names are managed by WINS. In Windows Server 2008 R2, you can rely on the GNZ in DNS to replace WINS.
Start of Authority (SOA) record	This is a special DNS record that outlines domain information such as the update schedule for the records it contains, the intervals that other DNS servers should use to verify updates, and the date and time of the last update, as well as other information such as contacts for the domain and so on. Only one SOA record can be contained within a specific zone file. Each zone file should contain a particular SOA record.

TERM	DESCRIPTION
Stub zone	This is a special zone type that contains only the records of other DNS servers that maintain the actual zone itself. This can speed name resolution and reduce the likelihood of errors because stub zones are used as referrals to other, authoritative DNS servers for a zone.
TTL	Each DNS record is given a Time-to-Live (TTL) value. This value determines the valid duration of the record. When it expires, the record can be deleted through scavenging. However, if the record is still valid before its TTL value expires, you can renew the record and, therefore, renew its TTL value.
Zone delegations	Delegations are used to help you manage different namespace sections. For example, Microsoft might want to delegate different sections of its namespace, notably the MSDN or TechNet sections of Microsoft.com, to have them administered by other divisions in the company. When managing DNS namespaces in AD DS, you must delegate new domain-based zones when you create the domain; otherwise, the zone will be managed at the forest level and not at the domain level as it should be. In Windows Server 2003, this delegation had to be created manually before creating the domain. In Windows Server 2008 R2, the Active Directory Domain Services Installation Wizard performs the delegation automatically when you create a child domain.
Zone scavenging	Scavenging scours the DNS server to remove stale or outdated records whose age has gone beyond their TTL value. Zone scavenging applies when scavenging is applied to a single zone as opposed to the entire server.
Zone transfers	These are the transactions that DNS servers use to replicate information from one server to another. Full zone transfers transfer the entire content of a zone to one or more other DNS servers. Incremental transfers send only a subset of the data. Traditionally, full transfers are referred to as Asynchronous Full Transfer (AXFR), whereas incremental transfers are dubbed Incremental Zone Transfer (IXFR). Windows Server 2008 R2 also supports secure zone transfers, which are performed through AD DS multimaster replication.

The Windows Server 2008 R2 DNS service supports three zone types, as shown in Figure 9-6:

- **Primary zones**   Zones that can be integrated with AD DS or that can be of the former, standard type. These zones are authoritative for the namespace they contain. Primary zones are read-write zones except when located on RODCs.

- **Secondary zones**   Zones that are of the former, standard type and are only a replica of the data maintained by a primary or authoritative server for a namespace. When you create a secondary zone, you must tell DNS the address of the primary zone or source of the zone data.

- **Stub Zones**   Zones that are nothing but pointers to other, authoritative servers for the namespace they maintain. Once again, when you create a stub zone, you must specify a list of servers that are authoritative for the namespace.

Each zone type can be stored either in a text file or within an Active Directory directory store partition.

FIGURE 9-6 The New Zone Wizard, which allows you to create any of the three supported zones

Zones are containers that include information about the objects they manage. This information is in the form of records. DNS can contain several types of records. Table 9-3 outlines the most common record types used in DNS in Windows Server 2008 R2.

TABLE 9-3 DNS Record Types in Windows Server 2008 R2

RECORD TYPE	USAGE
Alias (CNAME)	Used to create an alternate record or alias DNS name for a name that is already specified as another record type in a specific zone. This is also known as a canonical name (CNAME). For example, if you want to create a record such as intranet.contoso.com to point to a server or server farm hosting Microsoft Office SharePoint Server, you would create it as an alias record. This facilitates usage by providing a more functional name than the server name.

RECORD TYPE	USAGE
Host (A or AAAA) records	The most common record type in DNS. Host records represent computer objects in the namespace and are used to resolve a specific IP address to a device.
Mail exchanger (MX)	Routes email messages to a specific namespace. For example, the MX record for contoso.com would indicate that all email directed to contoso.com should pass through the host or hosts identified by this record.
Pointer (PTR)	Points to a specific location within the namespace. PTR records are usually used to provide reverse lookup capabilities within the namespace.
Service location (SRV)	Indicates the location of a specific TCP/IP service. For example, if you want to use Microsoft Office Communications Server, you must create a session initiation protocol (SIP) service location record to indicate to all the devices that rely on this service where it is situated in your network. Similarly, AD DS creates several service location records in support of the logon or the Group Policy distribution processes. Service location records usually consist of the IP address for the server and the TCP/IP port on which the service is available.

The records in Table 9-3 provide the main functionality of DNS in a Windows Server 2008 R2 implementation.

EXAM TIP

Table 9-3 lists the most common record types. However, you should review all the record types the Windows Server 2008 R2 DNS server supports in preparation for the exam.

Windows Server 2008 R2 DNS Features

The Windows Server 2008 R2 DNS server complies fully with the RFC generated by the Internet Engineering Task Force (IETF, found at *http://www.ietf.org*) for Internet technology standards, but it also includes a series of features designed to support the network operating system (NOS) features of AD DS. The DNS server in Windows Server 2008 R2 can also operate with non-Windows-based DNS servers because it complies with all the RFCs related to the DNS service.

When the DNS service is integrated with AD DS, you can store DNS data in different locations within the directory database. DNS data can be stored within the domain partition of the directory. You choose this option for data that references the domain itself. For example, a child domain within a forest would normally have its data stored within its own domain partition to make the data available to all DNS servers in the domain. You can also store data within application directory partitions. Unlike domain partitions, application directory partitions have a controllable replication scope. For example, forest DNS data is stored in an application directory partition that spans the entire forest, making this data available to any DNS server within the forest. By default, Windows Server 2008 R2 DNS creates two application directory partitions to host DNS data in each forest. These partitions are respectively named ForestDnsZones and DomainDnsZones. In addition, DomainDnsZones is created in each child domain within a forest to host data for that domain.

EXAM TIP

DNS replication scopes are a key section of the exam. Examine them in your DNS server implementations and understand the contents of each scope type.

In addition, the DNS service in Windows Server 2008 R2 has been improved to support background zone loading. When a DNS server hosts a large number of zones and records hosted in AD DS, it might take time for the server to boot because, traditionally, it needs to load all zone data before servicing requests. By using background loading, the DNS service can begin to respond to requests more quickly as it continues to load zone data in the background after the computer is started and logon is initiated.

To support the new read-only domain controller role, DNS has been updated to provide read-only DNS data for primary zones hosted on the RODC. This further secures the role and ensures that no one can create records from potentially unprotected servers to spoof the network.

EXAM TIP

Remember that DNS zones in RODCs are read-only *primary* DNS zones. Traditionally, read-only zones are secondary zones.

In an effort to support the removal of the WINS service from networks while still providing support for single-label names or names that do not include the parent name in their own name (for example, SERVER10 instead of SERVER10.Contoso.com), DNS has been updated to include a GNZ. This zone can be used to host a small number of names with static IP addresses.

EXAM TIP

Remember that you use GNZs to replace WINS implementations, but only when you have a small number of single-label names to manage. Single-label or NetBIOS names are often required for previous applications that cannot work with the more complex FQDN structure. In fact, single-label names stem from older Windows NT–based networks or applications. In most cases, organizations should have been able to deprecate these applications and remove them from their networks, but some exceptions might remain. GNZs are designed to support these few remaining applications. However, if an organization needs to run a multitude of single-label names, you will need to implement the WINS service along with DNS.

Finally, in an effort to provide further protection against spoofing, DNS now supports the addition of global query block lists. When clients use protocols such as the Web Proxy Automatic Discovery (WPAD) protocol or the Intra-site Automatic Tunnel Addressing Protocol (ISATAP) and rely on DNS to resolve host names, they can be vulnerable to malicious users who take advantage of dynamic updates to register computers that are not legitimate hosts.

WPAD is the protocol that web browsers usually rely on to discover network proxy server settings. Spoofing this address could lead users to malicious servers that impersonate legitimate proxy servers and potentially compromise a network. ISATAP is a transition protocol that enables IPv4 and IPv6 networks to work together. It does this by encapsulating IPv6 packets in IPv4 format to transmit them through routers. It does not support dynamic router discovery. Instead, it relies on a potential routers list to identify potential ISATAP routers. If this list is compromised, IPv6 packets could be routed to malicious routers and compromised in turn.

You can reduce the potential for these vulnerabilities by using global query block lists that contain specific blocked address ranges. Only the leftmost portion of an FQDN is included in global query block lists. When the DNS server receives a query that includes this name, it returns an answer as if no record existed. By default, the DNS server generates this list at installation or during an upgrade of an existing DNS service. If either of the two protocols exists, the one that exists will not be blocked. If they do not exist, they will both be blocked. In addition, you can add your own names to this list to block names that you do not want to be operational in your network.

> **MORE INFO   GLOBAL QUERY BLOCK LISTS**
>
> For more information on global query block lists, download the article titled "DNS Server Global Query Block List" from the Microsoft website at *http://download.microsoft.com/ download/5/3/c/53cdc0bf-6609-4841-a7b9-cae98cc2e4a3/DNS_Server_Global_%20Query_ Block%20List.doc.*

In short, the DNS service in Windows Server 2008 R2 provides full support for all the standard features you would expect in a DNS server but also includes custom features that are available in Windows only.

Integration with AD DS

Because of its special Windows features, always deploy the Windows DNS server when you deploy AD DS. You can rely on a third-party DNS server to provide name resolution support for AD DS also, but it is significantly more work to set up and prepare this DNS server than to use the one built into Windows. When you use the Windows DNS server with AD DS, all DNS content is configured by default. This is why DNS installation is integrated with the domain controller promotion wizard. Installing DNS with AD DS performs several tasks that are usually completely transparent to the administrator running the wizard. These operations occur only during the creation of a forest, a domain tree within an existing forest, or a new domain within an existing forest.

If the AD DS deployment is for a forest root domain, DNS creates placeholders for the forward lookup zones (FLZ), reverse lookup zones (RLZ), and conditional forwarders (CF). Then it generates two new zones within the FLZ. The first is a container for the entire forest for the namespace you created during the installation of AD DS. This zone is usually named _msdcs.*domainname*. For example, for the contoso.com domain, this zone is called _msdcs .contoso.com. In addition, it creates a zone within the FLZ for the root domain itself, as shown in Figure 9-7.

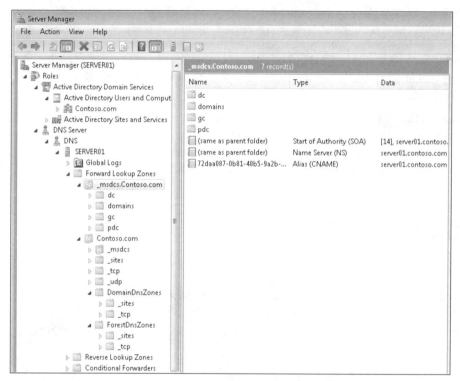

FIGURE 9-7 Forward lookup zones for the contoso.com forest

When the AD DS process creates a domain tree in an existing forest, it requires a manual delegation before the domain tree is created. Because the name of the domain tree is different from the root domain name—it must be different because that is the definition of a tree within a forest—the wizard cannot create the delegation on its own. When two DNS namespaces are different, neither has the authority to delegate information for the other, creating the need for a manual delegation. After the delegation has been created, the AD DS Installation Wizard creates the DNS namespace and stores it appropriately within the domain tree's new domain partition.

When the AD DS process creates a child domain in an existing forest, it automatically creates a delegation within the top-level root domain and then properly stores the DNS data for the child domain in the child domain's partition.

To remove a domain, you must run the Active Directory Domain Services Installation Wizard once again to remove the domain controller role, and then you can remove the AD DS role. However, because there is no interface to access the wizard, you must type **Dcpromo.exe** in the Search box of the Start menu to launch the wizard. When you remove the DC role, DNS data created for a domain is also removed if this DC is the last DC in a domain. Also, if the DC is a global catalog (GC) server, you receive a warning during the demotion because GCs support the search function in AD DS. During removal of the DC role, you are prompted to remove DNS delegations, as shown in Figure 9-8. If this is a top-level domain such as a forest or tree root domain, make sure you clear this option; otherwise, you receive an error because the wizard will ask you for credentials to delete the delegation. Because you do not have root-level credentials (for names such as .com, .net, .org, and so on), you cannot provide them and, therefore, cannot delete (or create, for that matter) root-level delegations. However, if it is a child domain, select to delete the DNS delegation and it will work properly.

FIGURE 9-8 Removing DNS delegations with the Active Directory Domain Services Installation Wizard

New DNS Features in Windows Server 2008 R2

Windows Server 2008 R2 includes several updates to DNS, including three features focused on security and one on ease of use. They include:

- DNS Security Extensions
- DNS Cache Locking
- DNS Socket Pool
- DNS Devolution

These enhancements are part of Microsoft's effort to continually improve the Windows DNS service and its integration with AD DS.

DNS Security Extensions

DNS is a critical service when it comes to the operation of a network. This is why it becomes more and more important for organizations to ensure that their DNS implementations are secure at all times. DNS does not really offer any form of security and because of this, it is vulnerable to spoofing, man-in-the-middle, and cache poisoning attacks. DNS Security Extensions (DNSSEC), defined in RFC 2535, provide additional security by supporting the cryptographic signature of a DNS zone and all of its contents. When you sign a DNS zone, its behavior changes when it receives a query. Instead of simply sending all of the records in the query, it sends the records along with their digital signatures. The DNS resolver must obtain the public key of the private/public key pair used to encrypt the records in order to resolve the records. The public key validates that the responses are authentic and have not been tampered with. Resolvers must be configured with a trust anchor or a private key for signed zones or for the parent of a signed zone to interpret signed records.

The Windows Server 2008 R2 implementation of DNSSEC supports both AD DS–integrated and file-backed zones. Signing is done offline through the dnscmd.exe tool. AD DS–integrated zones must be exported to a file before signing. In addition, DNSSEC must first be enabled in the registry before zones can be signed. Signed zones and records are replicated to other authoritative DNS servers. When configured with a trust anchor, the DNS server can validate DNSSEC responses received on behalf of DNS clients.

> **IMPORTANT** **SIGNING AD DS–INTEGRATED ZONES**
>
> AD DS-integrated zones no longer support dynamic updates after they are signed and therefore require manual updates.

DNS clients in Windows Server 2008 R2 or Windows 7 are non-validating security-aware stub resolvers; clients offload validation to a local DNS server and can then consume DNSSEC records. Query results are returned to an application only if the DNS server has successfully performed a validation of the response. DNS client behavior in regards to DNSSEC is controlled by a policy that determines whether the client should check for validation within a specific namespace.

Microsoft strongly recommends the use of Internet Protocol Security (IPSec) to secure communications between DNS clients and DNS servers in a DNSSEC implementation. This helps secure last hop communications, or direct communications between the client and its local DNS server, the last communication in a DNS request. DNSSEC also relies on Secure Sockets Layer (SSL) to ensure secure communications between the client and the server. This allows the client to verify the DNS server's certificate and prove its identity before requesting records. If a domain IPSec policy is in use, you must exclude TCP/UDP port 53 traffic (DNS traffic) from the policy, or certificate validation will not occur because the IPSec policy will be used instead.

DNS Cache Locking

DNS functionality is designed to rely on response caching to allow servers to quickly answer queries that have already been resolved once. A common attack on a DNS server is cache poisoning, or overwriting the cache with malicious records to redirect traffic to sites of the attacker's choosing. Cache locking, a new feature of DNS servers in Windows Server 2008 R2, does not allow the cache to be overwritten for the duration of the TTL value of the record. This helps protect the DNS cache from attackers.

Cache locking is configured as a percent value of the TTL. By default, the cache value is 100 percent, but because the value is stored in the CacheLockingPercent registry key in HKEY_LOCAL_MACHINE\SYSTEM\CurrentControlSet\services\DNS\Parameters settings, it can be changed to accommodate an organization's requirement. If this registry key is not present, the DNS server automatically relies on the default and retains cached records for 100 percent of their TTL. However, you should rely on the following command to modify the cache locking feature instead of editing it directly in the registry:

```
dnscmd /Config /CacheLockingPercent percentvalue
```

where *percentvalue* is the value you want to set. You must restart the DNS service after making the change.

DNS Socket Pool

Traditional DNS servers always use the same source port when resolving DNS queries. This makes it easier for attackers to poison DNS caches, because they already know which port the DNS server relies on. Windows Server 2008 R2 resolves this issue by supporting DNS Socket Pools, or pools of available sockets from which it picks a random port to perform its queries. When DNS Socket Pools are in use, attackers must both guess which port the DNS server is relying on as well as the random transaction ID for the request. This makes it more difficult for them to try poisoning the cache.

A Windows Server 2008 R2 DNS server can now use source port randomization to protect against DNS cache poisoning. The DNS Socket Pool is enabled by default. The default pool size is 2,500, but it can be configured between 0 and 10,000 sockets. Note that larger values provide more protection than smaller values. You can also configure a socket pool exclusion list in Windows Server 2008 R2. Socket pools are configured through registry keys, but like the cache locking feature, they should be configured through the following commands.

The first two provide information on the current value of the pool size or the excluded port ranges, the third configures the pool size, and the fourth configures pool exclusions.

```
dnscmd /Info /SocketPoolSize
dnscmd /Info /SocketPoolExcludedPortRanges
dnscmd /Config /SocketPoolSize value
dnscmd /Config /SocketPoolExcludedPortRanges value
```

where *value* is the value you want to set. You must restart the DNS service after the change has been made.

> **IMPORTANT   DNS SOCKET POOLS FOR OTHER VERSIONS OF WINDOWS SERVER**
>
> Older versions of Windows Server can also work with socket pools if they have Security Update MS08-037 (*http://go.microsoft.com/fwlink/?LinkID=148634*) installed. They cannot, however, support port exclusions. Port exclusions are available only in Windows Server 2008 R2.

DNS Devolution

Windows Server 2008 R2 and Windows 7 clients that are part of a child namespace— for example, a child domain within an AD DS forest—can access resources in the parent namespace without having to explicitly provide the FQDN of the resource. The DNS resolver automatically creates FQDNs by appending single-label, unqualified domain names with the parent DNS suffix name, the parent of that suffix, and so on until the request is resolved. The DNS server stops at a level determined by devolution settings or when the name is resolved. Basically, devolution is based on removing the left-most label and trying to also resolve the resulting parent suffix.

Take, for example, the primary DNS suffix of child.contoso.com. With a devolution setting of two, a query for a host name of FileServer01 automatically tries to resolve FileServer01.child.contoso.com and FileServer01.contoso.com; with a devolution setting of three, the resolver only attempts to resolve FileServer01.child.contoso.com. By default, Windows networks rely on a devolution level of two; however, in Windows Server 2008 R2 and Windows 7, administrators can configure devolution settings for their network.

Note that devolution will not work if a global suffix list is configured through Group Policy or if the Append parent suffixes of the primary DNS suffix check box is not selected in the Advanced TCP/IP Settings for the IPv4 or IPv6 properties of a network connection. Also note that DNS devolution control is available for previous versions of Windows through an update (see *http://support.microsoft.com/kb/957579*).

Devolution behavior varies with the DNS structure of a forest. For example, in a single forest root domain—a domain with a single name, such as contoso.net—devolution is not performed because there is only a single label in the DNS name. In a child domain—a domain with a forest root domain as a parent, such as child.contoso.net—devolution is automatically set at two. In a new tree—a domain with a suffix or name that is different from the forest root domain, such as treyresearch.net or lab.contoso.ms—devolution is not performed because the DNS name is not a subset of the forest root domain name.

Devolution settings are controlled through the registry. Two settings can be added to the registry:

- UseDomainNameDevolution is set to a value of 1 by default in HKEY_LOCAL_MACHINE\ SOFTWARE\Policies\Microsoft\Windows NT\DNSClient, which enables devolution. A value of 0 disables devolution.

- DomainNameDevolutionLevel can be set to values between 1 and 50 in HKEY_LOCAL_ MACHINE\SYSTEM\CurrentControlSet\Services\Dnscache\Parameters to control the devolution level in your network.

These registry keys do not exist if you are using the default DNS devolution behavior. Create these keys if you want to change the default behavior.

Devolution settings can also be controlled through Group Policy under Computer Configuration\Administrative Templates\Network\DNS Client (although they are not configured by default):

- Primary DNS Suffix Devolution
- Primary DNS Suffix Devolution Level

Note that the Group Policy will take precedence if devolution settings are configured in both the registry and in Group Policy.

> **MORE INFO** **DNS DEVOLUTION**
>
> For more information on devolution behavior in Windows Server 2008 R2 and Windows 7, go to *http://technet.microsoft.com/en-us/library/ee683928%28WS.10%29.aspx*.

EXAM TIP

Make sure you are familiar with these enhancements to DNS in Windows Server 2008 R2. They will be part of the updated exam.

 Quick Check

1. What are the most common address types in IPv6, and which type is used by default on Windows Server 2008 R2 and Windows 7 systems?

2. What is a major difference between the PNRP and DNS?

3. Which are the two types of read-only DNS servers supported by Windows Server 2008 R2?

4. What is the first step in an AD DS logon process?

5. Which type of delegations can the Active Directory Domain Services Installation Wizard automatically remove?

6. What are the new features found in DNS with Windows Server 2008 R2?

Quick Check Answers

1. The most common IPv6 address types are link-local, site-local, and global unicast. By default, Windows Server 2008 R2 and Windows 7 are designed to use dynamic IPv6 addresses. However, when no DHCPv6 servers are present in a network, IPv6 automatically assigns a link-local address to the interface.

2. One major difference between PNRP and DNS is the number of records each can contain. PNRP can scale to contain millions of name records; DNS is much more modest and relies on a hierarchy of servers to validate names.

3. The DNS server supports two read-only modes in Windows Server 2008 R2. The first is the traditional, or legacy, secondary DNS. Secondary DNS servers are subordinate to one or more primary servers and contain only a copy of the information provided to them by a read-write source. The second type of read-only server is the one included in an RODC. This DNS server, however, includes *primary* read-only zones.

4. The first step in an AD DS logon process is a DNS request sent to locate the SRV for the closest domain controller. When this record is resolved, the logon process can begin through exchanges with the domain controller.

5. The Active Directory Domain Services Installation Wizard supports the removal of any delegation you have control over. This means it will properly remove child domain delegations, but it cannot remove top-level delegations because the root servers are on the Internet, and you do not have access to these servers.

6. Windows Server 2008 R2 DNS includes four new features: support for DNSSEC, DNS Cache Locking, DNS Socket Pool, and DNS Devolution.

PRACTICE   **Installing the DNS Service**

In this practice, you install the DNS service. In the first exercise, you install the DNS service in stand-alone mode to explore how you would create a legacy primary server. Then you install AD DS and create a root domain in a new forest. This creates forest DNS zones in the DNS server. In the third exercise, you create a manual zone delegation to prepare for the integration of a new domain tree into your new forest. Then you install AD DS and create a new domain tree within the same forest as the first server. This creates tree-based zones in DNS by relying on the delegation you created. Finally, you install AD DS and create a child domain to view child domain zones in DNS. Note that in this case, the wizard properly creates the appropriate delegations for the child domain. This last exercise requires that SERVER10, SERVER20, and SERVER30 be running.

EXERCISE 1   Install a Primary DNS Server

In this exercise, you use a stand-alone computer to install the DNS service and view how it operates in nondynamic mode. This exercise is performed on SERVER10.

1.   Log on to SERVER10 with the local administrator account.

2.   In Server Manager, right-click the Roles node and click Add Roles.

3.   Review the Before You Begin page and click Next.

4.   On the Select Server Roles page of the Add Roles Wizard, select DNS Server and click Next.

5.   Review the information on the DNS Server page and click Next.

6.   Review your choices and click Install.

7.   Examine the installation results and click Close.

    Your installation is complete.

8.   Navigate to the DNS Server node in Server Manager and expand all its sections. You might need to close and reopen Server Manager to refresh the nodes.

    As you can see in Figure 9-9, the DNS installation creates all the containers required to run the DNS service in Windows Server 2008 R2, but because this is the process you would normally use to install a legacy DNS server, no information is created within the DNS container structure. Legacy DNS servers require manual input for the creation of zone information. You can automate the input process, but because Windows does not know why you want to use this DNS server, it does not create data for you.

FIGURE 9-9 Viewing the default DNS server containers

9.   Explore the DNS Server container structure before you move on to the next exercise.

EXERCISE 2   Install AD DS and Create a New Forest

In this exercise, you use a stand-alone computer to install the AD DS role and then create a new forest. After AD DS is installed, you use the Active Directory Domain Services Installation Wizard to create a root domain in a new forest.

1.   Log on to SERVER10 with the local administrator account.

2.   In Server Manager, right-click the Roles node and click Add Roles.

3.   Review the Before You Begin screen and click Next.

4. On the Select Server Roles page of the Add Roles Wizard, select Active Directory Domain Services and click Next. Add required features if they have not already been installed.

5. Review the information on the Active Directory Domain Services page and click Next.

6. Confirm your choices and click Install.

7. Examine the installation results and click Close.

   Your installation is complete.

8. Click the Active Directory Domain Services node in Server Manager.

9. Click Run The Active Directory Domain Services Installation Wizard in the details pane to launch the wizard.

10. Click Next.

11. Review the information on the Operating System Compatibility page and click Next.

12. On the Choose A Deployment Configuration page, select Create A New Domain In A New Forest and click Next.

13. On the Name The Forest Root Domain page, type **treyresearch.net** and click Next.

    You use a name with the .net extension because you do not want to use a split-brain DNS model. Trey Research uses a public name with the .com extension on the Internet but a name with the .net extension internally. Trey Research has purchased both domain names and knows that because it owns them, no one can use the names for AD DS structures. If Trey Research ever faces a merger or acquisition, it will be much easier for the company to integrate its own forest with another to streamline IT operations for the new organization.

14. On the Set Forest Functional Level page, select Windows Server 2008 R2 from the drop-down list and click Next.

15. On the Additional Domain Controller Options page, verify that DNS Server and Global Catalog are both selected and click Next. Note that the DNS Server service is already installed on this server.

16. If you did not assign a static IP address, the Active Directory Domain Services Installation Wizard gives you a warning because you are using a dynamic IP address. Click the Yes, The Computer Will Use An IP Address Automatically Assigned By A DHCP Server (Not Recommended) option.

17. The Active Directory Domain Services Installation Wizard warns you that it cannot create a delegation for this server. Click Yes.

    You get this error message for two reasons. First, because you assigned this server's own IP address as the DNS server in its network configuration, you cannot reach a proper DNS server to create the delegation. Second, even if you could reach a proper DNS server, you are using a name based on a top-level root name (.net), and you would not have the authorization to create the delegation in the server hosting root addresses for that extension.

18. On the Location For Database, Log Files And SYSVOL page, accept the default locations and click Next.

19. On the Directory Services Restore Mode Administrator Password page, type a strong password, confirm it, and click Next.

20. Confirm your settings on the Summary page and click Next.

21. Select the Reboot On Completion check box and wait for the operation to complete.

22. After the computer has rebooted, log on with the newly created domain credentials (TreyResearch\Administrator) and navigate to the DNS Server node in Server Manager.

Review the changes that the AD DS setup created within the forward lookup zones of this new forest. Note that DNS data is divided into two sections, one that affects the entire forest and another that affects only the root domain, as shown in Figure 9-10.

FIGURE 9-10 Active Directory Domain Services entries for a new forest

EXERCISE 3 Create a Manual Zone Delegation

In this exercise, performed on SERVER10, you use the newly created domain controller for the treyresearch.net domain to create a manual DNS zone delegation. This delegation will be used in Exercise 4, "Install AD DS and Create a New Domain Tree," to load DNS data for a domain tree. It will not contain any data when you create it and will point to a nonexistent server—a server that is not yet created; this is called a dummy DNS delegation. Also, because a domain tree uses a different DNS name than the forest, you must create a new FLZ for the tree; otherwise, you would not be able to use the new name in the delegation.

1. Log on to SERVER10 with the domain administrator account.

2. In Server Manager, expand the DNS Server node, expand the DNS node, and then expand the Server10 node. Click the Forward Lookup Zones node.

3. Right-click Forward Lookup Zones and click New Zone.

   This launches the New Zone Wizard.

4. Click Next.

5. On the Zone Type page, select Primary Zone and make sure that the Store The Zone In Active Directory check box is selected. Click Next.

   You must create a new zone to host the delegation because if you tried to store the delegation in an existing zone, it would automatically add the name suffix for the existing zone. Because a domain tree is distinguished from the forest namespace by its name suffix, you must create a new zone to host it.

6. On the Active Directory Zone Replication Scope page, select To All DNS Servers In This Domain: Treyresearch.net and click Next. This places the DNS data in the DomainDnsZones application directory partition for the treyresearch.net domain.

7. On the Zone Name page, type **northwindtraders.com** and click Next.

   Trey Research has decided to expand its operations and create a new division focused on new sportswear related to Trey's latest discoveries and inventions. Because of this, they need to create a new domain tree in their existing forest.

> **IMPORTANT**   **USING NAME EXTENSIONS OTHER THAN .COM**
>
> You would normally use a name extension other than .com to protect your internal network from possible name conflicts and to avoid the split-brain syndrome, but using a .com extension is valid for the purposes of this exercise.

8. On the Dynamic Update page, select Allow Only Secure Dynamic Updates (Recommended For Active Directory) and click Next.

   Dynamic updates are not really required for this zone because it will host a delegation only, but using this setting allows for eventual growth if the Trey Research strategy for this domain changes in the future.

9. Click Finish to create the zone.

10. Navigate to the northwindtraders.com zone in Server Manager and select it.

    The DNS server is peculiar in that it does not provide you with context menu options until you have selected the item first. You need to select the item with the left mouse button, and then you can use the right mouse button to view the context menu.

11. Right-click the northwindtraders.com zone and click New Delegation.

    This launches the New Delegation Wizard.

12. Click Next.

13. On the Delegated Domain Name page, type **SERVER20**, which should list SERVER20. northwindtraders.com as the FQDN, and click Next.

14. On the Name Servers page, click Add and type the FQDN of the server you will create for this zone, **SERVER20.northwindtraders.com**. In the IP Addresses Of This NS Record section of the dialog box, click <Click Here To Add An IP Address>, and then type the IP address you assigned to SERVER20. Click OK.

15. Click Next, and then click Finish to create the delegation.

> **IMPORTANT** **ADD NAME SERVERS TO A DELEGATION**
>
> In a production environment, you should have at least two or more name servers for this delegation. In this exercise, one is enough, but when you create any AD DS domain, always create at least two DCs. You should, therefore, return to this delegation after the second server is created and add it to the delegation to provide fault tolerance for it.

EXERCISE 4 Install AD DS and Create a New Domain Tree

In this exercise, you use a stand-alone computer to install the AD DS role and then create a new domain tree in an existing forest. This exercise is performed on SERVER20, but SERVER10 must also be running. After AD DS is installed, you use the Active Directory Domain Services Installation Wizard to create a new domain tree in an existing forest.

1. Log on to SERVER20 with the local administrator account.

2. In Server Manager, right-click the Roles node and click Add Roles.

3. Review the Before You Begin screen and click Next.

4. On the Select Server Roles page of the Add Roles Wizard, select Active Directory Domain Services and click Next. Add required features if they have not already been installed.

5. Review the information on the Active Directory Domain Services page and click Next.

6. Confirm your choices and click Install.

7. Examine the installation results and click Close.

   Your installation is complete.

8. Click the Active Directory Domain Services node in Server Manager.

9. Click Run The Active Directory Domain Services Installation Wizard in the details pane.

10. In the Active Directory Domain Services Installation Wizard, select the Use Advanced Mode Installation check box, and then click Next.

    This option enables you to create a new domain tree.

11. Review the information on the Operating System Compatibility page and click Next.

12. On the Choose A Deployment Configuration page, select Existing Forest, select Create A New Domain In An Existing Forest, select the Create A New Domain Tree Root Instead Of A New Child Domain check box, and click Next.

13. On the Network Credentials page, type **treyresearch.net**, and then click Set to enter alternate credentials. Type **Administrator** or the equivalent account name and the password. Click OK, and then click Next.

14. On the Name The New Domain Tree Root page, type **northwindtraders.com** and click Next.

15. On the Domain NetBIOS Name page, accept the proposed name and click Next.

    This page appears because you are running the wizard in advanced mode. Note that the name does not include the final *s* because it is limited to 15 characters. The sixteenth is always reserved by the system.

16. On the Select A Site page, accept the default and click Next. This page also appears because you are running the wizard in advanced mode.

17. On the Additional Domain Controller Options page, verify that the DNS Server check box is selected. Select the Global Catalog check box, and then click Next.

    Note that one authoritative DNS server has been found for this domain. This is the server in your delegation and the server you are now creating.

18. If you did not assign a static IP address, the Active Directory Domain Services Installation Wizard gives you a warning because you are using a dynamic IP address. Click the Yes, The Computer Will Use An IP Address Automatically Assigned By A DHCP Server (Not Recommended) option.

    The AD DS Installation Wizard warns you that it has detected an existing DNS infrastructure for this domain and, because of this, you now have two choices: to attempt to create a DNS delegation or to omit it. See Figure 9-11.

FIGURE 9-11 The Create DNS Delegation page

19. Select No, Do Not Create The DNS Delegation and click Next.

    You select No because you already created the delegation manually. The wizard cannot create this delegation because it would attempt to create it in a .com root name DNS server, and you do not have access rights to this server.

20. On the Source Domain Controller page, verify that Let The Wizard Choose An Appropriate Domain Controller is selected, and click Next.

21. On the Location For Database, Log Files And SYSVOL page, accept the default locations and click Next.

22. On the Directory Services Restore Mode Administrator Password page, type a strong password, confirm it, and click Next.

23. Confirm your settings on the Summary page and click Next. Select the Reboot On Completion check box and wait for the operation to complete.

24. After the computer has rebooted, log on with the new domain credentials (NorthwindTraders\Administrator or equivalent) and navigate to the DNS Server node in Server Manager. Review the changes that the AD DS setup created within the FLZs of this new domain tree. Note that DNS data includes a container for this tree only and not for the domain. (See Figure 9-12.)

    Any child domains created under this tree root would also create delegations of their own and would be listed in this zone.

FIGURE 9-12 Active Directory Domain Services entries for a new domain tree in an existing forest

EXERCISE 5   Install AD DS and Create a Child Domain

In this exercise, you use a stand-alone computer to install the AD DS role and then create a new child domain. This exercise is performed on SERVER30. Make sure both SERVER10 and SERVER20 are also running. After AD DS is installed, you use the Active Directory Domain Services Installation Wizard to create a child domain in the Trey Research forest.

1. Log on to SERVER30 with the local administrator account.

2. In Server Manager, right-click the Roles node and click Add Roles.

3. Review the Before You Begin screen and click Next.

4. On the Select Server Roles page of the Add Roles Wizard, select Active Directory Domain Services and click Next. Add required features if they have not already been installed.

5. Review the information on the AD DS page and click Next.

6. Confirm your choices and click Install.

7. Examine the installation results and click Close.

   Your installation is complete.

8. Click the Active Directory Domain Services node in Server Manager.

9. Click Run The Active Directory Domain Services Installation Wizard in the details pane to launch the wizard.

10. Click Next.

11. Review the information on the Operating System Compatibility page and click Next.

12. On the Choose A Deployment Configuration page, choose Existing Forest and Create A New Domain In An Existing Forest and click Next.

13. On the Network Credentials page, type **treyresearch.net** and click Set to add proper credentials.

14. In the Network Credentials dialog box, type **Administrator** or equivalent, type the password, click OK, and click Next.

15. On the Name The New Domain page, type **treyresearch.net** as the FQDN of the parent domain, type **intranet** in the single label of the child domain field, and click Next.

    The complete FQDN should be intranet.treyresearch.net.

    When you create a global child production domain, you name it with an appropriate name such as Intranet. This provides a clear demarcation for users and clearly shows that they are in an internal, protected network.

16. On the Select A Site page, use the default settings and click Next.

17. On the Additional Domain Controller Options page, verify that the DNS Server check box is selected and select the Global Catalog check box. Click Next.

    Note that there are no authoritative DNS servers for this domain name.

    If you did not assign a static IP address, the Active Directory Domain Services Installation Wizard gives you a warning because you are using a dynamic IP address. Click the Yes, The Computer Will Use An IP Address Automatically Assigned By A DHCP Server (Not Recommended) option.

18. On the Location For Database, Log Files And SYSVOL page, accept the default locations and click Next.

19. On the Directory Services Restore Mode Administrator Password page, type a strong password, confirm it, and click Next.

20. Confirm your settings on the Summary page and click Next.

    Note that in this case, the wizard creates a DNS delegation for this domain. (See Figure 9-13.) This is because the parent domain is authoritative for the treyresearch.net zone and can, therefore, create a proper delegation for the child domain.

FIGURE 9-13 The Active Directory Domain Services Installation Summary page

21. Select the Reboot On Completion check box and wait for the operation to complete.

22. After the computer has rebooted, log on with the newly created domain credentials (Intranet\Administrator or equivalent) and navigate to the DNS Server node in Server Manager.

23. Review the changes that the AD DS setup created within the FLZs of this new domain. Note that DNS data is in only one section that affects this particular domain, as shown in Figure 9-14. Also, if you return to SERVER10, you will see that a new DNS delegation (a gray icon instead of yellow) has been created for this child domain in the treyresearch.net FLZ.

FIGURE 9-14 Active Directory Domain Services entries for a new child domain in an existing forest

Lesson Summary

- DNS is a name resolution system that relies on a hierarchical naming structure to map IP addresses to FQDNs, which are in the *object.namespace.rootname* format.

- AD DS also relies on a hierarchical structure. In fact, the AD DS forest structure is based entirely on the hierarchical structure found in DNS.

- Because Windows Server 2008 R2 has been updated to support IPv6, and IPv6 is installed by default with link-local addresses, the DNS server in Windows Server 2008 R2 provides support for the longer 128-bit address format used by IPv6.

- DNS Server can host three types of zones. Primary zones are read-write zones that contain data in support of name resolution for a given namespace. Secondary zones are read-only zones that contain a copy of a primary zone. Stub zones are pointers to other DNS servers and contain only the authoritative servers for the namespace they point to. Each zone type can be integrated with AD DS to be stored in the directory database.

Lesson Review

You can use the following questions to test your knowledge of the information in Lesson 1, "Understanding and Installing Domain Name System." The questions are also available on the companion CD if you prefer to review them in electronic form.

> **NOTE** ANSWERS
>
> Answers to these questions and explanations of why each answer choice is right or wrong are located in the "Answers" section at the end of the book.

1. You are an administrator for Contoso, Ltd. Your organization has decided to move to Windows Server 2008 R2 and, because of your past experience, you have decided to create a new server implementation instead of upgrading your existing infrastructure. After the new infrastructure has been created, you will move all data—accounts, directory settings, and more—to the new forest that you will implement with Windows Server 2008 R2. You have been asked to create the initial forest structure. This forest includes a root domain, a global child production domain, and a domain tree. The forest is named with a .net extension, and the domain tree uses a .ms extension to differentiate it from the production forest. You successfully create the forest root domain and the child domain, but when you come to the domain tree, you find that you cannot locate the domain tree option. What could be the problem?

    A. You cannot create a domain tree with the Active Directory Domain Services Installation Wizard. You must use the command-line *Dcpromo.exe* command to do so.

    B. You are not logged on with the appropriate credentials.

    C. You must return to the Welcome page of the wizard to select the Advanced mode of the wizard.

    D. The server you are using is not a member of the forest root domain.

2. You are an administrator for Contoso, Ltd. Your organization has decided to move to Windows Server 2008 R2 and, because of your past experience, you have decided to create a new server implementation instead of upgrading your existing infrastructure. After the new infrastructure has been created, you will move all data—accounts, directory settings, and more—to the new forest that you will implement with Windows Server 2008 R2. You have been asked to create the initial forest structure. This forest includes a root domain, a global child production domain, and a domain tree. The forest is named with a .net extension, and the domain tree uses a .ms extension to differentiate it from the production forest. You successfully create the forest root domain and the child domain, but when you come to the domain tree, you find that you cannot create the delegation, no matter which options you try or which credentials you provide. What could be the problem? (Each correct answer presents a complete solution. Choose all that apply.)

    A. You must select the advanced mode of the wizard to create the delegation.

    B. You must create a manual delegation before creating the domain tree.

    C. You must tell the wizard to create the delegation during the creation of the domain tree and provide appropriate credentials.

    D. You must tell the wizard to omit the creation of the delegation during the creation of the domain tree.

    E. You must create the delegation manually after the domain tree has been created.

Lesson 2: Configuring and Using Domain Name System

When you install the DNS Server role with AD DS, there is little configuration to be done. FLZs are created automatically; replication is configured automatically because it rides on the AD DS multimaster replication system, and you don't even need to add records because all computer systems running Windows 2000 or later can register and update their own records in the dynamic DNS AD DS requires.

However, some operations are not performed automatically. For example, the DNS server configuration does not, by default, include RLZs. It is a good idea to add them to support reverse lookups. In addition, the DNS server needs configuration finalization. For example, you must set it to support record scavenging to automatically delete outdated records.

It is also a very good idea to review all the DNS server content to become familiar with it and ensure that all data and values correspond to your actual requirements.

After this lesson, you will be able to:

- Finalize the configuration of your DNS servers.
- Administer DNS servers and DNS replication.

Estimated lesson time: 40 minutes

Configuring DNS

The DNS configuration involves several activities. These include:

- Considering the security of your DNS servers to reduce their attack surface.
- Configuring scavenging settings for the server as a whole.
- Finalizing the configuration of your FLZs.
- Creating RLZs.
- Adding custom records to FLZs for specific services and resources.

It is also a good idea to make sure your DNS replication is working properly.

Security Considerations for the DNS Server Role

DNS servers that are exposed to the Internet are notorious targets for malicious users. The most common attack is a denial-of-service (DoS) attack that floods the DNS service with so many requests that the service cannot respond to valid requests. Another common attack form occurs when an attacker tries to obtain all the data contained within a DNS server, intending to use it to identify the object a network contains. This is called *footprinting the network*. Two more attack types attempt to modify data within the DNS server or redirect user queries from a valid DNS server to another DNS server that would be under the control of the attacker. The latter usually occurs through the modification of DNS data contained within the DNS cache. Remember that DNS uses in-memory caching to increase the speed of responses to queries. When this data is corrupted, users can receive invalid responses to their queries.

This is why it is important to apply common security measures to your DNS installations. When you use a whole-brain approach to DNS configuration and you rely on DNS integration with AD DS in your internal network, your internal DNS servers are much less prone to attack because they do not share a namespace with the outside world and are, therefore, protected by firewalls, which do not allow external users to access your internal DNS servers. This does not mean that internal servers do not need protection. Anytime an untrusted user can connect to your network either through wired connections or through wireless access, your infrastructure is at risk. This is why extensive screening is a good practice whenever you allow someone you are not familiar with to connect to your network. Being inside the firewall does not necessarily mean being protected.

Consider a different security approach with internal vs. external DNS servers. When servers are in an external or perimeter network, they should be highly secured. One good protection method is to use a secondary or subordinate server only whenever the server is exposed to the outside world. Then you configure the zone updates to occur only from known sources that are included within DNS itself.

In internal networks, tie the DNS Server role to the DC role and ensure that they support secure dynamic updates only. This helps protect them from obtaining or transmitting erroneous data. Verify DNS data on a regular basis to validate it, and monitor your DNS event logs to identify potential security issues quickly if they arise.

EXAM TIP

The exam focuses on DNS usage with AD DS. Be sure you fully understand DDNS and AD DS integration. DDNS and AD DS are most often used internally. If you find that you need to configure an external DNS server, you can read more about DNS security at *http://technet.microsoft.com/en-us/library/cc783606(WS.10).aspx*.

Working with DNS Server Settings

DNS stores name records for a specific period of time. Each name record is assigned a TTL value. When this value expires, the record should be removed to avoid providing false positive results to users performing lookups on the name. Fortunately, the DNS server in Windows Server 2008 R2 can perform this task automatically through server or zone scavenging. When applied to the server, scavenging cleans all active zones on the server. When applied to a particular zone, only the records for the zone are scavenged.

CONFIGURING SCAVENGING FOR ALL ZONES

To set scavenging for an entire server, you must assign the setting through the server's action menu:

1. Right-click the server name in the DNS node of Server Manager and click Set Aging/Scavenging For All Zones.

2. Select the Scavenge Stale Resource Records check box to enable the feature.

   No-Refresh Interval refers to the time between the most recent refresh of a record stamp and the moment when the system allows the timestamp to be refreshed again. Refresh Interval refers to the earliest moment when a record may be updated or when it may be scavenged if no updates have been applied. The default value of seven days is sufficient for most networks.

3. Leave the default values as is and click OK.

4. Because you set the values for existing zones, DNS also allows you to set it for any future zone you create, including Active Directory–integrated zones. Select the Apply These Settings To The Existing Active Directory-Integrated Zones check box and click OK.

Your DNS zones are set to remove stale records. Make sure you apply these settings to every DNS server in your network. Make this part of your default configuration for DNS servers. If you need to modify the setting for a single zone, you must use the Properties dialog box for that zone. Zone scavenging is performed on the General tab by clicking Aging.

You'll note that in the server's context menu, you can also manually initiate scavenging by choosing Scavenge Stale Resource Records. You use this operation if you discover that your servers are sending out stale data.

If you do discover that records are stale, you can also use the Clear Cache command from the same context menu. Because the DNS server relies heavily on the in-memory cache to improve performance, you might have scavenged records from the database but find they are still in the cache, which might still be providing false positives.

FINALIZING FLZ CONFIGURATION

When you examine the Properties dialog box for an FLZ, you'll find that there are several options you can set for each zone. Make a point of reviewing these options, and configure the following settings for each production DNS zone as a best practice:

- On the General tab, make sure each internal DNS zone is Active Directory–Integrated, uses the proper replication scope, and supports Secure Only dynamic updates. Set the scope by clicking Change next to the Replication field. Select an option in the Change Zone Replication Scope dialog box (shown here) as follows:

  - Domain-based DNS zones should replicate to all DNS servers in the domain. Each DC that also hosts the DNS role will include the zone.

  - Forest DNS zones should replicate to all DNS servers in the forest.

- If you maintain Windows 2000 Server DCs in your network, you must use the To All Domain Controllers In This Domain (For Windows 2000 Compatibility) option, because Windows 2000 Server does not support application directory partitions.

- You can also set replication to custom application directory partitions, but you must create the partition first.

- On the Name Servers tab, ensure that each DNS zone includes at least two name servers. Just as you would create at least two DCs for each domain, create two DNS servers for each zone as a best practice.

- On the WINS tab, assign WINS lookups only if you cannot use GNZs and you must deploy WINS. This lesson discusses single-label name management in a later section.

- On the Zone Transfers tab, set the name servers to which you allow this zone to be transferred upon request. If this zone is integrated with Active Directory, zone transfers are not required. This tab is mostly used for previous DNS server installations.

- On the Security tab, review the default security settings. These settings use the appropriate configuration for most networks, but in highly secure implementations they might need to be revised and modified.

- The final tab is the Start Of Authority (SOA) tab, shown in the following figure. SOA records identify the zone and its related information such as owner, operator, update schedules, and so on. These records include the following information:
  - Serial Number, which is assigned when your zone is created. You can increment the serial number if you need to change its value.
  - Primary Server, the master server for this zone. This is usually the server where the zone was first created.
  - Responsible Person, which should list the operator name for this server. Normally, this is a standard term such as Hostmaster or Operations. By default, Windows Server 2008 R2 assigns hostmaster.*dnszonename*, where *dnszonename* is the FQDN of the zone. Responsible Person entries are based on Responsible Person records. These records are not created by default. Create a proper Responsible Person

record for each zone or, at the very least, for each master DNS server and assign it to this value.

- Various intervals and time-based settings for the record. These include the Refresh Interval, the Retry Interval, the Expires After setting, and the Minimum (Default) TTL for the record. Default values are acceptable for most record types.

- TTL For This Record. This is assigned to the same value as the Minimum (Default) TTL value listed above it in the dialog box.

Finalize these settings for each zone you manage on your DNS servers.

CREATING A RESPONSIBLE PERSON RECORD

As mentioned earlier, each zone should be assigned a Responsible Person (RP) as a best practice. This means that you need at least one RP record in your DNS configuration. Use the context menu for the zone in which you want to host this record to create the record. Remember, you need the following items for the creation of this record:

- **A common group name** This name will be displayed in the record.

- **A group mailbox in the directory** It is best to use a group mailbox to make sure the messages sent to this address are treated in a timely fashion.

- **A text record** The text record can indicate information about your organization and its DNS management policies.

Use the following procedure to create the RP record. Begin with the Text Record.

1. Right-click the zone name and click Other New Records.

2. In the Select A Resource Record Type list, scroll down to select Text (TXT) and click Create Record.

3. In the New Resource Record dialog box, type the name of the record, such as **Disclaimer**. In the Text box, type your message and click OK to return to the Resource Record Type dialog box.

   Your message should include information about you and your DNS management practices. You might consider preparing the message in a word processor and then pasting it in this dialog box, because the text box does not offer proofing capabilities.

4. In the Select A Resource Record Type list, scroll up to select Responsible Person (RP), and then click Create Record.

5. In the New Resource Record dialog box, type the name of the record in the Host Or Domain text box (for example, **Operations**), and then click Browse next to the Mailbox field to locate the mailbox of the responsible person. You can also type the email address if you know it.

6. Click Browse next to the Optional Associated Text (TXT) Record field to locate your newly created text record. Navigate to the zone you are working with to locate the text record, select it, and click OK.

7. Click OK to create the record. Click Done to close the Resource Record Type dialog box.

8. Return to the zone Properties dialog box, or double-click the Start Of Authority record to assign the RP record to the SOA record.

Perform these operations for each zone you manage. It is always better to configure the zone completely than to have to figure out what to do if issues arise and nothing is configured.

Creating Reverse Lookup Zones

Small networks with few computers (fewer than 500, for example) might not require RLZs. RLZs provide resolution from an IP address to a name instead of a name to an IP address and are most often used by applications. For example, a secure web application might use a reverse lookup to verify that the computer it is communicating with is actually the right computer and not an impersonating computer. If you do not have any such application in your network, you can safely do without RLZs.

However, clients that have the ability to update their own DNS records dynamically will also create a PTR record—a reverse record that maps the IP address to the name—and try to store it within the RLZ that corresponds to the FLZ in which their name record is located. If there is no RLZ, these records will never be generated.

> **MORE INFO** **HOW DYNAMIC UPDATES WORK**
>
> For more information on dynamic updates and how they work, go to *http://technet.microsoft.com/en-us/library/cc753014.aspx*.

If you need RLZs, create them for the corresponding FLZs. Create a zone for each named FLZ. In an Active Directory–integrated DNS implementation, you would create an RLZ for each domain DNS zone. In a multidomain forest, this would include the root domain, any child domain, and any domain trees. Use the following procedure:

1. Navigate to the Reverse Lookup Zone section of the DNS node in Server Manager.

2. Right-click Reverse Lookup Zone and click New Zone.

3. Review the information on the Welcome page and click Next.

4. Select Primary Zone, make sure the Store The Zone In Active Directory check box is selected, and click Next.

5. Because RLZs are tied to a specific domain name, select To All DNS Servers In This Domain and click Next.

6. On the Reverse Lookup Zone Name page, select either IPv4 or IPv6 and click Next.

   Remember that reverse lookups map an IP address to a name. You need to create an RLZ for the type of IP addressing you are using in the network. If you are using both IPv6 and IPv4, you must create two zones.

   You generate the zone name on the next page. This page differs, depending on the IP version you are using.

   If you are using IPv4, type the network ID for the zone. Note that as you type the network address, the name is automatically generated in the lower part of the page under Reverse Lookup Zone Name.

   If you are using IPv6, you can add up to eight zones at a time. Remember that IPv6 addresses use hexadecimal format. For example, if you are using link-local addresses in your network, you might type **fe80::/64** as the address scope. This automatically generates the zone name in the Reverse Lookup Zones section of the page. If one zone is all you need, you can move on from this page.

Click Next.

7. On the next page, select which type of dynamic update you want to allow. In most cases, you should select Allow Only Secure Dynamic Updates. Click Next, and then click Finish to create the zone.

After the zones are created, they will begin supporting record hosting when the next dynamic update refresh occurs on your client systems.

EXAM TIP

Practice working with zones and zone properties, because they are an important part of the exam.

 Quick Check

1. Why should you configure scavenging and aging on a DNS server?

2. When should you create reverse lookup zones?

Quick Check Answers

1. Every DNS name record is assigned a TTL value when created. This value determines when the information in the record is no longer valid. If the record is not renewed, it becomes stale. Aging and scavenging on the DNS server automatically removes stale records to limit the possibility of false positives when users request data from the DNS server.

2. Reverse lookup zones are mostly useful for secure web applications, which must validate the IP address provided by the systems with which they communicate. If a network does not include any such application, reverse lookup zones are not required.

Creating Custom Records

The last step in a DNS server configuration is the creation of custom records for the FLZs. Custom records are created manually and provide a variety of services in your network. For example, you might need to create the following:

- An MX record to point to your email servers.

- An alias record, such as intranet.*domainname,* to point to an Office SharePoint Server server farm to support collaboration in your network.

- SRV records for various services in your network. For example, you must create SIP records for Microsoft Office Communication Server deployments.

Time will tell which custom records you need. In an internal network, manually created records should be infrequent because of the dynamic update process initiated by client systems.

EXAM TIP

Practice record creation, because it is also an important topic on the exam.

Forwarders vs. Root Hints

Name resolution is performed by two main methods. DNS servers either contain root hints that enable them to identify and locate authoritative DNS servers for root names or rely on forwarders to link them to another server that performs the lookup for them.

By default, Windows DNS Server relies on root hints to perform lookups. This means that if your users need to perform a lookup on the Internet, your DNS servers communicate with the name servers. In smaller organizations, this is quite acceptable, because even if your DNS servers expose themselves by communicating directly with the Internet, they are the ones who initiate the communication. External systems reply to the initiated communication only and cannot initiate the communication themselves.

However, in highly secure networks, you might prefer to rely on forwarders instead of root hints. For example, you might place two stand-alone DNS servers in your perimeter network and link the internal DNS servers to these servers through forwarders. Each time the internal servers need to resolve an Internet name, they link to one of the servers in the perimeter and ask it to perform the lookup for them. This way, the only servers to communicate outside the network are the more secure stand-alone servers in the perimeter.

Forwarders are configured as part of the properties of the DNS server and are accessed from the Forwarders tab in the DNS server Properties dialog box, shown in Figure 9-15. If you are configuring forwarders for security purposes, make sure you clear the Use Root Hints check box if no forwarders are available; otherwise, your internal DNS servers will communicate directly with the Internet if your servers in the perimeter do not respond.

FIGURE 9-15 Configuring forwarders in DNS

You can also use conditional forwarders in your DNS configuration. Conditional forwarders are used to forward DN requests when specific conditions are met. For example, if you want to link two namespaces but only when users request a particular name, you would use conditional forwarders.

For example, consider the following scenario. Your network includes two forests. The first is the production forest, the one that contains all the accounts that users use to work together in your organization. The second is a special forest that was created to test the AD DS integration of third-party applications with the AD DS forest schema before they are deployed in your production forest. Because of the schema changes, you do not want to link your forests together through a forest trust. Therefore, you create conditional forwarders in each forest so that users in the production domain, mostly developers and IT professionals, can link from the production domain to the staging domain.

Conditional forwarders include their own container in DNS Server. To create a new conditional forwarder:

1. Right-click the Conditional Forwarders node and click New Conditional Forwarder. The following dialog box appears.

2. Type the name of the DNS domain that you want to forward to.

3. Click <Click Here To Add An IP Address Or DNS Name> and type the server's IP address.

4. Add at least two servers to the list.

5. As a best practice, store the conditional forwarder in Active Directory and determine which replication scope to apply to the forwarder. Click OK.

In the preceding example, you would replicate the data only to the production domain because you do not need to replicate it to the entire forest. In other cases, you might need to replicate it to the entire forest.

Note that when you create a conditional forwarder, it creates a new container for the domain you will forward to under the Conditional Forwarders node. From now on, each time your users request a name resolution that contains this domain name, your DNS servers will automatically forward it to the DNS servers that you provided in the list.

Single-Label Name Management

When you want to manage single-label names, you must create a GNZ manually. A single GNZ is required for each forest. The basic process of creating a GNZ requires five steps, but it involves an operation on each DNS server in the forest. If you are using AD DS–integrated DNS servers and each of your DCs is also running the DNS service, you must perform this operation on each DC. This means using domain administrator credentials to complete the operation.

- Create the GlobalNames FLZ.
- Set its replication scope to all DNS servers in the forest.
- Do not enable dynamic updates for this zone.
- Enable GNZ support on each DNS server in the forest.
- Add single-label names to the DNS zone.

Configuration is performed through the command line because there is no graphical user interface to access this feature. You can create the GNZ through Server Manager, but enabling GNZ support in a DNS server requires a modification of the Windows Registry. This modification is performed with the Dnscmd.exe command and uses the following format:

```
dnscmd /config /enableglobalnamessupport 1
```

This command must be run on each DNS server in the forest. If you need to support single-label names and you do not want to use WINS, you might want to make this command part of your standard DNS server installation and configuration process. You need to restart the DNS service after the command has been run.

After you have enabled GNZ support, you can begin to add records. GNZ names are aliases because each object in your network already has a host name in DNS. You create an alias and point it to the corresponding FQDN for the object. GNZ aliases, like WINS names, cannot have more than 15 characters—they actually use 16 characters, but the system reserves the last character. If you want to create the names through a command file, use the following command format for each name:

```
dnscmd dnsservername /recordadd globalnames singlelabelname
   cname correspondingdnsname
```

where *dnsservername* is the name of the DNS server that you are adding the name to, *singlelabelname* is the 15-character name you want to add, and *correspondingdnsname* is the FQDN of the object whose GNZ name you are adding.

> **MORE INFO**   **GLOBALNAMES ZONES**
>
> For more information on GNZs, get the "DNS Server GlobalNames Zone Deployment" document from *http://download.microsoft.com/download/e/2/0/e2090852-3b7f-40a3-9883-07a427af1560/dns-globalnames-zone-deployment.doc*.

DNS and WINS

If your network requires a multitude of single-label names, and you cannot provide support for them through a GNZ because there are simply too many names to manage, install the WINS service on at least two servers in your network. WINS automatically generates and manages names for each object in the network. Remember that WINS services are a feature of Windows Server 2008 R2, not a role, and that WINS is an outdated technology that has not been updated since the original release of Windows Server 2003.

If you do deploy WINS, remember that:

- WINS does not appear in Server Manager. To administer WINS, you must use the WINS console in the Administrative Tools program group.
- WINS supports IPv4 addresses only and will not be updated to support IPv6.
- You need at least two WINS servers to provide fault tolerance for single-label names in your network. These two servers should be configured to use push/pull synchronization to make sure that both name databases are synchronized at all times.

- You must ensure that the values for WINS are specified in the DHCP settings that you send to computers requiring dynamic IPv4 addresses. Two settings are required. The first lists the name servers, and the second identifies which type of node each client will work with:
  - 044 WINS/NBNS Servers identifies which servers host the WINS service.
  - 046 WINS/NBT Node Type identifies how nodes interact with WINS. The most commonly used node type is 0x8, or the Hybrid node type. This minimizes the amount of broadcasting required in single-label name networks.
- You can also integrate WINS and DNS by modifying the properties of an FLZ. The Properties dialog box includes a WINS tab, shown in Figure 9-16, that is unused unless you have WINS servers in your network. This feature is useful in networks in which many clients rely on WINS and it is possible that some of the client device names will not be present in DNS. However, all Windows operating systems since Windows 2000 can participate in a dynamic DNS infrastructure. Networks that include clients running operating systems earlier than Windows 2000 are becoming very rare.

FIGURE 9-16 Linking DNS with WINS to provide both FQDN and single-label name resolution

DNS and DHCP Considerations

When you work with dynamic DNS and you integrate the DNS service with the AD DS directory store, you must change the traditional approach that network administrators use to configure DHCP settings provided to each client device that relies on dynamic IP addresses, whether they are IPv4 or IPv6.

Traditionally, network administrators provide as few as two central DNS servers in the server options of the DHCP settings. This provides all client devices with the DNS addresses they need to resolve both internal and external FQDNs, but because the servers are centrally located, any client in a remote site would need to perform a DNS lookup over the WAN.

However, with the integration of DNS, and especially DNS data with the directory store, DNS data is now available wherever there is a DC and, to provide authentication services wherever clients are located, DCs are distributed throughout a network. In fact, some organizations have DCs available wherever there are at least 20 clients. With the advent of server virtualization through Hyper-V, as well as DC hardening through the RODC, DCs can be even more prevalent in networks. This means that DNS data, even read-only DNS data, is available in each remote site or branch office. Clients can use servers in their local site to perform FQDN lookups.

However, for clients to perform the lookup locally, they must know about the presence of local DNS servers. Imagine the following scenario:

- A client in a remote site uses a dynamic IP address allocated through DHCP.
- There are two DCs in the remote site.
- DNS is integrated with the directory and is replicated with the domain partition.
- DHCP sends out values for only two DNS servers in a central site.
- When the client boots in the morning, it performs a DNS lookup to locate its closest DC to log on.
- The DNS lookup occurs over the WAN to request the name resolution from one of the two central DCs.
- The central DNS servers look up the client's site and find that there are two local DCs to support logon.
- The DNS server returns the location of the closest DC to the client, once again over the WAN.
- The client contacts its local DC to log on.

In this scenario, the client cannot log on if there is no WAN connectivity, even though the DNS data is stored locally within the two DCs!

Because of this, DHCP options must be modified as follows:

- For redundancy, the server scope should continue to provide at least two addresses for centrally located DNS servers. If the local DC is down, clients can still log on, albeit over the WAN.
- Each individual address scope should include options for name resolution servers, and these records should point to the DCs that are local to the site the scope is assigned to. This means adding the *006 DNS Servers* value to each individual scope in DHCP.

- All DCs should also be running the DNS Server role. That's all you have to do. If a DNS zone is stored in the AD DS directory store, it will be made available to the DNS service as soon as you install the DNS Server role on the DC. There is nothing more to configure except global DNS server settings.

Keep this in mind when planning to integrate DNS with DHCP.

Working with Application Directory Partitions

In certain circumstances, you will want to create custom application directory partitions in support of DNS data replication. Remember that application directory partitions control the replication scope of the data they contain. The DNS server creates two application directory partitions when it is installed with AD DS in a forest (one for forest data and one for domain data in each domain), but under certain conditions, these two scopes might not be appropriate, especially in complex forests.

Consider this scenario. Your forest includes three domains: the forest root, a global child production domain, and a development domain. You created the development domain because your developers have special access right requirements, and you do not want to grant them these access rights in the production domain. All production domain users except system administrators have standard user access rights. In the development domain, however, you can grant developers higher access rights—rights to create, modify, or delete objects— because this domain does not affect production operations.

In addition, you created only a single account for each developer. This account is located in the global child production domain and has standard user rights, but through the transitive trusts inherent in each forest, developers can use their accounts from the production domain to access objects in the development domain where their production domain accounts have higher access rights.

By default, name resolution between the two child domains passes through the forest root domain. Developers access this domain on a constant basis every day, so to provide them with faster name resolution, you create a custom application directory partition to share the DNS records between the development and production domains. This means that because the data is available in the partition, production DNS servers do not need to pass through the forest root domain to resolve development domain names. (See Figure 9-17.)

Creating and Assigning Custom Application Directory Partitions

Custom application directory partitions are created through the command line with the Dnscmd.exe command. There is no interface for creating these partitions. However, after they are created, the partitions can be assigned through the graphical user interface. You can perform each operation through the command line if you prefer. You must perform three tasks:

- Create the partition.
- Enlist DNS servers into the partition.
- Assign the zones whose replication scope you want to change to the newly created partition.

FIGURE 9-17 Relying on custom application directory partitions to share DNS data between two child domains

To create an application directory partition, you must be a member of the Enterprise Admins groups because you must have full access to the forest.

1. Log on to a DNS server with an account that is a member of the Enterprise Admins group for the forest.

2. Launch an elevated command prompt through the context menu and the Run As Administrator command.

3. Type the following command:

   dnscmd *dnsservername* /createdirectorypartition *partitionfqdn*

   where the *dnsservername* is the FQDN of your DNS server or its IP address and *partitionfqdn* is the FQDN of the partition you want to create.

   For example, if you want to create a new partition on SERVER10 and name it partition01.treyresearch.net, you would use the following command:

   dnscmd server10.treyresearch.net /createdirectorypartition
       partition01.treyresearch.net

4. Enlist the server into the partition. Once again, you use the Dnscmd.exe command. Type the following command:

   dnscmd *dnsservername* /enlistdirectorypartition *partitionfqdn*

   Repeat this command for each DNS server you want to enlist into the partition. Note that the server you use to create the partition is enlisted by default. In the preceding scenario, you would need to enlist all the DNS servers for the production domain as well as all the DNS servers for the development domain into the partition. For example, if you wanted to enlist SERVER30—a server of the child domain—as an additional server into the new partition named partition01.treyresearch.net, you would use the following command:

```
dnscmd server30.intranet.treyresearch.net /enlistdirectorypartition
    partition01.treyresearch.net
```

Now you can change the replication scope of the zones you want to make available to the members of the new application directory partition:

1. Return to the DNS node in Server Manager, right-click the name of the zone you want to change, and click Properties.

2. On the General tab, click Change to change the replication scope.

3. In the Change Zone Replication Scope dialog box shown here, select To All Domain Controllers In The Scope Of This Directory Partition and click the drop-down list to select your new partition. Click OK twice.

Be careful when you work with application directory partitions, because many of the commands must be manually entered. If you make a mistake, you could damage the replication scope of your servers and thereby disable name resolution.

MORE INFO   APPLICATION DIRECTORY PARTITIONS

For more information on application directory partitions, go to *http://technet2.microsoft*
.com/windowsserver2008/en/library/2e2e0678-1775-4cdd-8779-32d5c281540f1033
.mspx?mfr=true.

EXAM TIP

Replication scopes and application directory partitions are an important part of the exam. Be sure that you understand them fully.

Administering DNS Servers

You've already seen several tools in operation through practices and detailed step-by-step lists. However, you might need to work with other tools when working with your DNS servers. Table 9-4 outlines other tools you can use to support DNS operations and management.

TABLE 9-4 Common DNS Administration Tools

TOOL	TASK	LOCATION
DNS Manager	Perform initial configuration of a new server. Connect to and manage a local DNS server. Add and remove forward and reverse lookup zones. Add, remove, and update resource records in zones. Modify how zones are stored and replicated between servers. Modify how a server processes queries and handles dynamic update. Modify security for specific zones or resource records. Perform maintenance. Monitor contents of the server cache. Tune advanced server options. Configure and perform aging and scavenging of stale resource records.	Administrative Tools program group or Server Manager
Dnscmd	Manage all aspects of DNS servers. This is the most powerful command-line tool for DNS administration. Common switches include: */info* to obtain server information. */config* to modify server configuration parameters. */statistics* to obtain operational statistics from a server. */clearcache* to clear and reset the cache. */startscavenging* to initiate a scavenging operation. */directorypartitioninfo* for information about partitions. */exportsettings* to create a backup file of your server's settings.	Command line

TOOL	TASK	LOCATION
Dnslint	Diagnose common DNS name resolution issues. Common switches include: */d* to request domain name resolution tests. */ql* to verify DNS query tests from a list. */ad* to verify records specifically related to Active Directory.	Command line
Event Viewer	Two options are available for monitoring DNS servers: Default logging of DNS server event messages to the DNS server log. Debug options for trace logging to a text file on the DNS server. This option is enabled through the DNS server's Properties dialog box and is disabled by default. Use it only for debugging purposes.	Server Manager
Ipconfig	Display and modify IP configuration details. Common switches include: */all* to display all network configuration settings on a system. */renew* to request a dynamic IPv4 address renewal from DHCP. */renew6* to request a dynamic IPv6 address renewal from DHCP. */release* to release a dynamic IPv4 address. */release6* to release a dynamic IPv6 address. */flushdns* to clear the DNS resolver cache on a system. */registerdns* to renew a dynamic DNS registration for a system.	Command line
Nslookup	Perform query testing of the DNS domain namespace. *Nslookup* is also a command interpreter that is entered by typing **nslookup** at the command line. Type **exit** to return to the command line. It can also be used directly. To do so, type **nslookup** followed by the hostname or the IP address of the computer you are looking for.	Command line

TOOL	TASK	LOCATION
System Monitor	Create charts and graphs of server performance trends. Determine performance benchmarks.	Server Manager, Diagnostics, Reliability, and Performance
Windows PowerShell	Automates the control of the DNS service. Note, however, that there are no PowerShell cmdlets specific to the DNS service, and automating DNS administration through PowerShell requires a bit of preparatory work. Some simple cmdlets do exist and include: *sc stop dnscache* to stop the DNS cache service. *sc start dnscache* to restart the DNS cache service. For more information on how to automate DNS management through PowerShell, go to *http://blogs.technet.com/b/heyscriptingguy/ archive/2010/09/13/manage-dns-in-a-windows-environment-by-using-powershell.aspx.*	Administrative Tools program group

EXAM TIP

Run through each of these tools. DNS operation is an important part of the exam.

Little will go wrong with your internal DNS implementations if you follow the guidelines outlined here. However, there is always the possibility of uncontrolled issues. This is why you should become familiar with the tools listed in Table 9-4. Examine DNS events and understand them.

MORE INFO **DNS TROUBLESHOOTING AND POTENTIAL RESOLUTIONS**

For more information on DNS troubleshooting and potential resolutions to DNS issues, go to *http://technet.microsoft.com/en-us/library/cc787724(WS.10).aspx.* To obtain *Dnslint.exe*, go to *http://support.microsoft.com/kb/321045.*

PRACTICE **Finalizing a DNS Server Configuration in a Forest**

In this practice, you work with the DNS service to finalize its configuration. First you enable single-label name management in the Trey Research forest. Then you create single-label names to populate your GNZ. Finally, you modify a global query block list to protect your servers from dynamic entry spoofing.

EXERCISE 1 Enable Single-Label Name Management

In this exercise, you create and configure a GNZ for the treyresearch.net forest. This operation is manual and requires domain administrator credentials because your DNS servers are running on DCs. This exercise requires SERVER10, SERVER20, and SERVER30.

1. Log on to SERVER10 as treyresearch\Administrator.

2. In Server Manager, select the Forward Lookup Zones node in the DNS role.

3. Right-click Forward Lookup Zone and click New Zone.

4. Review the welcome information and click Next.

5. Select Primary Zone and make sure the Store The Zone In Active Directory check box is selected. Click Next.

6. Select To All DNS Servers In This Forest: TreyResearch.net and click Next.

7. On the Zone Name page, type **GlobalNames** and click Next.

8. On the Dynamic Update page, select Do Not Allow Dynamic Updates and click Next.

    You do not allow dynamic updates in this zone because all single-label names are created manually in DNS.

9. Click Finish to create the zone.

    Now, enable GNZ support on this DNS server. You need to do this through an elevated command line.

10. From the Start menu, right-click Command Prompt and click Run As Administrator.

11. Type the following command:

    dnscmd /config /enableglobalnamessupport 1

12. Close the command prompt and return to Server Manager. Right-click SERVER10 under the DNS node, point to All Tasks, and click Restart to recycle the DNS service on this server.

13. Repeat steps 10–12 on SERVER20 and SERVER30.

14. Return to SERVER10 to add single-label names.

EXERCISE 2 Create Single-Label Names

In this exercise, you create single-label names within the GNZ on SERVER10. This operation is manual and requires domain administrator credentials because your DNS servers are running on DCs. You add a single-label record for each of your three servers.

1. Log on to SERVER10 as treyresearch\Administrator.

2. In Server Manager, select the GlobalNames FLZ node in the DNS role.

3. Right-click GlobalNames and click New Alias (CNAME).

4. In the Alias Name field, type **SERVER10**. In the Fully Qualified Domain Name (FQDN) For Target Host field, type **SERVER10.treyresearch.net**.

Remember that like WINS names, single-label DNS names cannot have more than 15 characters—they actually use 16 characters, but the system reserves the last character. Also, single-label or NetBIOS names are almost always uppercase. Use uppercase to create your single-label names as a best practice.

5. Do not select the Allow Any Authenticated User To Update All DNS Records With The Same Name. This Setting Applies Only To DNS Records For A New Name check box.

6. Click OK to create the single-label name.

7. Use the command line to create the other two single-label names you need. From the Start menu, right-click Command Prompt and click Run As Administrator.

8. Type the following commands:

```
dnscmd server10.treyresearch.net /recordadd globalnames server20 cname
    server20.northwindtraders.com
```

```
dnscmd server10.treyresearch.net /recordadd globalnames server30 cname
    server30.intranet.treyresearch.net
```

9. Close the command prompt and return to the GNZ in Server Manager to view the new records. Click the Refresh icon on the toolbar to update the details view.

If you have many names to add, you might want to script this operation to simplify it.

EXERCISE 3 Modify a Global Query Block List

In this exercise, you modify an existing global query block list on SERVER10. This operation is manual and requires domain administrator credentials because your DNS server is running on a DC. You add a special DNS name (manufacturing) to the list to block name resolution for any object that uses this name.

1. Log on to SERVER10 as treyresearch\Administrator.

2. Use the command line to modify the block list. From the Start menu, right-click Command Prompt and click Run As Administrator.

3. Type the following command:

```
dnscmd /config /globalqueryblocklist wpad isatap manufacturing
```

You must add the existing names in the block list (WPAD and ISATAP) to the command to ensure that they continue to be blocked. Make a note of the new name to ensure that you continue to block it if you need to add another name at a later date.

4. Close the command prompt.

Your block list is configured.

Lesson Summary

- After the DNS server is installed, its configuration must be completed. DNS configuration settings include a review of the security parameters, scavenging and aging settings, zone configuration, and possible RLZ creations.

- Each forward lookup or stub zone includes a SOA record. This record should be properly configured to include the email addresses of the responsible parties for DNS operation as well as information about your DNS operating standards.

- If you require single-label name management in your network, you need to determine whether you will be using GNZs or the WINS service. GNZs are used when only a select list of names is required. If a multitude of names is required, you must deploy WINS.

- By default, DNS servers rely on root hints for name resolution. You can also use forwarders, which direct the DNS server to another DNS server under special circumstances.

- By default, replication scopes for DNS data integrated with Active Directory automatically span the proper number of DNS servers. However, under special circumstances, you can create manual application directory partitions to control the replication scope more precisely.

Lesson Review

You can use the following questions to test your knowledge of the information in Lesson 2, "Configuring and Using Domain Name System." The questions are also available on the companion CD if you prefer to review them in electronic form.

> **NOTE** **ANSWERS**
>
> Answers to these questions and explanations of why each answer choice is right or wrong are located in the "Answers" section at the end of the book.

1. You are the DNS administrator for the contoso.com internal forward lookup zone. You have been asked to complete the configuration of this zone now that it has been created. What should you do? (Each correct answer is a part of the solution. Choose all that apply.)

   A. Configure scavenging for the zone.

   B. Validate the replication scope for the zone.

   C. Create custom records for the zone.

   D. Create a text (TXT) record for the zone.

   E. Assign an email address to the zone.

   F. Delete unused records in the zone.

   G. Create a reverse lookup zone for the zone.

2. You are a system administrator for the treyresearch.net domain. Your organization has decided to create a new development domain to segregate development from the production domain. Because of compliance issues, all users of the production domain except operational staff must be granted only standard user rights. This means that for developers to be able to work, they must be granted rights other than in the production domain. However, because developers will be using the new domain

on a regular basis, it has been determined that a new application directory partition must be created to support faster DNS name resolution between the two domains. All forward lookup zones are Active Directory–integrated zones. You must assign this new partition to a forward lookup zone. However, when you try to assign it, it is not available, as shown in the following dialog box. What could be the problem? (Each correct answer presents a complete solution. Choose all that apply.)

A. You must log on with domain administrator credentials.

B. You must enlist the server you are using in the partition.

C. You must log on with enterprise administrator credentials.

D. You must use the command line to assign the zone to the partition.

E. You cannot change the replication scope of a forward lookup zone after it is created.

Chapter Review

To further practice and reinforce the skills you learned in this chapter, you can perform the following tasks:

- Review the chapter summary.
- Review the list of key terms introduced in this chapter.
- Complete the case scenario. This scenario sets up a real-world situation involving the topics of this chapter and asks you to create a solution.
- Complete the suggested practices.
- Take a practice test.

Chapter Summary

- The most common types of DNS structures are the dynamic DNS server, the primary DNS server, and the secondary DNS server. Dynamic DNS servers accept automatic name registration from authorized entities within their network. Primary DNS servers are read-write servers that are usually maintained by authorized administrators. Names can be entered manually or through automated processes but are not entered dynamically. Secondary DNS servers are usually subordinate servers that include read-only data that has originated from another DNS server, usually a primary DNS server. DNS in Windows Server 2008 R2 also includes another type of read-only DNS server, the RODC DNS server, which hosts read-only *primary* DNS zones.

- A typical Windows Server 2008 R2 DNS scenario can include up to four DNS server deployments. The first and most prolific is the dynamic DNS server, which is integrated with every DC in the network. Read-write DCs also contain read-write DNS servers. In remote sites that do not have local administrative staff but require a DC for availability purposes, RODCs also include read-only DNS servers. External networks include at least one primary stand-alone DNS, which is maintained manually. If more DNS servers are required, they should be secondary, read-only DNS servers. Read-only DNS servers are more secure than read-write servers and should be deployed in areas that demand the highest security levels.

- To support the move to IPv6, Windows Server 2008 R2 also supports the Peer Name Resolution Protocol and includes a PNRP server that can help promote name resolution. PNRP and DNS do not work the same way and do not include the same features. However, most organizations will continue to rely on DNS to support name resolution for some time. For example, AD DS hierarchies are not supported in PNRP. This is a good reason to continue using DNS for now.

Key Terms

The following terms were introduced in this chapter. Do you know what they mean?

- record
- zone

Case Scenario

In the following case scenario, you apply what you've learned about Domain Name System services. You can find answers to the questions in this scenario in the "Answers" section at the end of this book.

Case Scenario: Blocking Specific DNS Names

In the past, Trey Research has had problems with the Biometrics and the Biology departments when unauthorized users in these departments set up their own non-Windows servers to run their research programs. These servers were set up with little or no care for security and were quickly taken over by malicious users. After they were compromised, the servers started sending out dynamic updates for the Biometrics department, spoofing valid addresses. Now, Trey Research wants to ensure that this can never occur again. They have taken administrative measures to ensure that if other non-Windows operating systems are needed, they are installed according to proper IT guidelines.

- What other technical measure can Trey Research take to ensure that these two departments do not cause issues with DNS name resolution in the internal network?

Suggested Practices

To help you successfully master the exam objectives presented in this chapter, complete the following tasks.

Work with DNS

DNS in Windows Server 2008 R2 is tightly integrated with Active Directory Domain Services. Therefore, you should practice working with dynamic DNS systems that support AD DS. Use the following exercises to do so.

- **Practice 1** Practice installing and uninstalling DNS both on its own and through the Active Directory Domain Services Installation Wizard in as many scenarios as possible. In addition, create manual delegations and compare their interaction with the installation process to the automatically created delegations that the wizard generates. This will familiarize you with the various pages presented by the wizards.

- **Practice 2**   Work with zones, creating each of the three supported zone types one after another. Try as many configuration options as possible. Then create as many different record types as possible. This will familiarize you with the different dialog boxes and wizards used to configure zones and records.

- **Practice 3**   Work with the command-line tools and try as many different switches as possible for each tool. The Dnscmd.exe command, especially, will be present on the exam. Familiarity with this command will help you understand its function better.

- **Practice 4**   Work with the DNS event log and tracing log and examine their content. Familiarity with DNS logging is essential for any DNS operator.

Take a Practice Test

The practice tests on this book's companion CD offer many options. For example, you can test yourself on just one exam objective, or you can test yourself on all the 70-640 certification exam content. You can set up the test so that it closely simulates the experience of taking a certification exam, or you can set it up in study mode so that you can look at the correct answers and explanations after you answer each question.

MORE INFO   **PRACTICE TESTS**

For details about all the practice test options available, see the "How to Use the Practice Tests" section in this book's Introduction.

CHAPTER 10

Administering Domain Controllers

D omain controllers (DCs) host the directory service and perform the services that support identity and access management in an enterprise running Microsoft Windows. So far in this training kit, you have learned to support the logical and management components of an Active Directory Domain Services (AD DS) infrastructure: users, groups, computers, and Group Policy. Each of these components is contained in the directory database and in SYSVOL on domain controllers. In this chapter, you begin your exploration of the service-level components of Active Directory, starting with the domain controllers themselves. You learn how to add Windows Server 2008 R2 domain controllers to a forest or domain, how to prepare a Microsoft Windows Server 2003 forest or domain for its first Windows Server 2008 R2 DC, how to manage the roles performed by DCs, and how to migrate the replication of SYSVOL from the File Replication Service (FRS) used in earlier versions of Windows to the Distributed File System Replication (DFS-R) mechanism that provides more robust and manageable replications.

Exam objectives in this chapter:

- Configure a forest or a domain.
- Configure Active Directory replication.
- Configure operations masters.

Lessons in this chapter:

Before You Begin

To complete the practices in this chapter, you must have created a domain controller named SERVER01 in a domain named contoso.com and a member server named SERVER02, with a full installation of Windows Server 2008 R2. See Chapter 1, "Creating an Active Directory Domain," for detailed steps for this task.

 REAL WORLD

Dan Holme

Active Directory allows you to configure a domain and a forest with a single domain controller. But that's not enough. Domain controllers provide functionality critical to the identity and access management requirements of an enterprise, and if a domain controller fails, you must have a way to provide continuity of service. That's why it's very important to have at least two DCs in a domain. As soon as you start adding DCs to a domain, you start needing to consider replication, and in this chapter, you learn about one of the exciting features introduced in Windows Server 2008: DFS-R of SYSVOL. FRS, used by previous versions of Windows and supported by Windows Server 2008 and Windows Server 2008 R2 for backward compatibility, has been a notorious weak spot, prone to problems and difficult to troubleshoot. To take advantage of this feature, all domain controllers must be running Windows Server 2008 or later, so you'll need to know how to prepare an existing forest for its first Windows Server 2008 R2 DC—another objective of this chapter. Finally, as you add domain controllers to an enterprise, you need to consider the placement of single master operations, which are special roles assigned to one DC in a forest or domain. By the time you're through with this chapter, you'll have the skills to improve the redundancy, performance, and manageability of multiple domain controllers in your enterprise.

Lesson 1: Deploying Domain Controllers

In Chapter 1, you used the Add Roles Wizard in Server Manager to install Active Directory Domain Services (AD DS). Then you used the Active Directory Domain Services Installation Wizard to create the first DC in the contoso.com forest. Because DCs are critical to authentication, it is highly recommended that you maintain at least two domain controllers in each domain in your forest to provide a level of fault tolerance in the event that one DC fails. You might also need to add domain controllers to remote sites or create new domains or trees in your Active Directory forest. In this lesson, you learn user-interface, command-line, and unattended methods for installing domain controllers in a variety of scenarios.

> **After this lesson, you will be able to:**
> - Install a DC, using the Windows interface, Dcpromo.exe command-line parameters, or an answer file for unattended installation.
> - Add Windows Server 2008 R2 DCs to a domain or forest with Windows Server 2003 and Windows 2000 Server DCs.
> - Create new domains and trees.
> - Perform a staged installation of a read-only domain controller.
> - Install a DC from installation media to reduce network replication.
> - Remove a domain controller.
>
> **Estimated lesson time: 60 minutes**

Installing a Domain Controller with the Windows Interface

Using the Windows interface to install a domain controller requires two major steps. First, you must install the AD DS role, which, as you learned in Chapter 1, can be accomplished by using the Add Roles Wizard in Server Manager. After the AD DS role installation has copied the binaries required for the role to the server, you must install and configure AD DS by launching the Active Directory Domain Services Installation Wizard, using one of these methods:

- Click Start and, in the Start Search box, type dcpromo and click OK.
- When you complete the Add Roles Wizard, click the link to launch the Active Directory Domain Services Installation Wizard.
- After adding the AD DS role, links appear in Server Manager that remind you to run the Active Directory Domain Services Installation Wizard. Click any of those links.

The Active Directory Domain Services Installation Wizard is shown in Figure 10-1.

FIGURE 10-1 The Active Directory Domain Services Installation Wizard

NOTE **ALL-IN-ONE WIZARD**

Microsoft documentation for Windows Server 2008 R2 emphasizes the role-based model, so it recommends that you add the AD DS role and then run Dcpromo.exe (the Active Directory Domain Services Installation Wizard). However, you can simply run Dcpromo.exe and, as a first step, the wizard detects that the AD DS binaries are not installed and adds the AD DS role automatically.

Unattended Installation Options and Answer Files

You can also add or remove a domain controller in Command Prompt, using unattended installation supported by the Windows Server 2008 R2 version of Dcpromo.exe. Unattended installation options provide values to the Active Directory Domain Services Installation Wizard. For example, the NewDomainDNSName option specifies a fully qualified domain name (FQDN) for a new domain.

These options can be provided at the command line using dcpromo */unattendOption:value;* for example, type **dcpromo /newdomaindnsname:contoso.com**. Alternately, you can provide the options in an unattended installation answer file. The answer file is a text file that contains a section heading, [DCINSTALL], followed by options and their values in the *option=value* form. For example, the following file provides the NewDomainDNSName option:

```
[DCINSTALL]
NewDomainDNSName=contoso.com
```

The answer file is called by adding its path to the /unattend parameter. For example:

```
dcpromo /unattend:"path to answer file"
```

The options in the answer file can be overridden by parameters on the command line. For example, if the NewDomainDNSName option is specified in the answer file and the /NewDomainDNSName parameter is used on the command line, the value on the command line takes precedence.

If any required values are neither in the answer file nor on the command line, the Active Directory Domain Services Installation Wizard prompts for the answers, so you can use the answer file to partially automate an installation, providing a subset of configuration values for use during an interactive installation. The wizard is not available when running Dcpromo.exe from the command line in Server Core. In that case, the Dcpromo.exe command returns with an error code.

For a complete list of parameters that you can specify as part of an unattended installation of AD DS, open an elevated command prompt and type the following command:

```
dcpromo /?[:operation]
```

where *operation* is one of the following:

- **Promotion** Returns all parameters you can use when creating a domain controller.
- **CreateDCAccount** Returns all parameters you can use when creating a prestaged account for a read-only domain controller (RODC).
- **UseExistingAccount** Returns all parameters you can use to attach a new DC to a prestaged RODC account.
- **Demotion** Returns all parameters you can use when removing a domain controller.

MORE INFO   DCPROMO PARAMETERS AND UNATTENDED INSTALLATION

For a complete reference of Dcpromo parameters and unattended installation options, see *http://go.microsoft.com/fwlink/?LinkID=101181*.

NOTE   GENERATE AN ANSWER FILE

When you use the Windows interface to create a domain controller, the Active Directory Domain Services Installation Wizard gives you the option, on the Summary page, to export your settings to an answer file. If you need to create an answer file for use from the command line, such as on a Server Core installation, you can use this shortcut to create an answer file with the correct options and values.

Installing a New Windows Server 2008 R2 Forest

Chapter 1 discussed the installation of the first Windows Server 2008 R2 DC in a new forest, using the Windows interface. Exercise 3, "Install a New Windows Server 2008 R2 Forest with the Windows Interface," and Exercise 4, "Install a New Windows Server 2008 R2 Forest," of Lesson 1, "Installing Active Directory Domain Services," in that chapter detailed the steps to add the AD DS role to a server by using Server Manager and then running Dcpromo.exe to promote the server to a domain controller. When creating a new forest root domain, you must specify the forest root domain name system (DNS) name, its NetBIOS name, and the forest and domain functional levels. The first domain controller cannot be a read-only domain controller and must be a global catalog (GC) server. If the Active Directory Domain Services Installation Wizard detects that it is necessary to install or configure DNS, it does it automatically.

You can also use an answer file by typing **dcpromo /unattend:"*path to answer file*"**, where the answer file contains unattended installation options and values. The following example contains the minimum parameters for an unattended installation of a new Windows Server 2008 R2 domain controller in a new forest:

```
[DCINSTALL]
ReplicaOrNewDomain=domain
NewDomain=forest
NewDomainDNSName=fully qualified DNS name
DomainNetBiosName=domain NetBIOS name
ForestLevel={0=Windows 2000 Server Native;
             2=Windows Server 2003 Native;
             3=Windows Server 2008;
             4=Windows Server 2008 R2}
DomainLevel={0=Windows Server 2000 Native;
             2=Windows Server 2003 Native;
             3=Windows Server 2008;
             4=Windows Server 2008 R2}
InstallDNS=yes
DatabasePath="path to folder on a local volume"
LogPath="path to folder on a local volume"
SYSVOLPath="path to folder on a local volume"
SafeModeAdminPassword=password
RebootOnCompletion=yes
```

You can also specify one or more unattended installation parameters and values at the command line. For example, if you don't want the Directory Services Restore Mode password in the answer file, leave the entry blank and specify the */SafeModeAdminPassword:password* parameter when you run Dcpromo.exe.

You can also include all options on the command line itself. The following example creates the first domain controller in a new forest in which you don't expect to install any Windows Server 2003 domain controllers:

```
dcpromo /unattend /installDNS:yes /dnsOnNetwork:yes
    /replicaOrNewDomain:domain /newDomain:forest
    /newDomainDnsName:contoso.com /DomainNetbiosName:contoso
```

```
/databasePath:"e:\ntds" /logPath:"f:\ntdslogs" /sysvolpath:"g:\sysvol"
/safeModeAdminPassword:password /forestLevel:3 /domainLevel:3
/rebootOnCompletion:yes
```

Installing Additional Domain Controllers in a Domain

If you have a domain with at least one domain controller running Windows 2000 Server, Windows Server 2003, Windows Server 2008, or Windows Server 2008 R2 you can create additional domain controllers to distribute authentication, create a level of fault tolerance in the event that any one DC fails, or provide authentication in remote sites.

Installing the First Windows Server 2008 R2 Domain Controller in an Existing Forest or Domain

If you have an existing forest with domain controllers running a previous version of Windows Server, you must prepare them before you create your first Windows Server 2008 R2 domain controller. That's because Windows Server 2008 R2 adds objects and attributes to the directory that previous versions of Windows don't understand. Therefore, the schema must be updated. The schema is the definition of the attributes and object classes that can exist within a domain. It is like the catalog for what can be created in other directory partitions.

The ADPrep command prepares Active Directory for a DC that is running a version of Windows Server that is newer than the existing DCs in the forest or domain. Adprep.exe is a command-line tool that is included on the installation disk of each version of Windows Server. Adprep.exe performs operations that must be completed in an existing Active Directory environment before you can add a DC that runs that version of Windows Server.

Adprep.exe has parameters that perform a variety of operations to help prepare an existing Active Directory environment for a DC that runs a later version of Windows Server. Not all versions of Adprep.exe perform the same operations, but Adprep.exe can generally:

- Update the Active Directory schema.

- Update security descriptors.

- Modify access control lists (ACLs) on Active Directory objects and on files in the SYSVOL shared folder.

- Create new objects, as needed.

- Create new containers, as needed.

To prepare the forest schema for Windows Server 2008 R2, follow these steps:

1. Log on to the schema master as a member of the Enterprise Admins, Schema Admins, and Domain Admins groups.

   Lesson 2, "Managing Operations Masters," discusses operations masters and provides steps for identifying which domain controller is the schema master.

2. Copy the contents of the \Support\Adprep folder from the Windows Server 2008 R2 DVD to a folder on the schema master.

3. Open an elevated Command Prompt and change directories to the Adprep folder.

4. Type **adprep /forestprep** and press Enter.

You must allow time for the operation to complete. After the changes have replicated throughout the forest, you can continue to prepare the domains for Windows Server 2008 R2. To prepare a domain for the first Windows Server 2008 R2 domain controller, perform these steps:

1. Log on to the domain infrastructure operations master as a member of the Domain Admins group.

   Lesson 2 provides steps for identifying which domain controller is the infrastructure operations master.

2. Copy the contents of the \Support\Adprep folder from the Windows Server 2008 R2 DVD to a folder on the infrastructure master.

3. Open an elevated Command Prompt and change directories to the Adprep folder.

4. Type **adprep /domainprep /gpprep** and press Enter.

   On Windows Server 2003, you might receive an error message stating that updates were unnecessary. You can ignore this message.

Allow the change to replicate throughout the forest before you install a domain controller that runs Windows Server 2008 R2.

To prepare AD DS for the first RODC, follow these steps:

1. Log on to any computer as a member of the Enterprise Admins group.

2. Copy the contents of the \support\adprep folder from the Windows Server 2008 R2 DVD to a folder on the computer.

3. Open an elevated command prompt, and change directories to the adprep folder.

4. Type **adprep /rodcprep**, and then press ENTER.

NOTE RODCPREP, ANYTIME

If you plan to install an RODC in any domain in the forest, run adprep /rodcprep. You can run Adprep /rodcprep from any DC as long as you are logged on as a member of the Enterprise Admins group. Wait to allow its changes to replicate throughout the forest before you install the first RODC. You can run Adprep /rodcprep at any time in a Windows 2000 Server or Windows Server 2003 forest. It does not have to run in conjunction with /forestprep.

EXAM TIP

The Adprep /rodcprep command is required before installing an RODC into any domain in an existing forest with Windows Server 2003 or Windows 2000 Server domain controllers. It is not necessary if the forest is a new forest consisting only of Windows Server 2008 domain controllers.

Installing an Additional Domain Controller

You can add additional domain controllers by installing AD DS and launching the Active Directory Domain Services Installation Wizard. You are prompted to choose the deployment configuration, enter network credentials, select a domain and site for the new DC, and configure the DC with additional options such as DNS Server, Global Catalog, or Read-Only Domain Controller. The remaining steps are the same as for the first domain controller: configuring file locations and the Directory Services Restore Mode Administrator password.

If you have one domain controller in a domain, and if you select the Use Advanced Mode Installation check box on the Welcome To The Active Directory Domain Services Installation Wizard page, you can configure advanced options, which are:

- **Install From Media**   By default, a new domain controller replicates all data for all directory partitions it will host from other domain controllers during the Active Directory Domain Services Installation Wizard. To improve the performance of installation, particularly over slow links, you can use installation media created by existing domain controllers. Installation media is a form of backup. The new DC is able to read data from the installation media directly and then replicate only updates from other domain controllers. Install from Media (IFM) is discussed in the "Installing AD DS from Media" section.

- **Source Domain Controller**   If you want to specify the domain controller from which the new DC replicates its data, you can click Use This Specific Domain Controller.

> **NOTE   DCPROMO /ADV IS STILL SUPPORTED**
>
> In Windows Server 2003, Dcpromo /adv was used to specify advanced installation options. The /adv parameter is still supported; it simply pre-selects the Use Advanced Mode Installation check box on the Welcome page.

To use Dcpromo.exe with command-line parameters to specify unattended installation options, you can use the minimal parameters shown in the following example:

```
dcpromo /unattend /replicaOrNewDomain:replica
    /replicaDomainDNSName:contoso.com /installDNS:yes /confirmGC:yes
    /databasePath:"e:\ntds" /logPath:"f:\ntdslogs" /sysvolpath:"g:\sysvol"
    /safeModeAdminPassword:password /rebootOnCompletion:yes
```

If you are not logged on to the server with domain credentials, specify the /userdomain and /username parameters as well. A minimal answer file for an additional domain controller in an existing domain is as follows:

```
[DCINSTALL]
ReplicaOrNewDomain=replica
ReplicaDomainDNSName=FQDN of domain to join
UserDomain=FQDN of domain of user account
UserName=DOMAIN\username (in Administrators group of the domain)
Password=password for user specified by UserName (* to prompt)
InstallDNS=yes
```

```
ConfirmGC=yes
DatabasePath="path to folder on a local volume"
LogPath="path to folder on a local volume"
SYSVOLPath="path to folder on a local volume"
SafeModeAdminPassword=password
RebootOnCompletion=yes
```

Installing a New Windows Server 2008 Child Domain

If you have an existing domain, you can create a new child domain by creating a Windows Server 2008 R2 domain controller. If the forest includes domain controllers running Windows Server 2003, you must run Adprep /forestprep before installing the first domain controller running Windows Server 2008 R2. For details, see the section, "Installing the First Windows Server 2008 R2 Domain Controller in an Existing Forest or Domain."

Then install AD DS and launch the Active Directory Domain Services Installation Wizard and, on the Choose A Deployment Configuration page, click Existing Forest and Create A New Domain In An Existing Forest. You are prompted to select the domain functional level. Because it is the first DC in the domain, it cannot be an RODC, and it cannot be installed from media. If you select the Use Advanced Mode Installation check box on the Welcome page, the wizard presents you with a Source Domain Controller page on which you specify a domain controller from which to replicate the configuration and schema partitions.

Using Dcpromo.exe, you can create a child domain with the minimal options shown in the following command:

```
dcpromo /unattend /installDNS:yes
    /replicaOrNewDomain:domain /newDomain:child
    /ParentDomainDNSName:contoso.com
    /newDomainDnsName:subsidiary.contoso.com /childName:subsidiary
    /DomainNetbiosName:subsidiary
    /databasePath:"e:\ntds" /logPath:"f:\ntdslogs" /sysvolpath:"g:\sysvol"
    /safeModeAdminPassword:password /forestLevel:3 /domainLevel:3
    /rebootOnCompletion:yes
```

The following answer file reflects the same minimal parameters:

```
[DCINSTALL]
ReplicaOrNewDomain=domain
NewDomain=child
ParentDomainDNSName=FQDN of parent domain
UserDomain=FQDN of user specified by UserName
UserName= DOMAIN\username (in Administrators group of ParentDomainDNSName)
Password=password for user specified by UserName or * for prompt
ChildName=single-label prefix for domain
     (Child domain FQDN will be ChildName.ParentDomainDNSName)
DomainNetBiosName=Domain NetBIOS name
DomainLevel=domain functional level (not lower than current forest level)
InstallDNS=yes
CreateDNSDelegation=yes
DNSDelegationUserName=DOMAIN\username with permissions to create
     DNS delegation, if different than UserName, above
DNSDelegationPassword=password for DNSDelegationUserName or * for prompt
```

```
DatabasePath="path to folder on a local volume"
LogPath="path to folder on a local volume"
SYSVOLPath="path to folder on a local volume"
SafeModeAdminPassword=password
RebootOnCompletion=yes
```

Installing a New Domain Tree

You learned in Chapter 1 that in an Active Directory forest, a tree is composed of one or more domains that share a contiguous DNS namespace. So, for example, the contoso.com and subsidiary.contoso.com domains would be in a single tree. Additional trees are simply additional domains in the same forest that are not in the same namespace. For example, if Contoso, Ltd., bought Tailspin Toys, the tailspintoys.com domain would be in a separate tree in the domain. Very little functional difference exists between a child domain and a domain in another tree, and the process for creating a new tree is, therefore, very similar to creating a child domain.

First, you must run Adprep.exe /forestprep, as described in the "Installing the First Windows Server 2008 R2 Domain Controller in an Existing Forest or Domain" section. Then you can install AD DS and run the Active Directory Domain Services Installation Wizard. You must select Use Advanced Mode Installation on the Welcome page of the wizard. On the Choose A Deployment Configuration page, click Existing Forest, select Create A New Domain In An Existing Forest, and select Create A New Domain Tree Root Instead Of A New Child Domain. The rest of the process is identical to creating a new child domain.

The following options provided as parameters to Dcpromo.exe create a new tree for the tailspintoys.com domain within the contoso.com forest:

```
dcpromo /unattend /installDNS:yes
    /replicaOrNewDomain:domain /newDomain:tree
    /newDomainDnsName:tailspintoys.com /DomainNetbiosName:tailspintoys
    /databasePath:"e:\ntds" /logPath:"f:\ntdslogs" /sysvolpath:"g:\sysvol"
    /safeModeAdminPassword:password /domainLevel:2
    /rebootOnCompletion:yes
```

The domain functional level is configured at 2—Windows Server 2003 Native—so the domain could include Windows Server 2003 domain controllers. An unattended installation answer file that creates the same new tree would look similar to the following:

```
[DCINSTALL]
ReplicaOrNewDomain=domain
NewDomain=tree
NewDomainDNSName=FQDN of new domain
DomainNetBiosName=NetBIOS name of new domain
UserDomain=FQDN of user specified by UserName
UserName= DOMAIN\username (in Administrators group of ParentDomainDNSName)
Password=password for user specified by UserName or * for prompt
DomainLevel=domain functional level (not lower than current forest level)
InstallDNS=yes
ConfirmGC=yes
CreateDNSDNSDelegation=yes
```

```
DNSDelegationUserName=account with permissions to create DNS delegation
    required only if different than UserName, above
DNSDelegationPassword=password for DNSDelegationUserName or * for prompt
DatabasePath="path to folder on a local volume"
LogPath="path to folder on a local volume"
SYSVOLPath="path to folder on a local volume"
SafeModeAdminPassword=password
RebootOnCompletion=yes
```

Staging the Installation of an RODC

As you remember from Chapter 8, "Improving the Security of Authentication in an AD DS Domain," RODCs are designed to support branch office scenarios by providing authentication local to the site while mitigating the security and data integrity risks associated with placing a DC in a less controlled environment. Many times, there are few or no IT support personnel in a branch office. How, then, should a domain controller be created in a branch office?

To answer this question, Windows Server 2008 R2 allows you to create a staged, or delegated, installation of an RODC. The process includes two stages:

- **Create the account for the RODC** A member of Domain Admins creates an account for the RODC in Active Directory. The parameters related to the RODC are specified at this time: the name, the Active Directory site in which the RODC will be created, and, optionally, the user or group that can complete the next stage of the installation.

- **Attach the server to the RODC account** After the account has been created, AD DS is installed, and the server—which must be a member of a workgroup and not the domain—is joined to the domain as an RODC attached to the prestaged account. These steps can be performed by the users or groups specified when the RODC account was prestaged; these users do not require any privileged group membership. A server can also be attached by a member of Domain Admins or Enterprise Admins, but the ability to delegate this stage to a nonprivileged user makes it much easier to deploy RODCs in branches without IT support. The domain controller will replicate its data from another writable DC in the domain, or you can use the IFM method discussed in the "Installing AD DS from Media" section.

Creating the Prestaged Account for the RODC

To create the account for the RODC, using the Active Directory Users And Computers snap-in, right-click the Domain Controllers OU and choose Pre-Create Read-Only Domain Controller Account. A wizard appears that is very similar to the Active Directory Domain Services Installation Wizard. You are asked to specify the RODC name and site, and you can also configure the password replication policy, as detailed in Chapter 8.

On the Delegation Of RODC Installation And Administration page, you can specify one security principal—user or group—that can attach the server to the RODC account you create. The user or group will also have local administrative rights on the RODC after the installation. It is recommended that you delegate to a group rather than to a user. If you do not specify a user or group, only members of the Domain Admins or Enterprise Admins groups can attach the server to the account.

> **MORE INFO**   **CREATING PRESTAGED RODC ACCOUNTS**
>
> You can create prestaged RODC accounts by using Dcpromo.exe with numerous parameters or by creating an answer file for Dcpromo.exe. The steps for doing so are detailed at *http://technet2.microsoft.com/windowsserver2008/en/library/f349e1e7-c3ce-4850-9e50-d8886c866b521033.mspx?mfr=true.*

Attaching a Server to the RODC Account

After you have prestaged the account, the server can be attached to it.

To attach a server to a prestaged RODC account:

1. Ensure that the server is a member of a workgroup, not a member of the domain.

> **NOTE**   **PROMOTE FROM A WORKGROUP**
>
> When you create an RODC by using the staged approach—when you attach an RODC to a prestaged account—the server must be a member of a workgroup, not the domain, when you launch Dcpromo.exe or the Active Directory Domain Services Installation Wizard. The wizard looks in the domain for the existing account with its name and attaches to that account.

2. Type **dcpromo.exe /UseExistingAccount:attach**.

   The wizard prompts for network credentials and then finds the RODC account in the domain indicated by the credentials. Remaining steps are similar to other domain controller promotion operations.

To use an answer file, provide the following options and values:

```
[DCINSTALL]
ReplicaDomainDNSName=FQDN of domain to join
UserDomain=FQDN of user specified by UserName
UserName=DOMAIN\username (in Administrators group of the domain)
Password=password for user specified by UserName
InstallDNS=yes
ConfirmGC=yes
DatabasePath="path to folder on a local volume"
LogPath="path to folder on a local volume"
SYSVOLPath="path to folder on a local volume"
SafeModeAdminPassword=password
RebootOnCompletion=yes
```

Run Dcpromo.exe with the */unattend:"answer file path"* and the */UseExistingAccount:Attach* parameters, as in the following example:

```
dcpromo /useexistingaccount:attach /unattend:"c:\rodcanswer.txt"
```

All the options just shown in the answer file can also be specified or overridden directly on the command line. Just type a command similar to the following:

```
dcpromo /unattend /UseExistingAccount:Attach /ReplicaDomainDNSName:contoso.com
    /UserDomain:contoso.com /UserName:contoso\dan /password:*
    /databasePath:"e:\ntds" /logPath:"f:\ntdslogs" /sysvolpath:"g:\sysvol"
    /safeModeAdminPassword:Pa$$w0rd /rebootOnCompletion:yes
```

✔ **Quick Check**

- You administer a domain containing Windows Server 2003 domain controllers. You want to allow a manager at a remote site to promote a member server at a remote site to an RODC. You do not want to give the manager administrative credentials in the domain. What steps must you and the manager take?

Quick Check Answer

- You must run Adprep.exe /rodcprep to prepare the domain for the RODC. You must then prestage the RODC account, delegating to the manager the ability to attach the domain controller to the account. The manager will run Dcpromo.exe with the UseExistingAccount option to attach the server; but first, the server must be removed from the domain and placed in a workgroup.

Installing AD DS from Media

When you add domain controllers to a forest, data from existing directory partitions are replicated to the new DC. In an environment with a large directory or where bandwidth is constrained between a new DC and a writable DC from which to replicate, you can install AD DS more efficiently by using the IFM option. Installing from media involves creating *installation media*—a specialized backup of Active Directory that can be used by the Active Directory Domain Services Installation Wizard as a data source for populating the directory on a new DC. Then the new DC will replicate only updates from another writable DC, so if the installation media is recent, you can minimize the impact of replication to a new DC.

Remember that it is not only the directory that must be replicated to a new DC but SYSVOL as well. When you create your installation media, you can specify whether to include SYSVOL on the installation media.

Using IFM also allows you to control the timing of impact to your network bandwidth. You can, for example, create installation media and transfer it to a remote site during off hours, and then create the domain controller during normal business hours. Because the installation media is from the local site, the replication burden on the network is reduced, and only updates are replicated over the link to the remote site.

To create installation media:

1. Open an elevated Command Prompt on a writable domain controller, running Windows Server 2008 R2.

    The installation media can be used to create both writable and read-only DCs.

2. Type **ntdsutil.exe**, and then press Enter.

3. At the ntdsutil prompt, type **activate instance ntds**, and then press Enter.

4. Type **ifm**, and then press Enter.

5. At the **ifm:** prompt, type one of the following commands, based on the type of installation media you want to create:

- **create sysvol full *Path***   Creates installation media with SYSVOL for a writable domain controller in the folder specified by *Path*

- **create full *Path***   Creates installation media without SYSVOL for a writable domain controller or an Active Directory Lightweight Directory Services (AD LDS) instance in the folder specified by *Path*

- **create sysvol rodc *Path***   Creates installation media with SYSVOL for a read-only domain controller in the folder specified by *Path*

- **create rodc *Path***   Creates installation media without SYSVOL for a read-only domain controller in the folder specified by *Path*

When you run the Active Directory Domain Services Installation Wizard, select the Use Advanced Mode Installation check box, and you will be presented with the Install From Media page later in the wizard. Choose Replicate Data From Media At The Following Location. You can use the *ReplicationSourcePath* installation option in an answer file or on the Dcpromo.exe command line.

PRACTICE IT

Exercise 3, "Create Installation Media," in the practice at the end of this lesson, steps you through the process of creating installation media with Ntdsutil.exe.

Removing a Domain Controller

You can remove a domain controller by using Dcpromo.exe, either by launching the Active Directory Domain Services Installation Wizard or from a command prompt, specifying options at the command line or in an answer file. When a domain controller is removed while it has connectivity to the domain, it updates the forest metadata about the domain controller so that the directory knows the DC has been removed.

To use an answer file, provide the following options and values:

```
[DCINSTALL]
UserName=DOMAIN\username (in Administrators group of the domain)
UserDomain=FQDN of user specified by UserName
```

```
Password=password for user specified by UserName
AdministratorPassword=password will be assigned to local Administrator
RemoveApplicationPartitions=yes
RemoveDNSDelegation=yes
DNSDelegationUserName=DOMAIN\username with permissions to remove DNS delegation
DNSDelegationPassword=password for the account
```

Run Dcpromo.exe with the */unattend:"answer file path"* and the */UninstallBinaries* options, as in the following example:

```
dcpromo /uninstallbinaries /unattend:"c:\rodcanswer.txt"
```

All the options just shown in the answer file can also be specified or overridden directly on the command line. Just type a command similar to the following:

```
dcpromo /unattend /uninstallbinaries
    /UserName:contoso\dan /password:* /administratorpassword:Pa$$w0rd
```

> **MORE INFO** **REMOVING A DOMAIN CONTROLLER**
>
> For detailed steps for removing a domain controller, see *http://technet2.microsoft.com/windowsserver2008/en/library/9260bb40-a808-422f-b33b-c3d2330f5eb81033.mspx*.

If a domain controller must be demoted while it cannot contact the domain, you must use the */forceremoval* option of Dcpromo.exe. Type **dcpromo /forceremoval**, and the Active Directory Domain Services Installation Wizard takes you through the process. Warnings appear related to any roles that the domain controller hosts. Read each warning and, after you have mitigated or accepted the impact of the warning, click Yes. You can suppress warnings by using the *demotefsmo:yes* option of Dcpromo.exe. After removing the DC, you must manually clean up the forest metadata.

> **MORE INFO** **PERFORMING METADATA CLEANUP**
>
> See article 216498 in the Microsoft Knowledge Base for information about performing metadata cleanup. The article is located at *http://go.microsoft.com/fwlink/?LinkId=80481*.

PRACTICE Deploying Domain Controllers

In this practice, you perform the steps required to install an additional domain controller in the contoso.com domain. You install AD DS and configure an additional DC, using the Active Directory Domain Services Installation Wizard. *You will not complete the installation.* Instead, you save the settings as an answer file and use the settings to perform an unattended installation, using the *Dcpromo.exe* command with installation options.

To perform this exercise, you need a second server running Windows Server 2008 full installation. The server must be named SERVER02, and it should be joined to the contoso.com domain. Its configuration should be as follows:

- Computer Name: SERVER02
- Domain Membership: contoso.com
- IPv4 address: 10.0.0.12
- Subnet Mask: 255.255.255.0
- Default Gateway: 10.0.0.1
- DNS Server: 10.0.0.11

EXERCISE 1   Create an Additional DC with the Active Directory Domain Services Installation Wizard

In this exercise, you use the Active Directory Domain Services Installation Wizard (Dcpromo.exe) to create an additional domain controller in the contoso.com domain. You do not complete the installation, however. Instead, you save the settings as an answer file, which will be used in the next exercise.

1. Log on to SERVER02 as CONTOSO\Administrator.
2. Click Start, click Run, type **Dcpromo.exe**, and then press Enter.

   Active Directory binaries are installed.
3. Click Next.
4. On the Operating System Compatibility page, review the warning about the default security settings for Windows Server 2008 R2 domain controllers, and then click Next.
5. On the Choose A Deployment Configuration page, select Existing Forest, select Add A Domain Controller To An Existing Domain, and then click Next.
6. On the Network Credentials page, type **contoso.com** in the text box, select My Current Logged On Credentials, and then click Next.
7. On the Select A Domain page, select contoso.com and click Next.
8. On the Select A Site page, select Default-First-Site-Name and click Next.

   The Additional Domain Controller Options page appears. DNS Server and Global Catalog are selected by default.
9. Clear the Global Catalog and DNS Server check boxes, and then click Next.

   An Infrastructure Master Configuration Conflict warning appears. You will learn about the infrastructure master in Lesson 2, so you ignore this error.
10. Click Do Not Transfer The Infrastructure Master Role To This Domain Controller, I Will Correct The Configuration Later.

11. On the Location For Database, Log Files, And SYSVOL page, accept the default locations for the database file, the directory service log files, and the SYSVOL files and click Next.

   The best practice in a production environment is to store these files on three separate volumes that do not contain applications or other files not related to AD DS. This best practices design improves performance and increases the efficiency of backup and restore.

12. On the Directory Services Restore Mode Administrator Password page, type a strong password in both the Password and Confirmed Password boxes. Click Next.

   Do not forget the password you assigned to the Directory Services Restore Mode Administrator.

13. On the Summary page, review your selections.

   If any settings are incorrect, click Back to make modifications.

14. Click Export Settings.

15. Click Browse Folders.

16. Select Desktop.

17. In the File Name box, type **AdditionalDC** and click Save.

   A message appears, indicating that settings were saved successfully.

18. Click OK.

19. On the Active Directory Domain Services Installation Wizard Summary page, click Cancel.

20. Click Yes to confirm that you are cancelling the installation of the DC.

EXERCISE 2   Add a Domain Controller from the Command Line

In this exercise, you examine the answer file you created in Exercise 1, "Create an Additional DC with the Active Directory Domain Services Installation Wizard." You use the installation options in the answer file to create a Dcpromo.exe command line to install the additional domain controller.

1. Open the AdditionalDC.txt file you created in Exercise 1.

2. Examine the answers in the file. Can you identify what some of the options mean?

   Tip: Lines beginning with a semicolon are comments or inactive lines that have been commented out.

3. Open a command prompt.

   You will be building a command line, using the options in the answer file. Position the windows so you can see both Notepad and the command prompt, or print the answer file for reference.

4. Determine the command line to install the domain controller with the configuration contained in the answer file.

Parameters on the command line take the form */option:value,* whereas in the answer file they take the form *option=value.*

5. Type the following command and press Enter:

```
dcpromo /unattend /replicaornewdomain:replica
    /replicadomaindnsname:contoso.com /sitename:Default-First-Site-Name
    /installDNS:No /confirmGC:No /CreateDNSDelegation:No
    /databasepath:"C:\Windows\NTDS" /logpath:"C:\Windows\NTDS"
    /sysvolpath:"C:\Windows\SYSVOL" /safemodeadminpassword:password
    /transferimroleifnecessary:no
```

where *password* is a complex password.

6. Installation completes, and the server reboots.

EXERCISE 3 Create Installation Media

You can reduce the amount of replication required to create a domain controller by promoting the domain controller, using the IFM option. IFM requires that you provide installation media, which is, in effect, a backup of Active Directory. In this exercise, you create the installation media.

1. Log on to SERVER01 as Administrator.
2. Open a command prompt.
3. Type **ntdsutil** and press Enter.
4. Type **activate instance ntds** and press Enter.
5. Type **ifm** and press Enter.
6. Type **?** and press Enter to list the commands available in IFM mode.
7. Type **create sysvol full c:\IFM** and press Enter.

    The installation media files are copied to C:\Ifm.

Lesson Summary

- You can install AD DS by running Dcpromo.exe, which launches the Active Directory Domain Services Installation Wizard or, with the */unattend* parameter, can obtain installation options from the command line or an answer file.

- When you introduce the first Windows Server 2008 R2 domain controller into an existing forest, you must run Adprep.exe /forestprep. Before you introduce the first Windows Server 2008 R2 DC into an existing domain, you must run Adprep.exe /domainprep /gpprep.

- Before you install the first RODC in a domain containing Windows 2000 Server or Windows Server 2003 DCs, you must run Adprep.exe /rodcprep.

- To perform a staged installation of an RODC, you create the account for the RODC and specify the user or group that will be able to attach the RODC to the account.

- To reduce replication requirements, you can create installation media and use the media as a source when performing a domain controller promotion.

Lesson Review

You can use the following questions to test your knowledge of the information in Lesson 1, "Deploying Domain Controllers." The questions are also available on the companion CD if you prefer to review them in electronic form.

> **NOTE ANSWERS**
>
> Answers to these questions and explanations of why each answer choice is right or wrong are located in the "Answers" section at the end of the book.

1. You are an administrator at Trey Research. The Trey Research forest consists of three domains, each of which includes two domain controllers running Windows Server 2003. You want to upgrade one of the domain controllers to Windows Server 2008 R2. What must you do first?

   A. Upgrade the domain controller's operating system to Windows Server 2008 R2.

   B. Run the Adprep.exe /domainprep /gpprep command.

   C. Run the Active Directory Domain Services Installation Wizard.

   D. Run the Adprep.exe /forestprep command.

   E. Run the Adprep.exe /rodcprep command.

2. You are an administrator at Contoso, Ltd. The domain was built using Windows Server 2008 R2 domain controllers. You want to improve authentication at a remote site by promoting a member server at the site to a read-only domain controller. There is no IT support at the site, so you want the site's manager to perform the promotion. You do not want to give her administrative credentials in the domain. Which steps must you or the manager take? (Choose all that apply. Each correct answer is part of the solution.)

   A. Run Adprep.exe /rodcprep.

   B. Create the RODC account in the Domain Controllers OU.

   C. Run Dcpromo.exe with the UseExistingAccount option.

   D. Remove the server from the domain.

3. You want to promote a server to act as a domain controller, but you are concerned about the replication traffic that will occur during the promotion and its impact on the slow link between the server's site and the data center where all other domain controllers are located, so you choose to promote the server, using a backup of the directory from another domain controller. What must you do to create the installation media?

   A. Run Ntbackup.exe and select System State.

   B. Install the Windows Server Backup Features.

   C. Run Ntdsutil.exe in the IFM mode and use the Create Sysvol Full command.

   D. Copy ntds.dit and SYSVOL from a domain controller to a location in the remote site.

Lesson 2: Managing Operations Masters

In an Active Directory domain, all domain controllers are equivalent. They are all capable of writing to the database and replicating changes to other domain controllers. However, in any multimaster replication topology, certain operations must be performed by one and only one system. In an Active Directory domain, *operations masters* are domain controllers that play a specific role. Other domain controllers are capable of playing the role but do not. This lesson introduces you to the five operations masters found in Active Directory forests and domains. You learn their purposes, how to identify the operations masters in your enterprise, and the nuances of administering and transferring roles.

After this lesson, you will be able to:

- Define the purpose of the five single master operations in Active Directory forests.
- Identify the domain controllers performing operations master roles.
- Plan the placement of operations master roles.
- Transfer and seize operations master roles.

Estimated lesson time: 45 minutes

Understanding Single Master Operations

In any replicated database, some changes must be performed by one and only one replica because they are impractical to perform in a multimaster fashion. Active Directory is no exception. A limited number of operations are not permitted to occur at different places at the same time and must be the responsibility of only one domain controller in a domain or forest. These operations, and the domain controllers that perform them, are referred to by a variety of terms:

- *Operations masters*
- *Operations master roles*
- *Single master roles*
- *Operations tokens*
- *Flexible Single Master Operations (FSMOs)*

Regardless of the term used, the idea is the same. One domain controller performs a function, and while it does, no other domain controller performs that function.

Not Déjà Vu

I f you were an administrator in the days of Microsoft Windows NT 4.0, the concept of operations masters might sound similar to Windows NT primary domain controllers (PDCs). However, single master operations are characteristic of any replicated database, and Active Directory single master operations are strikingly different from Windows NT 4.0 PDCs in several ways:

- All Active Directory domain controllers are capable of performing single master operations. The domain controller that actually does perform an operation is the domain controller that currently holds the operation's token.
- An operation token, and thus the role, can be transferred easily to another domain controller without a reboot.
- To reduce the risk of single points of failure, the operations tokens can be distributed among multiple DCs.

AD DS contains five operations master roles. Two roles are performed for the entire forest:

- Domain naming
- Schema

Three roles are performed in each domain:

- Relative identifier (RID)
- Infrastructure
- PDC Emulator

Each of these roles is detailed in the following sections. In a forest with a single domain, there are, therefore, five operations masters. In a forest with two domains, there are eight operations masters because the three domain master roles are implemented separately in each of the two domains.

EXAM TIP

Commit to memory the list of forest-wide and domain single master operations. You are likely to encounter questions that test your knowledge of which roles apply to the entire forest and which are domain specific. Exam questions are cast in scenarios and, often, the scenarios provide so much detail that you can lose sight of what is really being asked. When you read items on the certification exam, always ask yourself, "What is really being tested?" Sometimes what is being tested is different from, and simpler than, what the scenario in the question would lead you to believe.

Forest-Wide Operations Master Roles

The schema master and the domain naming master must be unique in the forest. Each role is performed by only one domain controller in the entire forest.

Domain Naming Master Role

The domain naming role is used when adding or removing domains in the forest. When you add or remove a domain, the domain naming master must be accessible or the operation will fail.

Schema Master Role

The domain controller holding the schema master role is responsible for making any changes to the forest's schema. All other DCs hold read-only replicas of the schema. If you want to modify the schema or install an application that modifies the schema, it is recommended you do so on the domain controller holding the schema master role. Otherwise, changes you request must be sent to the schema master to be written into the schema.

Domain-Wide Operations Master Roles

Each domain maintains three single master operations: RID, Infrastructure, and PDC Emulator. Each role is performed by only one domain controller in the domain.

RID Master Role

The RID master plays an integral part in the generation of security identifiers (SIDs) for security principals such as users, groups, and computers. The SID of a security principal must be unique. Because any domain controller can create accounts and, therefore, SIDs, a mechanism is necessary to ensure that the SIDs generated by a DC are unique. Active Directory domain controllers generate SIDs by assigning a unique RID to the domain SID. The RID master for the domain allocates pools of unique RIDs to each domain controller in the domain. Thus, each domain controller can be confident that the SIDs it generates are unique.

> **NOTE THE RID MASTER ROLE IS LIKE DHCP FOR SIDS**
>
> If you are familiar with the concept that you allocate a scope of IP addresses for the Dynamic Host Configuration Protocol (DHCP) server to assign to clients, you can draw a parallel to the RID master, which allocates pools of RIDs to domain controllers for the creation of SIDs.

Infrastructure Master Role

In a multidomain environment, it is common for an object to reference objects in other domains. For example, a group can include members from another domain. Its multivalued *member* attribute contains the distinguished names of each member. If the member in the other domain is moved or renamed, the infrastructure master of the group's domain updates the group's *member* attribute accordingly.

> **NOTE** **THE INFRASTRUCTURE MASTER**
>
> You can think of the infrastructure master as a tracking device for group members from other domains. When those members are renamed or moved in the other domain, the infrastructure master identifies the change and makes appropriate changes to group memberships so that the memberships are kept up to date.

Phantoms of the Directory

Although you are not expected to understand the internals of the infrastructure master role for the certification exam, such understanding can be helpful in the production environment. When you add a member from another domain into a group in your domain, the group's *member* attribute is appended with the distinguished name of the new member. However, your domain might not always have access to a domain controller from the member's domain, so Active Directory creates a phantom object to represent the member. The phantom object includes only the member's SID, distinguished name (DN), and globally unique identifier (GUID). If the member is moved or renamed in its domain, its GUID does not change, but its DN changes. If the object is moved between domains, its SID also changes. The infrastructure master periodically—every two days by default—contacts a GC or a DC in the member domain. At that time, the infrastructure master looks for each phantom object, using the GUID of the phantom object. It updates the DN of the phantom objects with the current DN of the object. Any change is then propagated to the *member* attribute of groups.

After a member is moved or renamed in another domain, and until the infrastructure master has updated DNs, you might look at the membership of a group using the Active Directory Users And Computers snap-in, for example, and the group might appear not to include that member. However, the member continues to belong to the group. The member's *memberOf* attribute still refers to the group, so the *memberOf* attribute and the *tokenGroups* constructed attribute are unchanged. There is no compromise to security; only an administrator looking at that particular group membership would notice the temporary inconsistency.

PDC Emulator Role

The PDC Emulator role performs multiple, crucial functions for a domain:

- **Emulates a PDC for backward compatibility**   In the days of Windows NT 4.0 domains, only the PDC could make changes to the directory. Earlier tools, utilities, and clients written to support Windows NT 4.0 are unaware that all Active Directory domain controllers can write to the directory, so such tools request a connection to the PDC. The domain controller with the PDC Emulator role registers itself as a PDC so that down-level applications can locate a writable domain controller. Such applications are less common now that Active Directory is nearly 10 years old, and if your enterprise includes such applications, work to upgrade them for full Active Directory compatibility.

- **Participates in special password update handling for the domain**   When a user's password is reset or changed, the domain controller that makes the change replicates the change immediately to the PDC emulator. This special replication ensures that the domain controllers know about the new password as quickly as possible. If a user attempts to log on immediately after changing passwords, the domain controller responding to the user's logon request might not know about the new password. Before it rejects the logon attempt, that domain controller forwards the authentication request to a PDC emulator, which verifies that the new password is correct and instructs the domain controller to accept the logon request. This function means that anytime a user enters an incorrect password, the authentication is forwarded to the PDC emulator for a second opinion. The PDC emulator, therefore, should be highly accessible to all clients in the domain. It should be a well-connected, high-performance DC.

- **Manages Group Policy updates within a domain**   If a Group Policy object (GPO) is modified on two DCs at approximately the same time, there could be conflicts between the two versions that cannot be reconciled as the GPO replicates. To prevent this situation, the PDC emulator acts as the focal point for all Group Policy changes. When you open a GPO in Group Policy Management Editor (GPME), GPME binds to the domain controller performing the PDC emulator role. Therefore, all changes to GPOs are made on the PDC emulator by default.

- **Provides a master time source for the domain**   Active Directory, Kerberos, File Replication Service (FRS), and Distributed File System Replication (DFS-R) each rely on timestamps, so synchronizing the time across all systems in a domain is crucial. The PDC emulator in the forest root domain is the time master for the entire forest, by default. The PDC emulator in each domain synchronizes its time with the forest root PDC emulator. Other domain controllers in the domain synchronize their clocks against that domain's PDC emulator. All other domain members synchronize their time with their preferred domain controller. This hierarchical structure of time synchronization, all implemented through the Win32Time service, ensures consistency of time. Coordinated Universal Time (UTC) is synchronized, and the time displayed to users is adjusted based on the time zone setting of the computer.

- **Acts as the domain master browser**   When you open Network in Windows, you see a list of workgroups and domains, and when you open a workgroup or domain, you see a list of computers. These two lists, called *browse lists*, are created by the Browser service. In each network segment, a master browser creates the browse list: the lists of workgroups, domains, and servers in that segment. The domain master browser serves to merge the lists of each master browser so that browse clients can retrieve a comprehensive browse list.

Optimizing the Placement of Operations Masters

When you create the forest root domain with its first domain controller, all five operations master roles are performed by the domain controller. As you add domain controllers to the domain, you can transfer the operations master role assignments to other domain controllers to balance the load among domain controllers or optimize placement of a single master operation. The best practices for the placement of operations master roles are as follows:

- **Co-locate the schema master and domain naming master**   The schema master and domain naming master roles should be placed on a single domain controller that is a GC server. These roles are rarely used, and the domain controller hosting them should be tightly secured. The domain naming master must be hosted on a GC server, because when a new domain is added the master must ensure that there is no object of any type with the same name as the new domain. The GC's partial replica contains the name of every object in the forest. The load of these operations master roles is very light unless schema modifications are being made.

- **Co-locate the RID master and PDC Emulator roles**   Place the RID and PDC Emulator roles on a single domain controller. If the load mandates that the roles be placed on two separate domain controllers, those two systems should be physically well connected and have explicit connection objects created in Active Directory so that they are direct replication partners. They should also be direct replication partners with domain controllers that you have selected as standby operations masters. You will learn about connection objects in Chapter 11, "Managing Sites and Active Directory Replication."

- **Place the infrastructure master on a DC that is not a GC**   The infrastructure master should be placed on a domain controller that is not a GC server but is physically well connected to a GC server. The infrastructure master should have explicit connection objects in Active Directory to that GC server so that they are direct replication partners. The infrastructure master can be placed on the same domain controller that acts as the RID master and PDC emulator. You will learn about connection objects in Chapter 11.

> **NOTE   IT DOESN'T MATTER IF THEY'RE ALL GCS**
>
> If all DCs in a domain are GC servers—a best practices recommendation discussed in Chapter 11—you do not need to worry about which DC is the infrastructure master. When all DCs are GCs, all DCs have up-to-date information about every object in the forest, which eliminates the need for the infrastructure master role.

- **Have a failover plan**   In following sections, you learn to transfer single operations master roles between domain controllers, which is necessary if there is lengthy planned or unplanned downtime of an operations master. Determine, in advance, a plan for transferring operations roles to other DCs in the event that one operations master is offline.

Identifying Operations Masters

To implement your role placement plan, you must know which DCs are currently performing single master operations roles. Each role is exposed in an Active Directory administrative tool as well as in other user interface and command-line tools. To identify the current master for each role, use the following tools:

- **PDC Emulator: The Active Directory Users And Computers snap-in**   Right-click the domain and choose Operations Masters. Click the PDC tab. An example is shown in Figure 10-2, which indicates that SERVER01.contoso.com is currently the PDC operations master.

- **RID Master: The Active Directory Users And Computers snap-in**   Right-click the domain and choose Operations Masters. Click the RID tab.

- **Infrastructure Master: The Active Directory Users And Computers snap-in**   Right-click the domain and choose Operations Masters. Click the Infrastructure tab.

- **Domain Naming: The Active Directory Domains And Trusts snap-in**   Right-click the root node of the snap-in (Active Directory Domains And Trusts) and choose Operations Master.

- **Schema Master: The Active Directory Schema snap-in**   Right-click the root node of the snap-in (Active Directory Schema) and choose Operations Master.

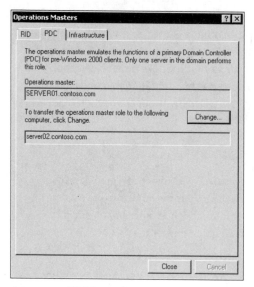

FIGURE 10-2 PDC Operations Master

You can also use several other tools to identify operations masters, including the following commands:

- **NTDSUtil** Type the following series of commands in Command Prompt to list the operations master roles of a domain controller:

```
ntdsutil
roles
connections
connect to server DomainControllerFQDN
quit
select operation target
list roles for connected server
quit
quit
quit
```

- **DCDiag** Type the following command to list the operations master roles of a domain controller:

```
dcdiag /test:knowsofroleholders /v
```

- **NetDom** Type the following command to list the operations master roles of a domain controller:

```
netdom query fsmo
```

> **PRACTICE IT**
>
> Exercise 1, "Identify Operations Masters," in the practice at the end of this lesson covers the identification of operations masters.

Transferring Operations Master Roles

You can transfer a single operations master role easily. You transfer roles in the following scenarios:

- When you establish your forest, all five roles are performed by the first domain controller you install. When you add a domain to the forest, all three domain roles are performed by the first domain controller in that domain. As you add domain controllers, you can distribute the roles to reduce single-point-of-failure risks and improve performance.
- If you plan to take a domain controller offline that is currently holding an operations master role, transfer that role to another domain controller before taking it offline.
- If you are decommissioning a domain controller that currently holds an operations master role, transfer that role to another domain controller before decommissioning. The Active Directory Domain Services Installation Wizard will attempt to do so automatically, but you should prepare for demoting a domain controller by transferring its roles.

To transfer an operations master role, follow these steps:

1. Make sure that the new role holder is up to date with replication from the former role holder. You can use skills introduced in Chapter 11 to force replication between the two systems.
2. Open the administrative tool that exposes the current master.

   For example, open the Active Directory Users And Computers snap-in to transfer any of the three domain master roles.
3. Connect to the domain controller to which you are transferring the role.

   This is accomplished by right-clicking the root node of the snap-in and choosing Change Domain Controller or Change Active Directory Domain Controller. (The command differs between snap-ins.)
4. Open the Operations Master dialog box, which displays the domain controller currently holding the role token for the operation. Click Change to transfer the role to the domain controller to which you are connected.

When you transfer an operations master role, both the current master and the new master are online. The token is transferred, the new master immediately begins to perform the role, and the former master immediately ceases to perform the role. This is the preferred method of moving operations master roles.

Recognizing Operations Master Failures

Several operations master roles can be unavailable for quite some time before their absence becomes a problem. Other master roles play a crucial role in the day-to-day operation of your enterprise. You can identify problems with operations masters by examining the Directory Service event log.

However, you will often discover that an operations master has failed when you attempt to perform a function managed by the master, and the function fails. For example, if the RID master fails, eventually you will be prevented from creating new security principals.

Seizing Operations Master Roles

If a domain controller performing a single master operation fails and you cannot bring the system back to service, you have the option of seizing the operations token. When you seize a role, you designate a new master without gracefully removing the role from the failed master.

Seizing a role is a drastic action, so before seizing a role, think carefully about whether it is necessary. Determine the cause and expected duration that the operations master will be offline. If the operations master can be brought online in sufficient time, wait. What is sufficient time? It depends on the impact of the role that has failed:

- **PDC emulator failure**   The PDC emulator is the operations master that has the most immediate impact on normal operations and on users if it becomes unavailable. Fortunately, the PDC Emulator role can be seized to another domain controller and then transferred back to the original role holder when the system comes back online.

- **Infrastructure master failure**   A failure of the infrastructure master is noticeable to administrators but not to users. Because the master is responsible for updating the names of group members from other domains, it can appear as if group membership is incorrect even though, as mentioned earlier in this lesson, membership is not actually affected. You can seize the infrastructure master role to another domain controller and then transfer it back to the previous role holder when that system comes online.

- **RID master failure**   A failed RID master eventually prevents domain controllers from creating new SIDs and, therefore, prevents you from creating new accounts for users, groups, or computers. However, domain controllers receive a sizable pool of RIDs from the RID master, so unless you are generating numerous new accounts, you can often go for some time without the RID master online while it is being repaired. Seizing this role to another domain controller is a significant action. After the RID master role has been seized, the domain controller that had been performing the role cannot be brought back online.

- **Schema master failure** The schema master role is necessary only when schema modifications are being made, either directly by an administrator or by installing an Active Directory integrated application that changes the schema. At other times, the role is not necessary. It can remain offline indefinitely until schema changes are necessary. Seizing this role to another domain controller is a significant action. After the schema master role has been seized, the domain controller that had been performing the role cannot be brought back online.

- **Domain naming master failure** The domain naming master role is necessary only when you add a domain to the forest or remove a domain from a forest. Until such changes are required to your domain infrastructure, the domain naming master role can remain offline for an indefinite period of time. Seizing this role to another domain controller is a significant action. After the domain naming master role has been seized, the domain controller that had been performing the role cannot be brought back online.

Although you can transfer roles by using the administrative tools, you must use *Ntdsutil.exe* to seize a role. To seize an operations master role, perform the following steps:

1. From the command prompt, type **ntdsutil** and press Enter.

2. At the ntdsutil prompt, type **roles** and press Enter.

   The next steps establish a connection to the domain controller that you want to perform the single master operation role.

3. At the fsmo maintenance prompt, type **connections** and press Enter.

4. At the server connections prompt, type **connect to server DomainControllerFQDN** and press Enter, where *DomainControllerFQDN* is the FQDN of the domain controller you want to perform the role.

   Ntdsutil responds that it has connected to the server.

5. At the server connections prompt, type **quit** and press Enter.

6. At the fsmo maintenance prompt, type **seize Role** and press Enter, where *Role* is one of the following:

   - schema master
   - domain naming master
   - RID master
   - PDC
   - infrastructure master

7. At the fsmo maintenance prompt, type **quit** and press Enter.

8. At the ntdsutil prompt, type **quit** and press Enter.

Returning a Role to Its Original Holder

To provide for planned downtime of a domain controller if a role has been transferred, not seized, the role can be transferred back to the original domain controller.

If, however, a role has been seized and the former master can be brought back online, you must be very careful. The PDC emulator and infrastructure master are the only operations master roles that can be transferred back to the original master after having been seized.

> **NOTE** **DO NOT RETURN A SEIZED SCHEMA, DOMAIN NAMING, OR RID MASTER TO SERVICE**
>
> After seizing the schema, domain naming, or RID roles, you must completely decommission the original domain controller.

If you have seized the schema, domain naming, or RID roles to another domain controller, you must not bring the original domain controller back online without first completely decommissioning it. That means you must keep the original role holder physically disconnected from the network, and you must remove AD DS by using the *Dcpromo /forceremoval* command. You must also clean the metadata for that domain controller, as described in *http://go.microsoft.com/fwlink/?LinkId=80481*.

After the domain controller has been completely removed from Active Directory, if you want the server to rejoin the domain, you can connect it to the network and join the domain. If you want it to be a domain controller, you can promote it. If you want it to resume performing the operations master role, you can transfer the role back to the DC.

> **NOTE** **BETTER TO REBUILD**
>
> Because of the critical nature of domain controllers, it is recommended that you completely reinstall the former domain controller in this scenario.

 Quick Check

- You need to upgrade the power supply and motherboard of SERVER01, the domain controller performing the PDC Emulator operations master role. You want to ensure continuity of services provided by the PDC emulator. Describe the process of transferring the role to SERVER02, another domain controller, and transferring it back after SERVER01 has been upgraded. Which tools will you use, and which steps will you perform?

Quick Check Answer

- Before performing the upgrade, make sure the standby operations master is up to date with replication from the PDC emulator. Then open the Active Directory Users And Computers snap-in, right-click the domain, and choose Change Domain Controller. Select SERVER02. Right-click the domain and choose Operations

Masters. Click the PDC tab and click Change. The role is transferred. When SERVER01 comes back online, right-click the domain, choose Change Domain Controller, and select SERVER01. Right-click the domain, choose Operations Masters, click the PDC tab, and click Change.

PRACTICE   Transferring Operations Master Roles

In this practice, you identify the operations masters in the contoso.com domain, and you transfer an operations master to another domain controller to take the current master offline for maintenance. To perform Exercise 2 in this practice, you must have completed "Practice: Installing Domain Controllers" in Lesson 1 so that you have a second domain controller, SERVER02, in the domain.

EXERCISE 1   Identify Operations Masters

In this exercise, you use both user interface and command-line tools to identify operations masters in the contoso.com domain.

1. Log on to SERVER01 as Administrator.
2. Open the Active Directory Users And Computers snap-in.
3. Right-click the contoso.com domain and choose Operations Masters.
4. Click the tab for each operations master.

   The tabs identify the domain controllers currently performing the single master operations roles for the domain: PDC emulator, RID master, and Infrastructure master.
5. Click Close.
6. Open the Active Directory Domains And Trusts snap-in.
7. Right-click the root node of the snap-in, Active Directory Domains And Trusts, and choose Operations Master.

   The dialog box identifies the domain controller performing the domain naming master role.
8. Click Close.

   The Active Directory Schema snap-in does not have a console of its own and cannot be added to a custom console until you have registered the snap-in.
9. Open a command prompt, type **regsvr32 schmmgmt.dll**, and press Enter.
10. Click OK to close the message that appears.
11. Click Start and, in the Start Search box, type **mmc.exe** and press Enter.
12. Choose Add/Remove Snap-In from the File menu.

13. From the Available snap-ins list, choose Active Directory Schema, click Add, and then click OK.

14. Right-click the root node of the snap-in, Active Directory Schema, and choose Operations Master.

    The dialog box that appears identifies the domain controller currently performing the schema master role.

15. Click Close.

16. Open a command prompt, type the command **netdom query fsmo**, and press Enter.

    All operations masters are listed.

EXERCISE 2   Transfer an Operations Master Role

In this exercise, you prepare to take the operations master offline by transferring its role to another domain controller. You then simulate taking it offline, bringing it back online, and returning the operations master role.

1. Open the Active Directory Users And Computers snap-in.

2. Right-click the contoso.com domain and choose Change Domain Controller.

3. In the list of directory servers, select SERVER02.contoso.com and click OK.

    Before transferring an operations master, you must connect to the domain controller to which the role will be transferred.

    The root node of the snap-in indicates the domain controller to which you are connected: Active Directory Users And Computers [SERVER02.contoso.com].

4. Right-click the contoso.com domain and choose Operations Masters.

5. Click the PDC tab.

    The tab indicates that SERVER01.contoso.com currently holds the role token. SERVER02 .contoso.com is listed in the second text box. It should appear similar to Figure 10-2.

6. Click Change.

    An Active Directory Domain Services dialog box prompts you to confirm the transfer of the operations master role.

7. Click Yes.

    An Active Directory Domain Services dialog box confirms the role was successfully transferred.

8. Click OK, and then click Close. Wait two minutes to ensure that the change has replicated.

9. Simulate taking SERVER01 offline for maintenance by shutting down the server.

10. Simulate bringing the server back online by starting the server.

    Remember that you cannot bring a domain controller back online if the RID, schema, or domain naming roles have been seized. But you can bring it back online if any of these roles was transferred.

11. Log back on to SERVER01 as Administrator. Wait two minutes to ensure that all services have started. Repeat steps 1–8, this time connecting to SERVER01 and transferring the operations master role back to SERVER01.

Lesson Summary

- Operations master roles are assigned to domain controllers to perform single master operations.
- There are five operations master roles. Two are unique to the entire forest: schema and domain naming. Three are unique to each domain: PDC Emulator, RID, and infrastructure.
- The infrastructure master must be placed on a domain controller that is not a GC unless all DCs in the domain are GC servers.
- You can transfer a role by using Windows tools or Ntdsutil.exe. Transferring a role is the preferred method for managing operations masters.
- You can seize a role by using Ntdsutil.exe. This should be done only when the former role holder cannot be brought back online in sufficient time. Only the PDC Emulator and infrastructure roles can be transferred back to the original holder when it comes back online. DCs that held schema, RID, or domain naming roles must be completely decommissioned if those roles are seized.

Lesson Review

You can use the following questions to test your knowledge of the information in Lesson 2, "Managing Operations Masters." The questions are also available on the companion CD if you prefer to review them in electronic form.

> **NOTE ANSWERS**
>
> Answers to these questions and explanations of why each answer choice is right or wrong are located in the "Answers" section at the end of the book.

1. You are an administrator at Contoso, Ltd. The contoso.com domain consists of two sites. At the headquarters, one domain controller, named SERVER01, is a GC server and performs all five operations master roles. The second domain controller at the headquarters is named SERVER02. SERVER02 is not a GC and performs no operations master roles. At the branch office, the domain controller is named SERVER03, and it is a GC server. Which change to the operations master role placement must you make?

   A. Transfer the infrastructure master to SERVER03.

   B. Transfer the RID master to SERVER02.

   C. Transfer the schema master to SERVER02.

D. Transfer the domain naming master to SERVER03.

E. Transfer the infrastructure master to SERVER02.

2. You are an administrator at Contoso, Ltd. The forest consists of two domains, contoso.com and windows.contoso.com. Currently, SERVER02.windows.contoso.com performs all five operations master roles. You are going to decommission the windows.contoso.com domain and move all accounts into contoso.com. You want to transfer all operations masters to SERVER01.contoso.com. Which operations masters do you transfer? (Choose all that apply. Each correct answer is part of the solution.)

A. Infrastructure master

B. PDC emulator

C. RID master

D. Schema master

E. Domain naming master

3. You are an administrator at Contoso, Ltd. The contoso.com domain has five domain controllers. You want to move all domain operations masters to SERVER02.contoso.com. Which masters do you move? (Choose all that apply. Each correct answer is part of the solution.)

A. Infrastructure master

B. PDC emulator

C. RID master

D. Schema master

E. Domain naming master

Lesson 3: Configuring DFS Replication of SYSVOL

SYSVOL, a folder located at %SystemRoot%\SYSVOL by default, contains logon scripts, group policy templates (GPTs), and other resources critical to the health and management of an Active Directory domain. Ideally, SYSVOL should be consistent on each domain controller. However, changes to Group Policy objects and logon scripts are made from time to time, so you must ensure that those changes are replicated effectively and efficiently to all domain controllers. In versions of Windows Server prior to Windows Server 2008, the FRS was used to replicate the contents of SYSVOL between domain controllers. FRS has limitations in both capacity and performance that cause it to break occasionally. Unfortunately, troubleshooting and configuring FRS is quite difficult. In Windows Server 2008 and Windows Server 2008 R2 domains, you have the option to use DFS-R to replicate the contents of SYSVOL. In this lesson, you learn how to migrate SYSVOL from FRS to DFS-R.

> **After this lesson, you will be able to:**
> - Raise the domain functional level.
> - Migrate SYSVOL replication from FRS to DFS-R.
>
> **Estimated lesson time: 60 minutes**

Raising the Domain Functional Level

In Chapter 12, "Managing Multiple Domains and Forests," you learn about forest and domain functional levels. A domain's functional level is a setting that both restricts the operating systems that are supported as domain controllers in a domain and enables additional functionality in Active Directory. A domain with a Windows Server 2008 R2 domain controller can be at one of four functional levels: Windows 2000 Native, Windows Server 2003 Native, Windows Server 2008, and Windows Server 2008 R2.

At Windows 2000 Native domain functional level, domain controllers can be running Windows 2000 Server or Windows Server 2003. At Windows Server 2003 Native domain functional level, domain controllers can be running Windows Server 2003. At Windows Server 2008 domain functional level, all domain controllers must be running Windows Server 2008 or Windows Server 2008 R2. And at Windows Server 2008 R2 domain functional level, all domain controllers must be running Windows Server 2008 R2.

As you raise functional levels, new capabilities of Active Directory are enabled. At Windows Server 2008 domain functional level, for example, you can use DFS-R to replicate SYSVOL. Simply upgrading all domain controllers to Windows Server 2008 is not enough: You must specifically raise the domain functional level. You do this by using Active Directory Domains And Trusts.

To raise the domain functional level:

1. Run the Active Directory Domains And Trusts snap-in.

2. Right-click the domain and choose Raise Domain Functional Level.

3. Select Windows Server 2008, or the desired functional level, and then click Raise.

After you've set the domain functional level to Windows Server 2008, you cannot add domain controllers running previous versions of Windows Server. The functional level is associated only with domain controller operating systems; member servers and workstations can be running Windows Server 2003, Windows 2000 Server, Windows Vista, Windows XP, or Windows 2000 Workstation.

 Quick Check

- You are the administrator of Northwind Traders. The domain consists of three domain controllers. You have upgraded two of them to Windows Server 2008 R2. The third is still running Windows Server 2003. You want to establish DFS-R as the replication mechanism for SYSVOL. What must you do?

Quick Check Answer

- You must upgrade the third domain controller to Windows Server 2008 R2 and then raise the domain functional level to Windows Server 2008 or higher.

Understanding Migration Stages

Because SYSVOL is critical to the health and functionality of your domain, Windows does not provide a mechanism with which to convert replication of SYSVOL from FRS to DFS-R instantly. In fact, migration to DFS-R involves creating a parallel SYSVOL structure. When the parallel structure is successfully in place, clients are redirected to the new structure as the domain's system volume. When the operation has proven successful, you can eliminate FRS.

Migration to DFS-R thus consists of four stages or *states*:

- **0 (start)** The default state of a domain controller. Only FRS is used to replicate SYSVOL.

- **1 (prepared)** A copy of SYSVOL is created in a folder called SYSVOL_DFSR and is added to a replication set. DFS-R begins to replicate the contents of the SYSVOL_DFSR folders on all domain controllers. However, FRS continues to replicate the original SYSVOL folders and clients continue to use SYSVOL.

- **2 (redirected)** The SYSVOL share, which originally refers to SYSVOL*domain*\sysvol, is changed to refer to SYSVOL_DFSR*domain*\sysvol. Clients now use the SYSVOL_DFSR folder to obtain logon scripts and Group Policy templates.

- **3 (eliminated)** Replication of the old SYSVOL folder by FRS is stopped. The original SYSVOL folder is not deleted, however, so if you want to remove it entirely, you must do so manually.

You move your domain controllers through these stages by using the Dfsrmig.exe command. You use the following three options with Dfsrmig.exe:

- **setglobalstate**   The setglobalstate option configures the current global DFSR migration state, which applies to all domain controllers. The state is specified by the *state* parameter, which is 0–3. Each domain controller is notified of the new DFSR migration state and migrates to that state automatically.

- **getglobalstate**   The getglobalstate option reports the current global DFSR migration state.

- **getmigrationstate**   The getmigrationstate option reports the current migration state of each domain controller. Because it might take time for domain controllers to be notified of the new global DFSR migration state, and because it might take even more time for a DC to make the changes required by that state, DCs are not synchronized with the global state instantly. The getmigrationstate option allows you to monitor the progress of DCs toward the current global DFSR migration state.

If there is a problem moving from one state to the next higher state, you can revert to previous states by using the setglobalstate option. However, after you have used the setglobalstate option to specify state 3 (eliminated), you cannot revert to earlier states.

Migrating SYSVOL Replication to DFS-R

To migrate SYSVOL replication from FRS to DFS-R, perform the following steps:

1. Open the Active Directory Domains And Trusts snap-in.

2. Right-click the domain and choose Raise Domain Functional Level.

3. If the Current Domain Functional Level box does not indicate Windows Server 2008 or Windows Server 2008 R2, choose either Windows Server 2008 or Windows Server 2008 R2 from the Select An Available Domain Functional Level list.

4. Click Raise. Click OK twice in response to the dialog boxes that appear.

5. Open an elevated Command Prompt.

6. Type **dfsrmig /setglobalstate 1**.

7. Type **dfsrmig /getmigrationstate** to query the progress of DCs toward the Prepared global state. Repeat this step until the state has been attained by all DCs.

   This can take 15 minutes to an hour or longer.

8. Type **dfsrmig /setglobalstate 2**.

9. Type **dfsrmig /getmigrationstate** to query the progress of DCs toward the Redirected global state. Repeat this step until the state has been attained by all DCs.

   This can take 15 minutes to an hour or longer.

10. Type **dfsrmig /setglobalstate 3**.

    After you begin migration from state 2 (redirected) to state 3 (eliminated), any changes made to the SYSVOL folder must be replicated manually to the SYSVOL_DFSR folder.

11. Type **dfsrmig /getmigrationstate** to query the progress of DCs toward the Eliminated global state. Repeat this step until the state has been attained by all DCs.

This can take 15 minutes to an hour or longer.

For more information about the Dfsrmig.exe command, type **dfsrmig.exe /?**.

PRACTICE   **Configuring DFS Replication of SYSVOL**

In this practice, you experience SYSVOL replication and migrate the replication mechanism from FRS to DFS-R. You then verify that SYSVOL is being replicated by DFS-R.

Other practices in the training kit require Windows Server 2008 R2 forest functional level. To perform the exercises in this practice, you need a domain running at Windows Server 2003 domain functional level, so you must create a new forest running at Windows Server 2003 forest functional level consisting of one domain at Windows Server 2003 domain functional level and two domain controllers. To prepare for this practice, perform the following tasks:

- Install a server running Windows Server 2008 R2 full installation. The server must be named SERVER01. Its configuration should be as follows:
  - Computer Name: SERVER01
  - Workgroup membership: WORKGROUP
  - IPv4 address: 10.0.0.11
  - Subnet Mask: 255.255.255.0
  - Default Gateway: 10.0.0.1
  - DNS Server: 10.0.0.11

  Use the procedures described in Lesson 1, "Installing Active Directory Domain Services," of Chapter 1 if you need assistance installing Windows Server 2008 R2.

- Promote SERVER01 as a domain controller in a new forest named contoso.com. Select Windows Server 2003 forest and domain functional levels. Allow the Active Directory Domain Services Installation Wizard to install DNS on the domain controller.

  Use the steps in Exercises 3 and 4 of Lesson 1 in Chapter 1 if you need assistance promoting the domain controller. Be certain, however, to select Windows Server 2003 forest and domain functional levels.

- Install a second server running Windows Server 2008 R2 full installation. The server must be named SERVER02. Its configuration should be as follows:
  - Computer Name: SERVER02
  - Workgroup membership: WORKGROUP
  - IPv4 address: 10.0.0.12
  - Subnet Mask: 255.255.255.0
  - Default Gateway: 10.0.0.1
  - DNS Server: 10.0.0.11

Use the procedures described in Lesson 1 of Chapter 1 if you need assistance installing Windows Server 2008 R2.

- Promote SERVER02 as an additional domain controller in the contoso.com domain. Do not make it a GC or DNS server.

  Refer to the steps in Exercise 1 of Lesson 1 of this chapter if you need assistance promoting SERVER02.

EXERCISE 1 Experience SYSVOL Replication

In this exercise, you experience SYSVOL replication by adding a logon script to the NETLOGON share and observing its replication to another domain controller.

1. Log on to SERVER01 as Administrator.
2. Open %SystemRoot%\Sysvol\Domain\Scripts.
3. Create a new text file called **Sample Logon Script**.
4. Log on to SERVER02 as Administrator.
5. Open %SystemRoot%\Sysvol\Domain\Scripts.
6. Confirm that the text file replicated to the SERVER02 Scripts folder.

EXERCISE 2 Prepare to Migrate to DFS-R

Before you can migrate replication of SYSVOL to DFS-R, the domain must contain only Windows Server 2008 R2 domain controllers, and the domain functional level must be raised to Windows Server 2008 or higher. In this exercise, you confirm the fact that DFS-R migration is not supported in other domain functional levels. You also install the DFS administrative tools.

1. On SERVER01, open the Active Directory Domains And Trusts snap-in.
2. Right-click the contoso.com domain and choose Raise Domain Functional Level.
3. Confirm that the Current Domain Functional Level is Windows Server 2003.
4. Cancel out of the dialog box without raising the functional level.
5. Open a command prompt.
6. Type **dfsrmig /getglobalstate** and press Enter.

   A message informs you that Dfsrmig.exe is supported only on domains at the Windows Server 2008 functional level or higher.
7. Open the Active Directory Domains And Trusts snap-in.
8. Right-click the contoso.com domain and choose Raise Domain Functional Level.
9. Confirm that the Select An Available Domain Functional Level list indicates Windows Server 2008.
10. Click Raise. Click OK to confirm your change.

    A message informs you that the functional level was raised successfully.

11. Click OK.

12. At the command prompt, type **dfsrmig /getglobalstate** and press Enter.

    A message informs you that DFSR migration has not yet initialized.

EXERCISE 3 Migrate Replication of SYSVOL to DFS-R

In this exercise, you migrate SYSVOL replication from FRS to DFS-R.

1. On SERVER01, open Command Prompt.

2. Type **dfsrmig /setglobalstate 0** and press Enter.

   The following message appears:

   ```
   Current DFSR global state: 'Start'
   New DFSR global state: 'Start'
   Invalid state change requested.
   ```

   The default global state is already 0, 'Start,' so your command is not valid. However, this does serve to initialize DFSR migration.

3. Type **dfsrmig /getglobalstate** and press Enter.

   The following message appears:

   ```
   Current DFSR global state: 'Start'
   Succeeded.
   ```

4. Type **dfsrmig /getmigrationstate** and press Enter.

   The following message appears:

   ```
   All Domain Controllers have migrated successfully to Global state
   ('Start').
   Migration has reached a consistent state on all Domain Controllers.
   Succeeded.
   ```

5. Type **dfsrmig /setglobalstate 1** and press Enter.

   The following message appears:

   ```
   Current DFSR global state: 'Start'
   New DFSR global state: 'Prepared'

   Migration will proceed to 'Prepared' state. DFSR service will
   copy the contents of SYSVOL to SYSVOL_DFSR
   folder.

   If any DC is unable to start migration then try manual polling.
   OR Run with option /CreateGlobalObjects.
   Migration can start anytime between 15 min to 1 hour.
   Succeeded.
   ```

6. Type **dfsrmig /getmigrationstate** and press Enter.

   A message appears that reflects the migration state of each domain controller. Migration can take up to 15 minutes. Repeat this step until you receive the following message that indicates migration has progressed to the 'Prepared' state and is successful:

```
All Domain Controllers have migrated successfully to Global state
('Prepared').
Migration has reached a consistent state on all Domain Controllers.
Succeeded.
```

When you receive the message just shown, continue to step 7.

During migration to the 'Prepared' state, you might see one of these messages:

```
The following Domain Controllers are not in sync with Global state
('Prepared'):


Domain Controller (Local Migration State) - DC Type
====================================================

SERVER01 ('Start') - Primary DC
SERVER02 ('Start') - Writable DC

Migration has not yet reached a consistent state on all Domain Controllers.
State information might be stale due to AD latency.
```

or

```
The following Domain Controllers are not in sync with Global state
('Prepared'):


Domain Controller (Local Migration State) - DC Type
====================================================

SERVER01 ('Start') - Primary DC
SERVER02 ('Waiting For Initial Sync') - Writable DC

Migration has not yet reached a consistent state on all Domain Controllers.
State information might be stale due to AD latency.
```

or

```
The following Domain Controllers are not in sync with Global state
('Prepared'):


Domain Controller (Local Migration State) - DC Type
====================================================

SERVER02 ('Waiting For Initial Sync') - Writable DC

Migration has not yet reached a consistent state on all Domain Controllers.
State information might be stale due to AD latency.
```

7. Open the Event Viewer console from the Administrative Tools program group.

8. Expand Applications And Services Logs and select DFS Replication.

9. Locate the event with event ID 8014 and open its properties.

You should see the details shown in Figure 10-3.

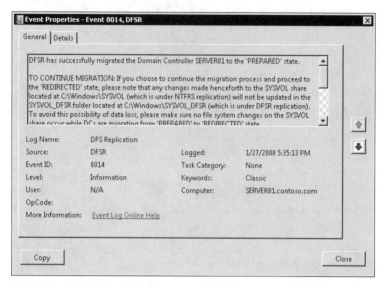

FIGURE 10-3 DFS-R event indicating successful migration to the 'Prepared' state

Type **dfsrmig /setglobalstate 2** and press Enter.

The following message appears:

```
Current DFSR global state: 'Prepared'
New DFSR global state: 'Redirected'

Migration will proceed to 'Redirected' state. The SYSVOL share will be
changed to SYSVOL_DFSR folder, which is replicated using DFSR.


Succeeded.
```

10. Type **dfsrmig /getmigrationstate** and press Enter.

A message appears that reflects the migration state of each domain controller. Migration can take up to 15 minutes. Repeat this step until you receive the following message that indicates migration has progressed to the 'Prepared' state and is successful:

```
All Domain Controllers have migrated successfully to Global state
('Redirected').
Migration has reached a consistent state on all Domain Controllers.
Succeeded.
```

When you receive the message just shown, continue to step 12.

During migration, you might receive messages like the following:

```
The following Domain Controllers are not in sync with Global state
```

```
('Redirected'):

Domain Controller (Local Migration State) - DC Type
=====================================================

SERVER02 ('Prepared') - Writable DC

Migration has not yet reached a consistent state on all Domain Controllers.
State information might be stale due to AD latency.
```

11. Type **net share** and press Enter.

12. Confirm that the NETLOGON share refers to the %SystemRoot%\SYSVOL_DFSR\Sysvol \contoso.com\Scripts folder.

13. Confirm that the SYSVOL share refers to the %SystemRoot%\SYSVOL_DFSR\Sysvol folder.

14. In Windows Explorer, open the %SystemRoot%\SYSVOL_DFSR\Sysvol\contoso.com \Scripts folder.

15. Confirm that the Sample Logon Script file was migrated to the new Scripts folder.

16. Create a new text file named **Sample Logon Script DFSR**.

17. On SERVER02, confirm that the file replicated to the %SystemRoot%\SYSVOL_DFSR \Sysvol\contoso.com\Scripts folder.

Lesson Summary

- You cannot use DFS-R to replicate SYSVOL until the domain is at Windows Server 2008 functional level or higher.

- The Dfsrmig.exe command manages the migration from the FRS-replicated SYSVOL folder to the DFS-R replicated SYSVOL_DFSR folder.

- There are four migration states: Start, Prepared, Redirected, and Eliminated. You can revert to previous states until you have configured the state as Eliminated.

Lesson Review

You can use the following questions to test your knowledge of the information in Lesson 3, "Configuring DFS Replication of SYSVOL." The questions are also available on the companion CD if you prefer to review them in electronic form.

> **NOTE ANSWERS**
>
> Answers to these questions and explanations of why each answer choice is right or wrong are located in the "Answers" section at the end of the book.

1. You are an administrator at Trey Research. Your domain consists of three domain controllers, two running Windows Server 2008 R2 and one running Windows Server 2003. The forest root domain has two domain controllers, both running

Windows Server 2003. You want to replicate SYSVOL in your domain, using DFS-R. What steps must you take? (Choose all that apply. Each correct answer is part of the solution.)

A. Upgrade the forest root domain controllers to Windows Server 2008 R2.

B. Configure the forest functional level to Windows Server 2008.

C. Upgrade your Windows Server 2003 domain controller to Windows Server 2008 R2.

D. Configure the domain functional level of your domain to Windows Server 2008.

E. Configure the domain functional level of the forest root domain to Windows Server 2008.

2. You want to configure Active Directory so that replication of logon scripts is managed using DFS-R. Which command do you use?

A. Dfsrmig.exe

B. Repadmin.exe

C. Dfsutil.exe

D. Dfscmd.exe

Chapter Review

To further practice and reinforce the skills you learned in this chapter, you can perform the following tasks:

- Review the chapter summary.
- Review the key term introduced in this chapter.
- Complete the case scenario. This scenario sets up a real-world situation involving the topics of this chapter and asks you to create a solution.
- Complete the suggested practices.
- Take a practice test.

Chapter Summary

- Domain controllers in an Active Directory domain replicate changes in a multimaster fashion; however, certain roles are performed by a single domain controller.
- When you add new domain controllers to a domain, you can transfer operations master roles to decrease single-point-of-failure risks, to increase performance, or to accommodate planned downtime.
- Before you add the first Windows Server 2008 R2 domain controller to a forest, you must run Adprep.exe /forestprep and Adprep.exe /domainprep /gpprep.
- After all domain controllers are running Windows Server 2008 or Windows Server 2008 R2, you can raise the domain functional level to Windows Server 2008, which allows you to begin migrating replication of SYSVOL to the more robust DFS-R technology.

Key Term

The following term was introduced in this chapter. Do you know what it means?

- operations master

Case Scenario

In the following case scenario, you apply what you've learned about installing domain controllers and configuring operations masters. You can find answers to these questions in the "Answers" section at the end of this book.

Case Scenario: Upgrading a Domain

You are a consultant who has been hired by Contoso, Ltd., to provide guidance during the upgrade of the contoso.com forest to Windows Server 2008 R2 domain controllers. The forest consists of two domains, contoso.com and subsidiary.contoso.com. Both domains contain three domain controllers running Windows Server 2003.

1. What must you do before installing any Windows Server 2008 R2 domain controllers in the contoso.com forest?

2. The subsidiary.contoso.com domain consists of three small branch offices, each with a domain controller. The management of Contoso wants all three branch office DCs to be read-only. Is this possible and, if so, how?

3. You are planning to upgrade SERVER01 in the forest root domain, which performs all forest and domain single master operations. What should you do prior to upgrading the server?

Suggested Practices

To help you successfully master the exam objectives presented in this chapter, complete the following tasks.

Upgrade a Windows Server 2003 Domain

In this practice, you upgrade a Windows Server 2003 domain to Windows Server 2008 R2. To perform these practices, you must have two servers available.

- **Practice 1** Install a server running Windows Server 2003. Promote it to a domain controller in a new forest. Configure its domain and forest functional levels to Windows Server 2003.

- **Practice 2** Run Adprep /forestprep and Adprep /domainprep /gpprep from the Windows Server 2008 R2 installation DVD \Support\Adprep folder.

- **Practice 3** Install a server running Windows Server 2008 R2 and join the domain. Promote the server to a domain controller, including DNS and global catalog.

- **Practice 4** Transfer all operations master roles to the new domain controller.

- **Practice 5 (Option 1)** Upgrade the first domain controller to Windows Server 2008 R2.

- **Practice 5 (Option 2)** Demote the Windows Server 2003 domain controller and remove it from the domain to a workgroup. Format the disk. Install Windows Server 2008 R2 and join the domain. Promote the server to a domain controller. Transfer all operations master roles back to the system.

Take a Practice Test

The practice tests on this book's companion CD offer many options. For example, you can test yourself on just one exam objective, or you can test yourself on all the 70-640 certification exam content. You can set up the test so that it closely simulates the experience of taking a certification exam, or you can set it up in study mode so that you can look at the correct answers and explanations after you answer each question.

MORE INFO **PRACTICE TESTS**

For details about all the practice test options available, see the "How to Use the Practice Tests" section in this book's Introduction.

Managing Sites and Active Directory Replication

You learned in previous chapters that domain controllers (DCs) in a Windows Server 2008 R2 domain are peers. Each maintains a copy of the directory, each performs similar services to support authentication of security principals, and changes made on any one domain controller are replicated to all other domain controllers. As an administrator of an enterprise running Microsoft Windows, one of your tasks is to ensure that authentication is provided as efficiently as possible and that replication between domain controllers is optimized. Active Directory Domain Services (AD DS) sites are the core component of the directory service that supports the goals of service localization and replication. In this chapter, you learn how to create a distributed directory service that supports domain controllers in portions of your network that are separated by expensive, slow, or unreliable links. You learn where domain controllers should be placed and how to manage replication and service utilization. You also learn how to control which data is replicated to each domain controller by configuring global catalogs (GCs) and application partitions.

Exam objectives in this chapter:

- Configure the global catalog.
- Configure sites.
- Configure Active Directory replication.
- Monitor Active Directory.

Lessons in this chapter:

Before You Begin

To complete the practices in this chapter, you must have created two domain controllers named SERVER01 and SERVER02 in a domain named contoso.com. Both domain controllers should be running a full installation of Windows Server 2008 R2, rather than a Server Core installation. See Chapter 1, "Creating an Active Directory Domain," and Chapter 10, "Administering Domain Controllers," for detailed steps for this task.

 REAL WORLD

Dan Holme

As you learned in the previous chapter, it is important to have more than one domain controller in a domain to provide continuity of service in the event that one domain controller fails. That general rule—at least two DCs per domain—assumes that all servers and clients in your environment are well connected to the DCs. But what happens if you have several network locations separated by links that are not LAN speed? And what must you do if those intersite links are unreliable? Well, then, you must determine whether to place domain controllers in remote locations and how to manage replication of the directory to those domain controllers. On the 70-640 exam, the focus on Active Directory sites is their relationship to replication, and you will certainly learn how to manage replication in this chapter. But sites are also important in highly connected environments because they allow you to manage *service localization*—that is, to ensure that when a service is available from multiple servers, a client uses the most efficient server. Throughout this chapter, be aware of the relationship between sites and service localization as well, because although it might not be as important on the exam, it is certainly important in your production environment.

Lesson 1: Configuring Sites and Subnets

Active Directory represents human beings as user objects in the directory service. It represents machines as computer objects. It represents network topology with objects called *sites* and *subnets*. Active Directory site objects are used to manage replication and service localization and, fortunately, in many environments, the configuration of sites and subnets can be quite straightforward. In this lesson, you learn the fundamental concepts and techniques required to configure and manage sites and subnets.

> **After this lesson, you will be able to:**
> - Identify the roles of sites and subnets.
> - Describe the process with which a client locates a domain controller.
> - Configure sites and subnets.
> - Manage domain controller server objects in sites.
>
> **Estimated lesson time: 45 minutes**

Understanding Sites

When administrators describe their network infrastructure, they often mention how many sites make up their enterprise. To most administrators, a site is a physical location, such as an office or a city. Sites are connected by links—network links that might be as basic as dial-up connections or as sophisticated as fiber links. Together, the physical locations and links make up the network infrastructure.

Active Directory represents the network infrastructure with objects called *sites* and *site links*, and although the words are similar, these objects are not identical to the sites and links described by administrators. This lesson focuses on sites, and Lesson 3, "Configuring Replication," discusses site links.

It's important to understand the properties and roles of sites in Active Directory to understand the subtle distinction between Active Directory sites and network sites. Active Directory sites are objects in the directory, specifically in the Configuration container (CN=Configuration,DC=*forest root domain*). These objects are used to achieve two service management tasks:

- To manage replication traffic
- To facilitate service localization

Replication Traffic

Replication is the transfer of changes between domain controllers. When you add a user or change a user's password, for example, the change you make is committed to the directory by one domain controller. That change must be communicated to all other domain controllers in the domain.

Active Directory assumes there are two types of networks within your enterprise: highly connected and less highly connected. Conceptually, a change made to Active Directory should replicate immediately to other domain controllers within the highly connected network in which the change was made. However, you might not want the change to replicate immediately over a slower, more expensive, or less reliable link to another site. Instead, you might want to manage replication over less highly connected segments of your enterprise to optimize performance, reduce costs, or manage bandwidth.

An Active Directory site represents a highly connected portion of your enterprise. When you define a site, the domain controllers within the site replicate changes almost instantly. Replication between sites can be scheduled and managed.

Service Localization

Active Directory is a distributed service; that is, assuming you have at least two domain controllers, multiple servers (domain controllers) provide the same services of authentication and directory access. If you have more than one network site, and if you place a domain controller in each, you want to encourage clients to authenticate against the domain controller in their site. This is an example of service localization.

Active Directory sites help you localize services, including those provided by domain controllers. During logon, Windows clients are automatically directed to a domain controller in their site. If a domain controller is not available in their site, they are directed to a DC in another site that can authenticate the client efficiently.

Other services can be localized as well. Distributed File System Namespaces (DFS Namespaces), for example, is a localized service. DFS clients obtain replicated resources from the most efficient server, based on their Active Directory site. In fact, because clients know what site they are in, any distributed service could be written to take advantage of the Active Directory site structure to provide intelligent localization of service usage.

Planning Sites

Because sites are used to optimize replication and to enable service localization, you must spend time designing your Active Directory site structure. Active Directory sites might not map one to one with your network's sites. Consider two scenarios:

- You have offices in two distinct locations. You place one domain controller in each location. The locations are highly connected, and to improve performance, you decide to configure a single Active Directory site that includes both locations.

- You have an enterprise on a large, highly connected campus. From a replication perspective, the enterprise could be considered a single site. However, you want to encourage clients to use distributed services in their location, so you configure multiple sites to support service localization.

Therefore, an Active Directory site can include more than one network site or be a subset of a single network site. The key is to remember that sites serve both replication management and service localization roles. Several characteristics of your enterprise can be used to help you determine which sites are necessary:

Connection Speed

An Active Directory site represents a unit of the network that is characterized by fast, reliable, inexpensive connectivity. Much documentation suggests that the slowest link speed within a site should be no less than 512 kilobits per second (kbps). However, this guidance is not immutable. Some organizations have links as slow as 56 or even 28 kbps within a site.

Service Placement

Because Active Directory sites manage Active Directory replication and service localization, it is not useful to create a site for a network location that does not host a domain controller or other Active Directory–aware service such as a replicated DFS resource.

> **NOTE SITES WHERE THERE ARE NO DOMAIN CONTROLLERS**
>
> Domain controllers are only one distributed service in a Windows enterprise. Other services, such as replicated DFS resources, are site-aware as well. You might configure sites to localize services other than authentication, in which case you will have sites without domain controllers.

User Population

Concentration of users can also influence your site design, although indirectly. If a network location has a sufficient number of users for whom the inability to authenticate would be problematic, place a domain controller in the location to support authentication within the location. After a domain controller or other distributed service is placed in the location to support those users, you might want to manage Active Directory replication to the location or localize service use by configuring an Active Directory site to represent the location.

Summarizing Site Planning Criteria

Every Active Directory forest includes at least one site. The default site created when you instantiate a forest with the first domain controller is creatively named *Default-First-Site-Name*. You should create additional sites when:

- A part of the network is separated by a slow link.
- A part of the network has enough users to warrant hosting domain controllers or other services in that location.
- Directory query traffic warrants a local domain controller.
- You want to control service localization.
- You want to control replication between domain controllers.

Server Placement

Network administrators often want to know when placing a domain controller in a remote site is recommended. The answer is, "It depends." Specifically, it depends on the resources required by users in the site and the tolerance for downtime. If users in a remote site perform all work tasks by accessing resources in the data center, for example, then if the link to the remote site fails, the users cannot access the resources they require and a local domain controller would not improve the situation. However, if users access resources in the remote site and the link fails, a local domain controller can continue to provide authentication for users and they can continue to work with their local resources.

In most branch office scenarios, users require certain resources in the branch office to perform their work tasks. Those resources, if not stored on the user's own computer, require domain authentication of the user. Therefore, a domain controller is generally recommended. The introduction of read-only domain controllers (RODCs) in Windows Server 2008 and Windows Server 2008 R2 reduces the risk and management burden of domain controllers in branch offices, so it will be easier for most organizations to deploy DCs in each network location.

Creating Sites

Sites and replication are managed using the Active Directory Sites And Services snap-in. To define an Active Directory site, you create an object of class *site*. The site object is a container that manages replication for domain controllers in the site. You also create one or more subnet objects. A subnet object defines a range of IP addresses and is linked to one site. Service localization is attained when a client's IP address can be associated with a site through the relationship between the subnet object and the site object.

To create a site:

1. Right-click the Sites node in Active Directory Sites And Services, and then click New Site.

2. In the New Object – Site dialog box, shown in Figure 11-1, enter a site name and select a site link.

   The default site link, DEFAULTIPSITELINK, is the only site link available to you until you create additional site links as discussed in Lesson 2, "Configuring the Global Catalog and Application Directory Partitions."

After creating a site, you can right-click it and click Rename to rename it. It is recommended that you rename the Default-First-Site-Name site to reflect a site name that is aligned with your business and network topology.

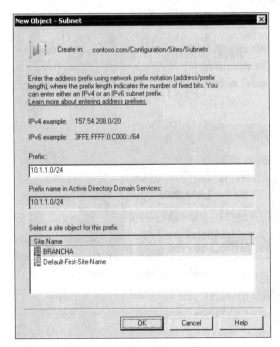

FIGURE 11-1 The New Object – Site dialog box

Sites are useful only when a client or server knows the site to which it belongs. This is typically achieved by associating the system's IP address with a site, and subnet objects achieve this association.

To create a subnet object:

1. Right-click the Subnets node in the Active Directory Sites And Services snap-in and click New Subnet. The New Object – Subnet dialog box shown in Figure 11-2 appears.

FIGURE 11-2 The New Object – Subnet dialog box

2. Enter the network prefix and subnet mask length.

The subnet object is defined as a range of addresses using network prefix notation. For example, for a subnet representing the addresses 10.1.1.1 to 10.1.1.254 with a 24-bit subnet mask, the prefix would be 10.1.1.0/24. For more information about entering addresses, click the Learn More About Entering Address Prefixes link in the New Object – Subnet dialog box.

3. After entering the network prefix, select the site object with which the subnet is associated. A subnet can be associated with only one site; however, a site can have more than one subnet linked to it. The Properties dialog box of a site, shown in Figure 11-3, shows the subnets associated with the site. You cannot change the subnets in this dialog box, however; instead, you must open the properties of the subnet, shown in Figure 11-4, to change the site to which the subnet is linked.

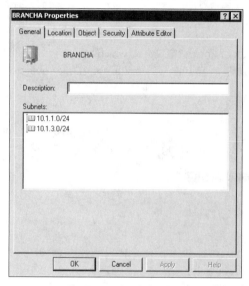

FIGURE 11-3 The Properties dialog box for a site

NOTE DEFINING EVERY IP SUBNET

In your production environment, be certain to define every IP subnet as an Active Directory subnet object. If a client's IP address is not included within a subnet range, the client is unable to determine which Active Directory site it belongs to, which can lead to performance and functionality problems. Don't forget backbone subnets and subnets used for remote access such as virtual private network (VPN) address ranges.

FIGURE 11-4 The Properties dialog box for a subnet

Managing Domain Controllers in Sites

There may be times when you need to manage domain controllers in Active Directory sites:

- You create a new site and move an existing domain controller to it.

- You demote a domain controller.

- You promote a new domain controller.

When you create your Active Directory forest, the first domain controller is automatically placed under the site object named *Default-First-Site-Name*. You can see the domain controller SERVER01.contoso.com in Figure 11-5. Additional domain controllers are added to sites based on their IP addresses. For example, if a server with IP address 10.1.1.17 is promoted to a domain controller in the network shown in Figure 11-4, the server is automatically added to the BRANCHA site, because the 10.1.1.0/24 subnet is associated with the BRANCHA site. Figure 11-5 shows SERVER02 in the BRANCHA site.

FIGURE 11-5 A domain controller in a site

Each site contains a Servers container, which itself contains an object for each domain controller in the site. The Servers container in a site should show only domain controllers, not all servers. When you promote a new domain controller, the domain controller is, by default, placed in the site associated with its IP address. However, the Active Directory Domain Services Installation Wizard allows you to specify another site. You can also pre-create the server object for the domain controller in the correct site by right-clicking the Servers container in the appropriate site, pointing to New, and then clicking Server.

Finally, you can move the domain controller to the correct site after installation by right-clicking the server and clicking Move. In the Move Server dialog box, select the new site and click OK. The domain controller is moved. It is a best practice to place a domain controller in the site object that is associated with the DC's IP address. If a DC is multihomed, it can belong to only one site. If a site has no domain controllers, users can still log on to the domain; their logon requests are handled by a domain controller in an adjacent site or another domain controller in the domain.

To remove a domain controller object, right-click it and click Delete.

Understanding Domain Controller Location

You started this lesson by examining AD DS as a distributed service, providing authentication and directory access on more than one domain controller. You learned to identify where, in your network topology, to define sites and place domain controllers. Now you are ready to examine how, exactly, service localization works—how Active Directory clients become site aware and locate the domain controller in their site. Although this level of detail is unlikely to appear on the certification examination, it can be extremely helpful when you need to troubleshoot authentication of a computer or of a user.

Service Locator Records

When a domain controller is added to the domain, it advertises its services by creating Service Locator (SRV) records, also called locator records, in DNS. Unlike host records (A records), which map host names to IP addresses, SRV records map services to host names. The domain controller advertises its ability to provide authentication and directory access by registering Kerberos and LDAP SRV records. These SRV records are added to several folders within the DNS zones for the forest. The first folder is within the domain zone. It is called _tcp, and it contains the SRV records for all domain controllers in the domain. The second folder is specific to this site, in which the domain controller is located, with the path _sites*sitename*_tcp, where *sitename* is the name of the site. In Figure 11-6, you can see the Kerberos and LDAP SRV records for SERVER02.contoso.com in its site, _sites\BRANCHA_tcp. You can also see the _tcp folder at the first level beneath the zone.

The same records are registered in several places in the _msdcs.*domainName* zone— for example, _msdcs.contoso.com in Figure 11-6. This zone contains records for Microsoft Domain Controller Services. The underscore characters are a requirement of RFC 2782.

FIGURE 11-6 The SRV records for SERVER02 in the BRANCHA site

Locator records contain:

- **The service name and port**   This portion of the SRV record indicates a service with a fixed port. It does not have to be a well-known port. SRV records in Windows Server 2008 R2 include LDAP (port 389), Kerberos (port 88), Kerberos Password protocol (KPASSWD, port 464), and GC services (port 3268).

- **Protocol**   TCP or UDP are indicated as a transport protocol for the service. The same service can use both protocols, in separate SRV records. Kerberos records, for example, are registered for both TCP and UDP. Microsoft clients use only TCP, but UNIX clients can use UDP.

- **Host name**   The name corresponds to the A (Host) record for the server hosting the service. When a client queries for a service, the DNS server returns the SRV record and associated A records, so the client does not need to submit a separate query to resolve the IP address of a service.

The service name in the SRV record follows the standard DNS hierarchy, with components separated by dots. For example, the Kerberos service of a domain controller is registered as:

```
kerberos._tcp.siteName._sites.domainName
```

Reading this SRV record name right to left like other DNS records, it translates to:

- *domainName*: the domain or zone—for example, contoso.com
- _sites: all sites registered with DNS

- *siteName*: the site of the domain controller registering the service
- _tcp: any TCP-based services in the site
- kerberos: a Kerberos Key Distribution Center (KDC) using TCP as its transport protocol

Domain Controller Location

Imagine that a Windows client has just been joined to the domain. It restarts, receives an IP address from a DHCP server, and is ready to authenticate to the domain. How does the client know where to find a domain controller?

It does not. Therefore, the client queries the domain for a domain controller by querying the _tcp folder, which, you'll remember, contains the SRV records for all domain controllers in the domain. DNS returns a list of all matching DCs, and the client attempts to contact all of them on this, its first startup. The first domain controller that responds to the client examines the client's IP address, cross-references that address with subnet objects, and informs the client of the site to which the client belongs. The client stores the site name in its registry, and then queries for domain controllers in the site-specific _tcp folder. DNS returns a list of all DCs in the site. The client attempts to bind with all, and the DC that responds first authenticates the client.

The client forms an affinity for this DC and will attempt to authenticate with the same DC in the future. If the DC is unavailable, the client queries the site's _tcp folder again and attempts to bind with all DCs in the site. But what happens if the client is a mobile computer—a laptop? Imagine that the computer has been authenticating in the BRANCHA site, and then the user brings the computer to the BRANCHB site. When the computer starts up, it is assigned an IP address appropriate for the BRANCHB site by a DHCP server that services the site. The computer then attempts to authenticate with its preferred DC in the BRANCHA site. That DC notices the client's IP address is associated with BRANCHB and informs the client of its new site. The client then queries DNS for domain controllers in BRANCHB.

You can see how, by storing subnet and site information in Active Directory and by registering services in DNS, a client is encouraged to use services in its site—the definition of service localization.

> **MORE INFO** **DOMAIN CONTROLLER LOCATION**
>
> For more information about domain controller location, see *http://www.microsoft.com/technet/prodtechnol/windows2000serv/reskit/distrib/dsbc_nar_jevl.mspx?mfr=true.*

Site Coverage

What happens if a site has no domain controller? Sites can be used to direct users to local copies of replicated resources such as shared folders replicated within a DFS namespace, so you might have sites without a DC. In this case, a nearby domain controller registers its SRV records in the site in a process called *site coverage*. To be precise, a site without a DC is generally covered by a domain controller in a site with the lowest cost to the site requiring coverage. You learn more about site link costs in the next lesson. You can also manually configure site coverage and SRV record priority if you want to implement strict control over authentication in sites without DCs. The domain controller location URL just listed contains details about the algorithm that determines which DC automatically covers a site without a DC.

PRACTICE **Configuring Sites and Subnets**

In this practice, you use best practices to implement a structure of sites and subnets for the contoso.com domain.

EXERCISE 1   Configure the Default Site

A new domain contains the Default-First-Site-Name site. In this exercise, you rename that site and associate two subnets with the site.

1. Open the Active Directory Sites And Services snap-in.
2. Expand Sites, right-click Default-First-Site-Name, and click Rename.
3. Type **HEADQUARTERS** and press Enter.

    Because site names are registered in DNS, you should use DNS-compliant names that avoid special characters and spaces.
4. Right-click Subnets and click New Subnet.
5. In the Prefix box, type **10.0.0.0/24**.
6. In the Select A Site Object For This Prefix list, select HEADQUARTERS.
7. Click OK.
8. Right-click Subnets and click New Subnet.
9. In the Prefix box, type **10.0.1.0/24**.
10. In the Select A Site Object For This Prefix list, select HEADQUARTERS.
11. Click OK.

EXERCISE 2   Create an Additional Site

Sites allow you to manage replication traffic and localize services such as the authentication and directory access provided by domain controllers. In this exercise, you create a second site and associate a subnet with it.

1. Open the Active Directory Sites And Services snap-in.
2. Right-click Sites and click New Site.
3. Type **BRANCHA** in the Name box.
4. Select DEFAULTIPSITELINK.
5. Click OK.

An Active Directory Domain Services dialog box appears, explaining the steps required to complete the configuration of the site.

6. Click OK.
7. Right-click Subnets and click New Subnet.
8. In the Prefix box, type **10.1.1.0/24**.
9. In the Select A Site Object For This Prefix list, select BRANCHA.
10. Click OK.
11. In the Active Directory Sites And Services snap-in, expand the Subnets node.
12. Right-click 10.1.1.0/24 and click Properties.
13. In the Description box, type **Primary subnet for branch office**.
14. In the Site drop-down list, select BRANCHA.
15. Click OK.

Lesson Summary

- Sites are Active Directory objects that are used to manage directory replication and service localization.
- To configure a site, you must create a site object and associate a subnet object with the site. A site can have more than one subnet, but a subnet can belong to only one site.
- Domain controllers are placed in sites as server objects.
- Domain controllers register service locator (SRV) records to advertise their Kerberos (authentication) and directory access services. These SRV records are created in site-specific nodes within the DNS zones for the domain and forest.
- Domain members discover their site during authentication. A domain controller uses a client's IP address and the domain's site and subnet information to determine the client's site and then sends that information to the client.

Lesson Review

You can use the following questions to test your knowledge of the information in Lesson 1, "Configuring Sites and Subnets." The questions are also available on the companion CD if you prefer to review them in electronic form.

> **NOTE ANSWERS**
>
> Answers to these questions and explanations of why each answer choice is right or wrong are located in the "Answers" section at the end of the book.

1. Client computers in a branch office are performing poorly during logon. You notice that the computers report that their logon server is a domain controller in a remote site rather than the domain controller in the branch office itself. Which of the following could cause this problem?

    A. The branch office domain controller is not assigned to a site.

    B. The branch office site is not assigned to a site link.

    C. The branch office IP address range is not associated with the site.

    D. The branch office subnet is assigned to two sites.

2. You are adding a read-only domain controller to a branch office location. You want to ensure that clients in the branch office are likely to authenticate with the RODC. What is required? (Choose all that apply. Each correct answer presents part of the solution.)

    A. A subnet object with the network prefix of the branch office IP address range

    B. An account for the domain controller in the organizational unit for the site

    C. A site link transport for the site

    D. A site object for the branch office

    E. A server object in the site object for the branch office

Lesson 2: Configuring the Global Catalog and Application Directory Partitions

As soon as you have more than one domain controller in your domain, you must consider replication of the directory database between domain controllers. In this lesson, you learn which directory partitions are replicated to each domain controller in a forest and how to manage the replication of the GC and application partitions.

> **After this lesson, you will be able to:**
> - Define the purpose of the global catalog.
> - Configure domain controllers as global catalog servers.
> - Implement universal group membership caching.
> - Understand the role of application directory partitions.
>
> **Estimated lesson time: 45 minutes**

Reviewing Active Directory Partitions

In Chapter 1, you learned that AD DS includes a data store for identity and management, specifically the directory database, Ntds.dit. Within that single file are directory partitions. Each directory partition, also called a naming context, contains objects of a particular scope and purpose. Three major naming contexts are discussed in this training kit:

- **Domain**   The Domain naming context (NC) contains all the objects stored in a domain, including users, groups, computers, and Group Policy containers (GPCs).

- **Configuration**   The Configuration partition contains objects that represent the logical structure of the forest, including domains, as well as the physical topology, including sites, subnets, and services.

- **Schema**   The Schema defines the object classes and their attributes for the entire directory.

Each domain controller maintains a copy, or *replica*, of several naming contexts. The Configuration is replicated to every domain controller in the forest, as is the Schema. The Domain NC for a domain is replicated to all domain controllers within a domain but not to domain controllers in other domains, so each domain controller has at least three replicas: the Domain NC for its domain, the Configuration, and the Schema.

Traditionally, replicas have been complete replicas, containing every attribute of an object, and replicas have been writable on all DCs. Beginning with Windows Server 2008, read-only domain controllers (RODCs) change the picture slightly. An RODC maintains a read-only replica of all objects in the Configuration, Schema, and Domain NCs of its domain. However, certain attributes are not replicated to an RODC—specifically, secrets such as user passwords—unless the password policy of the RODC allows such replication. There are also attributes that are domain and forest secrets that are never replicated to an RODC.

Understanding the Global Catalog

Imagine a forest with two domains. Each domain has two domain controllers. All four domain controllers maintain a replica of the Schema and Configuration for the forest. The domain controllers in Domain A have replicas of the Domain NC for Domain A, and the domain controllers in Domain B have replicas of the Domain NC for Domain B.

What happens if a user in Domain B is searching for a user, computer, or group in Domain A? The Domain B domain controllers do not maintain any information about objects in Domain A, so a domain controller in Domain B could not answer a query about objects in the Domain NC of Domain A.

That's where the global catalog comes in. The *global catalog* (GC) is a partition that stores information about every object in the forest. When a user in Domain B looks for an object in Domain A, the GC provides the results of the query. To optimize efficiency of the GC, it does not contain every attribute of every object in the forest. Instead, it contains a subset of attributes that are useful for searching across domains. That is why the GC is also called the *partial attribute set* (PAS). In terms of its role supporting search, you can think of the GC as a kind of index for the AD DS data store.

Placing Global Catalog Servers

The GC improves efficiency of the directory service tremendously and is required for applications such as Microsoft Exchange Server and Microsoft Office Outlook. Therefore, you want a GC to be available to these and other applications. The GC can be served only by a domain controller and, in an ideal world, every domain controller would be a GC server. In fact, many organizations are now configuring all of their domain controllers as GC servers.

The potential downside to such a configuration relates to replication. The GC is another partition that must be replicated. In a single domain forest, very little overhead is actually added by configuring all domain controllers as GC servers because all domain controllers already maintain a full set of attributes for all domain and forest objects. A large, multidomain forest has overhead related to replication of changes to the partial attribute set of objects in other domains. However, many organizations are finding that Active Directory replication is efficient enough to replicate the GC without significant impact to their networks and that the benefits far outweigh such impact. If you choose to configure all DCs as GC servers, you no longer need to worry about the placement of the infrastructure operations master; its role is no longer necessary in a domain where all DCs are GC servers.

It is particularly recommended to configure a GC server on a domain controller in a site where one or more of the following is true:

- A commonly used application performs directory queries against the GC.
- The connection to a GC server is slow or unreliable.
- The site contains a computer running Exchange Server.

Configuring a Global Catalog Server

When you create the first domain in the forest, the first domain controller is configured as a GC. You must decide for each additional DC whether it should be a GC server. The Active Directory Domain Services Installation Wizard and the Dcpromo.exe command both allow you to configure a GC server when promoting a domain controller. You can also add or remove the GC from a domain controller by using Active Directory Sites And Services.

To configure a DC as a GC:

1. In the Active Directory Sites And Services snap-in, expand the site, the Servers container within the site, and the domain controller's server object.

2. Right-click the NTDS Settings node and click Properties.

3. On the General tab, shown in Figure 11-7, select the Global Catalog check box.

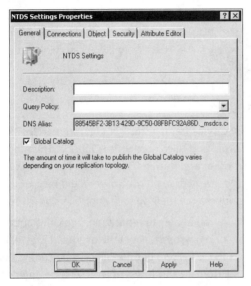

FIGURE 11-7 The NTDS Settings Properties dialog box, showing the Global Catalog check box

To remove the GC from a domain controller, perform the same steps, clearing the Global Catalog check box.

Universal Group Membership Caching

In Chapter 4, "Managing Groups," you learned that Active Directory supports groups of universal scope. Universal groups are designed to include users and groups from multiple domains in a forest. The membership of universal groups is replicated in the GC. When a user logs on, the user's universal group membership is obtained from a GC server. If a GC is not available, universal group membership is not available. It's possible that a universal group is used to deny the user access to resources, so Windows prevents a security incident by denying domain authentication to the user. If the user has logged on to his or her computer before, he or she can log on using cached credentials, but as soon as the user attempts to access network resources, access will be denied. To summarize: If a GC server is not available, users will effectively be unable to log on and access network resources.

If every domain controller is a GC server, this problem will not arise. However, if replication is a concern, and if you have, therefore, chosen not to configure a domain controller as a GC server, you can facilitate successful logon by enabling universal group membership caching (UGMC). When you configure universal group membership caching for a branch offsite, a domain controller obtains universal group membership information from a GC for a user when the user first logs on in the site, and the domain controller caches that information indefinitely, updating universal group membership information every eight hours. That way, if the user later logs on and a GC server is not accessible, the domain controller can use its cached membership information to permit logon by the user.

It is recommended, therefore, that in sites with unreliable connectivity to a GC server, you configure UGMC on the site's domain controllers.

To configure UGMC:

1. Open the Active Directory Sites And Services snap-in and select the site in the console tree.

2. In the details pane, right-click NTDS Site Settings and click Properties.

3. The NTDS Site Settings Properties dialog box, shown in Figure 11-8, exposes the Enable Universal Group Membership Caching option. When you select the option, the default of the the Refresh Cache From option, <Default>, uses the most efficient route to a site with a global catalog server. It is recommended to use <Default>. Alternately, you can select a site from which to refresh the membership cache. Ensure that the site contains a working global catalog server.

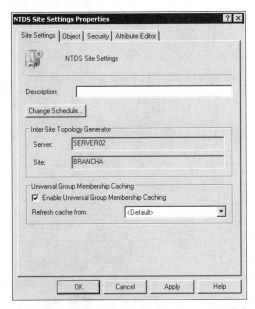

FIGURE 11-8 The NTDS Site Settings Properties dialog box with the option to enable Universal Group Membership Caching

Understanding Application Directory Partitions

In review, the Domain, Configuration, and Schema partitions of the directory are replicated to all DCs in a domain, the Configuration and Schema are further replicated to all DCs in the forest, and the partial attribute set is replicated by global catalog servers. In addition, Active Directory also supports *application directory partitions*. An application directory partition is a portion of the data store that contains objects required by an application or service that is outside of the core AD DS service. Unlike other partitions, application partitions can be targeted to replicate to specific domain controllers; they are not, by default, replicated to all DCs.

Application directory partitions are designed to support directory-enabled applications and services. They can contain any type of object except security principals such as users, computers, or security groups. Because these partitions are replicated only as needed, application directory partitions provide the benefits of fault tolerance, availability, and performance while optimizing replication traffic.

The easiest way to understand application directory partitions is to examine the application directory partitions maintained by Microsoft DNS Server. When you create an Active Directory–integrated zone, DNS records are replicated between DNS servers by using an application directory partition. The partition and its DNS record objects are not replicated to every domain controller, only to those acting as DNS servers.

To explore the application directory partitions in your forest:

1. Open ADSI Edit.

2. Right-click the root of the snap-in, ADSI Edit, and click Connect To.

3. In the Select A Well Known Naming Context drop-down list, choose Configuration, and then click OK.

4. Expand Configuration and the folder representing the Configuration partition, and then select the Partitions folder, CN=Partitions, in the console tree.

   The details pane displays the partitions in your AD DS data store, as shown in Figure 11-9.

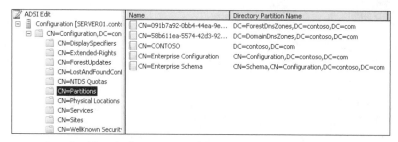

FIGURE 11-9 Partitions in the contoso.com forest

Note the two application partitions in Figure 11-9, ForestDnsZones and DomainDnsZones. Most application partitions are created by applications that require them. DNS is one example, and Telephony Application Programming Interface (TAPI) is another. Members of the Enterprise Admins group can also create application directory partitions manually by using *Ntdsutil.exe*.

An application partition can appear anywhere in the forest namespace that a domain partition can appear. The DNS partitions distinguished names—DC=DomainDnsZones, DC=contoso,DC=com, for example—place the partitions as children of the DC=contoso,DC=com domain partition. An application partition can also be a child of another application partition or a new tree in the forest.

Generally speaking, you use tools specific to the application to manage the application directory partition, its data, and its replication. For example, simply adding an Active Directory–integrated zone to a DNS server automatically configures the domain controller to receive a replica of the DomainDns partition. With tools such as Ntdsutil.exe and Ldp.exe, you can manage application directory partitions directly.

You should consider application partitions before demoting a domain controller. If a domain controller is hosting an application directory partition, you must evaluate the purpose of the partition, whether it is required by any applications, and whether the domain controller holds the last remaining replica of the partition, in which case, demoting the domain controller would result in permanent loss of all information in the partition. Although the Active Directory Domain Services Installation Wizard prompts you to remove application directory partitions, it is recommended that you manually remove application directory partitions before demoting a domain controller.

PRACTICE **Replication and Directory Partitions**

In this practice, you configure replication of the GC and examine the DNS application directory partitions. To complete the exercises in this practice, you must have completed the Lesson 1 practice, "Configuring Sites and Subnets."

EXERCISE 1 **Configure a Global Catalog Server**

The first domain controller in a forest acts as a GC server. You might want to place GC servers in additional locations to support directory queries, logon, and applications such as Exchange Server. In this exercise, you configure SERVER02 to host a replica of the partial attribute set—the GC.

1. Log on to SERVER01 as Administrator.
2. Open the Active Directory Sites And Services snap-in.
3. Expand HEADQUARTERS, Servers, and SERVER02.
4. Right-click NTDS Settings below SERVER02 and click Properties.
5. Select Global Catalog and click OK.

EXERCISE 2   Configure Universal Group Membership Caching

In sites without GC servers, user logon might be prevented if the site's domain controller is unable to contact a GC server in another site. To reduce the likelihood of this scenario, you can configure a site to cache the membership of universal groups. In this exercise, you create a site to reflect a branch office and configure the site to cache universal group membership.

1. Right-click Sites and click New Site.
2. In the Name box, type **BRANCHB**.
3. Select DEFAULTIPSITELINK.
4. Click OK.

   If this were a production environment, you would need to create at least one subnet object linked to the site and install a domain controller in BRANCHB.

5. Select BRANCHB in the console tree.
6. Right-click NTDS Site Settings in the details pane and click Properties.
7. On the Site Settings tab, select the Enable Universal Group Membership Caching check box.
8. Click OK.

EXERCISE 3   Examine Application Directory Partitions

In this exercise, you explore the DomainDnsZone application directory partition, using ADSI Edit.

1. Open ADSI Edit from the Administrative Tools program group.
2. Right-click the root node of the snap-in, ADSI Edit, and click Connect To.
3. In the Select A Well Known Naming Context drop-down list, choose Configuration. Click OK.
4. Select Configuration in the console tree, and then expand it.
5. Select CN=Configuration, DC=contoso, DC=com in the console tree, and then expand it.
6. Select CN=Partitions in the console tree.
7. Make a note of the Directory Partition Name of the DomainDnsZones partition: DC=DomainDnsZones,DC=contoso,DC=com.
8. Right-click ADSI Edit and click Connect To.
9. Select the Select Or Type A Distinguished Name Or Naming Context option.
10. In the combo box, type **DC=DomainDnsZones,DC=contoso,DC=com**. Click OK.
11. Select Default Naming Context in the console tree, and then expand it.
12. Select and then expand DC=DomainDnsZones,DC=contoso,DC=com.
13. Select and then expand CN=MicrosoftDNS.

14. Select DC=contoso.com.

15. Examine the objects in this container. Compare them to the DNS records for the contoso.com domain, which you can view by using DNS Manager.

Lesson Summary

- The global catalog (GC) contains a copy of every object in the forest but only a subset of object attributes. It is also called the partial attribute set (PAS).

- GC servers improve directory queries, support logon, and provide data for applications such as Exchange Server.

- The first domain controller in a forest is a GC server. You can configure a domain controller as a GC server by using the Dcpromo.exe command, the Active Directory Domain Services Installation Wizard, or the Active Directory Sites And Services snap-in after the domain controller has been installed.

- If a site does not contain a GC server, you can configure universal group membership caching (UGMC) to reduce the chance of a user's logon being denied when a GC server is not available.

- Application directory partitions are unique because they can be replicated to specific domain controllers throughout a forest. Active Directory–integrated DNS zones are stored in application partitions.

Lesson Review

You can use the following questions to test your knowledge of the information in Lesson 2, "Configuring the Global Catalog and Application Directory Partitions." The questions are also available on the companion CD if you prefer to review them in electronic form.

> **NOTE ANSWERS**
>
> Answers to these questions and explanations of why each answer choice is right or wrong are located in the "Answers" section at the end of the book.

1. A branch office is connected to the data center with a slow link that is not reliable. You want to ensure that the domain controller in the branch is able to authenticate users when it cannot contact a global catalog server. Which of the following should you configure?

    A. Read-only domain controller

    B. Application directory partition

    C. Intersite replication

    D. Universal group membership caching

2. You are the administrator at Contoso, Ltd. The Contoso forest consists of three domains, each with four domain controllers. You are preparing to demote a domain controller in the forest root domain. You want to be sure that you do not permanently destroy any Active Directory partitions. Which of the following Active Directory partitions might exist only on that domain controller? (Choose all that apply.)

   A. Schema

   B. Configuration

   C. Domain

   D. Partial attribute set

   E. Application directory partition

3. You want to configure all the existing domain controllers in your forest as global catalog servers. Which tool can you use to achieve this goal?

   A. Dcpromo.exe

   B. Active Directory Domain Services Installation Wizard

   C. Active Directory Sites And Services snap-in

   D. Active Directory Users And Computers snap-in

   E. Active Directory Domains And Trusts snap-in

Lesson 3: Configuring Replication

In Lesson 1, you learned how to create site and subnet objects that enable Active Directory and its clients to localize authentication and directory access; you decided *where* domain controllers should be placed. In Lesson 2, you configured GC servers and application directory partitions; you managed *what* will replicate between domain controllers. In this lesson, you learn *how* and *when* replication occurs. You discover why the default configuration of Active Directory supports effective replication and why you might modify that configuration so that replication is equally effective but more efficient, based on your network topology.

> **After this lesson, you will be able to:**
> - Create connection objects to configure replication between two domain controllers.
> - Implement site links and site link costs to manage replication between sites.
> - Designate preferred bridgehead servers.
> - Understand notification and polling.
> - Report and analyze replication with Repadmin.exe.
> - Perform Active Directory replication health checks with Dcdiag.exe.
>
> **Estimated lesson time: 90 minutes**

Understanding Active Directory Replication

In previous lessons, you learned how to place domain controllers in network locations and how to represent those locations with site and subnet objects. You also learned about the replication of directory partitions (Schema, Configuration, and Domain), the partial attribute set (GC), and application partitions. The most important thing to remember as you learn about Active Directory replication is that it is designed so that, in the end, each replica on a domain controller is consistent with the replicas of that partition hosted on other domain controllers. It is not likely that all domain controllers will have exactly the same information in their replicas at any one moment in time because changes are constantly being made to the directory. However, Active Directory replication ensures that all changes to a partition are transferred to all replicas of the partition. Active Directory replication balances accuracy (or *integrity*) and consistency (called *convergence*) with performance (keeping replication traffic to a reasonable level). This balancing act is described as *loose coupling*.

Key features of Active Directory replication are:

- **Multimaster replication**   Any domain controller can initiate and commit a change to Active Directory.
- **Pull replication**   A domain controller requests, or "pulls," changes from other domain controllers. As you learn more about replication, it may become easy to forget this,

because a DC notifies its replication partners that it has changes to the directory, or a DC can poll its partners to see if they have changes to the directory. But the changes themselves are, in the end, requested or "pulled" by the target DC.

- **Store-and-forward replication**   A domain controller can pull changes from one partner, and then make those changes available to another partner. For example, domain controller B can pull changes initiated by domain controller A. Then domain controller C can pull the changes from domain controller B.

- **Partitioning of the data store**   Domain controllers in a domain host only the domain naming context for their domain, which helps keep replication to a minimum, particularly in multidomain forests. Other data, including application directory partitions and the partial attribute set (GC), are not replicated to every domain controller in the forest, by default.

- **Automatic generation of an efficient and robust replication topology**   By default, Active Directory configures an effective, two-way replication topology so that the loss of any one domain controller does not impede replication. This topology is automatically updated as domain controllers are added, removed, or moved between sites.

- **Attribute-level replication**   When an attribute of an object is modified, only that attribute, and minimal metadata that describes that attribute, is replicated. The entire object is not replicated except when the object is created.

- **Distinct control of intrasite replication (within a single site) and intersite replication (between sites)**   Replication can be distinctly controlled in both of these situations.

- **Collision detection and management**   It is possible, although rare, for an attribute to be modified on two different domain controllers during a single replication window. In such an event, the two changes must be reconciled. Active Directory has resolution algorithms that satisfy almost every such situation.

It is easier to understand Active Directory replication by examining each of its components. The following sections examine the components of Active Directory replication.

Connection Objects

A domain controller replicates changes from another domain controller because of AD DS connection objects, also simply called *connection objects*. Connection objects appear in the administrative tools in the Active Directory Sites And Services snap-in as objects contained in the NTDS Settings container of a domain controller's server object. Figure 11-10 shows an example: A connection object in SERVER02 configures replication from SERVER01 to SERVER02. A connection object represents a replication path from one domain controller to another.

Connection objects are one-way, representing inbound-only replication. Replication in Active Directory is always a pull technology. In the domain illustrated in Figure 11-10, SERVER02 pulls changes from SERVER01. SERVER02 is considered, in this example, a downstream replication partner of SERVER01. SERVER01 is the upstream partner. Changes from SERVER01 flow to SERVER02.

> **NOTE FORCE REPLICATION**
>
> You can force replication between two domain controllers by right-clicking the connection object and clicking Replicate Now. Remember that replication is inbound only, so to replicate both domain controllers, you must replicate the inbound connection object of both domain controllers.

FIGURE 11-10 A connection object in the Active Directory Sites And Services snap-in

The Knowledge Consistency Checker

The replication paths built between domain controllers by connection objects create the replication topology for the forest. Luckily, you do not have to create the replication topology manually. By default, Active Directory creates a topology that ensures effective replication. The topology is two-way so that if any one domain controller fails, replication continues uninterrupted. The topology also ensures that there are no more than three hops between any two domain controllers.

You'll notice in Figure 11-10 that the connection object indicates it was automatically generated. On each domain controller, a component of Active Directory called the Knowledge Consistency Checker (KCC) helps generate and optimize the replication automatically between domain controllers within a site. The KCC evaluates the domain controllers in a site and creates connection objects to build the two-way, three-hop topology described earlier. If a domain controller is added to or removed from the site, or if a domain controller is not responsive, the KCC rearranges the topology dynamically, adding and deleting connection objects to rebuild an effective replication topology.

You can manually create connection objects to specify replication paths that should persist. Manually created connection objects are not deleted by the KCC.

To create a connection object:

1. In Active Directory Sites And Services, locate the server object for the downstream replication partner—the DC that will receive changes from a source DC. In the console tree, right-click the NTDS Settings container in the server object and click New Active Directory Domain Services Connection.

2. In the Find Active Directory Domain Controllers dialog box, select the upstream replication partner, and then click OK.

3. Give the new connection object a name, and then click OK.

4. Open the properties of the connection object; use the Description field to indicate the purpose of any manually created connection object.

Within a site, there are very few scenarios that would require creating a connection object. One such scenario is standby operations masters. Operations masters are discussed in Chapter 10. It is recommended that you select domain controllers as standby operations masters to be used in the event that the operations master role must be transferred or seized. A standby operations master should be a direct replication partner with the current operations master. Thus, if a domain controller named DC01 is the RID master, and DC02 is the system that will take the RID master role if DC01 is taken offline, then a connection object should be created in DC02 so that it replicates directly from DC01.

Intrasite Replication

After connection objects between the domain controllers in a site have been established—either automatically by the KCC or manually—replication can take place. Intrasite replication involves the replication of changes within a single site.

Notification

Consider the site shown in Figure 11-10. When SERVER01 makes a change to a partition, it queues the change for replication to its partners. SERVER01 waits 15 seconds, by default, to notify its first replication partner, SERVER02, of the change. *Notification* is the process by which an upstream partner informs its downstream partners that a change is available. SERVER01 waits three seconds, by default, between notifications to additional partners. These delays, called the *initial notification delay* and the *subsequent notification delay*, are designed to stagger network traffic caused by intrasite replication.

Upon receiving the notification, the downstream partner, SERVER02, requests the changes from SERVER01, and the directory replication agent (DRA) performs the transfer of the attribute from SERVER01 to SERVER02. In this example, SERVER01 made the initial change to Active Directory. It is the originating domain controller, and the change it made is the originating change. When SERVER02 receives the change from SERVER01, it makes the change to its directory. The change is not called a replicated change, but it is a change nonetheless. SERVER02 queues the change for replication to its own downstream partners.

Assume SERVER03 is a downstream replication partner of SERVER02. After 15 seconds, SERVER02 notifies SERVER03 that it has a change. SERVER03 makes the replicated change to its directory and then notifies its downstream partners. The change has made two hops, from SERVER01 to SERVER02 and from SERVER02 to SERVER03. The replication topology ensures that there are no more than three hops before all domain controllers in the site have received the change. At approximately 15 seconds per hop, that means the change fully replicates in the site within one minute.

Replication mechanisms ensure that changes are dampened, so that a change is not replicated to a domain controller that already received the change from another replication partner. You can learn more about the internals of AD DS replication in the *Windows Server 2008 Active Directory Resource Kit*.

Polling

It is possible that SERVER01 might not make any changes to the partitions it hosts for quite a long time, particularly during off hours. In this case, SERVER02, its downstream replication partner, will not receive notifications from SERVER01.

However, it is also possible that SERVER01 might be offline, which would also prevent it from sending notifications to SERVER02 and would break the two-way, three-hop replication topology that was generated by the KCC. The replication topology must be self-healing, so it's important for SERVER02 to determine whether its upstream partner is offline, or whether it is online and simply does not have any changes.

This is achieved through a process called *polling*. The downstream replication partner contacting the upstream replication partner with a query as to whether any changes are queued for replication. By default, the polling interval for intrasite replication is once per hour. It is possible, although not recommended, to configure the polling frequency from the properties of a connection object by clicking Change Schedule.

If an upstream partner fails to respond to repeated polling queries, the downstream partner assumes that its upstream partner is offline, so it triggers the KCC to check the replication topology. If the KCC determines that the upstream server is indeed offline, the site's replication topology is rebuilt to accommodate the change, to ensure that a two-way, three-hop topology is maintained.

Site Links

The KCC assumes that within a site, all domain controllers can reach each other. It builds an intrasite replication topology that is agnostic to the underlying network connectivity. Between sites, however, you can represent the network paths over which replication should occur by creating *site link* objects. A site link contains two or more sites. The Intersite Topology Generator (ISTG), a component of the KCC, builds connection objects between servers in each of the sites to enable intersite replication—replication between sites.

Site links are greatly misunderstood, and the important thing to remember about a site link is that it represents an available path for replication. A single site link does not control the network routes that are used. When you create a site link and add sites to it, you are telling Active Directory that it can replicate between any of the sites associated with the site link. The ISTG creates connection objects, and those objects determine the actual path of replication. Although the replication topology built by the ISTG effectively replicates Active Directory, it might not be efficient, given your network topology.

An example illustrates this concept: When you create a forest, one site link object is created—DEFAULTIPSITELINK. By default, each new site that you add is associated with the DEFAULTIPSITELINK. Consider an organization with a data center at the headquarters and three branch offices. The three branch offices are each connected to the data center with a dedicated link. You create sites for each branch office, Seattle (SEA), Amsterdam (AMS), and Beijing (PEK). The network and site topology is shown in Figure 11-11. The lightning bolts indicate physical connectivity between the sites.

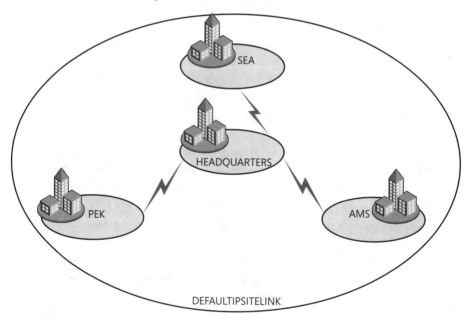

FIGURE 11-11 Network topology and a single site link

Because all four sites are on the same site link, you are instructing Active Directory that all four sites can replicate with each other. That means it is possible that Seattle will replicate changes from Amsterdam, Amsterdam will replicate changes from Beijing, and Beijing will replicate changes from Headquarters, which in turn replicates changes from Seattle. In several of these replication paths, the replication traffic on the network flows from one branch through the headquarters on its way to another branch. With a single site link, you have not created a hub-and-spoke replication topology, even though your network topology is hub-and-spoke.

Therefore, it is recommended that you manually create site links that reflect your physical network topology. Continuing the preceding example, you would create three site links:

- HQ-AMS, including the Headquarters and Amsterdam sites
- HQ-SEA, including the Headquarters and Seattle sites
- HQ-PEK, including the Headquarters and Beijing sites

You would then delete the DEFAULTIPSITELINK. The resulting topology is shown in Figure 11-12.

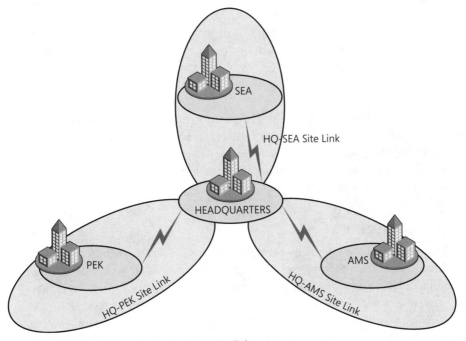

FIGURE 11-12 Network topology and a three-site link

The four Active Directory sites shown in Figure 11-12 (HEADQUARTERS, SEA, PEK, and AMS) are logical objects that represent portions of the network with strong connectivity. The lightning bolts represent physical connectivity between sites. Site links—for example, HQ-AMS—are logical objects that represent a potential path for replication between sites.

After you create site links, the ISTG uses the topology to build an intersite replication topology connecting each site. Connection objects are built to configure the intersite replication paths. These connection objects are created automatically, and although you can create connection objects manually, there are few scenarios that require manually creating intersite connection objects.

Replication Transport Protocols

You'll notice in the Active Directory Sites And Services snap-in that site links are contained within a container named IP that itself is inside the Inter-Site Transports container. Changes are replicated between domain controllers, using one of two protocols:

- **Directory Service Remote Procedure Call (DS-RPC)**   DS-RPC appears in the Active Directory Sites And Services snap-in as IP. IP is used for all intrasite replication and is the default, and preferred, protocol for intersite replication.

- **Inter-Site Messaging—Simple Mail Transport Protocol (ISM-SMTP)**   Also known simply as SMTP, this protocol is used only when network connections between sites are unreliable or are not always available.

In general, you can assume you will use IP for all intersite replication. Very few organizations use SMTP for replication because of the administrative overhead required to configure and manage a certificate authority (CA) and because SMTP replication is not supported for the domain naming context, meaning that if a site uses SMTP to replicate to the rest of the enterprise, that site must be its own domain.

EXAM TIP

Although, in the production environment, you are highly unlikely to use SMTP for replication, it is possible you will encounter SMTP replication on the exam. The most important thing to remember is that if two sites can replicate only with SMTP—if IP is not an option—then those two sites must be separate domains in the forest. SMTP cannot be used to replicate the domain naming context.

Bridgehead Servers

The ISTG creates a replication topology between sites on a site link. To make replication more efficient, one domain controller is selected as the *bridgehead server*. The bridgehead server is responsible for all replication into and out of the site for a partition. For example, if a data center site contains five DCs, one of the DCs will be the bridgehead server for the domain naming context. All changes made to the domain partition within the data center replicate to all DCs in the site. When the changes reach the bridgehead server, those changes are replicated to bridgehead servers in branch offices, which in turn replicate the changes to DCs in their sites. Similarly, any changes to the domain naming context in branch offices are replicated from the branches' bridgehead servers to the bridgehead server in the data center, which in turn replicates the changes to other DCs in the data center. Figure 11-13 illustrates intrasite replication within two sites and the intersite replication using connection objects between the bridgehead servers in the sites.

To summarize, the bridgehead server is the server responsible for replicating changes to a partition from other bridgehead servers in other sites. It is also polled by bridgehead servers in other sites to determine when it has changes that they should replicate.

Domain Controller

Domain Controller

HQ-AMS Site Link

HEADQUARTERS

AMS

Domain
Controller

Domain Controller
Bridgehead Server

Domain Controller
Bridgehead Server

Domain
Controller

FIGURE 11-13 Sites, intrasite replication, bridgehead servers, and intersite replication

Bridgehead servers are selected automatically, and the ISTG creates the intersite replication topology to ensure that changes are replicated effectively between bridgeheads sharing a site link. Bridgeheads are selected per partition, so it is possible that one DC in a site might be the bridgehead server for the schema and another might be the bridgehead server for the configuration. However, you will usually find that one domain controller is the bridgehead server for all partitions in a site unless there are domain controllers from other domains or application directory partitions, in which case bridgeheads will be chosen for those partitions.

> **MORE INFO** **LOAD BALANCING BRIDGEHEAD SERVER SELECTION**
>
> Windows Server 2008 R2 improves the algorithms with which bridgehead servers are selected, to create a load-balanced intersite replication topology. For more information, see "Bridgehead Server Selection" at *http://technet.microsoft.com/en-us/library/bridgehead_server_selection(WS.10).aspx.*

Preferred Bridgehead Servers

You can also designate one or more *preferred bridgehead servers*.

To designate a domain controller as a preferred bridgehead server:

1. Open the properties of the server object in the Active Directory Sites And Services snap-in.

2. Select the transport protocol, which is almost always IP, and then click Add.

You can configure more than one preferred bridgehead server for a site, but only one will be selected and used as the bridgehead. If that bridgehead fails, one of the other preferred bridgehead servers will be used.

It's important to understand that if you have specified one or more bridgehead servers and none of the bridgeheads is available, no other server is automatically selected, and replication does not occur for the site even if there are servers that could act as bridgehead servers. In an ideal world, you should not configure preferred bridgehead servers. However, performance considerations might suggest that you assign the bridgehead server role to domain controllers with greater system resources. Firewall considerations might also require that you assign a single server to act as a bridgehead instead of allowing Active Directory to select and possibly reassign bridgehead servers over time.

Configuring Intersite Replication

After you have created site links and the ISTG has generated connection objects to replicate partitions between bridgehead servers that share a site link, your work might be complete. In many environments, particularly those with straightforward network topologies, site links might be sufficient to manage intersite replication. In more complex networks, however, you can configure additional components and properties of replication.

Site Link Transitivity

By default, site links are transitive. That means, continuing the example from earlier, that if Amsterdam and Headquarters sites are linked, and Headquarters and Seattle sites are linked, then Amsterdam and Seattle are transitively linked. This means, theoretically, that the ISTG could create a connection object directly between a bridgehead in Seattle and a bridgehead in Amsterdam, again working at odds with the hub-and-spoke network topology.

You can disable site link transitivity by opening the properties of the IP transport in the Inter-Site Transports container and clearing the Bridge All Site Links option. Before you do this in a production environment, be sure to spend time reading the technical resources about replication in the Windows Server technical libraries on Microsoft TechNet at *http://technet.microsoft.com/en-us/library/bb625087.aspx*.

EXAM TIP

For the certification exam, you need to know that site links are transitive by default, that transitivity can be disabled, and that when transitivity is disabled, you might want to build site link bridges.

 Quick Check

- You want to create a hub-and-spoke topology for replication so that changes made to Active Directory in any branch office are replicated, first to the domain controllers in the data center, and then out to other branches. You have created a site link for each branch office that includes the branch office and the data center. However, you discover that connection objects have been created between domain controllers at several branch offices. What must you do to ensure that replication follows your desired hub-and-spoke topology?

Site Link Bridges

A site link bridge connects two or more site links in a way that creates a transitive link. Site link bridges are necessary only when you have cleared the Bridge All Site Links option for the transport protocol. Remember that site link transitivity is enabled by default, in which case, site link bridges have no effect.

Figure 11-14 illustrates the use of a site link bridge in a forest in which site link transitivity has been disabled. By creating a site link bridge, AMS-HQ-SEA, that includes the HQ-AMS and HQ-SEA site links, those two site links become transitive, so a replication connection can be made between a domain controller in Amsterdam and a domain controller in Seattle.

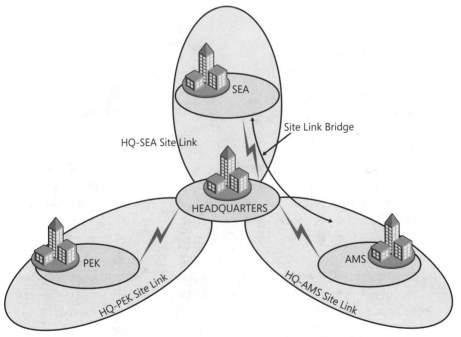

FIGURE 11-14 A site link bridge that includes the HQ-AMS and HQ-SEA site links

Site Link Costs

Site link costs are used to manage the flow of replication traffic when there is more than one route for replication traffic. You can configure site link cost to indicate that a link is faster, more reliable, or preferred. Higher costs are used for slow links, and lower costs are used for fast links. Active Directory replicates using the connection with the lowest cost.

By default, all site links are configured with a cost of 100. To change the site link cost, open the properties of a site link and change the value in the Cost box, shown in Figure 11-15.

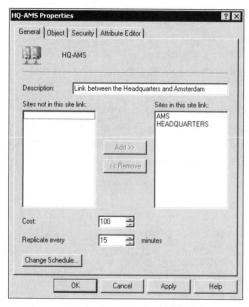

FIGURE 11-15 The properties of a site link

Returning to the example used earlier in the lesson, imagine that a site link was created between the Amsterdam and Beijing sites, as shown in Figure 11-16. Such a site link could be configured to allow replication between domain controllers in those two sites in the event that the links to the headquarters become unavailable. You might want to configure such a topology as part of a disaster recovery plan, for example.

With the default site link cost of 100 assigned to the AMS-PEK site link, Active Directory will replicate changes directly between Amsterdam and Beijing. If you configure the site link cost to 300, changes will replicate between Amsterdam and the Headquarters, then between the Headquarters and Beijing at a total cost of 200 rather than directly over the AMS-PEK site link at a cost of 300. This cost configuration is illustrated in Figure 11-16.

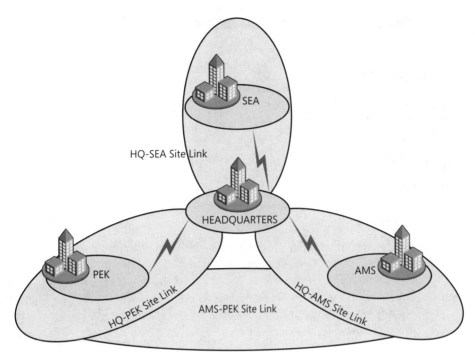

FIGURE 11-16 Site links

Replication Frequency

Intersite replication is based only on polling; by default, there is no notification in intersite replication, as there is with intrasite replication. Every three hours, by default, a bridgehead server polls its upstream replication partners to determine whether changes are available. This replication interval is too long for organizations that want changes to the directory to replicate more quickly.

To change the polling interval for a site link:

1. Open the site link's properties, shown in Figure 11-15.

2. Change the value in the Replicate Every box.

The minimum polling interval is 15 minutes. With this setting, and using Active Directory's default replication configuration, a change made to the directory in one site takes on average seven and a half minutes to replicate to domain controllers in another site.

Replication Schedules

By default, replication occurs 24 hours a day. However, you can restrict intersite replication to specific times by changing the schedule attributes of a site link. Open the properties of a site link and click Change Schedule. Using the Schedule For dialog box shown in Figure 11-17, you can select the times during which the link is available for replication. The link shown in the figure does not replicate between 8:00 A.M. and 6:00 P.M. Monday through Friday.

FIGURE 11-17 Site link schedule

You must be careful when scheduling site link availability. It is possible to schedule windows of availability that do not overlap, at which point replication will not happen. It's generally not recommended to configure link availability. If you do not require link scheduling, you should select the Ignore Schedules option in the properties of the IP transport protocol. This option causes any schedules for site link availability to be ignored, ensuring replication 24 hours a day over all site links.

Monitoring Replication

After you have implemented your replication configuration, you must be able to monitor replication for ongoing support, optimization, and troubleshooting. Two tools are particularly useful for reporting and analyzing replication: the Replication Diagnostics tool (Repadmin.exe) and Directory Server Diagnosis (Dcdiag.exe). This lesson introduces you to these powerful tools.

Repadmin.exe

The Replication Diagnostics tool, Repadmin.exe, is a command-line tool that allows you to report the status of replication on each domain controller. The information produced by Repadmin.exe can help you spot a potential problem before it gets out of control and troubleshoot problems with replication in the forest. You can view levels of detail down to the replication metadata for specific objects and attributes, helping you identify where and when a problematic change was made to Active Directory. You can even use Repadmin.exe to create the replication topology and force replication between domain controllers.

Like other command-line tools, you can type **repadmin /?** to see the usage information for the tool. Its basic syntax is as follows:

```
repadmin command arguments...
```

Repadmin.exe supports several commands that perform specific tasks. You can learn about each command by typing **repadmin /?:command**. Most commands require arguments. Many commands take a *DSA_LIST* parameter, which is simply a network label (DNS or NetBIOS name or IP address) of a domain controller. Some of the replication monitoring tasks you can perform with Repadmin are:

- **Displaying replication status**   To display the status of inboud replication of a domain controller, type **repadmin /showrepl *DSA_LIST***.

- **Displaying connection objects for a domain controller**   Type **repadmin /showconn *DSA_LIST*** to show the connection objects for a domain controller.

- **Displaying metadata about an object, its attributes, and replication**   You can learn a lot about replication by examining an object on two different domain controllers to find out which attributes have or have not replicated. Type **repadmin /showobjmeta *DSA_LIST Object***, where *DSA_LIST* indicates the domain controller(s) to query. (You can use an asterisk [*] to indicate all domain controllers.) *Object* is a unique identifier for the object, its DN, or its GUID, for example.

You can also make changes to your replication infrastructure by using Repadmin.exe. Some of the management tasks you can perform are:

- **Launching the KCC**   Type **repadmin /kcc** to force the KCC to recalculate the inbound replication topology for the server.

- **Forcing replication between two partners**   You can use Repadmin.exe to force replication of a partition between a source and a target domain controller. Type **repadmin /replicate *Destination_DSA_Name Source_DSA_Name Naming_Context***.

- **Synchronizing a domain controller with all replication partners**   Type **repadmin /syncall DSA /A /e** to synchronize a domain controller with all its partners, including those in other sites.

Dcdiag.exe

The Directory Service Diagnosis tool, Dcdiag.exe, performs several tests and reports on the overall health of replication and security for AD DS. Run by itself, Dcdiag.exe performs summary tests and reports the results. On the other extreme, Dcdiag.exe /c performs almost every test. The output of tests can be redirected to files of various types, including XML. Type **dcdiag /?** for full usage information.

You can also specify one or more tests to perform by using dcdiag /test:*TestName* parameter. Tests that are directly related to replication include:

- **FrsEvent**   Reports any operation errors in the file replication system (FRS).
- **DFSREvent**   Reports any operation errors in the DFS replication (DFS-R) system.
- **Intersite**   Checks for failures that would prevent or delay intersite replication.
- **KccEvent**   Identifies errors in the KCC.
- **Replications**   Checks for timely replication between domain controllers.
- **Topology**   Checks that the replication topology is fully connected for all DSAs.
- **VerifyReplicas**   Verifies that all application directory partitions are fully instantiated on all domain controllers hosting replicas.

PRACTICE Configuring Replication

In this practice, you manage intrasite and intersite replication in the contoso.com domain. To perform the exercises in this practice, you must have two domain controllers, SERVER01 and SERVER02, running in the domain. You must also have completed the Lesson 1 practice as well as the Lesson 2 practice, "Replication and Directory Partitions," in this chapter.

EXERCISE 1 Create a Connection Object

Configure direct replication between a domain controller that will be a standby operations master and the domain controller that is currently the operations master. As a result, if the current operations master needs to be taken offline, the standby operations master is as up to date as possible with the operations master. In this exercise, you create a connection object between SERVER01 and SERVER02, where SERVER02, the standby operations master, replicates from SERVER01, the current operations master.

1. Log on to SERVER01 as Administrator.

2. Open the Active Directory Sites And Services snap-in.

3. Expand Sites, HEADQUARTERS, Servers, and SERVER02.

4. Select the NTDS Settings node under SERVER02 in the console tree.

5. Right-click NTDS Settings and click New Active Directory Domain Services Connection.

6. In the Find Active Directory Domain Controllers dialog box, select SERVER01 and click OK.

   Because the KCC has already created a connection from SERVER01 to SERVER02, a warning appears asking if you want to create another connection.

7. Click Yes.

8. In the New Object – Connection dialog box, type the name **SERVER01 – OPERATIONS MASTER** and click OK.

9. Right-click the new connection object in the details pane and click Properties.

10. Examine the properties of the connection object and the partitions that are replicated from SERVER01. Do not make any changes.

11. Click OK to close the Properties dialog box.

12. Because the sample domain has only two DCs, and you will move the server in a later exercise, delete the connection object by right-clicking it and clicking Delete. Confirm the deletion by clicking Yes.

EXERCISE 2 Create Site Links

In this exercise, you create site links between the branch sites and the headquarters site.

1. In the Active Directory Sites And Services snap-in, expand Inter-Site Transports.
2. Select IP.
3. Right-click DEFAULTIPSITELINK and click Rename.
4. Type **HQ-BRANCHA** and press Enter.
5. Double-click HQ-BRANCHA.
6. In the Sites In This Site Link list, select BRANCHB and click Remove. Click OK.
7. Right-click IP and click New Site Link.
8. Type **HQ-BRANCHB** in the Name box.
9. In the Sites Not In This Site Link list, select Headquarters and click Add.
10. In the Sites Not In This Site Link list, select BRANCHB and click Add.
11. Click OK.

EXERCISE 3 Designate a Preferred Bridgehead Server

You can designate a preferred bridgehead server that will handle replication to and from its site. This is useful when you want to assign the role to a domain controller in a site with greater system resources or when firewall considerations require that the role be assigned to a single, fixed system. In this exercise, you designate a preferred bridgehead server for the site.

1. Expand Headquarters, Servers, and SERVER02.
2. Right-click SERVER02 and click Properties.
3. In the Transports Available For Inter-Site Data Transfer list, select IP.
4. Click Add, and then click OK.

   It is recommended that if a site has a GC server, the domain controller acting as a GC server should be the preferred bridgehead server. When Active Directory designates a bridgehead server automatically, it selects a GC server if one is available.

   If SERVER02 is not a DNS server and a GC server, you receive a warning that the preferred bridgehead server does not include all the directory partitions in the site. You can ignore the message for this exercise.

EXERCISE 4 Configure Intersite Replication

After you have created site links and, optionally, designated bridgehead servers, you can continue to refine and control replication by configuring properties of the site link. In this exercise, you reduce the intersite replication polling frequency and increase the cost of a site link.

1. Expand Inter-Site Transports.
2. Select the IP container in the console tree.

3. Double-click the HQ-BRANCHA site link.

4. In the Replicate Every box, type **15** and click OK.

5. Double-click the HQ-BRANCHB site link.

6. In the Replicate Every box, type **15**.

7. Click Change Schedule.

8. Examine the Schedule For HQ-BRANCHB dialog box. Experiment with configuring the schedule, but click Cancel when you are finished.

9. In the Cost box, type **200**.

10. Click OK.

Lesson Summary

- Connection objects represent paths of replication between two domain controllers.
- Site links represent available network connectivity between two or more sites.
- Bridgehead servers in each site are responsible for replication to and from the site.
- The Intersite Topology Generator (ISTG) creates connection objects between bridgehead servers that share a site link.
- If more than one connection is available, replication proceeds over the connection with the lowest cost.
- By default, site links are transitive. If you disable site link transitivity by clearing the Bridge All Site Links option in the properties of the intersite transport protocol, you might need to create site link bridges to create specific transitive links between two or more sites.

Lesson Review

You can use the following questions to test your knowledge of the information in Lesson 3, "Configuring Replication." The questions are also available on the companion CD if you prefer to review them in electronic form.

> **NOTE ANSWERS**
>
> **Answers to these questions and explanations of why each answer choice is right or wrong are located in the "Answers" section at the end of the book.**

1. You are an administrator at Adventure Works. The Active Directory forest consists of three sites: Site A, Site B, and Site C. Site A and Site C are connected to Site B with a fast connection. Sites A and C are connected to each other with a slow VPN connection. The Active Directory site link objects and their costs are as shown. You want to encourage replication to avoid the VPN connection. What should you do?

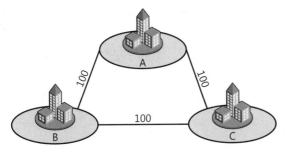

A. Increase the cost of link A-B to 250.

B. Increase the cost of link C-B to 250.

C. Decrease the cost of links A-B and C-B to 75.

D. Increase the cost of link A-C to 250.

2. You are an administrator at Adventure Works. The Active Directory forest consists of three sites: Site A, Site B, and Site C. The Active Directory site link objects and their costs are as shown. You want to ensure that all replication between Sites A and C goes to Site B before going to the other site. What should you do? (Choose all that apply. Each correct answer presents part of the solution.)

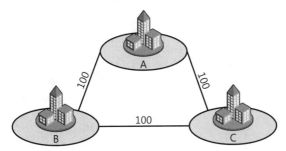

A. Increase the cost of site link A-C to 300.

B. Delete site link A-C.

C. Deselect Bridge All Site Links.

D. Reduce the costs of links A-B and B-C to 25.

3. The network infrastructure at Trey Research prevents direct IP connectivity between the data center and a research ship at sea. What must you do to support replication between the data center and the ship?

A. Configure a separate domain in the forest for the ship.

B. Increase the cost of the Active Directory site link containing the headquarters and the ship.

C. Configure the domain controller on the ship as a preferred bridgehead server.

D. Manually create a connection object between the domain controller on the ship and a domain controller at the headquarters.

4. You want to initiate replication manually between two domain controllers to verify that replication is functioning correctly. Which of the following tools can you use? (Choose all that apply.)

   A. The Active Directory Sites And Services snap-in

   B. Repadmin.exe

   C. Dcdiag.exe

   D. The Active Directory Domains And Trusts snap-in

Chapter Review

To further practice and reinforce the skills you learned in this chapter, you can perform the following tasks:

- Review the chapter summary.
- Review the list of key terms introduced in this chapter.
- Complete the case scenario. This scenario sets up a real-world situation involving the topics of this chapter and asks you to create a solution.
- Complete the suggested practices.
- Take a practice test.

Chapter Summary

- Domain controllers host replicas of Active Directory partitions: the Schema, Configuration, and Domain naming contexts. You can configure domain controllers to host the partial attribute set (global catalog) or application directory partitions.
- Within a site, domain controllers replicate quickly, using a topology generated by the Knowledge Consistency Checker (KCC), which is adjusted dynamically to ensure effective intersite replication.
- Between sites, the Intersite Topology Generator (ISTG) creates a topology of connection objects between bridgehead servers in sites that share site links. Intersite replication is based on polling only, by default, with an initial frequency of every three hours.
- You can modify intersite replication behavior, including the replication frequency, site link costs, and preferred bridgehead servers.
- Advanced configuration is not generally necessary, but you can modify site link transitivity, create site link bridges, and configure site link schedules.
- The Repadmin.exe and Dcdiag.exe commands allow you to monitor and troubleshoot replication.

Key Terms

The following terms were introduced in this chapter. Do you know what they mean?

- intrasite
- intersite
- partial attribute set or global catalog (GC)
- replica, partition, or naming context
- service localization

Case Scenario

In the following case scenario, you apply what you've learned about sites, subnets, partitions, and replication. You can find answers to these questions in the "Answers" section at the end of this book.

Case Scenario: Configuring Sites and Subnets

You are an administrator at Adventure Works. The Adventure Works network topology is illustrated as shown. Branch offices in Seattle, Chicago, and Miami are connected with fast, reliable links to the Denver site. Smaller branches in Portland and Fort Lauderdale are connected to Seattle and Miami, respectively. In Denver, the headquarters and the warehouse sites are connected with an extremely fast connection. There is one domain controller in each site except in the headquarters in Denver, where there are three. You are planning the Active Directory sites and replication for the domain.

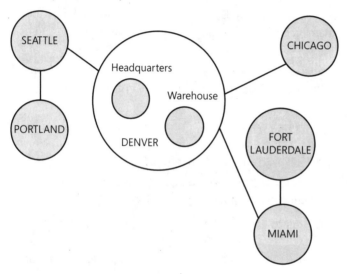

1. You want to ensure that, in Denver, any change to the directory replicates within one minute to all four domain controllers. How many Active Directory sites should you create for the Denver subnets?

2. A colleague recommends that you designate one of the domain controllers in the headquarters as a preferred bridgehead server. What are the advantages and disadvantages of doing so?

3. You want to ensure that replication follows a hub-and-spoke topology so that any change made to the directory in Denver replicates directly to all five branches and that any change made in one of the five branches replicates directly to Denver. Describe the site link changes you would make to support this goal.

4. For disaster planning purposes, you want the domain controller in the warehouse to be ready to take on forest and domain operations master roles performed by SERVER01 in the headquarters site. What change would you make to replication to support this goal?

Suggested Practices

To help you successfully master the exam objectives presented in this chapter, complete the following tasks.

Monitor and Manage Replication

In this practice, you perform replication management and monitoring tasks, using both user interface and command-line tools. To perform these practices, you must have completed the previous practices in this chapter.

- **Practice 1** Observe intersite replication by opening two instances of the Active Directory Users And Computers snap-in. In one instance, right-click the contoso.com domain, click Change Domain Controller, and select SERVER01. In the other instance, right-click the contoso.com domain, click Change Domain Controller, and select SERVER02. Using the SERVER01 snap-in, create an OU called User Accounts if it does not already exist. Within the User Accounts OU, create an OU called Temporary Employees. Using the SERVER02 snap-in, refresh the view to see that the objects were replicated successfully. Using the SERVER02 snap-in, create a new user named Replication Test. Confirm in the SERVER01 snap-in that the user object replicated.

- **Practice 2** Observe the KCC and the ISTG by opening the Active Directory Sites And Services snap-in. Expand BRANCHA and Servers. Expand Headquarters and Servers. Drag SERVER02 from the HEADQUARTERS\Servers container to the BRANCHA\Servers container. In the SERVER01 Active Directory Users And Computers snap-in, create a new user object called Intersite Test 1. Examine the SERVER02 Active Directory Users And Computers snap-in. It is likely that the object replicated because the connection object between SERVER02 and SERVER01 continues to be treated as an intrasite replication connection. In the Active Directory Sites And Services snap-in, expand SERVER01, right-click NTDS Settings, point to All Tasks, and then click Check Replication Topology. Repeat the process with SERVER02. Refresh the Active Directory Sites And Services snap-in view. Select NTDS Settings in the SERVER01 container. You should see that the connection object from SERVER02 now shows that SERVER02 is in the BRANCHA site.

- **Practice 3** Observe intersite replication and manual replication. In the SERVER01 Active Directory Users And Computers snap-in, add another user, named Intersite Test 2. In the SERVER02 snap-in, you should not see the object when you refresh the view. The servers are now replicated using intersite topology. In the Active Directory Sites And Services snap-in, select NTDS Settings under SERVER02. In the console details pane, right-click the connection object and click Replicate Now.

Take a Practice Test

The practice tests on this book's companion CD offer many options. For example, you can test yourself on just one exam objective, or you can test yourself on all the 70-640 certification exam content. You can set up the test so that it closely simulates the experience of taking a certification exam, or you can set it up in study mode so that you can look at the correct answers and explanations after you answer each question.

> **MORE INFO   PRACTICE TESTS**
>
> For details about all the practice test options available, see the "How to Use the Practice Tests" section in this book's Introduction.

CHAPTER 12

Managing Multiple Domains and Forests

In Chapter 1, "Creating an Active Directory Domain," you learned that Active Directory Domain Services (AD DS) provides the foundation for an identity and access management solution, and you explored the creation of a simple AD DS infrastructure consisting of a single forest and a single domain. In subsequent chapters, you mastered the details of managing an AD DS environment. Now you are ready to return to the highest level of an AD DS infrastructure and consider the model and functionality of your domains and forests. In this chapter, you learn how to raise the domain and forest functionality levels within your environment, how to design the optimal AD DS infrastructure for your enterprise, how to migrate objects between domains and forests, and how to enable authentication and resource access across multiple domains and forests.

Exam objectives in this chapter:

- Configure a forest or a domain.
- Configure trusts.

Lessons in this chapter:

Before You Begin

To complete the lessons in this chapter, you must have installed a domain controller named SERVER01 in the contoso.com domain. In the practices for this chapter, you create a new domain controller in a new domain, tailspintoys.com. See the practice at the end of Lesson 1 for specifications for this domain controller.

REAL WORLD

Dan Holme

In some organizations, there is a perception that domain controllers (DCs) should be the last systems to be upgraded. My experience, however, has been that domain controllers should be among the first systems that you upgrade (after testing the upgrade in a lab, of course). Domain controllers are the cornerstone of identity and access management in your enterprise AD DS forest. Because of that, you should ensure that, wherever possible, DCs are dedicated—serving only the AD DS role and related core services, such as DNS. If your DCs are dedicated, the risk associated with upgrading them diminishes significantly—there are far fewer moving parts that could cause problems during an upgrade. Additionally, the sooner you upgrade your DCs, the sooner you can raise the domain and forest functional levels.

Functional levels enable the newer capabilities added by Microsoft Windows Server 2008 and Windows Server 2008 R2. In return for added functionality, you are restricted as to the versions of Microsoft Windows that are supported for the domain controllers in the domain. (Member servers and workstations can run any version of Windows.) Some of the functionality, such as linked-value replication, last logon information, read-only domain controllers, fine-grained password policies, and Distributed File System Replication (DFS-R) of System Volume (SYSVOL), has a profound impact on the day-to-day security, management, and flexibility of AD DS. I encourage you to move with a reasonable but quick pace toward upgrading your domain controllers to Windows Server 2008 R2 so you can raise the domain and forest functional levels to take advantage of these capabilities. They make a big difference.

Lesson 1: Configuring Domain and Forest Functional Levels

As you introduce Windows Server 2008 and Windows Server 2008 R2 domain controllers into your domains and forest, you can begin to take advantage of new capabilities in AD DS. Domain and forest functional levels are operating modes of domains and forests, respectively. Functional levels determine the versions of Windows that you can use as domain controllers and the availability of Active Directory features.

> **After this lesson, you will be able to:**
> - Understand domain and forest functional levels.
> - Raise domain and forest functional levels.
> - Identify capabilities added by each functional level.
>
> **Estimated lesson time: 45 minutes**

Understanding Functional Levels

Functional levels are like switches that enable new functionality offered by each version of Windows. Windows Server 2003 added several features to Active Directory, and Windows Server 2008 and Windows Server 2008 R2 continue the evolution of AD DS. These features are not backward compatible: if you have DCs running Windows 2000 Server, you cannot enable the functionality offered by later versions of Windows, so the newer functionality is disabled. Similarly, until all DCs are running Windows Server 2008 R2, you cannot implement its enhancements to AD DS. Raising the functional level entails two major requirements:

- All domain controllers must be running the correct version of Windows Server.
- You must manually raise the functional level. It does not happen automatically.

> **NOTE   FUNCTIONAL LEVELS, OPERATING SYSTEM VERSIONS, DOMAIN CONTROLLERS, AND DOMAINS**
>
> Remember that only domain controllers determine your ability to set a functional level. You can have member servers and workstations running any version of Windows within a domain or forest at any functional level.
>
> It's important to note that raising a functional level is a one-way operation: you cannot lower a domain or forest functional level. Therefore, after you have raised the domain functional level to Windows Server 2008 R2, for example, you cannot at a later date add a domain controller running Windows Server 2003 to the same domain.
>
> It's also important to note that a forest can have domains running at different functional levels, but after the forest functional level has been raised, you cannot add a domain controller running an earlier version of Windows to any domain in the forest.

Domain Functional Levels

The domain functional level affects the Active Directory features available within the domain and determines the versions of Windows that are supported for domain controllers within the domain. In previous versions of Windows, domain functional levels and modes, as they were called in Windows 2000 Server, supported domain controllers running Microsoft Windows NT 4.0. That support ended with Windows Server 2008. All domain controllers must be running Windows 2000 Server or later before you can add the first Windows Server 2008 domain controller to the domain. Windows Server 2008 R2 Active Directory supports these domain functional levels:

- Windows 2000 Native
- Windows Server 2003
- Windows Server 2008
- Windows Server 2008 R2

Windows 2000 Native

The Windows 2000 Native domain functional level is the lowest functional level that supports a Windows Server 2008 domain controller. The following operating systems are supported for domain controllers:

- Windows 2000 Server
- Windows Server 2003
- Windows Server 2008
- Windows Server 2008 R2

If you have domain controllers running Windows 2000 Server, or if you expect that you might add one or more domain controllers running Windows 2000 Server, you should leave the domain at Windows 2000 Native functional level.

Windows Server 2003

After you have removed or upgraded all domain controllers running Windows 2000 Server, the domain functional level can be raised to Windows Server 2003. At this functional level, the domain can no longer support domain controllers running Windows 2000 Server, so all domain controllers must be running one of the following operating systems:

- Windows Server 2003
- Windows Server 2003 R2
- Windows Server 2008
- Windows Server 2008 R2

Windows Server 2003 domain functional level adds several new features to those offered at the Windows 2000 Native domain functional level. These features include the following:

- **Domain controller rename** The domain management tool, Netdom.exe, can be used to prepare for domain controller rename.

- **lastLogonTimestamp attribute** When a user or computer logs on to the domain, the *lastLogonTimestamp* attribute is updated with the logon time. This attribute is replicated within the domain.

- **userPassword attribute** Security principals in Active Directory include users, computers, and groups. A fourth object class, *inetOrgPerson*, is similar to a user and is used to integrate with several non-Microsoft directory services. At the Windows Server 2003 domain functional level, you can set the *userPassword* attribute as the effective password on both *inetOrgPerson* and *user* objects. This attribute is Write Only. You cannot retrieve the password from the *userPassword* attribute.

- **Default user and computer container redirection** In Chapter 5, "Configuring Computer Accounts," you learned that you can use the Redirusr.exe and Redircmp.exe commands to redirect the default user and computer containers. Doing so causes new accounts to be created in specific organizational units rather than in the Users and Computers containers.

- **Authorization Manager policies** Authorization Manager, a tool that can be used to provide authorization by applications, can store its authorization policies in AD DS.

- **Constrained delegation** Applications can take advantage of the secure delegation of user credentials by means of the Kerberos authentication protocol. Delegation can be configured to be allowed only to specific destination services.

- **Selective authentication** In Lesson 2, "Managing Multiple Domains and Trust Relationships," you learn to create trust relationships between your domain and another domain or forest. Selective authentication allows you to specify the users and groups from the trusted domain or forest who are allowed to authenticate to servers in your forest.

Windows Server 2008

After you have removed or upgraded all domain controllers running Windows Server 2003, Windows Server 2003 R2, and Windows 2000 Server, you can raise the domain functional level to Windows Server 2008. Windows Server 2008 domain functional level supports domain controllers running the following two operating systems:

- Windows Server 2008
- Windows Server 2008 R2

Windows Server 2008 domain functional level adds the following domain-wide features to AD DS:

- **DFS-R replication of SYSVOL** In Chapter 10, you learned to configure SYSVOL so that it is replicated with Distributed File System Replication (DFS-R) instead of with File Replication Service (FRS). DFS-R provides a more robust and detailed replication of SYSVOL contents.

- **Advanced Encryption Services** You can increase the security of authentication with Advanced Encryption Services (AES 128 and AES 256) support for the Kerberos protocol. AES replaces the RC4-HMAC (Hash Message Authentication Code) encryption algorithm.

- **Last interactive logon information**   When a user logs on to the domain, several attributes of the user object are updated with the time, the workstation to which the user logged on, and the number of failed logon attempts since the last logon.

- **Fine-grained password policies**   In Chapter 8, "Improving the Security of Authentication in an AD DS Domain," you learned about fine-grained password policies, which allow you to specify unique password policies for users or groups in the domain.

- **Access-based enumeration (ABE) of domain DFS namespaces**   ABE presents a view of a DFS namespace to a user that shows only the folders in the namespace to which the user has at least Read permission. Folders that the user cannot read are hidden. ABE for domain DFS namespaces also requires forest functional level of Windows Server 2003 or higher.

Windows Server 2008 R2

After all domain controllers in a domain have been upgraded to Windows Server 2008 R2, you can raise the domain functional level to Windows Server 2008 R2. Windows Server 2008 R2 domain functional level does not provide additional functionality. However, by raising the domain functional level, you ensure that no one can promote a domain controller running an earlier version of Windows Server. In addition, the domain functional level of every domain in the forest must be Windows Server 2008 R2 before you can raise the forest functional level to Windows Server 2008 R2.

Raising the Domain Functional Level

You can raise the domain functional level after all domain controllers are running a supported version of Windows and you are confident that you will not have to add domain controllers running unsupported versions of Windows. To raise the domain functional level, open the Active Directory Domains And Trusts snap-in, right-click the domain, and click Raise Domain Functional Level. The dialog box shown in Figure 12-1 allows you to select a higher domain functional level.

Figure 12-1 The Raise Domain Functional Level dialog box

You can also raise the domain functional level by using the Active Directory Users And Computers snap-in. Right-click the domain and click Raise Domain Functional Level, or right-click the root node of the snap-in, point to All Tasks, and then click Raise Domain Functional Level.

You must be a member of the Domain Admins group, and the domain controller running the PDC Emulator operations master must be accessible—it is the PDC emulator that is targeted by tools used to raise the domain functional level.

Forest Functional Levels

Just as domain functional levels enable certain domain-wide functionality and determine the versions of Windows that are supported for domain controllers in the domain, forest functional levels enable forest-wide functionality and determine the operating systems supported for domain controllers in the entire forest. Windows Server 2008 R2 Active Directory supports four forest functional levels:

- Windows 2000
- Windows Server 2003
- Windows Server 2008
- Windows Server 2008 R2

Each functional level is described in the following sections.

Windows 2000

Windows 2000 forest functional level is the baseline, default functional level. At Windows 2000 functional level, domains can be running at any supported domain functional level:

- Windows 2000 Native
- Windows Server 2003
- Windows Server 2008
- Windows Server 2008 R2

You can raise the forest functional level after all domains in the forest have been raised to the equivalent domain functional level.

Windows Server 2003

After all domains in the forest are at the Windows Server 2003 domain functional level, and when you do not expect to add any new domains with Windows 2000 Server domain controllers, you can raise the forest functional level to Windows Server 2003. At this forest functional level, domains can be running at the following domain functional levels:

- Windows Server 2003
- Windows Server 2008
- Windows Server 2008 R2

The following features are enabled at the Windows Server 2003 forest functional level:

- **Forest trusts**   In Lesson 2, you learn to create trust relationships between forests.
- **Domain rename**   You can rename a domain within a forest.
- **Linked-value replication**   At Windows 2000 forest functional level, a change to a group's membership results in the replication of the entire multivalued *member* attribute of the group. This can lead to increased replication traffic on the network and the potential loss of membership updates when a group is changed concurrently at different domain controllers. It also leads to a recommended cap of 5,000 members in any one group. Linked-value replication, enabled at the Windows Server 2003 forest functional level, replicates an individual membership change rather than the entire *member* attribute. This uses less bandwidth and prevents you from losing updates when a group is changed concurrently at different domain controllers.
- **Read-only domain controllers (RODCs)**   A forest must be at the Windows Server 2003 forest functional level before an RODC can be added. In addition, you must run Adprep /rodcprep, and at least one writable domain controller running Windows Server 2008 or Windows Server 2008 R2 must be in place. The RODC itself must be running Windows Server 2008 or Windows Server 2008 R2. There are additional requirements for adding an RODC to a domain. See Lesson 3 of Chapter 8 for details.

 Quick Check

- You want to add an RODC to a domain with Windows Server 2003 domain controllers. The domain is at the Windows Server 2003 functional level and already includes one Windows Server 2008 domain controller. The forest is at the Windows 2000 functional level. Which two things must you do prior to adding the RODC?

Quick Check Answer

- You must raise the forest functional level to Windows Server 2003, and you must run Adprep /rodcprep.

- **Improved Knowledge Consistency Checker (KCC) algorithms and scalability**   The Intersite Topology Generator (ISTG) uses improved algorithms that enable AD DS to support replication in forests with more than 100 sites. At the Windows 2000 forest functional level, you must manually intervene to create replication topologies for forests with hundreds of sites. Additionally, the election of the ISTG uses an algorithm that is more efficient than at Windows 2000 forest functional level.

■ **Conversion of inetOrgPerson objects to user objects**   You can convert an instance of an *inetOrgPerson* object, used for compatibility with certain non-Microsoft directory services, into an instance of class *user*. You can also convert a *user* object to an *inetOrgPerson* object.

■ **Support for dynamicObject auxiliary class**   The schema allows instances of the dynamic auxiliary class in domain directory partitions. This object class can be used by certain applications and by developers.

■ **Support for application basic groups and LDAP query groups**   Two added group types, called *application basic groups* and *LDAP query groups*, can be used to support role-based authorization in applications that use Authorization Manager.

■ **Deactivation and redefinition of attributes and object classes**   Although you cannot delete an attribute or object class in the schema, at Windows Server 2003 forest functional level you can deactivate or redefine attributes or object classes.

Windows Server 2008

The Windows Server 2008 forest functional level does not add new forest-wide features. However, after the forest is configured to Windows Server 2008 forest functional level, new domains added to the forest will operate at Windows Server 2008 domain functional level by default. At this forest functional level, all domains must be at Windows Server 2008 domain functional level, which means that all domain controllers must be running Windows Server 2008.

Windows Server 2008 R2

The Windows Server 2008 R2 forest functional level enables the Active Directory Recycle Bin, which is discussed in Chapter 13, "Providing Directory Service Continuity." In addition, new domains added to the forest will operate at Windows Server 2008 R2 domain functional level by default. At this forest functional level, all domains must be at Windows Server 2008 R2 domain functional level, which means that all domain controllers must be running Windows Server 2008 R2.

Raising the Forest Functional Level

Use the Active Directory Domains And Trusts snap-in to raise the forest functional level. Right-click the root node of the Active Directory Domains And Trusts snap-in and click Raise Forest Functional Level. The dialog box shown in Figure 12-2 allows you to choose a higher forest functional level.

Raise the forest functional level only when you are confident that you will not add new domains at unsupported domain functional levels. You cannot roll back to a previous forest functional level after raising it.

FIGURE 12-2 The Raise Forest Functional Level dialog box

EXAM TIP

Be sure to memorize the functionality that is enabled at each domain and forest functional level. Pay particular attention to the capabilities that affect you as an administrator.

PRACTICE **Raising the Domain and Forest Functional Levels**

In this practice, you raise domain and forest functional levels. To perform the exercises in this practice, you must prepare at least one domain controller in a new domain in a new forest. Install a new server running Windows Server 2008 R2 full installation. The server must be named SERVERTST. Its configuration should be as follows:

- Computer Name: SERVERTST
- IPv4 address: 10.0.0.111
- Subnet Mask: 255.255.255.0
- Default Gateway: 10.0.0.1
- DNS Server: 10.0.0.111

Run Dcpromo.exe and create a new forest and a new domain named tailspintoys.com. Set the forest functional level to Windows 2000 and the domain functional level to Windows 2000 Native. Install DNS on the server. You are warned that the server has a dynamic IP address. Click Yes. Also click Yes when you are informed that a DNS delegation cannot be created. Refer to Lesson 1, "Installing Active Directory Domain Services," of Chapter 1 for detailed instructions on installing Windows Server 2008 R2 and promoting a domain controller as a new domain in a new forest.

In the tailspintoys.com domain, create two first-level organizational units (OUs) named Clients and People.

EXERCISE 1   Experience Disabled Functionality

In this exercise, you attempt to take advantage of capabilities supported at higher domain functional levels and find that these capabilities are not supported.

1. Log on to SERVERTST as the domain's Administrator.

2. Open a command prompt.

3. Type **redircmp.exe "ou=clients,dc=tailspintoys,dc=com"** and press Enter.

    A message appears indicating that redirection was not successful. This is because the domain functional level is not at least Windows Server 2003.

4. Type **redirusr.exe "ou=people,dc=tailspintoys,dc=com"** and press Enter.

    A message appears, indicating that redirection was not successful. This is because the domain functional level is not at least Windows Server 2003.

5. Open the Active Directory Users And Computers snap-in.

6. On the View menu, click Advanced Features.

7. Navigate to and double-click the Administrator account in the Users container.

8. On the Attribute Editor tab, locate the *lastLogonTimestamp* attribute. Note that its value is *<not set>*.

EXERCISE 2   Raise the Domain Functional Level

In this exercise, you raise the domain functional level of the tailspintoys.com domain.

1. Open Active Directory Domains And Trusts.

2. Right-click the tailspintoys.com domain and click Raise Domain Functional Level.

3. Confirm that the Select An Available Domain Functional Level drop-down list indicates Windows Server 2003.

4. Click Raise. Click OK to confirm your change.

    A message appears informing you that the functional level was raised successfully.

5. Click OK.

EXERCISE 3   Test Windows Server 2003 Domain Functional Level

In this exercise, you discover that previously disabled functionality is now available.

1. Log off and log on as the domain Administrator.

2. Open a command prompt.

3. Type **redircmp.exe "ou=clients,dc=tailspintoys,dc=com"** and press Enter.

    A message appears, indicating that redirection was successful.

4. Type **redirusr.exe "ou=people,dc=tailspintoys,dc=com"** and press Enter.

    A message appears, indicating that redirection was successful.

5. Open the Active Directory Users And Computers snap-in.

6. On the View menu, ensure that Advanced Features is selected.

7. Double-click the Administrator account in the Users container.

8. On the Attribute Editor tab, locate the *lastLogonTimestamp* attribute. Note that its value is now populated.

9. At the command prompt, type **dfsrmig /setglobalstate 0** and press Enter.

   A message appears stating that this function is available only at Windows Server 2008 or higher domain functional level. In Chapter 10, you raised the domain functional level to Windows Server 2008 to configure DFS-R migration of SYSVOL.

Lesson Summary

- Domain and forest functional levels determine which capabilities of Active Directory are supported and which versions of Windows are supported on domain controllers.

- The Windows Server 2003 and Windows Server 2008 domain functional levels offer significant new functionality.

- The Windows Server 2003 forest functional level enables linked-value replication, supports RODCs, and provides other capabilities. The Windows Server 2008 R2 forest functional level adds the Active Directory Recycle Bin.

Lesson Review

You can use the following questions to test your knowledge of the information in Lesson 1, "Configuring Domain and Forest Functional Levels." The questions are also available on the companion CD if you prefer to review them in electronic form.

NOTE **ANSWERS**

Answers to these questions and explanations of why each answer choice is right or wrong are located in the "Answers" section at the end of the book.

1. You want to raise the domain functional level of a domain in the contoso.com forest. Which tools can you use? (Choose all that apply.)

   A. Active Directory Users And Computers

   B. Active Directory Schema

   C. Active Directory Sites And Services

   D. Active Directory Domains And Trusts

2. You are an administrator of the contoso.com domain. You want to add a read-only domain controller to a domain with one Windows Server 2003 domain controller and one Windows 2008 R2 domain controller. Which of the following must be done before

adding a new server as an RODC? (Choose all that apply. Each correct answer is part of the solution.)

A. Upgrade the Windows 2003 domain controller to Windows Server 2008.

B. Raise the domain functional level to Windows Server 2003.

C. Raise the domain functional level to Windows Server 2008.

D. Raise the forest functional level to Windows Server 2003.

E. Run Adprep /rodcprep.

F. Run Adprep /forestprep.

3. You have just finished upgrading all domain controllers in the contoso.com domain to Windows Server 2008 R2. Domain controllers in the subsidiary.contoso.com domain will be upgraded in three months. You want to configure fine-grained password policies for several groups of users in contoso.com. What must you do first?

A. Install a read-only domain controller.

B. Run Dfsrmig.exe.

C. Raise the forest functional level.

D. Install the Group Policy Management Console (GPMC) feature.

Lesson 2: Managing Multiple Domains and Trust Relationships

Previous chapters in this training kit have prepared you to configure, administer, and manage a single domain. However, your enterprise Active Directory infrastructure might include a multidomain forest or even more than one forest. You might need to move objects between domains or restructure your domain model entirely. You might also encounter requirements to enable authentication and access to resources across domains and forests. In this lesson, you learn the skills required to support multiple domains and forests.

> **After this lesson, you will be able to:**
> - Design an effective domain and tree structure for AD DS.
> - Identify the role of the Active Directory Migration Tool and the issues related to object migration and domain restructure.
> - Understand trust relationships.
> - Configure, administer, and secure trust relationships.
>
> **Estimated lesson time: 60 minutes**

Defining Your Forest and Domain Structure

With the perspective you have gained from the previous 11 chapters of this training kit, you are prepared to consider the design of your Active Directory forest, trees, and domains. Interestingly, the best practices guidance regarding forest and domain structure has evolved as enterprises around the world have put Active Directory into production in every conceivable configuration, and as the Active Directory feature set has grown.

Dedicated Forest Root Domain

In the early days of Active Directory, the recommendation was to create a dedicated forest root domain. You'll recall from Chapters 1 and 10 that the forest root domain is the first domain in the forest. A dedicated forest root domain's exclusive purpose is to administer the forest infrastructure. It contains, by default, the single master operations for the forest. It also contains highly sensitive groups, such as Enterprise Admins and Schema Admins, that can have a far-reaching impact on the forest. The theory was that the dedicated forest root would enhance the security around these forest-wide functions. The dedicated forest root domain would also be less likely to become obsolete and would provide easier transfer of ownership. Underneath the dedicated forest root, according to early recommendations, would be a single global child domain with all the objects one thinks of in a domain: users, groups, computers, and so on. The structure would look something like Figure 12-3.

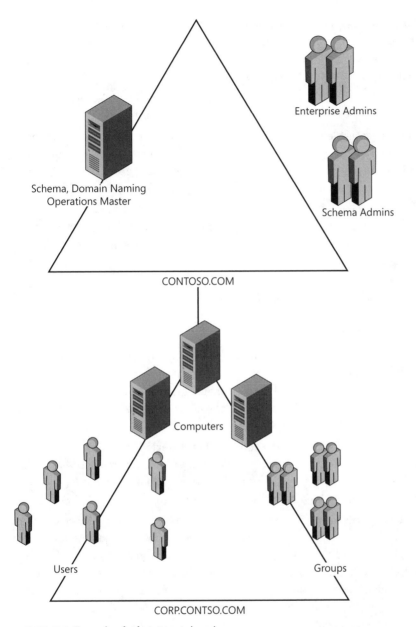

FIGURE 12-3 Example of a forest root domain

Single-Domain Forest

> **NOTE** **SINGLE-DOMAIN FOREST IS THE NEW RECOMMENDATION**
>
> It is no longer recommended to implement a dedicated forest root domain for most
> enterprises. A single-domain forest is the most common design recommendation. No
> single design is appropriate for every organization, so you must examine the characteristics
> of your enterprise against the design criteria presented later in this lesson.

After more than a decade on the market, Active Directory is better understood, and the former recommendation no longer applies. For most organizations, building a forest with a single domain is now recommended. The experience and knowledge that have led to the change in guidance include the following points:

- Any multidomain forest has risks and costs as you'll learn later in this lesson. A single domain bears the lowest hardware and support cost and reduces certain risks.

- Tools are not yet available that enable an enterprise to perform pruning and grafting of Active Directory trees. In other words, you cannot break a domain off of your tree and transplant it in the forest of another enterprise. If that were possible, a dedicated forest root that you could maintain while transferring domains in and out of your forest would make more sense.

- You can implement least-privilege security within a single domain that is at least as secure as, if not more secure than, security in a forest with a dedicated forest root and a child domain.

Therefore, when you consider your domain design, you should begin with the assumption that you will have a single domain in your forest.

Multiple-Domain Forests

In some scenarios, a multiple-domain forest is required. The important point to remember is that you should never create a multiple-domain forest simply to reflect the organizational structure of your business. That structure—the business units, divisions, departments, and offices—will change over time. The logical structure of your directory service should not be dependent solely on organizational characteristics.

Instead, your domain model should be derived from the characteristics of domains themselves. Certain properties of a domain affect all objects within the domain, and if that consistent effect is not appropriate for your business requirements, you must create additional domains. A domain is characterized by the following:

- **A single domain partition, replicated to all domain controllers**   The domain naming context contains the objects for users, computers, groups, policies, and other domain resources. It is replicated to every domain controller in the domain. If you need to partition replication for network topology considerations, you must create separate domains. Consider, however, that Active Directory replication is extremely efficient and can support large domains over connections with minimal bandwidth.

  If there are legal or business requirements that restrict replication of certain data to locations where you maintain domain controllers, you need to either avoid storing that data in the domain partition or create separate domains to segregate replication. In such cases, you should also ensure that the global catalog (GC) is not replicating that data.

Because legal and technical issues surrounding replication tend to affect the global catalog and potentially other data stores, organizations with these concerns are increasingly turning to multiple forest models.

- **A single Kerberos policy** The default Kerberos policy settings in AD DS are sufficient for most enterprises. If, however, you need distinct Kerberos policies, you will require distinct domains.

- **A single DNS namespace** An Active Directory domain has a single DNS domain name. If you need multiple domain names, you need multiple domains. However, give serious consideration to the costs and risks of multiple domains before modeling your directory service domains to match arbitrary DNS name requirements.

In domains running domain functional levels lower than Windows Server 2008, a domain can support only one password and account lockout policy. Therefore, in earlier versions of Windows, an organization requiring multiple password policies would need multiple domains to support that requirement. This is no longer the case in Windows Server 2008 R2, which, at the Windows Server 2008 domain functional level or higher, can support fine-grained password policies.

Adding domains to a forest increases administrative and hardware costs. Each domain must be supported by at least two domain controllers, which must be backed up, secured, and managed. Even more domain controllers might be required to support cross-domain resource access in a geographically distributed enterprise. Additional domains can result in the need to move users between domains, which is more complicated than moving users between OUs. Group Policy objects and access control settings that are common for the enterprise must be duplicated for each domain.

These are just a few of the costs associated with a multiple-domain environment. There are also security risks involved with having multiple domains. Most of these risks relate to the fact that a domain is not a security boundary—a forest is the security boundary. Within a forest, service administrators can cause forest-wide damage. There are several categories of vulnerability whereby a compromised administrative account, or an administrator with bad intent, could cause denial of service or damage to the integrity of the forest.

For example, an administrator in any domain can create universal groups, the membership of which is replicated to the GC. If an administrator creates multiple universal groups and overpopulates the *member* attribute, excessive replication could lead to denial of service on domain controllers in other domains. An administrator in any domain could also restore an outdated backup of the directory, which could corrupt the forest.

> **MORE INFO** **SECURITY CONSIDERATIONS FOR DOMAIN AND FOREST DESIGN**
>
> For more information about the security considerations related to domain and forest design, see "Best Practices for Delegating Active Directory Administration" at *http://technet.microsoft.com/en-us/library/cc773318(WS.10).aspx*.

Given the costs and risks of multiple domains, the construction of a single-domain forest is highly recommended. The most common driver to multiple-domain forests is a significant business requirement related to the replication of the domain naming context.

In a multidomain forest, it might make sense to create a dedicated forest root domain as an empty domain to act as the trust root for the forest. Trust roots are discussed later in this lesson.

Multiple Trees

Remember that a tree is defined as a contiguous DNS namespace. If you have more than one domain, you can decide whether those domains share a contiguous DNS namespace and form a single tree, as shown at the top of Figure 12-4, or are in a noncontiguous DNS namespace, thus forming multiple trees, as shown at the bottom of Figure 12-4.

FIGURE 12-4 Forests with a single tree or multiple trees

Multiple Forests

A forest is an instance of Active Directory. All domains and domain controllers in a forest share replicas of the schema and configuration. Domain controllers that are GC servers host partial attribute sets for all objects in other domains in the forest. Domains in a forest share transitive, two-way trusts, meaning that all users in the domain belong to the Authenticated Users special identity in every domain. The forest's Enterprise Admins, Schema Admins, and Administrators groups in the forest root domain wield significant power over all objects in the forest.

If any of these characteristics of a forest are in conflict with your business requirements, you might need multiple forests. In fact, given the market's current concerns with security, many consultants are recommending that organizations design either a single-domain forest or use multiple forests. Cross-forest trusts, discussed later in this lesson, and Active Directory Federation Services (AD FS) make it easier to manage authentication in multiple-forest enterprises.

MORE INFO **PLANNING THE ARCHITECTURE**

For more information about planning the architecture of an AD DS enterprise,
see *http://technet2.microsoft.com/windowsserver2008/en/library/b1baa483-b2a3-4e03-90a6-d42f64b42fc31033.mspx?mfr=true.*

Moving Objects Between Domains and Forests

In multidomain scenarios, you might need to move users, groups, or computers between
domains or forests to support business operations. You might need to move large quantities
of users, groups, or computers between domains or forests to implement mergers and
acquisitions or to restructure your domain model.

In each of these tasks, you move or copy the accounts from one domain (the *source* domain)
into another domain (the *target* domain). Domain restructuring terminology, concepts, and
procedures apply to *inter-forest migration*—between a Windows NT 4.0 or Active Directory
source domain and an Active Directory target domain in a separate forest—and to *intra-forest
migration*—that is, the restructuring or moving of accounts between domains in the same
forest.

An inter-forest domain restructure preserves the existing source domain, and clones
(or copies) accounts into the target domain. This nondestructive method enables
an enterprise to time the transition and even migrate in phases. Operations go uninterrupted
because both domains are maintained in parallel to support operations for users in either
domain. This method also provides a level of rollback because the original environment
remains unaltered in any significant way. After the migration is complete, you can simply
decommission the source domain by moving any remaining accounts, member servers,
and workstations into the new domain and then taking source DCs offline, at which point
you can redeploy those DCs for roles in the new domain.

An intra-forest migration involves moving objects from the source domain to the target
domain without decommissioning the source domain. After you have migrated objects, you
can restructure your domains to consolidate operations and build a domain and OU structure
that more accurately reflects your administrative model. Many organizations consolidate
multiple domains into one Active Directory domain. This consolidation can result in cost
savings and simplified administration by reducing administrative complexity and the cost of
supporting your Active Directory environment.

Understanding the Active Directory Migration Tool

The Active Directory Migration Tool (ADMT) version 3 can perform object migration
and security translation tasks. You can download ADMT v3 from *http://go.microsoft.com/
fwlink/?LinkID=75627.* On that page, you will also find a detailed guide to the tool.

You can use ADMT to migrate objects between a source and a target domain. The migration can take place between domains in the same forest (an intra-forest migration) or between domains in different forests (an inter-forest migration). The ADMT provides wizards that automate migration tasks such as migrating users, groups, service accounts, computers, and trusts and performing security translation. You can perform these tasks by using the ADMT console or the command line, at which you can simplify and automate the Admt.exe command with option files that specify parameters for the migration task. Then, with a simple text file, you can list objects to migrate rather than having to enter each object on the command line. ADMT also provides interfaces that allow you to script migration tasks with languages such as Microsoft Visual Basic Scripting Edition (VBScript). Run the ADMT console and open the online Help function for details about how to use ADMT from the command line and about scripting the ADMT.

When you are performing migration tasks, ADMT allows you to simulate the migration so that you can evaluate potential results and errors without making changes to the target domain. Wizards provide the Test The Migration Settings And Migrate Later option. You can then configure the migration task, test the settings, and review the log files and wizard-generated reports. After identifying and resolving any problems, you can perform the migration task. You repeat this process of testing and analyzing results as you migrate users, groups, and computers and perform security translations.

Security Identifiers and Migration

Uninterrupted resource access is the primary concern during any migration. Further, to perform a migration, you must be comfortable with the concepts of security identifiers (SIDs), tokens, access control lists (ACLs), and *sIDHistory*.

SIDs are domain-unique values that are assigned to the accounts of security principals—users, groups, and computers, for example—when those accounts are created. When a user logs on, a token is generated that includes the primary SID of the user account and the SIDs of groups to which the user belongs. The token thus represents the user with all the SIDs associated with the user and the user's group memberships.

Resources are secured using a security descriptor (SD) that describes the permissions, ownership, extended rights, and auditing of the resource. Within the SD are two ACLs. The system ACL (SACL) describes auditing. The discretionary ACL (DACL) describes resource access permissions. Many administrators and documents refer to the DACL as the ACL. The DACL lists permissions associated with security principals. Within the list, individual access control entries (ACEs) link a specific permission with the SID of a security principal. The ACE can be an Allow or Deny permission.

When a user attempts to access a resource, the Local Security Authority Subsystem (LSASS) compares the SIDs in the user's token against the SIDs in the ACEs in the resource's ACL.

When you migrate accounts to a new domain, the accounts are copied or cloned from the source domain to the target domain. New SIDs are generated for the accounts in the target domain, so the SIDs of new accounts will not be the same as the SIDs of the accounts in the source domain. That is, even though the cloned accounts have the same name and many of the same properties, because the SIDs are different, the accounts are technically different and will not have access to resources in the source domain. You have two ways to address this problem: *sIDHistory* or security translation:

- **sIDHistory**   Enterprises typically prefer to take advantage of the *sIDHistory* attribute to perform effective domain restructuring. The capitalization, which appears odd, reflects the capitalization of the attribute in the Active Directory schema. An Active Directory security principal (which can be a user, group, or computer) has a principal SID and a *sIDHistory* attribute, which can contain one or more SIDs that are also associated with the account. When an account is copied to a target domain, the unique principal SID is generated by Active Directory in the target domain. Optionally, the *sIDHistory* attribute can be loaded with the SID of the account in the source domain. When a user logs on to an Active Directory domain, the user's token is populated with the principal SID and the *sIDHistory* of the user account and groups to which the user belongs. The LSASS uses the SIDs from the *sIDHistory* just like any other SID in the token to maintain the user's access to resources in the source domain.

- **Security translation**   Security translation is the process of examining each resource's SD, including its ACLs, identifying each SID that refers to an account in the source domain and replacing that SID with the SID of the account in the target domain. The process of re-mapping ACLs (and other elements in the SD) to migrated accounts in the target domain is also called re-ACLing. As you can imagine, security translation or re-ACLing would be a tedious process to perform manually in anything but the simplest environment. Migration tools such as ADMT automate security translation. ADMT can translate the SDs and policies of resources in the source domain to refer to the corresponding accounts in the target domain. Specifically, ADMT can translate:
  - File and folder permissions.
  - Printer permissions.
  - Share permissions.
  - Registry permissions.
  - User rights.
  - Local profiles, which involves changing file, folder, and registry permissions.
  - Group memberships.

In most domain restructuring and migration projects, *sIDHistory* is used to maintain access and functionality during the migration; then, security translation is performed.

MORE INFO   DOMAIN MIGRATION

For more information about domain migration, SIDs, and SID history, see the "Domain Migration Cookbook" at *http://technet.microsoft.com/en-us/library/bb727135.aspx.*

Group Membership

The final concern related to resource access is that of group membership. Global groups can contain members only from the same domain. Therefore, if you clone a user to the target domain, the new user account cannot be a member of the global groups in the source domain to which the source user account belonged.

To address this issue in an inter-forest migration, first migrate global groups to the target domain. Those global groups will maintain the source groups' SIDs in their *sIDHistory* attributes, thus maintaining resource access. Then, migrate users. As you migrate users, ADMT evaluates the membership of the source account and adds the new account to the same group in the target domain. If the group does not yet exist in the target domain, ADMT can create it automatically. In the end, the user account in the target domain will belong to global groups in the target domain. The user and the user's groups will contain the SIDs of the source accounts in their *sIDHistory* attributes. Therefore, the user will be able to access resources in the source domain that have permissions assigned to the source accounts.

In an intra-forest migration, the process works differently. A global group is created in the target domain as a universal group so that it can contain users from both the source and the target domain. The new group gets a new SID, but its *sIDHistory* is populated with the SID of the global group in the source domain, thereby maintaining resource access for the new group. After all users have been migrated from the source to the target domain, the scope of the group is changed back to global.

Other Migration Concerns

You must address several issues when planning for and executing the migration of objects between domains and forests. Each issue is detailed in the ADMT user guide, available from the ADMT download page listed earlier. Among the greatest concerns are:

- **Password migration**   ADMT supports migrating user passwords; however, it cannot confirm that those passwords comply with the policies of the target domain regarding password length and complexity. Nonblank passwords will migrate regardless of the target domain password policy, and users will be able to log on with those passwords until they expire, at which time a new, compliant password must be created. If you are concerned about locking down the environment at the time of migration, this might not be a satisfactory process. You might, instead, want to let ADMT configure complex passwords or script an initial password and then force the user to change the password at the first logon.

- **Service accounts**   Services on domain computers might use domain-based user accounts for authentication. As those user accounts are migrated to the target domain, services must be updated with the new service account identity. ADMT automates this process.

- **Objects that cannot be migrated**   Some objects cannot be seamlessly migrated. ADMT cannot migrate built-in groups such as Domain Admins or the domain local Administrators group. The user guide provides details for working around this limitation.

MORE INFO   **MIGRATING A FOREST**

For information on creating a new forest and migrating its contents from one forest to another, look up *Windows Server 2008: The Complete Reference* by Ruest and Ruest (McGraw-Hill Osborne, 2008). This book describes how to build a complete infrastructure based on Microsoft Windows Server and migrate all of its contents from one location to another.

Understanding Trust Relationships

Whenever you are implementing a scenario involving two or more AD DS domains, it is likely that you will be working with *trust relationships*, or *trusts*. It is important that you understand the purpose, functionality, and configuration of trust relationships.

Trust Relationships Within a Domain

In Chapter 5, you were guided through what happens when a domain member server or workstation joins a domain. While in a workgroup, the computer maintains an identity store in the security accounts manager (SAM) database, it authenticates users against that identity store, and it secures system resources only with identities from the SAM database. When the computer joins a domain, it forms a trust relationship with the domain. The effect of that trust is that the computer allows users to be authenticated, not by the local system and its local identity store but by the authentication services and identity store of the domain: AD DS. The domain member also allows domain identities to be used to secure system resources. For example, Domain Users is added to the local Users group, giving Domain Users the right to log on locally to the system. Also, domain user and group accounts can be added to ACLs on files, folders, registry keys, and printers on the system. All domain members have similar trust relationships with the domain, enabling the domain to be a central store of identity and a centralized service providing authentication.

Trust Relationships Between Domains

With that foundation, you can extend the concept of trust relationships to other domains. A trust relationship between two domains enables one domain to trust the authentication service and the identity store of another domain and to use those identities to secure resources. In effect, a trust relationship is a logical link established between domains to enable pass-through authentication.

Every trust relationship has two domains: a trusting domain and a trusted domain. The trusted domain holds the identity store and provides authentication for users in that identity store. When a user in the directory of the trusted domain logs on to or connects to a system in the trusting domain, the trusting domain cannot authenticate that user because the user is not in its data store, so it passes the authentication to a domain controller in the trusted domain. The trusting domain, therefore, *trusts* the trusted domain to authenticate the identity of the user. The trusting domain *extends trust* to the authentication services and the identity store of the trusted domain.

Because the trusting domain trusts the identities in the trusted domain, the trusting domain can use the trusted identities to grant access to resources. Users in a trusted domain can be given user rights such as the right to log on to workstations in the trusting domain. Users or global groups in the trusted domain can be added to domain local groups in the trusting domain. Users or global groups in the trusted domain can be given permissions to shared folders by adding the identities to ACLs in the trusting domain.

The terminology can be confusing, and it is often easier to understand trust relationships with a figure. Figure 12-5 shows a diagram of a simple trust relationship. Domain A trusts Domain B. That makes Domain A the trusting domain and Domain B the trusted domain. If a user in Domain B connects to or logs on to a computer in Domain A, Domain A passes the authentication request to a domain controller in Domain B. Domain A can also use the identities from Domain B—users and groups, for example—to grant user rights and resource access in Domain A. A user or group in Domain B can, therefore, be added to an ACL on a shared folder in Domain A. A user or group in Domain B can also be added to a domain local group in Domain A.

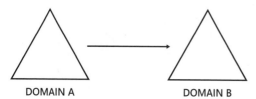

DOMAIN A   DOMAIN B

FIGURE 12-5 Diagram of a simple trust relationship

EXAM TIP

Trust relationships are highly likely to appear on the 70-640 exam. Be certain that you completely understand the terms *trusted*, *trusting*, and *trust*. It is helpful when taking the exam to draw trust relationships so that you can more easily analyze which domain is trusted and has users and groups that the trusting domain can use to grant access to resources. Always make sure that the trust is extended from the domain with resources, such as computers and shared folders, to the domain with users.

Characteristics of Trust Relationships

Trust relationships between domains can be characterized by three attributes of the trust:

- **Direction** A trust relationship can be one-way or two-way. In a one-way trust, such as the trusts illustrated in Figure 12-5, users in the trusted domain can be given access to resources in the trusting domain, but users in the trusting domain cannot be given access to resources in the trusted domain. In most cases, you can create a second, one-way trust in the opposite direction to achieve that goal. For example, you can create a second trust relationship in which Domain B trusts Domain A. Some trust relationships are by nature two-way. In a two-way trust, both domains trust the identities and authentication services of the other domain.

- **Transitivity** Some trusts are not transitive, and others are transitive. In Figure 12-6, Domain A trusts Domain B, and Domain B trusts Domain C. If the trusts are transitive, Domain A trusts Domain C. If they are not transitive, Domain A does not trust Domain C. In most cases, you could create a third trust relationship, specifying that Domain A trusts Domain C. With transitive trusts, that third relationship is not necessary; it is implied.

DOMAIN A DOMAIN B DOMAIN C

FIGURE 12-6 A trust relationship example

- **Automatic or Manual** Some trusts are created automatically. Other trusts must be created manually.

How Trusts Work

Within a forest, all domains trust each other. That is because the root domain of each tree in a forest trusts the forest root domain—the first domain installed in the forest—and each child domain trusts its parent domain. All trusts automatically created should never be deleted and are transitive and two-way. The net result is that a domain trusts the identity stores and authentication services of all other domains in its forest. Users and global groups from any domain in the forest can be added to domain local groups, can be given user rights, and can be added to ACLs on resources in any other domain in the forest. Trusts to other forests and to domains outside the forest must be manually established. With that summary, you can look at the details of trusts within and outside of an Active Directory forest.

Authentication Protocols and Trust Relationships

Windows Server 2008 R2 Active Directory authenticates users with one of two protocols—Kerberos version 5 (v5) or NT LAN Manager (NTLM). Kerberos v5 is the default protocol used by computers running Windows Server 2008 R2, Windows Server 2008, Windows Vista,

Windows Server 2003, Windows XP, and Windows 2000 Server. If a computer involved in an authentication transaction does not support Kerberos v5, the NTLM protocol is used instead. Group Policies can be used to disable NTLM authentication.

Kerberos Authentication Within a Domain

When a user logs on to a client running Kerberos v5, the authentication request is forwarded to a domain controller. Each Active Directory domain controller acts as a Key Distribution Center (KDC), a core component of Kerberos. After validating the identity of the user, the KDC on the domain controller gives the authenticated user what is known as a ticket-granting ticket (TGT).

When the user needs to access resources on a computer in the same domain, the user must first obtain a valid session ticket for the computer. Session tickets are provided by the KDC of a domain controller, so the user returns to a domain controller to request a session ticket. The user presents the TGT as proof that he or she has already been authenticated. This enables the KDC to respond to the user's session ticket request without having to re-authenticate the user's identity. The user's session ticket request specifies the computer and the service that the user wants to access. The KDC identifies that the service is in the same domain based on the service principal name (SPN) of the requested server. The KDC then provides the user with a session ticket for the service.

The user then connects to the service and presents the session ticket. The server determines that the ticket is valid and that the user has been authenticated by the domain. This happens through private keys, a topic that is beyond the scope of this lesson. The server, therefore, does not need to authenticate the user; it accepts the authentication and identity provided by the domain with which the computer has a trust relationship.

All these Kerberos transactions are handled by Windows clients and servers and are transparent to users themselves.

Kerberos Authentication Across Domains in a Forest

Each child domain in a forest trusts its parent domain with an automatic, two-way, transitive trust called a *parent-child trust*. The root domain of each tree in a domain trusts the forest root domain with an automatic, two-way, transitive trust called a *tree-root trust*.

These trust relationships create what is referred to as the *trust path* or *trust flow* in a forest. The trust path is easy to understand with a diagram, as shown in Figure 12-7. In this example, the forest consists of two trees, the tailspintoys.com tree and the wingtiptoys.com tree. The tailspintoys.com domain is the forest root domain. On the top of Figure 12-7 is the forest as seen from a DNS perspective. On the bottom of the figure is the trust path. It indicates that the wingtiptoys.com tree root domain trusts the tailspintoys.com domain.

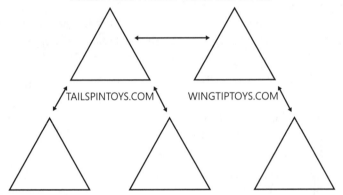

FIGURE 12-7 An Active Directory forest from a DNS perspective and from a trust path perspective

Kerberos authentication uses the trust path to provide a user in one domain a session ticket to a service in another domain. If a user in usa.wingtiptoys.com requests access to a shared folder on a server in europe.tailspintoys.com, the following transactions occur:

1. The user logs on to a computer in usa.wingtiptoys.com and is authenticated by a domain controller in usa.wingtiptoys.com, using the authentication process described in the previous section. The user obtains a TGT for the domain controller in usa.wingtiptoys.com.

   The user wants to connect to a shared folder on a server in europe.tailspintoys.com.

2. The user contacts the KDC of a domain controller in usa.wingtiptoys.com to request a session ticket for the server in europe.tailspintoys.com.

3. The domain controller in usa.wingtiptoys.com identifies, based on the SPN, that the desired service resides in europe.tailspintoys.com, not in the local domain.

The job of the KDC is to act as a trusted intermediary between a client and a service. If the KDC cannot provide a session ticket for the service because the service is in a trusted domain and not in the local domain, the KDC provides the client a *referral* to help it obtain the session ticket it is requesting.

The KDC uses a simple algorithm to determine the next step. If the KDC domain is trusted directly by the service's domain, the KDC gives the client a referral to a domain controller in the service's domain. If not, but if a transitive trust exists between the KDC and the service's domain, the KDC provides the client a referral to the next domain in the trust path.

4. The usa.wingtiptoys.com domain is not trusted directly by europe.tailspintoys.com, but a transitive trust exists between the two domains, so the KDC in the usa.wingtiptoys.com domain gives the client a referral to a domain controller in the next domain in the trust path, wingtiptoys.com.

5. The client contacts the KDC in the referral domain, wingtiptoys.com.

6. Again, the KDC determines that the service is not in the local domain and that europe .tailspintoys.com does not trust wingtiptoys.com directly, so it returns a referral to a domain controller in the next domain in the trust path, tailspintoys.com.

7. The client contacts the KDC in the referral domain, tailspintoys.com.

8. The KDC determines that the service is not in the local domain and that europe .tailspintoys.com trusts tailspintoys.com directly, so it returns a referral to a domain controller in the europe.tailspintoys.com domain.

9. The client contacts the KDC in the referral domain, europe.tailspintoys.com.

10. The KDC in europe.tailspintoys.com returns to the client a session ticket for the service.

11. The client contacts the server and provides the session ticket; the server provides access to the shared folder based on the permissions assigned to the user and the groups to which the user belongs.

This process might seem complicated, but recall that it is handled in a way that is completely transparent to the user.

The reverse process occurs if a user from usa.wingtiptoys.com logs on to a computer in the europe.tailspintoys.com domain. The initial authentication request must traverse the trust path to reach a KDC in the usa.wingtiptoys.com domain to authenticate the user.

Although it is not necessary to master the details of Kerberos authentication between domains in a forest for the 70-640 exam, it can help you in the real world to have a basic understanding that cross-domain authentication in a forest follows a trust path.

Manual Trusts

Four types of trusts must be created manually:

- Shortcut trusts
- External trusts

- Realm trusts
- Forest trusts

Each of these types of trusts is discussed in the following sections.

Creating Manual Trust Relationships

The steps for creating trusts are similar across categories of trusts. You must be a member of the Domain Admins or Enterprise Admins group to create a trust successfully.

To create a trust relationship, complete the following steps:

1. Open the Active Directory Domains And Trusts snap-in.

2. Right-click the domain that will participate in one side of the trust relationship and click Properties.

   You must be running Active Directory Domains And Trusts with credentials that have permissions to create trusts in this domain.

3. On the Trusts tab, click New Trust.

   The New Trust Wizard guides you through the creation of the trust.

4. On the Trust Name page, type the DNS name of the other domain in the trust relationship, and then click Next.

5. If the domain you entered is not within the same forest, you are prompted to select the type of trust, which will be one of the following:

   - Forest
   - External
   - Realm

   If the domain is in the same forest, the wizard knows it is a shortcut trust.

6. If you are creating a realm trust, you are prompted to indicate whether the trust is transitive or non-transitive. (Realm trusts are discussed later in this lesson.)

7. On the Direction Of Trust page, shown in Figure 12-8, select one of the following:

   - **Two-Way** Establishes a two-way trust between the domains.
   - **One-Way Incoming** Establishes a one-way trust in which the domain you selected in step 2 is the trusted domain, and the domain you entered in step 4 is the trusting domain.
   - **One-Way Outgoing** Establishes a one-way trust in which the domain you selected in step 2 is the trusting domain, and a domain you entered in step 4 is the trusted domain.

8. Click Next.

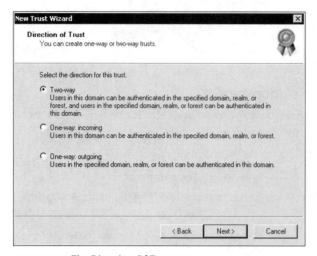

FIGURE 12-8 The Direction Of Trust page

9. On the Sides Of Trust page, shown in Figure 12-9, select one of the following:

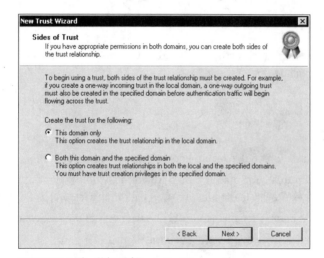

FIGURE 12-9 The Sides Of Trust page

- **Both This Domain And The Specified Domain**   Establishes both sides of the trust. This requires that you have permission to create trusts in both domains.

- **This Domain Only**   Creates the trust relationship in the domain you selected in step 2. An administrator with permission to create trusts in the other domain must repeat this process to complete the trust relationship.

The next steps depend on the options you selected in steps 7 and 9. The steps involve one of the following:

- If you selected Both This Domain And The Specified Domain, you must enter a user name and password with permissions to create the trust in the domain specified in step 4.
- If you selected This Domain Only, you must enter a trust password. A trust password is entered by administrators on each side of a trust to establish the trust. It should not be an administrator's user account password. Instead, it should be a unique password used only for the purpose of creating this trust. The password is used to establish the trust, and then the domains change it immediately.

10. If the trust is an outgoing trust, you are prompted to choose one of the following:

- Selective Authentication
- Domain-Wide Authentication or Forest-Wide Authentication, depending on whether the trust type is an external trust or a forest trust, respectively.

Authentication options are discussed in the section "Resource Access for Users from Trusted Domains," later in this chapter.

11. The New Trust Wizard summarizes your selections on the Trust Selections Complete page. Click Next.

The wizard creates the trust.

12. The Trust Creation Complete page appears. Verify the settings, and then click Next.

You then have the opportunity to confirm the trust. This option is useful if you have created both sides of the trust or if you are completing the second side of a trust.

If you selected Both This Domain And The Specified Domain in step 9, the process is complete. If you selected This Domain Only in step 9, the trust relationship will not be complete until an administrator in the other domain completes the process:

- If the trust relationship you established is a one-way, outgoing trust, an administrator in the other domain must create a one-way, incoming trust.
- If the trust relationship you established is a one-way, incoming trust, an administrator in the other domain must create a one-way, outgoing trust.
- If the trust relationship you established is a two-way trust, an administrator in the other domain must create a two-way trust.

MORE INFO   **PROCEDURES FOR CREATING TRUSTS**

You can find detailed procedures for creating each type of trust at *http://technet.microsoft .com/en-us/library/bb727050.aspx*.

Shortcut Trusts

In an earlier section, you followed 11 steps of the process used to grant a session ticket for a client to access a resource in another domain within a forest. Most of those steps involved referrals to domains on the trust path between the user's domain and the domain of the shared folder. When a user from one domain logs on to a computer in another domain, the authentication request must also traverse the trust path. This can affect performance, and, if a domain controller is not available in a domain along the trust path, the client cannot authenticate or access the service.

Shortcut trusts are designed to overcome those problems by creating a trust relationship directly between child domains in the forest trust path. Two shortcut trusts are illustrated in Figure 12-10.

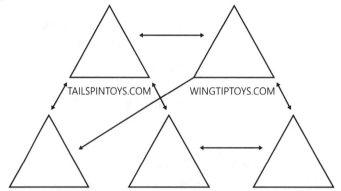

FIGURE 12-10 Shortcut trusts

Shortcut trusts optimize authentication and session ticket requests between domains in a multidomain forest. By eliminating the trust path, they eliminate the time required to traverse the trust path and, thereby, can significantly improve performance of session ticket requests.

Shortcut trusts can be one-way or two-way. In either case, the trust is transitive. In Figure 12-10, a one-way shortcut trust exists whereby wingtiptoys.com trusts asia.tailspintoys .com. When a user from asia.tailspintoys.com logs on to a computer in wingtiptoys.com or requests a resource in wingtiptoys.com, the request can be referred directly to a domain controller in the trusted domain, asia.tailspintoys.com. However, the reverse is not true. If a user in wingtiptoys.com logs on to a computer in asia.tailspintoys.com, the authentication request traverses the trust path up to tailspintoys.com and down to wingtiptoys.com.

A two-way shortcut trust is illustrated between usa.wingtiptoys.com and europe .tailspintoys.com. Users in both domains can be authenticated by and can request resources from computers in the other domain, and the shortcut trust path is used.

External Trusts

When you need to work with a domain that is not in your forest, you might need to create an external trust. An external trust is a trust relationship between a domain in your forest and a Windows domain that is not in your forest. Examples are shown in Figure 12-11.

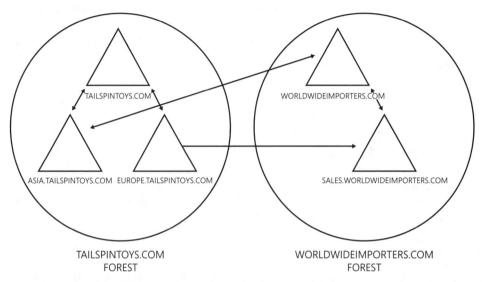

TAILSPINTOYS.COM
FOREST

WORLDWIDEIMPORTERS.COM
FOREST

FIGURE 12-11 An external trust to a domain in another forest

In Figure 12-11, you can see a one-way trust between the sales.worldwideimporters.com domain and the europe.tailspintoys.com domain. The Europe domain trusts the Sales domain, so users in the Sales domain can log on to computers in the Europe domain or connect to resources in the Europe domain.

Figure 12-11 also shows a two-way trust between the worldwideimporters.com domain and the asia.tailspintoys.com domain. Users in each domain can be given access to resources in the other domain. Technically, all external trusts are nontransitive, one-way trusts. When you create a two-way external trust, you are actually creating two one-way trusts, one in each direction.

When you create an outgoing external trust, Active Directory creates a foreign security principal object for each security principal in the trusted domain. Those users, groups, and computers can then be added to domain local groups or to ACLs on resources in the trusting domain.

To increase the security of an external trust relationship, you can choose Selective Authentication on the Outgoing Trust Authentication Level page of the New Trust Wizard. Additionally, domain quarantine, also called SID filtering, is enabled by default on all external trusts. Both of these configurations are detailed in the "Resource Access for Users from Trusted Domains" section, later in this chapter.

Realm Trusts

When you need cross-platform interoperability with security services based on other Kerberos v5 implementations, you can establish a realm trust between your domain and a UNIX Kerberos v5 realm. Realm trusts are one-way, but you can establish one-way trusts in each direction to create a two-way trust. By default, realm trusts are non-transitive, but they can be made transitive.

If a non-Windows Kerberos v5 realm trusts your domain, the realm trusts all security principals in your domain. If your domain trusts a non-Windows Kerberos v5 realm, users in the realm can be given access to resources in your domain; however, the process is indirect. When users are authenticated by a non-Windows Kerberos realm, Kerberos tickets do not contain all the authorization data needed for Windows. Therefore, an account mapping system is used. Security principals are created in the Windows domain and are mapped to a foreign Kerberos identity in the trusted non-Windows Kerberos realm. The Windows domain uses only these proxy accounts to evaluate access to domain objects that have security descriptors. All Windows proxy accounts can be used in groups and on ACLs to control access on behalf of the non-Windows security principal. Account mappings are managed through Active Directory Users And Computers.

Forest Trusts

When you require collaboration between two separate organizations represented by two separate forests, you can consider implementing a forest trust. A forest trust is a one-way or two-way transitive trust relationship between the forest root domains of two forests. Figure 12-12 shows an example of a forest trust between the tailspintoys.com forest and the worldwideimporters.com forest.

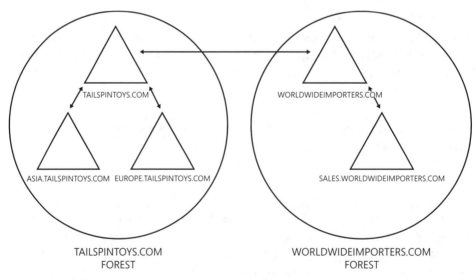

FIGURE 12-12 A forest trust

A single forest trust relationship allows the authentication of a user in any domain by any other domain in either forest, assuming that the forest trust is two-way. If the forest trust is one-way, any user in any domain in the trusted forest can be authenticated by computers in the trusting forest. Forest trusts are significantly easier to establish, maintain, and administer than are separate trust relationships between each of the domains in the forests. Forest trusts are particularly useful in scenarios involving cross-organization collaboration, mergers and acquisitions, or within a single organization that has more than one forest, to isolate Active Directory data and services.

When you establish a forest trust relationship, domain quarantine—also called SID filtering—is enabled by default. Domain quarantine is discussed in the "Domain Quarantine" section, later in this chapter. You can specify whether the forest trust is one-way, incoming or outgoing, or two-way. As mentioned earlier, a forest trust is transitive, allowing all domains in a trusting forest to trust all domains in a trusted forest. However, forest trusts are not themselves transitive. For example, if the tailspintoys.com forest trusts the worldwideimporters .com forest, and the worldwideimporters.com forest trusts the northwindtraders.com forest, those two trust relationships do not allow the tailspintoys.com forest to trust the northwindtraders.com forest. If you want those two forests to trust each other, you must create a specific forest trust between them.

Several requirements must be met before you can implement a forest trust. The forest functional level must be Windows Server 2003 or later. In addition, you must have a specific DNS infrastructure to support a forest trust.

> **MORE INFO**   **DNS REQUIREMENTS FOR A FOREST TRUST**
>
> You can learn about the DNS requirements for a forest trust at *http://technet.microsoft .com/en-us/library/ee307976(WS.10).aspx*.

Administering Trusts

If you are concerned that a trust relationship is not functioning, you can validate a trust relationship between any two Windows domains. You cannot validate a trust relationship to a Kerberos v5 realm. To validate a trust relationship, complete the following steps:

1. Open Active Directory Domains And Trusts.
2. In the console tree, right-click the domain that contains the trust that you want to validate, and then click Properties.
3. On the Trusts tab, select the trust you want to validate, and then click Properties.
4. Click Validate.
5. Do one of the following, and then click OK:
    - Click Yes, Validate The Incoming Trust. Enter credentials that are members of the Domain Admins or Enterprise Admins groups in the reciprocal domain.

- Click No, Do Not Validate The Incoming Trust. It is recommended that you repeat this procedure for the reciprocal domain.

You can also verify a trust from the command prompt by typing the following command:

```
netdom trust TrustingDomainName /domain:TrustedDomainName /verify
```

There can also be reason to remove a manually created trust. To do so, follow these steps:

1. Open Active Directory Domains And Trusts.

2. In the console tree, right-click the domain that contains the trust you want to validate, and then click Properties.

3. On the Trusts tab, select the trust you want to remove, and then click Remove.

4. Do one of the following, and then click OK:

    - Click Yes, Remove The Trust From Both The Local Domain And The Other Domain. Enter credentials that are members of the Domain Admins or Enterprise Admins groups in the reciprocal domain.

    - Click No, Remove The Trust From The Local Domain Only. It is recommended that you repeat this procedure for the reciprocal domain.

5. To delete a manually created trust by using the command prompt, use the Netdom.exe command with the following syntax:

```
netdom trust TrustingDomainName /domain:TrustedDomainName
    /remove [/force] /UserD:User /PasswordD:*
```

The *UserD* parameter specifies a user with credentials in the Enterprise Admins or Domain Admins group of the trusted domain. Specifying the *PasswordD:** parameter causes Netdom.exe to prompt you for the password to the account. The */force* switch is required when removing a realm trust.

> **NOTE COMMAND-LINE TOOLS TO MANAGE AND TEST TRUST RELATIONSHIPS**
>
> The Windows Domain Manager, *Netdom.exe*, and other command-line tools can be used to manage and test trust relationships. See *http://technet.microsoft.com/en-us/library/cc756944(WS.10).aspx* for details regarding these commands.

Resource Access for Users from Trusted Domains

When you configure a trust relationship that enables your domain to trust another domain, you open up the possibility for users in the trusted domain to gain access to resources in your domain. The following sections examine components related to the security of a trusting domain's resources.

Domain Quarantine

By default, domain quarantine, also called SID filtering, is enabled on all external and forest trusts. When a user is authenticated in a trusted domain, the user presents authorization data that includes the SIDs of the user's account in the groups to which the user belongs. Additionally, the user's authorization data includes security identifiers from other attributes of the user and his or her groups.

Some of the SIDs presented by the user from the trusted domain might not have been created in the trusted domain. For example, if a user is migrated from one domain into another, a new SID is assigned to the migrated account. The migrated account will, therefore, lose access to any resources that had permissions assigned to the SID of the user's former account. To allow the user to continue to access such resources, an administrator performing a migration can specify that the *sIDHistory* attribute of the user's migrated account include the former account's SID. When the user attempts to connect to the resource, the original SID in the *sIDHistory* attribute is authorized for access.

In a trusted domain scenario, it is possible that a rogue administrator could use administrative credentials in the trusted domain to load SIDs into the *sIDHistory* attribute of a user that are the same as SIDs of privileged accounts in your domain. That user would then have inappropriate levels of access to resources in your domain.

Domain quarantine prevents this problem by enabling the trusting domain to filter out SIDs from the trusted domain that are not the primary SIDs of security principals. Each SID includes the SID of the originating domain, so when a user from a trusted domain presents the list of the user's SIDs and the SIDs of the user's groups, SID filtering instructs the trusting domain to discard all SIDs without the domain SID of the trusted domain.

Domain quarantine is enabled by default for all outgoing trusts to external domains and forests. Disable domain quarantine only if one or more of the following are true:

- You have extremely high levels of confidence in the administrators of the trusted domain.
- Users or groups have been migrated to the trusted domain with their SID histories preserved, and you want to grant those users or groups permissions to resources in the trusting domain based on the *sIDHistory* attribute.

To disable domain quarantine, type the following command:

```
netdom trust TrustingDomainName /domain:TrustedDomainName /quarantine:no
```

To re-enable domain quarantine, type this command:

```
netdom trust TrustingDomainName /domain:TrustedDomainName /quarantine:yes
```

EXAM TIP

You might encounter either term—*domain quarantine* or *SID filtering*—on the 70-640 exam. Remember that this procedure is used so that users from a trusted domain are authorized using only the SIDs that originate in the trusted domain. An effect of domain quarantine is that the trusting domain ignores SIDs in the *sIDHistory* attribute, which typically contains the SIDs of accounts from a domain migration.

Authenticated Users

A trust relationship itself does not grant access to any resources; however, it is likely that by creating a trust relationship, users in the trusted domain will have immediate access to some of your domain's resources. This is because many resources are secured with ACLs that give permissions to the Authenticated Users group.

Membership in Domain Local Groups

As you learned in Chapter 4, "Managing Groups," the best practice for managing access to a resource is to assign permissions to a domain local group. You can then nest users and groups from your domain into the domain local group and, thereby, grant them access to the resource. Domain local security groups can also include users and global groups from trusted domains as members. Therefore, the most manageable way to assign permissions to users in a trusted domain is to make them or their global groups members of a domain local group in your domain.

ACLs

You can also add users and global groups from a trusted domain directly to the ACLs of resources in a trusting domain. This approach is not as manageable as the previous method, using a domain local group, but it is possible.

Transitivity

When you create a realm trust, the trust is non-transitive by default. If you make it transitive, you open up the potential for users from domains and realms trusted by the Kerberos v5 realm to gain access to resources in your domain. It is recommended that you use non-transitive trusts unless you have a compelling business reason for a transitive realm trust.

Selective Authentication

When you create an external trust or a forest trust, you can control the scope of authentication of trusted security principals. There are two modes of authentication for an external or forest trust:

- Selective authentication
- Domain-wide authentication (for an external trust) or forest-wide authentication (for a forest trust)

If you choose domain-wide or forest-wide authentication, all trusted users can be authenticated for access to services on all computers in the trusting domain. Trusted users can, therefore, be given permission to access resources anywhere in the trusting domain. With this authentication mode, you must have confidence in the security procedures of your enterprise and in the administrators who implement those procedures so that inappropriate access is not assigned to trusted users. Remember, for example, that users from a trusted domain or forest are considered Authenticated Users in the trusting domain, so any resource with permissions granted to Authenticated Users will be immediately accessible to trusted domain users if you choose domain-wide or forest-wide authentication.

If, however, you choose selective authentication, all users in the trusted domain are trusted identities; however, they are allowed to authenticate only for services on computers that you have specified. For example, imagine that you have an external trust with a partner organization's domain. You want to ensure that only users from the marketing group in the partner organization can access shared folders on only one of your many file servers. You can configure selective authentication for the trust relationship and then give the trusted users the right to authenticate only for that one file server.

To configure the authentication mode for a new outgoing trust, use the Outgoing Trust Authentication Level page of the New Trust Wizard. Configure the authentication level for an existing trust, open the properties of the trusting domain in Active Directory Domains And Trusts, select the trust relationship, click Properties, and then click the Authentication tab, shown in Figure 12-13.

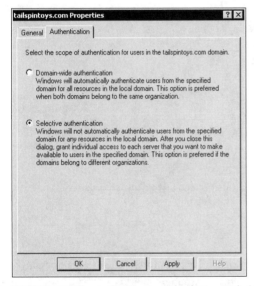

FIGURE 12-13 The Authentication tab of a trust relationship's Properties dialog box

After you have selected Selective Authentication for the trust, no trusted users will be able to access resources in the trusting domain, even if those users have been given permissions. The users must also be assigned the Allowed To Authenticate permission on the computer object in the domain.

To assign this permission:

1. Open the Active Directory Users And Computers snap-in and make sure that Advanced Features is selected on the View menu.

2. Open the properties of the computer to which trusted users should be allowed to authenticate—that is, the computer that trusted users will log on to or that contains resources to which trusted users have been given permissions.

3. On the Security tab, add the trusted users or a group that contains them and select the Allow check box for the Allowed To Authenticate permission, shown in Figure 12-14.

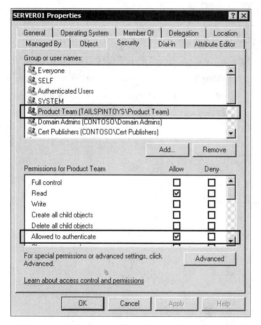

FIGURE 12-14 Assigning the Allowed To Authenticate permission to a trusted group

---

✔ Quick Check

- You have configured selective authentication for an outgoing trust to the domain of a partner organization. You want to give a group of auditors in the partner organization permission to a shared folder on SERVER32. Which two permissions must you configure?

Quick Check Answer

- You must assign the auditors the Allowed To Authenticate permission for the SERVER32 computer object. You must also give the auditors NTFS permissions to the shared folder.

In this practice, you create, secure, and administer a trust relationship between the contoso.com domain and the tailspintoys.com domain. In this scenario, Contoso, Ltd., is forming a partnership with Tailspin Toys. A team of product developers at Tailspin Toys requires access to a shared folder in the Contoso domain. To perform this practice, you must have completed the practice in Lesson 1, "Configuring Domain and Forest Functional Levels," so that you have two domain controllers, one in the contoso.com domain and forest and one in the tailspintoys.com domain and forest.

EXERCISE 1   Configure DNS

It is important for DNS to be functioning properly before you create trust relationships. Each domain must be able to resolve names in the other domain. In Chapter 9, "Integrating Domain Name System with AD DS," you learned how to configure name resolution. There are several ways to support name resolution between two forests. In this exercise, you create a stub zone in the contoso.com domain for the tailspintoys.com domain and a conditional forwarder in the tailspintoys.com domain to resolve contoso.com.

1. Log on to SERVER01.contoso.com as Administrator.

2. Open DNS Manager from the Administrative Tools program group.

3. Expand SERVER01 and select Forward Lookup Zones.

4. Right-click Forward Lookup Zones and click New Zone.

   The Welcome To The New Zone Wizard page appears.

5. Click Next.

6. On the Zone Type page, select Stub Zone and click Next.

   The Active Directory Zone Replication Scope page appears.

7. Click Next.

8. On the Zone Name page, type **tailspintoys.com** and click Next.

   The Master DNS Servers page appears.

9. Select Click Here To Add An IP Address Or DNS Name, type **10.0.0.111,** and press Tab.

10. Select the Use The Above Servers To Create A Local List Of Master Servers check box. Click Next, and then click Finish.

11. Log on to SERVERTST.tailspintoys.com as Administrator.

12. Open DNS Manager from the Administrative Tools program group.

13. Expand SERVERTST.

14. Right-click the Conditional Forwarders folder and click New Conditional Forwarder.

15. In the DNS Domain box, type **contoso.com**.

16. Select Click Here To Add An IP Address Or DNS Name, and type **10.0.0.11**.

17. Select the Store This Conditional Forwarder In Active Directory, And Replicate It As Follows check box.

18. Click OK.

EXERCISE 2 Create a Trust Relationship

In this exercise, you create the trust relationship to enable authentication of Tailspin Toys users in the Contoso domain.

1. Users in tailspintoys.com require access to a shared folder in contoso.com. Answer the following questions:

    ■ Which domain is the trusting domain, and which is the trusted domain?

    ■ Which domain has an outgoing trust, and which has an incoming trust?

    Answers: The contoso.com domain is the trusting domain with an outgoing trust to the tailspintoys.com domain, which is the trusted domain with an incoming trust.

2. Log on to SERVER01 as the Administrator of the contoso.com domain.

3. Open Active Directory Domains And Trusts from the Administrative Tools program group.

4. Right-click contoso.com and click Properties.

5. On the Trusts tab, click New Trust.

6. On the Welcome To The New Trust Wizard page, click Next.

    The Trust Name page appears.

7. In the Name box, type **tailspintoys**. Click Next.

    Because you did not configure DNS on SERVER01 to forward queries for the tailspintoys.com domain to the authoritative DNS service on SERVERTST.tailspintoys .com, you must use the NetBIOS name of the tailspintoys.com domain. In a production environment, it is recommended to use the DNS name of the domain in this step.

8. On the Trust Type page, select External Trust. Click Next.

9. On the Direction of Trust page, select One-way: Outgoing. Click Next.

10. On the Sides Of Trust page, select This Domain Only. Click Next.

11. On the Outgoing Trust Authentication Level page, select Domain-Wide Authentication. Click Next.

12. On the Trust Password page, enter a complex password in the Trust Password and Confirm Trust Password boxes. Remember this password, because you will need it to configure the incoming trust for the tailspintoys.com domain. Click Next.

13. On the Trust Selections Complete page, review the settings. Click Next.

14. On the Trust Creation Complete page, review the status of changes. Click Next.

    The Confirm Outgoing Trust page appears. You should not confirm the trust until both sides of the trust have been created. You create the other side of the trust later in the exercise. Click Next.

15. On the Completing The New Trust Wizard page, click Finish.

    A dialog box appears to remind you that SID filtering is enabled by default. Click OK.

16. Click OK to close the contoso.com Properties dialog box.

    Now you complete the incoming trust for the tailspintoys.com domain.

17. Log on to SERVERTST.tailspintoys.com as the Administrator of the tailspintoys.com domain.

18. Open Active Directory Domains And Trusts from the Administrative Tools program group.

19. Right-click tailspintoys.com and click Properties.

20. On the Trusts tab, click New Trusts.

21. On the Welcome To The New Trust Wizard page, click Next.

    The Trust Name page appears.

22. In the Name box, type **contoso**, and then click Next.

23. On the Direction Of Trust page, select One-way: Incoming. Click Next.

24. On the Sides Of Trust page, select This Domain Only. Click Next.

25. On the Trust Password page, enter the password you created in step 12 in the Trust Password and Confirm Trust Password boxes. Click Next.

26. On the Trust Selections Complete page, click Next.

27. On the Trust Creation Complete page, review the status of changes. Click Next.

    The Confirm Incoming Trust page appears. You validate the trust in the next exercise. Click Next.

28. On the Completing The New Trust Wizard page, click Finish.

29. Click OK to close the tailspintoys.com Properties dialog box.

EXERCISE 3 Validate the Trust

In step 28 of the previous exercise, you had the opportunity to confirm the trust relationship. You can also confirm or validate an existing trust relationship. In this exercise, you validate the trust between contoso.com and tailspintoys.com.

1. Log on to SERVER01.contoso.com as the Administrator of the contoso.com domain.

2. Open Active Directory Domains And Trusts from the Administrative Tools folder.

3. Right-click contoso.com and click Properties.

4. On the Trusts tab, select tailspintoys.com and click Properties.

5. Click Validate.

    A message appears, indicating that the trust has been validated and that it is in place and active.

6. Click OK.

7. Click OK twice to close the Properties dialog boxes.

EXERCISE 4   Provide Access to Trusted Users

In this exercise, you provide access to a shared folder in the Contoso domain to the product team from Tailspin Toys.

1. Create the following objects:
   - A global security group named Product Team in the tailspintoys.com domain
   - A global security group named Product Developers in the contoso.com domain
   - A domain local security group named ACL_Product_Access in the contoso.com domain

2. Create a folder named Project on the C drive of SERVER01.

3. Give the ACL_Product_Access group Modify permission to the Project folder.

4. Open the Active Directory Users And Computers snap-in for contoso.com.

5. Open the properties of the ACL_Product_Access group.

6. On the Members tab, click Add.

7. Type **Product Developers** and click OK.

8. Click Add.

9. Type **TAILSPINTOYS\Product Team** and click OK.

   A Windows Security dialog box appears. Because the trust is one-way, your user account as the administrator of contoso.com does not have permissions to read the directory of the tailspintoys.com domain. You must have an account in tailspintoys.com to read its directory. If the trust were a two-way trust, this message would not have appeared.

10. In the User Name box, type **TAILSPINTOYS\Administrator**.

11. In the Password box, type the password for the Administrator account in tailspintoys.com.

12. Click OK.

13. Note that the two global groups from the two domains are now members of the domain local group in the contoso.com domain that has access to the shared folder.

EXERCISE 5   Implement Selective Authentication

In this exercise, you restrict the ability of users from the tailspintoys.com domain to authenticate with computers in the contoso.com domain.

1. On SERVER01.contoso.com, open Active Directory Domains And Trusts.

2. Right-click contoso.com and click Properties.

3. On the Trusts tab, select tailspintoys.com and click Properties.

4. On the Authentication tab, click the Selective Authentication option, and then click OK twice.

With selective authentication enabled, users from a trusted domain cannot authenticate against computers in the trusting domain, even if they've been given permissions to a folder. Trusted users must also be given the Allow To Authenticate permission on the computer itself.

5. Open the Active Directory Users And Computers snap-in for contoso.com.

6. On the View menu, ensure that Advanced Features is selected.

7. Navigate to and select the Domain Controllers OU in the console tree.

8. In the details pane, right-click SERVER01 and click Properties.

9. On the Security tab, click Add.

10. Type **TAILSPINTOYS\Product Team** and click OK.

    A Windows Security dialog box appears. Because the trust is one-way, your user account as the administrator of contoso.com does not have permissions to read the directory of the tailspintoys.com domain. You must have an account in tailspintoys.com to read its directory. If the trust were a two-way trust, this message would not have appeared.

11. In the User Name box, type **TAILSPINTOYS\Administrator**.

12. In the Password box, type the password for the Administrator account in tailspintoys.com.

13. Click OK.

14. In the Permissions For Product Team list, select the check box under Allow and next to Allowed To Authenticate.

15. Click OK.

    Now the product team from tailspintoys.com can authenticate to SERVER01 and has been given permission to the shared folder through its membership in the ACL_Product_Access group. Those users cannot authenticate with any other computer in contoso.com, even if the group has been assigned permissions to folders on those computers. Also, no other users from tailspintoys.com can access resources on SERVER01.contoso.com.

Lesson Summary

- The best practices design for an Active Directory forest is a single domain. However, there are requirements, particularly related to replication of the domain naming context, that might necessitate multiple domains in a forest.

- The Active Directory Migration Tool (ADMT) migrates objects between domains or for intra-forest or inter-forest domain restructure. When an account is moved to another domain, it receives a new SID. The SID of the source account can be added to the target account's *sIDHistory* attribute so that the new account maintains access to resources that had been assigned to the original account's SID. Group membership can also be maintained by the ADMT.

- Trust relationships allow users in a trusted domain to be authenticated by computers in a trusting domain and, therefore, to be added to domain local groups or given access to resources in the trusting domain.

- Within a forest, there are two-way, transitive trusts between each child and parent domain and between each tree root and the forest root domain. You can create shortcut trusts within a forest to improve authentication.

- You can create trusts to external domains, forests, and Kerberos v5 realms. Those trusts can be one-way or two-way. Kerberos v5 trusts can be transitive or non-transitive. Forest trusts are always transitive, and external trusts are always non-transitive.

- Selective authentication allows you to manage which trusted users and groups can authenticate against which computers in the trusting domain.

- Domain quarantine, also known as SID filtering, is enabled by default on all external and forest trusts. It prevents trusted users from presenting in their authorization data SIDs from domains other than the primary domain of the account.

Lesson Review

You can use the following questions to test your knowledge of the information in Lesson 2, "Managing Multiple Domains and Trust Relationships." The questions are also available on the companion CD if you prefer to review them in electronic form.

> **NOTE ANSWERS**
>
> Answers to these questions and explanations of why each answer choice is right or wrong are located in the "Answers" section at the end of the book.

1. You are an administrator at Wingtip Toys, which has just acquired Tailspin Toys. You plan to restructure the forests of the two companies so that all objects are in the wingtiptoys.com domain. Until then, you want to allow users in the wingtiptoys.com and europe.wingtiptoys.com domains to log on to all computers in the tailspintoys .com domain. Which of the following describes the trust relationship you must configure in wingtiptoys.com? (Choose all that apply. Each correct answer is part of the solution.)

   A. Incoming

   B. Outgoing

   C. One-way

   D. Two-way

   E. Realm

   F. Shortcut

   G. Forest

   H. External

2. You are an administrator at Wingtip Toys, which has just acquired Tailspin Toys. You have created a one-way outgoing trust to allow users in the tailspintoys.com domain to access resources that have been moved into the wingtiptoys.com domain. Some users from tailspintoys.com can access the resources successfully, but other users are reporting that they cannot. You discover that the users having problems have worked for Tailspin Toys for eight or more years and that their accounts were migrated from a Windows NT 4.0 domain. What must you do to give them access to the resources? (Choose all that apply.)

   A. Create accounts in the wingtiptoys.com domain with the same user names and passwords as their accounts in the tailspintoys.com domain.

   B. Rebuild the Windows NT 4.0 domain and upgrade a domain controller to Windows Server 2008.

   C. Run the Netdom trust command with the /verify parameter.

   D. Run the Netdom trust command with the /quarantine:no parameter.

3. You are an administrator of the forest shown in the following figure. Domain controllers for the tailspintoys.com domain are located in Los Angeles. Domain controllers for the Asia domain are in Beijing. Domain controllers for the Europe domain are in Stockholm. Users in Europe and Asia report excessive delays when attempting to open shared folders on servers in each other's domain. Performance is reasonable for accessing resources in the users' own domains. What can you do to improve performance for these users?

ASIA.TAILSPINTOYS.COM   EUROPE.TAILSPINTOYS.COM

   A. Reinstall the operating systems on the users' computers.

   B. Change the IP address to a static address.

   C. Disable dynamic updates in DNS.

   D. Create a trust relationship between Europe and Asia.

Chapter Review

To further practice and reinforce the skills you learned in this chapter, you can perform the following tasks:

- Review the chapter summary.
- Complete the case scenario. This scenario sets up a real-world situation involving the topics of this chapter and asks you to create a solution.
- Complete the suggested practices.
- Take a practice test.

Chapter Summary

- Domain and forest functional levels enable features of Active Directory that have been added by each new version of the Windows operating system. Raising the domain or forest functional level is a one-way operation. After the functional level has been raised, you can no longer add domain controllers running previous versions of Windows.

- Trust relationships between domains allow users from a trusted domain to be authenticated by computers in a trusting domain. Trusted users and groups can be added to domain local groups in the trusting domain and can be given access to resources in the trusting domain.

- Within a forest, there are two-way, transitive trusts between each child domain and its parent, and between each domain tree root domain and the forest root domain. Those trusts result in each domain in a forest trusting each other domain in the forest. You can create shortcut trusts to improve the performance and reliability of authentication within a forest.

- An external trust is created between a domain in a forest and another Windows domain. You can also create a trust with a Kerberos v5 realm.

- A cross-forest trust is established between the forest roots of two AD DS forests. It creates a trust between all domains in the two forests.

- Selective authentication can be applied in the trusting domain to control which computers allow the authentication of trusted users.

- SID filtering, or domain quarantine, is enabled by default on all external and cross-forest trusts. It prevents users in the trusted domain from presenting SIDs that were not generated in the users' primary domain.

- The Active Directory Migration Tool (ADMT) is used to move or copy users, computers, or groups between domains. When you migrate an account, you must consider the fact that the new object will have a new SID, which can affect the object's access to resources and group membership. Use of the *sIDHistory* attribute and the migration of both users and groups can mitigate this risk.

Case Scenario

In the following case scenario, you apply what you've learned about domain functional levels and trust relationships. You can find answers to these questions in the "Answers" section at the end of this book.

Case Scenario: Managing Multiple Domains and Forests

You are an administrator at Tailspin Toys. Your company is partnering on new product development with Wingtip Toys. You want to establish a forest trust to allow users in the tailspintoys.com domain to be authenticated in the wingtiptoys.com domain and vice versa.

1. You upgrade your domain controllers directly from Windows 2000 Server to Windows Server 2008 R2. What must you do with the Active Directory Domains And Trusts snap-in before creating the trust relationship?

2. What type(s) of trust relationship(s) can you create in tailspintoys.com to achieve this goal? What must you ask administrators in wingtiptoys.com to do?

3. You want to control authentication so that users from wingtiptoys.com can access resources on only four servers in your domain. What must you do?

Suggested Practices

To help you successfully master the exam objectives presented in this chapter, complete the following tasks.

Configure a Forest or Domain

You are an administrator at Contoso, Ltd., which is expanding its operations to Europe and Asia. In this exercise, you perform trust management tasks within a multidomain forest. These exercises require multiple domains and domain controllers. To begin the practice, you also need two new servers, named SERVEREU.contoso.com and SERVERAS.contoso.com, with full installations of Windows Server 2008 R2, each a member of the contoso.com domain.

- **Practice 1** Promote SERVEREU.contoso.com to a domain controller in a new domain named europe.contoso.com in the existing contoso.com forest. Promote SERVERAS .contoso.com to a domain controller in a new domain named asia.contoso.com in the existing contoso.com forest. Install DNS on all servers and make sure that all forest zones are replicated to both new domain controllers. Ensure also that both domain controllers use their own DNS service to resolve names—that is, configure each DC's DNS server address to point to the DC's own IP address.

After creating the two domains, europe.contoso.com and asia.contoso.com, you must give users the right to log on to domain controllers in the new domains. In this and other practices in this training kit, you will log on to domain controllers with user accounts that are not a member of Domain Administrators or the domain's Administrators group. Follow the steps in the article, "Grant a Member the Right to Logon Locally," at *http://technet.microsoft.com/en-us/library/ee957044(WS.10).aspx* to grant the Allow Logon Locally right to the Administrators and Domain Users groups. If you will use Remote Desktop Services to connect to the domain controller—rather than logging on locally—grant the Allow Logon Through Remote Desktop Services right. Reboot the server or otherwise refresh Group Policy. Repeat the procedures for both the Europe and Asia domains. This is for the practice environment only. In a production environment, you should not grant users the right to log on to domain controllers.

- **Practice 2** Create a user account in the europe.contoso.com domain. Add the user to the Print Operators group in the Europe domain and the Asia domain so that the user can log on to the domain controllers for the purposes of this practice. Create a shared folder on SERVERAS.asia.contoso.com and give the Europe user permission to the folder. Log on to SERVEREU.europe.contoso.com as the user and connect to the shared folder on SERVERAS.asia.contoso.com.

- **Practice 3** Shut down SERVER01.contoso.com. Log on to SERVEREU.europe.contoso.com as the Europe user. Ping SERVERAS.asia.contoso.com. If you cannot ping the server, DNS or networking is not configured correctly. Troubleshoot the problem. When you can ping SERVERAS, attempt to connect to the shared folder. It should fail because a domain controller in the trust path is not available.

- **Practice 4** Power on SERVER01.contoso.com. Log on to SERVEREU as the Europe administrator. Create a trust relationship with the Asia domain.

- **Practice 5** Power down SERVER01. Log on to SERVEREU.europe.contoso.com as the Europe user. Ping SERVERAS.asia.contoso.com. If you cannot ping the server, DNS or networking is not configured correctly. Troubleshoot the problem. When you can ping SERVERAS, attempt to connect to the shared folder. The connection should succeed because the shortcut trust is in place.

Take a Practice Test

The practice tests on this book's companion CD offer many options. For example, you can test yourself on just one exam objective, or you can test yourself on all the 70-640 certification exam content. You can set up the test so that it closely simulates the experience of taking a certification exam, or you can set it up in study mode so that you can look at the correct answers and explanations after you answer each question.

> **MORE INFO** **PRACTICE TESTS**
>
> For details about all the practice test options available, see the "How to Use the Practice Tests" section in this book's Introduction.

CHAPTER 13

Directory Business Continuity

Business continuity is a hot topic, especially in light of the natural disasters that many organizations have faced all over the world. Hurricanes, tidal waves, and earthquakes are examples of catastrophic disasters that have a far-reaching impact on organizations. Several studies have shown that up to 40 percent of small to medium organizations that face a significant disaster and have no business continuity plan will fail. Don't let this happen to you. Prepare in advance and make sure you are ready for any eventuality.

Disasters don't have to be on a catastrophic scale to be devastating. A user whose Active Directory Domain Services (AD DS) account has been erased by mistake will be as devastated—albeit on a smaller scale—when he or she can't log on one morning without knowing why. That's why you need proactive plans that will keep you ready at all times and ensure that you can react to any situation, disastrous or not. To create these plans, you must address two key areas of business continuity: maintaining and protecting the directory and data store and managing directory performance.

Both of these areas address a facet of directory business continuity. A third area of business continuity, availability, is built into the AD DS operational model. Every domain controller (DC), except for the read-only domain controller (RODC), includes the capability to support multimaster replication. Because of this, each time you put two or more DCs in place for the same domain, you provide high availability for the service. Therefore, simple deployment rules guide the process of maintaining directory service availability.

Exam objectives in this chapter:

- Perform offline maintenance.
- Configure backup and recovery.
- Monitor Active Directory.

Lessons in this chapter:

Before You Begin

To complete the lessons in this chapter, you must have done the following:

- Installed Windows Server 2008 R2 on a physical or virtual computer, which should be named SERVER10. This computer hosts the DNS Server role as well as the Active Directory Domain Services role and is a DC for the treyresearch.net forest root domain. Add a second disk to this server. If the machine is virtual, make it a dynamically expanding disk of 10 GB, format it, and name it D: Data. Use the Disk Management feature in Server Manager to configure this additional drive.

- Performed the practice exercises outlined in Chapter 9, "Integrating Domain Name System with AD DS." These exercises set up a multidomain directory service named treyresearch.net. This forest includes a forest root domain, a domain tree, and a child domain. Exercises in this chapter reuse the forest root domain created in Chapter 9.

- Installed Windows Server 2008 R2 on a physical or virtual computer, which should be named SERVER11 and should be a stand-alone server. This computer hosts the DNS Server role and the Active Directory Domain Services role that you install and create through the exercises in this chapter. Assign an IPv4 address from one of the private ranges, such as 192.168.x.x, and map its DNS server address to the address you assigned to SERVER10.

Using virtual machines (VMs) is strongly recommended in support of the exercises. The DC and Domain Name System (DNS) server roles are ideal for virtualization through either Microsoft Virtual Server 2005 R2 or Hyper-V.

 REAL WORLD

Danielle Ruest and Nelson Ruest

In 2003, we were asked to write a follow-up book to *Windows Server 2003: Best Practices for Enterprise Deployments*. This book would be a pocket guide and would focus on systems administration instead of operating system deployment.

We collected and collated tasks that should be performed on Windows Server 2003 infrastructures, depending on the features deployed. We divided the tasks according to server role and created five categories, focusing only on roles available with the default installation files for Windows Server 2003, and we divided the list according to task frequency, finding four frequencies: daily, weekly, monthly, and ad hoc. The last would include both infrequent tasks and tasks needed to perform on a schedule longer than one month. Then we put it all together in a single spreadsheet.

Before we started writing, we wanted to validate the task list, so we asked our clients if they would help us supplement it. Twenty-five clients, with network sizes ranging from 50 to 25,000 nodes, responded. We sent the list to each one to look it over, evaluate whether the task was appropriate, validate the schedule we suggested, and suggest any missing tasks.

Responses were quite varied, but every client came back with the same general comment: "We never knew you had to do all those things in Windows!" Of all the clients, only a handful even touched on the task list, and those were in the largest networks. We were shocked, but this taught us a valuable lesson.

When clients deploy Windows, things work right away for the most part and, because of this, few organizations assign staff to focus on proactive network monitoring. IT professionals are mostly overworked in almost every organization. When requests come in, they are always high priority; system administrators usually don't have time to be proactive because they are almost always in reactive mode and already working overtime.

Since our *Pocket Administrator for Windows Server 2003* has been published, we have been giving one-day Windows Server administration classes, updating them each time a new version is released. In every case, attendees have come back to us to say that when they use our schedule, they no longer have to work overtime on a constant basis. Our new book, *Windows Server 2008: The Complete Reference*, contains an updated task list.

Monitoring—especially proactive monitoring—is a very important part of any Windows Server deployment, especially in terms of AD DS or DNS, which supports it. Every organization that relies on the identity and access solution AD DS provides should take measures to verify the system's proper operation at regular intervals. Running Microsoft Windows technologies while not performing proactive management for them is not practical. They will work, but users can often leave themselves exposed to potential issues and, perhaps worse, potential security holes. This is why this might be the most important chapter in this book for you.

Lesson 1: Proactive Directory Maintenance and Data Store Protection

One of the most important concepts administrators need to understand when working with a directory service such as AD DS is the division of responsibilities they face. A directory service is very much like a web service. IT administrators of a web service are responsible for the management of Microsoft Internet Information Services (IIS) and the underlying operating system, not for the maintenance of the content included in the websites the server will host. Imagine having to change a comma here, a word there, a picture here, or a phrase there in addition to having to perform all the other work required to maintain a network environment. You would never have time to do anything else but work!

In a web service, you must divide responsibilities based on data and service management. IT is responsible for service management, whereas the users are responsible for data or content management. The same applies to the directory service. AD DS is a distributed database that contains information about the users, computers, servers, services, and more that run in your network, hence its categorization as a network operating system (NOS) as well as a Lightweight Directory Access Protocol (LDAP) directory service. Because of this, administration activities are shared among several members of your organization:

- Users can update their own records. If a user uses the Search Active Directory feature to locate his or her own account record, he or she can change information such as phone number, location, and so on.

- Security and distribution group managers, when assigned the role in AD DS, can automatically manage group content if you assign this user right to them. This is a good approach for reducing the workload system administrators face when managing a NOS directory service. How would you know whether a user should be a member of a group? In every case, when you change group ownership, you respond to a request that was initiated by someone else. Why not cut out the middle person and make group managers directly responsible?

■ The help desk manages password resets. Each time a password must be reset, the help desk is involved.

■ System administrators should focus most of their efforts on directory and DNS service availability. After all, system administrators are there to manage the availability of services and the data the directory contains, not to manage the data itself.

When you plan your proactive management strategy, focus on the service aspect of operations management and delegate data management as much as possible. AD DS delegation capabilities further enhance this model by allowing you to assign object control to others in your organization discretely. This is the approach of this chapter and the focus of this lesson.

After this lesson, you will be able to

■ Understand which administrative tasks must be performed to maintain AD DS and DNS.

■ Understand the difference between online and offline maintenance tasks.

■ Perform offline maintenance tasks.

■ Recover data while online.

■ Recover data while offline.

Estimated lesson time: 90 minutes

Twelve Categories of AD DS Administration

When you consider it, Active Directory administration or management covers 12 major activities. These activities and their breadth of coverage are described in Table 13-1, which also outlines which tasks focus on data or content management and which are concentrated on service administration.

TABLE 13-1 AD DS Administration Activities

TASK	DESCRIPTION	SERVICE	DATA
User and group account administration	This includes user password resets, user creation and deactivation, user group creation, and membership management. Should be delegated to the help desk.	☐	☑
Endpoint device administration	All computers in a Windows network environment must have a computer account. This is how they interact with the directory and how the directory interacts with them. Should be delegated to technicians.	☐	☑
Networked service administration	This includes publication of network file shares, printers, Distributed File System (DFS) shares, application directory partitions, and so on. Should be delegated to the administrator of each service type.	☑	☑
Group Policy Object (GPO) management	GPOs provide the most powerful model for object management in Windows Server 2008 R2. Should be delegated to appropriate technicians, but a central GPO steward should control GPO proliferation.	☑	☐
DNS administration	DNS is now tied closely to the directory, and the operation is based on a properly functioning dynamic DNS service. Because DNS is integrated with the directory, DNS administration is the responsibility of the domain administrator.	☑	☐
Active Directory topology and replication management	Replication is at the very core of the directory service operation. It covers the configuration of subnets, sites, site links, site link bridges, and bridgehead servers. You should rely heavily on the Knowledge Consistency Checker (KCC)—a service that automatically generates replication topologies based on the rules and guidelines you give it—to control replication. This is the responsibility of the domain administrator.	☑	☐

TASK	DESCRIPTION	SERVICE	DATA
Active Directory configuration management	Configuration administration involves forest, domain, and organizational unit (OU) design and implementation. It also involves Flexible Single Master Operations (FSMO) roles, global catalog servers, and DCs, including RODCs because these servers define the configuration of each forest. One last activity that is related to configuration management is time synchronization. AD DS relies on the PDC Emulator role to synchronize time in the network. These tasks are the responsibility of the forest and domain administrators.	☑	☐
Active Directory schema management	AD DS is a database, albeit a distributed one. As such, it includes a database schema. Schema modifications are not done lightly because added objects cannot normally be removed, although they can be deactivated, renamed, and reused. This is the responsibility of the forest administrator.	☑	☐
Information management	This refers to the population of the directory with information about the objects it contains. User objects, shared folders, and computer objects can include owners; groups can include managers; printers and computers can include location tracking information. The Active Directory Schema Management console can be used to add or remove content from the global catalog and determine whether an object should be indexed. You can also assign NTDS quotas to make sure no one adds or extracts more information than permitted in the directory. Delegate as many of the information management tasks as possible.	☐	☑
Security administration	Security administration covers everything from setting Domain Account policies and assigning user rights to managing trusts and access control list (ACL) and access control entry (ACE) administration. This is the responsibility of the domain administrator or designated operators to whom it has been delegated.	☑	☐

TASK	DESCRIPTION	SERVICE	DATA
Database management	Database management involves Ntds.dit maintenance and AD DS object protection as well as GPO protection. Includes managing the LostandFound and LostandFoundConfig containers, which are designed to collect homeless objects in your directory. Also includes compacting the directory database on each DC. Although AD DS regularly compacts its own database automatically, it is good practice to compact it manually. This is the responsibility of the domain administrator.	☑	☐
AD reporting	Generate reports from your directory to know how it is structured, what it contains, and how it runs. There is no default centralized reporting tool, but you can export data at several levels of the directory. You can also generate GPO reports with the Group Policy Management console. This is the responsibility of the domain administrator and the GPO steward.	☑	☑

Depending on the size of your network, each of the activities included in Table 13-1 can be a job by itself. This is why you need to make sure you delegate as much of the work as you can so that you can enlist as much help as possible to ensure that the directory service is highly available at all times. A couple of tools can help in particular situations.

Using Specops Gpupdate

When you work with computer objects in the directory with Active Directory Users And Computers, you can right-click the object and click Manage to launch the Computer Management console with the computer as the focus for the console, but this does not give you access to simpler functions such as remote update of GPOs or the more common *Start*, Shut down, or Restart commands. However, you can obtain a simple and free add-on from Special Operations Software called Specops Gpupdate. Specops Gpupdate is used here only as an example and is by no means an endorsement. This tool automatically adds functionality to the Active Directory Users And Computers console and gives you control over the following activities:

- Remotely updating GPOs on an object in the directory
- Starting computers remotely, using Wake-on-LAN if enabled locally

- Remotely restarting or shutting down the selected computer
- Graphically reporting the results of an operation

In addition, Gpupdate allows you to perform these tasks on single computer objects or on a collection of objects by applying them to an entire OU. This is a good tool for administrators who must manage computers and servers remotely.

> **NOTE OBTAINING SPECOPS GPUPDATE**
>
> To obtain Specops Gpupdate, go to *http://www.specopssoft.com/products/ specops-gpupdate*. A one-time registration is required.

EXAM TIP

Although Specops Gpupdate is quite a useful tool for object management through AD DS, it is not part of the exam.

If you choose to implement Specops Gpupdate, use the following procedure. You need local administrator credentials if you are on a workstation or member server, but you need domain administrator credentials on a DC. Also, you need to be an Enterprise Administrator for the one-time Display Specifier registration in the forest. This step is part of the prerequisite setups for Specops Gpupdate. After the display specifiers have been added, you can run the Setup.exe file on any computer on which you want to install Specops Gpupdate.

1. Make sure the RSAT, especially the AD DS administration tools, are installed on your system.
2. Download the Specops Gpupdate tool from the Special Operations Software website and save it to the Documents folder on the system you want to install it to.
3. Run the self-extracting executable to extract the components to your Documents folder.
4. After the components are extracted, locate the setup.exe file. Double-click it to launch the setup.
5. On the welcome page, click the Start Installation link under Specops: GPUpdate.
6. Accept the license by clicking Accept.
7. Verify that the prerequisites are installed. These include the .NET Framework, PowerShell, and ADUC Menu Extensions. Add them if they are not installed. Click Install when ready.
8. Click OK when the installation is complete.

When you need to work with computer objects, you can simply use the shortcut menu to access the new administration features on either a computer object or an organizational unit containing computer objects. (See Figure 13-1.) This tool is free and a good addition to any directory service.

FIGURE 13-1 The shortcut menu commands added by Specops Gpupdate

Using AD DS Administration Tools

To perform the activities related to service administration in AD DS and DNS, you can use a series of tools. You've already seen many of these tools as you read through the previous lessons, but it is a good idea to review them here. Table 13-2 outlines which tools you can use for which task and where you can locate them. In this table, the focus is on service, not data administration. Many of these tools also work with Active Directory Lightweight Directory Services (AD LDS) because it is based on the same core code as AD DS.

TABLE 13-2 Common Service Administration Tools

TOOL	DESCRIPTION	LOCATION
Active Directory Domains And Trusts	Administer trusts, domain and forest functional levels, and user principal name suffixes.	Administrative Tools program group
Active Directory Schema Snap-in	Modify the schema for AD DS directories or AD LDS instances. You must use the Regsvr32.exe command to register the Schmmgmt.dll first.	Custom MMC
Active Directory Sites And Services	Configure and manage replication scopes for AD DS directories and AD LDS instances.	Administrative Tools program group
Active Directory Users And Computers	Configure and manage the domain-centric FSMO roles as well as RODC features.	Administrative Tools program group

TOOL	DESCRIPTION	LOCATION
ADSI Edit	Query, view, and edit directory objects and attributes.	Administrative Tools program group
Best Practices Analyzer	Verify the configuration of a role as well as potential dependency errors.	Server Manager
CSVDE.exe	Import data into AD DS directories or AD LDS instances.	Command line
DCDiag.exe	Diagnose AD DS directories or AD LDS instances.	Command line
Dcpromo.exe	Add or remove the DC service.	Start menu, Search
DFSRadmin.exe	Manage Distributed File System Replication, which is the system used when the forest runs in Windows Server 2008 R2 functional level.	Command line
DNS Manager	Perform general maintenance of DNS servers.	Administration Tools program group or Server Manager
Dnscmd.exe	Manage all aspects of DNS servers.	Command line
DSACLS.exe	Control access control lists on directory objects.	Command line
Dsadd.exe	Add specific types of objects (users, groups, computers).	Command line
Dsamain.exe	Mount Active Directory store (.dit) backups or snapshots to identify their contents.	Command line
DSDButil.exe (installed with AD LDS and AD DS)	Perform maintenance of the AD DS store. Configure AD LDS ports. View AD LDS instances.	Command line
Dsget.exe	View the selected properties of a specific object (user, computer).	Command line
Dsmgmt.exe	Manage application partitions and operations master roles.	Command line
Dsmod.exe	Modify an existing object of a specific type (user, computer).	Command line
Dsmove.exe	Move an object to a new location within a directory. Also rename an existing object.	Command line
Dsquery.exe	Query the directory for a specific object type according to specified criteria.	Command line

TOOL	DESCRIPTION	LOCATION
Dsrm.exe	Delete an object of a specific type or a collection of objects.	Command line
Event Viewer	Audit AD DS or AD LDS changes and log old and new values for both objects and attributes.	Administrative Tools program group
GPfixup.exe	Repair domain name dependencies in Group Policy objects. Also, relink Group Policy objects after a domain rename operation.	Command line
Group Policy Management Console	Create, manage, back up, and restore GPOs.	Administrative Tools program group
Ipconfig	Display and modify IP configuration details.	Command line
Ksetup.exe	Configure a client to use a Kerberos v5 realm instead of an AD DS domain.	Command line
Ktpass.exe	Configure a non-Windows Kerberos service as a security principal in AD DS.	Command line
LDIFDE.exe	Import data into AD LDS instances.	Command line
Ldp.exe	Perform LDAP operations against the directory.	Start menu, Search
Movetree.exe	Move objects between domains in a forest.	Download from Microsoft.com
Netdom.exe	Manage computer accounts, domains, and trust relationships.	Command line
Nltest.exe	Query replication status or verify trust relationships.	Command line
Nslookup.exe	View information on name servers to diagnose DNS infrastructure problems.	Command line
Ntdsutil.exe (installed with AD DS, not AD LDS)	Perform database maintenance on the AD DS store.	Command line
Repadmin.exe	Diagnose Active Directory replication problems between domain controllers running Microsoft Windows operating systems.	Command line
Server Manager	Manage existing AD DS domains or AD LDS instances.	Administrative Tools program group

TOOL	DESCRIPTION	LOCATION
System Monitor	Create charts and graphs of server performance trends. Determine performance benchmarks.	Server Manager, Diagnostics, Reliability, and Performance
Ultrasound (*Ultrasound.exe*)	Troubleshoot and diagnose replication between DCs that use FRS. Relies on Windows Management Instrumentation (WMI).	Download from Microsoft.com
W32tm.exe	View settings, manage configuration, or diagnose problems with Windows Time.	Command line
Windows PowerShell	Interact with and automate AD DS operations.	Administrative Tools program group
Windows Server Backup	Back up or restore AD DS directories or AD LDS instances and their contents.	Administrative Tools program group

> **MORE INFO** **FINDING AND DOWNLOADING TOOLS**
>
> To locate the Movetree.exe command, go to *http://www.microsoft.com/downloads/details.aspx?FamilyID=96a35011-fd83-419d-939b-9a772ea2df90&DisplayLang=en*. Obtain the .cab file and extract all files named movetree.* from the file. Note that not all tools contained within this file work with Windows Server 2008 R2; Windows Server 2003 support tools are not supported on Windows Server 2008 R2. For example, the *ReplMon.exe* tool simply will not launch.
>
> To obtain Ultrasound, go to *http://www.microsoft.com/Downloads/details.aspx?FamilyID=61acb9b9-c354-4f98-a823-24cc0da73b50&displaylang=en*.

Performing Online Maintenance

You performed many of the activities listed in Table 13-1 as you read through other lessons. Table 13-3 lists chapter locations for information about each of the 12 AD DS tasks in this book.

TABLE 13-3 AD DS Administration Activities

TASK	LOCATION
User and group account administration	Chapter 2
	Chapter 3
	Chapter 4
Endpoint device or computer object administration	Chapter 5

TASK	LOCATION
Networked service administration	Chapter 4
	Chapter 7
	Chapter 8
	Chapter 10
	Chapter 11
Group Policy Object (GPO) management	Chapter 6
	Chapter 7
Domain Name Service administration	Chapter 9
Active Directory topology and replication management	Chapter 10
	Chapter 11
Active Directory configuration management	Chapter 1
	Chapter 8
	Chapter 10
	Chapter 11
	Chapter 12
Active Directory schema management	Chapter 14
Information management	Chapter 2
	Chapter 3
	Chapter 4
	Chapter 5
	Chapter 11
Security administration	Chapter 2
	Chapter 7
	Chapter 8
	Chapter 12
Database management	Chapter 13
Active Directory reporting	Chapter 2
	Chapter 6
	Chapter 7
	Chapter 8
	Chapter 10
	Chapter 11
	Chapter 13

Performing Offline Maintenance

One significant change in AD DS from previous versions is the transformation of the DC role into a controllable service. In previous versions of Windows Server, the DC role was monolithic: to stop the service, you needed to stop the DC as a whole. This meant that when you needed to perform maintenance on the Ntds.dit database—the database that contains the directory store—you had to shut down a DC and restart it in Directory Services Repair Mode. Because of this, there was no way to automate the database maintenance operations. Consequently, most domain administrators never performed any database maintenance at all. Performing no maintenance is not a valid approach to systems management.

Every database works the same way: As new records are added, the database allocates additional space to store information associated with the record. However, when the record is deleted, the allocated space is not recovered. You need to perform database compaction activities to recover this space. The AD DS service does perform some automatic database compaction, but this compaction does not recover lost space within the database; it only rearranges data to make it easier to access. To recover lost space, you must take the database offline and run a compaction and defragmentation sequence against it.

However, with AD DS and Windows Server 2008 R2, the AD DS service is now a manageable service that can be started and stopped like all Windows Server services. This means that to perform database maintenance activities, you no longer need to shut down the DC to restart it in Directory Services Repair Mode. It also means that because the service behaves natively, you can script the defragmentation and compaction operations through basic command-line tools.

Note that to stop the AD DS service, the DC must be able to communicate with another DC that is running the service. If it cannot, you will not be able to stop the service. AD DS includes automatic checks and verifications that ensure that at least one DC is available at all times; otherwise, no one will be able to log on to the network.

You work with the defragmentation and compaction operation in the practice exercises at the end of this lesson.

EXAM TIP

Offline defragmentation and compaction and the restartable AD DS service are important parts of the exam.

Relying on Built-in Directory Protection Measures

Data protection is also a very important aspect of proactive systems management, and it is essential for AD DS. As you know, each account stored in the AD DS database is a unique object because it is tied to a specific and unique security identifier (SID). This means that when an account is deleted, you cannot simply re-create it. Although a re-created account appears the same to humans, it is a completely different object to AD DS and, as such, does not retain the properties or attributes of the formerly deleted object. Group memberships, passwords, attribute settings, and more are completely different for the object. This is one very good reason to reassign accounts rather than re-create them when people change positions in your network. Reassigning them automatically grants the new person the same rights as the previous account owner. Re-creating an account requires you to dig in and identify all the access rights required by the role in your network, which is a lot more work.

It is difficult to lose data within the directory because of the multimaster replication model—when a change is performed in one location, it is automatically replicated to all other locations. However, this same replication model can also cause issues. When an operator deletes an object, it is deleted in the entire directory. If an object is deleted by mistake, it might need to be restored from backup to be recovered. However, AD DS includes three features that allow you to recover information without resorting to backups:

- The new object protection option, which protects objects from deletion.
- The new AD DS Access auditing feature, which logs old and new values, allowing you to return to an original value when object properties are modified.
- The AD DS Recycle Bin. If you are running Windows Server 2008 R2 and your forest schema is updated to Windows Server 2008 R2, you can rely on the AD DS Recycle Bin to restore objects.

Each of these features provides a means of protecting and recovering the information in the directory database. Note that you can also rely on Windows Server Backup to restore AD DS objects.

Protecting AD DS Objects

By default, every new object in AD DS can be protected from deletion when it is created. In every case, you must specifically assign this feature to the object. When you create objects through batch processes or through a migration process, it is not protected unless you assign the feature during the creation process. When you create an object interactively, you must also assign protection explicitly. Object protection is assigned or removed on the Object tab (shown in Figure 13-2), which can be viewed only when you have Advanced Features turned on in the View menu of the Active Directory Users And Computers console. Note that container objects such as OUs have the object protection option enabled by default because they form part of your directory structure.

After object protection is assigned, you cannot delete the object accidentally. This also means that the object cannot be moved from one location to the other, as illustrated in this error message.

FIGURE 13-2 Protecting an object from deletion in AD DS

In fact, this option assigns two Deny permissions to the Everyone group: Deny::Delete and Deny::Delete subtree. Remember that in AD DS, deny permissions override every allow permission. The only way you can move or delete this object from this point on is if you clear the protection feature check box. This is a useful feature for organizations that delegate object administration to technical staff. In fact, you might consider making this feature part of the user account template that you create to assist in the creation of user accounts in your directory.

Auditing Directory Changes

When you audit directory changes in Windows Server 2008 R2, you automatically log old and new values of an attribute each time an object is modified. Further, because the AD DS audit policy in Windows Server 2008 R2 now logs four subcategories of service access, you can control the assignment of this policy at a more granular level than in previous versions of Windows Server. The subcategory that controls attribute change logging is Directory Service Changes. When enabled, it captures creation, modification, move, and undeletion operations on an object. Each operation is assigned a specific event ID in Directory Services Event Log.

This feature turns Event Log into a record-keeping system for directory changes, allowing you to maintain extensive records on the changes that have been made in your directory. It is also useful for fixing modifications that have been performed erroneously.

When an object is modified, at least two events are logged. The first event lists the former value, and the second—more recent—event lists the new value. Use the two to correct modifications that should not have been made.

Using the AD Recycle Bin

In earlier versions of Windows Server, you often had to perform authoritative restores to recover data that was deleted by mistake. The problem with this is that it placed the DC in Directory Services Restore Mode (DSRM), which made it unable to service logon requests during the operation. With Windows Server 2008 R2, you can rely on the AD Recycle Bin to restore deleted objects without having to take the DC offline. The Recycle Bin relies on the AD DS tombstone feature—a feature that does not immediately remove deleted objects from the directory database, but rather moves them to a special Deleted Objects container. Whereas you needed arcane tools and procedures to access tombstone information in previous versions of Windows Server, you can have immediate access to this information through the new AD Recycle Bin in Windows Server 2008 R2.

Note that the Recycle Bin is available for AD directory services. This means it is available for both AD DS and AD LDS. Also note that the Recycle Bin is not enabled by default. Instead, it must be activated to be made available.

When you rely on the Recycle Bin to restore a deleted object, the object is restored with both its link-valued and non-link-valued attributes. For example, a deleted user object that is restored through the Recycle Bin would retain its group memberships as well as all of its security descriptors. All attributes are restored both within a specific domain and across other domains in the forest.

The Recycle Bin is a feature of Windows Server 2008 R2, and as such cannot be activated unless the forest functional level is Windows Server 2008 R2. Remember that to achieve such a functional level in the forest, all DCs in all domains must be running Windows Server 2008 R2. Large organizations running thousands of DCs will likely not rely on the Recycle Bin for quite some time, until their entire forest is updated to Windows Server 2008 R2. Organizations in this situation should rely on LDP.exe to perform object restores without resorting to DSRM. For this reason, this procedure is described in the section titled "Restoring Deleted Objects with LDP.exe."

Smaller organizations or organizations that are implementing a new directory service will have more immediate access to this feature because it is easier for them to raise their forest functional level to Windows Server 2008 R2. Note that after you enable the Recycle Bin, you cannot disable it.

The AD Recycle Bin introduces new concepts in terms of deleted objects:

- **Logically deleted object** When you delete an object, its values—link-enabled and non-link-enabled—are retained, but its distinguished name is mangled and the object is moved to the Deleted Objects container. The object remains in a logically deleted state for the duration of its deleted lifetime.

- **Recycled object** After the deleted lifetime expires, the deleted object moves to a recycled state. Most of its attributes are stripped away and it remains in the Deleted Objects container for the duration of its recycled lifetime (formerly known as tomb-stone duration); however, the object is now hidden. After the recycled lifetime expires, the object is physically deleted through the AD DS garbage collection process. Note that a recycled object is not like a tombstone object in former versions of Windows Server. In former versions, the tombstone object could be recovered, but a recycled object cannot. Also note that all tombstone objects are immediately moved to the recycled state when you enable the AD Recycle Bin.

Both state durations are controllable. By default, the value of a logically deleted object lifetime is set to null and as such is set to the lifetime duration of a recycled object. By default, the recycled object lifetime is also set to null and lasts the same as a tombstone object, which is 180 days. The logically deleted object lifetime is controlled by the value of the *msDS-DeletedObjectLifetime* attribute. The recycled object lifetime is controlled by the value of the *tombstoneLifetime* attribute. When you modify either attribute, you change the default behavior. If 180 days of potential recovery is not sufficient, then you can set the value to something that works best for your organization, but you will be modifying the default behavior. Rely on a schema management console to locate the attribute and modify its value.

To enable the recycle bin, you must perform the following tasks. Remember that all DCs must be running Windows Server 2008 R2.

1. Update the forest schema. This procedure is required only if you are introducing new Windows Server 2008 R2 DCs in an existing forest. You must be a member of the Schema Admins group to perform this task. Run the following command on the DC that holds the Schema Master operations master role:

   ```
   adprep /forestprep
   ```

   Run the following commands on the DC that holds the Infrastructure Master operations master role:

   ```
   adprep /domainprep /gpprep
   ```

   ```
   adprep /rodcprep
   ```

2. Update the forest functional level to Windows Server 2008 R2. You must be a member of the Enterprise Admins group. Use the AD Domains And Trusts console to do so. You can also use the following PowerShell cmdlet in the AD Module For Windows PowerShell. Make sure you run the module as an administrator.

   ```
   Set-ADForestMode -Identity DNSForestName -ForestMode Windows2008R2Forest
   ```

   where *DNSForestName* is the DNS name of the forest you want to raise—for example, contoso.com. Note that if your forest is a new forest running only Windows Server 2008 R2 DCs, you should already be at the Windows Server 2008 R2 functional level.

3. Enable the Recycle Bin. Again, you need Enterprise Admins group membership and you use the AD Module For Windows PowerShell in administrator mode:

   ```
   Enable-ADOptionalFeature -Identity ADOptionalFeature -Scope ADOptionalFeatureScope
      -Target DNSForestName
   ```

For example, to enable the Recycle Bin in the contoso.com forest, use:

```
Enable-ADOptionalFeature -Identity 'CN=Recycle Bin Feature,CN=Optional Features,
    CN=Directory Service,CN=Windows NT,CN=Services,CN=Configuration,DC=contoso,
DC=com'
    -Scope ForestOrConfigurationSet -Target 'contoso.com'
```

Because this action is irreversible, the system asks you to confirm the action. Type **Y** and press Enter. The Recycle Bin is now enabled, or will be after replication has been completed to all DCs. You can force replication to speed up the process. This means that all existing tombstone objects have been changed to the recycled state and are no longer recoverable. However, all new deletions will be recoverable for 180 days by default. Now you can rely on the LDP.exe command to display and restore objects in the directory. You must be a member of Domain Admins to perform this procedure.

1. From an elevated command prompt, type **Ldp.exe**.

2. On the Connection menu, click Connect. Type the server's fully qualified domain name (FQDN), such as **Server10.TreyResearch.net**, and click OK.

3. On the Connection menu, click Bind. Make sure the Bind As Currently Logged On User option is selected and click OK.

4. On the Options menu, click Controls. In the Load Predefined drop-down list, select Return Deleted Objects. Make sure Server is selected in the Control Type section of the dialog box and click OK.

5. On the View menu, click Tree. Type the deleted object container's distinguished name (DN) and click OK.

   For example, the DN of the container in Trey Research would be:

   ```
   cn=Deleted Objects,dc=TreyResearch,dc=net
   ```

6. In the tree pane, double-click the deleted objects container to expand its contents.

   Remember that Ldp.exe returns only 1,000 objects by default.

7. Locate the object you want to restore in the tree pane and double-click it.

   This displays its information in the details pane. For example, if the object is a user account, it begins with cn=username. You may need to scroll through the details pane to locate the object you seek.

8. Right-click the object name in the tree pane and click Modify.

9. In the Modify dialog box, type **isDeleted** in the Edit Entry Attribute value, select Delete as the Operation, and then click the X button.

10. In the Modify dialog box, type **distinguishedName** in the Edit Entry Attribute value, type the object's new DN in the Attribute value, select Replace as the Operation, and then click the X button.

    For example, to restore John Kane's account to the People container in the Trey Research domain, the DN would be cn=John Kane,ou=People,dc=treyresearch,dc=net.

11. Make sure the Extended check box is selected in the bottom left of the dialog box, and then click Run. Then click Close.

12. Use Active Directory Users And Computers to move to the OU you restored the object to. Use the refresh button to refresh the OU contents if the console was already opened.

The object is restored. This procedure recovers the object and retains the original SID for the object as well.

You can also rely on the *Get-ADObject* and *Restore-ADObject* PowerShell cmdlets to restore objects. Obtain the object through the *Get-ADObject* cmdlet and pipe it to the *Restore-ADObject* cmdlet to perform the actual restore. Although the Recycle Bin is useful, its interface is left obscure by default because restoring AD objects is not an action you should perform lightly.

> **MORE INFO** **AD RECYCLE BIN**
>
> For more information on how to use the AD Recycle Bin, go to *http://go.microsoft.com/ fwlink/?LinkId=133971*.

Restoring Deleted Objects with LDP.exe

If your forest is not running at Windows Server 2008 R2 functional level, you cannot use the AD DS Recycle Bin. Therefore you must rely on the AD DS tombstone feature along with LDP. exe to perform restores of accidentally deleted objects. You can also rely on Quest Object Restore For Active Directory, a free utility. The procedure to install and use Quest Object Restore is described in the next section.

Perform this procedure with Domain Administrator access rights.

1. From Command Prompt, type **Ldp.exe**.

2. On the Connection menu, click Connect. Type the server's FQDN, such as **Server10. TreyResearch.net**, and click OK.

3. On the Connection menu, click Bind. Make sure the Bind As Currently Logged On User option is selected and click OK.

4. On the Option menu, click Controls. In the Load Predefined drop-down list, select Return Deleted Objects. Make sure Server is selected in the Control Type section of the dialog box and click OK.

5. On the View menu, click Tree. Type the deleted object container's DN and click OK.

For example, the DN of the container in Trey Research would be:

```
cn=Deleted Objects,dc=treyresearch,dc=net.
```

6. In the tree pane, double-click the deleted objects container to expand its contents. Remember that Ldp.exe returns only 1,000 objects by default.

7. Locate the object you want to restore in the tree pane and double-click it.

   This displays its information in the details pane. For example, if the object is a user account, it begins with cn=username. You may need to scroll through the details pane to locate the object you seek.

8. Right-click the object name in the tree pane and click Modify.

9. In the Modify dialog box, type **isDeleted** in the Edit Entry Attribute value, select Delete as the Operation, and then click the X button.

10. In the Modify dialog box, type **distinguishedName** in the Edit Entry Attribute value, type the object's new DN in the Attribute value, select Replace as the Operation, and then click the X button.

    For example, to restore John Kane's account to the People container in the Trey Research domain, the DN would be cn=John Kane,ou=People,dc=TreyResearch,dc=net.

11. Make sure the Synchronous and Extended check boxes are both selected in the bottom left of the dialog box, and then click Run. (See Figure 13-3.) Then click Close.

12. Use Active Directory Users And Computers to move to the OU you restored the object to. Use the refresh button to refresh the OU contents if the console was already opened.

13. Reset the newly restored object's password, group memberships, and any other values you need to reapply, and then click Enable.

    The object is restored. This procedure recovers the object and retains the original SID for the object as well, but it does not retain all group memberships and other values.

FIGURE 13-3 Recovering a deleted object with *Ldp.exe*

Using Quest Object Restore for Active Directory

As you can see from the previous procedure, objects are not immediately removed from the directory when they are deleted. Instead, they are tombstoned and moved to a special hidden container. You can access this container with special tools but not with the normal

Active Directory consoles. You can, however, use a utility from Quest Software, Quest Object Restore For Active Directory, to access the tombstone container through a graphical console and locate objects you want to restore. This utility is free; however, it expires every six months and must be removed and reinstalled to work again. Quest Object Restore For Active Directory is used here only as an example and is by no means an endorsement.

> **NOTE OBTAINING QUEST OBJECT RESTORE**
>
> To obtain the Quest Object Restore For Active Directory, go to *http://www.quest.com/ object-restore-for-active-directory/*. A one-time registration with a business email address is required.

EXAM TIP

Although Quest Object Restore For Active Directory is quite a useful tool for recovering deleted objects in AD DS, it is not part of the exam.

Proceed as follows to download and install Quest Object Restore For Active Directory. You need domain administrator credentials if you perform this procedure on a DC, or local administrator credentials if you do so on a workstation or member server.

1. Make sure the RSAT, especially the AD DS administration tools, are installed on your system.

2. Download the Quest Object Restore For Active Directory tool from the Quest Software website and save it to the Documents folder on the system on which you want to install it.

3. Extract the components from the executable.

4. After the tools are extracted, locate the Quest Object Restore For Active Directory.msi file. It should be in your Documents folder. Double-click the .msi file to launch the setup.

5. Click Run in the warning dialog box.

6. Click Next at the Welcome screen.

7. Accept the license and click Next.

8. Type your full name and organization, ensuring that Anyone Who Uses This Computer is selected, and click Next.

9. Accept the default installation location and click Next.

10. Click Next to install the application, and then click Finish when the installation is complete.

11. To use the tool, navigate to Start\All Programs\Quest Software\Quest Object Restore For Active Directory and click Quest Object Restore For Active Directory.

    This tool runs in its own Microsoft Management Console (MMC).

12. When the console is open, right-click Quest Object Restore For Active Directory and click Connect To.

13. Type the domain's FQDN or click Browse to locate it. Click OK to connect.

14. Click the domain name in the tree pane to see a list of deleted objects in the details pane.

15. If the objects do not appear, click Refresh.

16. To restore an object, right-click the object name in the details pane and click Restore, as shown in Figure 13-4. Click OK when the object has been restored.

FIGURE 13-4 Using Quest Object Restore For Active Directory to restore objects

Basically, Quest Object Restore For Active Directory displays the tombstone container in AD DS. Because all objects are tombstoned for a period of 180 days by default, you can restore these objects anytime before they are destroyed by directory database cleanup operations. However, as with the Ldp.exe tool, this procedure recovers the object and retains the original SID for the object, but it does not retain all group memberships and other values, so you must modify the object before you enable it. However, using this tool is much simpler than using the *Ldp.exe* procedure from the previous section.

Relying on Windows Server Backup to Protect the Directory

Although you can use special tools to access the tombstone data in the directory, doing so does not always provide the best method for data recovery. For example, objects that you restore from tombstone containers do not include all of their previous attributes. Because of this, you must know which contents and attributes were assigned to the object before deletion to be able to bring it back to its original state. However, when you restore the data from backup and reassign it to the directory, you restore all of an object's attributes at once, and you do not need to reassign attributes such as group memberships and so on. This saves time after the object is restored but requires a more complex operation to perform the restore.

In addition, restoring objects in AD DS was more or less a hit-or-miss operation in previous versions of Windows Server because it was impossible to view objects within a backup data set prior to the restore. It was and continues to be impossible to restore different backup sets to different DCs to view the data they contain. However, Windows Server 2008 R2 includes a new tool, the AD DS database mounting tool with which you can view backup data set contents prior to the restore operation. This tool can ensure that you recover the right version of the object and save you considerable time when you need to recover an object.

When you work with Active Directory backup and restore operations, you can perform several operations:

- You can back up the entire server, including its operating system.
- You can back up only the System State Data, data that includes the server's configuration data as well as the *Ntds.dit* directory store.
- You can restore nonauthoritative data—data that will be added to the DC but updated by multimaster replication when the DC is back online.
- You can restore authoritative data—data that will be added to the DC but will update all other DCs through multimaster replication when the DC is back online.
- You can perform Install From Media (IFM) DC setups that rely on a copy of the *Ntds.dit* from another DC to reduce the amount of replication required to create the DC during setup.

There are several ways to work with and use backup data sets when working with DCs in Windows Server 2008 R2. However, if you are familiar with DCs from previous versions of Windows, you will find that several operations are different in Windows Server 2008 R2:

- Backups are performed with Windows Server Backup or through its corresponding *Wbadmin.exe* command-line tool. Both are Windows Server 2008 R2 features and must be added to the server to be made available. They are not installed by default.
- Backups are not discrete. They capture critical volumes in their entirety. On a DC, these volumes include the following:
  - The system volume
  - The boot volume
  - The volume hosting the SYSVOL share
  - The volume that hosts the AD DS database
  - The volume that hosts the AD DS logs
- As with previous versions of Windows, backups can be automated or manual.
- Backups can be performed to network drives, removable hard drives configured as basic volumes, DVDs and CDs, dynamic disks, and even virtual hard drives (VHD). For more information on Windows Server Backup for Windows Server 2008 R2, go to http://technet. microsoft.com/en-us/library/ee344835%28WS.10%29.aspx..
- You cannot back up individual files. Windows Server Backup supports full volume backups only.
- If you want to protect only the system state data, you must use the Ntdsutil.exe command-line tool. To do so, you must use the new IFM subcommand available in *Ntdsutil.exe* to capture this information for Install From Media installations. If the installation is for a read-only DC, this tool automatically strips AD DS secrets from the data to create secure installation media.

- Backup operators can create scheduled backups in Windows Server 2008 R2.
- If a server is down, you must use a local copy of the Windows Recovery Environment (WinRE) to restore the system. WinRE can either be installed locally or found on the Windows Server 2008 R2 installation media.

These new capabilities affect the way you work with DCs in Windows Server 2008 R2. Use the following recommendations when building DCs to make them easier to recover:

- Run each DC as a single-purpose server and do not add any other roles except the DNS Server role to the server.
- Run DCs as virtual machines under Windows Server 2008 R2 Hyper-V. DCs are ideal candidates for Hyper-V because they mostly require network throughput and processing capability to manage logons. Even if your domains include thousands of users and have a high processor usage during key logon periods such as the morning and the afternoon after lunch, virtualize them and assign more resources to them.
- Do not store any other data on the DC, although you can use separate volumes for the DC database and logs if your AD DS database includes large numbers of objects.
- Transform the Windows Installation Media into an ISO file and make it available on your Hyper-V hosts so that it is readily available if you need to restore the DC. If not, install WinRE onto each DC you create. To do so, you will need access to the Windows Automated Installation Kit (WAIK).

MORE INFO   **WINDOWS AUTOMATED INSTALLATION KIT (WAIK)**

For more information about the Windows Automated Installation Kit, go to
http://go.microsoft.com/fwlink/?LinkId=90643.

- Perform regular, automated backups of your DCs. These can be to a dedicated basic volume or to a mapped network drive.
- Protect the Directory Services Restore Mode password carefully. This password must be used to restore data to a DC, and, because it is a highly privileged password, it must be protected at all times.

MORE INFO   **AD DS BACKUP AND RECOVERY**

For more information about AD DS backup and recovery, see "Step-by-Step Guide for Windows Server 2008 Active Directory Domain Services Backup and Recovery" at
http://technet.microsoft.com/en-us/library/cc771290(WS.10).aspx.

Working with the System State Only

On a server running the AD DS role, system state data includes the following data:

- Registry
- COM+ Class Registration database
- Boot files
- System files that are under Windows Resource Protection
- Active Directory Domain Services database
- SYSVOL directory

When other server roles are installed on a system, the system state includes the first four objects listed previously plus the following files:

- For the Active Directory Certificate Services role: AD CS database
- For the Failover Cluster feature: cluster service information
- For the Web Server role: IIS configuration files

System state information is important, although it cannot be captured as-is through Windows Server Backup. It can, however, be restored because Windows Server Backup supports three restore modes:

- Full server restore
- System state only restore
- Individual file or folder restore

Each mode enables you to recover the information you need when you need it. Remember that backups generated by Windows Server Backup are always backed up to the same file and added to file content as changes are identified on the source system. However, each time a backup is generated, a new catalog file is created. This catalog file is used to locate data for a particular backup.

EXAM TIP

Using Windows Server Backup to back up volumes and system state data to removable media is an important part of the exam. Make sure you understand it fully.

Creating Installation From Media Data Sets

When you need to stage DCs in large networks, you might prefer to use removable media to create the initial directory content rather than filling up bandwidth to replicate directory contents during the DC installation process. To do this, you rely on Installation From Media (IFM), but to create the media, you must use the Ntdsutil.exe command with the IFM subcommand.

Ntdsutil.exe is a command interpreter and can be used either interactively or through a single command line that provides all options. Table 13-4 describes the options available in the IFM subcommand.

TABLE 13-4 Ntdsutil.exe IFM Subcommand Options

DC TYPE	OPTION	DESCRIPTION
Writable DC	Create Full *destination*	Create media for a normal DC or for an AD LDS instance in a destination folder.
RODC	Create RODC *destination*	Create secure media for an RODC in a destination folder.
Writable DC with SYSVOL data	Create SYSVOL Full *destination*	Create media for a normal DC, including the entire SYSVOL folder, in a destination folder.
RODC with SYSVOL data	Create SYSVOL RODC *destination*	Create media for an RODC, including the entire SYSVOL folder, in a destination folder.

Ntdsutil.exe is the only tool that supports the creation of media for installation. You work with this tool in the practice at the end of this lesson.

Performing a Full System Backup

You perform a full system backup in one of two ways: interactively and through a scheduled task. Either method can be performed through the graphical interface or the command line. Begin with the graphical interface. Remember that Windows Server Backup is a feature that must be installed before you create any backups.

CREATING AN INTERACTIVE FULL SYSTEM BACKUP WITH WINDOWS SERVER BACKUP

Use the following procedure to protect AD DS data with Windows Server Backup. This procedure applies to both the full installation and Server Core, but when applied to Server Core, it must be performed remotely. Use the Connect To Another Computer option in the action pane to connect to a server running Server Core.

1. Log on to a DC with domain administrator credentials, and launch Windows Server Backup from the Administrative Tools program group.

2. If a User Account Control dialog box appears, confirm the action and click Continue.

3. Click Backup Once in the Actions pane. This launches the Backup Once Wizard.

4. If this is the first time you have run the Backup Once Wizard, click Different Options and click Next. If not, you can also click The Same Options.

5. Click Full Server (Recommended), and then click Next.

   Note that you can also select Custom, where you can omit anything, including specific volumes. You can omit folders and even select only the System State, as shown in Figure 13-5. Remember that your DCs should be single-purpose servers and, as such, you would not need to exclude any volumes. However, if you are backing up to a local disk, you should exclude this target volume from the backup operation. Note that when you use the custom option, you can select an option called Bare Metal Recovery, which automatically captures all the data required to recover a full system.

6. Choose the destination (either Local Drives or Remote Shared Folder) and click Next.

   You can target DVDs, CDs, local drives, locally attached removable hard drives, or network shares.

7. If you targeted a local drive, select the drive, make sure it has enough space, and click Next.

8. If you selected Full Server, Windows Backup warns you that the target drive is also included in the list of items to back up and asks if you want to exclude it from the backup items. Click OK.

9. Click Backup to perform the backup.

10. Click Close.

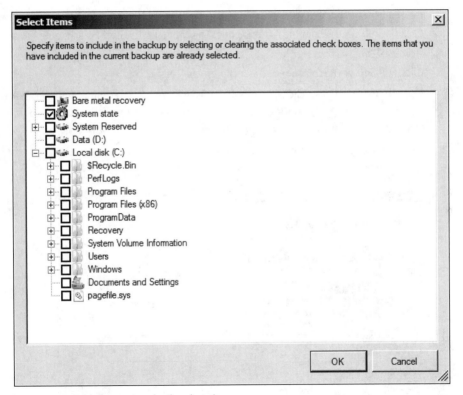

FIGURE 13-5 Selecting custom backup locations

You do not need to keep the backup window open for the backup to complete because it will continue in the background; however, it is useful to watch the progress of the backup operation at least once.

CREATING AN INTERACTIVE FULL SYSTEM BACKUP WITH WBADMIN.EXE

You can also perform this operation at the command line through the Wbadmin.exe command. This procedure applies directly to either the full installation or Server Core. In the full installation, you must use an elevated command prompt—in Server Core, the command prompt is always elevated by default—and use the following command syntax:

```
wbadmin start backup -allcritical -backuptarget:location -quiet
```

where *location* is the drive letter or path to the target drive. Also, you use the *–quiet* option to avoid having to type **Y** for the operation to proceed.

SCHEDULING A BACKUP WITH WINDOWS SERVER BACKUP

Use the following procedure to protect AD DS data automatically with Windows Server Backup.

1. Log on to a DC with domain administrator credentials and launch Windows Server Backup from the Administrative Tools program group.

2. If a User Account Control dialog box appears, confirm the action and click Continue.

3. Click Backup Schedule in the Actions pane. This launches the Backup Schedule Wizard; click Next.

4. Click Full Server (Recommended), and then click Next.

    Note that you can also click Custom, but this will not let you omit anything other than specific volumes. You cannot omit folders. Also note that in this wizard, when you use the Custom option, you cannot select the Enable System Recovery option.

5. On the Specify Backup Time page, choose the time of day for the backup. You can alternatively choose to back up the system more than once a day. Click Next.

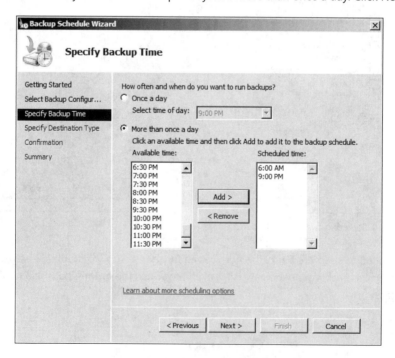

6. On the Specify Destination Type page, click Back Up To A Hard Disk That Is Dedicated For Backups (Recommended) and click Next. You can also select to back up to a volume or a network share, but a dedicated disk is by far the best option.

7. On the Select Destination Disk page, click Show All Available Disks, select the remote storage device, and click OK. Select the disk and click Next. If you selected Full Backup, Windows Backup prompts you to remove the disk from the selected items list. Click OK.

> **IMPORTANT USING VIRTUAL HARD DISKS FOR BACKUP**
>
> Consider using virtual hard disk (VHD) drives as backup targets because of their portability. You can store all VHDs in a central location and place them on a single removable drive to send to an offsite location. This lets you combine multiple backups on one disk as opposed to using multiple removable disks, one per protected system.

8. When you click Next, the wizard tells you that the target disk will be reformatted. Click Yes. Windows Server Backup requires exclusive access to the target device and, therefore, must format it when the scheduled backup is created.

9. Confirm your options and click Finish.

10. Click Close to create the schedule.

The target disk is formatted, and the task is added to the system's Scheduled Tasks list.

SCHEDULING A BACKUP WITH WBADMIN.EXE

You can also perform this operation at the command line through the Wbadmin.exe command. In this case, you must use an elevated command prompt and rely on several commands. Begin by identifying the ID of the target disk:

```
wbadmin get disks >diskidentifiers.txt
```

This returns a list of the disks attached to a system and places it in the Diskidentifiers. txt file. The Wbadmin.exe command relies on disk identifiers or globally unique identifiers (GUIDs) to locate a disk. You pipe the results of the command into a text file so that you can copy the target disk's GUID to the clipboard and reuse it in later commands.

To capture the disk GUID, type:

```
notepad diskidentifiers.txt
```

Highlight the disk identifier you need, including the brackets, and copy it to the clipboard. Close Notepad.

You are ready to create the schedule. Type the following commands:

```
wbadmin enable backup -addtarget:diskid -schedule:times -include:sourcedrives
```

where *diskid* is the GUID you copied. (Right-click, and then click Paste to add it.) *Times* is the times when you want the backup to run in HH:MM 24-hour format. If more than one time is required, separate each with a comma. *Sourcedrives* are the drive letters of the drives to protect. For example:

```
wbadmin enable backup -addtarget:{f0e2788d-0000-0000-0000-000000000000}
-schedule:21:00,06:00 -include:C:
```

![Administrator: Command Prompt window showing wbadmin enable backup command output]

will schedule a backup of drive C at 9:00 P.M. and 6:00 A.M. to the target drive identified by the GUID. You must confirm the command after you enter it.

The result is a new scheduled task in the Microsoft\Windows\Backup node of the Task Scheduler. (See Figure 13-6.)

FIGURE 13-6 The scheduled task created by `Wbadmin.exe`

You can use this procedure to generate batch files to create these jobs, but you must pipe the results into a text file; otherwise, you will have no record of the labels for the removable disks.

Also note that the target drive is reformatted each time the backup is run. If you need more granular schedules or if you want to change from a daily to a weekly schedule, you can modify the task in Task Scheduler after the Wbadmin.exe command has created it.

Performing Proactive Restores

Backup data sets are only as good as the restores and recoveries they support. This is why it is essential for you to test the restoration procedure and to test as many scenarios as possible to ensure that when you do face a disaster, you can recover the data or systems you lost by relying on your backups.

When working with a DC, there are several restoration scenarios:

- Restoring nonauthoritative data to the directory to reduce the replication required to update a DC that has been off for some time
- Restoring authoritative data because the data in the directory has been destroyed
- Restoring a complete DC from a backup

When you need to restore data to a system, you cannot do so when the DC is running, despite the fact that in Windows Server 2008 R2 you can control the AD DS service as you would other services. In fact, you must restart the server and run WinRE, or you must restart the server in Directory Services Restore Mode (DSRM). Each method supports different restoration procedures. DSRM supports data restores to the directory; WinRE supports recovery of the entire system.

Restarting in DSRM

There are two ways to launch a server into DSRM. The first relies on a server reboot and, during the reboot process, pressing F8 to view startup options. Note that if you are running the DC in a virtual machine on Hyper-V, you must press the F5 key while the machine is starting to access the Windows Boot Manager screen first, then press F8 to access Advanced Boot Options. This allows you to choose the Directory Services Restore Mode. Remember that you need to have access to the DSRM password to use this mode.

```
                          Advanced Boot Options

Choose Advanced Options for: Windows Server 2008 R2
(Use the arrow keys to highlight your choice.)

    Repair Your Computer

    Safe Mode
    Safe Mode with Networking
    Safe Mode with Command Prompt

    Enable Boot Logging
    Enable low-resolution video (640x480)
    Last Known Good Configuration (advanced)
    Directory Services Restore Mode
    Debugging Mode
    Disable automatic restart on system failure
    Disable Driver Signature Enforcement

    Start Windows Normally

Description: Start Windows in Directory Services Repair Mode (for Windows
            domain controllers only).

 ENTER=Choose                                               ESC=Cancel
```

You can also force the reboot directly into DSRM by changing the boot order in the boot file of the OS. This is done with the Bcdedit.exe command. To use the command line to change the boot order, type the following command in an elevated command prompt:

bcdedit /set safeboot dsrepair

Then, when you need to restart the server normally, use the following command:

bcdedit /deletevalue safeboot

If you need to perform the operation only once, it might be best simply to rely on the F8 key at system startup.

> **IMPORTANT RESETTING THE DSRM PASSWORD**
>
> To reset the DSRM password—an activity you should perform on a regular basis—you must first boot into DSRM and then use the standard password changing methods.

> **MORE INFO RUNNING DCS AS VMS**
>
> For more information on working with DCs as VMs, go to *http://technet.microsoft.com/pt-pt/library/dd363545%28WS.10%29.aspx*.

Identifying the Appropriate Backup Data Set

One of the challenges faced by organizations who used AD DS in previous versions of Windows was the ability to identify properly whether the data they required was located in a particular backup data set. In Windows Server 2008 R2, you can rely on the AD DS database mounting tool to view the contents of a data set before you perform a recovery operation. This prevents the previous hit-or-miss approach that system administrators needed to rely on.

The mounting tool works with database snapshots. Snapshots can easily be created with the Ntdsutil.exe tool. For example, to generate regular snapshots of a directory, you would use the following command:

```
ntdsutil "activate instance NTDS" snapshot create quit quit
```

This generates a snapshot on the same volume as the database. Be careful how you use this command, because it will quickly fill up the disk on which the Ntds.dit database file is located.

Perform the following steps to view backup data set or snapshot contents:

1. Launch an elevated command prompt by right-clicking Command Prompt in the Start menu and choosing Run As Administrator.

2. Begin by listing the available snapshots. Snapshots are created each time a backup is run or through the Ntdsutil.exe create subcommand, but you need to have the snapshot GUID to mount it. Use the following command to pipe all snapshot GUIDs into a text file.

   ```
   ntdsutil "activate instance NTDS" snapshot "list all" quit quit >snapshot.txt
   ```

3. Now, look into the text file to locate and copy the GUID you need:

   ```
   notepad snapshot.txt
   ```

4. Locate the GUID you need and copy it to the clipboard. The snapshot GUID is always preceded by the date and time you created the snapshot. Remember to include the brackets in the selection. Minimize Notepad in case you need a different GUID.

5. Mount the snapshot you need to use. Remember to right-click and then click Paste to paste the GUID at the mount command.

   ```
   ntdsutil
   activate instance NTDS
   snapshot
   ```

```
mount guid
quit
quit
```

Note the path listed for the mounted database.

6. Use the AD DS database mounting tool to load the snapshot as an LDAP server.

```
dsamain -dbpath c:\$SNAP_datetime_VOLUMEC$\windows\ntds\ntds.dit
    -ldapport portnumber
```

Be sure to use ALL CAPS for the *-dbpath* value and use any number beyond 40,000 for the *-ldapport* value to ensure that you do not conflict with AD DS. Also note that you can use the minus (–) sign or the slash (/) for the options in the command. The database is mounted and will stay mounted until you have completed your operations. *Do not close the command prompt.* In fact, you might want to use two command prompts, one for mounting the snapshot in Ntdsutil.exe and one for the Dsamain.exe command. Then you can mount and unmount different snapshots until you locate the one that contains the information you need to recover.

Note that if the dsamain command gives you errors, you must restart the server to clear reserved TCP ports. After the server is restarted, the operation should work properly.

7. Now use Ldp.exe or Active Directory Users And Computers to access the instance. For example, launch Active Directory Users And Computers from the Administrative Tools program group.

8. Right-click Active Directory Users And Computers and click Change Domain Controller.

9. In the Change Directory Server dialog box, click <Type A Directory Server Name[:Port] Here>, type the *servername:portnumber*, such as **Server10:40000**, and press Enter. (Use the port number you specified in step 6.) The status column should indicate that the server is online. Click OK.

10. Search the loaded instance to locate the information you need and view its properties. If it is the instance you need, make note of its name. Close Active Directory Users And Computers.

11. Return to the dsamain command prompt and press Ctrl+C to stop Dsamain.exe.

12. Unmount the database snapshot. Use the following command. Remember to paste in the GUID from the clipboard.

```
ntdsutil
activate instance NTDS
snapshot
unmount guid
quit
quit
```

13. Close the command prompt.

If the selected database snapshot was not the one you were looking for, repeat the procedure. If it was, proceed to a restore.

> **IMPORTANT USING ARROW KEYS IN COMMAND PROMPTS**
>
> You can use the up and down arrow keys when you are in a command prompt to return to previous commands. Also, note that there are different buffers in the command prompt. For example, there is a buffer in the command prompt itself and a different buffer in the Ntdsutil.exe command. You can use both to return to previous commands and save typing.

Performing Nonauthoritative or Authoritative Restores

As mentioned earlier, performing a restore requires that you restart the directory in DSRM. This means shutting down the DC. Remember that you can perform either nonauthoritative or authoritative restores on both the full installation and Server Core. A nonauthoritative restore addresses a DC rebuild when no data was lost because it is still found on other DCs. An authoritative restore restores data that was lost and updates the Update Sequence Number (USN) for the data to make it authoritative and ensure that it is replicated to all other servers. You can use the same procedure for both types of restores, but you can also perform authoritative restores without using DSRM. Make sure you have connected the removable media on which you stored the backup that you want to restore.

1. Repair the server, if required, and start it. During startup, press F8 to view the startup modes. Remember that if you are using a virtual machine, you must press F5 before you can press F8.

2. Select Directory Services Restore Mode and press Enter.

3. This will boot into Windows. Press Ctrl+Alt+Delete, and then log on with the DSRM account using the *servername\accountname* format and password. You will need to switch users to log on because the last logged on user account will be displayed by default. Use the DSRM password you set when you created the DC.

    You can restore the data either through the command line or with Windows Server Backup. Note, however, that when you want to restore directory data, you must perform a System State restore and, to do so, you must use the command line or the graphical interface.

4. Launch an elevated command prompt by right-clicking Command Prompt on the Start menu and choosing Run As Administrator.

5. Type the following command:

    ```
    wbadmin get versions -backuptarget:drive -machine:servername
    ```

    For example, to list the available backups located on D drive on SERVER10, type:

    ```
    wbadmin get versions -backuptarget:d: -machine:server10
    ```

    Note the version identifier information, because you need the exact name for the next command.

6. To recover system state information, type the following command:

    ```
    wbadmin start systemstaterecovery -version:datetime -backuptarget:drive
        -machine:servername -quiet
    ```

    For example, to recover the system state from a backup dated February 15, 2008, from D drive on SERVER10, type:

    ```
    wbadmin start systemstaterecovery -version:02/15/2008-19:38
        -backuptarget:d: -machine:server10 -quiet
    ```

    You use the *-quiet* option to avoid having to confirm the backup operation. Note that the restore takes time to complete.

Administrator: Command Prompt - wbadmin start systemstaterecovery -version:02/15/2008-19:38 -backupt...

```
C:\Users\Administrator>wbadmin get versions -backuptarget:D: -machine:Server10
wbadmin 1.0 - Backup command-line tool
(C) Copyright 2004 Microsoft Corp.

Backup time: 2/15/2008 11:38 AM
Backup target: Fixed Disk labeled Data(D:)
Version identifier: 02/15/2008-19:38
Can Recover: Volume(s), File(s), Application(s), Bare Metal Recovery, System Sta
te

C:\Users\Administrator>wbadmin start systemstaterecovery -version:02/15/2008-19:
38 -backuptarget:D: -machine:Server10 -quiet
wbadmin 1.0 - Backup command-line tool
(C) Copyright 2004 Microsoft Corp.

NOTE: The recovery operation will cause all replicated content on the local
machine to re-sync after recovery. This may cause potential latency or outage
issues.
Starting System State Restore [2/15/2008 4:25 PM]
Processing files to restore (This may take a few minutes)...
Processed (39) files
```

7. When prompted, press **Y** to restart the DC in its normal operating mode. When you restart the server, AD DS knows that it has recovered from a restore and performs an integrity check of the database as it starts.

If you are performing a nonauthoritative restore, you are finished. AD DS replication will bring this server up to date when the restart is complete.

> **IMPORTANT** **USING DFS REPLICATION**
>
> If your forest is in Windows Server 2008 R2 functional level, you will be using DFS replication. In this case, the restore creates a nonauthoritative version of the SYSVOL share. If you want to avoid additional replication, add the *authsysvol* switch to the Wbadmin.exe command.

If you are performing an authoritative restore, you must mark the restored data as authoritative. The best approach is to perform this restore with an online DC. Use the following steps:

1. With the server restarted in normal mode, log on with domain administrator credentials. Launch Server Manager, expand the Configuration node, and click Services. Locate the Active Directory Domain Services service, select it, and then click Stop in the details pane. Click Yes when prompted to stop dependent services.

2. Launch Command Prompt as an administrator and type the following commands:

```
ntdsutil
activate instance NTDS
authoritative restore
restore object database
quit
quit
```

The restore object database subcommand marks all the data in the Ntds.dit database of this DC as authoritative. When you use this command, you are prompted to confirm the restore. Click Yes to do so.

If you want to restore only a portion of the directory, use the restore subtree subcommand in Ntdsutil.exe, as follows:

```
restore subtree ou=ouname,dc=dcname,dc=dcname
```

where you must supply the distinguished name of the OU or object that you want to restore.

3. Close the command prompt and restart the AD DS service.

After the service is restarted, the replication process starts and the restored information that has been marked as authoritative is replicated to all other DCs. AD DS replication brings the server up to date when the service is restarted by replicating data from this DC to others because the restore was authoritative.

```
Administrator: Command Prompt                                              _ □ ×
Overall progress - 99% (Currently restoring files reported by 'WMI Writer')
Restore of files reported by 'WMI Writer' completed
Overall progress - 99% (Currently restoring additional system state files)
Restoring Registry (This may take a few minutes)...
Finalizing restore...

Summary of recovery:
------------------------

Restore of system state completed successfully [2/15/2008 5:49 PM]

Log of files successfully restored
'C:\Windows\Logs\WindowsServerBackup\SystemStateRestore 15-02-2008 16-25-03.log'

Please restart the machine to complete the operation.
NOTE: When you restart your server, System State Recovery will attempt to
recover many system files which may take several minutes to complete depending
on the number of files that are getting replaced. The machine might reboot multi
ple
times in the process. Please be patient and do not interrupt the reboot process.

C:\Users\Administrator>
```

EXAM TIP

Performing an authoritative or nonauthoritative Active Directory restore, working with the restartable AD DS service, and working in Directory Services Recovery Mode are important parts of this topic on the exam.

Restoring from a Complete Backup

When the DC is completely down and needs to be rebuilt, but you have access to a full server backup, you can perform a complete system restore. You need access to the full server backup files. If they are on a removable drive, make sure this drive is connected to the server before you begin the restore; otherwise, you must restart the server. If the files are on a network drive, make note of the path. Also, obtain the Windows Installation Media DVD or, if your new DC is a virtual machine, link its DVD drive to an ISO file containing the Windows Installation Media.

Full server recoveries can be performed through the graphical interface or the command line.

PERFORMING A GRAPHICAL FULL SERVER RECOVERY

To perform a full server recovery with the graphical interface, use the following procedure. This procedure applies to both the full installation and Server Core.

1. Insert or connect the Windows Server 2008 R2 installation DVD, restart the computer, and, when prompted, press a key to start from the DVD.

2. On the initial Windows screen, accept or select the language to install, the time and currency format, and a keyboard layout, and then click Next.

3. In the Install Now window, click the Repair Your Computer link.

4. In the System Recovery Options dialog box, click anywhere to clear any operating systems that are selected for repair and click Next.

5. Under Choose A Recovery Tool, click System Image Recovery.

6. If the backup is stored on a remote server, click Cancel on the warning message.

7. Choose Select A System Image and click Next.

8. In the Select The Location Of The Backup page, perform the following steps, depending on whether the backup is stored locally or on a network share:

   a. If the backup is stored on the local computer, select the location of the backup and click Next. Proceed to step 9.

   b. If the backup is stored on a network share, click Advanced, and then click Search For A System Image On The Network. Click Yes to confirm.

   c. In the Network Folder, type the path for the network share and click OK.

   d. Type the appropriate credentials and click OK.

   e. In the Select The Location Of The Backup page, select the backup image and click Next.

9. Select the date and time of the image to restore and click Next.

10. If you want to replace all data on all volumes, on the Choose Additional Restore Options page, select Format And Repartition Disks.

11. To prevent volumes that are not included in the restore from being deleted and re-created, click Exclude Disks, select each disk you want to exclude, and then click OK.

12. Click Next, and then click Finish. Click Yes to confirm that all selected disks will be reformatted and replaced with the data in the image backup.

    When the restore is complete, the server should restart as a new image of the server you restored in the backup set you used.

PERFORMING A COMMAND-LINE FULL SERVER RECOVERY

To perform a full server recovery with the command line, use the following procedure. This procedure applies to both the full installation and Server Core.

1. Insert or connect the Windows Server 2008 R2 installation DVD, restart the DC, and, when prompted, press a key to start from the DVD.

2. On the initial Windows screen, accept or select the language to install, the time and currency format, and a keyboard layout, and then click Next.

3. In the Install Now window, click the Repair Your Computer link.

4. In the System Recovery Options dialog box, click anywhere to clear any operating systems that are selected for repair and click Next.

5. Under Choose A Recovery Tool, select Command Prompt.

6. At the command prompt, type **diskpart** and press Enter.

7. At the diskpart prompt, type **list vol** and press Enter.

   Identify from the list the drive letter for the volume that corresponds to the location of the full server backup you want to restore. The drive letters in WinRE do not necessarily match the volumes as they appeared in Windows Server 2008 R2.

8. Type exit and press Enter.

9. At the Sources prompt, type the following command and press Enter:

   ```
   wbadmin get versions -backuptarget:drive -machine:servername
   ```

   For example, to list the available backups located on the D drive on SERVER10, type:

   ```
   wbadmin get versions -backuptarget:D: -machine:SERVER10
   ```

   Note the version identifier information, because you need the exact name for the next command.

10. At the command prompt, type the following command and press Enter:

    ```
    wbadmin start sysrecovery -version:datetime -backuptarget:drive
      -machine:servername -quiet
    ```

    For example, to recover the system state from a backup dated February 15, 2009, from D drive on SERVER10, type:

    ```
    wbadmin start sysrecovery -version:02/15/2009-19:38 -backuptarget:d:
      -machine:server10 -quiet
    ```

    You use the *-quiet* option to avoid having to confirm the backup operation.

11. After the recovery operation has completed, minimize the command window and, in the System Recovery Options dialog box, click Restart.

    The server should restart and operate normally.

MORE INFO   **WBADMIN COMMAND**

For more information on the switches you can use with the WBAdmin command, go to *http://technet.microsoft.com/en-us/library/cc754015%28WS.10%29.aspx*.

Protecting DCs as Virtual Machines

When a server is created as a VM instead of being installed on a physical computer, it becomes nothing more than a set of files on a disk because the disk drives for the computer are hosted in virtual hard drives. DCs running both AD DS and DNS are ideal candidates for virtualization on Hyper-V because they focus on providing a single, network-oriented service.

When a machine is virtual, it becomes much easier to protect it, restore it, and otherwise manipulate it. Note, however, that even if the DC is a virtual machine, it should be protected with traditional approaches just as if it were a physical DC. This means backing up the System State on a regular basis. If the machine fails, restore it like you would any other DC.

> **MORE INFO**   **PROTECTING DCS AS VIRTUAL MACHINES**
>
> For more information on how to protect a DC in a virtual machine, go to *http://technet. microsoft.com/en-us/library/dd363545%28WS.10%29.aspx*.

PRACTICE   Working with the AD DS Database

In this practice, you work with a variety of utilities to protect and manage the AD DS database. First you generate a backup of directory data, and then you use this backup to create a new DC, using offline data to speed the process and reduce replication over the network. You work with the AD DS database to perform a manual defragmentation and compaction and then automate the process. Finally, you rely on the Group Policy Management Console (GPMC) to protect Group Policy objects. This practice relies on SERVER10 and SERVER11, which you prepared in the "Before You Begin" section at the beginning of this chapter.

EXERCISE 1   Use Ntdsutil.exe to Capture System State Data

In this exercise, you use the Ntdsutil.exe command to capture the data required to perform an installation from media for a DC.

1. Log on to SERVER10 with the domain administrator account.
2. Verify that this server includes a formatted D drive, and create a folder named IFM on this drive.
3. Launch an elevated command prompt by right-clicking Command Prompt on the Start menu and clicking Run As Administrator.
4. Type the following commands:

    ```
    ntdsutil
    activate instance NTDS
    ifm
    create sysvol full d:\ifm
    ```

    The system displays a Creating Snapshot message while the operation is in progress and then lists a series of other information as it completes the operation. Note that the system defragments the newly captured snapshot.

```
Administrator: Command Prompt - ntdsutil ifm /?                    _ □ X

ifm: create sysvol full d:\ifm
Creating snapshot...
Snapshot set {3b38a62c-e6d1-4518-9026-0c31398055e0} generated successfully.
Snapshot {ddd9dc0d-0549-42c9-92ce-a2a3d4b77af3} mounted as C:\$SNAP_200802150638
_VOLUMEC$\
Snapshot {ddd9dc0d-0549-42c9-92ce-a2a3d4b77af3} is already mounted.
Snapshot {ddd9dc0d-0549-42c9-92ce-a2a3d4b77af3} is already mounted.
Initiating DEFRAGMENTATION mode...
      Source Database: C:\$SNAP_200802150638_VOLUMEC$\Windows\NTDS\ntds.dit
      Target Database: d:\ifm\Active Directory\ntds.dit

                 Defragmentation  Status (% complete)

          0    10   20   30   40   50   60   70   80   90  100
          !----!----!----!----!----!----!----!----!----!----!
          ..................................................

Copying registry files...
Copying d:\ifm\registry\SYSTEM
Copying d:\ifm\registry\SECURITY
Copying SYSVOL...
Copying d:\ifm\SYSVOL
Copying d:\ifm\SYSVOL\TreyResearch.net
Copying d:\ifm\SYSVOL\TreyResearch.net\Policies
```

5. Type:

   quit
   quit

6. Use Windows Explorer to view the results of the snapshot you created with Ntdsutil. exe.

7. Share the IFM folder by right-clicking the folder, pointing to Share With, and clicking Specific People.

8. In the drop-down list, choose Everyone; click Add, and then assign Read/Write permissions in the Permission Level column.

9. Click Share to create the share.

10. Click Done.

    Your IFM data is now ready to use to stage a new DC.

EXERCISE 2   Create a DC from Backup Data

In this exercise, you install a new DC in the treyresearch.net domain, using IFM data.

1. Log on to SERVER 11 with the local administrator account.

2. Launch Windows Explorer, and create a new folder on the C drive called IFM.

3. In the Windows Explorer address bar, type **\\server10\ifm** and press Enter.

4. If the credentials dialog box appears, type **TreyResearch\Administrator** or its equivalent and the required password.

   If you use the same account name and password on both servers, even though SERVER11 is not a member of the domain, you will not be prompted for credentials because of pass-through authentication.

5. Copy the entire contents from the IFM folder on SERVER10 to the C:\IFM folder on SERVER11.

6. Verify that all items have been copied.

7. Install the Active Directory Domain Services role. In Server Manager, right-click the Roles node and click Add Roles.

8. Review the Before You Begin page of the wizard and click Next.

9. On the Select Server Roles page of the Add Roles Wizard, select Active Directory Domain Services, click Add Required Features, and then click Next.

10. On the Active Directory Domain Services page, review the information and click Next.

11. Review your choices and click Install.

12. Examine the installation results and click Close. Your installation is complete.

13. Click the Active Directory Domain Services node in Server Manager.

14. Click Run The Active Directory Domain Services Installation Wizard in the details pane. This launches the Active Directory Domain Services Installation Wizard.

15. Select the Use Advanced Mode Installation check box and click Next.

    You need this option to install from media.

16. On the Operating System Compatibility page, review the information and click Next.

17. On the Choose A Deployment Configuration page, choose Existing Forest, select Add A Domain Controller To An Existing Domain, and click Next.

18. On the Network Credentials page, type **treyresearch.net**.

    Because you logged on locally to the server and this account does not have access rights to the treyresearch.net domain, you must provide alternate credentials.

19. Click Set. Type **treyresearch.net\Administrator** or the equivalent account name and add the password. Click OK, and then click Next.

20. On the Select A Domain page, click treyresearch.net (forest root domain) and click Next.

21. On the Select A Site page, accept the default and click Next.

    This page also appears because you are running the wizard in advanced mode.

22. On the Additional Domain Controller Options page, verify that DNS Server and Global Catalog are both selected and click Next.

    If you did not assign a static IP address, the AD DS Active Directory Domain Services Installation Wizard gives you a warning because you are using a dynamic IP Address.

23. Click the Yes, The Computer Will Use An IP Address Automatically Assigned By A DHCP Server (Not Recommended) option.

    The wizard warns you that it cannot create a delegation for the domain.

24. Click Yes.

25. On the Install From Media page, click Replicate Data From Media At The Following Location, type **C:\IFM** or click Browse to locate the IFM folder on the C drive, and click Next.

Note that the wizard indicates that the media must have been created from a writable DC because you did not select the RODC mode for this DC.

26. On the Source Domain Controller page, accept the defaults and click Next.

27. On the Location For Database, Log Files, And SYSVOL page, accept the default locations and click Next.

28. Type a strong password, confirm it, and click Next.

29. Confirm your settings on the Summary page and click Next. Select Reboot On Completion and wait for the operation to complete.

   Your new DC has been created from local media. This reduces replication and then updates the data through replication after the DC has been created.

EXERCISE 3 Perform Database Maintenance

In this exercise, you perform interactive database maintenance, using the restartable Active Directory Domain Services mode. You can perform this operation now because there are two DCs in the treyresearch.net domain. You must have at least two DCs to use restartable AD DS.

1. Log on to SERVER11 with the domain administrator account.

2. Use Windows Explorer to create a C:\Temp and a C:\OrignalNTDS folder.

   You use these folders as temporary locations for the compacted and original databases.

3. In Server Manager, expand the Configuration node and click Services.

4. Locate the Active Directory Domain Services service (it should be first on the list), right-click it, and click Stop.

5. In the Stop Other Services dialog box, click Yes.

The server stops the service.

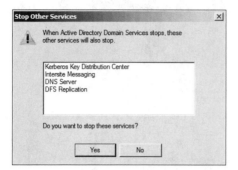

Remember that if the service cannot contact another writable DC, it cannot stop; otherwise, no one would be able to log on to the domain.

6. Launch an elevated command prompt by right-clicking Command Prompt on the Start menu and clicking Run As Administrator.

7. Begin by compacting the database. Type the following commands:

```
ntdsutil
activate instance NTDS
files
compact to C:\temp
```

The Ntdsutil.exe utility compacts the database and copies it to the new location. In very large directories, this operation can take some time.

8. Type the following after the compaction operation is complete:

```
quit
quit
```

9. Delete all the log files. Type the following:

```
cd %systemroot%\ntds
del *.log
```

You delete the log files because you will be replacing the Ntds.dit file with the newly compacted file, and the existing log files will not work with the newly compacted database.

10. Back up the Ntds.dit file to protect it in case something goes wrong. Type the following:

```
copy ntds.dit \originalntds
```

11. Copy the newly compacted database back to the NTDS folder. To do so, make sure you are still within the %SystemRoot%\NTDS folder and type the following:

```
copy c:\temp\ntds.dit
y
```

12. Verify the integrity of the new Ntds.dit file, and then perform a semantic database analysis to verify the data within the database. To do so, type the following:

```
ntdsutil
activate instance NTDS
files
integrity
quit
semantic database analysis
go fixup
quit
quit
```

Note that if the integrity check fails, you must recopy the original Ntds.dit back to this folder because the newly compacted file is corrupt. If you do not do so, your DC will no longer be operational.

13. Return to Server Manager, expand the Configuration node, and click Services.

14. Locate the Active Directory Domain Services service (it should be first on the list), right-click it, and click Start.

Your server is back online and ready to deliver authentication services to the network. It can take several minutes for the dependent services to restart. Delete the Ntds.dit located in the Original NTDS folder because it is no longer valid. You can also empty the Temp folder.

EXERCISE 4 Automate Database Maintenance

You can script the entire database compaction operation from the command line if you want to automate it. You should, however, make sure that all the operational results are captured in a text file so that you can review them if something goes wrong.

1. Log on to SERVER11 with the domain administrator account.

2. Make sure both a C:\Temp folder and a C:\originalntds folder exist on your server and that both folders are empty.

You use the C:\Temp folder as a temporary location for the compacted database. You are ready to automate the compaction process.

3. Move to the C:\Temp folder, right-click in the details pane, and click New; then click Text Document.

4. Name the text document **Compaction.cmd**.

   If you cannot see the .txt extension of the file, in Windows Explorer, click Folder And Search Options on the Organize menu. On the View tab, clear Hide Extensions For Known File Types and click OK. Remove the .txt extension on your file name. Confirm the name change.

5. Right-click Compaction.cmd and click Edit. Type the following commands:

```
del C:\temp\*.dit
del C:\originalntds\*.dit
net stop ntds /y
ntdsutil "activate instance NTDS" files "compact to C:\temp" quit quit
cd \windows\ntds
del *.log
copy ntds.dit \originalntds
del ntds.dit
copy c:\temp\ntds.dit
ntdsutil "activate instance NTDS" files integrity quit
   "semantic database analysis" "go fixup" quit quit
net start ntds
```

6. Save and close the Compaction.cmd file.

   Note that you can add a pause command after each command in your text file to verify the proper operation of the commands while testing.

7. Test the file by launching an elevated command prompt by right-clicking Command Prompt on the Start menu and clicking Run As Administrator.

8. Type:

```
cd \temp
compaction
```

9. If at any time the file does not work, use Ctrl+C to cancel the batch file and correct the errors.

   If the file works properly, you can use it to automate the compaction process.

10. Remove any pause statements you entered in the file and save it again.

    You can reuse this command file each time you want to run the compaction on your systems. It is recommended that you run this command file interactively to address any errors or issues during the process. Be very wary of putting this file into a scheduled task. You should never run compaction in unattended mode because errors could destroy your DC.

If a DC is nonfunctioning, you can use the following command to remove the DC role:

```
dcpromo /forceremoval
```

Run the Active Directory Domain Services Installation Wizard again to re-create the DC.

Perform the Ntds.dit compaction operation at least once a month.

EXERCISE 5 Protect Group Policy Objects

In this exercise, you use the GPMC to back up GPOs.

1. Log on to SERVER11 with the domain administrator account.

2. Verify the existence of a folder named Temp on the C drive.

3. Launch the Group Policy Management console from the Administrative Tools program group.

4. Expand Forest\Domains\treyresearch.net\Group Policy Objects.

5. Right-click Group Policy Objects and click Back Up All.

6. Type the location as **C:\Temp** or use the Browse button to locate the folder.

7. Type a description, in this case **First GPO Backup**, and click Back Up.

    The GPO backup tool shows the progress of the backup.

8. Click OK after the backup is complete.

    Your GPOs are now protected.

9. Back up the Temp folder.

    You can rely on this folder to copy the GPOs from one domain to another. Perform this operation at least once a week.

EXAM TIP

Backing up and restoring GPOs are both important parts of the exam. Practice these operations thoroughly to prepare for this topic.

Lesson Summary

- To maintain your directory service, you must perform proactive maintenance tasks. These tasks fall into 12 categories, many of which should be delegated to others. Domain administrators are responsible for the AD DS service and should focus on core directory operations such as database administration tasks.

- Several tools are available for AD DS administration. The most commonly used tools are the three main Active Directory consoles: Active Directory Users And Computers, Active Directory Sites And Services, and Active Directory Domains And Trusts.

- With Windows Server 2008 R2, AD DS is now a manageable service like all other servers and can be started and stopped without having to restart the server in Directory Services Restore Mode.

- When you delete an object in AD DS, you must restore the object to re-create its properties. If you simply re-create the object, it will not have the same SID and, therefore, will not retain any of the deleted object's properties. Restoring an object restores the original SID and, therefore, automatically restores most of the access rights associated with the object.

- You can protect information in the directory in several ways:
  - You can protect objects from deletion.

- You can audit AD DS changes to view previous and changed values when changes are made.
- You can rely on the tombstone container to recover deleted objects.
- You can rely on backup and restore to recover lost information.

- To restore objects from the deleted objects container in AD DS, you must use a tool that exposes this container and allows you to modify the state of the object. Two tools are available for this operation: *Ldp.exe* and Quest Object Restore For Active Directory. After the object is restored, you must reassign its password, group memberships, and other informational attributes and then enable the object.

- When you restore an object from backup, the object is restored with all its previous attributes. No additional changes are required.

Lesson Review

You can use the following questions to test your knowledge of the information in Lesson 1, "Proactive Directory Maintenance and Data Store Protection." The questions are also available on the companion CD if you prefer to review them in electronic form.

> **NOTE ANSWERS**
>
> Answers to these questions and explanations of why each answer choice is right or wrong are located in the "Answers" section at the end of the book.

1. You are a systems administrator for contoso.com. You have been asked to compact the database on one of the two DCs for the forest root domain. However, when you try to stop the AD DS service, you find that you cannot stop it on the server you are working on. What could be the problem?

   A. You cannot stop the AD DS service on a Windows Server 2008 R2 DC.

   B. Someone else is working on another DC in this domain.

   C. You must restart the server in Directory Services Restore Mode.

   D. You must use the Net Stop command to stop the AD DS service.

2. You are the network administrator of a large network. One of your DCs recently failed. You need to restore the DC to a working state. You have several backups of the server that were created with Windows Server Backup. Which of the following steps should you perform? (Choose all that apply.)

   A. Restart the server in Directory Services Restore Mode.

   B. Perform an authoritative restore using the Ntdsutil.exe command.

   C. Reinstall Windows Server 2008 R2.

   D. Restart the server in WinRE.

   E. Perform a nonauthoritative restore using the Ntdsutil.exe command.

   F. Perform a full server recovery using the command line.

Lesson 2: Proactive Directory Performance Management

The second activity you must master to maintain your DCs proactively is performance management. When you use proper installation and creation procedures, your DCs should just work. Remember that the Domain Controller role is now in its fifth iteration since it appeared in Microsoft Windows NT, and it has evolved with each release of the Microsoft server operating system. This means that it is now a very solid and stable service.

However, you'll find that despite this stability, things can still go wrong, whether they are related to system or human errors. And when they do, you need to be ready to identify the issues quickly and take appropriate steps to correct the situation. When you perform proactive performance management, you are forewarned when untoward events might occur. This is the crux of this lesson.

> **After this lesson, you will be able to**
> - Work with system performance indicators.
> - Use the Windows Server performance and reliability tools.
> - Use the Windows System Resource Monitor.
> - Generate and view performance reports.
>
> **Estimated lesson time: 45 minutes**

Managing System Resources

Windows Server includes several tools that help identify potential issues with system resources. When systems are not configured properly and are not assigned appropriate resources such as CPU, RAM, or disk space, systems monitoring helps you identify where bottlenecks occur. After you identify these bottlenecks, you assign additional resources to the system. If the system is physical, this most often means shutting down the system, installing new resources (for example, additional memory chips), and restarting the system. If the system is virtual, you might be able to allocate new resources while the virtual machine is still running, depending on the virtualization engine you use. If not, shut it down, allocate new resources (for example, an additional CPU and additional RAM), and restart it. After the system is restarted, monitor its performance again to identify whether the new resources solved the problem.

The tools you can rely on to identify performance bottlenecks in Windows Server 2008 R2 include:

- Task Manager, which displays current system resource usage.
- Event Viewer, which logs specific events, including performance-related events.

- Reliability Monitor, which tracks changes brought to the system, allowing you to identify whether a change could be the cause of a new bottleneck.

- Performance Monitor, which collects data in either real time or at specific intervals to identify potential issues.

- Windows System Resource Manager (WSRM), which can be used to profile specific applications to indicate which resources they need at which time. You can also use it to manage application resource allocation based on the profiles you generate.

You can use other tools as well, such as Microsoft System Center Operations Manager, to monitor the state of a system continuously and automatically correct well-known issues. Operations Manager relies on custom management packs to monitor specific applications.

Using Task Manager

The simplest of all tools to use is Task Manager. This tool provides real-time system status information and covers several key aspects of a system's performance, including:

- Running applications

- Running processes

- Running services

- Performance, including CPU and memory usage

- Networking, including network interface card (NIC) utilization

- Currently logged-on users

You can access Task Manager in a variety of ways, the most common of which is to right-click the taskbar and click Task Manager. Another common method is to use the Ctrl+Alt+Delete key combination and click Task Manager when the menu choices appear. For example, this is how you would access Task Manager on Server Core because it does not include a taskbar. You can also type **Taskmgr.exe** at the Command Prompt.

When you need information regarding system performance, the Performance tab, shown in Figure 13-7, is the most useful tab. This tab displays complete information about your system's key resource usage. It details physical and kernel memory usage. This tab also includes a button that gives you access to Resource Monitor. Clicking this button launches Resource Monitor while keeping Task Manager open.

Resource Monitor is a *super* Task Manager because it brings together the CPU, disk, memory, and network usage graphs in a single view. (See Figure 13-8.) In addition, it includes expandable components for each resource, displaying details of each component so that you can identify which processes might be the culprit if issues are evident. These two tools are ideal for on-the-spot verification of resource usage. You should rely on them if you need to identify immediately whether something is wrong with a server.

FIGURE 13-7 Viewing real-time performance information in Task Manager

FIGURE 13-8 Viewing real-time performance information in Resource Monitor

For example, if the system does not have enough memory, you immediately see that memory usage is constantly high. In this case, Windows is forced to use on-disk virtual memory and must swap or page memory contents constantly between physical and virtual memory. Constant paging is a typical issue that servers with insufficient physical memory face and is often indicated by slow system behavior. One good indicator of insufficient memory is slow Server Manager operation.

> **MORE INFO** **RESOURCE MONITOR**
>
> For more information on Resource Monitor, see Scenario 1 in "Windows Server 2008 Performance and Reliability Monitoring Step-by-Step Guide" at *http://technet.microsoft. com/en-us/library/cc771692(WS.10).aspx.*

Working with Event Viewer

Another excellent indicator of system health are the Windows event logs, which you can explore using Event Viewer. Windows maintains several event logs to collect information about each of the services running on a server. By default, these include the Application, Security, Setup, System, and Forwarded Events logs, all located in the Windows Logs folder. However, on a DC, you also have additional logs that are specifically related to AD DS operation. These are located in the Applications and Services Logs folder and include:

- DFS Replication, which is available in domains and forests operating in Windows Server 2008 R2 functional level. If you are running your domains or forests in one of the earlier modes, the log is for the FRS replication service.

- Directory Service, which focuses on the operations that are specifically related to AD DS.

- DNS Server, which lists all events related to the naming service that supports AD DS operation.

However, one of the best features of Event Log is related to Server Manager. Because it acts as the central management location for each of the roles included in Windows Server 2008 R2, Server Manager provides custom log views that percolate all the events related to a specific server role. For example, if you click the Active Directory Domain Services role, Server Manager provides a log view that includes, among other things, a summary view of key events related to this service, shown in Figure 13-9.

Event Log lists three types of events: Information, Warning, and Errors. By default, the Summary view displayed under the server role lists Errors with a high priority, Warnings with a medium priority, and Information messages with the lowest priority. Therefore, Errors always appear at the top of the summary, alerting you immediately if there is an issue with your system. To drill down and see the event details, either double-click the event itself or move to the Event Viewer section under the Diagnostics node of the tree pane in Server Manager.

> **MORE INFO** **ACTIVE DIRECTORY SERVICES EVENTS AND ERRORS**
>
> To learn about specific events and errors related to Active Directory Services roles go to *http://technet.microsoft.com/en-us/library/cc754424(WS.10).aspx.*

FIGURE 13-9 Viewing Summary events for AD DS in Server Manager

Events provide much more information in Windows Server 2008 R2 and Windows 7 than ever before. In previous versions of Windows, events were arcane items that provided very little information about an issue. Today, you get a full explanation on an event in Event Viewer, and you can link to an online database maintained by Microsoft for each event. You can look up an event in this database by clicking the Event Log Online Help link in the event's Properties dialog box. You are prompted to send information about the event to Microsoft. Click Yes if you want information specifically about this event.

This database does not provide information about every event in Windows, but it covers the most frequently viewed events. You can also use third-party event log databases to view information about events.

MORE INFO **WINDOWS EVENT IDS**

To access a free database of Windows event IDs, go to *http://kb.prismmicrosys.com/index.asp*.

The more you know about Windows events, the easier it will be to deal with issues. You can rely on the Microsoft online event database and free third-party event databases, and you can supplement this information with online searches by using tools such as Windows Live Search to locate information about an issue. Searching on the event ID returns the most results.

Working with Windows Reliability Monitor

Another useful tool to identify potential issues on a system is Reliability Monitor. This tool, located under the Diagnostic\Reliability and Performance\Monitoring Tools node in Server Manager, tracks changes made to a system. Each time a change is performed on the system, it is logged in Reliability Monitor. (See Figure 13-10.) Tracked changes include system changes, software installs or uninstalls, application failures, hardware failures, and Windows failures.

FIGURE 13-10 Viewing system changes in Reliability Monitor

If an issue arises, one of the first places you should check is Reliability Monitor because it tracks every change to your system and reveals what might have happened to make your system unresponsive. For example, if the change is a new driver for a device, it might be a good idea to roll back the device installation to see whether the system becomes more responsive. Verify Reliability Monitor whenever an issue affecting performance arises on a server.

Working with Windows Performance Monitor

Sometimes problems and issues are not immediately recognizable, requiring further research
to identify them. In such cases, you need to rely on Performance Monitor. This tool, located
under the Diagnostic\Reliability and Performance\Monitoring Tools node in Server Manager,
tracks performance data on a system. You use Performance Monitor to track particular system
components either in real time or on a scheduled basis.

If you are familiar with previous versions of Windows Server, you'll quickly note that
Windows Server 2008 R2 Performance Monitor brings together several tools that you might
be familiar with: Performance Logs And Alerts, Server Performance Advisor, and System
Monitor. If you are new to Windows Server with the 2008 R2 release, you'll quickly find that
when it comes to performance management and analysis, Performance Monitor is the tool to
use. Using Performance Monitor, you create interactive collections of system counters or create
reusable data collector sets. Performance Monitor is part of Windows Reliability And
Performance Monitor (WRPM). Table 13-5 describes each of the tools in WRPM that support
performance monitoring and the access rights required to work with them.

TABLE 13-5 WRPM Tools and Access Rights

TOOL	DESCRIPTION	REQUIRED MEMBERSHIP
Monitoring Tools, Performance Monitor	For viewing performance data in real time or from log files. The performance data can be viewed in a graph, histogram, or report.	Local Performance Log Users group
Monitoring Tools, Reliability Monitor	For viewing the system stability and the events that affect reliability.	Local Administrators group
Data collector sets	Groups data collectors into reusable elements that can be used to review or log performance. Contains three types of data collectors: performance counts, event trace data, and system configuration information.	Local Performance Log Users group with the Log On As A Batch Job user right
Reports	Includes preconfigured performance and diagnosis reports. Can also be used to generate reports from data collected using any data collector set.	Local Performance Log Users group with the Log On As A Batch Job user right

Windows Server 2008 R2 includes a new built-in group called Performance Log Users,
which allows server administrators who are not members of the local Administrators group

to perform tasks related to performance monitoring and logging. For this group to be able to initiate data logging or modify data collector sets, it must have the Log On As A Batch Job user right. Note that this user right is assigned to this group by default.

In addition, Windows Server 2008 R2 creates custom Data Collector Set templates when a role is installed. These templates are located under the System node of the Data Collector Sets node of WRPM. For example, with the AD DS role, four collector sets are created:

- The Active Directory Diagnostics set collects data from registry keys, performance counters, and trace events related to AD DS performance on a local DC.

- The LAN Diagnostics set collects data from network interface cards, registry keys, and other system hardware to identify issues related to network traffic on the local DC.

- The System Diagnostics set collects data from local hardware resources to generate data that helps streamline system performance on the local DC.

- The System Performance set focuses on the status of hardware resources and system response times and processes on the local DC.

Of the four, the most useful for AD DS is the first. This should be the data set you rely on the most. You can create your own personalized data set. If you do, focus on the items in Table 13-6 as the counters you should include in your data set.

TABLE 13-6 System Monitor Common Counters for AD DS

COUNTER	DESCRIPTION	REASON
Network Interface: Bytes Total/Sec	Rate at which bytes are sent and received over each network adapter, including framing characters.	Track network interfaces to identify high usage rates per NIC. This helps you determine whether you need to segment the network or increase bandwidth.
Network Interface: Packets Outbound Discarded	Number of outbound packets that were chosen to be discarded even though no errors had been detected to prevent transmission.	Long queues of items indicate that the NIC is waiting for the network and is not keeping pace with the server. This is a bottleneck.
NTDS: DRA Inbound Bytes Total/Sec	Total bytes received through replication. It is the sum of both uncompressed and compressed data.	If this counter does not have any activity, it indicates that the network could be slowing down replication.
NTDS: DRA Inbound Object Updates Remaining In Packet	Number of object updates received through replication that have not yet been applied to the local server.	The value should be low on a constant basis. High values show that the server is not capable of adequately integrating data received through replication.

COUNTER	DESCRIPTION	REASON
NTDS: DRA Outbound Bytes Total/Sec	Total bytes sent per second. It is the sum of both uncompressed and compressed data.	If this counter does not have any activity, it indicates that the network could be slowing down replication.
NTDS: DRA Pending Replication Synchronizations	The replication backlog on the server.	The value should be low on a constant basis. High values show that the server is not capable of adequately integrating data received through replication.
NTDS: DS Threads In Use	Number of threads in use by AD DS.	If there is no activity, the network might be preventing client requests from being processed.
NTDS: LDAP Bind Time	Time required for completion of the last LDAP binding.	High values indicate either hardware or network performance problems.
NTDS: LDAP Client Sessions	Number of connected LDAP client sessions.	If there is no activity, the network might be causing problems.
NTDS: LDAP Searches/Sec	Number of LDAP searches per second.	If there is no activity, the network might be causing problems.
NTDS: LDAP Successful Binds/Sec	Number of successful LDAP binds per second.	If there is no activity, the network might be causing problems.
NTDS: LDAP Writes/Sec	Number of successful LDAP writes per second.	If there is no activity, the network might be causing problems.
Security System-Wide Statistics: Kerberos Authentications	Number of Kerberos authentications on the server per second.	If there is no activity, the network might be preventing authentication requests from being processed.
Security System-Wide Statistics: NTLM Authentication	Number of NTLM authentications on the server per second.	If there is no activity, the network might be preventing authentication requests from being processed.
DFS Replicated Folders: All Counters	Counters for staging and conflicting data.	If there is no activity, the network might be causing problems.

COUNTER	DESCRIPTION	REASON
DFS Replication Connections: All Counters	Counters for incoming connections.	If there is no activity, the network might be causing problems.
DFS Replication Service Volumes: All Counters	Counters for update sequence number (USN) journal records and database processing on each volume.	If there is no activity, the processor might be causing problems.
DNS: All Counters	DNS Object Type handles the Windows NT DNS service on your system.	If there is no activity, the network might be causing problems, and clients might not be able to locate this DC.

To add counters to Performance Monitor, simply click the plus (+) sign on the toolbar at the top of the details pane. This displays the Add Counters dialog box shown in Figure 13-11. Scroll through the counters to identify which ones you need. In some cases, you need subcounters under a specific heading (as shown in Table 13-6); in others, you need the entire subset of counters. When you need a subcounter, click the down arrow beside the heading, locate the subcounter, and click Add. When you need the entire counter, click the counter and click Add. This adds the counter with a star heading below it, indicating that all subcounters have been added.

> **IMPORTANT THE WINDOWS SERVER 2008 R2 INTERFACE**
>
> When using the classic interface in Windows Server 2008 R2, subcounters are accessed by clicking plus signs. When using the Desktop Experience feature in Windows Server 2008 R2, which simulates the Windows 7 interface, subcounters are accessed through down arrows.

To obtain information about a counter, click Show Description. Then, when you click any counter or subcounter, a short description appears at the bottom of the dialog box.

As soon as you are finished adding counters and you click OK, Performance Monitor starts tracking them in real time. Each counter you added is assigned a line of a specific color. To remove a counter, click the counter, and then click the Delete button (X) on the toolbar at the top of the details pane.

You can start and stop Performance Monitor much like a media player, using the same type of buttons. When Performance Monitor runs, it automatically overwrites data as it collects more; therefore, it is more practical for real-time monitoring.

If you want to capture the counters you added into a custom data set, right-click Performance Monitor and click New; then choose New Data Collector Set. Follow the prompts to save your counter selections so that you can reuse them later.

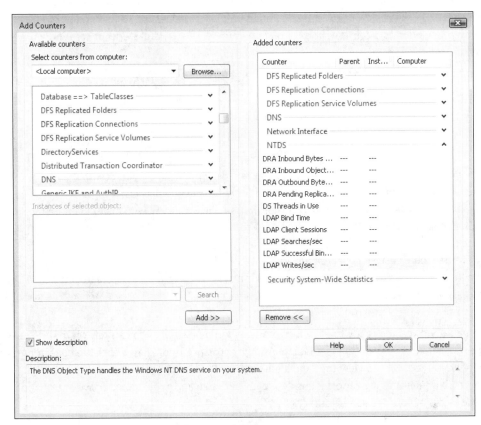

FIGURE 13-11 Adding counters to Performance Monitor

EXAM TIP

Practice working with Performance Monitor, because it is an important part of the exam. Also, note that there is no Server Performance Advisor (SPA) in Windows Server 2008 R2. This Windows Server 2003 tool has been rolled into Windows Reliability And Performance Monitor. Don't get caught on questions regarding SPA on the exam.

Creating Baselines for AD DS and DNS

For long-term system monitoring, you must create data collector sets. These sets run automated collections at scheduled times. When you first install a system, it is a good idea to create a performance baseline for that system. Then as load increases on the system, you can compare the current load with the baseline to see what has changed. This helps you identify whether additional resources are required for your systems to provide optimal performance. For example, when working with DCs, it is a good idea to log performance at peak and nonpeak times. Peak times would be when users log on in the morning or after lunch, and nonpeak times would be periods such as mid-morning or mid-afternoon. To create a performance baseline, you need to take samples of counter values for 30 to 45 minutes for at least a week during peak, low, and normal operations. The general steps for creating a baseline include:

1. Identify resources to track.
2. Capture data at specific times.
3. Store the captured data for long-term access.

> **IMPORTANT PERFORMANCE MONITORING AFFECTS PERFORMANCE**
>
> Taking performance snapshots also affects system performance. The object with the worst impact on performance is the logical disk object, especially if logical disk counters are enabled. However, because this affects snapshots at any time, even with major loads on the server, the baseline is still valid.

You can create custom collector sets, but with Windows Server 2008 R2, use the default templates that are added when the server role is installed. For example, to create a baseline for a DC, simply create a user-defined data collector set that is based on the Active Directory Diagnostics template and run it on a regular basis.

Then, when you are ready to view the results of your collection, you can rely on the Reports section of the Windows Reliability And Performance node. Right-click the collector set for which you want to view the report (either User Defined or System) and click Latest Report. This generates the report if it isn't already available and provides extensive information on the status of your DC. (See Figure 13-12.)

> **MORE INFO PERFORMANCE MONITOR SCENARIOS**
>
> For more information on Performance Monitor, see the scenarios in the "Windows Server 2008 Performance and Reliability Monitoring Step-by-Step Guide" at *http://technet.microsoft. com/en-us/library/cc771692(WS.10).aspx*.

Working with Windows System Resource Manager

Windows Server 2008 R2 includes an additional tool for system resource management, WSRM, a feature that can be added through Add Features in Server Manager. WSRM can be used in two ways. First, it can be used to profile applications. This means that it helps identify how many resources an application requires on a regular basis. When operating in this mode, WSRM logs events in the application event log only when the application exceeds its allowed limits. This helps you fine-tune application requirements.

The second mode offered by WSRM is the manage mode. In this mode, WSRM uses its allocation policies to control how many resources applications can use on a server. If applications exceed their resource allocations, WSRM can even stop the application from executing and make sure other applications on the same server can continue to operate. However, WSRM does not affect any application if combined processor resources do not exceed 70 percent utilization. This means that when processor utilization is low, WSRM does not affect any application.

FIGURE 13-12 Viewing an Active Directory diagnostics report

WSRM also supports Alerts And Event Monitoring. This is a powerful tool that helps you control processor and memory usage on large multiprocessing servers. By default, the WSRM includes four built-in management policies, but it also includes several custom resources that you can use to define your own policies. Basically, WSRM ensures that high-priority applications always have enough resources available to them for continued operation, making it a good tool for DCs.

IMPORTANT DCS AND WSRM

If you use single-purpose DCs, you will not need WSRM as much as if you use multipurpose DCs. Multipurpose DCs usually run other workloads at the same time that they run the AD DS service. Using WSRM in this case can ensure that the AD DS service is available during peak hours by assigning it more resources than other applications. However, consider your choices carefully when deciding to create a multipurpose DC. DCs are secure servers by default and should remain this way at all times. If you add workloads to a DC, you must grant access rights to the DC to application administrators, administrators who do not need domain administration access rights.

Use WSRM to first evaluate how your applications are being used; then apply management policies. Make sure you thoroughly test your policies before applying them in your production environment. This way, you can get a feel for WSRM before you fully implement it in your network. When you're ready, you can use WSRM Calendar to determine when each policy should be applied.

> **IMPORTANT   WSRM RESOURCE REQUIREMENTS**
>
> If you are managing several servers with WSRM, you might need to dedicate resources to it because it is resource-intensive. You might consider placing it on a dedicated management server if this is the case.

WSRM can be used for the following scenarios:

- Use predefined or user-defined policies to manage system resources. Resources can be allocated on a per-process, per-user, or per-IIS application pool basis.

- Rely on calendar rules to apply your policies at different times and dates without any manual intervention.

- Automate the resource policy selection process based on server properties, events, or even changes to available physical memory or processor count.

- Collect resource usage information in local text files or store them in a SQL database. You can also create a central WSRM collection system to collate resource usage from several systems running their own instances of WSRM.

Table 13-7 describes the default policies included in WSRM as well as the custom resources you can use to create custom policies.

TABLE 13-7 WSRM Policies and Custom Resources

BUILT-IN POLICY	DESCRIPTION
Equal per process	Assigns each application an equal amount of resources.
Equal per user	Groups processes assigned to each user who is running them and assigns equal resources to each group.
Equal per session	Allocates resources equally to each session connected to the system.
Equal per IIS application pool	Allocates resources equally to each running IIS application pool.
CUSTOM RESOURCE	**DESCRIPTION**
Process Matching Criteria	Used to match services or applications to a policy. Can be selected by file name, command, specified users, or groups.
Resource Allocation Policies	Used to allocate processor and memory resources to the processes that match criteria you specify.

CUSTOM RESOURCE	DESCRIPTION
Exclusion lists	Used to exclude applications, services, users, or groups from management by WSRM. Can also use command-line paths to exclude applications from management.
Scheduling	Uses a calendar interface to set time-based events to resource allocation. Supports policy-based workloads because you can set policies to be active at specific times of day, specific days, or other schedules.
Conditional policy application	Used to set conditions based on specific events to determine whether policy will run.

WSRM can completely control how applications can and should run.

 Quick Check

1. You want to view potential error messages about the directory service. Where can you find this information?

2. You are using WSRM to control processor and memory resources for several applications on a server. However, after investigation, you see that none of your policies are applied. What could be the problem?

3. What objects can you use to allocate resources in WSRM?

Quick Check Answers

1. View potential error messages about the directory service in Event Log. You can view this information in two places. The first is by clicking the server role name in the tree pane of Server Manager to display a summary view of directory service events. The second is by going to the Directory Service log itself, under Event Viewer, to display all the events related to the directory service.

2. WSRM does not apply any policies if the processor usage does not reach 70 percent.

3. WSRM resource allocations can be assigned to three objects: processes, users, and IIS application pools.

PRACTICE **AD DS Performance Analysis**

In this practice, you use both WRPM and WSRM to view the performance of your servers. First you create a custom collector set, and then you run it and view the diagnostics report. In the second exercise, you install WSRM to view the policies it provides. These exercises rely on SERVER10, but SERVER11 should also be running.

EXERCISE 1   Create a Data Collector Set

A data collector set is the core building block of performance monitoring and reporting in WRPM. You can create a combination of data collectors and save them as a single data collector set.

1. Log on to SERVER10 with the domain Administrator account.

    You need to be a member only of the Performance Log Users group with the Log On As A Batch Job user right, but for the purpose of these exercises, you use the domain administrator account.

2. In Server Manager, expand Diagnostics\Performance\Data Collector Sets, right-click User Defined, point to New, and then click Data Collector Set.

3. On the Template page, type **Custom AD DS Collector Set**, make sure Create From A Template (Recommended) is selected, and click Next.

4. On the next page, select the Active Directory Diagnostics template and click Next.

5. By default, the wizard selects %systemdrive%\PerfLogs\Admin as the root directory; however, you might prefer to keep your collector sets on a separate drive if one exists. In this case, click Browse, choose drive D, and create a new folder named **AD DS Collector Sets**. Press Enter and click OK to close the dialog box, and then click Next.

6. On the Create The Data Collector Set page, click Change next to the Run As field, and type the account name **TreyResearch\Administrator** and the password to run the data collector set.

When you create collector sets for long-term use, use a special account that is a member of the Performance Log Users group and has the Log On As A Batch Job user right to run your collector sets. Note that the Performance Log Users group has this right assigned to it by default.

On this final page of the New Collector Set Wizard, you have three options:

- Open Properties Data For This Data Collector Set to view the properties of the data collector set or to make additional modifications.

- Start This Data Collector Set Now to run the data collector set immediately.

- Save And Close to save the data collector set without starting the collection.

Leave the defaults and click Finish.

Your custom data collector set has been created. Notice that it is stopped. To schedule the Start condition for your data collector set, use the following procedure (steps 7 through 10):

7. Right-click Custom AD DS Collector Set and click Properties.

8. On the Schedule tab, click Add to create a start date, time, or day schedule.

9. In the Folder Action dialog box, make sure that today's date is the beginning date, select the Expiration Date check box, and set it as one week from today. Also, make sure that the Start Time is set to the current time. Click OK.

You must set the start date of the schedule to the current time for the collection set to work. If not, you will not be able to generate reports in later steps.

Note that you can create quite a modular schedule in this dialog box. Also note that selecting an expiration date will not stop data collection in progress on that date. It only prevents new instances of data collection from starting after the expiration date. You must use the Stop Condition tab to configure how data collection is stopped.

10. On the Stop Condition tab, select the Overall Duration check box, make sure it lists 5 minutes, and select the Stop When All Data Collectors Have Finished check box. Click OK and type the password for the account you assigned to this collector set, and then click OK again.

You select the Stop When All Data Collectors Have Finished check box to enable all data collectors to finish recording the most recent values before the data collector set is stopped if you have also configured an overall duration.

You can also set limits on your collection. However, note that when an overall duration is configured, it overrides any limits you set. If you do want to set limits, make sure the Overall Duration check box is cleared and define the following limits:

- To segment data collections into separate logs, select the Restart The Data Collector Set At Limits check box.

- To configure a time period for data collection to write to a single log file, select the Duration check box and set its value.

■ To restart the data collector set or to stop collecting data when the log file reaches a specific limit, select the Maximum Size check box and set its value.

Collector sets generate a large amount of data if you allow them to run unmonitored. To configure data management for a data collector set, use the following procedure (steps 11 through 14):

11. Right-click Custom AD DS Data Collector Set and click Data Manager.

12. On the Data Manager tab, you can accept the default values or change them according to your data retention policy. Keep the defaults.

   ■ Select the Minimum Free disk or Maximum Folders check boxes to delete previous data according to the resource policy you choose from the drop-down list (Delete Largest or Delete Oldest).

   ■ Select the Apply Policy Before The Data Collector Set Starts check box to delete previous data sets according to your selections before the data collector set creates its next log file.

   ■ Select the Maximum Root Path Size check box to delete previous data according to your selections when the root log folder size limit is reached.

13. On the Actions tab, you can set specific data management actions for this collector set. Note that three policies already exist. Click the 1 Day(s) policy and click Edit.

   Folder actions allow you to specify how data is archived before it is permanently deleted. You can decide to disable the Data Manager limits in favor of managing all data according to these folder action rules. For example, you could copy all collection sets to a central file share before deleting them on the local server.

14. Click OK, and then click OK again. Type the password for the account you assigned to the collector set and click OK.

Your collector set is ready to run. Wait until the scheduled time occurs for the report to run. However, if you want to view an immediate report, proceed as follows:

15. Right-click your new collector set and click Start. This generates a new report.

16. Expand Diagnostics/Performance/Reports/User Defined/Custom AD DS Collector Set in the tree pane of Server Manager; you see that the collection set has generated a report. Click the report name in the tree pane to view it.

You can also use the other default templates to generate immediate reports. For example, if you want to run a report from the Systems Diagnostics template, right-click the template name under the System node and select Latest Report. If no report exists, it runs the collector set and then displays the report in the details pane.

EXERCISE 2   Install WSRM

In this exercise, you install the WSRM service and view how it operates. This exercise is performed on SERVER10; ensure that it is running.

1. Log on to Server10 with the domain Administrator account.

2. In Server Manager, right-click the Features node and click Add Features.

3. On the Select Features page of the Add Features Wizard, select Windows System Resource Manager.

4. Server Manager prompts you to add Windows Internal Database. Click Add Required Feature, and then click Next.

    Note that Windows Internal Database is a locally used database only and does not accept remote connections. To collect data from other servers, you must use Microsoft SQL Server 2005 or later.

5. Review the information on the Confirm Installation Selections page and click Install.

6. Examine the installation results and click Close.

    Your installation is complete.

7. You can now use WSRM on this system. Windows System Resource Manager is a stand-alone console that can be found in the Administrative Tools program group.

8. When you open the console, it asks you which computer to connect to. Select This Computer and click Connect.

    Now you can tour the WSRM interface. (See Figure 13-13.) Note that it uses the standard Microsoft Management Console format. Explore the features of this console.

FIGURE 13-13 Using Windows System Resource Monitor

Lesson Summary

- In Windows Server 2008 R2, you can use a series of tools to manage and monitor resource usage on a computer. These include Task Manager, event logs, Reliability Monitor, and Performance Monitor.

- Performance Monitor is now the single tool that regroups other tools used in previous versions of Windows. These tools included Performance Logs And Alerts, Server Performance Advisor, and System Monitor.

- You can use Windows System Resource Manager to control how resources behave on a scheduled basis. In fact, it provides two functions: It can monitor resource usage over time and log activity, and it can control access to resources based on specific policies.

Lesson Review

You can use the following questions to test your knowledge of the information in Lesson 2, "Proactive Directory Performance Management." The questions are also available on the companion CD if you prefer to review them in electronic form.

> **NOTE ANSWERS**
>
> Answers to these questions and explanations of why each answer choice is right or wrong are located in the "Answers" section at the end of the book.

1. You are the systems administrator for contoso.com. You have been assigned the task of verifying data collector sets on a DC. You did not create the collector sets. When you check the collector sets, you find that they are continuously running and that the allocated storage area is full. What could be the problem? (Choose all that apply.)

   A. The collector sets do not have an expiration date.

   B. The collector sets have not been set to run on a schedule.

   C. The collector sets do not have a stop condition.

   D. The collector sets have been scheduled improperly.

2. You are a systems administrator at contoso.com. As you log on to a DC to perform maintenance, you get the impression that server response is sluggish. You want to verify what is going on. Which tool should you use? (Choose all that apply.)

   A. Reliability Monitor

   B. Event Viewer

   C. Task Manager

   D. Performance Monitor

Chapter Review

To further practice and reinforce the skills you learned in this chapter, you can perform the following tasks:

- Review the chapter summary.
- Review the list of key terms introduced in this chapter.
- Complete the case scenario. This scenario sets up a real-world situation involving the topics of this chapter and asks you to create a solution.
- Complete the suggested practices.
- Take a practice test.

Chapter Summary

- Active Directory Domain Services is a set of complex services that interact with each other to provide a highly available identity and access solution. Because of this, there are several aspects to AD DS administration. In fact, 12 activities are required to manage the environment both online and offline, although many of the 12 can be delegated to others.
- As domain administrators, operators of the directory service must concentrate on making sure the AD DS service is always available and performs optimally. Many of the operations required to do this involve offline database administration tasks. With the release of Windows Server 2008 R2, these tasks can be performed without having to shut down the server because the AD DS service can be started and stopped like any other service.
- There are several ways to protect AD DS data in Windows Server 2008 R2 and several ways to restore it. One easy way to restore data is to recover it from the Deleted Items container, but when you do so, you must update the recovered item and then enable it.
- Two tools support backups of directory data in Windows Server 2008 R2. *Ntdsutil.exe* supports both the creation of offline installation media and the protection of the system state data required by the DC. Windows Server Backup protects entire volumes of the system and even protects and supports the restore of an entire computer system.
- Because the DC role is ideal for virtualization, you can also protect DCs by using simple services such as the Volume Shadow Copy Service on host servers. This protects the virtual hard drives that comprise the virtual machine the DC is running on.
- When performance issues arise, Windows Server 2008 R2 provides a series of tools for analysis and problem correction. These include both real-time and scheduled analysis tools. Real-time tools include Task Manager, Resource Monitor, and Performance Monitor. Scheduled or tracking tools include Event Log, Reliability Monitor, and scheduled data collection sets in Performance Monitor.
- Windows Server 2008 R2 also includes Windows System Resource Manager, a powerful tool by which you can manage policy-based workloads. You must first use it to analyze running processes and then assign policies to these processes.

Key Terms

The following terms were introduced in this chapter. Do you know what they mean?

- **compaction**
- **data collector set**
- **Ntds.dit**
- **tombstone**

Case Scenario

In the following case scenario, you apply what you've learned about subjects of this chapter. You can find answers to the questions in this scenario in the "Answers" section at the end of this book.

Case Scenario: Working with Lost and Found Data

You are a domain administrator with Contoso, Ltd. During a routine verification, you notice that some of the accounts that should be contained within a specific OU have disappeared. You know that a local technician was assigned to work on these accounts recently to add information in the account properties. In addition, new accounts needed to be created in this OU. The technician was assigned to add information such as the user's address, manager, and office location in each of the accounts. You contact the technician and verify that he made the modifications as expected.

You examine your directory event logs to locate the answer. Fortunately, you configured a central collection server to which you forward AD DS events from all the DCs in your domain. After some time, you discover that another administrator from a remote office was working on the same OU at the same time as the technician. More examination shows that the administrator moved the OU from its original location and then moved it back at the same time as the technician was working on the accounts.

Where are the missing accounts?

Suggested Practices

To help you successfully master the exam objectives presented in this chapter, complete the following tasks.

Practice Proactive Directory Maintenance

Working with AD DS means working with a central repository that provides two key services: user authentication and object management, hence the classification of AD DS as a NOS directory service. To become even more familiar with the exam objectives covered by this chapter, perform the following additional practices.

- **Practice 1** Practice working with the various backup and restore tools found in Windows Server 2008 R2. If you can, perform a complete server backup and then a complete server restore. Work with the DSRM, and practice changing the DSRM password as well as performing nonauthoritative and authoritative restores. Make sure you examine as many of the options available to you in each of the supported DC backup and restore scenarios as possible.

- **Practice 2** Work with the DC monitoring tools. Use Task Manager, Event Viewer, and the Windows Reliability and Performance Monitor views. Try as many of the options as possible to become familiar with how they work. Look up the suggested article for Event Log management and apply its principles to your DCs.

- **Practice 3** Work with Windows System Resource Manager. WSRM includes many options. Examine as many as possible and test out their operation. Try assigning different policies to your DCs to see how they affect system operation. View the event logs to see how WSRM logs information about the system.

Take a Practice Test

The practice tests on this book's companion CD offer many options. For example, you can test yourself on just one exam objective, or you can test yourself on all the 70-640 certification exam content. You can set up the test so that it closely simulates the experience of taking a certification exam, or you can set it up in study mode so that you can look at the correct answers and explanations after you answer each question.

> **MORE INFO** **PRACTICE TESTS**
>
> For details about all the practice test options available, see the "How to Use the Practice Tests" section in this book's Introduction.

CHAPTER 14

Active Directory Lightweight Directory Services

Of the five Active Directory technologies available in Windows Server 2008 R2, the one that most resembles Active Directory Domain Services (AD DS) is Active Directory Lightweight Directory Services (AD LDS). That's because AD LDS is really nothing more than a subset of AD DS functionality. Both use the same core code, and both provide a very similar feature set.

AD LDS, formerly called Active Directory Application Mode (ADAM), is a technology that is designed to support directory-enabled applications on an application-by-application basis without requiring modification of the database schema of your network operating system (NOS) directory running on AD DS. AD LDS is a boon to administrators who want to use directory-enabled applications without integrating them in their NOS directory.

Active Directory Domain Services can also support the use of directory-enabled applications. One very good example is Microsoft Exchange Server 2007. All user information in Exchange Server is provided by the directory. When you install Exchange Server in your network, it begins by extending the AD DS schema, practically doubling its size. As you know, schema modifications are not taken lightly because, when you add an object or an attribute to the AD DS schema, it is added forever; it cannot be removed. You can deactivate or rename and reuse these objects, but who wants defunct objects in their NOS directory? Adding to the schema for an application such as Exchange Server is appropriate because it provides a core networking service: email.

> **MORE INFO** **BEST PRACTICES FOR ACTIVE DIRECTORY DESIGN**
>
> For a guide outlining best practices for the design of Active Directory as well as AD DS schema management guidelines, download the free "Chapter 3: Designing the Active Directory" from *Windows Server 2003: Best Practices for Enterprise Deployments*, available at *http://www.reso-net.com/Documents/007222343X_Ch03.pdf*.
>
> For information on creating a new forest and migrating its contents from one forest to another, look up *Windows Server 2008: The Complete Reference* by Ruest and Ruest (McGraw-Hill Osborne, 2008). This book describes how to build a complete infrastructure based on Microsoft Windows Server and migrate all of its contents from one location to another.

However, when it comes to other applications, especially applications that are provided by third-party software manufacturers, carefully consider whether you should integrate them into your AD DS directory. Remember, your production AD DS structure will be with you for a very long time. You don't want to find yourself in a situation in which you integrated a product to your directory and then, several years later when the third-party manufacturer is out of business, have to figure out what to do with the extensions this product added to your AD DS structure, increasing replication timings and adding unused content in the directory.

This is why AD LDS is such a boon. Because it can support multiple AD LDS instances on a single server (unlike AD DS, which can support only one instance of a directory on any given server), AD LDS can meet the requirements of any directory-enabled application and even provide instances on an application-by-application basis. In addition, you do not need Enterprise Administrator or Schema Administrator credentials to work with AD LDS, as you would with AD DS. AD LDS runs on member or stand-alone servers and requires only local administration access rights to manage it. Because of this, it can also be used in a perimeter network to provide application or web authentication services. AD LDS is one of the four Active Directory technologies that allow you to extend your organization's authority beyond the firewall and into the Internet cloud. (See Figure 14-1.)

FIGURE 14-1 AD LDS can be used internally or externally in support of applications

Exam objectives in this chapter:

- Configure Active Directory Lightweight Directory Services (AD LDS).

Lessons in this chapter:

Before You Begin

To complete the lessons in this chapter, you must have installed Windows Server 2008 R2 on:

- A physical or virtual computer, which should be named SERVER01 and should be a domain controller in the contoso.com domain. The details for this setup are presented in Chapter 1, "Creating an Active Directory Domain." Use the same range of IP addresses as outlined in this chapter.

- Another physical or virtual computer. The machine should be named SERVER03 and should be joined to the contoso.com domain as a member server. This computer will host the AD LDS instances you install and create through the exercises in this chapter. Make sure this computer also includes a D drive (10 GB is recommended) to store the data for the AD LDS instances. Use the Disk Management feature in Server Manager to configure this additional drive.

- A third physical or virtual computer. The computer should be named SERVER04 and should be joined to the contoso.com domain as a member server. This computer will be used to configure replication scopes for AD LDS. Make sure this computer also includes a D drive (10 GB is recommended) to store the data for the AD LDS instances.

> **MORE INFO**   **SETUP FOR FOLLOWING CHAPTERS**
>
> You should rely on the Enterprise edition of Windows Server 2008 R2 for all new server creations for the exercises in the remainder of the chapters of this book. Many of the exercises rely on the same servers and will therefore require Enterprise features. However, in production, you do not always need the Enterprise edition. The actual edition you require is noted at the beginning of each exercise.

Danielle Ruest and Nelson Ruest

In late 2003, we were asked by *Redmond Magazine* (then *MCP Magazine*) to put together a review of the various products on the market that would help system administrators manage Active Directory environments. We were thrilled by the request because Active Directory was one of our favorite technologies. Besides being a true Lightweight Directory Access Protocol (LDAP) directory service, Active Directory is also a very powerful NOS directory that can manage millions of objects. In addition, Active Directory includes Group Policy, a potent object management platform that extends the NOS capabilities of the directory service. Finally, through Group Policy Software Delivery, you could manage the delivery of Windows Installer–based software packages throughout the entire structure of the directory. There was no doubt, for us, that Active Directory was one of the best products ever to come out of *Redmond's* development labs.

After scouring the Internet and polling our customers, we came up with a short list that included six products:

- Quest FastLane Active Roles
- Aelita Enterprise Directory Manager
- NetIQ Security Administration Suite
- Javelina ADvantage
- NetPro Active Directory Lifecycle Suite
- Bindview Secure Active Directory LifeCycle Suite

Of the six, only four were available to review for the article. Bindview declined to give us an evaluation copy of their product, so we had to omit it by default. NetPro, which seemed to have a great set of tools, wasn't ready to go to market yet, so we had to omit this product as well. We did, however, have a chance to write about NetPro's suite of Active Directory products later (see *http://mcpmag.com/reviews/products/article.asp?EditorialsID=454*), and it did very well indeed. So, we were left with four products to write about. The result was an article titled "The 12 Mighty Labors of Active Directory Management" (see *http://mcpmag.com/Features/article.asp?EditorialsID=359*). Readers everywhere seemed to like the article quite a bit. But we received some very biting comments from a couple of sources about one key point we made in the article.

Two of the four products we reviewed, the NetIQ Security Administration Suite and Quest FastLane Active Roles, modified the database schema for Active Directory to work. At that time, we had consulted in quite a few Active Directory implementations, and each one faced one single difficult question: how to manage schema modifications? That's because, when the schema is modified, you can't undo it. Of course, in Windows Server 2003, Microsoft allowed you to deactivate or rename and reuse schema modifications, but for our customers and for us, that was a poor second choice. It's best to leave the schema alone, if at all possible. In addition, Microsoft had just released ADAM in support of organizations that needed to integrate applications to a directory service but didn't want to modify the schema of their NOS directory.

In the end, we chose the Aelita product as the best choice for one major reason: Aelita had opted to store all of its database requirements in Microsoft SQL Server instead of modifying the Active Directory schema, yet its tool was as powerful as the other major contenders.

To make a long story short, about two months after we published the article, Quest bought Aelita and transformed Enterprise Directory Manager (EDM) into the next version of Active Roles. The original Active Roles, which was produced by FastLane, a small company from Ottawa, Canada, which was also bought by Quest, was rolled into EDM. The new version of Active Roles no longer required schema modifications to be implemented, yet still offered a powerful set of Active Directory management features. Did our article have anything to do with this? Who knows? One thing is sure: You should never take a NOS directory schema modification lightly, not when you have powerful tools like ADAM, now AD LDS, at your fingertips.

Lesson 1: Understanding and Installing AD LDS

Even though it is based on the same code as AD DS, AD LDS is much simpler to work with. For example, when you install AD LDS on a server, it does not change the configuration of the server in the same way that AD DS does when you create a domain controller. AD LDS is an application and nothing more. When you install it, you are not required to reboot the server because the application installation process only adds functionality to the server and does not change its nature.

However, before you begin, you must first understand what makes up an AD LDS instance, how AD LDS instances should be used, and what their relationship is or can be with AD DS directories. Then you can proceed to the installation of the AD LDS service.

> **After this lesson, you will be able to:**
> - Understand when to use AD LDS.
> - Install AD LDS on a member server.
> - Locate and view the AD LDS directory store.
>
> **Estimated lesson time: 30 minutes**

Understanding AD LDS

Like AD DS, AD LDS instances are based on the Lightweight Directory Access Protocol (LDAP) and provide hierarchical database services. Unlike relational databases, LDAP directories are optimized for specific purposes and should be used whenever you need to rely on fast lookups of information that support given applications. Table 14-1 outlines the major differences between an LDAP directory and a relational database such as Microsoft SQL Server. This comparison helps you understand when to choose an LDAP directory in support of an application over a relational database.

TABLE 14-1 Comparing LDAP Directories to Relational Databases

LDAP DIRECTORIES	RELATIONAL DATABASES
Fast reads and searches.	Fast writes.
Hierarchical database design often based on the Domain Name System (DNS) or the X.500 naming system.	Structured data design relying on tables containing rows and columns. Tables can be linked together.
Relies on a standard schema structure, a schema that is extensible.	Does not rely on schemas.
Decentralized (distributed) and relies on replication to maintain data consistency.	Centrally located data repositories.

LDAP DIRECTORIES	RELATIONAL DATABASES
Security is applied at the object level.	Security is applied at the row or column level.
Because the database is distributed, data consistency is not absolute—at least not until replication passes are complete.	Because data input is transactional, data consistency is absolute and guaranteed at all times.
Records are not locked and can be modified by two parties at once. Conflicts are managed through update sequence numbers (USNs).	Records are locked and can be modified by only one party at a time.

Although AD LDS is based on AD DS, it does not include all the features of AD DS. Table 14-2 outlines the differences in features between AD LDS and AD DS.

TABLE 14-2 Comparing AD LDS with AD DS

FEATURE	AD LDS	AD DS
Includes more than one instance on a server.	☑	☐
Includes independent schemas for each instance.	☑	☐
Runs on client operating systems such as Windows 7 or Windows Server 2008 R2 member servers.	☑	☐
Runs on domain controllers.	☑	☑
Directory partitions can rely on X.500 naming conventions.	☑	☐
Can be installed or removed without a reboot.	☑	☐
Service can be stopped or started without reboot.	☑	☑
Supports Group Policy.	☐	☑
Includes a global catalog.	☐	☑
Manages objects such as workstations, member servers, and domain controllers.	☐	☑
Supports trusts between domains and forests.	☐	☑
Supports and integrates with public key infrastructures (PKIs) and X.509 certificates.	☐	☑
Supports DNS service (SRV) records for locating directory services.	☐	☑
Supports LDAP application programming interfaces (APIs).	☑	☑
Supports Active Directory Services Interface (ADSI) API.	☑	☑
Supports the Messaging API (MAPI).	☐	☑
Supports object-level security and delegation of administration.	☑	☑

FEATURE	AD LDS	AD DS
Relies on multimaster replication for data consistency.	☑	☑
Supports schema extensions and application directory partitions.	☑	☑
Can install a replica from removable media.	☑	☑
Can include security principals to provide access to a Windows Server network.	☐	☑
Can include security principals to provide access to applications and Web Services.	☑	☑
Is integrated into the Windows Server 2008 R2 backup tools.	☑	☑

As you can see from the contents of Table 14-2, there are several similarities and differences between AD LDS and AD DS. For example, it is easy to see why Exchange Server must integrate with AD DS as opposed to relying on AD LDS; Exchange Server requires access to the global catalog service to run. Without it, email users could not look up recipients. Because AD LDS does not support the global catalog, Exchange Server cannot rely on it. However, Exchange Server is an application that requires access to directory data in each site of the domain or forest. As such, it also relies on your domain controller positioning to ensure that each user can properly address emails.

AD LDS, however, provides much of the same functionality as AD DS. For example, you can create instances with replicas distributed in various locations in your network, just as with the location of domain controllers, and then use multimaster replication to ensure data consistency. In short, AD LDS is a lightweight, portable, and more malleable version of the directory service offered by AD DS.

AD LDS Scenarios

Now that you have a better understanding of AD LDS and its feature set, you can begin to identify scenarios in which you would need to work with this technology. Consider these scenarios when you decide whether to rely on AD LDS or AD DS:

- When your applications need to rely on an LDAP directory, consider using AD LDS instead of AD DS. AD LDS can often be hosted on the same server as the application, providing high-speed and local access to directory data. This reduces network traffic because all required data is local. In addition, you can bundle the AD LDS instance with the application when you deploy it. For example, if you have a human resources application that must rely on custom policies to ensure that users can access only specific content when their user object contains a set of particular attributes, you can store these attributes and policies within AD LDS.

- Rely on AD LDS to provide data associated with user accounts in AD DS but requiring extensions to the AD DS schema to support it. Using AD LDS in this scenario provides the additional user data without modifying the AD DS schema. For example, if you have a centralized application that provides a photograph of each employee in your organization and associates the photographs with the users' AD DS accounts, you can store the photographs in an AD LDS instance. By storing the photographs in AD LDS in a central location, they are associated with the user accounts in AD DS, but because they are in AD LDS, they are not replicated with all other AD DS data, reducing bandwidth requirements for replication.

- Rely on an AD LDS instance to provide authentication services for a web application such as Microsoft SharePoint Portal Server in a perimeter network or extranet. AD LDS can query the internal AD DS structure through a firewall to obtain user account information and store it securely in the perimeter network. This avoids having to deploy AD DS in the perimeter or having to include domain controllers from the internal network in the perimeter. Note that you can also rely on Active Directory Federation Services (AD FS) to provide this access. AD FS is discussed in further detail in Chapter 17, "Active Directory Federation Services."

- Consolidate various identity repositories into a single directory store. Using a metadirectory service such as Forefront Identity Manager (FIM) or the free Identity Integration Feature Pack (IIFP), you can obtain data from various sources and consolidate it within an AD LDS instance. FIM and IIFP support the provisioning of data from a wide variety of sources such as AD DS forests, SQL Server databases, third-party LDAP services, and much more. IIFP is a subset of Microsoft Identity Integration Server (MIIS) and supports data integration between AD DS, AD LDS, and Exchange Server. Using these solutions reduces your identity management overhead by designating a single master source and provisioning all other repositories from this source.

> **MORE INFO** **FIM AND IIFP**
>
> For more information on FIM, go to *http://www.microsoft.com/forefront/identitymanager/en/us/default.aspx*.
>
> For more information on and to download IIFP, go to *http://www.microsoft.com/downloads/details.aspx?familyid=d9143610-c04d-41c4-b7ea-6f56819769d5&displaylang=en*.

- Provide support for departmental applications. In some cases, departments might require additional identity information, information that is of no relevance to any other department within the organization. By integrating this information in an AD LDS instance, you give the department access to it without affecting the directory service for the entire organization.

- Provide support for distributed applications. If your application is distributed and requires access to data in several locations, you can also rely on AD LDS because AD LDS provides the same multimaster replication capabilities as AD DS.

- Migrate legacy directory applications to AD LDS. If your organization is running legacy applications that rely on an LDAP directory, you can migrate the data to an AD LDS instance and standardize it on Active Directory directory technologies.

- Provide support for local development. Because AD LDS can be installed on client workstations, you can provide your developers with portable single-instance directories that they can use to develop custom applications that require access to identity data. Developing with AD LDS is much simpler and easier to manage and contain than developing with AD DS.

- When evaluating directory-enabled commercial applications, you should always give preference to an application that relies on AD LDS or its predecessor, ADAM, rather than select one that relies on AD DS schema modifications. Deploying commercial applications with portable directories is much easier and has much less impact on your network than deploying applications that will modify your NOS directory schema forever.

Each of these scenarios represents a possible use of AD LDS. Typical applications should include white-page directories, security-oriented applications and network configuration, and policy store applications.

As you can see, AD LDS is much more portable and malleable than AD DS will ever be. Whenever you need to think about schema modifications in AD DS, think of AD LDS instead. On almost every occasion, AD LDS provides a better choice because AD DS should always be reserved as a NOS directory and should include integration only with applications that add functionality to the NOS directory functions.

> **MORE INFO**   **AD LDS**
>
> For more information on AD LDS, go to *http://technet2.microsoft.com/windowsserver2008/en/library/b7fb96ec-3f3f-4860-a1ab-eb43e54bbefc1033.mspx*.

EXAM TIP

Pay attention to the scenarios outlined previously in this chapter. Although few exam questions are about AD LDS, you can be sure that when they do arise, they will be related to choosing AD LDS over other Active Directory technologies.

New AD LDS Features in Windows Server 2008 R2

Microsoft has provided several updates to AD LDS with the release of Windows Server 2008 R2. All of these updates are also included in AD DS, and some have already been covered in previous chapters.

- **Active Directory Recycle Bin**   This feature is made available by a schema update and offers administrators the ability to recover accidentally deleted items. This feature is also included in AD DS and is covered in Chapter 13, "Directory Business Continuity."

- **Active Directory Web Services (ADWS)**   This feature offers a web service interface that connects to AD LDS instances. This feature is automatically installed and available when installing the AD LDS role. This feature is also available for AD DS and is introduced in Chapter 3, "Administering User Accounts."

- **Active Directory Module for Windows PowerShell**   This feature provides a command-line interface for administrators. You can use PowerShell to perform administrative tasks interactively or automate repetitive tasks. This feature is also available for AD DS and is also introduced in Chapter 3.

All three updates have been discussed before and can be used with AD LDS in very much the same way they are used with AD DS.

Installing AD LDS

As part of Windows Server 2008 R2, AD LDS can be installed and configured in both the full installation and in Server Core. In addition, AD LDS is an ideal candidate for virtualization through Windows Server 2008 R2 Hyper-V. Because of its light requirements, AD LDS can easily run within a virtual instance of the Windows Server 2008 R2 operating system and should be considered as such unless the application that is tied to the AD LDS instance has specific requirements for physical installation.

In addition, avoid installing AD LDS on domain controllers as much as possible. Although AD LDS can fully coexist with the domain controller (DC) role, and even the read-only domain controller (RODC) role, domain controllers should be considered special roles within your network and should be tied only to the DNS service and nothing else, if at all possible. Because DCs are also good candidates for virtualization, any network that can rely on host servers running Hyper-V and virtualized instances of other services should virtualize DCs as much as possible. With a virtual DC, it is much easier to ensure that no other roles are hosted on the server because all other roles can also be virtualized within their own instances of Windows Server 2008 R2.

Also, consider running AD LDS in scenarios in which high security is required. A good example is one in which you need to run an authentication directory service in extranets or perimeter networks. Relying on Server Core installations within these environments can help reduce the attack surface of servers you expose outside of your corporate network.

Identifying AD LDS Requirements

As mentioned earlier, AD LDS has very light installation requirements. They include:

- A supported operating system such as Windows Server 2008 R2, Standard edition, Enterprise edition, or Datacenter edition.
- An account with local administration access rights.

Removing AD LDS from a server requires two activities:

- First, uninstall any instance of AD LDS that you created after the role installation, using Programs And Features in Control Panel.
- Second, use Server Manager to remove the AD LDS role.

As you can see, both installation and removal requirements are straightforward. The major caveat is that you must ensure that all instances have been removed from a server before you remove the role.

 EXAM TIP

Remember that you need to remove all instances of AD LDS from a server before you can remove the role from the server.

Installing AD LDS on Server Core

Installing AD LDS is very similar to installing AD DS. First you must install the server role; then you must create the AD LDS instances you want to use. Installing AD LDS on the full installation of Windows Server 2008 R2 is covered in the practice later in this lesson.

The installation process for AD LDS is as simple on Server Core as it is on a full installation of Windows Server 2008 R2. Use the following process:

1. Log on with local administrative credentials to a Windows Server 2008 R2 stand-alone or member server running Server Core.

2. Begin by identifying the service name for AD LDS. Use the following command:

    ```
    oclist | more
    ```

    This name should appear after several screens of information and should be DirectoryServices-ADAM-ServerCore.

3. Proceed to the installation of the role. Use the following command:

    ```
    Dism /online /enable-feature /featurename:DirectoryServices-ADAM-ServerCore
    ```

    Role names are case-sensitive, so ensure that you type the role name exactly as displayed; otherwise, the command will not work. Also, using the Start /w command ensures that the command prompt does not return until the role installation is complete.

> **NOTE THE DISM COMMAND**
>
> **Windows Server 2008 R2 administrators should get used to the DISM command, which is designed to replace OCSetup in future Server Core versions of Windows Server. For more information on DISM and additional installation and control options, go to http://technet.microsoft.com/en-us/library/dd744382%28WS.10%29.aspx.**

If you run the oclist command again, you see that the AD LDS role has been added to this server. You can also navigate to the %SystemRoot%\ADAM folder to view the new AD LDS files. Your server is ready to host AD LDS instances.

PRACTICE **Installing AD LDS**

In this practice, you install the AD LDS role on a server running the full installation of Windows Server 2008 R2. Then you browse the contents of the installation folder to identify which files have been installed.

EXERCISE 1 **Install AD LDS**

In this exercise, you install the AD LDS server role.

1. Make sure your Active Directory Domain Server, SERVER01.contoso.com, is running, and start your member servers, SERVER03.contoso.com and SERVER04.contoso.com.

2. Log on to SERVER03.contoso.com with the CONTOSO\Administrator account.

   You do not need domain administrator rights to work with AD LDS. Because each AD LDS installation is independent of AD DS, you need only local administrator rights to work with it, but using the domain administrator account is acceptable for the purpose of this exercise.

3. In Server Manager, right-click the Roles node and click Add Roles.

4. Review the Before You Begin screen and click Next.

5. In the Select Server Roles dialog box, select Active Directory Lightweight Directory Services, click Add Required Features, and then click Next.

6. Review the information in the Active Directory Lightweight Directory Services window and click Next.

7. Confirm your choices and click Install.

8. Review the installation results and click Close.

9. Repeat the operation on SERVER04.contoso.com.

   AD LDS is installed on both member servers.

   The AD LDS installation installs the service and generates a directory store called Adamntds.dit located in the %SystemRoot%\Adam folder. It also adds the tools to configure and manage AD LDS as well as the PowerShell Module for Active Directory.

When the installation is complete, the role appears in Server Manager, as shown in Figure 14-2.

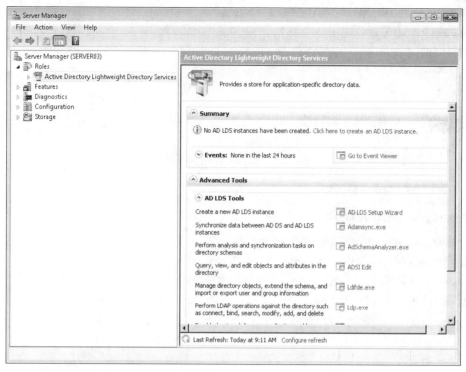

FIGURE 14-2 Viewing the AD LDS role within Server Manager

EXERCISE 2   Review the Installed AD LDS Files

In this exercise, you review the files that AD LDS installs on servers.

1. Log on to your member server, SERVER03.contoso.com, using the CONTOSO\Administrator account.

2. From the Start menu, right-click Computer and click Open to open a Windows Explorer window.

3. Navigate to the %SystemRoot%\ADAM folder.

4. Review the files created by the AD LDS installation process.

   On a full installation of Windows Server 2008 R2, AD LDS creates the ADAM folder and populates it with 21 files and two subfolders. The two subfolders include localization information. In this case, they are in U.S. English. As shown in Figure 14-3, the files contained in the ADAM folder include:

   - The AD LDS program files, including .dll, .exe, .cat, .ini, and .xml files.

   - The AD LDS directory store, Adamntds.dit.

   - Lightweight directory format (.ldf) files that are used to populate AD LDS instances when they are created.

You work with these file types when you configure AD LDS in the next lesson.

FIGURE 14-3 AD LDS installs into the %SystemRoot%\Adam folder and creates the AD LDS database

The installation of AD LDS on Server Core does not include the same files and folders as the installation on a full installation of Windows Server 2008 R2. Server Core creates only one folder for localization, whereas the full installation creates two. In addition, the full installation includes an additional tool: the Active Directory Schema Analyzer, which is not installed on Server Core.

Lesson Summary

- As its name suggests, AD LDS is a lightweight version of AD DS. AD LDS supports all the features of AD DS except for the network operating system capabilities. As such, it is a directory service that can be tied to applications and support their need for custom configurations and authentication services in environments that are not secured, such as perimeter networks.

- The installation requirements for AD LDS are very simple: All you need is a server running a supported version of Windows Server 2008 R2. This server can be a member, a stand-alone server, or even a domain controller, although you should endeavor to keep your DCs separate from all other roles.

- To install AD LDS, you select the role in the Add Roles Wizard. The installation process is probably the most basic installation process of all the roles in Windows Server 2008 R2.

- To remove AD LDS, you must first remove all instances through Programs And Features in Control Panel and then remove the role in Server Manager.

Lesson Review

You can use the following question to test your knowledge of the information in Lesson 1, "Understanding and Installing AD LDS." The question is also available on the companion CD if you prefer to review them in electronic form.

> **NOTE ANSWERS**
>
> Answers to these questions and explanations of why each answer choice is right or wrong are located in the "Answers" section at the end of the book.

1. You are a server administrator for contoso.com. Your manager has asked you to repurpose SERVER04 with a new role as soon as possible. SERVER04 currently hosts five AD LDS instances. You must uninstall AD LDS from this server. You log on to SERVER04 with local administrative rights and launch an elevated command prompt. You use the ocsetup command with the /uninstall switch, and it does not work. Which of the following options should you use to resolve the problem?

    A. You must restart the server to make sure all running setup processes are complete and then run the ocsetup /uninstall command again.

    B. You must use Server Manager to remove all AD LDS instances and the role.

    C. You must uninstall all existing instances of AD LDS first, using Programs And Features in Control Panel, and then execute ocsetup /uninstall from the command prompt.

    D. You must use the oclist command to verify the syntax of the option you are trying to remove with the ocsetup command. You retry the ocsetup command with the correct syntax.

Lesson 2: Configuring and Using AD LDS

Now that you have installed AD LDS, you can begin to work with it to store directory-related data for various applications. The first thing you should do is become familiar with the AD LDS tool set. After you understand which tools you can use to manage AD LDS, you can begin to create your first instances. After you've created your instances, you can secure them to ensure that they are properly protected. You can then move on to the creation of replicas for these instances so that you can install them on various other systems and control replication so that instances located on different computers can be updated through multimaster replication.

This lesson illustrates the value that AD LDS offers when you combine it with applications and integrate it with the other Active Directory technologies contained within Windows Server 2008 R2.

> **After this lesson, you will be able to:**
> - Create AD LDS instances.
> - Work with AD LDS tools.
> - Work with application partitions.
> - Manage replication between AD LDS instances.
>
> **Estimated lesson time: 30 minutes**

Working with AD LDS Tools

You can work with AD LDS through a selection of tools, many of which will be familiar to you because they are the same tools you use for AD DS administration. Table 14-3 describes each of these tools and the purpose they serve in managing the AD LDS service.

TABLE 14-3 AD LDS Tools and AD DS Tools

TOOL NAME	USAGE	LOCATION
Active Directory Schema Snap-in	Modify the schema for AD LDS instances. You must use the Regsvr32.exe command to register the schmmgmt.dll first.	Custom MMC
Active Directory Sites And Services	Configure and manage replication scopes for AD LDS instances. AD LDS instances must be updated to support replication objects first.	Administrative Tools program group
AD LDS Setup	Create AD LDS instances.	Administrative Tools program group

TOOL NAME	USAGE	LOCATION
ADAMInstall.exe	Command-line tool for the creation of AD LDS instances.	%SystemRoot% \ADAM folder
ADAMSync.exe	Command-line tool for synchronizing data from AD DS forest to AD LDS instance. AD LDS instance must be updated to AD DS schema first.	%SystemRoot% \ADAM folder
ADAMUninstall.exe	Command-line tool for the removal of AD LDS instances.	%SystemRoot% \ADAM folder
ADSchemaAnalyzer .exe	Command-line tool for copying schema contents from AD DS to AD LDS or from one AD LDS instance to another. Supports third-party LDAP directory schema copies.	%SystemRoot% \ADAM folder
ADSI Edit	Interactively manage AD LDS content through ADSI.	Administrative Tools program group
CSVDE.exe	Import data into AD LDS instances.	Command line
DSACLS.exe	Control access control lists on AD LDS objects.	Command line
DSAMain.exe	Mount Active Directory store (.dit) backups or snapshots to identify their contents.	Command line
DSDBUtil.exe	Perform database maintenance, configure AD LDS ports, and view existing instances. Also, create one-step installations for transporting AD LDS instances through the Install from Media (IFM) generation process.	Command line
Dcdiag.exe	Diagnose AD LDS instances. Must use the /n:*NamingContext* switch to name the instance to diagnose.	Command line
DSMgmt.exe	Supports application partition and AD LDS policy management.	Command line
Event Viewer	Audit AD LDS changes and log old and new values for both objects and attributes.	Administrative Tools program group
LDAP Data Interchange Format (LDIF) files	AD LDS installations can dynamically import LDIF files (.ldp) during instance creation, automatically configuring the instance.	%SystemRoot% \ADAM folder
LDIFDE.exe	Import data into AD LDS instances.	Command line
LDP.exe	Interactively modify content or AD LDS instances through LDAP.	Command line

TOOL NAME	USAGE	LOCATION
Ntdsutil.exe	Manage AD LDS instances, but only if AD DS is also installed. (Not recommended; use DSDBUtil.exe instead.)	Command line
RepAdmin.exe	Analyze replication to view potential issues.	Command line
Server Manager	Manage existing AD LDS instances.	Administrative Tools program group
Windows PowerShell	Create, manage, and delete AD LDS instances.	Administrative Tools program group
Windows Server Backup	Back up or restore AD LDS instances and their contents.	Administrative Tools program group

You'll use a variety of the tools listed in Table 14-3 to perform the configuration and administration operations required when you run AD LDS services.

> **MORE INFO** **AD LDS AUDITING**
>
> For more information on auditing AD LDS instances or AD DS domains, go to *http://go.microsoft.com/fwlink/?LinkId=94846*.

Creating AD LDS Instances

The AD LDS role installation process is very similar to the AD DS installation process. You begin by installing the AD LDS binaries, and then, after they are installed, you create AD LDS instances to use the service. In the same way, when you deploy AD DS, you begin by installing the binaries, and then you use the Active Directory Domain Services Installation Wizard to create the AD DS instance you will use. Because of their same roots, many of the tools you use to manage them are the same.

Preparing for AD LDS Instance Creation

You create AD LDS instances by using the Active Directory Lightweight Directory Services Setup Wizard. However, you need to prepare several items before you create the instance. Make note of the values you choose as you prepare each item because you will need these values to create and manage the instance. These items include:

- A data drive created for your server. Because this server will be hosting directory stores, place these stores on a drive that is separate from the operating system.
- The name you will use to create the instance. Use meaningful names, such as the name of the application that will be tied to an instance, to identify instances. This name is

used to identify the instance on the local computer as well as to name the files that make up the instance and the service that supports it.

- The ports you intend to use to communicate with the instance. Both AD LDS and AD DS use the same ports for communication. These ports are the default LDAP (389) and LDAP over the Secure Sockets Layer (SSL), or Secure LDAP (636), ports. AD DS uses two additional ports, 3268, which uses LDAP to access the global catalog, and 3269, which uses Secure LDAP to access the global catalog. Because AD DS and AD LDS use the same ports, this is another good reason for not running both roles on the same server. However, when the wizard detects that ports 389 and 636 are already in use, it proposes 50,000 and 50,001 for each port and then uses other ports in the 50,000 range for additional instances.

✔ **Quick Check**

1. Which ports are used to work with AD LDS instances?
2. How do the ports in an AD LDS instance differ from ports used by AD DS?

Quick Check Answers

1. The ports used by an AD LDS instance can be the standard LDAP port, 389, or the LDAP over SSL or Secure LDAP port, 636. In addition, AD LDS can use any port over 1025. However, use ports in the 50,000 range as a best practice.
2. Both AD DS and AD LDS can use ports 389 (LDAP) or 636 (Secure LDAP). In addition, AD DS uses ports 3268 (LDAP) and 3269 (Secure LDAP) to communicate with the global catalog service. However, reserve ports 389 and 636 for AD DS as a best practice.

IMPORTANT USING PORTS 389 AND 636

If you are creating AD LDS instances within a domain, do not use ports 389 or 636 even if you are not creating the first instance on a domain controller. AD DS uses these ports by default, and, because of this, some consoles, such as those using the Active Directory Schema snap-in, will not bind to local instances because they bind to the AD DS directory by default. As a best practice, always use ports beyond the 50,000 range for your AD LDS instances.

EXAM TIP

Make note of the default ports. They are sure to be on the exam, even though you should avoid them in production environments.

- The Active Directory application partition name that you intend to use for the instance. You must use a distinguished name (DN) to create the partition. For example, you could use CN=AppPartition1,DC=Contoso,DC=com. Depending on how you intend to use the instance, you might or might not need the application partition. Application partitions control the replication scope for a directory store. For example, when you integrate DNS data within the directory, AD DS creates an application partition to make DNS data available to appropriate DCs. Application partitions for AD LDS can be created in one of three ways: when you create the instance, when you install the application that will be tied to the instance, or when you create the partition manually through the LDP.exe tool. If your application will not create application partitions automatically, create them with the wizard.

- A service account to run the instance. You can use the Network Service account, but if you intend to run multiple instances, it might be best to use named service accounts for each instance. If you choose not to use a managed service account and decide to set up your service accounts manually, remember to follow the service accounts guidelines and requirements as listed here. Create a domain account if you are in a domain; otherwise, use a local account (for example, in a perimeter network).

NOTE MANAGED SERVICE ACCOUNT

To create a Managed Service Account, use the procedures outlined in Chapter 8, Lesson 4.

- Name the account with the same name you gave to the instance.
- Assign a complex password to this account.
- Set User Cannot Change Password in the account properties. You assign this property to ensure that no one can appropriate the account.
- Set Password Never Expires in the account properties. You assign this property to ensure that the service does not fail because of a password policy.
- Assign the Log On As A Service user right in the Local Security Policy of each computer that will host this instance.
- Assign the Generate Security Audits user right in the Local Security Policy of each computer that will host this instance to support account auditing.
- A group that will contain the user accounts that will administer the instance. The best practice for permission assignments is always to use groups even if only one account is a member of the group. If personnel changes, you can always add or change group members without having to add or change permissions. Create a domain group if you are in a domain; otherwise, create a local group. Name the group the same as the instance. This way, it will be easy to track the group's purpose. Add your own account to the group as well as to the service account you created earlier.
- Any additional LDIF files you need for the instance. Place these files in the %SystemRoot% \ADAM folder. These files are imported during the creation of the instance. Importing LDIF files extends the schema of the instance you are creating to support additional opera-

tions. For example, to synchronize AD DS with AD LDS, you would import the MS-Adam-SyncMetadata.ldf file. If your application requires custom schema modifications, create the LDIF file ahead of time and import it as you create the instance. Note that you can always import LDIF files after the instance is created. Default LDIF files are listed in Table 14-4.

TABLE 14-4 Default AD LDS LDIF Files

FILE NAME	PURPOSE
MS-ADAM-Upgrade-1.ldf	To upgrade the AD LDS schema to the latest version.
MS-ADAM-Upgrade-2.ldf	To upgrade the AD LDS schema to support the AD Recycle Bin.
MS-adamschemaw2k3.ldf	Required as a prerequisite for synchronizing an instance with Active Directory in Windows Server 2003.
MS-adamschemaw2k8.ldf	Required as a prerequisite for synchronizing an instance with Active Directory in Windows Server 2008 R2.
MS-AdamSyncMetadata.ldf	Required to synchronize data between an AD DS forest and an AD LDS instance through ADAMSync.
MS-ADLDS-DisplaySpecifiers.ldf	Required for the Active Directory Sites And Services snap-in operation.
MS-AZMan.ldf	Required to support the Windows Authorization Manager.
MS-InetOrgPerson.ldf	Required to create *inetOrgPerson* user classes and attributes.
MS-User.ldf	Required to create user classes and attributes.
MS-UserProxy.ldf	Required to create a simple *userProxy* class.
MS-UserProxyFull.ldf	Required to create a full *userProxy* class. MS-UserProxy.ldf must be imported first.

After you have all these items in hand, you are ready to create your instance. Make sure the account you use has local administrative rights. You can create instances in one of two ways. The first is through the Active Directory Lightweight Services Setup Wizard, and the second is through the command line. You use the wizard during the practice in this lesson. Using the command line is explained in the next section.

IMPORTANT **AD LDS LOG FILES**

AD LDS creates log files during the creation of an instance. These files are located in the %SystemRoot%\Debug folder and are named ADAMSetup.log and ADAMSetup_loader.log. You can review the content of these files to debug instance creation issues.

Performing an Unattended AD LDS Instance Creation

You can also perform unattended AD LDS instance creations. For example, to create instances on Server Core installations, you must use an unattended instance creation process because there is no graphical interface to run the wizard. Unattended instance creations are also useful when you need to create an instance for a distributed application on multiple servers. Make sure you prepare all the prerequisites for the instance as outlined in the "Preparing for AD LDS Instance Creation" section earlier in this lesson.

The %SystemRoot%\ADAM folder includes an additional command, AdamInstall.exe, which can be run to perform unattended instance setups. As with the Dcpromo.exe command, this command requires a text file as input for the creation of the instance. You can run AdamInstall.exe on either a full installation or Server Core. Begin by creating an answer file, as follows:

1. Launch Notepad.

2. Type the text for the answer file. Include the following items:

   ```
   [ADAMInstall]
   InstallType=Unique
   InstanceName=InstanceName
   LocalLDAPPortToListenOn=PortNumber
   LocalSSLPortToListenOn=PortNumber
   NewApplicationPartitionToCreate=PartitionName
   DataFilesPath=D:\ADAMInstances\InstanceName\Data
   LogFilesPath=D:\ADAMInstances\InstanceName\Data
   ServiceAccount=DomainOrMachineName\AccountName
   ServicePassword=Password
   Administrator=DomainOrMachineName\GroupName
   ImportLDIFFiles="LDIFFilename1" "LDIFFilename2" "LDIFFilename3"
   SourceUserName=DomainorMachineName\AccountName
   SourcePassword=Password
   ```

   Replace all names in italics with appropriate values. Refer to the "Preparing for AD LDS Instance Creation" section earlier in this lesson to identify the required values. Use caution with this file because it includes passwords, and these passwords are displayed in clear text. The passwords are removed as soon as the file is used by the AD LDS instance creation tool.

3. Save the file in the %SystemRoot%\ADAM folder, and name it with the name of the instance you want to create.

4. Close Notepad.

MORE INFO **AD LDS INSTANCE CREATION**

For more information on AD LDS instance creation, go to *http://technet2.microsoft.com/ windowsserver2008/en/library/141900a7-445c-4bd3-9ce3-5ff53d70d10a1033 .mspx?mfr=true.*

Now you're ready to create your instance. Remember that you need local administrative rights.

1. Open an elevated command prompt from the Start menu by right-clicking Command Prompt and clicking Run As Administrator.

2. In the command prompt window, move to the %SystemRoot%\ADAM folder. Type the following command, and then press Enter.

   ```
   cd windows\adam
   ```

3. Type the following command. Use quotation marks for the file name if it includes spaces.

   ```
   adaminstall /answer:filename.txt
   ```

4. Close the command prompt window.

Your instance is ready. You can verify that the instance files have been created by going to the target folder and viewing its contents.

Migrating a Previous LDAP Instance to AD LDS

You can also migrate existing LDAP directories to AD LDS or upgrade instances of ADAM to AD LDS. You can do this by importing the contents of the older instances into a new instance of AD LDS.

You can import data either when you create the instance or after the instance is created. Both processes use the same approach because both rely on LDIF files or files with the .ldf extension. If you choose to import data after the instance is created, you must use the LDIFDE.exe command. Remember that you must first export the data from the previous instance and place it in a file in LDIF format before you can import the data.

You can use LDIFDE to export contents from legacy instances. Remember that you need local administrative rights as well as administrative rights to the instance to perform these operations. Also make sure you run the command prompt with elevated credentials. Use the following command syntax:

```
ldifde -f filename -s servername:portnumber -b username domainname password
```

where *filename* is the name of the file to create (use quotation marks if the path includes spaces); *servername* is the name of the server hosting the instance; *portnumber* is the communications port; and *username, domainname,* and *password* are the credentials of an instance administrator.

Use a similar command to import the data into the new instance:

```
ldifde -i -f filename -s servername:portnumber -b username domainname password
```

Note that to import passwords from the legacy instance, you must use the *–h* switch. This switch encrypts all passwords, using Simple Authentication And Security Layer (SASL).

Enabling the AD Recycle Bin in AD LDS

By default, the AD Recycle Bin is not enabled in AD LDS instances just as it is not available in AD DS until it is enabled. Enabling the Recycle Bin in AD LDS requires a schema update. Use the following command to update the schema:

```
ldifde -i -f MS-ADAM-Upgrade-2.kdf -s servername:portnumber -b username
    domainname password -j . -$ adamschema.cat
```

This action is irreversible and cannot be undone. Note that it is easiest to perform this update after Windows Server 2008 R2 is installed and the AD LDS role is enabled, because the required LDF and CAT files are easy to locate (in the %SystemRoot%\ADAM folder). If you try to update an AD LDS instance before updating the server to Windows Server 2008 R2, you must locate these files on another server and copy them to the server where you are performing the update.

 Quick Check

1. What are the three ways to create application partitions for AD LDS instances?

2. What is the purpose of the LDIF files included with AD LDS?

3. How can you debug an AD LDS instance creation process that goes awry?

Quick Check Answers

1. You can create application partitions for AD LDS instances in three ways:

   ■ During the creation of an instance with AD LDS Setup

   ■ Through the installation of the application that will be tied to an AD LDS instance

   ■ Manually through the LDP.exe tool

2. The LDIF files included with AD LDS serve several purposes, depending on the actual file, but generally they are used to extend the schema of an instance to support specific functionality.

3. AD LDS creates log files during the creation of the instance. These files are located in the %SystemRoot%\Debug folder and are named ADAMSetup.log and ADAMSetup_loader.log. You can review them to find and resolve issues during the creation of the instance.

MORE INFO   **LDIFDE**

For more information on the *LDIFDE.exe* command, refer to Chapter 3.

Working with AD LDS Instances

Table 14-3, presented earlier, lists all the tools you can use to work with AD LDS instances. Of these, the most useful are the graphical tools such as ADSI Edit, LDP.exe, the Schema snap-in, and Active Directory Sites And Services. They control how you view and edit content in your instances. Command-line tools are more useful for automating processes and data input for AD LDS instances.

Using ADSI Edit to Work with Instances

ADSI Edit is a general administration tool for AD LDS instances. Each time you want to work with an instance, you must first connect and bind to the instance. Remember that you must be an administrator of the instance to perform administrative operations on them. Use the following procedure:

1. Launch ADSI Edit from the Administrative Tools program group.

2. In the tree pane, right-click ADSI Edit, and then select Connect To. This opens the Connection Settings dialog box. Enter the following values as shown in Figure 14-4:

   ▪ Name: This should be the name of the instance to which you want to connect.

   ▪ Connection Point: Choose Select Or Type A Distinguished Name Or Naming Context, and type the distinguished name of the instance.

   ▪ Computer: Choose Select Or Type A Domain Or Server, and type the server name with the port number—for example, SERVER03:50000.

   ▪ Computer: Select the Use SSL-Based Encryption check box if you are using a Secure LDAP port.

3. Click OK.

   This connects you to the instance. Expand all entries to view the instance contents. Explore the shortcut menus to understand the operations you can perform with ADSI Edit on AD LDS instances.

FIGURE 14-4 Connecting to an AD LDS instance with ADSI Edit

Now that you are bound to the instance, you can create and manage objects within the instance. Use the following procedure:

1. Right-click the application partition distinguished name, point to New, and click Object. This opens the Create Object dialog box, which lists all the available object classes in the instance's schema.

2. Begin by creating a user group. Scroll to the Group object, select it, and then click Next.

3. Type the name of the group, such as **AD LDS Users**, and click Next.

4. On the next screen of the dialog box, you can click More Attributes to assign more values to this new object. For example, you can assign a description to the group. From the Select A Property To View drop-down list, select AdminDescription. Type a description in the Edit Attribute field, such as **Group to contain AD LDS users**, click Set, and then click OK.

5. Click Finish to create the group. By default, this creates a security group.

6. Create a user: Right-click the application partition distinguished name, point to New, and then click Object.

7. Scroll to the User object, select it, and then click Next.

8. Type the name of the user and click Next.

9. Once again, you can click More Attributes to assign more values to this new object.

10. Click Finish to create the user.

11. Add the user to the group: Select the partition in the tree pane, locate the group in the details pane, right-click it, and then click Properties.

12. In the Properties dialog box, locate the member property and click Edit.

13. In the Multi-Valued Distinguished Name With Security Principal Editor dialog box, click Add DN.

14. In the Add Distinguished Name dialog box, type the distinguished name of the user you created. For example, type **cn=John Kane,cn=Instance1,dc=contoso,dc=com**. Click OK. The user is now listed in the members list.

15. Click OK to complete the operation.

If you view the properties of the group again, you see that your user has been added to the group. It is quite cumbersome to add users and groups to an instance in this manner, but you can use it for single modifications. Ideally, you should create user and group lists and then use either CSVDE.exe or LDIFDE.exe to add them in batches. Refer to Chapter 3 to review the automation of user creation and Chapter 4, "Managing Groups," to review the automation of group creation for more information.

Using LDP.exe to Work with Instances

Similarly, the LDP.exe console allows you to view and edit instance contents. As with the ADSI Edit tool, you must connect and then bind to the instance you need to work with. Remember that you must be an administrator of the instance to perform administrative operations on it. Use the following procedure:

1. Launch LDP.exe from the command line or from Server Manager under the Active Directory Lightweight Directory Service, Advanced Tools section.

2. On the Connection menu, click Connect.

3. Type the name of the server you want to connect to and the port number to use. Select SSL if you are using a Secure LDAP port. Click OK.

4. On the Connection menu, click Bind.

5. If your account has the required permissions, select Bind As Currently Logged On User. If not, select Bind With Credentials and type the appropriate credentials. Click OK.

6. On the View menu, click Tree to fill the tree pane.

7. In the BaseDN dialog box, click the down arrow to view the list of distinguished names, and select the name of your instance. Click OK.

   From this point, you can use the tree pane to identify where you want to work inside the instance. Explore the various menus to see which operations you can perform with LDP.exe, and then close LDP.exe.

> **MORE INFO** **USING LDP.EXE WITH AD LDS INSTANCES**
>
> For more information on using LDP.exe with AD LDS instances, see *http://technet2.microsoft .com/windowsserver2008/en/library/141900a7-445c-4bd3-9ce3-5ff53d70d10a1033.mspx.*

Using the Schema Snap-in to Work with Instances

You can also use the Active Directory Schema snap-in to create custom consoles to manage AD LDS instance schemas. Remember that to use this snap-in, you must first register it on the server (this was previously covered in Chapter 2, "Administering Active Directory Domain Services"). Use the following command in an elevated command prompt:

```
regsvr32 schmmgmt.dll
```

You're now ready to load the Schema snap-in and view the schema of your instances. Remember to use administrative credentials for the instance.

1. Click Start, and then type **mmc** in the Search box. Press Enter.

2. In the empty MMC, click Add/Remove Snap-in on the File menu.

3. Locate the Active Directory Schema snap-in in the Available Snap-ins list, click Add, and then click OK.

4. Save the console with an appropriate name. Make sure you save it in an appropriate location.

5. The Schema snap-in binds to the Active Directory Domain Services directory by default. To bind to an AD LDS instance, right-click Active Directory Schema in the tree pane and click Change Active Directory Domain Controller.

6. In the Change Directory Server dialog box, select This Domain Controller Or AD LDS Instance, click <Type A Directory Server Name[:Port] Here>, type the server name with the port number separated by a colon, and then press Enter. Click OK.

7. In the warning dialog box, click Yes to change servers.

You can now view the schema for this instance. Save this console again to save these settings. Note the similarities between the schema of an AD LDS instance and the one for an AD DS directory.

> **NOTE CREATING A MULTI-AD LDS CONSOLE**
>
> If you want to create one console with multiple AD LDS instance schemas, just add additional Schema snap-ins to your console. Use one snap-in for each instance you want to connect to. When you reopen the console it links to each instance, saving you time.

Using Active Directory Sites And Services to Work with Instances

As with the other Active Directory tools, you can manage AD LDS instances with the Active Directory Sites And Services console. However, before you can do so, you must import the MS-ADLDS-DisplaySpecifiers.ldf file to update the instance's schema to support the appropriate objects. This must be done for each instance you want to manage with this console. To do so, perform the following steps:

1. Begin by adding the LDIF file to your instance if it hasn't already been done. To do so, start by opening an elevated command prompt.

2. Move to the %SystemRoot%\ADAM folder. For example, type **cd \windows\adam**.

3. Import the LDIF file into the instance:

```
ldifde -i -f MS-ADLDS-DisplaySpecifiers.ldf -s servername:portnumber
    -b username domainname password
```

4. Close the command prompt.

5. Launch Active Directory Sites And Services from the Administrative Tools program group.

6. The console binds to the Active Directory Domain Services directory by default. To bind to an AD LDS instance, right-click Active Directory Sites And Services in the tree pane and click Change Domain Controller.

7. In the Change Directory Server dialog box, select This Domain Controller Or AD LDS Instance and click <Type A Directory Server Name[:Port] Here>. Type the server name with the port number separated by a colon, and then press Enter. Click OK.

8. In the warning dialog box, click Yes to change servers.

   You can now work with the replication parameters for the instance. Note that the server name uses the Servername$InstanceName format to illustrate that it is not a domain controller.

> **MORE INFO** **AD LDS TOOLS AND INSTANCES**
>
> For more information on AD LDS tools and instances, go to *http://technet2.microsoft.com/ windowsserver2008/en/library/141900a7-445c-4bd3-9ce3-5ff53d70d10a1033.mspx.*

EXAM TIP

You cannot use graphical tools on Server Core. Use the graphical tools from a full Windows installation or from a client system running Remote Server Administration Tools (RSAT) to remotely manage instances located on Server Core installations.

Working with AD LDS instances requires care and attention, because almost every activity is performed either through the command line or by using distinguished names. As you probably have seen when working with AD DS, typographical errors are the bane of any administrator working with these tools. The same applies to AD LDS. Be sure to double-check all your entries before you run any command or create and manage any object by using its distinguished name.

Using Active Directory Module for Windows PowerShell to Work with Instances

You can also use Windows PowerShell to interact with or automate AD LDS administration. AD LDS administration with PowerShell is very much like the administration of AD DS through the same tool. Many of the same cmdlets are available. To administer AD LDS with PowerShell, perform the following steps:

1. Launch Windows PowerShell. To do so, open Active Directory Module For Windows PowerShell from the Administrative Tools program group.

2. You are ready to work with an AD LDS instance. You can perform several activities. For example:

   ■ Get information from an AD LDS instance:

   ```
   Get-ADGroupMember -identity 'distinguishedname of the group' -server
       'servername:port' -partition 'distinguishedname of the partition' |
       FT Name,DistinguishedName -A
   ```

   This provides a list of the members of a specific group within the instance. Remember that you need to provide the name of the group, the server name, and the port for the

AD LDS instance, as well as the name of the partition where the group is located. Also remember that all names are distinguished names.

- Create objects within an AD LDS instance:

```
New-ADUser -name 'username' -DisplayName 'display name'
  -server 'servername:port'
  -path 'distinguishedname of the path where the user will be located'
```

This creates a new user in a specific location within an AD LDS instance. Remember that you need to provide the name of the user, the display name for the user, the server name, and the port for the AD LDS instance, as well as the name of the location for the user. All names are distinguished names.

- Remove objects within an AD LDS instance:

```
Remove-ADUser -identity 'username' -server 'servername:port'
  -path 'distinguishedname of the path where the user is located'
```

This removes a user from a specific location within an AD LDS instance. Remember that you need to provide the name of the user, the server name, and the port for the AD LDS instance, as well as the name of the location for the user. All names are distinguished names.

As you can see, you can use many of the AD DS PowerShell cmdlets to work with AD LDS instances. The major difference is that you need to provide the path to the instance—server name and port number—to access it with PowerShell.

PRACTICE   Working with AD LDS Instances

In this practice, you create your first AD LDS instance, as well as a replica. Then you manage replication between the two instances. For this, you need the two servers listed in the "Before You Begin" section of this chapter.

EXERCISE 1   Create an AD LDS Instance

In this exercise, you create your first AD LDS instance. You previously installed the AD LDS service on both of the member servers mentioned in the "Before You Begin" section of this chapter. Use the values in Table 14-5 to perform this exercise.

TABLE 14-5 Instance Creation Values

ITEM	VALUE
Instance Name	ADLDSInstance
Ports	50,004 for LDAP 50,005 for Secure LDAP
Application Partition Name	CN=ADLDSInstance,dc=contoso,dc=com
Data Paths	D:\ADLDS\ADLDSInstance\Data

ITEM	VALUE
Service Account	Network Service
Administration Account	Contoso\Administrator
LDIF Files for Import	MS-AdamSyncMetadata.ldf
	MS-ADLDS-DisplaySpecifiers.ldf
	MS-AZMan.ldf
	MS-InetOrgPerson.ldf
	MS-User.ldf
	MS-UserProxy.ldf
	MS-UserProxyFull.ldf

Make a practice of filling out a table similar to Table 14-5 each time you create a new instance of AD LDS. Because a server can host a multitude of AD LDS instances, it is a very good practice to document each one.

1. Begin by making sure your domain controller, SERVER01.contoso.com, and your member servers, SERVER03.contoso.com and SERVER04.contoso.com, are running.

2. Log on to SERVER03.contoso.com with the domain Administrator account.

   Remember that, in production, you need only local administrative rights for operations with AD LDS.

3. Launch the Active Directory Lightweight Directory Services Setup Wizard from the Administrative Tools program group.

4. Review the information on the Welcome page and click Next.

5. On the Setup Options page, select A Unique Instance and click Next.

6. On the Instance Name page, type **ADLDSInstance** and click Next.

   When you name the instance, you also name the service that will run that instance. Note that the service name will be ADAM_*instancename*, but the name listed in the Services console will be *instancename* alone.

7. On the Ports page, provide the ports to use to communicate with this instance. Use 50,004 for LDAP and 50,005 for the SSL port number. Click Next.

8. On the Application Directory Partition page, click Yes, Create An Application Directory Partition. Provide the application partition name, in this case **CN=ADLDSInstance, dc=contoso,dc=com**, and click Next.

   You must always supply a distinguished name.

9. On the File Locations page, change the paths to D:\ADLDS\ADLDSInstance\Data and click Next.

   Because this is a directory store, it should be placed on a disk that is separate from the operating system, such as the D drive. You can also use separate subfolders for the data files and the data recovery files.

10. On the Service Account Selection page, select Network Service Account and click Next.

   Microsoft Windows selects the Network Service account by default. This account has limited local access rights and is a protected account. You should usually use a proper service account, but Network Service suffices for the purpose of the exercise.

11. On the AD LDS Administrators page, select Currently Logged On User and click Next.

   You should usually use a predefined group, but the Administrator account suffices for the purpose of this exercise.

12. On the Importing LDIF Files page, select all the listed LDIF files and click Next.

13. On the Ready To Install page, review your selections and click Next.

   AD LDS installs the new instance.

14. Click Finish.

   Your first instance has been created. Open Server Manager and expand the Roles\Active Directory Lightweight Directory Services node to view the results of your operation.

   AD LDS creates log files during the creation of the instance. These files are located in the %SystemRoot%\Debug folder and are named ADAMSetup.log and ADAMSetup_loader.log. You can review them if you find issues during the creation of the instance. Also, creating an instance creates a service for the instance. You can launch the Services console from the Administrative Tools program group to verify the existence of this service.

EXERCISE 2   Create an AD LDS Replica Instance

In this exercise, you create your first AD LDS replica instance, on the second member server you created.

1. Make sure your domain controller, SERVER01.contoso.com, and your member servers, SERVER03.contoso.com and SERVER04.contoso.com, are running.

2. Log on to SERVER04.contoso.com with the domain Administrator account.

3. Launch the Active Directory Lightweight Directory Services Setup Wizard from the Administrative Tools program group.

4. Review the information on the Welcome page and click Next.

5. Under Setup Options, select A Replica Of An Existing Instance and click Next.

6. On the Instance Name page, type **ADLDSInstance** and click Next.

7. On the Ports page, provide the ports to communicate with this instance. Use 50,004 for LDAP and 50,005 for the SSL port number. Click Next.

8. On the Joining A Configuration Set page, under Server, click Browse to locate SERVER03. Type **SERVER03**, and then click Check Names. Click OK, and then type **50004** in the LDAP Port field. Click Next.

9. On the Administrative Credentials For The Configuration Set page, select Currently Logged On User and click Next.

   You should usually use a group, but the Administrator account suffices for the purpose of this exercise.

10. On the Copying Application Directory Partitions page, select the CN=ADLDSInstance, dc=contoso,dc=com partition and click Next.

11. On the File Locations page, change the paths to D:\ADLDS\ADLDSInstance\Data and click Next.

12. On the Service Account Selection page, select Network Service Account and click Next.

    You should usually use a proper service account, but Network Service suffices for the purpose of the exercise.

13. On the AD LDS Administrators page, select Currently Logged On User and click Next.

    You should usually use a group, but the Administrator account suffices for the purpose of this exercise.

14. On the Ready to Install page, review your selections and click Next.

    AD LDS installs the new instance.

15. Click Finish.

    Your replica has been created.

EXERCISE 3   Manage Replication Between AD LDS Replicas

In this exercise, you view the replication parameters between your two instances. You do not need to update the instances to support Active Directory Sites And Services objects because you imported all LDIF files in Exercise 1 when you created the source instance.

1. Begin by making sure your domain controller, SERVER01.contoso.com, and your member servers, SERVER03.contoso.com and SERVER04.contoso.com, are running.

2. Log on to SERVER04.contoso.com with the domain Administrator account.

3. Launch Active Directory Sites And Services from the Administrative Tools program group.

   The console binds to the Active Directory Domain Services directory by default.

4. To bind to the AD LDS instance, right-click Active Directory Sites And Services in the tree pane and click Change Domain Controller.

5. In the Change Directory Server dialog box, select This Domain Controller Or AD LDS Instance and click <Type A Directory Server Name[:Port] Here>. Type **SERVER03:50004** and press Enter. Click OK.

6. In the warning dialog box, click Yes to change servers.

7. Expand the Active Directory Sites And Services tree completely. You can do so by pressing the asterisk key (*) on your numerical keypad several times. This displays the replication structure for this instance.

   Next you create a new site and move one of the instance objects into this site.

8. Right-click Sites in the tree pane and click New Site.

9. Name the site **Replication01**, select the DEFAULTIPSITELINK object and click OK.

   Your new site link is created, and Active Directory Sites And Services outlines the next steps you must perform. (See Figure 14-5.)

10. Click OK to close the dialog box.

    In this case, you do not perform all activities. You only move SERVER04 to the new site link.

11. Expand Replication01.

12. Click SERVER04$ADLDSInstance, located under Default-First-Site-Name, and drag it to the Servers container under Replication01.

13. In the Moving Objects warning box, click Yes to move the object. The object now appears under the Replication01 site.

   This exercise shows you how to work with instances and control replication. In the real world, you must perform all the tasks listed in Figure 14-5 to create proper replication partnerships.

FIGURE 14-5 Required tasks to complete a replication partnership

---

MORE INFO   **AD LDS REPLICATION**

For more information on AD LDS replication, go to *http://technet2.microsoft.com/ windowsserver2008/en/library/9d4b4004-9f26-4545-a1e4-8e527102f0a71033.mspx*.

Lesson Summary

- The toolset used to control AD LDS instances is very similar to the toolset used for AD DS. Refer to the tools listed in Table 14-3 for a complete list of the tools you can use with AD LDS instances.

- You can create instances both with the graphical interface through the AD LDS Setup tool and through the command line with the ADAMInstall.exe command. In both cases, you must plan for all the instance prerequisites first. When using the ADAMInstall.exe tool, you must first prepare an answer file with these values.

- Working with AD LDS instances means working with distinguished names. Distinguished names use a hierarchical structure that is similar to the hierarchical structure of AD DS forests.

- Working with AD LDS instances means working with server names and port numbers. As a best practice, note each server name and each port number for the instances you create. In fact, always document each instance you create, listing all the values you use to create it.

Lesson Review

You can use the following question to test your knowledge of the information in Lesson 2, "Configuring and Using AD LDS." The question is also available on the companion CD if you prefer to review them in electronic form.

> **NOTE ANSWERS**
>
> Answers to these questions and explanations of why each answer choice is right or wrong are located in the "Answers" section at the end of the book.

1. You are a local server administrator with contoso.com. One of your jobs is to manage AD LDS instances on SERVER03. Recently, you had to install four instances on SERVER03. SERVER03 is a member server of your domain. You began with the default settings for the port selections of each instance. Now you need to modify the schema of the first instance you installed, Instance1. You register the Active Directory Schema snap-in on the server and create a custom Active Directory Schema console. Yet, when you try to connect to the schema of the first instance, you keep getting an error message. Which of the following is most likely to be the problem?

   A. Instance1 does not include a schema, and you cannot edit it.

   B. You cannot modify the schema of an instance with the Active Directory Schema snap-in. You must use the LDP.exe command to do so.

   C. You cannot modify the schema of an instance with the Active Directory Schema snap-in. Modifying the schema of an instance is performed by importing LDIF files with the LDIFDE.exe command.

   D. You cannot connect to the instance with the Active Directory Schema snap-in because, by default, it uses the same port as your Active Directory Domain Services directory.

Chapter Review

To further practice and reinforce the skills you learned in this chapter, you can perform the following tasks:

- Review the chapter summary.
- Review the list of key terms introduced in this chapter.
- Complete the case scenario. This scenario sets up a real-world situation involving the topics of this chapter and asks you to create a solution.
- Complete the suggested practices.
- Take a practice test.

Chapter Summary

- As its name suggests, AD LDS is a very portable and malleable directory service. It should always be considered first when you are faced with a schema modification of your network operating system, AD DS. If it is possible to use AD LDS instead of AD DS to integrate an application, use AD LDS. There are, however, occasions when you cannot replace AD DS with AD LDS.

- AD LDS runs on both the full installation and the Server Core installation of Windows Server 2008 R2. Because of its light weight, AD LDS is a prime candidate for virtualization through Hyper-V.

- AD DS and AD LDS use the same installation process. Begin by installing the role, and then create the directory service instance through a custom wizard or an unattended setup process. To remove AD LDS, you must first remove the instances you create, and then you can remove the role from the server.

- After you have installed the AD LDS service, you can begin to work with it to store directory-related data for different applications. Begin by becoming familiar with the AD LDS tool set. Then, after you understand which tools you can use to manage AD LDS, you can begin to create your first instances. When you've created your instances, you can secure them to ensure that they are properly protected. Then move on to the creation of replicas for these instances so that you can install them on various other systems and control replication so that instances located on different computers can be updated through multimaster replication.

Key Terms

The following terms were introduced in this chapter. Do you know what they mean?

- application partitions
- instances

Case Scenario

In the following case scenario, you apply what you've learned about Active Directory Lightweight Directory Services. You can find answers to the questions in this scenario in the "Answers" section at the end of this book.

Case Scenario: Determining AD LDS Instance Prerequisites

Contoso, Ltd., has been working with several custom applications that rely on custom information stores. Recently, Contoso managers decided to move to Active Directory Domain Services, and they have also decided to standardize on Windows Server 2008 R2 technologies. Because of this, they want to move the information stores in their former applications to Active Directory Lightweight Directory Services instances.

They turn to you as the potential administrator of AD LDS within the organization to help them address some specific questions in relation to instance prerequisites. Specifically, they want to know:

1. Where should the files for each instance be stored?
2. How should each instance be named?
3. Which ports should be used to connect to the instances?
4. Should application directory partitions be used, and why?
5. How should each instance be run?

Suggested Practices

To help you successfully master the exam objectives presented in this chapter, complete the following tasks.

Work with AD LDS Instances

Because there is only one exam objective for this topic, focus on three key tasks to help you prepare for the exam:

- Installing the AD LDS server role
- Configuring an AD LDS instance
- Accessing the AD LDS instance through its administration tools

    Also, perform the following practices.

- Practice 1 On a server—virtual or physical—that is running either Windows Server 2008 R2 Standard edition or Windows Server 2008 R2 Enterprise edition, install the AD LDS server role. This server should not be a domain controller and should be a member server of an Active Directory Domain Services domain.

- Practice 2 Create an AD LDS instance named MyADLDSInstance. Make sure you run through the AD LDS instance prerequisites preparation before you create the instance. Choose ports 50,010 and 50,011 for your instance. Create an application partition within the instance and assign a service account to it. Use an AD DS security group to manage the instance, and make sure your account is a member of that group. Store the instance on a data drive that is separate from the operating system. Make sure you import all LDIF files into the instance when you create it.

- Practice 3 After the instance is created, practice connecting and working with the instance. Use the following tools:
  - Active Directory Schema snap-in
  - Active Directory Sites And Services
  - *LDP.exe*
  - ADSI Edit
  - Windows PowerShell

Use these tools to explore the instance and view its content. You can also practice creating objects within the instance. For example, create an OU and add both a group and a user within the OU.

Take a Practice Test

The practice tests on this book's companion CD offer many options. For example, you can test yourself on just one exam objective, or you can test yourself on all the 70-640 certification exam content. You can set up the test so that it closely simulates the experience of taking a certification exam, or you can set it up in study mode so that you can look at the correct answers and explanations after you answer each question.

> **MORE INFO** **PRACTICE TESTS**
>
> For details about all the practice test options available, see the "How to Use the Practice Tests" section in this book's Introduction.

CHAPTER 15

Active Directory Certificate Services and Public Key Infrastructures

Public key infrastructures (PKIs) are becoming core infrastructure elements for all modern organizations. Almost every organization today has some use for public key certificates. Whether it is to secure wireless communications, to offer secure commercial services on websites, to integrate Secure Sockets Layer (SSL) virtual private networks, or even just to sign email and identify themselves in web environments, organizations everywhere are using PKI certificates.

With PKI certificates comes the infrastructure itself—an infrastructure you must first create and then manage. Microsoft has included the ability to generate and maintain PKIs directly in the OS for some years now. In the case of Windows Server 2008 R2, this ability is provided by Active Directory Certificate Services (AD CS), known simply as Certificate Services in previous versions of Microsoft Windows. Because of this, organizations are now choosing to implement and manage their own infrastructures.

> **MORE INFO**   **PUBLIC KEY INFRASTRUCTURES**
>
> For more information on the various aspects of a PKI, look up the PKI white paper series at *http://www.reso-net.com/articles.asp?m=8* under the Building A World Of Trust section.

However, the very nature of PKIs is that they are not based on software alone. Because PKI certificates are designed to prove to others that you are who you say you are, you must implement administrative processes that are designed to demonstrate effectively that each person who receives a certificate from you is really who he or she claims to be. By providing certificates to everyone in your organization, you provide them with an undeniable tool—a tool that guarantees the identity of each person. Public key infrastructures are designed to build a world of trust in an untrustworthy environment.

In fact, PKIs can be used to extend the authority that your organization has beyond the borders of the network it controls. Although Active Directory Domain Services (AD DS), as a network operating system (NOS) directory, is primarily intended for providing authentication and authorization within the corporate network boundaries, AD CS is designed, like the remaining three Active Directory technologies, to provide these services to both internal and external networks. However, when you extend your organization's authority beyond your network boundaries with AD CS, you should rely on a third-party commercial certificate authority (CA) to support the claims you establish through the certificates you publish. (See Figure 15-1.)

FIGURE 15-1 Active Directory Certificate Services providing services both inside and outside a network

For example, when you go to a website using the Secure Hypertext Transfer Protocol (HTTPS) that contains an SSL certificate, the certificate proves to you that you really are where you intend to be. When you verify the certificate, you see that it includes the server name, the organization name, and the issuing certificate authority. The certificate works with your browser because browsers such as Microsoft Internet Explorer or Firefox already include a list of trusted commercial CAs that manage the certification process as a business, as shown in Figure 15-2.

FIGURE 15-2 Browsers such as Internet Explorer and Firefox listing trusted CAs

The trusted CAs list is automatically updated through the update mechanisms for your operating system. In Windows 7 and Windows Server 2008 R2, this update is controlled through a Group Policy setting that is turned on by default. In earlier Windows operating systems, the update of Trusted Root Certificates was a component of Windows, accessed through Control Panel.

MORE INFO **CERTIFICATE SUPPORT IN WINDOWS 7**

For more information on Windows 7 certificate support, go to *http://technet.microsoft .com/en-us/library/dd631686(WS.10).aspx*. For a list of Trusted Root Certificates in Windows, go to *http://support.microsoft.com/kb/931125*.

When you issue your own certificates—certificates that do not originate from external CAs—you must include your own organization as a trusted CA on the computers of the people who will be using these certificates. You can do this when you work with the users of your own organization because you control their computers, but when the users are people whose computers you do not control, this becomes problematic. Asking them to accept your certificate is like asking them to trust you when they don't know you.

This is one of the reasons that PKI architectures are built the way they are. Essentially, all members of a public key infrastructure are chained together in a hierarchy that ends at the topmost CA. This CA is ultimately responsible for each of the certificates included in the chain. For example, if you obtain a certificate from your organization and your organization obtained its master certificate from a trusted commercial CA (as shown in Figure 15-3), your certificate is automatically trusted because each browser already trusts the commercial CA. As you can imagine, this external CA must use a stringent validation program; otherwise, that certificate provider won't be in business for long.

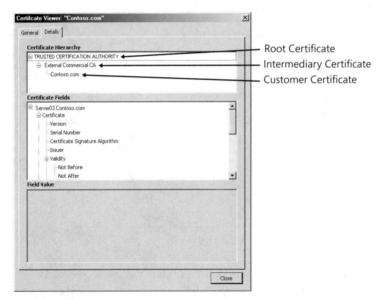

FIGURE 15-3 A trusted certificate chain

Several technologies rely on PKI certificates for operation. One very good example is Microsoft Exchange Server 2007. Because Exchange Server is divided into several roles—Hub Transport, Client Access, Mailbox, and more—and because it transports private information over TCP/IP connections, each server automatically generates a self-signed certificate at installation. Then, through the use of these certificates, email is transported over secure connections. This works well for internal communications, but as soon as you open the doors to communicate with the outside world, such as by providing Microsoft Outlook Web Access (OWA) to employees outside your internal network, you must replace the self-signed certificate with one purchased from a valid vendor. Otherwise, none of your users will be able to access OWA from external Internet locations.

In some cases, implementing an internal-only PKI makes sense because you are proving who you are only to yourself, but it becomes more difficult and even redundant when dealing with the Internet. How can you prove to others that you are who you claim to be when you are the only one saying so? If you are the one who issues the certificates that you use for e-commerce, no one will trust you. You must always keep this in mind whenever you are considering the use of AD CS.

Exam objectives in this chapter:

- Install Active Directory Certificate Services.
- Configure CA server settings.
- Manage certificate templates.
- Manage enrollments.
- Manage certificate revocations.

Lessons in this chapter:

Before You Begin

To complete the lessons in this chapter, you must have installed:

- Windows Server 2008 R2 on a physical or virtual computer. The machine should be named SERVER01 and should be a domain controller in the contoso.com domain. The details for this setup are presented in Chapter 1, "Creating an Active Directory Domain."
- Windows Server 2008 R2 Enterprise edition on a physical or virtual computer that should be named SERVER03 and should be a member server within the contoso.com domain. This machine will host the AD CS CAs that you will install and create through the exercises in this chapter. Ideally, this computer would also include a D drive (10 GB recommended) to store the data for AD CS. SERVER03 should have at least 1024 MB RAM.

- Windows Server 2008 R2 Enterprise edition on a physical or virtual computer named SERVER04 that should be a member server within the contoso.com domain. This computer will be used to host an issuing CA for AD CS. Ideally, this computer would also include a D drive (10 GB recommended) to store the data for AD CS. SERVER04 should have at least 1024 MB RAM.

This setup is sufficient to test basic AD CS installation and configuration. Testing all AD CS capabilities requires up to five computers, and even if they are installed as virtual machines, this might be beyond the laboratory capabilities of some readers.

Note that if you installed SERVER03 and SERVER04 for use in the exercises in Chapter 14, "Active Directory Lightweight Directory Services," you can reuse them here without impact.

 REAL WORLD

Danielle Ruest and Nelson Ruest

In 2003, the Canadian government issued a mandate regarding youthful offenders. Several problems and incorrect decisions had been made when judging youthful offender cases in court because some government representatives—federal, provincial, and municipal police; parole officers; and Ministry of Youth or Social Services representatives—would have information about the youth that was not available to the judging party. To resolve this issue, the government passed a law requiring all parties interacting with youthful offenders to share data among themselves so that the judging party would have all pertinent information on hand to make a more informed decision.

As infrastructure architects, we were hired to develop a system to facilitate this information sharing. Because each party affected by the law did not trust the others, the task held challenges. The police especially did not want their information to transit on the Internet nor even leave their premises. In addition, each party used different technologies to store the data. We needed to devise a solution that would provide complete security for information transfer yet also provide absolute proof that the data was not compromised in any way.

At the same time, various Canadian governmental entities were in the process of implementing PKIs to provide a secure identity process for their employees and any vendors who interacted with them. We decided to rely on this infrastructure for our solution. In fact, our clients were among the very first to take advantage of this new PKI implementation.

We instructed the developers to use Microsoft SQL Server and the .NET Framework to create the application that would act as a central repository for all the collected information. Then we created routines in each local data repository to extract the information on a regular basis. That's when the PKI became important. Because we wanted to create extraction files and then send them over the Internet, each partner needed two PKI certificates. The first was a personal certificate that would be used to identify each partner. The second was a server authentication certificate that would be used to identify the start and end points of all communication links. To obtain these certificates, each partner had to first undergo a training program from the governmental PKI agency to learn about its responsibilities when a certificate was assigned to it and then visit an official governmental representative for an identity verification process before it could obtain the certificates.

When everyone had certificates, we implemented them into the solution. First, we used public and private keys to sign the compressed extraction files digitally. Each partner signed the compressed file with its private key, and then the other partners used the signing partner's public key to decrypt it. When the file was signed and encrypted, it was transported over the Internet through an IP Security (IPSec) tunnel that was created using the server authentication certificates. Each certificate was validated against the Certificate Revocation Lists maintained by the governmental PKI agency every time the process was used. Any invalid certificates were automatically dropped by the application.

The result was a .NET web-based application. Because the solution was based on PKI and the PKI agency was a trusted authority, each partner could now trust the others without reservation. This is the value of PKI and certificate services: They provide a foundation for trust in an untrustworthy world. Five years later, the application is still running.

Lesson 1: Understanding and Installing Active Directory Certificate Services

Active Directory Certificate Services provide a variety of services regarding public key infrastructures and certificate usage in general. Using Windows Server 2008 R2 and AD CS, you can support the following certificate usage scenarios:

- You can encrypt all data files. One of the most common problems in IT today is the loss or theft of mobile computer systems. If data is encrypted, the loss is minor, but if data is unprotected, it could affect your ability to do business. With Windows Server 2008 R2 and Windows 7, you can encrypt all user data files automatically through Group Policy objects and enforce the strong passwords required to protect them further. The Encrypting File System (EFS) relies on certificates to lock and unlock encrypted files.

- You can encrypt all remote communications. Windows Server 2008 R2 includes both IPSec and Secure Sockets Tunneling Protocol (SSTP) virtual private network connections. Both rely on certificates to authenticate the start and end points of the communication.

- You can secure all email messages. Windows Server 2008 R2 includes support for Secure Multipurpose Internet Mail Extensions (S/MIME), the standard email security protocol. Signed messages are protected from tampering and prove they originate from the correct person.

- You can secure all logons. Using smart cards, you can use certificates to support the logon process and ensure that all users, especially administrators, are who they say they are.

- You can secure all websites. Using Windows Server 2008 R2 and Internet Information Services (IIS) 7.0, you can secure all communications to your websites, ensuring the safety of all your client transactions.

- You can secure servers to validate their authenticity. For example, when you assign certificates to servers in a Network Access Protection (NAP) infrastructure or in any other secure service, computers in your network know they are working with your own servers and not with other servers trying to impersonate yours.

- You can secure all wireless communication. Using Windows Server 2008 R2 and Windows 7, you can ensure that all wireless communication originates from trusted endpoints.

- You can protect all data from tampering. Using Active Directory Rights Management Services (AD RMS), you can rely on Windows Server 2008 R2 to protect from tampering with or misuse of the information you generate.

In addition, consider issuing a certificate to all your employees to help them certify who they are in all their Internet transactions. Remember that all external certificates should include a trusted CA within them to allow them to work automatically with any browser.

Understanding AD CS

Active Directory Certificate Services is the engine that Windows Server 2008 R2 relies on to manage public key certificates. By using AD CS, you can build a comprehensive PKI hierarchy that can be used to issue and manage certificates within your organization. AD CS is composed of several components:

- **Certificate authorities**   CAs are the servers that you use to issue and manage certificates. Because of the hierarchical nature of a PKI, AD CS supports both root and subordinate or child CAs. The root CA usually issues certificates to subordinate CAs, which enables them in turn to issue certificates to users, computers, and services. The subordinate CA can issue certificates only while its own certificate is valid. When this certificate expires, the subordinate CA must request a certificate renewal from its root CA. For this reason, root CAs often have certificate durations that are much longer than any of their subordinates. In turn, subordinate CAs usually have certificate durations that are longer than those they issue to users, computers, or services.

- **CA Web Enrollment**   By using Web Enrollment, users can connect to the CA through a web browser to request certificates, perform smart card enrollments, or obtain Certificate Revocation Lists (CRLs). CRLs provide users of your public key infrastructure with a list of certificates that have been invalidated or revoked by your organization. Systems that rely on PKI poll CA servers to obtain CRLs each time a certificate is presented to them. If the certificate presented to them is on this list, it is automatically refused.

- **Online responder**   This service is designed to respond to specific certificate validation requests through the Online Certificate Status Protocol (OCSP). Using an online responder (OR), the system relying on PKI does not need to obtain a full CRL and can submit a validation request for a specific certificate. The online responder decodes the validation request and determines whether the certificate is valid. When it determines the status of the requested certificate, it sends back an encrypted response containing the information to the requester. Using online responders is much faster and more efficient than using CRLs. AD CS includes online responders as a new feature in Windows Server 2008 R2.

MORE INFO   **ONLINE RESPONDERS**

Online responders are often an alternative to or an extension of CRLs that support the certificate revocation process. Microsoft online responders comply with request for comments (RFC) 2560 for OCSP. For more information about this RFC, go to *http://go.microsoft.com/fwlink/?LinkID=67082.*

■ **Network Device Enrollment Service**   Devices that use low-level operating systems, such as routers and switches, can also participate in a PKI through the Network Device Enrollment Service (NDES) by using the Simple Certificate Enrollment Protocol (SCEP), a protocol developed by Cisco Systems, Inc. These devices usually do not participate in an AD DS directory and, therefore, do not have AD DS accounts. However, through the NDES and the SCEP, they can also become part of the PKI hierarchy that is maintained and managed by your AD CS installation.

These four components form the core of the AD CS service in Windows Server 2008 R2.

MORE INFO   **NEW FEATURES IN AD CS**

For more information on the new features that AD CS supports in Windows Server 2008 R2, go to *http://technet.microsoft.com/en-us/library/dd448537%28WS.10%29.aspx.*

Stand-alone vs. Enterprise CAs

Your biggest concern when preparing to deploy an AD CS is how to structure the four basic services that AD CS offers. Initially, you should be concerned about the first role: the CAs you need to deploy. AD CS supports two CA types:

■ **Stand-alone CA**   A CA that is not necessarily integrated in an AD DS directory service. A stand-alone CA is a CA running either on a member server or on a stand-alone server—a server in a workgroup. Stand-alone CAs are often used as internal root CAs and are taken offline for security purposes after they have been used to generate certificates for subordinate servers. Certificate issuing and approval are performed manually, and certificates are based on standard templates, which you cannot modify. The clients of a stand-alone CA can be members of an AD DS directory, but AD DS directory membership is not a requirement. Stand-alone CAs can run Windows Server 2008 R2 Standard edition, Windows Server 2008 R2 Enterprise edition, or Windows Server 2008 R2 Datacenter edition.

■ **Enterprise CA**   A CA that is integrated in an AD DS directory service. Enterprise CAs are usually member servers and are often used as issuing CAs—CAs that are subordinate to another CA in a hierarchy but that actually provide certificates to end users and endpoint devices. Issuing CAs are usually online at all times and must be highly available. Because they are integrated in AD DS directories, enterprise CAs automatically issue and approve certificates when requested by members of the directory. Certificate templates are more advanced and can be edited to meet specific requirements. All encryption keys are protected through directory integration. Enterprise CAs can run only on Windows Server 2008 R2 Enterprise edition or Windows Server 2008 R2 Datacenter edition.

Table 15-1 outlines the features supported by stand-alone versus enterprise CAs.

TABLE 15-1 Comparing Standalone and Enterprise CAs

FEATURE	STAND-ALONE	ENTERPRISE
Publish CA configuration to Active Directory Domain Services directories.	Optional	Mandatory
CA certificate data integration with AD DS forests.	Optional (manual process)	Mandatory and Automatic
Certificate Revocation List publication in AD DS forests.	Optional (manual process)	Mandatory and Automatic; also includes Delta CRLs and cross certificates
AD DS forest publication assigned on a per-template level as an attribute of the template.	n/a	Supported
Web enrollment for certificate requests and validation.	Supported	Supported
Certificate Microsoft Management Console (MMC) for certificate requests and validation.	n/a	Supported
Certificate requests through HTTP or HTTPS.	Supported	Supported
Certificate requests through the remote procedure call (RPC) along with the Distributed Component Object Model (DCOM).	n/a	Default mode
V1 templates with custom object identifiers (OID) as source for certificates.	Default	n/a
V2 and V3 customizable templates as source for certificates. Templates can also be duplicated.	n/a	Default
User input during certificate requests.	Manual	Retrieved from AD DS
Supported enrollment methods.	Automatic or Pending for all templates	Automatic or Pending and applied on a template basis

FEATURE	STAND-ALONE	ENTERPRISE
Certificate approval process.	Manual	Manual or Automatic through AD DS authentication and access control
Certificate publishing.	Manually to client or CA; can be to AD DS but only through custom policy module	Depends on certificate type and template settings but can be automatically enrolled in client's certificate store and published in AD DS
Certificate publishing and management through AD DS.	n/a	Supported
Deployment options.	Domain controller (DC), member server, or stand-alone server	DC or member server only

As you can see in Table 15-1, stand-alone CAs are focused on delivering specific services and should be considered mostly for stand-alone environments where automation is not required. Good examples are root CAs or CAs located in a perimeter network and offering services to the Internet.

Enterprise CAs should be considered mostly as issuing CAs in internal networks that also include AD DS forest structures. Enterprise CAs automate the certificate allocation process and are very useful when you need to issue certificates to devices for wireless networks or to users for smart card integration. Imagine managing the entire request and approval process manually when you have thousands of users and devices. It could easily become overwhelming.

 EXAM TIP

Learn the differences between stand-alone and enterprise CAs well. These topics are an important part of the AD CS coverage on the exam.

Creating the CA Hierarchy

A second consideration when planning your CA hierarchy is security. Because a CA hierarchy is based on certificate chaining, any compromise of a top-level or root CA automatically compromises all the certificates that are based on it. This is one reason you must secure root CAs as much as possible. In fact, a common practice is to create a tiered CA hierarchy and take the top members of a tiered architecture offline. The logic is that if a server is offline, it is as secure as it can be.

However, determining the number of tiers in your AD CS architecture depends on several other factors as well. You need to consider the size and geographic distribution of your network. You also need to identify the trust relationship that you require between CAs and the certificate holders. Keep in mind that each time a certificate is presented, it must be validated through either a CRL or an online responder, so to use certificates, you must have connectivity of some sort.

Consider also the potential scenarios you intend to support with your AD CS deployment. Will you be interacting with people or partners outside your network? Will you be using smart cards? Will you be using wireless networks? Will you be using IPSec or the new SSTP? Basically, anytime you need to certify the identity of a device, an application, or a user, you must rely on AD CS and, potentially, third-party commercial certificate authorities.

When you have the answers to these questions, you can proceed with the planning of your AD CS hierarchy. When you do so, consider:

- Creating a single-tiered hierarchy with a single root CA only in very rare situations in which you feel the root CA will not be compromised under any circumstance.

- Creating a two-tiered hierarchy with a root CA and issuing CAs when you need to protect the root CA but your organization size and the purpose of the hierarchy does not warrant a more complex hierarchy. In this model, you can take the root CA offline to protect it. (See Figure 15-4.)

FIGURE 15-4 A two-tiered hierarchy

- Creating a three-tiered hierarchy with a root CA, intermediate CAs, and issuing CAs when you need higher levels of security and high availability for the issuing CAs, and your administration model, user population, and geographic scope warrant the extra cost of the additional tier. Multiple intermediate CAs are often used to support different policies in different environments in this model. If you use this model, take both the root and intermediate CAs offline to protect them, as shown in Figure 15-5.

FIGURE 15-5 A three-tiered hierarchy in a geographic deployment

- Creating more than three tiers only in highly complex environments that require the utmost security where the CA infrastructure must be protected at all times.

As you can see, the more tiers you create in a hierarchy, the higher the level of complexity in terms of management and administration. However, the more complex your hierarchy, the more secure it can be. In addition, consider which type of CA you need to deploy in each tier. Table 15-2 outlines the CA type based on the tier model.

TABLE 15-2 Assigning CA Type Based on Tier Model

CA TYPE	ONE-TIER HIERARCHY	TWO-TIER HIERARCHY	THREE-TIER HIERARCHY
Root CA	Enterprise CA (online)	Stand-alone CA (offline)	Stand-alone CA (offline)
Intermediate CA			Stand-alone CA (offline)
Issuing CA		Enterprise CA (online)	Enterprise CA (online)

EXAM TIP

Keep these hierarchies in mind when you take the exam. CA hierarchies are an important aspect of any AD CS deployment.

Best Practices for AD CS Deployments

Architectures using two or more tiers represent the most common deployments of AD CS. When you plan for your AD CS infrastructure, keep the following in mind:

- Avoid single-tiered hierarchies as much as possible, because they are very difficult to protect.
- Root and intermediate CAs (if implemented) should be taken offline as soon as possible after the infrastructure is in place. For this reason, these CAs are excellent candidates for virtualization through Windows Server 2008 R2 Hyper-V. Create a virtual machine (VM), install the AD CS Stand-alone CA role, and then save the machine state as soon as you can.
- Consider removing the VM files for the root CA from the host server as soon as it is taken offline. Store the secured VM in a vault of some type.
- If you use virtualization in support of your AD CS deployment, secure the VMs as much as possible. It is a lot easier to walk away with a VM than with a physical server.
- Consider creating VMs that do not have network connections or that have disabled network connections for the root and intermediate CAs. This ensures an even higher level of protection. Certificates are transferred from these servers through either USB devices or floppy disks.
- Control the removable devices on root and intermediate CAs through device protection settings in the Local Security Policy console. This adds a further layer of protection.
- Make sure your CA administrators are highly trustworthy individuals. They control the entire CA hierarchy and, because of this, they are in a very high position of trust.
- Thoroughly secure the data center that hosts the CAs. Control access to the data center, and use smart card administrative logons as much as possible.

- Consider using a single root CA, but adding availability through multiple CA installations as soon as you reach the intermediate and issuing tiers of the hierarchy.

- You cannot change the name of a server after the AD CS service is installed, so plan your server names carefully and make sure you can keep them for a very long time.

- You cannot change a CA from stand-alone to enterprise or vice versa after AD CS is installed. Once again, plan accordingly.

- As a general practice, do not install AD CS on a DC. Although it can be done, endeavor to keep the AD DS server role independent of all other roles except the Domain Name System (DNS) role.

These guidelines will assist you in your AD CS deployment planning phase.

> **MORE INFO** **BEST PRACTICES FOR PKI DEPLOYMENTS**
>
> For additional information on PKI deployments with Windows infrastructures, read "Best Practices for Implementing a Microsoft Windows Server 2003 Public Key Infrastructure" at *http://technet.microsoft.com/en-us/library/cc772670(WS.10).aspx*, or "Designing and Implementing a PKI: Part 1 Design and planning" at *http://blogs.technet.com/b/askds/archive/2009/09/01/designing-and-implementing-a-pki-part-i-design-and-planning.aspx*. They refer to Windows Server 2003 rather than Windows Server 2008 R2, but the practices are valid for any newer version of Windows.

Additional Planning Requirements

You're almost ready to proceed. However, as mentioned earlier, planning and deploying a CA hierarchy is not only a technical activity. You need to have the appropriate administrative processes to support the use of certificates in your network. Three additional considerations must be covered before you can move on to installing AD CS:

- You must consider how you will support certificate enrollment.

- You must consider how you will renew certificates.

- You must create a certificate practice statement (CPS).

The first consideration focuses on how you plan to support certificate requests and distribution. As mentioned earlier, a certificate identifies its holder thoroughly whether it is a user, a machine, or an application. Therefore, you must put in place a requester identification validation process. You don't want to issue a certificate to John Kane when you're not sure the requester is actually John Kane. Third-party certificate authorities use several types of processes for this validation, the most stringent of which involves a visit to the person requesting the certificate by an authorized legal representative of the CA. This means a face-to-face meeting; after the requester is validated, you can provide him or her with a certificate in that name. To protect the certificate further, you can store it on a hardware token such as a smart card and provide that to the requester. It then becomes the responsibility of the requester to protect the certificate and the token that contains it.

However, if you plan to use automatic enrollment through enterprise CAs, you need to make sure that users are properly validated before giving them access to your network. Rely on some form of official identification such as a passport or other governmental ID mechanism. This should already be part of your human resources processes and policies.

The second consideration involves certificate lifetimes. Certificates usually include two key pairs: a private key and a public key. When you encrypt data, you use the private key. When others decrypt the data, they usually use your public key. The longer you use a certificate key pair, the more prone it is to attack or compromise. When you renew a certificate, the renewal generates a new key pair for the certificate. Therefore, you must plan certificate lifetimes and renewals carefully. In fact, you must temper key pair life with the risk of compromise.

In addition, you must ensure that your tiered hierarchy also includes tiered lifetimes. Root CAs should have the longest lifetime, then intermediate CAs if you use them, then issuing CAs, and then issued certificates. For example, you might use a gap of 10 years for each tier in your architecture; that is, assign 10 years per each level in the tier. In a three-tier architecture, use 30 years for the root CA, 20 years for the intermediate CAs, and 10 years for issuing CAs. Then you can assign one or two years to the certificates you issue. The reason for this hierarchy of durations is that each time a certificate expires for a server, all subordinate certificates expire as well. To protect against this eventuality, you give very long durations to servers.

Finally, you must plan and prepare your certificate practice statement. CPSs are based on the certificate policies you create. Policies define the issuing organization's responsibilities in terms of each of the certificate types it issues. The issuing organization is ultimately responsible for any wrongdoing or misuse of the certificates it issued. Because of this, involve the legal, human resources, and security departments of your organization to assist you in defining the policies you use for each certificate type, and then generate your CPS from that. The CPS should include several items, such as a clear definition of who you are; a list of your certificate policies; a general statement of the procedures you use to issue, assign, and revoke certificates; a description of the method used to protect your CAs; and so on.

Another important item that must be included in your CPS is the revocation policy you use. Revocation occurs when you need to cancel a certificate for any reason, usually when someone does not adhere to the policy you defined for that particular certificate type. Remember that revocation is the only method you have of invalidating a certificate when it is misused.

The CPS should be publicly available to both your internal and external CA users. This usually means making it available in some form on the Internet or through intranets.

EXAM TIP

Familiarize yourself with certificate policies and certificate practice statements, because they are a definite part of the exam topics for AD CS.

New AD CS Features in Windows Server 2008 R2

As with other AD technologies in Windows Server 2008 R2, AD CS has been updated to include additional features. Three new features are available:

- Certificate Enrollment and Certificate Enrollment Policy Web Services
- Certificate enrollment across forests
- Better support for high-volume CAs

Each of these features is focused on either better administration of your AD CS deployment or better support for large AD CS deployments.

New AD CS Web Services

The new Web Services for AD CS feature provides support for certificate enrollment over the Hypertext Transfer Protocol (HTTP). The Web Service acts as a proxy between the client and the Certificate Authority. This makes direct communication between the two unnecessary and facilitates certificate enrollment over the Internet as well as across AD DS forests. Mobile workers, business partners, and remote users can now enroll for certificates directly over the Internet, making it simpler to support them. Large organizations or organizations that must interact across AD DS forest boundaries can also enjoy a simpler enrollment process through these Web Services.

> **IMPORTANT CERTIFICATE ENROLLMENT WEB SERVICE IN EXTRANETS**
>
> For the Certificate Enrollment Web Service to submit and support requests for new certificates on behalf of clients, it must be trusted for delegation. When you deploy the Web Service in an extranet, it may increase the threat of a network attack. To protect your network, configure the Web Service and the issuing CA to accept only renewal requests signed with existing certificates. This provides a more secure deployment because it no longer requires delegation. However, this configuration does not support clients without existing certificates.

To work with the new AD CS Web Services, your network configuration must meet the following requirements:

- The forest functional level must be Windows Server 2008 R2.
- Your enterprise CA must be running Windows Server 2008 R2, Windows Server 2008, or Windows Server 2003.
- Client computers must run Windows 7.
- To support cross-forest enrollment, the enterprise CAs in each forest must run either the Enterprise or Datacenter edition of Windows Server.

Rely on this feature if you need either cross-forest enrollment or enrollment over the Internet.

Enrollment across Forests

As mentioned earlier, cross-forest enrollment is provided by the new AD CS Web Services.
However, for cross-forest enrollment to work, the forests must also include a two-way trust
relationship and the forest functional level must be at least Windows Server 2003. If your
organization must rely on multiple forests, and you have PKI deployments within each forest,
you can rely on this feature to facilitate enrollments across your forests. Note that CAs can
now issue certificates across forests with a forest functional level of Windows Server 2003, but
for enrollment to work you need a forest functional level of Windows Server 2008 R2. Client
computers do not need an update to work with this feature.

However, you can simplify your CA deployments by removing CAs from other forests and
centralizing the issuing CA in one single forest. This provides support for certificate use in
multiple forests while running only one AD CS deployment.

High-Volume CAs

Some organizations, such as those that have deployed the Windows Server Network Access
Protection (NAP) feature, may require higher volume certificate management than others.
When you use a technology such as NAP, your CAs issue a vast number of health certificates.
These are used each time a client tries to connect to your network. NAP health certificates are
very short-lived and usually last only a matter of hours before they expire. Because of this,
a CA might issue several different certificates per computer each day. This high volume of
certificates can slow down the CA and have an impact on performance overall.

With Windows Server 2008 R2, organizations can choose to bypass certain CA database
operations to improve CA performance in these scenarios. By default, CAs store both a record
of each certificate request and the issued certificate in the CA database. This means that the
CA database can become quite bulky in large NAP deployments. By bypassing the storage
of certificates in the database—in fact, not storing either the request records or the issued
certificates in the CA database—you can improve the CA's performance and reduce CA
operational costs. This feature is called non-persistent certificate processing.

When you bypass certificate storage in the CA database, you can no longer revoke issued certificates. Although NAP health certificates are short-lived and the potential damage an unrevoked certificate can cause is minimal, be aware that you cannot manage Certificate Revocation Lists after enabling the high-volume feature on a CA.

For more information about high-volume CAs, go to *http://technet.microsoft.com/en-us/ library/ff934598%28WS.10%29.aspx.*

✔ Quick Check

1. What are the types of certificate authorities supported by AD CS?

2. You are planning to install a root CA in a two-tier architecture. Which type of CA should you install?

3. How is the trusted CA list updated in Windows 7 and Windows Server 2008 R2?

4. What are the new features of AD CS in Windows Server 2008 R2?

Quick Check Answers

1. AD CS supports two types of certificate authorities. The stand-alone CA is used in environments that do not need integration with Active Directory Domain Services because it does not interact with AD DS by default. Enterprise CAs are directly integrated into the AD DS directory and can provide automated user or device enrollment.

2. You should install a stand-alone CA. Root CAs are usually taken offline as soon as possible after the deployment of your public key infrastructure. Therefore, it makes sense to use the simplest form of CA supported by AD CS.

3. The trusted root CA list in Windows 7 and Windows Server 2008 R2 is updated through Group Policy settings, which are turned on by default. In previous versions of Windows, the trusted root CA list was a component of Windows controlled through Control Panel.

4. Windows Server 2008 R2 includes three new features for AD CS: new Certificate Enrollment Web Services, cross-forest enrollment, and better support for high-volume CAs.

Installing AD CS

Installing AD CS is a much more involved process than installing Active Directory Lightweight Directory Services (AD LDS). This is because of the choice between stand-alone and enterprise CAs and the subsequent choices that ensue from this original decision.

In most cases, you will install at least a two-tiered structure, installing first a stand-alone CA, then an enterprise CA. In larger organizations, you will deploy several tiers and install several servers in each tier except the root.

Servers hosting the AD CS role should be configured with the following capabilities, whether they are physical or virtual:

- Multiple processors, because this accelerates the certificate allocation process.
- Minimal amounts of RAM, because RAM has little effect on certificate processing. VMs need no more than 512 MB of RAM.
- Separate disks for the certificate store. Ideally, you should have at least one data disk and store the database on it. Issuing servers for large communities should also have a separate disk for log files.
- Key lengths kept to medium sizes, to obtain the best performance from the server. Key lengths have an impact on CPU and disk usage. Short keys require more disk overhead. Long keys require more CPU usage and less disk activity.
- If using physical systems, a redundant array of inexpensive disks (RAID) level that is balanced between reliability and improved performance.

> **IMPORTANT**   **INSTALLATION ON WINDOWS SERVER 2008 R2**
>
> The AD CS role can now be installed on Server Core in Windows Server 2008 R2. The installation is provided by a Visual Basic script and installs all of the required components to run a CA. This means that if you install CAs in perimeter networks, you should consider installing it on a Server Core installation to keep it more secure. Find out more at *http://technet.microsoft.com/en-us/library/ff849263%28WS.10%29.aspx*. In addition, AD CS cannot be installed on Itanium-based systems.

Different editions of Windows Server 2008 R2 offer different features in support of AD CS. Table 15-3 outlines the supported features based on the selected edition.

TABLE 15-3 AD CS Features per Windows Server 2008 R2 Edition

SUPPORTED COMPONENTS AND FEATURES	WEB	STANDARD	ENTERPRISE	DATACENTER
Stand-alone certificate authority	☐	☑	☑	☑
Enterprise certificate authority	☐	☐	☑	☑
Network Device Enrollment Service (NDES)	☐	☐	☑	☑

SUPPORTED COMPONENTS AND FEATURES	WEB	STANDARD	ENTERPRISE	DATACENTER
Online responder service	☐	☐	☑	☑
Key archival	☐	☐	☑	☑
Role Separation	☐	☐	☑	☑
Certificate Manager restrictions	☐	☐	☑	☑
Delegated enrollment agent restrictions	☐	☐	☑	☑

Preparing for AD CS Installation

You must prepare your environment before installing AD CS. The prerequisites for a typical AD CS installation include the following:

- An AD DS forest with at least a forest root domain. Preferably, you also have a child production domain.

- Computers to run the certificate authorities used in your hierarchy. In the simplest typical deployment, this means at least two computers: one for the root CA and one for the issuing CA. The issuing CA can also host the online responder service and NDES. The issuing CA requires the installation of IIS, but the AD CS installation process automatically adds this feature during installation. Both computers should be members of the production domain. In addition, these computers should include the following settings:

  - Remember that the root CA can run Windows Server 2008 R2 Standard edition. In addition, it should be disconnected from the network after the installation is complete, for security purposes.

  - The enterprise issuing CA must run on either Windows Server 2008 R2 Enterprise edition or Windows Server 2008 R2 Datacenter edition.

  - The root CA needs at least two drives, and the issuing CA should have three drives to store the certificate database and its logs.

- A special user account, if you choose to install the NDES service. Create a domain account and make it a member of the local IIS_IUSRS group on each server that will host this service. For example, you could name this account NDESService. Because this account will be shared among several computers, it should not be a managed service account.

- Client computers, ideally running Windows 7, to request and obtain certificates.

> **MORE INFO   DEPLOYING AD CS**
>
> For more information on deploying AD CS, go to *http://technet2.microsoft.com/ windowsserver2008/en/library/a8f53a9b-f3f6-4b13-8253-dbf183a5aa621033.mspx?mfr=true.*

Now you can move on to the actual installation. To install a stand-alone root CA, use the procedure described in the following practice.

Installing a CA Hierarchy

In this practice, you create a two-tier AD CS hierarchy and install the NDES feature of AD CS. To perform this practice, you must have prepared at least three virtual servers as outlined in the "Before You Begin" section at the beginning of this chapter.

> **NOTE** **WORKING WITH VIRTUAL MACHINES**
>
> It is easier to perform these exercises with virtual machines than with physical machines, at least for most readers. Note that when working with virtual machines, many users tend to save the machine state instead of shutting it down. It is a convenient way to work. However, for these exercises to work best, it is highly recommended that you work with machines that have been restarted rather than restored from a saved state. If you use machines restored from saved states, you may experience erratic behavior during these exercises.

EXERCISE 1 Install AD CS as a Stand-alone Root CA

In this exercise, you create a stand-alone root CA, which will be used as the root of your CA hierarchy. This task is performed on SERVER03. Make sure that SERVER01, your DC, is also running and that SERVER03 is a member of the domain.

1. Log on to SERVER03 with the domain Administrator account.

   You need local administrative credentials only, but for the purposes of this exercise, it is fine to use the domain administrator account. This server can be running Windows Server 2008 R2 Standard edition, Windows Server 2008 R2 Enterprise edition, or Windows Server 2008 R2 Datacenter edition.

> **NOTE** **STANDARD OR ENTERPRISE EDITION**
>
> To conserve costs in production, the server you use for the root CA that will be taken offline should be Standard edition. However, if you are using a virtual machine, Enterprise edition can actually cost less. For the purposes of this exercise, you should use Enterprise, because it allows you to reuse the server installation for the exercises in later chapters.

2. Launch Server Manager from the Administrative Tools program group.
3. Right-click the Roles node in the tree pane and click Add Roles.
4. Review the Before You Begin information and click Next.
5. On the Select Server Roles page, select Active Directory Certificate Services and click Next.

6. On the Introduction to Active Directory Certificate Services page, review the information about the selected role and click Next.

7. On the Select Role Services page, select Certification Authority and click Next.

   Because this will be a root CA and you will take it offline as soon as you create the issuing CA, you do not assign any other role features or services.

8. On the Specify Setup Type page, select Standalone and click Next.

9. On the CA Type page, select Root CA and click Next.

10. On the Set Up Private Key page, select Create A New Private Key and click Next.

    You need to create a new private key because you are creating a new root CA. However, if you were reinstalling a CA because of a system failure, you would use an existing key, one that was generated during the initial installation of the root CA. In addition, if you were creating a root CA to be chained with an external third-party CA, you would use the last option, to use the key provided by the third-party CA. You must install the key on the server before you begin the AD CS installation for the option to be available. Use the instructions provided by your third-party CA to install the certificate.

11. On the Configure Cryptography For CA page, select the suggested cryptographic service provider (CSP). Select a key character length of 2048. Select the sha1 hash algorithm for signing certificates issued by this CA. Also select Allow Administrator Interaction When The Private Key Is Accessed By The CA.

    There are several options on this page:

    - CSPs are the engines that the Microsoft Crypto application programming interface (API) uses to generate the key pair for this root CA. CSPs can be either software or hardware based. For example, the RSA#Microsoft Software Key Storage Provider is software based, and the RSA#Microsoft Smart Card Key Storage Provider is hardware based.

    - Key character length determines the length of the keys in the pair. Four lengths are possible. Remember that the longer the key, the more processing the server will require to decode it.

    - Hash algorithms produce and assign a hash value on the keys in the pair. Because they are assigned to the keys, any tampering of the key will change the hash value and invalidate the key. Hash values provide further key protection. The algorithm you select will simply use a different calculation method to generate the hash value.

    - The last option on the page provides further protection for the root CA. By selecting this option, you ensure that use of the CA will require administrative access and will work only with this level of access. In addition, using this option will allow administrators to work with third-paty CPSs.

    Click Next.

12. On the Configure CA Name page, type **Contoso-Root-CA** as the common name, leave the distinguished name suffix as is, and click Next.

    The name you use will be embedded in every subordinate certificate issued by the chain.

13. On the Set Validity Period page, change the year value to **20** and click Next.

14. On the Configure Certificate Database page, specify the storage locations for the certificate database and the certificate database log.

    Because this is a root CA that should be taken offline and should be used only to generate certificates for the issuing CAs, you can place both on the D drive.

    For the database location, click Browse, navigate to the D drive, click Make New Folder, type **CertData,** and press Enter. Click OK. For the logs, click Browse, similarly create a folder on the D drive and name it **CertLogs,** and then click OK. Click Next.

15. Review the information available on the AD CS page and click Install. When the installation completes, review the installation results and click Close.

    Your root CA is installed.

    Note that you can no longer change the name of this server unless you uninstall AD CS first. This is a good reason for not using a server name in the CA name in step 12.

EXAM TIP

Make sure you fully understand these installation choices, because they are part of the exam.

After your root CA is installed, return to Server Manager and click Active Directory Certificate Services under the Roles node to view the results of the installation. For example, you should have an event ID 103, as shown in Figure 15-6, listed on the summary page of the AD CS role. This event shows that the CA name will be added to the Certificate Authorities container in your AD DS domain. It also displays the command that you can use to view the information in the directory after the name has been added.

In a production environment, you should disconnect this CA from the network after the Group Policy cycle has been updated (you can force it with the gpudate.exe command) to provide further protection for this server.

You can now move on to installing your first issuing CA. You should install more than one issuing CA to provide high availability for your AD CS infrastructure, but each installation uses the same process. Although you do this through network connections in these exercises, in production you should use manual transfer methods such as USB devices.

NOTE   REVIEW THE AD CS INSTALLATION PROCESS

For a step-by-step guide to the installation of AD CS, go to *http://go.microsoft.com/ fwlink/?LinkId=90856.*

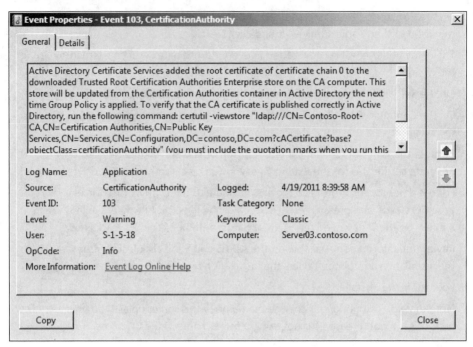

FIGURE 15-6 Viewing the contents of Event ID 103

EXERCISE 2 Install AD CS as an Enterprise Issuing CA

You should normally install more than one issuing CA to provide high availability for your AD CS infrastructure, but for the purposes of this exercise, one issuing CA is sufficient. Make sure that SERVER01, SERVER03, and SERVER04 are all running.

1. Log on to SERVER04 using the domain Administrator account.

    You need local administrative access rights only, but for the purposes of this exercise, the domain administrator account will also work. This server can be running Windows Server 2008 R2 Enterprise edition or Windows Server 2008 R2 Datacenter edition.

2. Launch Server Manager from the Administrative Tools program group.

3. Right-click the Roles node and click Add Roles.

4. Review the Before You Begin information and click Next.

5. On the Select Server Roles page, select Active Directory Certificate Services and click Next.

6. On the Introduction to Active Directory Certificate Services page, review the information about the selected role and click Next.

7. On the Select Role Services page, select Certificate Authority and Online Responder. When you select Online Responder, the wizard asks you to add the Web Server role with the required features. Click Add Required Role Services.

You do not select Certificate Authority Web Enrollment, because this is an internal enterprise CA, and enterprise CAs rely on AD DS to distribute certificates to users and devices. If you were installing this CA in an external network, you might consider using Web Enrollment to allow users to request certificates from your CA.

You cannot choose the Network Device Enrollment Service (NDES) installation at this time because AD CS does not support installing a CA at the same time as you install NDES. If you want to install NDES, you must select Add Roles from Server Manager after the CA installation has completed.

8. Click Next.

9. On the Specify Setup Type page, select Enterprise and click Next.

10. On the Specify CA Type page, select Subordinate CA and click Next.

11. On the Set Up Private Key page, select Create A New Private Key and click Next.

12. On the Configure Cryptography For CA page, accept the default values and click Next.

    Note that you do not select the Allow Administrator Interaction When The Private Key Is Accessed By The CA option for this installation, because it is an issuing CA and must be able to interact with end users to issue certificates.

13. On the Configure CA Name page, type **Contoso-Issuing-CA01** as the common name, leave the default distinguished name suffix as is, and click Next.

    You use a valid name—one that has meaning for the people who interact with the machine—and a number, because you should create additional issuing CAs for redundancy purposes. For example, by naming one server Root-CA and others Issuing-CA, you are aware of the CA's role in the hierarchy simply by looking at its name.

14. On the Request Certificate From A Parent CA page, select Save A Certificate Request To File And Manually Send It Later To A Parent CA.

15. Select the certificate request name (excluding the path) from the File Name field and copy it to the clipboard, and then click Browse and navigate to your Documents folder. Paste the name in the File Name box, click Save, and then click Next. You must do this; if you do not, the wizard will place the request file on the root of the C: drive.

16. On the Configure Certificate Database page, specify the storage locations for the certificate database and the certificate database log.

    Because this is an issuing CA that will be used for testing only, you can place the data and the logs together on the D drive. However, in a production environment, issuing CAs are used heavily, so you should place the data on the D drive and the logs on an E drive.

    For the database location, click Browse, navigate to the D drive, click Make New Folder, and name it **CertData**. Click OK.

    For the logs, click Browse, create a folder on the D drive, name it **CertLogs,** and click OK. Click Next when ready.

17. Review the installation of IIS. Click Next.

18. On the Web Server Role Services page, review the required services and click Next.

19. Review the information in the Confirm Installation Selections page and click Install. When the installation completes, review the installation results and click Close.

   The subordinate CA setup is not usable until it has been issued a root CA certificate and this certificate has been used to complete the installation of this subordinate CA.

EXAM TIP

Remember that you cannot install the CA and the NDES role features at the same time.

EXERCISE 3 Obtain and Install the Issuing CA Certificate

Now you obtain the certificate to complete the installation of the issuing CA. You should normally perform this procedure offline using a removable storage device such as a floppy disk or a USB flash drive, but for the purpose of this exercise, you use a shared folder to transfer the certificate request and the certificate after it is issued.

1. On SERVER04, launch Windows Explorer and navigate to the C drive. Create a new folder and name it **Temp**.

2. Right-click the Temp folder, point to Share With, and click Specific People.

3. In the File Sharing dialog box, select Everyone in the drop-down list, and then click Add.

4. In the Permission Level column, from the drop-down list, assign the Read/Write permission to Everyone and click Share. Click Done.

5. Copy the certificate request you generated from your Documents folder to the Temp folder.

6. On SERVER03, launch the Certification Authority console from the Administrative Tools program group.

7. In the Certification Authority console, right-click the root CA name in the tree pane, point to All Tasks, and then click Submit New Request.

8. In the Open Request File dialog box, in the File Name box, type **\\SERVER04\Temp**. Click Open, select the request, and then click Open again.

9. Navigate to the Pending Requests node in the tree pane, right-click the pending request in the details pane, point to All Tasks, and then click Issue.

10. Move to the Issued Certificates node in the tree pane, right-click the issued certificate in the details pane, and click Open.

11. In the Certificate dialog box, click the Details tab, and then click Copy To File at the bottom of the dialog box.

   This launches the Certificate Export Wizard.

12. Click Next.

13. Select Cryptographic Message Syntax Standard – PKCS #7 Certificates (.P7B), select Include All Certificates In The Certification Path If Possible, and click Next.

There are several supported formats:

- Distinguished Encoding Rules (DER) Encoded Binary X.509 is often used for computers that do not run the Windows operating system. This creates certificate files in the DER format.

- Base-64 Encoded X.509 supports S/MIME, which is the format used to transfer secured email messages over the Internet. On servers, it is usually used for non-Windows operating systems. This also creates certificate files in the DER format.

- Cryptographic Message Syntax Standard (PKCS #7) is the format used to transfer certificates and their chained path from one computer to another. This format uses the P7B file format.

- Personal Information Exchange (PKCS #12) is also used to transfer certificates and their chained path from one computer to another, but in addition, this format supports the transfer of the private key as well as the public key. Use this format with caution, because transporting the private key can jeopardize it. This format uses the PFX file format.

- Microsoft Serialized Certificate Store is a custom Microsoft format that should be used when you need to transfer root certificates from one computer to another. This uses the SST file format.

14. In the File To Export dialog box, click Browse and save the certificate in the \\SERVER04\Temp folder. Name the file **Issuing-CA01.p7b** and click Save.

15. Click Next when you return to the wizard.

16. Review your settings and click Finish.

17. Click OK when the wizard tells you that the export was successful. Return to SERVER04.

Remember that, normally, you would use a removable device to transport this certificate from one server to another.

18. Go to Server Manager and select Contoso-Issuing-CA01 in the tree pane (Server Manager\Roles\Active Directory Certificate Services\Contoso-Issuing-CA01).

19. Right-click Contoso-Issuing-CA01, point to All Tasks, and then click Install CA Certificate.

20. Move to the C:\Temp folder, select the certificate, and click Open.

21. The first time you enable an issuing CA, AD CS warns you that the root certificate server is not trusted. Click OK to trust the root certificate. This imports the certificate and enables the server. The trusted root will now be registered in AD DS and you will no longer get this message when you enable other issuing CAs.

22. Right-click the server name, Contoso-Issuing-CA01, point to All Tasks, and then click Start Service.

Your issuing CA is ready to issue certificates. At this point, you should normally take SERVER03 offline, but this is not necessary in a test environment.

EXERCISE 4   Prepare to Install the NDES Feature

Now you install the NDES feature. Again, this task is performed on SERVER04, but you must use SERVER01 to create a user account first.

1. Log on to SERVER01 using the domain Administrator account.
2. Launch Active Directory Users And Computers from the Administrative Tools program group.
3. Create the following OU structure: Contoso.com\Admins\Service Identities.
4. Right-click Service Identities, point to New, and then click User.
5. Name the user **NDESService,** and use this name for both the logon and the pre-Windows 2000 logon names. Click Next.
6. Assign a strong password. Clear User Must Change Password At Next Logon and select Password Never Expires.

NOTE **LEGACY SERVICE ACCOUNTS**

You must create the service account according to the steps outlined here, because you cannot use a managed service account in this instance. Managed service accounts do not work when the account is shared by multiple computers or when the account is used for a service running on multiple computers, such as for a cluster. Managed service accounts are discussed in Lesson 4 of Chapter 8, "Improving the Security of Authentication in an AD DS Domain."

7. Click Next, and then click Finish to create the account.
8. Return to SERVER04 and log on as the domain Administrator.
9. Launch Server Manager from the Administrative Tools program group.
10. Expand Configuration\Local Users And Groups, and then click Groups.
11. Double-click the IIS_IUSRS group.
12. Add the NDESService account to this group and click OK.

EXERCISE 5   Install the NDES Feature

Now you're ready to install the NDES service.

1. Right-click Active Directory Certificate Services in the tree pane of Server Manager and click Add Role Services.

2. On the Select Role Services page, select Network Device Enrollment Service.

   This requires the addition of Windows Authentication to your IIS installation.

3. Click Add Required Role Services and click Next.

4. On the Specify User Account page, click Select User, enter **NDESService** with its password, and click OK. Click Next.

5. On the Specify Registration Authority Information page, you must enter the information for your registration authority or the authority that will assign and manage certificates assigned to network devices. Type **Contoso-MSCEP-RA01** as the RA Name, select your country from the drop-down list, and leave all other information blank. Click Next.

   Normally, you should enter all the required and optional information, but for the purpose of this exercise, leaving them blank is fine.

6. On the Configure Cryptography For Registration Authority page, keep the defaults and click Next.

   Keep in mind that key length affects CPU usage; therefore, unless you have stringent security requirements, keep the 2048 key length.

7. Review the information about the installation of IIS. Click Next.

8. On the Web Server Role Services page, review the required services and click Next.

9. On the Confirm Installation Services page, click Install.

10. Review the status and progress of the installation.

11. Click Close.

    Your NDES service is now installed and ready to work. Your installation of the issuing server is complete.

> **MORE INFO   SIMPLE CERTIFICATE ENROLLMENT PROTOCOL (SCEP)**
>
> For more information on SCEP, go to *http://www3.ietf.org/proceedings/07jul/slides/pkix-3.pdf*.

Lesson Summary

- AD CS is composed of four elements: certificate authorities, CA Web Enrollment, online responders, and Network Device Enrollment Service. These are the core elements of any AD CS deployment.

- Certificate authorities are the servers you use to issue and manage certificates. Because of the hierarchical nature of a PKI, AD CS supports both root and subordinate or child

CAs. The root CA usually issues certificates to subordinate CAs, which enables them in turn to issue certificates to users, computers, and services. The subordinate CA can issue certificates only while its own certificate is valid. When this certificate expires, the subordinate CA must request a certificate renewal from its root CA. For this reason, root CAs often have certificate durations that are much longer than any of their subordinates. In turn, subordinate CAs usually have certificate durations that are longer than those they issue to users, computers, or services.

■ ORs are designed to respond to specific certificate validation requests through the Online Certificate Status Protocol (OCSP). Using an OR, the system relying on a PKI does not need to obtain a full CRL and can submit a validation request for a specific certificate. The OR decodes the validation request and determines whether the certificate is valid. When it determines the status of the requested certificate, it sends back an encrypted response containing the information to the requester. Using ORs is much faster and more efficient than using CRLs.

■ Devices that use low-level operating systems, such as routers and switches, can also participate in a PKI through the NDES by using the SCEP, a protocol developed by Cisco Systems, Inc. These devices usually do not participate in an AD DS directory and, therefore, do not have AD DS accounts. However, through the NDES and the SCEP, they can also become part of the PKI hierarchy that is maintained and managed by your AD CS installation.

■ CA server types are tied to the version of Windows Server 2008 R2 you use. Stand-alone CAs can be created with Windows Server 2008 R2 Standard edition, Windows Server 2008 R2 Enterprise edition, or Windows Server 2008 R2 Datacenter edition. Enterprise CAs can be created with Windows Server 2008 R2 Enterprise edition or Windows Server 2008 R2 Datacenter edition only.

Lesson Review

You can use the following question to test your knowledge of the information in Lesson 1, "Understanding and Installing Active Directory Certificate Services." The question is also available on the companion CD if you prefer to review it in electronic form.

NOTE ANSWERS

The answer to this question and explanations of why each answer choice is right or wrong are located in the "Answers" section at the end of the book.

1. You are an administrator for the Contoso domain. Your manager has decided to deploy Active Directory Certificate Services, and he wants it done today. You tell him that you investigated AD CS and, from what you've learned, deploying a public key infrastructure is not usually done in one day. After some discussion, your manager agrees that perhaps you should install this role in a laboratory first, but he wants to be there to see how it works. He wants you to install an enterprise certificate authority.

You make sure that the server you are using is running Windows Server 2008 R2 Enterprise edition, and you launch the installation through Server Manager. When you get to the Specify Setup Type page of the Add Roles Wizard, the Enterprise CA option is not available. (See Figure 15-7.) What could be the problem? (Choose all that apply.)

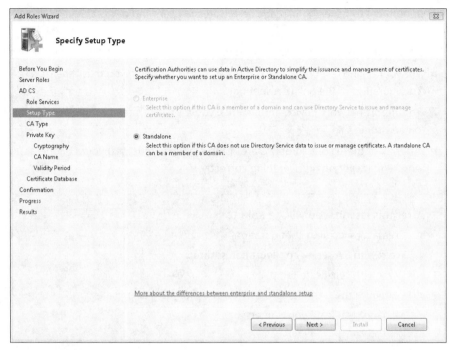

FIGURE 15-7 The Specify Setup Type page of the Add Roles Wizard

A. Your server is not running Windows Server 2008 R2 Enterprise edition.

B. You are logged on with an account that is not part of the domain.

C. Your server is not a member of an AD DS domain.

D. You cannot install an enterprise CA with Server Manager.

Lesson 2: Configuring and Using Active Directory Certificate Services

After you have deployed your servers, you still need to complete several configurations to begin using them to issue and manage certificates to users and devices. Several activities are required:

- To issue and maintain certificates, you must finalize the configuration of your issuing CAs.
- For your online responder to issue responses to requests, you must finalize the configuration of the online responder.
- To support network device enrollments, you must finish the configuration of the NDES on an issuing CA.
- After all of these configurations are completed, you must test your CA operations to ensure that everything is working correctly.

After this lesson, you will be able to:
- Create a revocation configuration.
- Work with CA server configuration settings.
- Work with certificate templates.
- Configure the CA to issue OCSP Response Signing certificates.
- Manage certificate enrollments.
- Manage certificate revocations.

Estimated lesson time: 40 minutes

Finalizing the Configuration of an Issuing CA

Finalizing the configuration of an issuing CA includes the following actions:

- Creating a certificate revocation configuration
- Configuring and personalizing certificate templates with specific attention to the following factors:
  - If you want to use the EFS to protect data, you must configure certificates for use with EFS. This also involves planning for the recovery agent or the agent that will be able to recover data if a user's EFS key is lost.
  - If you want to protect your wireless networks with certificates, you must configure wireless network certificates. This enforces strong authentication and encrypts all communication between wireless devices.
  - If you want to use smart cards to support two-factor authentication, you must configure smart card certificates.

- If you want to protect websites and enable e-commerce, you must configure web server certificates. You can also use this certificate type to protect DCs and encrypt all communication to and from them.

  - Configuring enrollment and issuance options

You perform each of these actions on the issuing CA itself or remotely through a workstation, using the Remote Server Administration Tools (RSAT).

Creating a Revocation Configuration for a CA

Revocation is one of the only methods available to you for controlling certificates when they are misused or when you need to cancel deployed certificates. This is one reason your revocation configuration should be completed before you begin to issue certificates.

To create a revocation configuration, perform the following actions:

- Specify Certificate Revocation List (CRL) distribution points.
- Configure CRL and Delta CRL overlap periods.
- Schedule the publication of CRLs.

Begin with the CRL distribution point. Revocation configurations are performed in the Certification Authority console.

1. Log on to an issuing CA with a domain account that has local administrative rights.
2. Launch the Certification Authority console from the Administrative Tools program group.
3. Right-click the issuing CA name and click Properties.
4. In the Properties dialog box, click the Extensions tab and verify that the Select Extension drop-down list is set to CRL Distribution Point (CDP). Also make sure that the Publish CRLs To This Location and the Publish Delta CRLs To This Location check boxes are selected.
5. Click OK.

   If you made any changes to the CA's configuration, you are prompted to stop and restart the AD CS service. Click Yes to do so.

Now configure CRL and Delta CRL overlap periods, using the Certutil.exe command.

1. On the issuing CA, open an elevated command prompt and execute the following commands:

```
certutil -setreg ca\CRLOverlapUnits value
certutil -setreg ca\CRLOverlapPeriod units
certutil -setreg ca\CRLDeltaOverlapUnits value
certutil -setreg ca\CRLDeltaOverlapPeriod units
```

Value is the value you want to use to set the overlap period, and *units* is minutes, hours, or days. For example, you could set the CRL overlap period to 24 hours and the Delta CRL publication period to 12 hours. For this, you would use the following commands:

```
certutil -setreg ca\CRLOverlapUnits 24
certutil -setreg ca\CRLOverlapPeriod hours
certutil -setreg ca\CRLDeltaOverlapUnits 12
certutil -setreg ca\CRLDeltaOverlapPeriod hours
```

2. Go to the Certification Authority console and right-click the issuing CA server name to stop and restart the service.

Finally, configure the publication of the CRLs.

1. In the Certification Authority console, expand the console tree below the issuing CA server name.

2. Right-click Revoked Certificates and click Properties.

3. On the CRL Publishing Parameters tab, configure the CRL and Delta CRL publication periods.

    By default, both values are set to one week and one day, respectively. If you expect to have a high throughput of certificates and need to ensure high availability of the CRLs, decrease both values. If not, keep the default values.

    You can also view existing CRLs on the View CRLs tab.

4. Click OK.

Your revocation configuration is complete.

Configuring and Personalizing Certificate Templates

Certificate templates are used to generate the certificates you use in your AD CS configuration. Enterprise CAs use version 2 and 3 templates. You can configure and personalize these templates. To prepare templates for various uses, you must first configure each template you intend to use and, after each is configured, deploy each to your CAs. After templates are deployed, you can use them to issue certificates. Begin by identifying which templates you want to use, and then move on to the following procedure.

1. Log on to an issuing CA, using domain administrative credentials.

2. Launch Server Manager from the Administrative Tools program group.

3. Expand Roles\Active Directory Certificate Services and select Certificate Templates (*servername*).

4. Note that all the existing templates are listed in the details pane.

> **IMPORTANT** **UPGRADING CERTIFICATE AUTHORITIES**
>
> If you are upgrading an existing CA infrastructure to Windows Server 2008 R2, the first time you log on to a new server running AD CS, you are prompted to update the existing certificate templates. Answer Yes. This upgrades all templates to Windows Server 2008 R2 versions.

5. Note that you are connected to a DC by default.

   To work with templates, you must be connected to a DC so that the templates can be published to AD DS.

6. If you are not connected, use the More Actions\Connect To Another Writable Domain Controller command in the Action pane to connect to a DC.

   You are ready to create the templates you require.

7. Select the source template, right-click the template, click Duplicate Template, and then select the version of Windows Server to support.

   This should always be Windows Server 2008 unless you are running in a mixed PKI hierarchy.

8. Name the new template, customize it, and save the customizations.

   Customize templates according to the following guidelines:

   - To create an EFS template, select the Basic EFS template as the source, duplicate it for Windows Server 2008, and name it. Use a valid name, such as Basic EFS WS08, and then move through the property tabs to customize its content. Pay particular attention to key archival on the Request Handling tab, and make sure you select the Archive Subject's Encryption Private Key check box. Also, use advanced Symmetric Algorithm to send the key to the CA. Archival storage of the private key allows you to protect it if the user ever loses it. You can also use the Subject Name tab to add information such as Alternate Subject Name values. Click OK.

   - If you plan to use EFS, you must also create an EFS Recovery Agent template. Duplicate it for Windows Server 2008. Name it with a valid name such as EFS Recovery Agent WS08. Publish the recovery agent certificate in Active Directory by selecting the Publish Certificate In Active Directory checkbox. Note that the recovery agent certificate is valid for a much longer period than the EFS certificate itself. Also, use the same settings on the other property tabs as you assigned to the Basic EFS duplicate.

MORE INFO **USING EFS**

For more information on the implementation of EFS, see the white paper "Working with the Encrypting File System" at *http://www.reso-net.com/articles.asp?m=8* under the Building A World Of Trust section.

   - If you plan to use wireless networks, create a Network Policy Server (NPS) template for use with your systems. Basically, you create the template and configure it for autoenrollment. Then, the next time the NPS servers in your network update their Group Policy settings, they will be assigned new certificates. Use the RAS and IAS Server templates as the sources for your new NPS template. Duplicate it for Windows Server 2008. Name it appropriately, such as NPS Server WS08. Publish it in Active Directory. On the Security tab, select the RAS and IAS Servers group to assign the Autoenroll and Enroll permissions. Review other tabs as needed and save the new template.

- If you want to use smart card logons, create duplicates of the Smartcard Logon and Smartcard User templates. Set the duplicates for Windows Server 2008. Name them appropriately and publish them in Active Directory. You do not use Autoenrollment for these certificates because you need to use smart card enrollment stations to distribute the smart cards to the users.

- If you want to protect web servers or DCs, create duplicates of the Web Server and Domain Controller Authentication templates. Do not use the Domain Controller template; it is designed for earlier versions of the operating system. Duplicate them for Windows Server 2008, publish them in Active Directory, and verify their other properties.

> **NOTE   CONFIGURING DUPLICATE TEMPLATES**
>
> The configuration of each template type often includes additional activities that are not necessarily tied to AD CS. Make sure you view the AD CS online help to review the activities associated with the publication of each certificate type.

Now that your templates are ready, you must issue the template to enable the CA to issue certificates based on these customized templates.

 9. In Server Manager, expand Roles\Active Directory Certificate Services*Issuing CA Name* and select Certificate Templates.

10. To issue a template, right-click Certificate Templates, point to New, and then click Certificate Template To Issue.

11. In the Enable Certificate Templates dialog box, shown in Figure 15-8, hold down the Ctrl key and click to select all the templates you want to issue, and then click OK.

FIGURE 15-8 Enable Certificate Templates dialog box

Now you're ready to configure enrollment. This is done through Group Policy. You can choose either to create a new Group Policy for this purpose or modify an existing Group Policy object. This policy must be assigned to all members of the domain; therefore, the Default Domain Policy might be your best choice; if you do not want to modify this policy, create a new policy and assign it to the entire domain by using the Group Policy Management Console (GPMC).

1. Log on to a DC, and then launch Group Policy Management from the Administrative Tools program group.

2. Locate or create the appropriate policy, right-click it, and then click Edit.

3. To assign autoenrollment for computers, expand Computer Configuration\Policies\Windows Settings\Security Settings and select Public Key Policies.

4. Double-click Certificate Services Client – Auto-Enrollment.

5. Enable the policy and select the Renew Expired Certificates, Update Pending Certificates, And Remove Revoked Certificates check box.

6. Select the Update Certificates That Use Certificate Templates check box if you have already issued some certificates manually. Click OK to assign these settings.

7. To assign autoenrollment for users, expand User Configuration\Policies\Windows Settings\Security Settings and select Public Key Policies.

8. Enable the Certificate Services Client – Auto-Enrollment policy and select the same options as for computers.

9. Notice that you can enable Expiration Notification for users. Enable it and set an appropriate value.

    Users will be notified when their certificates are about to expire.

10. Click OK to assign these settings.

> **IMPORTANT   COMPUTER AND USER GROUP POLICY SETTINGS**
>
> Normally, you should not apply both user and computer settings in the same Group Policy object. This is done here only to illustrate the settings you need to apply to enable autoenrollment.

11. Close the GPMC.

12. Return to the issuing CA and move to Server Manager to set the default action that your issuing CA will use when it receives certificate requests.

13. Right-click the issuing CA server name under AD CS and click Properties.

14. On the Policy Module tab, click Properties.

15. To have certificates issued automatically, select Follow The Settings In The Certificate Template, If Applicable. Otherwise, Automatically Issue The Certificate. Click OK.

16. Click OK again to close the Properties dialog box.

Your issuing CA is now ready for production and will begin to issue certificates automatically when they are requested either by devices or by users.

Finalizing the Configuration of an Online Responder

If you decided to use online responders, you need to finalize their configuration. You can link online responders to create an array of systems that provides high availability for the service. An array can be as simple as two CAs acting as ORs, or it can include many more servers.

To finalize the configuration of an online responder, you must configure and install an OCSP Response Signing certificate and configure an Authority Information Access (AIA) extension to support it. After this is done, you must assign the template to a CA and then enroll the system to obtain the certificate. Use the following procedure to configure the OCSP Response Signing certificate.

1. Log on to an issuing CA server, using a domain account with local administrative access rights.

2. In Server Manager, expand Roles\Active Directory Certificate Services and select Certificate Templates (*servername*).

3. Right-click the OCSP Response Signing template and click Duplicate Template. Select a Windows Server 2008 Enterprise template and click OK.

4. Type a valid name for the new template, such as **OCSP Response Signing WS08**.

5. Select the Publish Certificate In Active Directory check box.

6. On the Security tab, under Group Or User Names, click Add, click Object Types to enable the Computer object type, and click OK.

7. Type the server name, and then click Check Names or browse to find the computer that hosts the online responder. Click OK.

8. Click the computer name and then, in the Permissions section of the dialog box, select the Read and Enroll permissions in the Allow column.

9. Click OK to create the duplicate template.

Your certificate template is ready. Now you must configure the AIA extension to support the OR.

> **IMPORTANT** **ASSIGNING ACCESS RIGHTS**
>
> Normally, you should assign access rights to groups and not to individual objects in an AD DS directory. Because you will have several ORs, using a group makes sense. Ideally, you should create a group in AD DS, name it appropriately (for example, Online Responders), and add the computer accounts of each OR to this group. After you do that, you assign the access rights of the OCSP Response Signing template to the group instead of to the individual systems. This way, you have to assign these access rights only once.

1. Log on to an issuing CA, using a domain account with local administrative credentials.

2. Launch Server Manager from the Administrative Tools program group.

3. Expand Roles\Active Directory Certificate Services*Issuing CA servername*.

4. Right-click the issuing CA server in the tree pane and click Properties.

5. On the Extensions tab, click the Select Extension drop-down list, and then choose Authority Information Access (AIA).

6. Specify the locations to obtain certificate revocation data. In this case, select the location beginning with http://.

7. Select the Include In The AIA Extension Of Issued Certificates and the Include In The Online Certificate Status Protocol (OCSP) Extension check boxes.

8. Click OK to apply the changes.

9. Note that you must stop and restart the AD CS service because of the change. Click Yes in the Certification Authority dialog box to do so.

10. Move to the Certificate Templates node under the issuing CA name in the tree pane, right-click Certificate Templates, point to New, and then click Certificate Template To Issue.

11. In the Enable Certificate Templates dialog box, select the new OCSP Response Signing template that you created earlier and click OK.

    The new template should appear in the details pane.

12. You now need to verify that the OCSP certificate has been assigned to the server. You do so with the Certificates snap-in. By default, this snap-in is not in a console. You must create a new console to use it.

13. Open the Start menu, type **mmc** in the search box, and press Enter.

14. In the MMC, click Add/Remove Snap-in on the File menu to open the Add Or Remove Snap-ins dialog box.

15. Select the Certificates snap-in and click Add.

16. Select Computer Account and click Next.

17. Select Local Computer and click Finish.

18. Click OK to close the Add Or Remove Snap-ins dialog box.

19. On the File menu, click Save to save the console and place it in your Documents folder. Name the console **Computer Certificates** and click Save.

20. Expand Certificates\Personal and select Certificates.

21. Right-click Certificates under Personal, point to All Tasks, and then click Request New Certificate.

22. On the Certificate Enrollment page, make sure the Active Directory Enrollment Policy is selected and click Next.

23. Select the new OCSP certificate and click Enroll.

24. On the next page, click the down arrow to the right of Details, and then click View Certificate. Browse through the tabs to view the certificate details. Note the certificate name. Click OK.

25. Click Finish to complete this part of the operation.

26. Right-click the new Certificate, point to All Tasks, and then click Manage Private Keys.

27. On the Security tab, under Group Or User Names, click Add.

28. In the Select Users, Computers, Service Accounts, Or Groups dialog box, click Locations and select the local server name. Click OK.

29. Type **Network Service** and click Check Names.

30. Click OK.

31. Click Network Service, and then, in the Permissions section of the dialog box, make sure the Allow::Full Control permission is selected.

32. Click OK to close the dialog box.

Your OR is ready to provide certificate validation information.

MORE INFO **ONLINE RESPONDER**

For more information on the OR service, go to *http://technet2.microsoft.com/windowsserver2008/en/library/045d2a97-1bff-43bd-8dea-f2df7e270e1f1033.mspx?mfr=true.*

You'll note that the Online Responder node in Server Manager also includes an Array Configuration node. When you add other ORs, you can add them to this array configuration to provide high availability of the OR service. Complex environments using multitiered hierarchies have large OR arrays to ensure that all their users and devices can easily validate their certificates.

Adding a Revocation Configuration for an Online Responder

When the OR is ready, add a revocation configuration. Because each CA that is an OR in an array includes its own certificate, each also requires a revocation configuration. The revocation configuration serves requests for specific CA key pairs and certificates. In addition, you need to update the revocation configuration for a CA each time you renew its key pair. To create a Revocation Configuration, perform the following steps:

1. Log on to an issuing CA, using a domain account that has local administrative rights.

2. Launch Server Manager from the Administrative Tools program group.

3. Expand Roles\Active Directory Certificate Services\Online Responder and select Revocation Configuration.

4. Right-click Revocation Configuration and click Add Revocation Configuration.

5. On the Welcome page, click Next.

6. On the Name The Revocation Configuration page, assign a valid name.

Because each revocation configuration is tied to a particular CA, it makes sense to include the CA's name in the name of the configuration—for example, RCSERVER04.

7. Click Next.

8. On the Select CA Certificate Location page, identify the location from which the certificate can be loaded.

   You can choose from Active Directory, a local certificate store, or a file. Choose Select A Certificate For An Existing Enterprise CA and click Next.

   Now, the OR must validate that the issuer of the certificate, in this case the root CA, has a valid certificate. Two choices are possible: in Active Directory or by computer name.

9. Because your root CA is offline, choose Browse CA Certificates Published In Active Directory and click Browse.

10. Locate the root CA and click OK.

    After the certificate is selected, the wizard loads the Online Responder signing templates.

11. Click Next.

    On the Select Signing Certificate page, you must select a signing method because the OR signs each response to clients before it sends it. Three choices are available:

    - Automatic selection loads a certificate from the OCSP template you created earlier.
    - Manually, you can choose the certificate to use.
    - CA Certificate uses the certificate from the CA itself.

    Choose Automatically Select A Signing Certificate and select Auto-Enroll For An OCSP Signing Certificate.

12. Browse for a CA and select the issuing CA. Click OK.

    This should automatically select the certificate template you prepared earlier.

13. Click Next.

    The wizard initializes the revocation provider. If for some reason it cannot find it, you must add the provider manually, as described in the next steps.

14. Click Provider, and then click Add under Base CRLs. For example, you could use the following HTTP address: http://localhost/ca.crl.

15. Click OK. Repeat the preceding step for the Delta CRLs using the same HTTP address, and click OK. However, because you are obtaining the certificate from Active Directory, the listed provider is an address in ldap:// format and should be provided automatically by the wizard. AD CS relies on Lightweight Directory Access Protocol (LDAP) to obtain information from the AD DS directory store.

16. Click Finish to complete the revocation configuration.

You should now have a new revocation configuration listed in the details pane. Repeat this procedure for each CA that is an OR.

EXAM TIP

Take note of the operations required to enable ORs because they are part of the exam.

Considerations for the Use and Management of AD CS

Active Directory Certificate Services role services are managed by using MMC snap-ins. Table 15-4 lists the tools you have used throughout this chapter, most of which are available from within Server Manager.

TABLE 15-4 AD CS Management Tools

TOOL	USAGE	LOCATION
Certification Authority	To manage a certificate authority.	Server Manager
Certificates	To manage certificates. This snap-in is installed by default.	Custom MMC snap-in
Certificate Templates	To manage certificate templates.	Server Manager
Online Responder	To manage an OR.	Server Manager
Enterprise PKI	To manage the entire PKI infrastructure.	Server Manager
Certutil	To manage PKI functions from the command line.	Command prompt
Windows PowerShell	To automate PKI functions in your AD CS deployment.	Administrative Tools program group

> **NOTE** **INSTALL THE SNAP-IN WITHOUT INSTALLING AD CS**
>
> The snap-in listed in Table 15-4 can be installed by using Server Manager and selecting the AD CS tools under Remote Server Administration Tools. If the computer from which you want to perform remote administration tasks is running Windows 7, you can obtain the Remote Server Administration Tools from the Microsoft Download Center at *http://www.microsoft.com/downloads/en/details.aspx?FamilyID=7d2f6ad7-656b-4313-a005-4e344e43997d.*

> **MORE INFO** **WINDOWS POWERSHELL AND AD CS**
>
> Windows PowerShell provides some support for the automation of AD CS operations. For examples of the types of operations you can perform through Windows PowerShell with AD CS, go to *http://social.technet.microsoft.com/wiki/contents/articles/active-directory-certificate-services-ad-cs-powershell-examples.aspx.*

As you work with AD CS, you will see that it provides a great amount of information through the Event Log. Table 15-5 lists the most common events for AD CS certificate authorities.

TABLE 15-5 Common Certificate Authority Event IDs

CATEGORY	EVENT ID	DESCRIPTION
AD CS Access Control	39, 60, 92	Related to insufficient or inappropriate use of permissions.
AD CS and AD DS	24, 59, 64, 91, 93, 94, 106, 107	Related to access (read or write) for AD DS objects.
AD CS Certificate Request (Enrollment) Processing	3, 7, 10, 21, 22, 23, 53, 56, 57, 79, 80, 97, 108, 109, 128, 132	One element for certificate enrollment to succeed is missing: valid CA certificate, certificate templates with proper configuration, client accounts, or certificate requests.
AD CS Certification Authority Certificate and Chain Validation	27, 31, 42, 48, 49, 51, 58, 64, 100, 103, 104, 105	Related to availability, validity, and chain validation for a CA certificate.
AD CS Certification Authority Upgrade	111, 112, 113, 114, 115, 116, 117, 118, 119, 120, 121, 122, 123, 125, 126	Related to upgrading certificate authorities from an earlier version of Windows to Windows Server 2008 R2, and can indicate configuration options or components that need to be reconfigured.
AD CS Cross-Certification	99, 102	Related to the cross-CA certificates created to establish relationships between the original certificate and the renewed root.
AD CS Database Availability	17	Related to CA database access issues.
AD CS Exit Module Processing	45, 46	Related to the exit module functions: publish or send email notification.
AD CS Key Archival and Recovery	81, 82, 83, 84, 85, 86, 87, 88, 96, 98, 127	Related to key recovery agent certificates, exchange (XCHG) certificates and keys, or that one or all of these components are missing.
AD CS Performance Counters Availability	110	Related to performance counters that cannot be started.

CATEGORY	EVENT ID	DESCRIPTION
AD CS Policy Module Processing	9, 43, 44, 77, 78	Related to problems detected with a policy module.
AD CS Program Resource Availability	15, 16, 26, 30, 33, 34, 35, 38, 40, 61, 63, 89, 90	Related to the availability of system resources and operating system components.
AD CS Registry Settings	5, 19, 20, 28, 95	Related to the corruption or deletion of configuration settings in the registry.
AD CS Online Responder	16, 17, 18, 19, 20, 21, 22, 23, 25, 26, 27, 29, 31, 33, 34, 35	Related to Online Responder service dependencies.

Rely on the contents of Table 15-5 to quickly identify the area that an issue relates to so that you can resolve it faster.

> **MORE INFO**   **AD CS EVENT IDs**
>
> To find more information on event types, read the information at *http://technet2.microsoft* *.com/windowsserver2008/en/library/688d1449-3086-4a79-95e6-5a7f620681731033.mspx.*

Working with Enterprise PKI

One of the most useful tools in an AD CS infrastructure is Enterprise PKI, or PKIView from the command line, which is the Enterprise PKI node under Active Directory Certificate Services in Server Manager. Enterprise PKI can be used for several AD CS management activities. Basically, Enterprise PKI gives you a view of the status of your AD CS deployment and allows you to view the entire PKI hierarchy in your network and drill down into individual CAs to quickly identify issues with the configuration or operation of your AD CS infrastructure.

Enterprise PKI is mostly used as a diagnostic and health view tool because it displays operational information about the members of your PKI hierarchy. In addition, you can use Enterprise PKI to link to each CA quickly by right-clicking the CA name and clicking Manage CA. This launches the Certification Authority console for the targeted CA.

From the Actions pane, you can also gain access to the Templates console (Manage Templates) as well as the Certificate Containers in Active Directory Domain Services (Manage AD Containers). The latter, shown in Figure 15-9, allows you to view the contents of each of the containers in a directory used to store certificates for your PKI architecture.

Rely on Enterprise PKI to check AD CS health status visually. Its icons give you immediate feedback on each component of your infrastructure, showing green when all is healthy, yellow when minor issues are found, and red when critical issues arise.

FIGURE 15-9 Viewing the AD containers through Enterprise PKI

Protecting Your AD CS Configuration

Along with the security measures you must perform for your root and intermediate CAs, you must also protect each CA, especially issuing CAs through regular backups. Backing up a CA is very simple. In Server Manager, expand Roles\Active Directory Certificate Services*CA Server Name*. Right-click the server name, point to All Tasks, and click Back Up CA. When you launch the backup operation, it launches the Certification Authority Backup Wizard. To back up the CA, use the following operations:

1. Launch the Certification Authority Backup Wizard and click Next.

2. On the Items To Back Up page, select the items you want to back up.

   - The Private Key And CA Certificate option protects the certificate for this server.

   - The Certificate Database And Certificate Database Log option protects the certificates that this CA manages. You can also perform incremental database backups.

3. Identify the location to back up to.

   For example, you could create the backup to a file share on a central server location. Remember, however, that you are backing up highly sensitive data and transporting it over the network, which might not be the best solution. A better choice might be to back up to a local folder and then copy the backup to removable media.

4. Identify the location and click Next. Note that the target location must be empty.

5. Assign a strong password to the backup. Click Next.

6. Review the information and click Finish.

   The wizard performs the backup. Protect the backup media thoroughly because it contains very sensitive information.

You can also perform automated backups through the command line with the Certutil.exe command with the appropriate switches to back up and restore the database.

To restore information, use the Certification Authority Restore Wizard. When you request a restore operation by right-clicking the server name, pointing to All Tasks, and clicking Restore CA, the wizard immediately prompts you to stop the CA service before the restore operation can begin. Click OK. After the service is stopped, the Welcome page of the wizard appears.

1. Click Next.

2. Select the items you want to restore. You can restore the private key and the CA certificate as well as the database and log.

3. Type the location of the backup files or click Browse to locate the backup data. Click Next.

4. Type the password to open the backup and click Next.

5. Verify your settings and click Finish.

   After the restore operation is complete, the wizard offers to restart the AD CS service.

6. Click Yes. Verify the operation of your CA after the restore is complete.

Configuring and Using AD CS

In this practice, you perform five key tasks. In the first, you finalize the configuration of an Online Responder. In the second, you work with Enterprise PKI to correct the errors in an AD CS implementation. Then you create a custom certificate template to publish certificates. You also enable autoenrollment for certificates to ensure that your users can obtain them automatically. Finally, you ensure that your issuing CA will automatically enroll clients.

EXERCISE 1 Finalizing the Configuration of an Online Responder

As mentioned earlier, to finalize the configuration of an online responder, you must configure and install an OCSP Response Signing certificate and configure an Authority Information Access (AIA) extension to support it. Use the following procedure:

1. Log on to SERVER04 using the domain administrator account.

2. In Server Manager, expand Roles\Active Directory Certificate Services and select Certificate Templates. When you click it, the node displays the server name in parentheses, in this case SERVER01.contoso.com.

3. Right-click the OCSP Response Signing template and click Duplicate Template. Select Windows Server 2008 Enterprise and click OK.

4. Type a valid name for the new template, such as **OCSP Response Signing WS08**.

5. Select the Publish Certificate In Active Directory check box.

6. On the Security tab, under Group Or User Names, click Add, click Object Types to enable the Computer object type, and click OK.

7. Type **SERVER04**, and then click Check Names. Click OK.

8. Under Group Or User Names, click the computer name you just added, and then, in the Permissions section of the dialog box, select the Read, Enroll, and Autoenroll permissions in the Allow column.

9. Click OK to create the duplicate template.

Your certificate template is ready. Now you must configure the AIA extension to support the OR. Continue with these steps:

1. Remain on SERVER04.

2. Launch Server Manager from the Administrative Tools program group.

3. Expand Roles\Active Directory Certificate Services\Contoso-Issuing-CA01.

4. Right-click Contoso-Issuing-CA01 in the tree pane and click Properties.

5. On the Extensions tab, click the Select Extension drop-down list and choose Authority Information Access (AIA).

6. Specify the locations to obtain certificate revocation data. In this case, select the location beginning with http://.

7. Select the Include In The AIA Extension Of Issued Certificates and the Include In The Online Certificate Status Protocol (OCSP) Extension check boxes.

8. Click OK to apply the changes.

9. Note that you must stop and restart the AD CS service because of the change. Click Yes in the Certification Authority dialog box to do so.

10. Move to the Certificate Templates node under Contoso-Issuing-CA01 in the tree pane, right-click Certificate Templates, point to New, and then click Certificate Template To Issue.

11. In the Enable Certificate Templates dialog box, select the new OCSP Response Signing template that you created earlier and click OK.

    The new template should appear in the details pane.

12. You now need to verify that the OCSP certificate has been assigned to the server. You do so with the Certificates snap-in. By default, this snap-in is not in a console. You must create a new console to use it.

13. Open the Start menu, type **mmc** in the search box, and then press Enter.

14. In the MMC, click Add/Remove Snap-in on the File menu to open the Add Or Remove Snap-ins dialog box.

15. Select the Certificates snap-in and click Add.

16. Select Computer Account and click Next.

17. Select Local Computer and click Finish.

18. Click OK to close the Add Or Remove Snap-ins dialog box.

19. On the File menu, click Save to save the console and place it in your Documents folder. Name the console **Computer Certificates** and click Save.

20. Expand Certificates\Personal and select Certificates.

21. Right-click Certificates under Personal, point to All Tasks, and then click Request New Certificate. Click Next.

22. On the Certificate Enrollment page, make sure the Active Directory Enrollment Policy is selected and click Next.

23. Select the new OCSP certificate and click Enroll.

24. On the next page, click the down arrow to the right of Details, and then click View Certificate. Browse through the tabs to view the certificate details, noting the certificate name. Click OK.

25. Click Finish to complete this part of the operation.

26. Right-click the new certificate, point to All Tasks, and then click Manage Private Keys.

27. On the Security tab, under Group Or User Names, click Add.

28. In the Select Users, Computers, Service Accounts, Or Groups dialog box, click Locations, select SERVER04, and click OK.

29. Type **Network Service** and click Check Names. Click OK.

30. Click Network Service, and then, in the Permissions section of the dialog box, make sure the Allow::Full Control permission is selected. Click OK to close the dialog box.

Your OR is ready to provide certificate validation information. Now that it is ready, add a revocation configuration. Perform the following steps:

1. Remain on Server04.

2. Launch Server Manager from the Administrative Tools program group.

3. Expand Roles\Active Directory Certificate Services\Online Responder and select Revocation Configuration.

4. Right-click Revocation Configuration and click Add Revocation Configuration.

5. On the Welcome page, click Next.

6. On the Name The Revocation Configuration page, type **RCSERVER04**.

7. Click Next.

8. On the Select CA Certificate Location page, identify the location from which the certificate can be loaded. You can choose from Active Directory, a local certificate store, or a file. Choose Select A Certificate For An Existing Enterprise CA and click Next.

9. Because your root CA is offline, choose Browse CA Certificates Published In Active Directory and click Browse.

10. Locate the root certification authority (Contoso-Root-CA) and click OK.

After the certificate is selected, the wizard loads the Online Responder signing templates.

11. Click Next.

On the Select Signing Certificate page, you must select a signing method because the OR signs each response to clients before it sends it. Three choices are available:

- Automatic selection loads a certificate from the OCSP template you created earlier.
- Manually, you can choose the certificate to use.
- CA Certificate uses the certificate from the CA itself.

Choose Automatically Select A Signing Certificate and select Auto-Enroll For An OCSP Signing Certificate.

12. Click Browse to browse for a CA and select Contoso-Issuing-CA01. Click OK.

This should automatically select the certificate template you prepared earlier.

13. Click Next.

The wizard initializes the revocation provider. If for some reason it cannot find it—it is not displayed in the dialog box—you must add the provider manually, as described in steps 14 and 15; otherwise, skip to step 16. For the purposes of this exercise, perform steps 14 through 16.

14. Click Provider, and then click Add under Base CRLs. Use the following HTTP address: **http://localhost/ca.crl**. Click OK.

15. Repeat the preceding step for the Delta CRLs and use the same HTTP address. Note, because you are obtaining the certificate from Active Directory, the listed provider is an address in ldap:// format and should be provided automatically by the wizard. AD CS relies on Lightweight Directory Access Protocol (LDAP) to obtain information from the AD DS directory store. In production, however, you might need to add a second source such as from an HTTP address. Click OK.

16. Click Finish to complete the revocation configuration.

You should now have a new revocation configuration listed in the details pane, however it will not be working because of the HTTP addresses you added in step 14 and 15, which you will correct in the next exercise.

In production you would repeat this procedure for each CA that is an OR.

EXERCISE 2   Correct an AD CS Implementation with Enterprise PKI

In this exercise, you rely on Enterprise PKI to identify and then correct configuration issues with your AD CS implementation. This exercise demonstrates the value of working with Enterprise PKI.

1. Make sure that SERVER01, SERVER03, and SERVER04 are running.

2. Log on to SERVER04, using the domain Administrator account.

3. Launch Server Manager from the Administrative Tools program group.

4. Expand Roles\Active Directory Certificate Services and select Enterprise PKI. Expand Enterprise PKI\Contoso-Root-CA. Click Contoso-Issuing-CA01 and note the errors. (See Figure 15-10.) These errors exist if you added HTTP locations in the preceding exercise. If you did not, your configuration will not include any errors.

These errors refer to the web-based download locations for the CRL Distribution Point and for the AIA. These errors appear because they refer to locations that do not exist. These locations must be created manually in IIS. However, because you are using an AD DS–integrated AD CS deployment, you do not need to add web-based download locations even if they are indicated by default in the configuration of AD CS. In an AD DS–integrated deployment, the directory service is responsible for AIA and CRL distribution, and, because this service is highly available, no secondary location is required. In fact, you need to add secondary locations only if you want to make them available to mobile or external users who are outside your internal network. If you do so, the URLs you specify must be available externally.

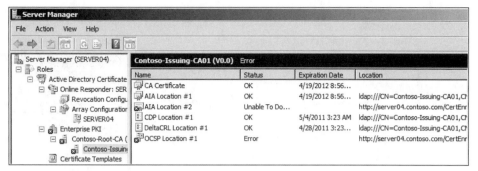

FIGURE 15-10 Viewing configuration errors in Enterprise PKI

5. Right-click Contoso-Issuing-CA01 under AD CS in Server Manager and click Properties.

6. On the Extensions tab, verify that CRL Distribution Point (CDP) is selected in the drop-down list.

7. Select http://<ServerDNSName>/CertEnroll/<CaName><CRLNameSuffix> <DeltaCRLAllowed>.crl in the Locations section of the dialog box, and make sure that Include In CRLs, Clients Use This To Find Delta CRL Locations, as well as Include In The CDP Extension Of Issued Certificates are cleared. (They may already be cleared.)

8. Select Authority Information Access (AIA) from the drop-down list.

9. Select http://<ServerDNSName>/CertEnroll/<ServerDNSName>_<CaName> <CertificateName>.crt and clear Include In The AIA Extension Of Issued Certificates as well as Include In The Online Certificate Status Protocol (OCSP) Extension. Click OK to apply your changes.

   AD CS automatically points to a CertEnroll virtual directory under the default website as the CDP. However, the installation process for AD CS does not create this virtual directory by default. If you need to provide web support for CRLs, even if this is only an internal deployment, you must create the virtual directory in IIS. However, in this case, it is not required. Also, as a best practice, you do not remove the HTTP location. If you need to add it later, the proper format for the URL will already be there, and you need only to reselect the appropriate options.

10. Because you modified the configuration of the AD CS server, the console asks you to restart AD CS on this server. Click Yes.

11. Return to Enterprise PKI in Server Manager.

12. On the toolbar, click the Refresh button to update Enterprise PKI.

    There should no longer be any errors in the Enterprise PKI view.

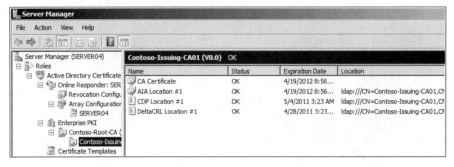

You must verify Enterprise PKI in your production network to make sure no errors are displayed. Use this procedure to correct them if errors are present.

EXERCISE 3 Create a Duplicate Certificate Template for EFS

In this exercise, you create a duplicate certificate to enable EFS and publish it so it can use autoenroll and use EFS to protect the system data.

1. Make sure SERVER01 and SERVER04 are both running.

2. Log on to SERVER04, using the domain Administrator account.

3. Launch Server Manager from the Administrative Tools program group.

4. Expand Roles\Active Directory Certificate Services. Click Certificate Templates (*servername*).

   Note that all the existing templates are listed in the details pane.

   Also note that you are connected to a DC (SERVER01) by default. To work with templates, you must be connected to a DC so that the templates can be published to AD DS. If you are not connected, you must click the More Actions\Connect To Another Writable Domain Controller link in the action pane to do so.

5. Select the Basic EFS template in the details pane, right-click it, and click Duplicate Template.

6. Select the version of Windows Server to support—in this case, Windows Server 2008—and click OK.

7. Name the template **Basic EFS WS08** and set the following options. Leave all other options as is.

   - On the Request Handling tab, select the Archive Subject's Encryption Private Key and Use Advanced Symmetric Algorithm To Send The Key To The CA check boxes. Archival storage of the private key allows you to protect it if the user loses it.

   - On the Subject Name tab, add information to the Alternate Subject Name values. Select the E-mail Name and User Principal Name (UPN) check boxes.

8. Click OK.

9. Right-click the EFS Recovery Agent template and click Duplicate.

10. Select the version of Windows Server to support—in this case, Windows Server 2008—and click OK.

11. Name the template **EFS Recovery Agent WS08** and set the following options. Leave all other options as is.

   ■ On the General tab, select the Publish Certificate In Active Directory check box. Note that the recovery agent certificate is valid for a much longer period than the EFS certificate itself.

   ■ On the Request Handling tab, make sure you select the Archive Subject's Encryption Private Key and Use Advanced Symmetric Algorithm To Send The Key To The CA check boxes. Archival storage of the private key allows you to protect it if the user loses it.

   ■ On the Subject Name tab, add information to the Alternate Subject Name values. Select the E-mail Name and User Principal Name (UPN) check boxes.

12. Click OK.

13. In Server Manager, expand Roles\Active Directory Certificate Services*Issuing CA Name* and select Certificate Templates.

14. To issue a template, right-click Certificate Templates, point to New, and then click Certificate Template To Issue.

15. In the Enable Certificate Templates dialog box, hold down the Ctrl key and click to select both Basic EFS WS08 and EFS Recovery Agent WS08. Click OK.

   Your templates are ready.

EXERCISE 4   Configure Autoenrollment

In this exercise, you use Group Policy to configure autoenrollment. This exercise uses the Default Domain policy for simplicity, but in your environment, you should create a custom policy for this purpose and for all other custom settings you need to apply at the entire domain level.

1. Move to SERVER01 and log on as a domain administrator.

2. Launch Group Policy Management from the Administrative Tools program group.

3. Expand all the nodes to locate the Default Domain Policy. Right-click it and click Edit.

4. To assign autoenrollment for computers, expand Computer Configuration\Policies\ Windows Settings\Security Settings and select Public Key Policies.

5. Double-click Certificate Services Client – Auto-Enrollment.

6. Enable the policy and select the Renew Expired Certificates, Update Pending Certificates, And Remove Revoked Certificates check box.

7. Click OK to assign these settings. Close the GPMC.

   Your policy is ready.

EXERCISE 5   Enable the CA to Issue Certificates

Now you need to set the default action that the CA performs when it receives certificate requests.

1. Return to SERVER04 and log on, using the domain Administrator account.
2. Move to Server Manager.
3. Right-click the issuing CA server name under AD CS, Contoso-Issuing-CA01, and click Properties.
4. On the Policy Module tab, click Properties.
5. To have certificates issued automatically, verify that Follow The Settings In The Certificate Template, If Applicable. Otherwise, Automatically Issue The Certificate is selected. Click OK. Click OK again to close the Properties dialog box.

   Your issuing CA is now ready for production and will begin to issue EFS certificates automatically when they are requested either by your users or by computers.

Lesson Summary

- Revocation configurations for issuing CAs include several components. The first is a list of the Certificate Revocation List distribution points. The second is the overlap between the CRL and the Delta CRLs you send to requesters. The third is the schedule you use to publish CRLs.

- Issuing CAs should be enterprise CAs because of their capability to support autoenrollment and modify and personalize certificate templates.

- You can link online responders to create an array of systems that provides high availability for the service. An array can be as simple as two CAs acting as ORs, or it can include many more servers.

- ORs must rely on the Online Certificate Status Protocol (OCSP) certificates to sign the responses they send to requesters. These certificates encrypt the content of the response sent from the OR.

- ORs also require the configuration of the Authority Information Access extension before they can be fully functional. This extension is part of the properties of the certificate authority.

- Each CA that is an OR must have its own revocation configuration because each has its own certificate. To operate in an array, each of these certificates must be trusted. The revocation configuration is used to allow other array members to trust each particular CA in the array.

- Protection of every CA in your infrastructure is essential. This is why you should perform regular backups of all CA data, including the CA's certificates. Protect these backups very carefully because they contain highly sensitive data.

Lesson Review

You can use the following question to test your knowledge of the information in Lesson 2, "Configuring and Using Active Directory Certificate Services." The question is also available on the companion CD if you prefer to review it in electronic form.

> **NOTE   ANSWERS**
>
> The answer to this question and explanations of why each answer choice is right or wrong are located in the "Answers" section at the end of the book.

1. You are a PKI administrator for Contoso, Ltd. You want to configure your OR. You have already configured your OCSP Response Signing certificates, configured the Authority Information Access extension, and restarted the server. Now you are ready to verify that the certificate has been automatically loaded onto the server. You create a custom console to contain the Certificates snap-in, but when you view the certificates in the Personal node of the computer, the snap-in does not appear. You decide to import the certificate manually, but when you use the Request New Certificate Wizard, you find that the certificate is not available to you. What could be the problem?

   A. You cannot request this certificate through the wizard. You must use the Certutil. exe command.

   B. The security properties of the certificate template are not set properly.

   C. You cannot load an OCSP Response Signing certificate on this server.

   D. You do not need to load this certificate manually. It will be loaded automatically at the next Group Policy refresh cycle.

Chapter Review

To further practice and reinforce the skills you learned in this chapter, you can perform the following tasks:

- Review the chapter summary.
- Review the list of key terms introduced in this chapter.
- Complete the case scenario. This scenario sets up a real-world situation involving the topics of this chapter and asks you to create a solution.
- Complete the suggested practices.
- Take a practice test.

Chapter Summary

- You can use public key infrastructures to extend the authority of your organization beyond the borders of the network it controls. The role of AD DS is focused on network operating system directory services and should be contained within the internal boundaries of your network. AD CS, however, can run both within a corporate network and outside the corporate network. When used within the network, it can be integrated with AD DS to provide automated certificate enrollment. When used outside your network, it should be installed as stand-alone certificate authorities and linked to a third-party trusted certificate authority to ensure that your certificates are trusted by computer systems over which you do not have control.

- You can rely on certificates for a variety of purposes, including data encryption on PCs, communication encryption between two endpoints, information protection, two-factor authentications, wireless communication, and more. All are based on the AD CS role.

- AD CS deployments are hierarchical in nature and form a chain of trust from the lowest to the topmost point of the hierarchy. If certificates are invalidated or expire at any point in the chain, every certificate that is below the invalidated certificate in the chain is invalidated as well.

- You can link Online Responders (ORs) to create an array configuration that provides high availability for the OR service. The more complex your AD CS deployment becomes, the more likely you are to create these arrays to ensure that all users and devices have constant access to the certificate validation services that the OR provides.

- When you deploy ORs, you must ensure that each contains its own revocation configuration. This step is necessary because each OR relies on its own certificate for validation purposes. Each revocation configuration supports a specific certificate key pair and is published to each OR in an array. If you need to renew the OR's certificate, you must update its revocation configuration.

- One of the most useful management tools you have for AD CS is Certutil.exe. This tool supports almost every possible operation on a CA and allows you to automate maintenance and administration tasks.

Key Terms

The following terms were introduced in this chapter. Do you know what they mean?

- hierarchy
- key pair
- revocation

Case Scenario

In the following case scenario, you apply what you have learned about AD CS. You can find answers to the questions in this scenario in the "Answers" section at the end of this book.

Case Scenario: Managing Certificate Revocation

You are a system administrator for Contoso, Ltd. Contoso has deployed an AD CS infrastructure and has published certificates for a wide number of uses. One of these is to create software signing certificates for the software it distributes to its clients. These certificates are used to ensure that the software actually originates from Contoso. Contoso clients are pleased with this new approach because it guarantees that the source of the software is valid and free of malicious code.

As administrator, one of your duties is to perform weekly reviews of the event logs of your servers. Because you're using Windows Server 2008 R2, you have configured event forwarding on each of the certificate authorities in your network. This makes administration easier, eliminating the need to log on to individual servers to view the event logs. You have to verify only one central location.

During a routine check, you notice that the root CA of your AD CS infrastructure has sent events to your central logging server. You think this is very odd, because the root CA should be offline at all times except for very rare instances requiring maintenance operations or in the rare instance when you need to issue a certificate for a new subordinate CA. As system administrator, you know that neither instance has occurred in the recent past.

You look at the events that were forwarded and see that the CA was turned on about a week ago. During that time, it was used to generate two new root certificates under the Contoso name. Fortunately, you also included the security logs in the forwarding configuration. You look them up to see who logged on to the root CA. Because logons require smart cards, your event logs can be used to validate who used the server. You find out to your surprise that the logons belong to two employees who were fired last week. These employees should not have had access to this server.

You check on the Internet and find that the two root certificates are being used to sign software that does not originate from Contoso. In fact, it appears that the two ex-employees are currently offering software signing certificates using the Contoso name for sale on the Internet.

What do you do?

Suggested Practices

To help you successfully master the exam objectives presented in this chapter, complete the following tasks.

Work with AD CS

There are several exam objectives for this topic. Because of this, you should focus your practices on the following areas:

- Identifying the differences between stand-alone and enterprise CAs
- Working with the installation and configuration process for AD CS CAs
- Installing and configuring the Online Responder service
- Installing Network Device Enrollment Service
- Working with certificate templates

You should also practice using the management tools and consoles for AD CS. Most of the consoles are available in Server Manager. The only console you need to create is the Certificates console.

- **Practice 1** Prepare two servers—virtual or physical—as member servers of an AD DS domain. Then install a stand-alone root CA and follow with the installation of an enterprise issuing CA. Run through each of the operations outlined in this chapter for the installation and configuration of both servers. For the purpose of the exercise, keep the root CA online and allow it to communicate with the issuing CA.

- **Practice 2** Use the issuing CA to install the Online Responder service. Then follow each of the steps outlined in Lesson 2 to finalize the configuration of the Online Responder service. Pay attention to each step. ORs are new to AD CS and, therefore, will likely be on the exam.

- **Practice 3** Follow the instructions in the practice in Lesson 1 to install and configure the NDES. This is also a new feature of AD CS and, thus, will be on the exam.

- **Practice 4**   Modify a few template duplicates. Make sure you review the tabs of each template's property sheets thoroughly. Version 2 and 3 templates include many options and features.

- **Practice 5**   Perform backups and restores, and explore both Enterprise PKI and the options available through the Certutil.exe tool. Don't forget to study AD CS as well as PKI implementations with Windows Server 2003. The Microsoft TechNet website includes much more information on PKI in Windows Server 2003 than in Windows Server 2008 R2.

Take a Practice Test

The practice tests on this book's companion CD offer many options. For example, you can test yourself on just one exam objective, or you can test yourself on all the 70-640 certification exam content. You can set up the test so that it closely simulates the experience of taking a certification exam, or you can set it up in study mode·so that you can look at the correct answers and explanations after you answer each question.

> **MORE INFO   PRACTICE TESTS**
>
> For details about all the practice test options available, see the "How to Use the Practice Tests" section in this book's Introduction.

CHAPTER 16

Active Directory Rights Management Services

Active Directory Rights Management Services (AD RMS), formerly known simply as Rights Management Services, is designed to extend the reach of your internal network to the outside world. However, now the extension applies to intellectual property. People have been struggling with Digital Rights Management (DRM) ever since they started working with computers. In the first days of computing, software manufacturers went to great lengths to protect their software from theft. Even today, some vendors require the use of hardware keys for their software to run. Others have resorted to a web-based approval and validation process. For example, with the release of Windows 7, Microsoft introduced a new licensing scheme, one option of which is a Key Management Server (KMS) to validate the licensed versions of Microsoft Windows you use.

Software creation isn't the only industry struggling with rights management. The music industry is also under pressure to determine the best way to protect digital music, sometimes even using questionable methods to do so. For instance, in 2005, Mark Russinovich, now a technical fellow at Microsoft Corporation, discovered that Sony BMG installed a root kit with its CD player that activated when users loaded it onto their PCs. This root kit sent playlist information back to a central server managed by Sony through the Internet. This led to a series of articles and a flurry of activity on the Internet about the approaches that music vendors were using to protect content.

> **MORE INFO** **MARK RUSSINOVICH AND SONY BMG**
>
> For more information on Mark's adventure with Sony, go to *http://blogs.technet.com/b/ markrussinovich/archive/2005/10/31/sony-rootkits-and-digital-rights-management-gone- too-far.aspx*.

Now many record labels have decided to sell their music in MP3 format without data protection. When you buy the song, you become responsible for protecting it; however, you can play it on any device. It might or might not be related to Mark's story with Sony BMG, but the move displays just how complex DRM can become.

Music and software are not the only items that need protection. In data centers everywhere, people are starting to look to new technologies to protect their intellectual property. For example, email messages automatically keep a trail of conversations. Each time you respond to a message, the original message is embedded into your message, and so on. Without DRM, anyone can change the content of this embedded response at any time, changing the tone or nature of the conversation. Even worse, anyone can forward the conversation and change its content, and you won't even know about it. Implementing DRM to protect email content ensures that your responses can never be modified, even if they are embedded in another message.

The same applies to other intellectual property—Microsoft Office Word documents, Microsoft Office PowerPoint presentations, and other content. Many organizations rely on the value of their intellectual property. Losing this property or having it misused, copied, or stolen can cause untold damage to their operations. You don't have to be a major enterprise to profit from some form of rights management. If you earn a living from the information you generate or you maintain competitive leadership through the use of internal information, consider DRM.

AD RMS helps you protect your intellectual property through the integration of several features. In fact, in addition to a direct integration with Active Directory Domain Services (AD DS), AD RMS can also rely on both Active Directory Certificate Services (AD CS) and Active Directory Federation Services (AD FS). AD CS can generate the public key infrastructure (PKI) certificates that AD RMS can embed in documents. AD FS extends your AD RMS policies beyond the firewall and supports the protection of your intellectual property among your business partners, as illustrated in Figure 16-1.

Exam objective in this chapter:

- Configure Active Directory Rights Management Services (AD RMS).

Lessons in this chapter:

FIGURE 16-1 AD RMS extending the reach of authority beyond network boundaries

Before You Begin

To complete the lessons in this chapter, you must have installed:

- Windows Server 2008 R2 on a physical or virtual computer. The computer should be named SERVER01 and should be a domain controller in the contoso.com domain. The details for this setup are presented in Chapter 1, "Creating an Active Directory Domain."

- Windows Server 2008 R2 Enterprise edition on a physical or virtual computer. The computer should be named SERVER04 and should be a member server within the contoso.com domain. This computer will host the AD RMS policy servers that you install and create through the exercises in this chapter. Ideally, this computer also includes a D drive to store the data for AD RMS. Microsoft recommends 80 GB for the D drive on a working AD RMS server, but 40 GB is sufficient for these exercises.

A thorough test of AD RMS would require quite a few computers. For this reason, using a virtual infrastructure makes the most sense. If you can, you should also add a client computer running Windows 7 and Microsoft Office 2010 so you can test the AD RMS infrastructure after it is deployed.

REAL WORLD

Danielle Ruest and Nelson Ruest

In 2007, we were asked to create a book as part of a complete series on a specific technology, covering architectures, deployment, administration, and so on. Several author teams would participate in the project, each focusing on one book.

We rushed to prepare our table of contents (TOC) and deliver it on the due date. Having recently installed Microsoft Office 2007, we decided to use one of the new templates in Word 2007. It gave our TOC a nice, polished look. The publisher was impressed with our format and sent it to the other teams, asking them to use the same format. When all the TOCs were in, the project was presented to the board and approved.

The author teams started working on their text. As it turned out, however, one of the teams was very far behind on its schedule and would not be able to complete its chapters on time. Could we help the team out and write a couple of its chapters? We agreed to look at the team's TOC.

When we received the other authors' TOC, we were not surprised to see our original format. However, as we examined the TOC to determine which chapters we could help with, we found that 33 percent of our content appeared verbatim in the other authors' TOC.

We quickly called our publisher. It was never determined whether they had performed the plagiarism on purpose or by mistake, but if we had used a digital rights management technology such as AD RMS in our own TOC, this could never have happened. Although copyrights protect content ownership, they will never be as far-reaching as DRM, which ensures that content can be used only in the manner intended. No other technology or principle can protect information in the same way.

Lesson 1: Understanding and Installing Active Directory Rights Management Services

Many organizations choose to implement AD RMS in stages.

- The first stage focuses on internal use of intellectual property. In this stage, you concentrate on implementing proper access rights for the documentation you produce. Employees can view, read, and manage only content they are involved with. Content cannot be copied except under strict conditions.

- The second stage involves sharing content with partners. Here you begin to provide protected content to partner firms. Partners can view and access protected documents but cannot copy or otherwise share the information.

- The third stage involves a wider audience. Your intellectual property can be distributed outside the boundaries of your network in a protected mode. Because it is protected, it cannot be copied or distributed electronically unless you give the required authorizations.

In each case, you must be sure to communicate your document protection policy fully to the people who will be working with your data. Employees must be fully trained on the AD RMS solution to understand the impact of divulging information to unauthorized audiences. Partners should be provided with policy statements so they can understand how to protect your information. Then, when you reach wider audiences, you must make sure that they also fully understand your protection policies so they can work with your information properly.

Each stage of the implementation requires additional components to further the reach of your protection strategies.

After this lesson, you will be able to:

- Understand the components that make up AD RMS services.
- Understand different AD RMS deployment scenarios.
- Understand AD RMS prerequisites for deployment.
- Install AD RMS in various scenarios.

Estimated lesson time: 40 minutes

Understanding AD RMS

As mentioned earlier, AD RMS is an updated version of the Rights Management Services available in Microsoft Windows Server 2003. With the latest release, Microsoft has included several new features that extend the functionality included in AD RMS. However, the scenarios you use to deploy AD RMS remain the same.

AD RMS works with a special AD RMS client to protect sensitive information. Protection is provided through the AD RMS server role, which is designed to provide certificate and licensing management. Information—configuration and logging—is persisted in a database. In test environments, you can rely on the Windows Internal Database (WID) included in Windows Server 2008 R2, but in production environments, you should rely on a formal database engine such as Microsoft SQL Server 2005 or Microsoft SQL Server 2008 running on a separate server. This provides the ability to load balance AD RMS through the installation of multiple servers running this role. WID does not support remote connections; therefore, only one server can use it. Internet Information Services (IIS) 7.0 provides the web services upon which AD RMS relies, and the Microsoft Message Queuing service ensures transaction coordination in distributed environments. The AD RMS client provides access to AD RMS features on the desktop. In addition, an AD DS directory provides integrated authentication and administration. AD RMS relies on AD DS to authenticate users and verify that they are allowed to use the service. This makes up the AD RMS infrastructure, shown in Figure 16-2.

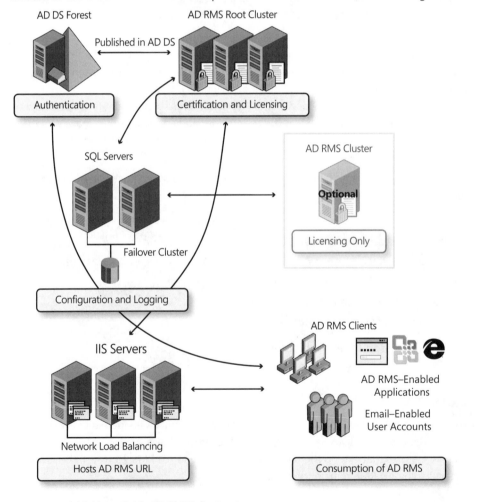

FIGURE 16-2 A highly available AD RMS infrastructure

The first time you install an AD RMS server, you create an AD RMS root cluster by default. A root cluster is designed to handle both certification and licensing requests. Only one root cluster can exist in an AD DS forest. You can also install licensing-only servers, which automatically form a licensing cluster. Clusters are available only if you deploy the AD RMS database on a separate server. Each time you add a new AD RMS server with either the root or the licensing role, it is automatically integrated into the corresponding existing cluster. Microsoft recommends that you rely on the root role more than the licensing-only role for two reasons:

- Root clusters handle all AD RMS operations and are, therefore, multifunctional.
- Root and licensing-only clusters are independent; that is, they cannot share load balancing of the service. If you install all your servers as root servers, they automatically load balance each other.

After the infrastructure is in place, you can enable information-producing applications such as word processors, presentation tools, email clients, and custom in-house applications to rely on AD RMS to provide information protection services. As users create information, they define who can read, write, modify, print, transfer, and otherwise electronically manipulate the information. In addition, you can create policy templates that can apply a given configuration to documents as they are created.

EXAM TIP

Remember that any server installation in AD RMS automatically creates a cluster. This cluster should not be confused with the Failover Clustering or Network Load Balancing services that are included in Windows Server 2008 R2. The AD RMS cluster is designed to provide high availability and load balancing to ensure that the service is always available.

Usage rights are embedded directly within the documents you create so that the information remains protected even if it moves beyond your zone of authority. For example, if a protected document leaves your premises and arrives outside your network, it will remain protected because AD RMS settings are persistent. AD RMS offers a set of web services that allow you to extend AD RMS and integrate its features in your own information-producing applications. Because they are web services, organizations can use them to integrate AD RMS features even in non-Windows environments.

MORE INFO   **AD RMS**

Find out more about AD RMS at *http://go.microsoft.com/fwlink/?LinkId=80907.*

AD RMS Features

Active Directory Rights Management Services includes several new features:

- AD RMS is now a server role that is integrated into Windows Server 2008 R2. In previous releases, the features supported by AD RMS were in a package that required a separate download. In addition, the Server Manager installation provides all dependencies and required component installations. Also, if no remote database is indicated during installation, Server Manager automatically installs Windows Internal Database.

- As with most of the Windows Server 2008 R2 server roles, AD RMS is administered through a Microsoft Management Console (MMC). Previous versions provided administration only through a web interface.

- AD RMS includes direct integration with Active Directory Federation Services, allowing you to extend your rights management policies beyond the firewall with your partners. This means that your partners do not need their own AD RMS infrastructures and can rely on yours through AD FS to access AD RMS features. In previous releases, you could rely on only Windows Live IDs to federate RMS services. With the integration of AD RMS and AD FS, you no longer need to rely on a third party to protect information. However, to use federation, you must have an established federated trust before you install the AD RMS extension that integrates with AD FS, and you must use the latest RMS client—the Windows 7 client or the RMS client with SP2 for versions of Windows earlier than Windows 7. For information on AD FS, see Chapter 17, "Active Directory Federation Services."

- AD RMS servers are self-enrolled when they are created. Enrollment creates a server licensor certificate (SLC), which grants the server the right to participate in the AD RMS structure. Earlier versions required access to the Microsoft Enrollment Center through the Internet to issue and sign the SLC. AD RMS relies on a self-enrollment certificate that is included in Windows Server 2008 R2. Because of this, you can now run AD RMS in isolated networks without requiring Internet access of any kind.

- Finally, AD RMS includes administration roles so that you can delegate specific AD RMS tasks without having to grant excessive administration rights. Four local administrative roles are created:

  - AD RMS Enterprise Administrators, which can manage all aspects of AD RMS. This group includes the user account used to install the role as well as the local administrators group.

  - AD RMS Template Administrators, which supports the ability to read information about the AD RMS infrastructure as well as list, create, modify, and export rights policy templates.

  - AD RMS Auditors, which allows members to manage logs and reports. Auditors have read-only access to AD RMS infrastructure information.

  - AD RMS Service, which contains the AD RMS service account that is identified during the role installation.

Because each of these groups is local, create corresponding global groups in your AD DS directory and insert these groups within the local groups on each AD RMS server. Then, when you need to grant rights to an administrative role, all you need to do is add the user's account to the global groups in AD DS.

EXAM TIP

Delegation is an important aspect of AD RMS administration. Pay close attention to the various delegation roles and the groups that support them.

MORE INFO   FEATURES AVAILABLE IN PREVIOUS RELEASES

For information on features released in RMS before Windows Server 2008 R2, go to *http://go.microsoft.com/fwlink/?LinkId=68637*.

Basically, when you protect information through AD RMS, you rely on the AD RMS server to issue rights account certificates. These certificates identify the trusted entities—users, groups, computers, applications, or services—that can create and publish rights-enabled content. After a content publisher has been trusted, it can assign rights and conditions to the content it creates. Each time a user establishes a protection policy on a document, AD RMS issues a publishing license for the content. By integrating this license in the content, AD RMS binds it so that the license becomes permanently attached and no longer requires access to an AD RMS system to provide document or content protection.

Usage rights are integrated in any form of binary data that supports usage within or outside your network, as well as online or offline. When content is protected, it is encrypted with special encryption keys, much like the keys created when using AD CS. To view the data, users must access it through an AD RMS–enabled browser or application. If the application is not AD RMS enabled, users cannot manipulate the information because the application cannot read the protection policy to decrypt the data properly.

When other users access the rights-protected content, their AD RMS clients request a usage license from the server. If the user is also a trusted entity, the AD RMS server issues this use license. The use license reads the protection license for this document and applies these usage rights to the document for the duration of its lifetime.

To facilitate the publishing process, trusted users can create protection licenses from predefined templates that can be applied with the tools they are already familiar with, such as word processors and email clients. Each template applies a specific predefined usage policy, as shown in Figure 16-3.

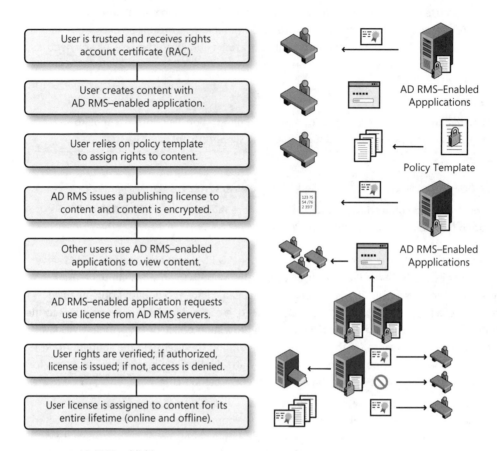

User is trusted and receives rights account certificate (RAC).	
User creates content with AD RMS–enabled application.	AD RMS–Enabled Appplications
User relies on policy template to assign rights to content.	Policy Template
AD RMS issues a publishing license to content and content is encrypted.	
Other users use AD RMS–enabled applications to view content.	AD RMS–Enabled Appplications
AD RMS–enabled application requests use license from AD RMS servers.	
User rights are verified; if authorized, license is issued; if not, access is denied.	
User license is assigned to content for its entire lifetime (online and offline).	

FIGURE 16-3 AD RMS publishing process

AD RMS Installation Scenarios

Each organization has its own needs and requirements for information protection. For this reason, AD RMS supports several deployment scenarios. These scenarios include:

- **Single-server deployment** Install AD RMS on a single server. This installs the WID as the support database. Because all the components are local, you cannot scale this deployment to support high availability. Use the single-server deployment only in test environments. If you want to use this deployment to test AD RMS beyond the firewall, you must add appropriate AD RMS exceptions.

- **Internal deployment** Install AD RMS on multiple servers tied to an AD DS directory. You must use a separate server to host the AD RMS database; otherwise, you will not be able to load balance the AD RMS role.

- **Extranet deployment** When users are mobile and do not remain within the confines of your network, you must deploy AD RMS in an extranet—a special perimeter network that provides internal services to authorized users. In this scenario, you must configure appropriate firewall exceptions and add a special extranet URL on an external-facing web server to allow external client connections.

MORE INFO **AD RMS CONFIGURATION IN AN EXTRANET**

For more information on how to configure AD RMS to collaborate outside of the organizational network, see the "AD RMS Deployment in an Extranet Step-by-Step Guide" at *http://technet.microsoft.com/en-us/library/cc753490(WS.10).aspx*.

- **Multiforest deployment** When you have existing partnerships that are based on AD DS forest trusts, you must perform a multiforest deployment. In this case, you must deploy multiple AD RMS installations, one in each forest. Then, assign a Secure Sockets Layer (SSL) certificate to each website that hosts the AD RMS clusters in each forest. You must also extend the AD DS forest schema to include AD RMS objects. However, if you are using Microsoft Exchange Server in each forest, the extensions will already exist. Finally, your AD RMS service account—the account that runs the service—will need to be trusted in each forest.

MORE INFO **MULTIFOREST AD RMS DEPLOYMENTS**

For more information on this deployment model, see *http://technet.microsoft.com/ en-us/library/cc772182(WS.10).aspx*.

- **AD RMS with AD FS deployment** You can also extend the AD RMS root cluster to other forests through Active Directory Federation Services. To do so, you must prepare the following:
  - Assign an SSL certificate to the website hosting the AD RMS root cluster. This ensures secure communications between the cluster and the AD FS resource server.
  - Install the root cluster.
  - Prepare a federated trust relationship before you install the Identity Federation Support role service of AD RMS.
  - Create a claims-aware application on the AD FS resource partner server for both the certification and the licensing pipelines of AD RMS.
  - Assign the Generate Security Audits user right to the AD RMS service account.
  - Define the extranet cluster URL in AD RMS, and then install the AD RMS Identity Federation Support role service through Server Manager. Have the federation URL available during installation.

MORE INFO **AD RMS AND AD FS DEPLOYMENT**

For more information on the AD RMS and AD FS deployment, see *http://technet .microsoft.com/en-us/library/cc771425(WS.10).aspx*.

- **Licensing-only server deployment** In complex forest environments, you might want to deploy a licensing-only AD RMS cluster in addition to the root cluster. In this case, you must first assign an SSL certificate to the website hosting the AD RMS root cluster and then install the root cluster. After you meet these conditions, you can install licensing-only servers.

> **MORE INFO** **SET UP A LICENSING-ONLY AD RMS CLUSTER**
>
> For more information on how to set up a licensing-only AD RMS cluster,
> see *http://technet.microsoft.com/en-us/library/cc730671(WS.10).aspx*.

- **Upgrade Windows RMS to AD RMS** If you upgrade from an existing Windows RMS installation, you must perform the following activities:
  - Make sure your RMS systems are upgraded to RMS Service Pack 1 prior to the upgrade.
  - Back up all servers, and back up the configuration database. Store it in a secure location.
  - If you are using offline enrollment to set up your Windows RMS environment, make sure the enrollment is complete before the upgrade.
  - If you already have service connection points in Active Directory directory service, make sure you use the same URL for the upgrade.
  - If your Windows RMS database is running Microsoft SQL Server Desktop Engine (MSDE), you must upgrade to SQL Server before you upgrade to AD RMS.
  - Clear the RMS Message Queuing queue to make sure all messages are written to the RMS logging database prior to upgrade.
  - Upgrade the root cluster before upgrading the licensing-only server. This provides the root cluster's self-signed SLC to the licensing server when you upgrade it.
  - Upgrade all other servers in the RMS cluster.

These scenarios provide the most common deployment structures for AD RMS.

Installing Active Directory Rights Management Services

A full installation of AD RMS can be quite complex. Remember that a single cluster can exist within an AD DS forest, and make sure you have all the prerequisites in place before you proceed. Also, because of the AD RMS dependencies, these prerequisites are comprehensive. During this preparation process, you decide how to deploy your AD RMS systems. Will you be using only root cluster members, or will you be dividing tasks between root and licensing-only clusters? Do you need interaction with outside partners? Will your deployment be internal only? Answers to each of these questions will help form the architecture of your AD RMS deployment and implementation.

After you have all the prerequisites in place, you can proceed to the actual installation. This is a multistep operation that requires care and attention.

> **MORE INFO** **AD RMS CLUSTER INSTALLATION INSTRUCTIONS**
>
> For more information on the installation of AD RMS clusters, go to *http://technet.microsoft* *.com/en-us/library/cc726041.aspx*.

Preparing AD RMS Installation Prerequisites

There are several prerequisites to AD RMS installation. If you are setting up only a test environment, you have few items to consider, but when you are ready to deploy AD RMS into a production environment, you should take the utmost care to deploy it correctly. For this reason, endeavor to make your test environment match the requirements of your production environment to prevent surprises when you perform the actual deployment.

> **IMPORTANT** **ADDITIONAL AD RMS INSTALLATION OPTIONS**
>
> Note that AD RMS is not supported and does not run in Server Core installations of Windows Server 2008 R2. However, AD RMS is a good candidate for virtualization under Hyper-V, especially in test environments. Keep this in mind when you plan and prepare your AD RMS deployment.

Begin with the prerequisites. Table 16-1 outlines the basic requirements for an AD RMS deployment. Table 16-2 outlines other matters to consider when preparing for AD RMS.

TABLE 16-1 RMS System Requirements

HARDWARE/ SOFTWARE	REQUIREMENT	RECOMMENDED
Processor	One Pentium, 4.3 GHz or higher	Two Pentium, 4.3 GHz or higher
RAM	512 MB	1024 MB
Hard disk space	40 GB	80 GB
Operating system	Any Windows Server 2008 R2 edition except Windows Server Web edition and Itanium-based systems	Windows Server Enterprise edition or Windows Server Datacenter edition
File system	FAT32 or NTFS	NTFS
Messaging	Message Queuing	
Web Services	IIS with ASP.NET enabled	

TABLE 16-2 AD RMS Considerations

COMPONENT	CONSIDERATION
Web Server URL	Reserve URLs that will not change and do not include a computer name or use localhost.
	Also, use different URLs for internal and external connections.
Active Directory Domain Services	An AD DS domain running on Windows 2000 SP3, Windows Server 2003, Windows Server 2008, or Windows Server 2008 R2.
	Upgrade or run a new AD DS domain on Windows Server 2008 R2 if possible.
Installation location	AD RMS must be installed in the same domain as its potential users.
	If possible, install a multidomain forest and install AD RMS in the child production domain.
Domain User accounts	Email address configured in AD DS.
Service account	Standard domain user account that is a member of the local Administrators group.
	Domain-based service account that is assigned the Generate Security Audits user right.
Installation account	A domain-based account.
	Must not be on a smart card.
	Must have local administrator privileges.
	To generate service connection points, must be a member of Enterprise Admins.
	To use an external database, must be a member of System Administrators role on the database server.
Database server	Windows Internal Database or SQL Server 2005 with SP2 or later, including stored procedures to perform operations.
	For fault tolerance, use SQL Server 2005 with SP2 or later installed on a separate computer.
Database instance	Create and name the AD RMS database instance and start the SQL Server Browser service before installation of AD RMS.
Installation certificate	Obtain an SSL certificate for the AD RMS cluster.
	Use self-signed certificates only in testing environments.
	Obtain a trusted certificate from an external third-party commercial CA, and install the certificate prior to the AD RMS installation.

COMPONENT	CONSIDERATION
Cluster key protection	Store the cluster key in the AD RMS configuration database.
	If possible, use a hardware protection device to store the cluster key and install it on each server before you install the AD RMS role.
DNS configuration	Create custom CNAME records for the root cluster URL and the database server.
	Use separate CNAME records for the AD RMS cluster URL and the database server to protect against system loss.
Server licensor certificate name	Prepare an official name before you install.
	Use an official name, such as the name of your organization.
AD RMS–enabled client	AD RMS–enabled browser or application (Word, Microsoft Office Outlook, or PowerPoint in Office 2010 Enterprise edition, Office 2010 Professional Plus, or Office 2010 Ultimate edition).
Smart card usage	Can be integrated in AD RMS but not for setup.
	Do not use a smart card for the installation account, or the account will fail.
Client OS	Windows 7 includes AD RMS client by default; XP requires Windows RMS Client with SP2.

EXAM TIP

Pay attention to the installation prerequisites in Table 16-1 as well as the considerations in Table 16-2. They are complex and, because of this, will certainly appear on the exam.

NOTE   AD RMS CLIENT

To obtain the AD RMS client, go to *http://support.microsoft.com/kb/917275/pl*.

As you can see from Table 16-1, installing AD RMS in a production environment is not a trivial matter.

MORE INFO   HARDWARE AND SOFTWARE CONSIDERATIONS FOR AD RMS

For more information, see "Pre-installation Information for Active Directory Rights Management Services" at *http://technet.microsoft.com/en-us/library/cc771789.aspx*.

Understanding AD RMS Certificates

Because it encrypts and signs data, AD RMS, like AD CS, relies on certificates and assigns these certificates to the users in the AD RMS infrastructure. It also uses licenses that are in an eXtensible rights Markup Language (XrML) format. Because these licenses are embedded in the content that users create, they are also a form of certificate. Like AD CS, the AD RMS hierarchy forms a chain of trust that validates the certificate or license when it is used. Table 16-3 outlines the certificates you require in an AD RMS infrastructure.

TABLE 16-3 AD RMS Certificates

CERTIFICATE	CONTENT
Server licensor certificate (SLC)	The SLC is a self-signed certificate generated during the AD RMS setup of the first server in a root cluster. Other members of the root cluster share this SLC. If you create a licensing-only cluster, it will generate its own SLC and share it with members of its cluster. The default duration for an SLC is 250 years.
Rights account certificate (RAC)	RACs are issued to trusted users who have an email-enabled account in AD DS. RACs are generated when the user first tries to open rights-protected content. Standard RACs identify users in relation to their computers and have a duration of 365 days. Temporary RACs do not tie the user to a specific computer and are valid for only 15 minutes. The RAC contains the public key of the user as well as his or her private key. The private key is encrypted with the computer's public key. (See "Machine certificate," listed later in this table.)
Client licensor certificate (CLC)	After the user has a RAC and launches an AD RMS–enabled application, the application automatically sends a request for a CLC to the AD RMS cluster. The client computer must be connected for this process to work, but after the CLC is obtained, the user can apply AD RMS policies even offline. Because the CLC is tied to the client's RAC, it is automatically invalidated if the RAC is revoked. The CLC includes the client licensor public key, the client licensor private key that is encrypted by the user's public key, and the AD RMS cluster's public key. The CLC private key is used to encrypt content.
Machine certificate	The first time an AD RMS–enabled application is used on a client, a machine certificate is created. The AD RMS client in Windows automatically manages this process with the AD RMS cluster. This certificate creates a lockbox on the computer to correlate the machine certificate with the user's profile. The machine certificate contains the public key for the activated computer. The private key is contained within the lockbox on the computer.

CERTIFICATE	CONTENT
Publishing license	The publishing license is created when the user saves content in a rights-protected mode. This license lists which users can use the content and under which conditions as well as the rights each user has to the content.
	This license includes the symmetric content key for decrypting content as well as the public key of the cluster.
Use license	The use license is assigned to a user who opens rights-protected content. It is tied to the user's RAC and lists the access rights the user has to the content. If the RAC is not available, the user cannot work with rights-protected content.
	The use license contains the symmetric key for decrypting content. This key is encrypted with the public key of the user.

EXAM TIP

Pay attention to the different certificates and licenses used in AD RMS. They are good candidates for exam questions.

Installation Procedure

Now that you understand the requirements and processes that make up an AD RMS installation, you are ready to proceed. Ensure that you have prepared all the requirements listed in Table 16-1, and then perform the following steps.

1. Log on to a member server running Windows Server 2008 R2, using Enterprise Administrative credentials.

   In production, this server can be running Windows Server 2008 R2 Standard edition, Windows Server 2008 R2 Enterprise edition, or Windows Server 2008 R2 Datacenter edition.

> *IMPORTANT* **USE MEMBER SERVERS**
>
> Do not install AD RMS on a domain controller. Use a member server only! With the advent of virtualization, aside from the operating system licensing aspect, there is no longer any reason to create multipurpose domain controllers. Each virtual machine can have its own purpose and run independently of all other services.

2. Launch Server Manager from the Administrative Tools program group.
3. Right-click the Roles node in the tree pane and click Add Roles.
4. Review the Before You Begin information and click Next.

5. On the Select Server Roles page, select Active Directory Rights Management Services and click Next.

   The Add Role Wizard asks you to add the Web Server (IIS) role with the required features, Message Queuing and Remote Server Administration Tools.

6. Click Add Required Role Services if these services were not installed prior to the installation of AD RMS. Click Next.

7. On the Active Directory Rights Management Services page, review the information about the selected role and click Next.

8. On the Select Role Services page, make sure the Active Directory Rights Management Server check box is selected and click Next.

   Do not choose the Identity Federation Support option at this time. You cannot install this option until the AD FS federation relationship has been created. Federations are discussed in Chapter 17.

9. On the Create Or Join An AD RMS Cluster page, select Create A New AD RMS Cluster option and click Next.

   If the cluster were already created and you were installing a second server, you would select Join An Existing AD RMS cluster because there can be only one cluster per forest.

10. On the Select Configuration Database page, select the Use A Different Database Server.

    If you choose to use Windows Internal Database to host the AD RMS databases for a single-server installation, steps 11 and 12 are not required. Remember that when you use a WID instance, you cannot join other servers to this cluster. Use WID only in test environments if you do not have the resources to create a proper database server.

11. Click Select to locate the server that hosts the database, type the server name, and then click Check Names. Click OK.

12. In the Database Instance drop-down list, select the appropriate instance, click Validate, and then click Next.

13. On the Specify Service Account page, click Specify, type the domain user account and password that should be used as the AD RMS service account, click OK, and then click Next.

    Remember that this account must be a member of the local Administrators group.

14. On the Configure AD RMS Cluster Key Storage page, select Use CSP Key Storage and click Next.

    You choose to protect the AD RMS cluster key by using a cryptographic storage provider because it is a more secure protection method. You must select the storage provider and then install this certificate on each new AD RMS server before you can add them to the root cluster. You can also store the key in the AD RMS database, but doing so is less secure than with a cryptographic service provider (CSP).

15. On the Specify AD RMS Cluster Key page, select the CSP to use. You can select either software or hardware cryptographic service providers. Use the one that best fits your security policy guidelines, and select Create A New Key With The Selected CSP. Click Next.

   You can also use an existing key, but do so only when you are recovering from an unrecoverable configuration database.

16. On the Select AD RMS Cluster Web Site page, select the website where you want to install the AD RMS web services and click Next. If you did not prepare the website before, the name of the website will be Default Web Site.

17. On the Specify Cluster Address page, select Use An SSL-Encrypted Connection (Https://).

   As a security best practice, the AD RMS cluster should be provisioned by using an SSL-encrypted connection. You should be using a certificate provided by a third-party commercial certification authority (CA) so that it can be automatically trusted by all parties. This certificate should already be installed on the server so that you can select it as you proceed through the installation.

   Do not use an unencrypted connection. You cannot rely on open connections if you intend to use Identity Federation for your AD RMS implementation.

18. In the Internal Address section of the Specify Cluster Address page, type the fully qualified domain name (FQDN) of the AD RMS cluster and click Validate. If validation succeeds, the wizard updates the preview of the cluster address at the bottom of the page. Click Next.

   This must be a valid FQDN, and it cannot be changed later. If you want to change the default port on which AD RMS communicates, you can do so on this page of the wizard. You must do so now, because you will not be able to change the port at a later date.

19. On the Choose A Server Authentication Certificate For SSL Encryption page, select Choose An Existing Certificate For SSL Encryption (Recommended), select the certificate you installed, and then click Next.

   If you did not install the certificate prior to setup, you can click Import to import the certificate now. You can also use a self-signed certificate, or, if you did not obtain the certificate prior to installation, you can select the third option, to choose encryption later. Note, however, that if you choose this last option, you cannot complete your installation until you obtain and install this certificate.

> **IMPORTANT   SELF-SIGNED CERTIFICATES**
>
> Self-signed certificates should be used for test environments only. In a production environment, use a proper SSL certificate issued from a commercial certification authority.

20. On the Name The Server Licensor Certificate page, type a valid name to identify the AD RMS cluster and click Next.

21. On the Register AD RMS Service Connection Point page, select Register The AD RMS Service Connection Point Now and click Next.

    This action registers the AD RMS service connection point (SCP) in the AD DS.

> **IMPORTANT** **ACCESS RIGHTS FOR SCP CREATION**
>
> To register the AD RMS SCP, you must be logged on to the AD RMS server, using a user account with write access to the Services container in AD DS—that is, a member of the Enterprise Admins group.

    If you are preparing the cluster and need to install additional cluster members before it starts servicing requests, select Register The AD RMS Service Connection Point Later. Then join the other cluster member and, when you are ready, create the SCP.

22. On the Web Server (IIS) page, review the information about IIS and click Next.

    The pages mentioned in steps 23 and 24 are available only if IIS is not preinstalled on the server.

23. On the next page, keep the Web Server default selections and click Next.

24. On the Confirm Installation Selections page, review your choices and click Install.

25. When the installation is complete, click Close to close the installation wizard. Log off and log back on to update the permissions granted to the logged-on user account.

    The user account logged on when the AD RMS server role was installed is automatically made a member of the AD RMS Enterprise Administrators group. This gives this account access to all AD RMS operations.

    The installation is complete. (See Figure 16-4.)

> **MORE INFO** **AD RMS CLUSTER**
>
> For more information on how to install an AD RMS cluster, see *http://technet.microsoft .com/en-us/library/cc726041.aspx*. For a step-by-step installation guide, see *http://technet .microsoft.com/en-us/library/cc753531(WS.10).aspx*. To provide high availability for the cluster, you must install additional cluster members. For information on this installation, go to *http://technet.microsoft.com/en-us/library/cc753417.aspx*.

FIGURE 16-4 After the installation is complete, the entire AD RMS tree structure becomes available in Service Manager

Moving AD RMS to Windows Server 2008 R2

If your organization is already running AD RMS on Windows Server 2008 and wants to move its installation to Windows Server 2008 R2, you have two options:

- Upgrade the installation.
- Migrate the installation.

Upgrading the installation means performing an operating system upgrade to Windows Server 2008 R2, then upgrading the AD RMS installation after the operating system upgrade is complete. Most organizations and IT administrators balk at the idea of performing an operating system upgrade. Upgrades are more reliable now that Microsoft has changed the operating system installation process—this change occurred with the release of Windows Vista—but many administrators still don't trust them. If this is the case in your organization, you'll have to rely on the second option to move to an AD RMS installation on Windows Server 2008 R2.

Migrating the installation is often simpler than upgrading. That's because you begin with a brand-new operating system installation on either a physical or virtual machine. Use the following process:

1. Install Windows Server 2008 R2 on a new computer.
2. Add the AD RMS role and join the existing AD RMS cluster. This makes all of the core components of your AD RMS available on the new server.

3. Add new servers running Windows Server 2008 R2 to the AD RMS cluster. This provides high availability and further protection for the core components of the AD RMS installation.

4. Decommission and remove the AD RMS cluster members that are not running Windows Server 2008 R2.

As you can see, migrating is as simple as upgrading and may provide better results. However, consider the following when you perform the move with whichever procedure you decide to rely on:

- Back up the AD RMS configuration database prior to the move. This provides additional protection during the move.

- Export the server licensor certificate. The SLC decrypts all encrypted content. Place it in a safe location.

- Export and install the CSP key. The CSP key stores the AD RMS private key and therefore is required on all cluster members. Export it from an existing server, and import it on all new cluster members running Windows Server 2008 R2.

Using these measures during a move protects your installation and allows you to roll back to the existing installation should a mishap occur during the move.

After the move is complete, you must also perform the following tasks:

1. Update the CNAME record for the AD RMS cluster. Make sure that you remove the decommissioned server names from this record and add the new server names running Windows Server 2008 R2.

2. Run the AD RMS console to make sure everything is okay with the updated cluster.

3. Test AD RMS connectivity by using an AD RMS client.

Performing these final tasks ensures that your new AD RMS cluster is ready for business.

> **MORE INFO** **MOVING FROM AN AD RMS INSTALLATION ON WINDOWS SERVER 2008 TO WINDOWS SERVER 2008 R2**
>
> For more information on how to upgrade AD RMS on Windows Server 2008 to Windows Server 2008 R2, go to *http://technet.microsoft.com/en-us/library/ ff770805%28WS.10%29.aspx*.

Working with Windows PowerShell

AD RMS can be both installed and administered with Windows PowerShell on Windows Server 2008 or Windows Server 2008 R2. There are two modules for AD RMS:

- AdRmsInstall, which supports the installation and configuration of AD RMS components

- AdRmsAdmin, which controls the administration of installed AD RMS components

Run the following cmdlets to import both modules:

```
Import-Module AdRms
```

```
Import-Module AdRmsAdmin
```

You can also import all available PowerShell modules to gain access to AD RMS cmdlets.

After the modules are imported, you can manage and administer AD RMS installations and components through PowerShell. One great advantage of PowerShell is that you can easily automate AD RMS administration and deployment through its cmdlets.

> **MORE INFO** **AD RMS AND WINDOWS POWERSHELL**
>
> For more information on how to use PowerShell to work with AD RMS, see *http://go.microsoft.com/fwlink/?LinkId=136806*.

PRACTICE   Installing AD RMS

In this practice, you install AD RMS into a new cluster. First you must add a DNS record. In the following exercises, you create the service account and the AD RMS role groups in the directory, create and install a Web Server certificate, and then proceed to the installation. Be sure the computers listed in the "Before You Begin" section of this chapter are running before you proceed. You need SERVER01 and SERVER04 for this practice.

EXERCISE 1   Prepare the DNS Record

In this exercise, you create a CNAME record to prepare for the AD RMS cluster URL.

1. Log on to SERVER01, using the domain Administrator account.
2. Launch Server Manager from the Administrative Tools program group.
3. Expand Roles\DNS Server\DNS\SERVER01\Forward Lookup Zones and select contoso.com.
4. Right-click in the details pane and click New Alias (CNAME).
5. In the New Resource Record dialog box, type the alias name **RightsManagement** and assign it to SERVER04.contoso.com in the Fully Qualified Domain Name (FQDN) For Target Host section of the dialog box. Click OK.

   You have created a new record for the AD RMS cluster URL. It will be updated to other servers as you perform the other exercises.

EXERCISE 2   Prepare the Directory

In this exercise, you create a service account and four groups for AD RMS administration delegation.

1. Log on to SERVER01, using the domain Administrator account, if you haven't done so already.
2. Launch Server Manager from the Administrative Tools program group.

3. Expand Roles\Active Directory Domain Services\Active Directory Users and Computers\contoso.com. Create the Admins\Service Identities OU structure if it doesn't already exist.

4. Right-click the Service Identities OU, point to New, and then click User.

5. Name the user **ADRMSService,** and use this name for both the logon and the pre–Windows 2000 logon names. Click Next.

6. Assign a complex password, clear User Must Change Password At Next Logon, and select Password Never Expires. Click Next, and then click Finish to create the account.

> **NOTE   LEGACY SERVICE ACCOUNTS**
>
> You must create the service account as directed in these steps because you cannot use a managed service account in this instance. Managed service accounts do not work when the account is shared by multiple computers or when the account is used for a service running on multiple computers, such as for a cluster. Managed service accounts are discussed in Lesson 4 of Chapter 8, "Improving the Security of Authentication in an AD DS Domain."

7. Create the AD RMS administration groups under the contoso.com\Admins\ Server Delegations OU. Create these OUs if they are not already created.

8. Create four global security groups. Right-click in the details pane, point to New, and then click Group. Type the name and click OK. Create the following four groups:
   - AD RMS Enterprise Administrators
   - AD RMS Template Administrators
   - AD RMS Auditors
   - AD RMS Service Account

9. Right-click the AD RMS Service Account group and click Properties. On the Members tab, add the ADRMSService account to this group and click OK.

10. Log on to SERVER04, using the domain Administrator account, if you have not done so already.

11. Launch Server Manager from the Administrative Tools program group.

12. Expand Configuration\Local Users And Groups and select Groups.

13. Double-click the Administrators group to open it.

14. Add the AD RMS Service Account group to this group, and click OK.

EXERCISE 3   Prepare a Web Server Certificate

Because AD RMS requires SSL-encrypted web connections, you must create and install a web server certificate before you can proceed with the installation. Note that for this practice to work, you must have performed the practices in Chapter 15, "Active Directory Certificate Services and Public Key Infrastructures," first. You can use a self-signed certificate, but by using real certificates you learn to integrate AD CS with AD RMS.

1. Log on to SERVER04, using the domain Administrator account.

   This grants you Enterprise Administrator credentials, which are required to create the SCP. These rights are required for Exercise 4.

2. Launch Server Manager from the Administrative Tools program group.

3. Expand Roles\Active Directory Certificate Services and select Certificate Templates. The node shows that you are connected to SERVER01.contoso.com.

   Note that all the existing templates are listed in the details pane.

4. Select the Web Server template in the details pane, right-click it, and then click Duplicate Template.

5. Select the version of Windows Server to support, in this case Windows Server 2008 Enterprise, and click OK.

6. Name the template **Web Server WS08** and set the following options. Leave all other options as they are.

   a. On the General tab, select Publish Certificate In Active Directory.

   b. On the Security tab, add the computer account for SERVER04. To do so, click Add, click Object Types, select Computers, and then click OK. Type **SERVER04**, click Check Names, and then click OK again.

   c. Grant SERVER04 the Allow::Read and Allow::Enroll permissions.

7. Click OK.

   Template issuance is performed in the Certification Authority console section of Server Manager.

8. Expand Roles\Active Directory Certificate Services\Contoso-Issuing-CA01 and click Certificate Templates.

9. To issue a template, right-click Certificate Templates, point to New, and then click Certificate Template To Issue.

10. In the Enable Certificate Templates dialog box, select Web Server WS08 and click OK.

    You are ready to proceed with the installation.

EXERCISE 4   Install a Web Server Certificate

Now you need to request and install the certificate.

1. Staying on SERVER04, click the Start menu, type **mmc** in the Search box, and then press Enter.

2. On the File menu, click Add/Remove Snap-in. In the Add or Remove Snap-ins dialog box, select the Certificates snap-in and click Add.

3. Choose Computer Account and click Next.

4. Make sure Local Computer is selected, click Finish, and then click OK.

5. On the File menu, click Save As, navigate to your Documents folder, and name it **Computer Certificates02**. Click Save.

6. Expand Certificates (Local Computer)\Personal and select Certificates.

7. Right-click Certificates, point to All Tasks, and then click Request New Certificate. Click Next. Make sure Active Directory Enrollment Policy is selected and click Next.

8. Select the Web Server WS08 certificate, and then click the More Information Is Required To Enroll For This Certificate link.

9. In the Certificate Properties dialog box, on the Subject tab:

    a. In the Subject Name area, ensure that Full DN is selected, type **CN=SERVER04,DC=Contoso,DC=com** as the Value, and then click Add.

    b. In the Alternative Name area, choose URL in the Type drop-down list, type **RightsManagement.contoso.com** in the Value field, and then click Add.

    c. On the General tab, type **Contoso DRM** in the Friendly Name field and **Web Server Certificate** in the Description field.

    d. On the Private Key tab, click the double down arrow icon on the right to expand the Key Options section and select the Make Private Key Exportable and Allow Private Key To Be Archived check boxes.

10. Click OK, and then click Enroll. Click Finish.

11. To verify that the certificate has been issued, click Certificates under the Personal node in the tree pane and view the certificate in the details pane. The certificate will be named with the server name only.

12. Close the Certificates console.

    You are ready to install AD RMS.

EXERCISE 5   Install an AD RMS Root Cluster

Ensure that you have at least SERVER01 and SERVER04 running.

1. Log on to SERVER04, using the domain Administrator account. This grants you Enterprise Administrator credentials, which are required to create the SCP.

2. Launch Server Manager from the Administrative Tools program group.

3. Right-click the Roles node in the tree pane and click Add Roles.

4. Review the Before You Begin information and click Next.

5. On the Select Server Roles page, select Active Directory Rights Management Services.

    The Add Role Wizard asks you to add the Web Server (IIS) role with the required features, and Message Queuing.

6. Click Add Required Role Services if these services weren't installed prior to the installation of AD RMS. Click Next.

7. On the Active Directory Rights Management Services page, review the information about the selected role and click Next.

8. On the Select Role Services page, ensure that Active Directory Rights Management Server is selected and click Next.

9. On the Create Or Join An AD RMS Cluster page, select Create A New AD RMS Cluster and click Next.

10. On the Select Configuration Database page, select Use Windows Internal Database On This Server and click Next.

    You choose to use Windows Internal Database to host the AD RMS database because this is a single-server installation. Remember: Using WID is valid for test purposes only.

11. On the Specify Service Account page, click Specify, type **ADRMSService** and its password, click OK, and then click Next.

12. On the Configure AD RMS Cluster Key Storage page, select Use AD RMS Centrally Managed Key Storage and click Next.

    You choose to protect the AD RMS cluster key by using this option because it simplifies the exercise and does not require additional components; however, normally, you should provide the best protection for this key, through a CSP provider.

13. On the Specify AD RMS Cluster Key Password page, type a strong password, confirm it, and then click Next.

14. On the Select AD RMS Cluster Web Site page, select Default Web Site and click Next.

15. On the Specify Cluster Address page, select Use An SSL-Encrypted Connection (Https://).

    As a security best practice, the AD RMS cluster should be provisioned by using an SSL-encrypted connection.

16. In the Internal Address section, type **RightsManagement.contoso.com**, leave the port number as is, and click Validate. When the validation succeeds, the wizard updates the preview of the cluster address at the bottom of the page. Click Next.

17. On the Choose A Server Authentication Certificate For SSL Encryption page, select Choose An Existing Certificate For SSL Encryption (Recommended), select the SERVER04 certificate, and click Next.

18. On the Name The Server Licensor Certificate page, type **Contoso DRM** to identify the AD RMS cluster and click Next.

19. On the Register AD RMS Service Connection Point page, select Register The AD RMS Service Connection Point Now and click Next.

    This action registers the AD RMS service connection point (SCP) in AD DS.

20. On the Web Server (IIS) page, review the information about IIS and click Next.

21. On the Select Role Services page, keep the Web Server default selections and click Next.

22. On the Confirm Installation Selections page, review your choices and click Install.

23. When the installation is complete, click Close to close the installation wizard.

24. Log off and log back on to update the permissions granted to the logged-on user account.

    The user account that is logged on when the AD RMS server role is installed is automatically made a member of the AD RMS Enterprise Administrators group. This gives you access to all AD RMS operations. Your installation is complete.

Lesson Summary

- AD RMS is designed to provide support for data protection services through digital rights management. To do so, it relies on a complex infrastructure that requires additional services such as AD DS, SQL Server, Internet Information Services, and, potentially, AD FS for interforest partnerships.

- Users must have an email-enabled account in an AD DS domain to use AD RMS services.

- Users must also rely on AD RMS–enabled applications to protect content. These applications can be productivity tools such as Word, Outlook, PowerPoint, Internet Explorer, or a custom AD RMS–enabled application. Without an AD RMS–enabled application, you cannot view or work with protected content.

- Windows 7 includes the AD RMS client by default, as does Windows Vista, but Windows XP does not. In Windows XP, you must download and install Windows Rights Management Client with SP2.

Lesson Review

You can use the following question to test your knowledge of the information in Lesson 1, "Understanding and Installing Active Directory Rights Management Services." The question is also available on the companion CD if you prefer to review it in electronic form.

1. You are an administrator for the contoso.com domain. You have just finished installing AD RMS, and now you want to configure AD RMS. Setup has completed without any errors. However, when you begin working with the AD RMS server, you get the following error message. What could be the problem?

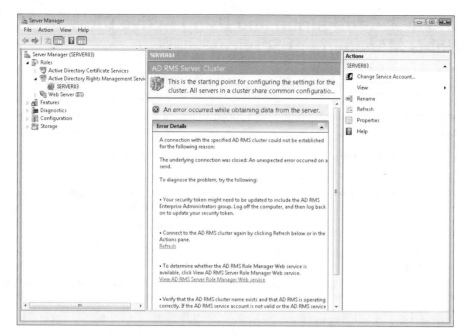

A. Your server is not running AD RMS.

B. The server certificate is invalid, and, because of this, the AD RMS server will not start.

C. Your server is not a member of an AD DS domain.

D. Your account does not have appropriate privileges to manage AD RMS.

Lesson 2: Configuring and Using Active Directory Rights Management Services

AD RMS installations can be complex to prepare, but after you have worked with the proper installation preparation process, your installations will be flawless. After your servers are installed, however, you must complete the configuration of the AD RMS cluster and prepare the usage policies you want to implement in your network. This involves several tasks:

- If you want to make AD RMS available outside your network, you must add an extranet cluster URL to your configuration.

- If you want to integrate AD RMS services with partners, you must configure proxy settings and install Identity Federation Support. Remember that you must have a working AD FS implementation to add these components to your infrastructure. You must also configure trust policies for the interoperation of your AD RMS cluster with other clusters.

- You must configure the AD RMS certificates to ensure that you set up proper validation periods.

- If your organization has decided that your rights-protection policies will not affect the entire organization and will target only a specific group of users or departments, such as the legal department, you must configure exclusion policies.

- You must prepare user accounts for integration with AD RMS.

- You must prepare policy templates for your organization to use. These templates facilitate the rights-protection process for your users.

- You must be familiar with the various AD RMS clients so that you can support them if your users experience problems.

- AD RMS relies on three databases for operation. You must be aware of these databases and maintain them for a proper AD RMS operation.

These tasks finalize the deployment of your AD RMS cluster.

> **After this lesson, you will be able to:**
> - Configure extranet URLs.
> - Prepare for integration with partners.
> - Work with AD RMS certificates.
> - Prepare user accounts for AD RMS.
> - Prepare exclusion policies.
> - Work with policy templates.
> - Work with the AD RMS databases.
>
> **Estimated lesson time: 30 minutes**

Configuring AD RMS

AD RMS configuration, unlike Windows Rights Management Services, is performed through the MMC. This console is integrated in Server Manager but is also available as a stand-alone console through Remote Server Administration Tools (RSAT). Each of the tasks you need to perform to finalize your configuration is available through this console.

> **MORE INFO** **CONFIGURE AD RMS**
>
> For more information on configuring AD RMS, go to *http://technet.microsoft.com/en-us/library/cc771603.aspx*.

Creating an Extranet URL

When you want to extend your AD RMS infrastructure to mobile users or teleworkers outside your internal network, you must configure an extranet URL. Use the following procedure:

1. Log on to a server that is a member of the root cluster, using AD RMS Enterprise Administrators credentials.
2. Launch Server Manager from the Administrative Tools program group.
3. Expand Roles\Active Directory Rights Management Services*servername*.
4. Right-click the server name and click Properties.
5. On the Cluster URLs tab, enable Extranet URLs and add the appropriate URL data for both Licensing and Certification.

   These URLs must point to a valid IIS installation in the extranet and should be permanent. Proper DNS registration should also be implemented for these URLs. Use SSL encryption for the communication through Secure HTTP or HTTPS connections. Finally, remember to create the appropriate virtual directories to host the AD RMS data.
6. Click OK to close the dialog box and apply the change.

   Your extranet URLs are ready.

Configuring Trust Policies

Although you can't enable federation support until you have a working AD FS infrastructure in place, you can learn about the models that AD RMS supports to provide federation of your DRM policies. AD RMS can support four trust models:

- Trusted user domains enable your AD RMS cluster to process requests for other AD RMS clusters located in different AD DS forests. Trusted user domains are added by importing the server licensor certificate from the AD RMS cluster you want to trust into your own cluster.

- Trusted publishing domains enable your own AD RMS cluster to issue use licenses for content that was protected by another AD RMS cluster. To create a trusted publishing domain, you must import the publishing cluster's SLC as well as its private key into your own cluster.

- Windows Live ID trusts allow users who have a valid Windows Live ID (formerly known as Microsoft Passport) to use rights-protected content but not to create it.
- Federated trusts are established through AD FS and extend the operation of your AD RMS cluster to the forests with which you have established a federated trust.

Each of these trust types extends your AD RMS authority beyond the limits of your own forest.

> **MORE INFO**   **CREATE AD RMS TRUSTS**
>
> To learn more about working with AD RMS trusts, go to *http://technet.microsoft.com/en-us/library/cc754459.aspx*.

Exporting the Server Licensor Certificate

To work with either trusted publishing domains or trusted user domains, you must export the server licensor certificate from your root cluster or from the root cluster to be trusted. Certificates are exported to be used in establishing trusts. To perform this procedure, you must be a member of the local AD RMS Enterprise Administrators or its equivalent.

1. Log on to a server that is a member of the root cluster, using AD RMS Enterprise Administrators credentials.
2. Launch Server Manager from the Administrative Tools program group.
3. Expand Roles\Active Directory Rights Management Services*servername*.
4. Right-click the server name and click Properties.
5. On the Server Certificate Tab, click Export Certificate.
6. In the Export Server Certificate As dialog box, type a valid name, such as the name of your cluster, and select a proper location (such as your Documents folder) to create the .bin file. Click Save.
7. Close the Properties dialog box.

   Protect this certificate thoroughly, because it controls access to your AD RMS cluster.

Preparing AD RMS Certificates

Certificates are created by default during the installation of AD RMS. However, you must configure appropriate certificate duration based on your rights-protection policies. Four activities can be performed in terms of certificate administration:

- Specify the duration of rights account certificates.
- Enable certification for mobile devices.
- Enable certification of server services.
- Authenticate clients through smart cards.

Of these, the one you must absolutely set is the validation period for the RAC. Others are optional operations that depend on your rights-protection policies. To modify the duration of the RAC, use the following procedure:

1. Log on to a server that is a member of the root cluster, using AD RMS Enterprise Administrators credentials.

2. Launch Server Manager from the Administrative Tools program group.

3. Expand Roles\Active Directory Rights Management Services*servername* and click Rights Account Certificate Policies.

4. In the details pane, click the Change Standard RAC Validity Period link.

5. On the Standard RAC tab, in the Standard RAC Validity Period box, set the number of days to enable the certificate.

6. On the Temporary RAC tab, in the Temporary RAC Validity Period box, set the number of minutes to enable the certificate.

7. Click OK to close the dialog box.

Note that standard RACs are valid for 365 days by default, and temporary RACs last only 15 minutes. You might want to extend the duration of a temporary RAC, but be careful about extending the validity of a standard RAC because one year is already a considerable time.

Note that if you are using federated trusts, you will need to modify the RAC validity period under the Federated Identity Support node, not under the Rights Account Certificate Policies.

> **MORE INFO** **MANAGING CERTIFICATES**
>
> For more information on working with the other certificate types, go to *http://technet .microsoft.com/en-us/library/cc730842.aspx*.

Preparing Exclusion Policies

When you decide the scope of your rights-protection policy implementation, you can configure exclusion policies, or policies that exclude users and computers from participating in your AD RMS implementation. You can create exclusion policies for four entities: users, applications, lockboxes, and Windows operating systems. When you do so, the list of the specified exclusion members is included in the use license for the content. You can remove an excluded entity from an exclusion list, but remember that if you remove the entity from the list, it will no longer be added to the use licenses. Existing content, however, will already contain it because use licenses are issued only once, by default. Because of this, follow these recommendations when preparing exclusion lists:

- Assign only exclusions that will be as permanent as possible.

- If you change your mind, wait until existing use licenses have expired before removing entities from an exclusion list.

- Rely on exclusion lists if the credentials of one of the supported entities, such as a user, have been compromised and your rights-protected content is at risk.

When you have decided to create an exclusion list, use the following procedure. In this case, you exclude users from AD RMS.

1. Log on to a server that is a member of the root cluster, using AD RMS Enterprise Administrators credentials.

2. Launch Server Manager from the Administrative Tools program group.

3. Expand Roles\Active Directory Rights Management Services*servername*\Exclusion Policies and click Users.

4. In the Actions pane, click the Enable User Exclusion link. This enables exclusion.

5. To exclude users, click the Exclude User link in the Actions pane. This launches the Exclude User Account Wizard.

   You can exclude a user either through the email address or through the public key assigned to the user. The first is for users included in your AD DS directory, and the second is for external users who might not have an account in your AD DS directory. If you exclude users in your AD DS directory, make sure you exclude a group so that it is easier to manage as time goes on.

6. Select the appropriate exclusion method and either locate the user account or type in the public key string, and then click Next.

7. Click Finish to close the wizard.

Use the same node to remove the exclusion if you need to. Use the same process for other exclusion types.

✔ Quick Check

1. How many AD RMS root clusters can you deploy in an Active Directory Domain Services forest?

2. What is the difference between a root cluster and a licensing-only cluster, and which is preferable to use?

3. Which delegation roles does AD RMS support?

Quick Check Answers

1. You can deploy only a single AD RMS root cluster per AD DS forest. This is because AD RMS creates an SCP during installation, and only one SCP can exist per forest.

2. The root cluster offers all AD RMS capabilities, whereas the licensing-only cluster simply manages licenses. Licensing-only clusters are designed to support the root cluster role, but if you are given a choice, you should deploy only root clusters. This creates a single AD RMS cluster on your network and simplifies management while providing all the functionality you require. Use licensing-only clusters in rare occasions when root-only deployments are not practical.

3. AD RMS supports four delegation roles:

- AD RMS Enterprise Administrators can manage every aspect of AD RMS.

- AD RMS Template Administrators can prepare and modify protection templates.

- AD RMS Auditors have read-only access to AD RMS logs.

- AD RMS Service Account grants proper access rights to the AD RMS service account.

MORE INFO   **EXCLUSION POLICIES**

To learn more about exclusion policies, go to *http://technet.microsoft.com/en-us/library/ cc771228.aspx*.

Preparing Accounts and Access Rights

To ensure that your users can work with AD RMS, you must prepare their accounts. When you do so, AD RMS includes the account within its own database. However, when you remove an account, AD RMS disables the account but does not automatically remove it from its database. Because of this, the database can become large and contain obsolete data. To protect against this, either create a stored procedure in SQL Server that automatically removes the account when you delete it or create a script that does this on a scheduled basis.

In addition, you might need to create a special Super Users group that contains operators who have full access to all the content protected by your AD RMS implementation. Members of this Super Users group are much like the recovery agents you would use for the Encrypting File System (EFS). These users can recover or modify any data that is managed by your AD RMS infrastructure and can, therefore, recover data from users who have left the organization. You should usually assign a Universal Group from your directory to this role. Prepare the Universal Group before enabling Super Users in AD RMS. To configure a Super Users group to work with AD RMS, use the following procedure:

1. Log on to a server that is a member of the root cluster, using AD RMS Enterprise Administrators credentials.

2. Launch Server Manager from the Administrative Tools program group.

3. Expand Roles\Active Directory Rights Management Services*servername* and click Security Policies.

4. Click the Change Super Users Settings link in the details pane.

5. In the Actions pane, click the Enable Super Users link.

6. Click the Change Super User Group link in the details pane to view the Super User Group property sheet.

7. Type the email address of a mail-enabled universal distribution group from your forest or use the Browse button to locate it.

8. Click OK to close the property sheet.

Members of this group will now have access to all AD RMS content. Select these members very carefully and ensure that they are completely trustworthy. In fact, for security purposes you might prefer to keep the Super Users group disabled and enable it only when you need it.

MORE INFO **ACCOUNT PREPARATION**

To learn more about account preparation, go to *http://technet.microsoft.com/en-us/library/cc754120.aspx.*

Preparing Policy Templates

To facilitate the rights-protection application by your users, prepare policy templates. These templates will save considerable time for your users and ensure that you maintain the standards you set in your rights-protection policies. You must perform several activities with policy templates. First, you must create the template. Next, you must specify a location for the template.

Locations are usually shared folders contained within your network. However, for users to rely on the template to create content, they must have access to it. Offline users will not have access to the templates unless you configure the offline folder settings for the shared folder so that the content of the folder will automatically be available locally to the user. In addition, relying on offline folders will ensure that when you modify, add, or update templates, they will automatically be updated on the client computer the next time the user connects to the network. Offline folders, however, will not work for external users who do not have access to your internal network. You will have to consider an alternate delivery method if you choose to allow external users to create content. Users who have access only to pre-created content do not require access to the policy templates. To create a policy template, use the following procedure:

1. Log on to a server that is a member of the root cluster, using AD RMS Template Administrators credentials.

2. Launch Server Manager from the Administrative Tools program group.

3. Expand Roles\Active Directory Rights Management Services*servername* and click Rights Policy Templates.

4. In the Actions pane, click the Create Distributed Rights Policy Template link. This launches the wizard.

5. On the Add Template Identification Information page, click Add.

6. Specify the language, type the name and description for the new template, click Add, and then click Next.

7. On the Add User Rights page, you must perform several activities:

   a. Click Add to select the user or group that will have access to the template.

   Selecting Anyone allows any user to request a use license for the content. If you want to select a specific group, use the Browse button.

   Click OK when done.

   b. Under Users And Rights, you must first select the user and then assign the rights to that particular user or group in the Rights For *user* area. You can also create a custom right for the user.

   c. Note that the Grant Owner (Author) Full Control Right With No Expiration check box is selected by default.

   d. In the Rights Request URL, type the appropriate URL. This gives users the ability to request additional rights by going to the URL.

8. Click Next.

9. On the Specify Expiration Policy page, select one of the three available options and type a value in days. If you need to ensure that content expires automatically after a number of days, select Expires After The Following Duration (Days) and type the number of days. Click Next.

10. On the Specify Extended Policy page, you can assign the following settings:

    - Choose Enable Users To View Protected Content Using A Browser Add-On. This allows users who do not have AD RMS–enabled applications to view protected content by automatically installing the required add-on.

    - Select Require A New Use License Every Time Content Is Consumed (Disable Client-Side Caching) if you need authentication against the AD RMS servers each time content is consumed. Note that this will not work for offline users.

    - Select If You Would Like To Specify Additional Information For Your AD RMS-Enabled Applications, You Can Specify Them Here As Name-Value Pairs if you need to add specific data to the protected content. This option is usually reserved for developers, however.

11. Click Next. On the Specify Revocation Policy page, you can enable revocation by selecting the Require Revocation check box and then:

    a. In the URL Of The Location Where The Revocation List Is Published area, specifying http:// or https:// and typing the revocation URL.

    If you use a URL and you have both internal and external users, the URL should be accessible from both network locations.

b. In the Refresh Interval For Revocation List (Days) box, typing the number of days the revocation list will be maintained.

This determines when users must update their revocation list when viewing content.

c. In the File Containing Public Key Corresponding To The Signed Revocation List, specifying a file.

12. Click Finish.

Note that when you implement revocation, you must be careful with its settings. To make revocation practical, you must publish the revocation list on a regular basis.

MORE INFO   POLICY TEMPLATES

To learn more about policy templates, go to *http://technet.microsoft.com/en-us/library/cc731599.aspx.*

Working with AD RMS Clients

AD RMS relies on a local client to give users access to its capabilities. Two clients exist: the built-in client included in Windows 7, Windows Vista, and Windows Server 2008 R2, and a client that runs on Windows 2000, Windows 2003, and Windows XP. The last of these must be downloaded and installed on each client computer to work. Three versions of this client exist: x86, x64, and Itanium to support all Windows version platforms.

Clients automatically discover the AD RMS cluster through one of three methods:

- They can rely on the AD DS Service Connection Point created during the AD RMS installation.
- In complex, multiforest AD RMS deployments, they must rely on registry overrides, which are placed directly on the client computer. This is especially true for earlier versions of Windows operating systems.
- They can rely on the URLs included in the issuance licenses for the content.

Each of these methods provides redundancy to ensure that clients can always access content.

MORE INFO   AD RMS AND WINDOWS RMS CLIENTS

To learn more about AD RMS clients and obtain the Windows RMS clients, go to *http://technet.microsoft.com/en-us/library/dd772753(WS.10).aspx.*

 Quick Check

1. What is a server licensor certificate?
2. Which trust policies does AD RMS support?

Managing Databases

AD RMS relies on three databases to operate. Familiarize yourself with these databases and their operation to ensure the proper functioning of your AD RMS cluster. These databases include:

■ The configuration database, which is used to store all AD RMS configuration data. This database is accessed by AD RMS servers to provide rights-protection services and information to clients.

■ The logging database, which stores data about every activity in either a root or a licensing-only cluster. This database is useful for auditing AD RMS events.

■ The directory services database, which stores information about users and all their corresponding data. This information is accessed from AD DS directories through the Lightweight Directory Access Protocol (LDAP). This database requires regular maintenance if you remove users from AD RMS, as mentioned earlier in this lesson.

In addition to these databases, AD RMS relies on the Message Queuing service to send events to the logging database. If you are concerned about auditing AD RMS usage (and you should be), perform regular checks and verifications of this service to ensure its proper operation.

In addition to the different functionalities available within the AD RMS console, Microsoft provides a special RMS toolkit that contains a series of utilities for AD RMS administration and operation. Download this toolkit and add it to your AD RMS administration kit to control your deployment fully.

> **MORE INFO**   **RIGHTS MANAGEMENT SERVICES ADMINISTRATION TOOLKIT**
>
> To download the RMS toolkit with utilities for RMS management, go to *http://www.microsoft.com/downloads/details.aspx?FamilyID=bae62cfc-d5a7-46d2-9063-0f6885c26b98&DisplayLang=en*.

> **MORE INFO**   **ADDITIONAL AD RMS RESOURCES**
>
> To access additional AD RMS resources, go to *http://technet.microsoft.com/en-us/library/cc771334.aspx*.

PRACTICE   Creating a Rights Policy Template

In this practice, you create a customized rights policy template. You use the AD RMS installation you created in Lesson 1 to create a new template.

EXERCISE 1   Create a New Template

Templates allow users to apply rights policies in a quick, standardized manner. To create a template, you must use the AD RMS Template Administrators access right or the AD RMS Enterprise Administrators access right. To perform this exercise, you should have SERVER01 and SERVER04 running.

1. Log on to a server that is a member of the root cluster, using AD RMS Template Administrators credentials. The Domain Administrator account has these privileges.

2. Launch Server Manager from the Administrative Tools program group.

3. Expand Roles\Active Directory Rights Management Services\SERVER04 and click Rights Policy Templates.

4. In the Actions pane, click the Create Distributed Rights Policy Template link.
   This launches the wizard.

5. On the Add Template Identification Information page, click Add.

6. Specify the language, type **Contoso Legal Template** for the name and **Template to protect legal documents at Contoso Ltd**. for the description for the new template, and click Add. Click Next.

7. On the Add User Rights page, you must perform several activities:

   a. Click Add to select the user or group that will have access to the template. Select Anyone and click OK. This allows any user to request a use license for the content.

> **b.** Under Users And Rights, select Anyone, and then assign the View rights in the Rights For *user* area.
>
> **c.** Make sure that the Grant Owner (Author) Full Control Right With No Expiration check box is selected.
>
> **d.** In the Rights Request URL, type the following URL: **https://RightsManagement.Contoso.com**.
>
> This allows users to request additional rights by going to the URL.

8. Click Next. On the Specify Expiration Policy page, select Never Expires. Make sure you do not select Expires After The Following Duration (Days). Click Next.

9. On the Specify Extended Policy page, make the following settings:

   - Select Enable Users To View Protected Content Using A Browser Add-On. This allows users who do not have AD RMS–enabled applications to view protected content by automatically installing the required add-on.

   - Do not select Require A New Use License Every Time Content Is Consumed (Disable Client-Side Caching).

   - Do not select If You Would Like To Specify Additional Information For Your AD RMS-Enabled Applications, You Can Specify Them Here As Name-Value Pairs. This option is usually reserved for developers.

10. Click Next. On the Specify Revocation Policy page, do not enable revocation. Click Finish.

    Note that the template now appears in the details pane. It is ready for distribution.

Lesson Summary

- When you work with AD RMS, you need to perform several configuration tasks to complete your installation. These tasks include creating an extranet URL if you want to give external users access to your DRM system. They also include configuring trust policies in support of additional external access.

- If you want to work with other AD RMS installations, each installation must exchange server licensor certificates with the other. This means exporting certificates from the source cluster and importing them in the target cluster.

- If you need to exclude users from your DRM system, you must create exclusion policies.

- To facilitate user content creation, create rights policy templates. These templates simplify users' work and ensure that your DRM strategy is used in a standard manner.

Lesson Review

You can use the following question to test your knowledge of the information in Lesson 2, "Configuring and Using Active Directory Rights Management Services." The question is also available on the companion CD if you prefer to review it in electronic form.

> **NOTE** **ANSWERS**
>
> The answer to this question and explanations of why each answer choice is right or wrong are located in the "Answers" section at the end of the book.

1. You are an administrator for the contoso.com domain. You have just finished installing AD RMS, and now you want to configure AD RMS. You've configured an extranet URL and tested the operation from the AD RMS server you were using to set up the URL. This URL relies on SSL to secure HTTP traffic. However, when users try to access AD RMS from outside your network, they can't. What could be the problem?

A. Your users should be using a URL address in the HTTP:// format.

B. The server certificate is invalid, and, because of this, users cannot access the URL.

C. Users must have AD DS domain accounts to access the URL.

D. The URL you provided to users is wrong.

Chapter Review

To further practice and reinforce the skills you learned in this chapter, you can perform the following tasks:

- Review the chapter summary.
- Review the list of key terms introduced in this chapter.
- Complete the case scenario. This scenario sets up a real-world situation involving the topics of this chapter and asks you to create a solution.
- Complete the suggested practices.
- Take a practice test.

Chapter Summary

- AD RMS is designed to support the extension of your organization's authority beyond the firewall. The extension applies to the protection of intellectual property.
- To protect your intellectual property, AD RMS must rely on several technologies: Active Directory Domain Services, Active Directory Certificate Services, Active Directory Federation Services, and SQL Server. AD DS provides a central authentication service, AD CS provides the public key infrastructure certificates used in AD RMS, AD FS allows you to integrate AD RMS policies with partners and external users, and SQL Server stores all AD RMS data.
- Many organizations choose to implement AD RMS in stages:
  - The first stage focuses on internal use of intellectual property.
  - The second involves sharing content with partners.
  - The third involves a wider audience; your intellectual property is distributed outside the boundaries of your network in a protected mode.
- When you install AD RMS, you create a root cluster. This cluster can supply both certification and licensing services. Each AD DS forest can host only a single root cluster; however, in large implementations, you can separate the certification and licensing roles by creating an additional licensing cluster. To consume the AD RMS services, you need AD RMS–enabled applications. These can be tools such as word processors, pre-

sentation tools, email clients, or custom in-house applications. Each time a user creates new information, AD RMS templates determine usage rights for the information. These include who will be able to read, open, write, modify, print, transfer, and otherwise electronically manipulate the information.

Key Terms

The following terms were introduced in this chapter. Do you know what they mean?

- enrollment
- publishing license
- root cluster

Case Scenario

In the following case scenario, you apply what you've learned about Active Directory Rights Management Services. You can find answers to the questions in this scenario in the "Answers" section at the end of this book.

Case Scenario: Preparing to Work with an External AD RMS Cluster

You are a systems administrator with Contoso, Ltd. You have recently finished implementing an AD RMS deployment within your organization, and everything is running smoothly. Users both inside and outside of your network have access to your rights management policies to ensure the protection of your content.

Now your organization wants to share rights protection policies with a partner organization, but it does not want to put a federation services infrastructure in place. What are your options?

Suggested Practices

To help you successfully master the exam objectives presented in this chapter, complete the following tasks.

Work with AD RMS

There is only one exam objective for this topic. Because of this, you should focus your practices on the following areas:

- Identifying the requirements for an AD RMS installation
- Working with the installation and configuration process for AD RMS root clusters
- Finalizing the configuration process for a root cluster
- Working with rights policy templates
- Working with Windows PowerShell to control AD RMS components

You should also practice using the various console sections for AD RMS. All of these are available in Server Manager.

- **Practice 1** Use the instructions in the "Before You Begin" section of this chapter to prepare your test environment. If at all possible, rely on an external database server to support the installation. This allows you to configure a true root cluster. When you're ready, create the cluster and add a second server to it so that you can see how clusters operate.

- **Practice 2** After the cluster is installed, use Server Manager to run through all the activities required to create or modify a rights policy template. These templates are an important part of the AD RMS administration process.

Don't forget to study DRM implementations with Windows Server 2008 R2. The Microsoft TechNet website includes more information on AD RMS; run through as much of it as you can.

Take a Practice Test

The practice tests on this book's companion CD offer many options. For example, you can test yourself on just one exam objective, or you can test yourself on all the 70-640 certification exam content. You can set up the test so that it closely simulates the experience of taking a certification exam, or you can set it up in study mode so that you can look at the correct answers and explanations after you answer each question.

> *MORE INFO*   **PRACTICE TESTS**
>
> For details about all the practice test options available, see the "How to Use the Practice Tests" section in this book's Introduction.

CHAPTER 17

Active Directory Federation Services

O rganizations have been struggling with securing their networks from the outside world ever since the Internet was invented. The basic principle is that every organization that has an interface between its network and the Internet also has a perimeter network of some sort. In many cases, organizations spend great effort implementing special security technologies such as intrusion detection systems, and yet, the basic premise of a perimeter network is to keep the firewalls it contains as secure as possible. But how does that affect potential partnerships?

In the early days of Microsoft Windows domains with Microsoft Windows NT, Microsoft provided the capability to create trusts between domains to support domain interactions. With the release of Active Directory Domain Services (AD DS) in Windows 2000, Microsoft brought forward the concept of the trust and supported interdomain trusts. Domains within the same forest would use automatic transitive trusts, and domains from different forests would use explicit trusts when they wanted to share security contexts. With the release of Microsoft Windows Server 2003, Microsoft extended the concept of the transitive trust to forests with the introduction of forest trusts. Using a forest trust, partners could extend the security contexts of their own internal forest to trust other partner forests. However, implementing forests trusts has two significant impacts:

- It requires opening specific ports in a firewall to support AD DS traffic.
- If the partnerships grow too large, it can become extremely cumbersome to manage multiple trusts. (See Figure 17-1.)

Using trusts might not be the best way to implement partnerships.

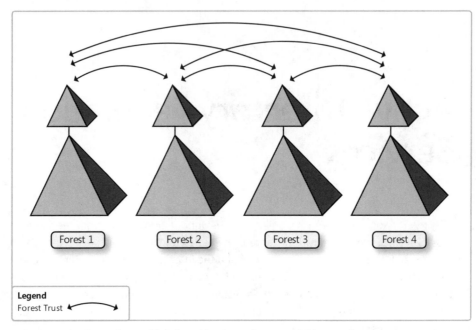

FIGURE 17-1 Implementing multiple forest trusts can become highly complex

The Purpose of a Firewall

Although forest trusts can become highly complex, they also have an impact on your protection mechanisms. For example, AD DS traffic transits through the Lightweight Directory Access Protocol (LDAP) on TCP/IP port 389 or, preferably, through secure LDAP (LDAP/S) on port 636. In addition, if you need to transit global catalog (GC) traffic, you must use port 3268 or, once again preferably, port 3269 on LDAP/S.

However, firewalls are designed to keep unwanted traffic out. Perforating them by opening endless numbers of TCP/IP ports is not a solution. Traditional perimeter networks have two layers of protection. The first protects perimeter networks from external access. The second protects internal networks from the perimeter. The perimeter itself provides a series of services such as Active Directory Certificate Services (AD CS), Active Directory Rights Management Services (AD RMS), and, in some circumstances, Active Directory Lightweight Directory Services (AD LDS). AD DS is reserved exclusively for internal networks.

The ideal external firewall uses one set of key ports only. These include:

- Port 53, which is used for Domain Name System (DNS) traffic. DNS traffic is usually provided in a read-only manner.
- Port 80, which is used by open Hypertext Transfer Protocol (HTTP) data. Port 80 is usually used for read-only access because it is not secured.

- Port 443 for Secure HTTP or Hypertext Transfer Protocol Secure (HTTPS). Communications on port 443 are secured through Secure Sockets Layer (SSL) or Transport Layer Security (TLS), which both rely on Certificate Authority (CA) certificates to encrypt data. Because of this, communications on port 443 support read-write or secure data read operations.

- Port 25, which is used for Simple Mail Transfer Protocol (SMTP), a necessary risk because no one can work without access to email.

All other ports should ideally be closed. The internal firewall will have a few more open ports, depending on the technologies you have running in the perimeter. (See Figure 17-2.) For example, if you are using AD LDS to provide authentication services for web applications in the perimeter, you might want to have one-way synchronizations from your internal AD DS directory to provision your own user accounts. If you are using Internet Information Services (IIS), you might want to push and pull data to the websites in the perimeter. In addition, you want to get the email messages from your SMTP relays in the perimeter into your internal network. This is the basis of a secure perimeter design.

FIGURE 17-2 The basis of a secure perimeter is a set of secure firewalls

Active Directory Federation Services

In comes Active Directory Federation Services (AD FS), one of the Active Directory technologies included in Windows Server 2008 R2. This Active Directory technology serves to extend the authority of your internal network to the outside world. (See Figure 17-3.) AD FS is designed to provide similar functionality to the forest trust or the explicit trust—not through the traditional LDAP TCP/IP ports, but rather through the common HTTP ports. In fact, AD FS uses port 443 because all AD FS trust communications are secured and encrypted. In this manner, it can rely on AD CS to provide certificates for each server in the AD FS implementation. AD FS can also extend your AD RMS deployment and provide federation services for intellectual property management between partners.

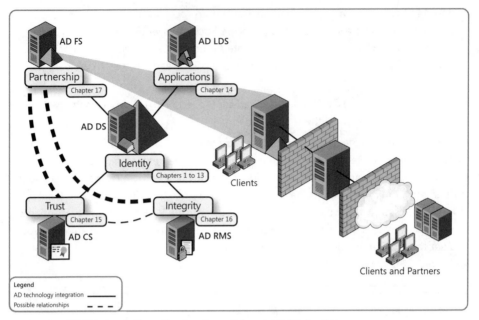

FIGURE 17-3 AD FS extends the authority of your internal AD DS directory

To extend your internal authority, AD FS provides extensions to internal forests and enables organizations to create partnerships without having to open any additional port on their firewalls. Basically, AD FS relies on each partner's internal AD DS directory to provide authentication for extranet or perimeter services. When a user attempts to authenticate to an application integrated to AD FS, the AD FS engine polls the internal directory for authentication data. If the user has access provided through the internal directory, he or she is granted access to the external application. The major advantage of this is that each partner organization needs to manage authentication data only in their internal network. The federation services of AD FS do all the rest.

In short, AD FS should be used whenever you want to implement a partnership with other organizations that also rely on internal AD DS directories. When you need to provide authentication services in your perimeter network, but the users or organizations you want to interact with do not have internal AD DS directories or the nature of the partnership does not warrant an AD FS deployment (for example, if it is temporary and will not last beyond a single project), you should rely on AD LDS.

Exam objective in this chapter:

- Configure Active Directory Federation Services (AD FS).

Lessons in this chapter:

Before You Begin

To complete the lessons in this chapter, you must have performed the installations shown in the following list. It is highly recommended that you use virtual machines for this chapter because it requires access to so many computers. If you performed the exercises in the previous chapters, you already have several of these computers in place.

- Windows Server 2008 R2 installed on a physical or virtual machine. The machine should be named SERVER01 and should be a domain controller in the contoso.com domain. The details for this setup are presented in Chapter 1, "Creating an Active Directory Domain."

- Windows Server 2008 R2 Enterprise edition installed on a physical or virtual machine, which should be named SERVER03 and should be a member server within the contoso.com domain. This computer will host the contoso.com internal AD FS role that you install and create through the exercises in this chapter.

- Windows Server 2008 R2 installed on a physical or virtual machine, which should be named SERVER06 and should be a domain controller in the woodgrovebank.com domain and include the DNS server role. No special setup is required other than having a new Windows Server 2008 R2 forest named woodgrovebank.com.

- Windows Server 2008 R2 Enterprise edition installed on a physical or virtual machine, which should be named SERVER07 and should be a member server within the woodgrovebank.com domain. This computer will host the woodgrovebank.com internal AD FS role that you install and create through the exercises in this chapter.

This setup is sufficient to test basic AD FS installation and configuration. Testing all of AD FS capabilities requires client machines as well as firewalls, and even if you are using virtual machines this might be beyond the laboratory capabilities of most readers.

Note that you can also create an AD FS environment with other computer roles, as outlined in "How to Setup the AD FS 2.0 VM Lab Setup Environment for Federated Collaboration," which is available at *http://www.microsoft.com/downloads/details.aspx? displaylang=en&familyid=f6d6eda6-374b-4e82-b739-d436c2a801f2*.

 REAL WORLD

Danielle Ruest and Nelson Ruest

In 2005, one of our clients, a major health care organization, needed to put together an identity federation solution. Their goal was to have their entire health care system—doctors, pharmacists, health care workers, hospitals, social services workers, private clinics, and so on—work together through a single integrated identity and access (IDA) solution. Because most of the organizations involved used internal Active Directory for authentication and network access, this solution was to be based on Windows technologies.

The goal was to make sure that all members of the system had a verifiable identity within the system. The challenge was considerable. Although many larger partners had their own internal Active Directory forests, many of the smaller partners did not. For example, pharmacies did not have any way of linking themselves together to have a single identity authority. Private clinics or doctors did not have this capability either.

The initial solution was to create a multitude of forest trusts between each of the existing Active Directory forests. Then, to provide support for the members of the system that did not have their own directory service, a completely new directory would be created that would be located within a perimeter network hosted by a hosting firm as an outsourced service to the health care provider for a per-user fee to maintain the directory service.

The customer had several concerns about the potential solution. The first was long-term costs. When all the members of the system were tallied, they added up to over 500,000 users, more than half of them without a directory service. Maintaining an external directory for these users would become very expensive very quickly. Second, the client did not want to perforate firewalls by supporting all the ports required for forest trusts. However, the cost of a private network was prohibitive. Third, although the client wanted each of the system members to interact through a single IDA solution, it did not want to be responsible for all the accounts linked to the new solution.

Although Windows Server 2008 was not available yet, Windows Server 2003 R2 was, and with it came the initial release of Microsoft Federation Services. In addition, Microsoft had released Active Directory Application Mode (ADAM) a couple of years earlier. This case seemed like a perfect candidate for the integration of the three technologies. We suggested the following:

- Use the Federation Services to link all existing directory services and make centralized applications available through the web.
- Allow each partner to manage its own internal directory services without external intervention.
- Use ADAM instances to provide authentication services in the perimeter network. The client could even create a self-service portal that would allow members to update their own records, change passwords, and so on.
- Reduce the number of open ports on the firewall down to the most common ports that were already open.

This proposal met the customer's needs and would not cost a fortune to implement. In fact, implementation could start with a pilot project focusing on one or two key applications and then adding new system members as the solution was implemented. What's even better is that with the release of Windows Server 2008, Microsoft brought many of the technologies we proposed under a single banner: Active Directory.

Lesson 1: Understanding Active Directory Federation Services

In general terms, AD FS is a single sign on (SSO) engine that allows users of your external web-based applications to access and authenticate through a browser. That's not so different from using an external AD LDS directory store that is linked with your internal directory. However, the key feature of AD FS is that to authenticate a client, it uses the internal authentication store of the user's own domain and does not have a store of its own. It also uses the original authentication the client performed in its own network and passes this authentication to all the web applications that are AD FS–enabled.

The advantages are clear. Organizations need to manage only a single authentication store for their own users and don't need to manage secondary stores at all. Using an AD LDS directory for extranet authentication adds administrative overhead because the organization needs to manage its own internal store and the external store or stores as well. Users also often must remember several access codes and passwords to log on to each of these stores. AD FS simplifies this because it federates the user's internal AD DS identity and projects it to the external world. Users need to authenticate only once: when they log on to their own network.

Using AD FS, you can form business-to-business (B2B) partnerships with very little overhead. In these B2B partnerships, organizations fit into two categories:

- **Resource organization**   When organizations that have exposed resources such as websites—for example, for e-commerce or collaboration—decide to use AD FS to simplify the authentication process to these resources, they form partnerships with other organizations—suppliers, partners, and so on. The organization that forms the partnership is deemed the resource organization because it hosts the shared resources in its perimeter network.

- **Account organization**   When organizations enter into an AD FS relationship with resource organizations, they are deemed the account organizations because they manage the accounts used to access the shared resources in SSO designs.

AD FS supports one additional authentication mode. In a web SSO design, it authenticates users from anywhere on the Internet. After users have been authenticated, AD FS examines the users' attributes in AD DS directories to identify which claims the users have to the application they are authenticating to.

To support this identity federation, AD FS relies on two role services:

- **Federation Service**   This service is created from the servers that share a trust policy. The federation server routes authentication requests to the appropriate source directory to generate security tokens for the user requesting access.

- **Federation Service Proxy**   To obtain the authentication requests from the user, the federation server relies on a proxy server that is located in the perimeter network. The proxy collects authentication information from the user's browser through the WS-Federation Passive Requestor Profile (WS-F PRP), an AD FS web service, and passes it on to the federation service.

Because it is based on a standard web service, AD FS does not need to rely on AD DS alone to support federated identities. Any directory service that adheres to the WS-Federation standard can participate in an AD FS identity federation.

Although Federation Services existed in Windows Server 2003 R2, AD FS has been improved significantly in Windows Server 2008 R2 to facilitate the installation and administration processes. AD FS 2.0 also supports more web-based applications than the original release did.

> **MORE INFO** **AD FS**
>
> For more information on AD FS, go to *http://technet.microsoft.com/en-ca/library/ cc772128%28WS.10%29.aspx.*

> **NOTE** **AD FS 2.0**
>
> AD FS 2.0 was not released with Windows Server 2008 R2. The version of AD FS included with the release of Windows Server 2008 R2 is AD FS 1.1. AD FS 2.0 is available as a separate download. For an evaluation version of AD FS 2.0, go to *http://technet.microsoft .com/en-ca/evalcenter/ee476597.aspx. Make sure you obtain the version for Windows Server 2008 R2.*

> **After this lesson, you will be able to:**
> - Understand the AD FS authentication process.
> - Understand the components that make up an AD FS implementation.
> - Install AD FS.
>
> **Estimated lesson time: 40 minutes**

Working with AD FS Designs

AD FS supports three configurations or architectural designs, depending on the type of B2B partnership you need to establish. Each configuration includes its own particularities, and each supports a particular partnership scenario.

- **Federated Web SSO** This model usually spans several firewalls because it links applications contained within an extranet in a resource organization to the internal directory stores of account organizations. The only trust that exists in this model is the federation trust, which is always a one-way trust from the resource organization to an account organization. This is the most common AD FS configuration. (See Figure 17-4.)

- **Web SSO**   When some of the users for an extranet application are external and do not have accounts within an AD DS domain, you must deploy Web SSO only. The Web SSO model allows the users to authenticate only once to multiple web applications. This means that external users who do not have an account in your internal AD DS and internal users who have an account within the internal AD DS both have access to your web applications. Your internal users rely on their own accounts, and external users rely on accounts stored either within an external AD DS or a SQL Server store. (See Figure 17-5.)

- **Federation with Cloud Services**   When you require access to cloud-based services such as Windows Azure and services such as SharePoint Online or Exchange Online, you can rely on AD FS to provide single sign on. AD FS provides SSO support for both Microsoft and non-Microsoft cloud services.

Ideally, all members of your identity federation deployment will have their own AD DS directory and act as account organizations to simplify your deployment strategy. However, AD FS can also be used to provide individual Internet users with access to your external web-based applications.

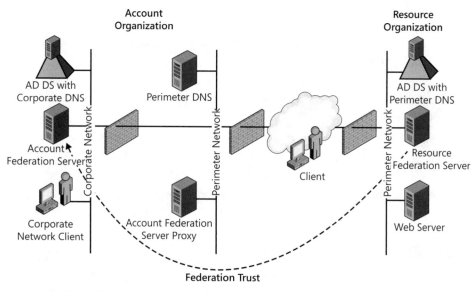

FIGURE 17-4 Using a Federated Web SSO federation configuration

---

EXAM TIP

Pay attention to the three AD FS configurations. Exam questions will be based on a specific configuration.

FIGURE 17-5 Using a Web SSO federation configuration

In fact, AD FS can be used in three deployment scenarios:

- **Scenario 1** Provide SSO to your internal AD DS users. In this scenario, your users log in to AD DS and rely on their AD DS account to grant them access to your own federated applications.

- **Scenario 2** Provide SSO to partner applications to your own users. This scenario includes all of the features of scenario 1 and can also support remote access over the Internet.

- **Scenario 3** Provide access to your web-based applications to others. This scenario allows users of either a partner organization or the Internet to access your own web-based applications.

Each scenario is not exclusive. For example, scenario 2 includes the capabilities of scenario 1, and scenario 3 can easily be added on to either scenario 1 or 2.

Understanding AD FS Components

As you have seen, AD FS relies on a special terminology of its own. To gain a better understanding of the AD FS components, it is important to review and understand this terminology as well as to review and understand the basic functionality of the AD FS components.

Understanding AD FS Terminology

Table 17-1 outlines the most common terms used in AD FS. Many of these terms are explained more fully in the sections that follow.

TABLE 17-1 Common AD FS Terms

TERM	DESCRIPTION
Account federation server	The federation server that is hosted in the account organization's internal network. This server issues security tokens to users based on prior user authentication. Basically, this server authenticates the user, extracts federation attributes and group memberships from the attribute store, creates a claim containing this information, and then generates and signs the security token that is returned to the user. This token can then be used within the internal organization or sent to a partner organization for application access.
AD FS configuration database	The database used to store all of the configuration data that defines an AD FS 2.0 instance or Federation Service. This database can be stored either within SQL Server or within the Windows Internal Database (or WID—a feature of Windows Server 2008 R2). If stored within WID, the database is created through the AD FS 2.0 Federation Server Configuration Wizard. If stored within SQL Server, the database must be created using the Fsconfig.exe command-line tool.
Account partner organization	The partner that hosts the AD DS directory that contains the accounts of the users who access extranet applications contained within the resource organization's web servers. This partner is represented by a claims provider trust in the Federation Service.
Attribute store	A container—either a database such as SQL Server or a directory such as AD DS—that includes attributes about clients.
Claim	The statement the federation server makes about a user or client.
Claims-aware application	A web-based application that can interpret claims to grant user access.
Claims provider	The organization that provides claims to its users, usually the account partner organization.
Claims provider trust	The one-way trust between a resource organization and the account organizations which with it wants to partner. This trust is composed of identifiers, names, and rules that provide the account partner organization's identity to the Federation Service.

TERM	DESCRIPTION
Federated user	Any user who has been granted appropriate claims in the account organization to access applications in the resource organization.
Federation	Any two organizations that have established a federation trust.
Federation metadata	The format used to communicate data between the members of a Federation Service. The data format stems from Security Assertion Markup Language (SAML) 2.0 and is extended within the WS-Federation.
Federation server	The internal server that performs claims mapping and issues access security tokens for users who need to work with an application.
Federation server proxy	A server located in a perimeter network. Its purpose is to forward client requests from the Internet to a Federation Service that is located on the internal corporate network.
Primary federation server (WID configuration database only)	A computer running the Windows Server 2008 R2 federation server role that has read and write access to the Federation Service configuration database contained within the Windows Internal Database. This server is created when you first run the AD FS 2.0 Federation Server Configuration Wizard and choose to create a new Federation Service. The primary federation server (PFS) is the first server in a federation farm. All other servers have read-only access to the database and must replicate changes made on the PFS to their own internal copy of the database. Note: A PFS exists only when you are using a WID configuration database. When you are using a SQL Server configuration database, all federation servers have read and write access.
Identity Metasystem Interoperability Protocol (IMIP)	The protocol hat outlines how to provision Information Cards. AD FS 2.0 implements version 1.1 of the protocol. IMIP is approved by the Organization for the Advancement of Structured Information Standards (OASIS) Identity Metasystem Interoperability Technical Committee.
Information Card	Represents digital identities. Users see Information Cards as a picture of an identity card on their computer screen. Administrators see them as containing the details of the Federation Service to obtain claims. Information Cards can either be managed—issued by a claims provider—or personal—issued by users themselves.

TERM	DESCRIPTION
Information Card Group Policies	AD FS 2.0 issues two Group Policy objects that outline how to provision and how to use Information Cards within an AD DS directory.
Relying party	The resource organization that processes claims sent by partners.
Relying party trust	Composed, like the claims provider trust, of identifiers, names, and rules that provide the partner organization's or web application's identity to the Federation Service. Relying party trusts are used in two situations: — Within account partner organizations to identify the source of the trusted accounts that a resource organization will rely on to grant access. — Within a resource organization to identify the trust between a web-based application and the Federation Service.
Resource federation server	The federation server within the resource organization. This server issues access tokens to web-based applications when it receives valid user account tokens from the account organization. After it receives the account security token, it verifies the signature of the token, applies a claim rule set to the appropriate access rights within the web application, and generates a new signed token to be sent out with the outgoing claims to both the user and the web application.
Resource partner organization	The organization that hosts the federated applications in its perimeter network and accepts access requests from account partners.
Security Assertion Markup Language (SAML)	Defines the web SSO protocol that outlines how to use HTTP web browser redirects to exchange assertion data used to authenticate and authorize clients across firewalls.
SAML security token	A special data format used to exchange claims between claims providers and relying parties. Members of a Federation Service based on AD FS 2.0 can use either SAML 1.1 or 2.0 tokens.
Web services (WS-*)	A standards-based Internet service that forms part of an SOA. Commonly known web services include the Simple Object Access Protocol (SOAP), Extensible Markup Language (XML), and Universal Description, Discovery, and Integration (UDDI). Web services are language-agnostic so they can interoperate between different IT infrastructures, such as UNIX, Linux, and Windows.
WS-Federation	The web server specification that outlines the standards to be used when implementing federation.

Core AD FS Components

To operate, AD FS relies on several core components:

- Attribute store
- AD FS configuration database
- Claims
- Claim rules

Each of these components provides additional support to the AD FS process.

The AD FS Attribute Store

As mentioned in Table 17-1, attribute stores can be a database or a directory. They are used to store user accounts and their associated attribute values. AD FS reads user attributes values from the store and relies on this information to create claims. These claims are provided to web-based applications so that they can grant appropriate authorizations to federated users.

Attribute stores can be used to provide authorization to web-based applications located either within an intranet or the Internet. Stores can be databases running on any edition of SQL Server 2005 or 2008, directories running AD DS, or custom attribute stores.

EXAM TIP

Note that AD FS 2.0 no longer supports AD LDS as an attribute store.

The AD FS Configuration Database

The configuration database determines the scope of a single instance of AD FS. The database can be contained within the Windows Internal Database, in which case it is configured using the AD FS Federation Server Configuration Wizard, or it can be contained within SQL Server, in which case it must be created through the Fsconfig.exe utility.

When running the configuration database in WID, you cannot configure additional parameters through a database user interface. Instead, you must rely on the AD FS management snap-in, FSconfig.exe, or PowerShell cmdlets. SQL Server databases can be modified through any of these user interfaces or the SQL Server management tools. WID configuration databases highly resemble the old Windows NT directory service in that a primary read-write database is created on the initial federation server—the primary federation server—in an AD FS deployment; then it is replicated as a read-only database on all other, secondary, federation servers within the same deployment. Secondary servers poll the primary server for database changes every five minutes. This value can be adjusted through the *Get-ADFSSyncProperties* and *Set-ADFSSyncProperties* PowerShell cmdlets.

WID databases can be used for either stand-alone or federation server farm deployments. In stand-alone deployments, the WID database is only configured to maintain a single instance and cannot be shared with other servers. Use this only for test deployments. In farm deployments, the WID database is configured for replication and growth as new servers are added to the AD FS farm.

SQL Server configuration databases are located centrally and do not need to be placed on a federation server. Each server within the deployment has read-write access to this database. SQL Server also provides performance enhancements to AD FS in situations of high traffic. In large deployments, the SQL Server database should be protected either through mirroring or clustering services. SQL Server also provides support for SAML artifact resolution and SAML/WS-Federation token replay detection. This means that your federation servers automatically discard token replays when they are detected. Token replays occur when a user continually tries to authenticate using the same credentials to the server by using the Back button on a web page. For example, a malicious user could try to impersonate a valid user by using web browser history to attempt to log in. Therefore, you should rely on SQL Server whenever security is a high concern for your web-based applications.

Claims

In their most basic form, claims are statements that each partner in an AD FS relationship makes about its users. Claims can be based on several values—for example, user names, certificate keys, group memberships, specific privileges, and so on. Claims are the basis of the authorization that AD FS sends to the web application. Claims can be sourced in two ways:

- The value can originate from an AD DS attribute store, such as a group membership of a user account.
- The value can be transformed into another by applying a rule.

AD FS can support several types of claims:

- A user principal name (UPN) representing the user's identity in a format that resembles an email address (*username@accountdomain*).
- A standard email address (*username@emaildomain*).
- Common names, which are really nothing more than arbitrary strings of characters.
- The group memberships a user belongs to can also be used in a claim. Because a user can belong to several groups, you can provide several group claim types in a claim. For example, the same user can belong to the Tester, Developer, and User groups for an application.
- Claim types also include roles, private personal identifiers (PPID), SAML name identifiers, user account or group account SIDs, and Windows account names.

Claims are transported through the claims pipeline within the Federation Service. The claims pipeline is detailed in the next section.

> **MORE INFO**   **AD FS CLAIM TYPES**
>
> For more information on AD FS claim types, go to *http://technet.microsoft.com/en-ca/library/ee913589%28WS.10%29.aspx*.

Claim Rules

Claim rules represent business logic that takes incoming claims, apply conditions to them, and generate outgoing claims. They are actual administrative representations of how you can customize the flow of claims through a Federation Service implementation. Claim rules are processed through the *claims engine*—the actual AD FS component that applies business logic to claims. Administrators rely on rules to determine how claims within the *claims pipeline*—the Federation Service implementation—will be processed and released to the relying parties within the pipeline. Rules also support the permission or denial of access to resources within the Federation Service.

The claims engine, together with claim rules associated to a particular federated trust, determines how claims are processed. Claims can be processed in one of three ways:

- They can be passed through as they are.
- They can be filtered to meet specific conditions.
- They can be transformed into completely new claims.

Administrators rely on *claim rule templates*—preconfigured generic rules—to generate custom claim rules within their Federation Service deployment. Claim rule templates also contain the claim rule language that is required to apply a rule through the claims engine. The exception is the custom rule template: Other templates represent common administrative tasks within an AD FS deployment and the corresponding claim rule language, but this template does not contain any claim rule language and should be used only when you are ready to generate the rule language syntax on your own.

Templates included with AD FS 2.0 allow for the generation of rules supporting the following tasks:

- Pass through or filter an incoming claim
- Transform an incoming claim
- Send LDAP attributes as claims
- Send group membership as claims
- Send claims using a custom rule
- Permit or deny users based on an incoming claim
- Permit all users

Templates can be used within the AD FS management snap-in or through the *New-ADFSClaimRuleSet* cmdlet. After they are generated, claim rules can be used singly or as a set (a group of one or more rules). Claim rule sets are processed in the order specified by the administrator and generate a result based on the cumulative application of each rule within the set. Claim rule sets are applied to specific federated trusts. A single federated trust can include several claim rule sets.

Basically, AD FS allows you to generate a partnership that supports access to applications through the generation of claims. Claims can originate from within your own organization or from within partner organizations and are transformed when processed by the claims engine through claim rule sets.

> **MORE INFO** **AD FS CLAIMS AND CLAIM RULES**
>
> For more information on AD FS claims and claim rules, go to *http://technet.microsoft.com/ en-ca/library/ee913586%28WS.10%29.aspx*.

> **EXAM TIP**
>
> Pay attention to AD FS claims and claim rules. Because AD FS relies entirely on the claims pipeline to process claims, they are a core part of this exam topic.

Understanding AD FS Certificates

To ensure secure communication, the AD FS implementation uses several certificate types. In fact, AD FS can rely on your AD CS deployment to obtain the certificates it needs, especially if your AD CS deployment relies on a trusted root. Each server role within an AD FS deployment relies on certificates. The type of certificate required by the role depends on its purpose.

- **Federation servers** The federation server must have both a server authentication certificate and a token-signing certificate installed before it can perform any AD FS operations and become fully functional. In addition, the trust policy that forms the basic tenet of the federation relationship must rely on a verification certificate. The latter is nothing more than the public key of the token-signing certificate.

  - The server authentication certificate is an SSL authentication certificate that secures web traffic between the federation server and the Federation Service Proxy or the web clients. This certificate must be bound to the Default Web Site in IIS. Ideally, this certificate originates from a trusted root, which facilitates client operation with the AD FS servers. The subject name for the certificate should reflect your Federation Service name, usually your organization's name. Note that the server authentication certificate is referred to as the Service Communication Certificate in the AD FS 2.0 management console.

  - Each time the federation server generates a security token, it must digitally sign the token with its token-signing certificate. Signing certificates ensures that it cannot be tampered with during transit. The token-signing certificate is made up of a private and public key pair. AD FS issues a self-signed certificate at installation. Replace this certificate with one from a trusted root in a production deployment.

  - Each time a federation server must decrypt an incoming token, it must rely on a token decryption certificate. This certificate is included with the incoming tokens as well as in the federation metadata. AD FS issues a self-signed certificate at installation. Replace this certificate with one from a trusted root in a production deployment.

- **Federation Service proxies** Proxies must have a server authentication certificate to support SSL-encrypted communication with web clients.

AD FS can easily rely on AD CS to obtain and manage these certificates. Keep in mind, however, that because many of the AD FS roles are outward-facing, your certificates must be from a trusted certification authority; otherwise, you must modify the Trusted CA store on each web client. In addition, remember that because certificates are such an important part of AD FS operation, they should be backed up and protected regularly.

AD FS 2.0 vs. AD FS 1.1

The major difference between AD FS 1.1 released with Windows Server 2008 R2 and AD FS 2.0 is the reliance on standards. AD FS 2.0 is completely built on the interoperability standards set out by the OASIS Technical Committee and, as such, its features and its terminology have changed to match the elements outlined in this standard.

As mentioned earlier, AD FS allows you to deploy three different scenarios, all built one upon the other. You can provide access to web-based applications for your own AD DS users, you can add Internet user support, and you can add partner user support. Each of these requires different configurations within your organization. In addition, AD FS 2.0 can now be integrated with third-party attribute stores including Computer Associates' Federation Manager, Oracle's Identity Federation, IBM's Tivoli, and any other product that supports both the WS* and the SAML standards.

Organizations already using AD FS 1.0 (from Windows Server 2003 R2) or 1.1 can migrate their installations to 2.0 or simply continue using the 1.*x* version along with a new deployment of 2.0. Remember that, in AD FS 2.0:

- AD LDS is no longer supported as an attribute store.
- The Windows NT token-based web agent is no longer supported.
- The AD FS 1.*x* claims-aware web agent for Microsoft Office SharePoint Server 2007 is no longer supported. Rely on SharePoint 2010 instead.
- The Federated Web Single Sign On with Forest Trust deployment scenario is no longer supported.

Overall, AD FS 2.0 deployment scenarios are simpler and easier to support than AD FS 1.*x* deployment scenarios, yet they provide more functionality and full support for cloud interoperability.

> **MORE INFO**   **AD FS 1.1 AND 2.0**
>
> For more information on migrating AD FS 1.1 to 2.0, go to *http://technet.microsoft.com/en-ca/library/ff678035%28WS.10%29.aspx*. For information on 1.1 and 2.0 interoperability, go to *http://technet.microsoft.com/en-ca/library/ff678322%28WS.10%29.aspx*.

Installing Active Directory Federation Services 2.0

A complete installation of AD FS requires a series of computers. Ideally, you would have two AD DS domains, two perimeter networks, and AD FS servers distributed within each environment. The account organization or claims provider should host AD DS and at least one federation server internally as well as a federation server proxy (FSP) in its perimeter network. Note that the FSP is required only if you intend to allow users to work with the Federation Service from the Internet. The resource organization or relying party should host AD DS and at least one internal federation server. Its perimeter network should include at least one AD FS–enabled web server and one FSP. However, the full deployment you design should be based on considerations such as the number of partner organizations, the type of applications to share, the requirement for high availability and load balancing, and other considerations of this type.

Test environments can be set up with as few as four computers: one client, one AD FS–enabled web server, and two federation servers to participate in AD FS federation between two organizations. Because of the nature of AD FS, computer clocks should be synchronized to the same time or should never have more than five minutes of difference between one and the other; otherwise, the process will not work because the token time stamps will be invalid. Because many of the computers are not part of an AD DS domain, you cannot rely on the PDC Emulator Operations Master for clock synchronization. The best way to ensure time synchronization is to use the Network Time Protocol (NTP) to link each server to an external clock server.

> **MORE INFO** **RELY ON NTP FOR TIME SYNCHRONIZATION**
>
> For information on how to set up NTP on your servers to ensure time synchronization in the perimeter and the internal networks, look up *Windows Server 2008: The Complete Reference* by Ruest and Ruest (McGraw-Hill Osborne, 2008).

 Quick Check

1. What are the two role services and features that make up the AD FS server role?
2. What are the three deployment configurations supported by AD FS?
3. What are the three deployment scenarios supported by AD FS?

Quick Check Answers

1. AD FS includes the following two role services:

   - The Federation Service provides the core AD FS functionality, managing resource access, filtering claims, and generating security tokens.

   - The Federation Service Proxy is an Internet relay that passes requests on to internal Federation Service servers.

2. AD FS supports Federated SSO, Web SSO, and Cloud SSO.

3. AD FS supports the following three deployment scenarios, which build upon each other:

- Providing SSO to your internal AD DS users.
- Providing SSO to your internal AD DS users as well as to Internet users.
- Providing SSO to your internal AD DS users, Internet users, and partner users.

AD FS Installation Requirements

To prepare for an AD FS deployment, you must begin with its prerequisites. Table 17-2 lists requirements for AD FS 2.0 for both the Web SSO and the Federated Web SSO designs.

TABLE 17-2 AD FS Deployment Requirements

HARDWARE/SOFTWARE	REQUIREMENT	NOTE
CPU speed	1 GHz for single core, 2 GHz for quad core	Because of the low processor, memory, and disk space requirements for AD FS server roles, you can easily virtualize this role through Hyper-V.
RAM	1 GB	Recommended: 4 GB. AD FS is not a memory-intensive process, but it is always best to allocate as much RAM as possible.
Hard disk space	50 MB for the AD FS installation	Recommended: a large system volume of at least 100 GB to ensure space for growth.
Operating system	Windows Server 2008 R2 Enterprise edition or Datacenter edition or Windows Small Business Server 2008	The Federation Service and the Federation Service Proxy are designed for the latest Windows Server editions. All required hotfixes are also installed during AD FS 2.0 installation.
Web services	IIS with ASP.NET enabled and .NET Framework 3.5 SP1	Use IIS 7.0 or 7.5 with the latest .NET Framework.
Installation location	Default location on the system drive	The federation service and Federation Service Proxy cannot coexist on the same server.
AD DS account store requirements	At least a single domain forest	Recommended: a minimum of two forests.

HARDWARE/SOFTWARE	REQUIREMENT	NOTE
Installation certificate for TLS/SSL and token signing	An SSL server authentication certificate for each deployed AD FS server role	Rely on an external third-party commercial CA to obtain a trusted certificate or enterprise CAs. Use self-signed certificates only in testing environments. Each of the federation servers and the Federation Service Proxy needs an authentication certificate from a trusted root chain.
TCP/IP network connectivity	IPv4 or IPv6 connectivity, ideally static address assignments	Network connectivity must exist between client, domain controller, and computers hosting the federation server and the federation server proxy.
Web browser	Microsoft Internet Explorer 7.0 or 8.0, Mozilla Firefox 3.0, or Safari 3.1	JavaScript and at least trusted cookies must be enabled for browser to work with the federation service.
Client operating system	Windows XP, Windows Vista, or Windows 7	Recommended: Windows 7.
Domain membership	AD DS domain membership	Federated servers must be members of the domain. Proxies do not require AD DS membership. Do not install AD FS on a domain controller.
Attribute store	AD DS or SQL Server	An AD DS attribute store is created by default at installation. You can also rely on a custom attribute store.
Windows Identity Foundation (WIF)	Downloadable component	WIF is required to externalize user access from applications via claims.
Windows PowerShell	PowerShell feature	PowerShell is required to facilitate AD FS management.

MORE INFO   **AD FS REQUIREMENTS**

For more information on AD FS 2.0 requirements, go to *http://technet.microsoft.com/ en-ca/library/ff678034%28WS.10%29.aspx.*

MORE INFO   **AD FS STEP-BY-STEP GUIDES**

For access to AD FS step-by-step guides, go to *http://technet.microsoft.com/en-ca/library/ dd727938%28WS.10%29.aspx.*

EXAM TIP

Because of its nature, the AD FS server role is ideal for virtualization through Windows Server 2008 R2 Hyper-V.

✔ Quick Check

1. Which ports must be open in a firewall to support AD FS operations?
2. Which claim types are supported by AD FS?

Quick Check Answers

1. AD FS relies on a single port for all its operations: port 443, the SSL/TLS HTTP or HTTPS port.

2. AD FS supports several claim types:
   - User principal name, email address, and common name
   - Group claims, which are nothing more than membership in specific distribution or security groups in AD DS
   - Claim types can also include roles, private personal identifiers (PPIDs), SAML name identifiers, user account or group account SIDs, and Windows account names

---

PRACTICE Prepare an AD FS Deployment

In this practice, you create a complex AD FS environment that consists of several computers. The computers you need for this practice are outlined in the "Before You Begin" section of this chapter. Table 17-3 outlines the roles that each domain and computer plays in your AD FS deployment.

TABLE 17-3 AD FS Computer Roles

DOMAIN NAME	ROLE
contoso.com	Account domain
woodgrovebank.com	Resource domain
COMPUTER NAME	**ROLE**
SERVER01	AD DS domain controller for contoso.com, the account domain
SERVER03	The federation server for contoso.com, the account domain; must be a member of the contoso.com domain
SERVER06	AD DS domain controller for woodgrovebank.com, the resource domain
SERVER07	The federation server for woodgrovebank.com, the resource domain; must be a member of the woodgrovebank.com domain

You begin by preparing the DNS in each forest in the first exercise, and then install the federation servers in each forest in the second exercise.

> **IMPORTANT** **PERIMETER NETWORKS**
>
> Note that this layout does not include perimeter networks. Perimeter networks require a complex TCP/IP configuration, which is not required for the purpose of this practice. However, make sure that your AD FS production deployments include proper server placement within perimeter networks as outlined in Lesson 1, "Understanding Active Directory Federation Services."

EXERCISE 1   Configure Cross-DNS References

In this exercise, you configure the DNS servers in both forests to refer to the servers in the other forest. Because each forest is independent of the other, their DNS servers do not know about the other. To exchange information between one forest and the other, you must implement cross-DNS references in both forests. The easiest way to do this is to use forwarders from one domain to the other and vice versa. Make sure SERVER01 and SERVER06 are running.

1. Log on to SERVER01 with the domain Administrator account.
2. Launch Server Manager from the Administrative Tools program group.
3. Expand Roles\DNS Server\DNS\SERVER01.
4. Right-click SERVER01 in the tree pane and select Properties.
5. On the Forwarders tab, click Edit.
6. Type the IP address of SERVER06 and click OK twice.
7. Repeat the procedure in reverse on SERVER06; that is, add the SERVER01 IP address as a forwarder for SERVER06.
8. Test the operation by pinging each server from the other. For example, use the following command to ping SERVER01 from SERVER06:

   ```
   ping server01.contoso.com
   ```

   You should receive a response stating the IP address of SERVER01. If you experience problems, try restarting SERVER06.
9. Finally, add a host (A) resource record for the federation servers and the federation proxy servers within both domains. On SERVER01, expand Roles\DNS Server\DNS\SERVER01\Forward Lookup Zones and select contoso.com. Right-click the details pane and click New Host (A Or AAAA).
10. Add FS (for SERVER03) and its corresponding IP address. Click Add Host, click OK, and then click Done. Repeat steps 9 and 10 on SERVER06 for woodgrovebank.com to add FS (for SERVER07) and its corresponding IP address.

EXERCISE 2   Install the Federation Servers

In this exercise, you install the federation servers. This involves the installation of the server role plus the required support services for the role. Make sure SERVER01, SERVER03, SERVER06, and SERVER07 are running.

> **IMPORTANT**   **DOWNLOAD AD FS 2.0**
>
> AD FS 2.0 is not included with Windows Server 2008 R2. You must download it from *http://www.microsoft.com/downloads/en/details.aspx?familyid=118c3588-9070-426a-b655-6cec0a92c10b&displaylang=en* to perform this exercise. Make sure you obtain the version for Windows Server 2008 R2.

1.   Log on to SERVER07 with the domain Administrator account.

    Your privileges need not be as high as the domain administrator to install and work with AD FS, but using these credentials here facilitates the exercise. Only local administrative privileges are required to work with AD FS.

2.   Locate the ADFSSetup.exe file that you downloaded, and launch the AD FS setup process. Click Run in the Open File – Security Warning dialog box. Click Next in the Welcome screen.

3.   Accept the License Agreement and click Next.

4.   On the Server Role page, select Federation Server. Click Next.

5.   The installation warns you that it will check for and install any missing prerequisite software. Click Next to begin the installation.

6.   When the installation is complete, make sure the Start The AD FS 2.0 Management Snap-in When This Wizard Closes check box is selected, and click Finish to close the installation wizard.

7.   Repeat the same procedure for SERVER03.

    This process can take considerable time if the prerequisites were not installed prior to the installation of AD FS.

    You can also install the federation server role through the command line with the following command:

    ```
    adfssetup.exe /quiet
    ```

Lesson Summary

- AD FS extends your internal authentication store to external environments through identity federation and federation trusts.
- Federation partnerships always involve a resource and an account organization. A resource or relying organization can be a partner of several account organizations, but an account organization can be a partner with only a single resource organization.

- AD FS relies on secure HTTP communications by using SSL authentication certificates to verify the identity of both the server and the client during communications. Because of this, all communications occur through port 443 over HTTPS.

- AD FS is a Web services implementation that relies on standards-based implementations to ensure that it can interact with partners using different operating systems, such as Windows, UNIX, and Linux.

Lesson Review

You can use the following question to test your knowledge of the information in Lesson 1, "Understanding Active Directory Federation Services." The question is also available on the companion CD if you prefer to review it in electronic form.

> **NOTE ANSWERS**
>
> The answer to this question and explanations of why each answer choice is right or wrong are located in the "Answers" section at the end of the book.

1. You are a systems administrator for Contoso, Ltd. Your organization already has a federation relationship with Woodgrove Bank, which was implemented using Federation Services 1.1. To improve security, you deployed the federation service with named accounts running the service. Now you're ready to upgrade to AD FS 2.0, but when you perform the upgrade, you find out that the named account used to run the service has been removed and replaced with the Network Service account. Why did this happen?

   A. You cannot use named service accounts to run the AD FS service.

   B. The default service account used in an AD FS installation or upgrade is Network Service.

   C. Woodgrove has a policy that states that all federation services must run with the Network Service account.

   D. Microsoft prefers to use the Network Service account to run federation services and resets it as a best practice.

Lesson 2: Configuring and Using Active Directory Federation Services

As you saw in Lesson 1, servers in an AD FS relationship must rely on certificates to create a chain of trust between each other and to ensure that all traffic transported over the trust relationships is encrypted at all times. As discussed in Chapter 15, "Active Directory Certificate Services and Public Key Infrastructures," the best way to ensure that this chain of trust is valid and trusted in all locations is to obtain certificates from a trusted third-party CA or through the creation of a linked AD CS implementation that uses a third-party CA as its root.

This is only one of the aspects of the AD FS configuration that must be completed. When you deploy AD FS, you also must configure your AD FS–aware applications, configure trust policies between partner organizations, and configure claims for your users and groups. Then you can begin to run and manage AD FS.

> **MORE INFO   AD FS OPERATIONS**
>
> For more information on AD FS operations, look up "Active Directory Federation Services" on the TechNet WIKI at *http://social.technet.microsoft.com/wiki/contents/articles/ active-directory-services-overview.aspx*.

> **After this lesson, you will be able to:**
> - Manage AD FS certificates.
> - Finalize AD FS server configurations.
> - Work with AD FS claims policies.
>
> **Estimated lesson time: 40 minutes**

Finalizing the Configuration of AD FS

When you deploy AD FS, you must perform the following actions to complete the configuration:

- Import a server authentication certificate to the default website on the servers in your configuration. This certificate is essential to the operation of AD FS. You use a self-signed certificate for the purposes of this exercise.
- Configure the federation servers and the federation server proxies (FSPs) in each AD DS domain.
- Configure the token-signing and token-decrypting certificates on the federation servers.
- Verify that the Federation Service is operational.

Each of these operations requires the computers in your setup to be operational.

Using and Managing AD FS

When the configuration of the identity federation is complete, you move on to regular administration and management of the AD FS services and server roles. You rely on the Active Directory Federation Services console to perform these tasks. Administration tasks include:

- Configuring the federation service or federation server farm
- Managing the trust policy that is associated with the federation service by:
  - Administering attribute stores in either AD DS or SQL Server
  - Managing the account partners, resource partners, or both that trust your organization
  - Managing claims on federation servers
  - Managing certificates used by federation servers
  - Managing certificates in AD FS–protected web applications

Other operations include adding or removing web-based applications, adding or removing federation partners, and general monitoring of the AD FS processes.

When you work with FSPs, you can rely on the AD FS console to configure:

- The federation service with which the FSP is working
- The manner in which the FSP collects user credential information from browsers and web applications

Preparing and putting in place an identity federation through AD FS requires care and planning. Because of this, take the time to practice and prepare thoroughly in a laboratory before you move this technology into production.

Working with Windows PowerShell

AD FS is administered with Windows PowerShell on Windows Server 2008 or Windows Server 2008 R2. AD FS 2.0 automatically registers the PowerShell module for AD FS during installation. Run the following cmdlet to add AD FS support in your PowerShell session:

```
Add-PSSnapin Microsoft.Adfs.Powershell
```

After the module is imported, you can manage and administer AD FS components through PowerShell. One great advantage PowerShell gives you is that you can easily automate AD FS administration through its cmdlets. The AD FS module for Windows PowerShell includes 15 cmdlet objects that let you manage everything from the attribute store to AD FS certificates and trusts.

MORE INFO   AD FS AND WINDOWS POWERSHELL

For more information on how to use PowerShell to work with AD FS, see *http://technet .microsoft.com/en-us/library/adfs2-help-using-windows-powershell%28WS.10%29.aspx*.

Ongoing AD FS 2.0 Administration

You can and will use the AD FS 2.0 Management Console to administer your AD FS 2.0 implementation after it is complete, but you also have to rely on Windows PowerShell. For example, the console does not provide any means to manage or update federation server proxies; these can be managed only through PowerShell. Become familiar with the PowerShell cmdlets for AD FS 2.0. Table 17-4 describes the PowerShell cmdlets for AD FS 2.0. Note that AD FS 2.0 includes both cmdlets and resources—convenience utilities that gather a set of control functions within a single cmdlet.

TABLE 17-4 AD FS 2.0 PowerShell cmdlets

CMDLET	PURPOSE
ADFSRelyingPartyTrust	Administer trusts with relying parties
ADFSClaimsProviderTrust	Administer trusts with claims providers
ADFSAttributeStore	Control the attribute store within an AD FS implementation
ADFSClaimDescription	Manage claim types supported by AD FS 2.0
ADFSEndpoint	Manage endpoints in a Federation Service
ADFSCertificate	Manage certificates in an AD FS 2.0 implementation
ADFSProxyProperties	Manage the properties of a federation server proxy
ADFSProperties	Manage the properties of a federation server
RESOURCE	**PURPOSE**
ADFSClaimRuleSet	Authors and updates AD FS policies
ADFSSAMLEndpoint	Encapsulates SAML endpoints and endpoint bindings
ADFSContactPerson	Encapsulates the contact information for a trust partner
ADFSOrganization	Encapsulates organization information for a trust partner
ADFSCertSharingContainer	Manages the service account that is used to share private keys of token signing and token decrypting certificates, as well as the SSL certificates used in an AD FS 2.0 deployment
ADFSSyncProperties	Controls the frequency of configuration database synchronization when using the Windows Internal Database instead of SQL Server

PRACTICE Finalizing the AD FS 2.0 Configuration

In this practice, you finalize the AD FS installation you performed in Lesson 1, and you rely on the same computers you used in that practice. You begin by configuring the IIS server on each of the federation servers and completing the AD FS configuration on each server. Then you configure the federation servers for each partner organization. You finish the AD FS configuration by creating the federation trust.

EXERCISE 1 Configure the Default Web Sites on Each Server

In this exercise, you configure the default websites on each server. Make sure that all servers are running. This includes SERVER01, SERVER03, SERVER06, and SERVER07.

1. Log on to SERVER03 with the domain Administrator account.

2. Launch IIS Manager (Start, All Programs, Administrative Tools, Internet Information Services (IIS) Manager), select the server name, and then scroll down and select Server Certificates in the Features view of the details pane.

3. In the Action pane, click the Open Feature link. In the Action pane, click the Create Self-signed Certificate link.

4. Type a friendly name for the certificate and click OK. In this instance, use the service name for each certificate. For example, use **FS.contoso.com** for SERVER03 and **FS.woodgrovebank.com** for SERVER07.

5. Bind the certificate to the default website on port 443. To do so, expand SERVER03 in the tree pane and click Sites. Click Default Web Site in the details pane. Click the Bindings link in the Actions pane. Click Add. Choose HTTPS from the Type drop-down list and All Unassigned from the IP Address drop-down list. Make sure 443 is entered as the Port value. Choose your self-signed certificate in the SSL Certificate drop-down list. Click OK, and then click Close.

   Repeat this operation for SERVER07.

EXERCISE 2 Configure the Federation Servers

In this exercise, you configure the federation servers for operation. Make sure that all servers are running. This includes SERVER01, SERVER03, SERVER06, and SERVER07.

1. Log on to SERVER03 with the domain Administrator account.

2. If it isn't already open, launch the AD FS Management Console (Start, All Programs, Administrative Tools, AD FS 2.0 Management), and then launch the AD FS 2.0 Federation Server Configuration Wizard from the details pane.

3. On the Welcome page, select Create A New Federation Service. Click Next.

4. On the Select Stand-Alone Or Farm Deployment page, select Stand-Alone Federation Server. Note that this deployment will rely on the WID as a database. Click Next.

> **IMPORTANT** **USING SQL SERVER IN PRODUCTION DEPLOYMENTS**
>
> You use WID in this exercise, but in production deployments you should rely on SQL Server for the AD FS configuration database. For information on how to configure a SQL Server database with AD FS 2.0, go to *http://social.technet.microsoft.com/ wiki/contents/articles/ad-fs-2-0-migrate-your-ad-fs-configuration-database-to-sql- server.aspx.*

5. The Federation Service Name is automatically obtained from the certificate you assigned to the default website. Click Next.

   Note that in a production environment, you would require a certificate from a trusted root.

6. On the Ready To Apply Settings page, click Next to begin the configuration.

7. When the Configuration Results page appears, click Close.

   Repeat the process for SERVER07.

EXERCISE 3 Prepare the Certificate Share Location

One of the most important factors in setting up federation partnerships is integrating certificates from the servers in the Federation Service to link the servers that must communicate with each other. To do this, you need to perform several tasks:

- Create a file share that each server can access to simplify the transfer of certificate files from one server to another.
- Export the server authentication certificate of the account federation server (SERVER03) to a file.
- Export the server authentication certificate of the resource federation server (SERVER07) to a file.
- Assign a token-signing certificate to the account federation server (SERVER03).
- Assign a token-decrypting certificate to the account federation server (SERVER03).

  You perform these tasks mostly because you are using self-signed certificates. If you were using trusted root certificates, you would only need to assign them to the federation servers.

First you must create the file share you will use to store the certificates. The other actions are performed in the exercises that follow.

1. Log on to SERVER03 with the domain Administrator account.

2. Launch Windows Explorer and move to the C drive. Create a new folder and name it **Temp**.

3. Right-click the Temp folder, point to Share With, and click Specific People.

4. In the File Sharing dialog box, select Everyone in the drop-down list, click Add, and assign Read/Write permission.

5. Click Share, and then click Done.

   Your shared folder is ready. Proceed with the remaining exercises.

EXERCISE 4 Export the SSL Server Certificate

Beginning with SERVER03, you will export the SSL server and client authentication certificates to a file on each server.

1. Log on to SERVER03 with domain Administrator credentials.

2. Launch Internet Information Services (IIS) Manager from the Administrative Tools program group.

3. In the tree pane, click the server name.

4. In the details pane in the Features view, scroll to the IIS section and double-click Server Certificates.

5. Double-click the FS.contoso.com certificate.

6. On the Details tab, click Copy To File. Click Next.

7. On the Export Private Key page, select No, Do Not Export The Private Key and click Next.

8. On the Export File Format page, ensure that DER Encoded Binary X.509 (.CER) is selected and click Next.

9. On the File To Export page, click Browse and move to the C:\Temp folder. Name the certificate **SERVER03SSL.cer** and click Save. Click Next.

10. On the Completing The Certificate Export Wizard page, verify the information and click Finish.

11. Click OK when you get the Certificate Export Was Successful message. Click OK again to close the Certificate dialog box.

   Now move to SERVER07 and repeat the procedure, as follows:

1. Log on to SERVER07 with domain Administrator credentials.

2. Launch Internet Information Services (IIS) Manager from the Administrative Tools program group.

3. In the details tree pane, click the server name.

4. In the details pane in Features view, scroll to the IIS section and double-click Server Certificates.

5. Double-click the FS.woodgrovebank.com certificate.

6. On the Details tab, click Copy To File. Click Next.

7. On the Export Private Key page, select No, Do Not Export The Private Key and click Next.

8. On the Export File Format page, ensure that DER Encoded Binary X.509 (.CER) is selected and click Next.

9. On the File To Export page, click Browse and in the address bar at the top of the Browse window, type **\\SERVER03.Contoso.com\temp**, and then press Enter. Name the certificate **SERVER07SSL.cer**, click Save, and then click Next.

10. On the Completing The Certificate Export Wizard page, verify the information and click Finish.

11. Click OK when you get the Certificate Export Was Successful message. Click OK again to close the Certificate dialog box.

    Your certificates are now all in a shared folder.

EXERCISE 5 Assign and Export Federation Certificates

Proceed to the assignment of certificates. Perform this operation on SERVER03.

1. Launch Windows PowerShell Modules from the Administrative Tools program group. If this is the first time you have used this module on this server, PowerShell will import all existing modules, including the module for AD FS. If the module is not present, execute the following cmdlet:

   ```
   Add-PSSnapin Microsoft.ADFS.PowerShell
   ```

   You must disable the AD FS Automatic Certificate Rollover feature to manually add certificates to your configuration. This feature allows AD FS to automatically manage the certificates it requires to operate. Remember to turn this feature back on when you are done. Execute the following cmdlet:

   ```
   Set-ADFSProperties -AutoCertificateRollover $false
   ```

   Minimize the PowerShell window when done.

2. Launch the AD FS 2.0 Management Console from the Administrative Tools program group. Double-click Service in the console tree and click Certificates.

3. In the Action pane, click the Add Token-Signing Certificate link.

4. Select the FS.Contoso.Com certificate in the Windows Security dialog box and click OK.

   In production, you would ensure that the private key for this certificate is exported and available to other servers you configure in an AD FS farm. In this case, you did not export the private key because your configuration includes only a single server. Click OK in the warning message dialog box.

5. In the Action pane, click the Add Token-Decrypting Certificate link.

6. Select the FS.Contoso.Com certificate in the Windows Security dialog box and click OK. Click OK again to close the warning dialog box.

7. Note that AD FS automatically assigned a Service Communications Certificate. This certificate is the same as the SSL certificate assigned to the default website.

8. Reactivate the Automatic Certificate Rollover feature. Return to the Windows PowerShell Modules window and execute the following cmdlet:

```
Set-ADFSProperties –AutoCertificateRollover $true
```

Close the PowerShell window.

9. Repeat this procedure on SERVER07, this time selecting the FS.Woodgrovebank.com certificate for each service.

EXERCISE 6   Configure the Federation Servers

You are now ready to configure both of your federation servers. The configuration for account partners (claims providers) and resource partners (relying parties) is very similar, with only minor differences. Table 17-5 describes the activities that you must perform for each partner.

TABLE 17-5   Configuring Federation Servers

ACTIVITY	ACCOUNT PARTNER	RESOURCE PARTNER
Determine your federated application strategy.	None	The resource partner must determine how shared applications will be accessed.
Add an attribute store.	The attribute store is required by both parties.	The attribute store is required by both parties.
Create a trust policy.	The trust policy is required to form the partnership. The account partner requires a Claims Provider trust.	The trust policy is required to form the partnership. The resource partner requires a Relying Party trust.
Create claim rules.	Claim rules are required to properly issue claims.	Claim rules are required to properly process claims.
Prepare client computers.	The account partner must prepare client computers to have them interoperate with the claims partnership.	No action required

> **MORE INFO**   **PREPARING FEDERATION SERVERS**
>
> Microsoft provides a complete checklist for the preparation of federation servers. For the preparation of a relying party federation server, go to *http://technet.microsoft.com/en-ca/library/dd807047%28WS.10%29.aspx*. For the preparation of a claims provider federation trust, go to *http://technet.microsoft.com/en-ca/library/dd807112%28WS.10%29.aspx*.

Begin with the federated application strategy in the resource partner. AD FS 2.0 supports ASP.NET applications as well as Windows Communications Foundation services. Applications can be accessed through Windows Integrated Authentication, simplifying access for end users. AD FS 2.0 also supports WS* standards and, because of this, supports a wide range of both Windows-based and non-Windows-based applications. When you configure a federated trust in your organization, you should determine the following:

- Which applications will be accessed through federation?
- What type of applications are they?
- Will your internal, corporate users have access to these applications?
- Will non-corporate users (Internet users) have access?
- Will partner users have access?

The answer to these questions will help determine your application strategy.

After you have determined the application strategy, you are ready to configure the federation servers. At this point, you normally configure the attribute store, but because AD FS 2.0 automatically generates an AD DS attribute store by default, you do not need to perform this operation in either environment.

Therefore, you can move on to create the trust policies. You will create the trusts manually, but in production, you can obtain a metadata file from your partners to create the trust automatically. These files might be available on the web as well. Begin with the account partner and claims provider, or SERVER03.

1. Log on to SERVER03 with the domain Administrator account.

   In this step, you need to use domain administrator credentials to identify the attribute store.

2. Launch AD FS 2.0 Management from the Administrative Tools program group.

3. Note that the Overview in the Details pane indicates that you must perform a required task before the configuration of your AD FS server is complete. Click the Required: Add A Trusted Relying Party link.

4. On the Welcome page, click Start.

5. On the Select Data Source page, select Enter Data About The Relying Party Manually and click Next.

6. Type **Woodgrove Bank** under Display Name, enter a description in the Notes section, and then click Next.

7. Select AD FS 2.0 Profile and click Next.

8. Click Browse on the Configure Certificate page, move to the C:\Temp folder, select SERVER07SSL, click Open, and then click Next.

9. Do not make any selections on the Configure URL page; click Next.

   AD FS 2.0 supports WS-Trust, WS-Federation, and SAML Web SSO protocols for trusts. You select either WS-Federation and/or SAML Web SSO if your partners are relying on them and enter the appropriate URLs. But because WS-Trust is enabled by default, you do not need to select either of the other protocols for your trust to work in this exercise.

10. Specify the relying party's URL, in this case **HTTP://woodgrovebank.com/adfs/services/trust**, click Add, and then click Next.

11. Choose the issuance authorization rules. Select Permit All Users To Access This Relying Party and click Next.

    In production environments, you might choose to deny all users and then assign specific authorization rules afterward. In this exercise, to simplify the process we allow all users.

12. On the Ready To Add Trust page, click Next, make sure that the Open The Edit Claim Rules Dialog For This Relying Party Trust When The Wizard Closes check box is selected, and then click Close.

    The Edit Claim Rules dialog box opens, allowing you to finalize the trust and add mappings between the claims and the data within AD DS.

13. Click Add Rule. Choose Send LDAP Attributes As Claims from the drop-down list and click Next.

14. Type a name for the rule, in this case **Group Membership Rule**, and make sure the attribute store is set to Active Directory. Then choose Token-Groups – Unqualified Names from the drop-down list under LDAP Attribute and choose Role under Outgoing Claim Type; then click Finish and click OK.

Your relying party trust is configured. Proceed to the configuration of the resource provider. Repeat the same operation, but this time on SERVER07, as follows:

1. Log on to SERVER07 with the domain Administrator account.

   In this step, you need to use domain administrator credentials to identify the attribute store.

2. Launch AD FS 2.0 Management from the Administrative Tools program group.

3. Note once again that you must still complete the configuration of the server for the Federation Service to work properly. Click the Required: Add A Trusted Relying Party link.

4. On the Welcome page, click Start.

5. On the Select Data Source page, select Enter Data About The Relying Party Manually and click Next.

6. Type **Contoso** under Display Name, enter a description in the Notes section, and then click Next.

7. Select AD FS 2.0 Profile and click Next.

8. Click Browse on the Configure Certificate page, and in the address bar at the top of the Browse window type **\\SERVER03.Contoso.com\temp**; then press Enter. Select SERVER03SSL, click Open, and then click Next.

9. Do not make any selections on the Configure URL page; click Next.

10. Specify the relying party's URL, in this case **HTTP://contoso.com/adfs/services/trust**, click Add, and then click Next.

11. Choose the issuance authorization rules. Select Permit All Users To Access This Relying Party and click Next.

    In production environments, you might choose to deny all users, and then assign specific authorization rules afterward. In this exercise, to simplify the process we allow all users.

12. On the Ready To Add trust page, click Next, make sure the Open The Edit Claim Rules Dialog For This Relying Party Trust When The Wizard Closes check box is selected, and then click Close.

    The Edit Claim Rules dialog box opens, allowing you to finalize the trust and add mappings between the claims and the data within AD DS.

13. Click Add Rule. Choose Send LDAP Attributes As Claims from the drop-down list and click Next.

14. Type a name for the rule, in this case **Group Membership Rule**, and make sure the attribute store is set to Active Directory. Then select Token-Groups – Unqualified Names from the drop-down list under LDAP Attribute and choose Role from the Outgoing Claim Type drop-down list; then click Finish and click OK.

Your AD FS 2.0 trust is almost complete. AD FS 2.0 is working, but your clients do not yet have access to the service. You must configure your client computers in the claims provider to grant them access to the Federation Service.

Preparing client computers requires two major actions: You must enable Internet Explorer to access and trust the account federation server, and you must distribute the federation certificates to your client computers. Both operations are performed through Group Policy.

Configuring Internet Explorer to trust the federation server is performed through the user configuration section of Group Policy and relies on the Security section of Internet Explorer Maintenance (User Configuration, Policies, Windows Settings, Internet Explorer Maintenance, Security). It is a matter of adding the federation server URL to the intranet sites in Internet Explorer. Ideally, you will perform this operation on a management computer running a client operating system such as Windows 7, because you must import the settings from the current computer to be able to modify the Security Zones And Content Ratings setting. Import the settings, click Modify Settings, move to the Security tab, and click Local Intranet. Click Sites and add the URL for the federation servers.

Distribution of the federation certificates to client computers is also performed through Group Policy, but through the Computer Configuration section under Policies\Windows Settings\Security Settings\Public Key Policies. Select Trusted Root Certification Authorities, right-click in the details pane, and click Import. This launches the Certificate Import Wizard that you use to import the certificates into the Trusted Root Certification Authorities container. The certificate for each federation server in the Federation Service must be added to this store for client computers to trust each member server of the service.

After clients are configured and your new Group Policy settings have been applied, your Federation Service will be functional and users will have access to federated applications and services.

> **MORE INFO** **PREPARING CLIENT COMPUTERS**
>
> For more information on configuring client computers for account federation, go to *http://technet.microsoft.com/en-ca/library/dd807114%28WS.10%29.aspx*.

EXAM TIP

Make note of the procedures required to prepare AD FS 2.0 trusts, because they differ significantly from the procedures for AD FS 1.1 trusts. Configuring trusts and mapping user and group claims will be included in the exam.

Lesson Summary

- Because AD FS relies on secure communication, you must ensure that each server in an AD FS partnership trusts the root certificate that was used to issue certificates for each of the servers in the deployment. If you use self-signed certificates, you must export each certificate and then import it in the corresponding server's trusted CA stores.

- When you configure a partnership, you must first create claims-aware applications and assign specific claims to each partner in the partnership.

- You also need to identify which attribute store will be used by each federation server in the deployment.

- You create a federation trust between the two partners. This involves preparing the trust on each server and linking the trust metadata to the servers in the claims provider. Then you can use this trust policy to assign claims to the account organization. At this point, your partnership has been created.

Lesson Review

You can use the following question to test your knowledge of the information in Lesson 2, "Configuring and Using Active Directory Federation Services." The question is also available on the companion CD if you prefer to review it in electronic form.

> **NOTE** **ANSWERS**
>
> The answer to this question and explanations of why each answer choice is right or wrong are located in the "Answers" section at the end of the book.

1. You are an administrator for the contoso.com domain. Your organization has decided to create a federation partnership with Woodgrove Bank so that you can use identity federation to access a new application in the bank's perimeter network. The federation servers and Federation Service proxies are already in place, but you need to configure the federation trust to enable identity federation. Which steps must you perform? (Choose all that apply.)

   A. Communicate with your counterpart at Woodgrove Bank to establish how you will exchange information.

   B. Determine the federated application strategy in contoso.com.

   C. Determine the federated application strategy in Woodgrove Bank.

   D. Configure client computers at Woodgrove Bank.

   E. Configure client computers in contoso.com.

   F. Assign an attribute store in each partner.

Chapter Review

To further practice and reinforce the skills you learned in this chapter, you can perform the following tasks:

- Review the chapter summary.
- Review the list of key terms introduced in this chapter.
- Complete the case scenario. This scenario sets up a real-world situation involving the topics of this chapter and asks you to create a solution.
- Complete the suggested practices.
- Take a practice test.

Chapter Summary

- As a network operating system directory service, AD DS is mainly designed to work within the boundaries of your network. When you need to extend its identity and access (IDA) services to the outside world, you must rely on additional technologies. This is where AD FS comes in. AD FS provides external support for the internal IDA services you run, without having to open any special port on the firewall. Because of this, AD FS is an excellent tool for the foundation of partnerships. Organizations partner through AD FS but continue to manage only their internal AD DS service.

- AD FS is composed of two role services: the Federation Service and the Federation Service Proxy. Note that the two services cannot coexist on the same server.

- In addition to the basic technologies included in AD FS, the federation processes rely on claims to identify which access has been granted to users, cookies to simplify the logon process and support for single sign-on, and certificates to validate all transactions and secure all communication.

- AD FS supports two designs: Federated Web SSO and Web SSO. Of the two, the more common deployment type is Federated Web SSO. In fact, the very existence of AD FS can help avoid the requirement for forest trusts that pass through firewalls.

Key Terms

The following terms were introduced in this chapter. Do you know what they mean?

- claim mapping
- claims provider
- federation trust
- relying party
- Web services

Case Scenario

In the following case scenario, you apply what you've learned about AD FS. You can find answers to the questions in this scenario in the "Answers" section at the end of this book.

Case Scenario: Choosing the Right AD Technology

You are a systems administrator for Contoso, Ltd. Your organization has decided to deploy Windows Server 2008 R2 and wants to implement several of its technologies. Specifically, your implementation goals are to:

- Update your central authentication and authorization store.
- Ensure the protection of your intellectual property, especially when you work with partners.
- Support three applications running in the extranet. These are web-based applications that rely on the authentication models supported by IIS.
- Support extranet clients from three types of locations, which include the internal network, partner organizations, and the general public on the Internet.
- Ensure secure communications at all times.

Your goal is to identify which Windows Server 2008 R2 technologies are required and how they should be implemented. What do you recommend?

Suggested Practices

To help you successfully master the exam objectives presented in this chapter, complete the following tasks.

Prepare for AD FS

The best way to practice for AD FS questions on the exam is to run through each of the practice exercises included in this chapter. They expose you to each of the elements required to understand the exam objective for this topic.

In addition, you can also run through the exercises outlined in "Microsoft Step-by-Step Guide for Active Directory Federation Services," which is available at *http://technet.microsoft.com/en-ca/library/dd727938%28WS.10%29.aspx*.

Take a Practice Test

The practice tests on this book's companion CD offer many options. For example, you can test yourself on just one exam objective, or you can test yourself on all the 70-640 certification exam content. You can set up the test so that it closely simulates the experience of taking a certification exam, or you can set it up in study mode so that you can look at the correct answers and explanations after you answer each question.

> **MORE INFO** **PRACTICE TESTS**
>
> For details about all the practice test options available, see the "How to Use the Practice Tests" section in this book's Introduction.

Answers

Chapter 1

Lesson 1

1. **Correct Answers: A and B**

   A. **Correct:** A domain controller will create or join an Active Directory domain, which must have a valid DNS name.

   B. **Correct:** A domain must have a NetBIOS name to support earlier applications that use NetBIOS names.

   C. **Incorrect:** A DHCP server is not necessary. In fact, a domain controller should have statically assigned IP addresses.

   D. **Incorrect:** Although a DNS server is required for the functionality of a domain, if a DNS server does not exist, the Active Directory Installation Wizard will install and configure DNS service on the domain controller.

2. **Correct Answer: D**

   A. **Incorrect:** Windows Server 2008 R2 forest functional level requires that all domains operate at Windows Server 2008 R2 domain functional level. Because the Litware domain might include Windows Server 2003 domain controllers, that domain must remain at the Windows Server 2003 domain functional level. Therefore, the forest must also remain at Windows Server 2003 forest functional level.

   B. **Incorrect:** Windows Server 2008 R2 forest functional level requires that all domains operate at Windows Server 2008 R2 domain functional level. Because the Litware domain might include Windows Server 2003 domain controllers, that domain must remain at the Windows Server 2003 domain functional level. Therefore, the forest must also remain at Windows Server 2003 forest functional level.

   C. **Incorrect:** A domain operating at Windows Server 2008 R2 domain functional level cannot include Windows Server 2003 domain controllers.

   D. **Correct:** The Litware domain might include Windows Server 2003 domain controllers and, therefore, must operate at Windows Server 2003 domain functional level. The forest functional level cannot be raised until all domains are operating at Windows Server 2008 R2 domain functional level.

Lesson 2

1. **Correct Answer: A**

   A. Correct: A password is required so that it can be assigned to the local Administrator account on the server after AD DS is removed.

   B. Incorrect: SERVER02 is currently a domain controller, and you are logged on as Administrator. Therefore, you already have the credentials required to perform the demotion operation.

   C. Incorrect: SERVER02 is currently a domain controller, and you are logged on as Administrator. Therefore, you already have the credentials required to perform the demotion operation. The Domain Controllers group contains computer accounts for domain controllers.

   D. Incorrect: No DNS name resolution is required to perform this task.

2. **Correct Answer: D**

   A. Incorrect: AD CS not required on the same server as AD FS

   B. Incorrect: AD FS is not supported on Server Core.

   C. Incorrect: AD RMS is not supported on Server Core.

   D. Correct: AD FS is not supported on Server Core, so you must reinstall the server with the full installation of Windows Server 2008 R2.

Case Scenario: Creating an Active Directory Forest

- Yes. Server Core supports Active Directory Domain Services. You do not need a full installation of Windows Server 2008 R2 to create a domain controller.

- Use the *Netsh* command to configure IP addresses.

- Use *Ocsetup.exe* to add server roles. Alternately, there are parameters for the *Dcpromo.exe /unattend* command that can install the DNS service.

- Use *Dcpromo.exe* to add and configure AD DS.

Chapter 2

Lesson 1

1. **Correct Answer: C**

   A. Incorrect: The Active Directory snap-in in Server Manager, if launched, will run with the same credentials as the custom console. An Access Denied error will continue to occur.

   B. Incorrect: Although dsa.msc is a shortcut to opening the Active Directory Users And Computers console, it will run with the same credentials as the custom console. An Access Denied error will continue to occur.

C. Correct: An Access Denied error indicates that your credentials are not sufficient to perform the requested action. The question indicates that you are certain that you have permission. The answer introduces the assumption that you have a secondary account. Even though that account is not the Administrator, it is administrative. This is the best answer to the question.

D. Incorrect: *DSMOD USER* with the *-p* switch can be used to reset a user's password; however, the question is targeting the Access Denied error. There is no suggestion that Command Prompt was launched with different credentials; therefore, you will continue to receive Access Denied errors.

Lesson 2

1. **Correct Answer: D**

   A. Incorrect: An Active Directory task, whether performed using command-line commands, scripts, or remote server administration tools, can be performed by any user who has been delegated permission to the task.

   B. Incorrect: Domain Admins are members of the Administrators group in the domain, so any permissions assigned to Administrators would also be assigned to you as a member of the Domain Admins group.

   C. Incorrect: The ability to delete an OU or any object in Active Directory is related to permissions, not to ownership.

   D. Correct: New organizational units are created with protection from deletion. You must remove the protection before deleting the OU. Protection can be removed by using the Active Directory Users And Computers snap-in, with Advanced Features view, on the Object tab of an OU's properties dialog box.

Lesson 3

1. **Correct Answers: A, B, and D**

   A. Correct: The Delegation Of Control Wizard masks the complexities of object ACEs by guiding you through the assignment of permissions to groups.

   B. Correct: DSACLs can be used to manage Active Directory permissions from Command Prompt.

   C. Incorrect: DSUTIL is used to manage the domain and directory service properties but not object permissions.

   D. Correct: Assigning an administrative task requires modifying the DACL of an object such as an OU. The Advanced Security Settings dialog box provides the most direct user interface access to the permissions in the DACL.

Case Scenario: Managing Organizational Units and Delegation

1. The best design for computer objects at Contoso would be a single parent OU, within which child OUs would be created for each site. The support team at each site would be delegated control for computer objects in that site's OU. The parent OU would be used to delegate permissions so that the team at headquarters can manage computer objects in any site.

2. Even though each site has only one or two members of support personnel, it is always a best practice to create a group, place the users in that group, and delegate permissions to the group. As the organization and support teams grow and as users enter and leave the organization, managing permissions assigned to user accounts becomes very difficult. If the permission is assigned to a group on the other hand, support personnel can simply be added to or removed from the group.

3. Because users at any site might request assistance from a support person in another site, users should remain within a single OU. There is no need to divide users into OUs by site based on delegation or manageability. The OU containing the users would be delegated to a group that includes all support personnel. In fact, you could create a group that includes the groups of each site's support teams.

Chapter 3

Lesson 1

1. **Correct Answer: C**

   A. Incorrect: Although a user account template will enable you to copy several dozen of its attributes to a new user account, you would have to copy the template 2,000 times to complete this task.

   B. Incorrect: The LDIFDE command imports objects from LDIF files, which are not the format natively managed by Microsoft Office Excel.

   C. Correct: The CSVDE command imports objects from comma-delimited text files. Excel can open, edit, and save these files.

   D. Incorrect: The DSAdd command enables you to create a user from the command.

2. **Correct Answer: A**

   A. Correct: LDIFDE supports adding, modifying, or deleting Active Directory objects.

   B. Incorrect: DSMod modifies properties of an existing object.

   C. Incorrect: DEL is a command that erases a file.

   D. Incorrect: CSVDE can import users but cannot delete them.

Lesson 2

1. **Correct Answer: C**

   A. Incorrect: The *New-Item* cmdlet creates a new object in the current location. Because you have just opened the Windows PowerShell console, you are in the default location, and you have not navigated to Active Directory using the Active Directory PSDrive. Therefore, *New-Item* will not be able to create a new Active Directory object.

   B. Incorrect: The *New-SPUser* cmdlet creates a new user in a SharePoint site collection.

   C. Correct: The *New-ADUser* cmdlet creates an Active Directory user object.

   D. Incorrect: The *Set-ADUser* cmdlet configures properties of an existing user object.

2. **Correct Answers: B or D**

   A. Incorrect: LDIFDE imports users from LDIF files. Excel cannot save a workbook as an LDIF file.

   B. Correct: The *Import-CSV* cmdlet can import a comma-separated values file produced by Excel and pipe the data source to the *New-ADUser* cmdlet.

   C. Incorrect: The *DSAdd* command cannot import from a file.

   D. Correct: The *CSVDE* command can import from a comma-separated values file produced by Excel.

3. **Correct Answers: A and B**

   A. Correct: The *-AccountPassword* parameter of the *New-ADUser* cmdlet specifies the password of the new account.

   B. Correct: You must convert a plain text password to a secure string before it can be passed to the *-AccountPassword* parameter.

   C. Incorrect: There is no cmdlet named *Reset-ADPassword*.

   D. Incorrect: The *Remove-ADUser* cmdlet deletes a user account.

Lesson 3

1. **Correct Answers: C or D**

   A. Incorrect: You can use the Ctrl key to multiselect users, but they must be in a single OU. The 10 users in this scenario are in different OUs.

   B. Incorrect: DSMod will let you change the *Description* property, but DSGet will not locate the objects. DSGet is used to display attributes, not locate objects.

   C. Correct: You can use the DSQuery command to identify users whose Description property is set incorrectly and pipe the results to the DSMod command to change the *Description* property.

   D. Correct: The *Get-ADUser* cmdlet returns users that match a filter or LDAP query. The collection can be piped to the *Set-ADUser* cmdlet, which can modify the *description* attribute.

2. **Correct Answers: A, B, and C**

   A. Correct: The *Move-Item* cmdlet moves objects in a namespace.

   B. Correct: The *Move-ADObject* cmdlet can move a user.

   C. Correct: You can use the DSMove command to move an object in Active Directory.

   D. Incorrect: Redirusr.exe is used to configure Active Directory so that new user objects created without specifying an OU will go to a container other than the default Users container.

   E. Incorrect: The Active Directory Migration Tool is used to migrate accounts between domains.

3. **Correct Answer: A**

   A. Correct: Computer restrictions limit the computers that a user can log on to. On the Account tab of her user account, you can click the Log On To button and add the computer by name to the list of allowed workstations.

   B. Incorrect: When a computer account is created, you can control who is allowed to join the computer to the domain with this button, but it has nothing to do with who can log on to the computer after it is a domain member.

   C. Incorrect: DSMove is used to move an object in Active Directory.

   D. Incorrect: Although the user right to log on locally is required, the error message that she reports is not the message that would be received if she did not have the right to log on locally.

Case Scenario: Import User Accounts

1. You should use Windows PowerShell, which is capable of taking advantage of a database, such as an Excel file saved as a comma-separated values (.csv) file, as the source of data for user account creation. Windows PowerShell allows you to add attributes to user accounts as they are being created, even if those attributes are not specified in the data source. Although CSVDE also enables you to import .csv files, it simply imports only those attributes in the file.

2. You can disable the accounts until the students arrive.

3. In the Active Directory Users And Computers snap-in, you can select all users and change the *company* attribute one time. In Command Prompt, you can use DSQuery to pipe the DNs of all users to DSMod, which can change the *company* attribute. In Windows PowerShell, you can use the *Get-ADUser* cmdlet to pipe users to the *Set-ADUser* cmdlet.

Chapter 4

Lesson 1

1. **Correct Answer: B**

   A. **Incorrect:** Universal security groups cannot contain users or groups from trusted external domains. They can contain users, global groups, and other universal groups from any domain in the forest.

   B. **Correct:** Domain local security groups can contain members from trusted external domains.

   C. **Incorrect:** Global security groups cannot contain users or groups from trusted external domains. They can contain users and other global groups from the same domain only.

   D. **Incorrect:** Distribution groups cannot be assigned permissions to resources.

2. **Correct Answer: D**

   A. **Incorrect:** The group is a distribution group, which cannot be assigned permission. Changing the scope will not address that limitation.

   B. **Incorrect:** The group is a distribution group, which cannot be assigned permission. Changing the scope will not address that limitation.

   C. **Incorrect:** The group is a distribution group. Adding it to the Domain Users group will not give its members access to the shared folder.

   D. **Correct:** The *-secgrp yes* parameter changes the group type to a security group, after which you can add it to the ACL of the shared folder.

3. **Correct Answers: E, and F**

   A. **Incorrect:** Global groups cannot contain global groups from other domains.

   B. **Incorrect:** Global groups cannot contain global groups from other domains.

   C. **Incorrect:** Global groups can contain users in the same forest.

   D. **Incorrect:** Global groups can contain users in trusted domains.

   E. **Correct:** Global groups can contain users in the same domain.

   F. **Correct:** Global groups can contain global groups in the same domain.

   G. **Incorrect:** Global groups cannot contain domain local groups.

   H. **Incorrect:** Global groups cannot contain universal groups.

Lesson 2

1. **Correct Answers: C and D**

   A. **Incorrect:** The *Remove-Item* cmdlet in Windows PowerShell cannot be used to remove members of a group. However, the *Remove-ADGroupMember* cmdlet can be used to remove a member of a group.

   B. **Incorrect:** DSRm is used to delete a group.

   C. **Correct:** DSMod with the *-remmbr* option can remove members from a group.

   D. **Correct:** LDIFDE with a *changeType* of *modify* and a *delete:member* operation can remove members from a group.

   E. **Incorrect:** CSVDE can import new groups. It cannot modify existing groups.

2. **Correct Answer: B**

   A. **Incorrect:** DSRm deletes a group. Deleting a group will not solve the problem.

   B. **Correct:** You can use DSMod with the *-scope* switch to change the scope of GroupA to a universal group, then to a global group. You will then be able to add GroupA to GroupB. This is a tricky question. Sometimes test questions are not about what they appear to be about. This question was not about using commands or even about adding one group to another—it was about group scope.

   C. **Incorrect:** DSQuery searches Active Directory for objects. It cannot make a change, so it will not solve the problem.

   D. **Incorrect:** DSGet retrieves an attribute of an object. It cannot make a change, so it will not solve the problem.

3. **Correct Answers: A and D**

   A. **Correct:** *Get-ADGroupMember*, with the *-recursive* parameter, can enumerate the membership of a group, including nested groups.

   B. **Incorrect:** DSQuery queries Active Directory for objects matching a search filter. It does not list group membership.

   C. **Incorrect:** LDIFDE can be used to export a group and thereby its members, but only direct members.

   D. **Correct:** DSGet can return an attribute of an object, including the *member* attribute of group objects. With the *-expand* parameter, DSGet can return the full membership of a group.

Lesson 3

1. **Correct Answer: D**

   A. **Incorrect:** The team members already have permission. This permission will not prevent them from accessing the folder from other computers.

B. **Incorrect:** The team members already have permission. This permission will not prevent them from accessing the folder from other computers.

C. **Incorrect:** This permission will not prevent users from accessing the folder from other computers.

D. **Correct:** A Deny permission overrides Allow permissions. If a team member attempts to connect to the folder from another computer, he or she will be a member of the Network special identity group and will be denied access. If the same team member logs on locally to the conference room computer, he will be a member of Interactive and not Network, so the permissions assigned to him as a member of the team will allow access.

2. **Correct Answer: D**

A. **Incorrect:** The Members tab of the group lets you add and remove members but not delegate the administration of membership.

B. **Incorrect:** The Security tab of Mike Danseglio's user object determines who is delegated the ability to perform tasks on his object, not what Mike is able to do.

C. **Incorrect:** The Member Of tab of Mike Danseglio's user object determines the groups to which Mike belongs, not the groups to which Mike has been delegated control.

D. **Correct:** The Managed By tab of a group lets you specify the group's manager and allow the manager to update group membership.

3. **Correct Answers: A, B, C, and D**

A. **Correct:** Account Operators does not have the right to shut down a domain controller.

B. **Correct:** Print Operators has the right to shut down a domain controller.

C. **Correct:** Backup Operators has the right to shut down a domain controller.

D. **Correct:** Server Operators has the right to shut down a domain controller.

E. **Incorrect:** The Interactive special identity group does not have the right to shut down a domain controller.

Case Scenario: Implementing a Group Strategy

1. Global security groups should be used to represent user roles at both Trey Research and Woodgrove Bank.

2. Domain local security groups should be used to manage Read and Write access to the Sliced Bread folders.

3. The Marketing and Research global groups will be members of the domain local group that manages Write access. The group that manages Read access will have the following members: Finance, the CEO, her assistant, and the Auditors global group from the Woodgrove Bank domain.

Chapter 5

Lesson 1

1. **Correct Answer: D**

   A. Incorrect: DSMove is a command-line utility that moves existing objects in Active Directory. It does not control the default location for new objects.

   B. Incorrect: *Move-Item* is a Windows PowerShell cmdlet that moves existing objects in a namespace.

   C. Incorrect: NetDom is a command-line utility that allows you to join a domain, rename a computer, and perform other computer-related activities, but it does not control the default location for new computers.

   D. Correct: RedirCmp is a command-line utility that redirects the default computer container to an alternate OU.

2. **Correct Answer: A**

   A. Correct: The *ms-DS-MachineAccountQuota* attribute of the domain by default allows all authenticated users the ability to join 10 computers to the domain. This quota is checked when a user is joining a computer to the domain without a prestaged account. Set this attribute to zero.

   B. Incorrect: This attribute configures the default quota for all Active Directory objects, not just for new computer accounts.

   C. Incorrect: Removing this user right does not prevent Authenticated Users from joining computers to the domain.

   D. Incorrect: Setting this permission will prevent all users, including administrators, from creating computer accounts.

3. **Correct Answer: B**

   A. Incorrect: DSAdd creates new objects, including computer objects, but does not join a computer to the account.

   B. Correct: NetDom Join can join the local computer or a remote computer to the domain.

   C. Incorrect: DCTest tests various components of a domain controller.

   D. Incorrect: System.cpl is the System Properties control panel application. It allows you to join the local computer to a domain, but not to join a remote computer to a domain.

Lesson 2

1. **Correct Answers: C and D**

   A. Incorrect: CSVDE can import one or more computers but requires you first to create a comma-separated values file.

B. Incorrect: LDIFDE can import one or more computers but requires you first to create an LDIF file.

C. Correct: DSAdd creates a computer object with a single command.

D. Correct: Windows PowerShell lets you create a computer object with the *New-ADComputer* cmdlet.

2. **Correct Answers: A and D**

A. Correct: CSVDE can import one or more computers from a .csv file, and Excel can save a worksheet as a .csv file.

B. Incorrect: LDIFDE can import one or more computers, but the LDIF format cannot be created using Excel.

C. Incorrect: DSAdd creates computer objects one at a time.

D. Correct: Windows PowerShell lets you create computers using a .csv file as a data source. Use the *Import-CSV* command to consume the data source, and pipe the resulting objects to the *New-ADComputer* cmdlet.

Lesson 3

1. **Correct Answer: A**

A. Correct: Such events are symptomatic of a broken secure channel. Resetting the computer's account is the correct step to take to address the issue.

B. Incorrect: The event does not reflect user authentication problems.

C. Incorrect: Disabling the server account will prevent the server from authenticating. Enabling it will not fix the problem.

D. Incorrect: The event does not reflect user authentication problems.

2. **Correct Answers: C, D, and E**

A. Incorrect: Deleting the computer account will cause its SID to be removed and its group memberships to be lost. You will be forced to add the new account to the same groups and assign permissions to the new account.

B. Incorrect: Creating a new account for the new system creates a new SID. Permissions will have to be reassigned and group memberships re-created.

C. Correct: Resetting the computer account makes it available for a system to join the domain using the account. The account's SID and group memberships are preserved.

D. Correct: You must rename the account so that it can be joined by the new system using its name.

E. Correct: After resetting and renaming the account, you must join the new system to the domain.

3. **Correct Answer: C**

    A. Incorrect: A down arrow indicates that computer accounts are disabled. It is not necessary to reset the accounts.

    B. Incorrect: A down arrow indicates that computer accounts are already disabled.

    C. Correct: A down arrow indicates that the accounts are disabled. You need to enable them.

    D. Incorrect: A down arrow indicates that computer accounts are disabled. It is not necessary to delete the accounts.

Case Scenario 1: Creating Computer Objects and Joining the Domain

1. Computers are added to the Computers container because it is the default computer container. When a computer is joined to the domain and an account has not been prestaged in a specific OU, Windows creates the account in the default computer container.

2. The *Redircmp.exe* command can redirect the default computer container to the Clients OU.

3. You can reduce the *ms-DS-MachineAccountQuota* attribute to zero. By default, the value is 10, which allows all authenticated users to create computers and join up to 10 systems to the domain.

Case Scenario 2: Automating the Creation of Computer Objects

1. CSVDE can import .csv files, which can be exported from Excel.

2. DSQuery computer *"DN of new OU"* | dsmod computer -disabled yes.

3. You can select 100 systems, right-click any one system, and choose Properties. You can change the *Description* attribute for all objects at one time in the Properties For Multiple Items dialog box.

Chapter 6

Lesson 1

1. **Correct Answers: B and D**

    A. Incorrect: The central store is used to centralize administrative templates so that they do not have to be maintained on administrators' workstations.

    B. Correct: To create GPOs, the business unit administrators must have permission to access the Group Policy Objects container. By default, the Group Policy Creator Owners group has permission, so adding the administrators to this group will allow them to create new GPOs.

C. Incorrect: Business unit administrators require permission to link GPOs only to their business unit OU, not to the entire domain. Therefore, delegating permission to link GPOs to the domain grants too much permission to the administrators.

D. Correct: After creating a GPO, business unit administrators must be able to scope the GPO to users and computers in their OU; therefore, they must have the Link GPOs permission.

2. **Correct Answer: B**

   A. Incorrect: The path indicated is the correct path, but ADM files are not language independent.

   B. Correct: ADML files are the localized portion of administrative templates in Windows Server 2008 R2. The path shown is the network, UNC path to the PolicyDefinitions folder.

   C. Incorrect: The path indicated is the correct path, but ADMX files specify the settings, not the localization, of administrative templates.

   D. Incorrect: The Boot.wim file is used during installation of Windows Server 2008 R2.

3. **Correct Answer: D**

   A. Incorrect: A saved report is an HTML or XML description of a GPO and its settings. It cannot be imported into another GPO.

   B. Incorrect: The Restore From Backup command is used to restore a GPO in its entirety.

   C. Incorrect: You cannot paste settings into a GPO.

   D. Correct: You can import settings to an existing GPO from the backed-up settings of another GPO.

Lesson 2

1. **Correct Answers: B and C**

   A. Incorrect: If you configure a domain to block inheritance, GPOs linked to sites will not be applied to users or computers in the domain. The Northwind Lockdown GPO is linked to the domain and will apply to all users, including those in the Domain Admins group.

   B. Correct: By blocking inheritance on the OU that contains all the users in the Domain Admins group, you prevent the policy settings from applying to those users.

   C. Correct: The Deny Apply Group Policy permission, assigned to Domain Admins, exempts Domain Admins from the scope of the GPO, which otherwise applies to the Authenticated Users group.

   D. Incorrect: All user accounts in the domain belong to the Domain Users group as their primary group. Therefore, the GPO will apply to all users, including those in the Domain Admins group.

2. **Correct Answers: A and D**

    A. **Correct:** Because the desktop restrictions are in the User Configuration node but are being applied when users log on to specific computers, loopback policy processing is required.

    B. **Incorrect:** Linking the GPO to the OU containing user accounts causes the restrictions to apply to all users at all times, not only when they log on to conference and training room systems.

    C. **Incorrect:** The Block Inheritance option is not necessary and will prevent the application of all other GPOs from parent OUs, from the domain, and from sites.

    D. **Correct:** To scope the GPO correctly, you must link it to the OU containing the computer objects of conference and training room systems.

Lesson 3

1. **Correct Answers: B and D**

    A. **Incorrect:** The Group Policy Modeling Wizard simulates Group Policy application; it does not report its actual application.

    B. **Correct:** The Group Policy Results Wizard can report Group Policy application on a remote system.

    C. **Incorrect:** Gpupdate.exe initiates a manual policy refresh.

    D. **Correct:** Gpresult.exe can be used with the /s switch to gather RSOP information remotely.

    E. **Incorrect:** Msconfig.exe gathers system information and controls system startup.

2. **Correct Answer: A**

    A. **Correct:** Gpresult.exe produces an RSOP report that indicates when the GPO was applied. Screen saver policy settings are user configuration settings, so you must run Gpresult.exe for user settings.

    B. **Incorrect:** There is no -*computer* option for the Gpresult.exe command.

    C. **Incorrect:** Screen saver settings are user, not computer, configuration.

    D. **Incorrect:** Gpupdate.exe is used to trigger a policy refresh, not to report policy application.

Case Scenario: Implementing Group Policy

1. The settings that control the user's desktop environment are found in the User Configuration node.

2. Link the GPO to the OU containing the training computers. If you link the GPO to the OU containing users, the settings will affect users on all computers at Northwind Traders.

3. You must enable loopback policy processing. By linking the GPO to the OU containing training room computers and enabling loopback processing, the training room computers will apply settings in the User Configuration node of the GPO.

4. Loopback policy processing must be configured in the Replace mode. In the Replace mode, user settings in GPOs scoped to the user are ignored. Only the user settings in GPOs scoped to the computer are applied.

5. You must exclude training room computers from the scope of the screen saver GPO. You can do this in one of two ways. You can block inheritance on the training room computer OU, or you can use security group filtering on the domain GPO. Create a group containing training room computers and assign the Deny Apply Group Policy permission to the screen saver GPO to that group.

Chapter 7

Lesson 1

1. **Correct Answers: A, B, C, and D**

    A. **Correct:** The local Administrator account is a default member of Administrators. It cannot be removed.

    B. **Correct:** Domain Admins is added to Administrators when a computer joins the domain. The Member Of policy settings add specified groups to Administrators and do not remove existing members.

    C. **Correct:** Sydney Support is added to the Administrators group by the Sydney Support GPO. The Member Of policy settings add specified groups to Administrators and do not remove existing members.

    D. **Correct:** Help Desk is added to the Administrators group by the Corporate Help Desk GPO. The Member Of policy settings add specified groups to Administrators and do not remove existing members.

    E. **Incorrect:** The Remote Desktop Users group is not a default member of Administrators and is not added to Administrators by any of the GPOs.

2. **Correct Answers: A and C**

    A. **Correct:** The local Administrator account is a default member of Administrators. It cannot be removed.

    B. **Incorrect:** Domain Admins is added to Administrators when a computer joins the domain but is removed by the Sydney Support GPO, which specifies the authoritative membership of the group.

    C. **Correct:** Sydney Support is added to the Administrators group by the Sydney Support GPO.

D. Incorrect: Help Desk is specified as a member of the Administrators group by the Corporate Help Desk GPO, but the Sydney Support GPO has higher precedence because it is linked to the OU in which DESKTOP234 exists. Therefore, the membership specified by the Sydney Support GPO's Members Of This Group setting is authoritative.

E. Incorrect: The Remote Desktop Users group is not a default member of Administrators and is not added to Administrators by any of the GPOs.

3. **Correct Answers: A, C, and D**

   A. Correct: The local Administrator account is a default member of Administrators. It cannot be removed.

   B. Incorrect: Domain Admins is added to Administrators when a computer joins the domain but is removed by the Corporate Help Desk GPO, which specifies the membership of Administrators using the Members Of This Group setting.

   C. Correct: Sydney Support is added to the Administrators group by the Sydney Support GPO. Because the Sydney Support GPO has higher precedence than the Corporate Help Desk GPO, DESKTOP234 applies the Sydney Support GPO after applying the Corporate Help Desk GPO; thus, the Sydney Support GPO's members are added to the Administrators group.

   D. Correct: Help Desk is specified as a member of the Administrators group by the Corporate Help Desk GPO. When this GPO is applied, all other members of Administrators, except the Administrator account itself, are removed.

   E. Incorrect: The Remote Desktop Users group is not a default member of Administrators and is not added to Administrators by any of the GPOs.

Lesson 2

1. **Correct Answer: B**

   A. Incorrect: You use Local Security Policy to configure the settings on a single server.

   B. Correct: You can use Security Configuration And Analysis to compare the test environment configuration to a template, reconcile discrepancies, and export the resulting settings to a security template. The security template can then be imported into a GPO.

   C. Incorrect: The Security Configuration Wizard does not manage user rights.

   D. Incorrect: The Security Templates snap-in can create a security template but cannot export the settings of the test environment server. Security Configuration And Analysis is a better answer.

2. **Correct Answer: C**

   A. Incorrect: You use Local Security Policy to configure the settings on a single server.

   B. Incorrect: Security Configuration And Analysis allows you to create security templates that can be imported into a GPO, but the tool is not role-based. The Security Configuration Wizard is a better answer.

C. **Correct:** The Security Configuration Wizard creates role-based security policies that manage services, firewall rules, and audit policies as well as certain registry settings.

D. **Incorrect:** Security Templates allows you to create security templates that can be imported into a GPO, but the tool is not role-based. The Security Configuration Wizard is a better answer.

3. **Correct Answers: A and D**

A. **Correct:** The Scwcmd.exe Transform command creates a GPO that includes the settings in the specified security policy.

B. **Incorrect:** You do not need to create a GPO. The Scwcmd.exe command does that automatically.

C. **Incorrect:** You do not import settings from a security policy into a GPO. You can import the settings from a security template into a GPO.

D. **Correct:** The GPO created must be linked to an appropriate site, domain, or OU before its settings are applied to computers in that container.

Lesson 3

1. **Correct Answers: B and D**

A. **Incorrect:** The goal is to deploy the application to computers, not to users. Therefore, the User Configuration node is not the correct place on which to create the software package.

B. **Correct:** To deploy the application to computers, the software package must be created in the Computer Configuration node of the GPO.

C. **Incorrect:** The software installation extension does not apply settings if a slow link is detected. Because the application is deployed to computers, not to users, configuring the connection speed in the User Configuration node does not change the default connection speed in the Computer Configuration node, 500 kbps. The connection from that branch office is less than 500 kbps, so computers in the branch office will not install the application.

D. **Correct:** The software installation extension does not apply settings if a slow link is detected. By configuring the slow link detection threshold to 256, you ensure that clients connecting over the 364-kbps connection from the branch office will detect the link as a fast link, so clients will install the application.

E. **Incorrect:** The software installation extension does not apply settings if a slow link is detected. The connection from that branch office is less than 1,000 kbps, so computers in the branch office will not install the application.

2. **Correct Answers: A and D**

A. **Correct:** You want to deploy the application to users, so you must create the package in the User Configuration policies of a GPO. The GPO must then be scoped to apply only to Sales users. Because all users are in a single OU, you must create a security group with which to filter the GPO.

B. **Incorrect:** The GPO is not correctly scoped. Only computers exist in the Sales OU of each site. Computers will not process settings in the User Configuration policies under normal Group Policy processing.

C. **Incorrect:** You want to deploy the application to users. Policies in the Computer Configuration node apply to computers. Because no computers are in the Sales group, the policy will not be applied by any system.

D. **Correct:** If a computer is configured to perform loopback policy processing, it applies settings in the User Configuration policies of GPOs scoped to the computer. The GPO is scoped to the sales computers by being linked to the Sales OU. Loopback processing enables the User Configuration software package to be installed by the computers.

3. **Correct Answers: A, C, D, and E**

   A. **Correct:** The software deployment GPO must be scoped to apply to all users in the four branch offices. Although you could link the GPO to each of the four selected branches, that was not presented as an option.

   B. **Incorrect:** The application must be fully installed before the user launches it for the first time. When you publish an application, the user must install it by using Programs And Features in Control Panel on Window Server 2008 and Windows Vista or by using Add/Remove Programs in Control Panel on Windows XP.

   C. **Correct:** For the application to be fully installed before the user opens it the first time, you must select the Install This Application At Logon option. Otherwise, the application will be installed when the user opens the application the first time or opens a file type associated with the application.

   D. **Correct:** A shadow group is a group that contains users based on a characteristic such as the OU in which the user account exists. Because the GPO is linked to the Employees OU, it must be filtered with a security group that contains the users in the four branches.

   E. **Correct:** For the application to be fully installed before the user opens it the first time, you must assign the application.

   F. **Incorrect:** The Required Upgrade For Existing Packages option is used only in upgrade scenarios.

Lesson 4

1. **Correct Answer: D**

   A. **Incorrect:** Logon Event auditing captures local interactive and network logon to workstations and servers.

   B. **Incorrect:** Directory Service Access auditing monitors changes to objects and attributes in Active Directory.

   C. **Incorrect:** Privilege Use auditing relates to program execution and termination.

D. **Correct:** Account Logon Event auditing creates events when a user attempts to log on with a domain user account to any computer in the domain.

E. **Incorrect:** Account Management auditing creates events related to the creation, deletion, and modification of users, computers, and groups in Active Directory.

2. **Correct Answer: B**

A. **Incorrect:** Account Management auditing creates events related to the creation, deletion, and modification of users, computers, and groups in Active Directory, but it does not show the previous and changed values of attributes.

B. **Correct:** The Auditpol.exe command can be used to enable Directory Service Changes auditing, which logs the details of changes made to attributes as defined in the SACL of Active Directory objects. The previous and changed values of the attribute are included in the event log entry.

C. **Incorrect:** Privilege Use auditing relates to program execution and termination.

D. **Incorrect:** Directory Service Access auditing monitors changes to objects and attributes in Active Directory, but it does not report the previous and changed values of attributes.

3. **Correct Answers: E, F, and G**

A. **Incorrect:** You have configured permissions that prevent access by consultants. Therefore, there will be no successful access attempts to audit.

B. **Incorrect:** File system access events will be logged on the file servers, not on the domain controllers.

C. **Incorrect:** Directory Service Access audit policy relates to changes to objects in Active Directory, not to a folder on a disk subsystem.

D. **Incorrect:** The audit policy setting must apply to the file servers, not to domain controllers.

E. **Correct:** You must enable Object Access auditing on the file servers. The Server Configuration GPO is scoped to apply to all file servers.

F. **Correct:** File system access events will appear in the Security log of each file server.

G. **Correct:** Auditing entries must be configured on the Confidential Data folder. Auditing failures to Full Control access will create audit events for any type of access that failed.

Case Scenario 1: Installing Software with Group Policy Software Installation

1. The application package should be created in the Computer Configuration node so that it is installed on computers used by the mobile sales force. If the package is created in the User Configuration node, the application is associated with users and will be installed on any computer to which the users log on, including conference-room computers.

2. Advanced. Because the application package is created in the Computer Configuration node, Publish is not an available option. The available options are Assign and Advanced. You must choose Advanced to associate a transform with the package.

3. The GPO deploys the application in the Computer Configuration node, so the GPO must be scoped to computers. It can be linked to the domain or, better yet, to the Clients OU in which all client computers exist. The GPO must be further filtered to apply only to the computers used by the mobile sales force. This is accomplished by creating a global security group that contains the computers and using that group to filter the GPO. You must also remove the Authenticated Users group, which is given the Apply Group Policy permission by default.

Case Scenario 2: Configuring Security

1. Add an auditing entry that audits for failed attempts by the Everyone group to access the folder at the Full Control access level, which includes all other access levels. A second auditing entry must audit successful attempts by the Administrators group to access the folder at the Full Control access level, again to capture activities at any access level.

2. Restricted groups policies allows you to manage the membership of groups. A restricted groups policy setting for the Administrators group should be configured to specify that Members Of This Group are your account and the account of the VP of Human Resources. This policy setting is called the Members setting. It lists the final, authoritative membership of the specified group. The Administrator account cannot be removed from the Administrators group.

3. You must enable the Audit Object Access and Audit Privilege Use audit policies. Audit Object Access must be defined to audit Success and Failure events because the auditing entries on the Salaries folder are for both successful and failed access. Audit Privilege Use must be defined to audit Success events to log events when a member of the Administrators group takes ownership of a folder.

4. You can use security templates to manage the configuration of the seven servers. Security templates can be created on one system by using the Security Templates snap-in and imported to a database, and thereafter applied to the servers by using the Security Configuration And Analysis snap-in.

5. Policy settings in Active Directory–based GPOs can override your security settings because domain-based GPOs override the configuration of local GPOs. You can monitor your server's configuration by running RSoP reports to identify settings in domain GPOs that conflict with your desired configuration or by using the Security Configuration And Analysis snap-in to compare the servers' configuration against the security template.

Chapter 8

Lesson 1

1. **Correct Answers: C, D, and E**

   A. **Incorrect:** The password policies in the Default Domain Policy GPO define policies for all users in the domain, not just for service accounts.

   B. **Incorrect:** PSOs cannot be linked to organizational units, only to groups and users.

   C. **Correct:** PSOs can be linked to groups, so you must create a group that contains the service accounts.

   D. **Correct:** The PSO must be applied to the Service Accounts group; otherwise, the settings contained in the PSO will not take effect.

   E. **Correct:** PSOs can be linked to groups, and the group must contain the service accounts.

2. **Correct Answer: D**

   A. **Incorrect:** The Account Lockout Duration policy setting is specified in minutes. This setting will lock out an account for 100 minutes, after which time the account will be unlocked automatically.

   B. **Incorrect:** The Account Lockout Duration policy setting is specified in minutes. This setting will lock out an account for 1 minute, after which time the account will be unlocked automatically.

   C. **Incorrect:** The Account Lockout Threshold policy setting specifies how many invalid logon attempts result in account lockout. It does not determine the length of time for which an account is locked out.

   D. **Correct:** An Account Lockout Duration policy setting of 0 locks the account indefinitely until an administrator unlocks the account.

3. **Correct Answer: C**

   A. **Incorrect:** Although PSO1 has the highest precedence value, a PSO that applies to groups is overridden by a PSO that applies directly to the user, even if the user PSO has lower precedence.

   B. **Incorrect:** A precedence value of 99 is lower than the precedence value of 1.

   C. **Correct:** Although PSO3 does not have the highest precedence value (PSO1 is higher), it is linked to the user account, so it takes precedence.

   D. **Incorrect:** PSO4 is a user-linked PSO, but its value, 200, is lower than PSO3.

Lesson 2

1. **Correct Answer: B**

   A. Incorrect: This setting will generate event log entries when a user successfully logs on with a domain account. A successful logon does not generate account lockout.

   B. Correct: Failed logons to a domain account can generate account lockout. Auditing for failed account logon events will generate event log entries that identify when the failed logons occur.

   C. Incorrect: Logon events generate event log entries on the computer to which a user logs on or connects over the network. Local logons are not associated with account lockout.

   D. Incorrect: Logon events generate event log entries on the computer to which a user logs on or connects over the network. Local logons are not associated with account lockout.

2. **Correct Answer: C**

   A. Incorrect: Account logon events are generated when a user logs on with a domain account to any computer in the domain.

   B. Incorrect: Audit policies are settings in the Computer Configuration node of a GPO. These settings do not apply to user accounts.

   C. Correct: Logon events are generated in the event log of a computer when a user logs on interactively to the computer or connects to the computer over the network—for example, to a shared folder on the computer.

   D. Incorrect: Account logon events are generated by domain controllers when they authenticate a user logging on to any computer in the domain. This GPO is not scoped to domain controllers.

Lesson 3

1. **Correct Answer: B**

   A. Incorrect: An RODC requires only one writable Windows Server 2008 domain controller. Such a domain controller already exists in your domain.

   B. Correct: You must run ADPrep /RODCPrep to configure the forest so that the RODC can replicate DNS application partitions.

   C. Incorrect: The DSMgmt command is used to configure administrator role separation on an RODC after the RODC has been installed.

   D. Incorrect: You use the DCPromo command to perform an installation of a domain controller, including an RODC.

2. **Correct Answer: A**

   A. Correct: The Policy Usage tab of the Advanced Password Replication Policy dialog box reports the accounts whose passwords are stored on an RODC.

   B. Incorrect: The Allowed RODC Password Replication Group specifies users whose credentials will be cached on all RODCs in the domain.

C. **Incorrect:** The Denied RODC Password Replication Group specifies users whose credentials will not be cached on any RODC in the domain.

D. **Incorrect:** The Resultant Policy tab evaluates the password replication policy for a user or computer; it does not indicate whether that user's or computer's credentials are yet cached on the RODC.

3. **Correct Answers: B and D**

A. **Incorrect:** The Allowed RODC Password Replication Group specifies users whose credentials will be cached on all RODCs in the domain. The five users need to log on to only one of the branch offices.

B. **Correct:** The Password Replication Policy tab of the branch office RODC is used to specify the credentials that can be cached by the RODC.

C. **Incorrect:** The users do not require the right to log on locally to the branch office domain controller.

D. **Correct:** By prepopulating the credentials of the five users, you ensure that the RODC will be able to authenticate the users without forwarding the authentication to the data center on the far side of the WAN link.

Lesson 4

1. **Correct Answers: B and D**

A. **Incorrect:** Active Directory Users And Computers cannot be used to create a new managed service account.

B. **Correct:** Windows PowerShell is used to create a new managed service account, and also to install the account on SERVER02.

C. **Incorrect:** Regedit is not used to configure managed service accounts.

D. **Correct:** The Services console is used to assign an identity to a service. The identity can be an installed managed service account.

2. **Correct Answers: A, D, and E**

A. **Correct:** A server must run Windows Server 2008 R2 (or Windows 7) to use managed service accounts.

B. **Incorrect:** You do not need to raise domain functional level to use managed service accounts.

C. **Incorrect:** You do not need to raise forest functional level to use managed service accounts.

D. **Correct:** The schema must be updated to Windows Server 2008 R2 to use managed service accounts. You must run adprep /forestprep first.

E. **Correct:** The schema must be updated to Windows Server 2008 R2 to use managed service accounts. You must run adprep /domainprep after running adprep /forestprep.

Case Scenario 1: Increasing the Security of Administrative Accounts

1. Fine-grained password policies can be configured only in a domain at the domain functional level of Windows Server 2008 or higher. Before you can raise the domain functional level to Windows Server 2008, you must upgrade all Windows Server 2003 domain controllers to Windows Server 2008.

2. ADSI Edit.

3. You should assign a value between 1 and 9. Values closer to 1 have higher precedence. In addition, ensure that the new PSOs are not directly linked to the user account.

4. Define audit policy settings in the Default Domain Controllers GPO that configure auditing of failed account logon events.

Case Scenario 2: Increasing the Security and Reliability of Branch Office Authentication

1. Ensure that all domains are at the Windows Server 2003 domain functional level and that the forest is at the Windows Server 2003 forest functional level. On the schema master, run Adprep /rodcprep. Upgrade at least one Windows Server 2003 domain controller to Windows Server 2008.

2. You can delegate the installation of an RODC by pre-creating the computer accounts of the RODC in the Domain Controllers OU. When you do so, you can specify the user credentials that will be used to promote the RODC using the prestaged account, and then that user can successfully install the RODC without domain administrative privileges.

3. You can use the Dsmgmt.exe command to give the user local administrative privileges on the RODC.

Chapter 9

Lesson 1

1. **Correct Answer: C**
   A. **Incorrect:** You can use the command-line tool to create a domain tree. To do so, it is best to pre-create an answer file so that all values are passed automatically to the command during setup. However, you can also use the wizard to perform this task.
   B. **Incorrect:** Most often, you use stand-alone servers to create a new domain. This means you must log on with local administrative rights and then provide appropriate forest credentials to add the domain during the installation.
   C. **Correct:** The option to create a domain tree is not available in the wizard unless you select the advanced mode of the wizard at the very beginning.

D. Incorrect: Credentials are requested by the wizard during the preparation process for the installation. Using a stand-alone or member server has no effect on the operation.

2. **Correct Answers: B and D**

A. Incorrect: You must select the advanced mode of the wizard to create the domain tree, but selecting this mode has no impact on the wizard's ability to create the delegation.

B. Correct: Because the delegation uses a top-level root name (.ms), you must create the delegation manually in your forest root domain. The wizard cannot create it automatically because you do not have credentials for the root DNS server that maintains this name.

C. Incorrect: Because you create the delegation manually, you must tell the wizard to omit the creation.

D. Correct: Because you created a manual delegation, you must tell the wizard to omit the delegation creation.

E. Incorrect: You can create the delegation manually after the domain tree has been installed; however, it is a best practice to create it beforehand and then add components to its configuration after additional domain controllers have been created in the domain tree.

Lesson 2

1. **Correct Answers: A, B, C, D, and E**

A. Correct: Your DNS server administrator might have already configured scavenging for all zones, but it is good practice to validate that it has been applied to your zone.

B. Correct: By default, replication scopes are assigned properly when you create the zone, but it is always good practice for your zone to use the appropriate replication scope.

C. Correct: You might have other custom records to create, but you should create at least two: a text (TXT) record and a responsible person (RP) record. These will be used to update the Start of Authority record.

D. Correct: The text (TXT) record will contain the information for the DNS operating standards you will apply to the zone.

E. Correct: An email address is assigned to a Responsible Person (RP) record to enable others to communicate with the operator in case of issues or problems with name resolution.

F. Incorrect: Because the zone is new, there should be no unused records in the zone.

G. Incorrect: Reverse lookup zones are required only when your zone hosts secure web applications. No information about such an application has been provided.

2. **Correct Answers: A and B**

A. Correct: Because all zones are located on domain controllers, you must use domain administrator credentials to manage DNS.

B. Correct: If the server is not enlisted into the partition, the partition will not be available to the server.

C. Incorrect: Enterprise administrator credentials are required only to create the application directory partition, not to assign it.

D. Incorrect: You can use the command line to assign zones to partitions, but it is not mandatory.

E. Incorrect: You can always change the replication scope of a partition in DNS after it has been created. It is one of the basic operations DNS zone administrators must perform.

Case Scenario: Blocking Specific DNS Names

Trey Research can add the two problematic names to the global query block list on their DNS servers. This is done through the command line. The corresponding command is:

```
dnscmd /config /globalqueryblocklist wpad isatap biometrics biology
```

This command ensures that the Web Proxy Automatic Discovery protocol and the Intra-site Automatic Tunneling Addressing Protocol that are blocked by default continue to be blocked, and it adds the two problematic department names. Now, even if the administrative policies are not followed, the possibility of spoofing from these departments will be greatly limited.

Remember that this command affects all the FLZs hosted on a particular DNS server. If you have other DNS servers hosting other zones, such as a DNS server in a child domain, you must run the command on those servers as well.

Chapter 10

Lesson 1

1. **Correct Answer: D**

    A. Incorrect: Because you are upgrading the operative system of a domain controller, you must perform another step prior to the upgrade.

    B. Incorrect: You must run the Adprep.exe /domainprep /gpprep command before you upgrade the domain controller, but you must perform another step before running this command.

    C. Incorrect: The server is already a domain controller, so it is not necessary to run the Active Directory Domain Services Installation Wizard.

    D. Correct: You must run Adprep.exe /forestprep on the schema master of the forest as the first step to prepare the forest for a Windows Server 2008 R2 domain controller.

    E. Incorrect: You must run the Adprep.exe /rodcprep command before installing a read-only domain controller.

2. **Correct Answers: B, C, and D**

   A. **Incorrect:** Because the domain was built using only Windows Server 2008 R2 domain controllers, it is not necessary to run Adprep.exe /rodcprep.

   B. **Correct:** To allow a nonadministrative user to attach an RODC to the domain, an account must be prestaged in the Domain Controllers OU.

   C. **Correct:** The UseExistingAccount option of the Dcpromo.exe command allows you to attach a server to a prestaged RODC account.

   D. **Correct:** To attach a server to a prestaged RODC account, you must remove the server from the domain before running Dcpromo.exe.

3. **Correct Answer: C**

   A. **Incorrect:** NTBackup and system state backups are not supported in Windows Server 2008 R2.

   B. **Incorrect:** Adding the Windows Server Backup Features is not sufficient to create installation media.

   C. **Correct:** The Ntdsutil.exe command allows you to create installation media. The Sysvol and Full options create installation media that include SYSVOL for a writable domain controller.

   D. **Incorrect:** A copy of the directory and SYSVOL is not used for installation of a domain controller.

Lesson 2

1. **Correct Answer: E**

   A. **Incorrect:** The infrastructure master should not be placed on a domain controller that is a GC server unless all domain controllers in the domain are GC servers.

   B. **Incorrect:** Although there can be benefits to transferring the RID master role, it is not the required change in this scenario.

   C. **Incorrect:** Although there can be benefits to transferring the schema master role, it is not the required change in this scenario.

   D. **Incorrect:** Although there can be benefits to transferring the domain naming master role, it is not the required change in this scenario.

   E. **Correct:** The infrastructure master should not be placed on a domain controller that is a GC server unless all domain controllers in the domain are GC servers. Because SERVER02 is not a GC server, you should transfer the infrastructure master role to SERVER02.

2. **Correct Answers: D and E**

   A. **Incorrect:** The infrastructure master role is specific to each domain. You do not need to transfer it and, in fact, you cannot transfer it to a domain controller in another domain.

   B. **Incorrect:** The PDC Emulator role is specific to each domain. You do not need to transfer it and, in fact, you cannot transfer it to a domain controller in another domain.

C. **Incorrect:** The RID master role is specific to each domain. You do not need to transfer it and, in fact, you cannot transfer it to a domain controller in another domain.

D. **Correct:** The schema master role is a forest role. It should be transferred to the contoso.com domain before you decommission the domain.

E. **Correct:** The domain naming master role is a forest role. It should be transferred to the contoso.com domain before you decommission the domain.

3. Correct Answers: A, B, and C

A. **Correct:** The infrastructure master is a domain operations master.

B. **Correct:** The PDC emulator is a domain operations master.

C. **Correct:** The RID master is a domain operations master.

D. **Incorrect:** The schema master is a forest operations master, not a domain operations master.

E. **Incorrect:** The domain naming master is a forest operations master, not a domain operations master.

Lesson 3

1. Correct Answers: C and D

A. **Incorrect:** The replication of SYSVOL by using DFS-R within a domain is dependent upon the domain controllers of that domain, not on domain controllers in other domains.

B. **Incorrect:** The replication of SYSVOL by using DFS-R within a domain is dependent upon the domain functional level of that domain, not on the forest functional level.

C. **Correct:** All domain controllers must be running Windows Server 2008 or Windows Server 2008 R2 before you can replicate SYSVOL by using DFS-R within that domain.

D. **Correct:** The domain must be at Windows Server 2008 domain functional level or higher before you can replicate SYSVOL by using DFS-R within that domain.

E. **Incorrect:** The replication of SYSVOL by using DFS-R within a domain is dependent upon the domain functional level of that domain, not on the domain functional level of other domains.

2. Correct Answer: A

A. **Correct:** The Dfsrmig.exe command is used to migrate the replication of SYSVOL from FRS to DFS-R.

B. **Incorrect:** The Repadmin.exe command is used to manage Active Directory replication, not SYSVOL replication.

C. **Incorrect:** The Dfsutil.exe command is used to perform administrative tasks on a DFS namespace, not to configure SYSVOL replication.

D. **Incorrect:** The Dfscmd.exe command is used to perform administrative tasks on a DFS namespace, not to configure SYSVOL replication.

Case Scenario: Upgrading a Domain

1. You must run Adprep /forestprep before installing any Windows Server 2008 R2 domain controllers in a forest.

2. It is not possible for all domain controllers in a domain to be read-only. There must be at least one writable domain controller, so it is not possible to have all three branches served by read-only domain controllers. One DC must be writable. Alternately, one writable DC could be maintained in a central location, and three RODCs could be deployed to the three branches.

3. When there is planned downtime for a server performing single master operations, you should transfer the operations to another domain controller. When the original master comes back online, you can transfer the operations back to it.

Chapter 11

Lesson 1

1. **Correct Answer: C**

   A. **Incorrect:** Every domain controller is assigned to a site. It might be in the wrong site, but it is reflected as a server object in a site.

   B. **Incorrect:** You cannot create a site without a site link, so the branch office site is on a site link. It might be the wrong site link, but it is assigned to a site link.

   C. **Correct:** If the branch office IP address range is not represented by a subnet object, which is then associated with the site, computers might authenticate against domain controllers in another site.

   D. **Incorrect:** It is not possible to assign a subnet to two different sites.

2. **Correct Answers: A, D, and E**

   A. **Correct:** A subnet object with the IP address range of the branch enables clients to be informed of their site.

   B. **Incorrect:** The computer account for each domain controller should be in the Domain Controllers OU.

   C. **Incorrect:** Two site link transports are supported by Active Directory: IP and SMTP. No additional site link transport is necessary.

   D. **Correct:** A site object for the branch office is required to manage service localization, such as authentication, within the branch office.

   E. **Correct:** A server object for the domain controller must be in the site object.

Lesson 2

1. **Correct Answer: D**

   A. **Incorrect:** A read-only domain controller must still be able to contact a global catalog server.

   B. **Incorrect:** Application directory partitions are not involved with user authentication.

   C. **Incorrect:** Intersite replication does not address the problem caused when the branch domain controller cannot contact a global catalog server.

   D. **Correct:** Universal group membership caching, implemented for the branch office site, causes the domain controller to cache users' universal group memberships from a global catalog server, so that logon is not denied.

2. **Correct Answers: D and E**

   A. **Incorrect:** The Schema partition is replicated to all domain controllers in the forest. However, you should make sure that the domain controller you are demoting is not the schema operations master.

   B. **Incorrect:** The Configuration partition is replicated to all domain controllers in the forest.

   C. **Incorrect:** The Domain naming context is replicated to all domain controllers in the domain.

   D. **Correct:** A global catalog is on only one domain controller, by default. It is possible that the domain controller you want to demote is the only global catalog server, in which case you should configure another global catalog server before demoting the domain controller.

   E. **Correct:** Application directory partitions can be hosted on one or more domain controllers. It is possible for an application directory partition to exist only on the domain controller you are planning to demote.

3. **Correct Answer: C**

   A. **Incorrect:** You can use Dcpromo.exe to specify that a new domain controller should be a global catalog server, but you cannot use Dcpromo.exe to modify existing domain controllers.

   B. **Incorrect:** You can use the Active Directory Domain Services Installation Wizard to specify that a new domain controller should be a global catalog server, but you cannot use the wizard to modify existing domain controllers.

   C. **Correct:** Use the Active Directory Sites And Services snap-in to configure a global catalog server by opening the properties of the *NTDS Settings* object within the server object representing the domain controller.

   D. **Incorrect:** The Active Directory Users And Computers snap-in cannot be used to configure global catalog servers.

   E. **Incorrect:** The Active Directory Domains And Trusts snap-in cannot be used to configure global catalog servers.

Lesson 3

1. **Correct Answer: D**

   A. **Incorrect:** The total cost of replication from Site A to Site C over the links to Site B would be 350. The cost of replication over link A-C is only 100. Replication will use link A-C.

   B. **Incorrect:** The total cost of replication from Site A to Site C over the links to Site B would be 350. The cost of replication over link A-C is only 100. Replication will use link A-C.

   C. **Incorrect:** The total cost of replication from Site A to Site C over the links to Site B would be 150. The cost of replication over link A-C is only 100. Replication will use link A-C.

   D. **Correct:** The total cost of replication from Site A to Site C over the links to Site B is 200. If the cost of replication over link A-C is over 200, replication will use links A-B and C-B.

2. **Correct Answers: B and C**

   A. **Incorrect:** If there is a site link from sites A to C, it is possible that replication might occur between sites on that link. You have not prevented replication directly between Sites A and C.

   B. **Correct:** To prevent replication between Sites A and C, you must delete the site link that contains those two sites.

   C. **Correct:** Site links are transitive by default, so Site A can replicate directly with Site C, using links A-B and B-C. You must disable site link transitivity.

   D. **Incorrect:** Reducing site link costs encourages replication to avoid creating a connection over link A-C. However, it does not ensure that changes are sent, first, to Site B.

3. **Correct Answer: A**

   A. **Correct:** When IP connectivity is not available, SMTP must be used for replication, and SMTP cannot be used to replicate the domain naming context. Therefore, the ship must be a separate domain in the forest.

   B. **Incorrect:** Increasing the cost of the site link will not enable replication between the ship and headquarters.

   C. **Incorrect:** Designating a bridgehead server will not enable replication between the ship and headquarters.

   D. **Incorrect:** Manually creating a connection object will not enable replication between the ship and headquarters.

4. **Correct Answers: A and B**

   A. **Correct:** In the Active Directory Sites And Services snap-in, you can right-click NTDS Settings and force replication.

   B. **Correct:** The Replication Diagnostics tool, Repadmin.exe, allows you to force replication from the command line.

   C. **Incorrect:** The Directory Service Diagnosis tool, Dcdiag.exe, is a command-line tool that helps you test the health of replication and security for Active Directory Domain Services.

   D. **Incorrect:** The Active Directory Domains And Trusts snap-in is used to create and manage user, group, and computer objects. It does not allow you to force replication.

Case Scenario: Configuring Sites and Subnets

1. Create one Active Directory site for Denver. Intrasite replication topology, created by the KCC, generates a two-way topology with a maximum of three hops. Replication will occur within one minute. If the headquarters and the warehouse are in separate sites, intersite replication frequency is, at best, every 15 minutes.

2. Designating a preferred bridgehead server is useful for ensuring that the role is performed by a server with the most available system resources. It can also be useful if network configuration, such as firewalls, requires that replication traffic be directed to a single IP address. However, if the preferred bridgehead server is not available, the ISTG does not automatically designate a temporary bridgehead. Therefore, replication stops if the preferred bridgehead server is offline.

3. To achieve a true hub-and-spoke topology, you must create five site links. Each site link contains the Denver site and one of the branches. Therefore, the five site links would be: Denver–Portland, Denver-Seattle, Denver-Chicago, Denver-Miami, and Denver-Fort Lauderdale. You must also disable site link transitivity so that replication cannot build connections that skip over the Denver site.

4. Create a manual connection object for the warehouse domain controller so that it receives replication from SERVER01. A manual connection object will not be deleted by the KCC when it builds the intrasite replication topology.

Chapter 12

Lesson 1

1. **Correct Answers: A and D**

   A. Correct: In Active Directory Users And Computers, you can right-click the root node of the snap-in or the domain to find the Raise Domain Functional Level command.

   B. Incorrect: Active Directory Schema is not used to raise the domain functional level.

   C. Incorrect: Active Directory Sites And Services is not used to raise the domain functional level.

   D. Correct: You can right-click the domain in the Active Directory Domains And Trusts snap-in and click Raise Domain Functional Level.

2. **Correct Answers: B, D, and E**

   A. Incorrect: You must have one writable domain controller running Windows Server 2008 before adding an RODC to a domain. You already have a Windows Server 2008 domain controller in the contoso.com domain.

   B. Correct: The domain functional level must be at least Windows Server 2003 before adding an RODC.

C. Incorrect: You cannot raise the domain functional level to Windows Server 2008 because you have a domain controller running Windows Server 2003.

D. Correct: The forest functional level must be at least Windows Server 2003 before adding an RODC.

E. Correct: You must run Adprep /rodcprep before adding the first RODC to a domain.

F. Incorrect: You already have a Windows Server 2008 domain controller, so you have already run Adprep /forestprep.

3. **Correct Answer: C**

   A. Incorrect: RODCs are not required to implement fine-grained password policies.

   B. Incorrect: The Dfsrmig.exe command configures DFS-R of SYSVOL.

   C. Correct: Windows Server 2008 domain level or higher is required for fine-grained password policies. When you raise the forest functional level, you must also raise the domain functional level, making answer C the best answer.

   D. Incorrect: Fine-grained password policies are not managed with the GPMC.

Lesson 2

1. **Correct Answers: A, C, and G**

   A. Correct: The users in wingtiptoys.com will authenticate with computers in the tailspintoys.com domain. That makes wingtiptoys.com the trusted domain. The trust you must configure in wingtiptoys.com is an incoming trust.

   B. Incorrect: An outgoing trust would allow users in tailspintoys.com to authenticate with computers in wingtiptoys.com.

   C. Correct: The users in wingtiptoys.com are required to log on to computers in tailspintoys.com, but there is no requirement for users in tailspintoys.com to authenticate with computers in wingtiptoys.com.

   D. Incorrect: The users in tailspintoys.com are not required to log on to computers in wingtiptoys.com.

   E. Incorrect: Realm trusts are created with Kerberos v5 realms, not with Windows domains.

   F. Incorrect: A shortcut trust is used between domains in a multidomain forest.

   G. Correct: Because users in both the europe.wingtiptoys.com and wingtiptoys.com domains will authenticate with computers in tailspintoys.com, a forest trust is required. Forest trusts are transitive.

   H. Incorrect: An external trust would not provide the ability for users in the europe.wingtiptoys.com domain to authenticate with computers in the tailspintoys.com domain.

2. **Correct Answers: D**

   A. Incorrect: Creating duplicate accounts for the users will not allow the users to access resources.

B. **Incorrect:** Rebuilding the Windows NT 4.0 domain will not allow the users to access resources.

C. **Incorrect:** The */verify* parameter verifies the health of an existing trust relationship. Some trusted users can access the resources, so the trust relationship is known to be healthy.

D. **Correct:** The fact that the problematic accounts were migrated from Windows NT 4.0 suggests that there are SIDs in the users' *sIDHistory* attributes that are being filtered out because SID filtering is enabled by default on all external trusts. The */quarantine:no* parameter disables SID filtering.

3. **Correct Answer: D**

A. **Incorrect:** Reinstalling the operating systems is unlikely to solve the problem because performance is reasonable for accessing resources in the users' own domains.

B. **Incorrect:** Whether the IP address is assigned dynamically or statically is not relevant to the problem.

C. **Incorrect:** Dynamic updates of DNS records is not relevant to the problem.

D. **Correct:** A shortcut trust can improve performance by allowing domain controllers in one domain to refer clients to the other domain directly rather than through the forest root domain.

Case Scenario: Managing Multiple Domains and Forests

1. You must raise the domain and forest functional level to at least Windows Server 2003 or higher. Forest trusts are allowed only at forest functional levels of Windows Server 2003 or higher.

2. Because you do not have an account in the wingtiptoys.com domain, you can create only one-way incoming and one-way outgoing trusts. Administrators in wingtiptoys.com must create the reciprocal one-way outgoing and one-way incoming trusts.

3. You must enable selective authentication on the outgoing trust. Then you must give those users the Allowed To Authenticate permission on the computer objects of the four servers.

Chapter 13

Lesson 1

1. **Correct Answer: B**

A. **Incorrect:** Restartable AD DS is one of the best features of Windows Server 2008.

B. **Correct:** If someone is working on the other DC in the forest root domain and has stopped the AD DS service, you will not be able to stop it on this server because at least one DC for each domain must be operational before the service will stop.

C. Incorrect: You do not need to use DSRM in Windows Server 2008 to perform database operations on a DC.

D. Incorrect: You can stop the AD DS service through the command line or through the Services console.

2. **Correct Answers: D and F**

A. Incorrect: If the server has failed, you cannot restart it in DSRM.

B. Incorrect: You do not need to perform an authoritative restore because there is no indication that the server contained lost data that was not found in the other DCs.

C. Incorrect: You do not need to reinstall the operating system if you have access to full server backups.

D. Correct: You must restart the server in WinRE to launch the full server recovery operation.

E. Incorrect: You cannot perform a nonauthoritative restore with Ntdsutil.exe in Windows Server 2008. You must use Windows Server Backup or Wbadmin.exe.

F. Correct: You can perform a full server recovery with either the command line or the graphical interface.

Lesson 2

1. **Correct Answers: C and D**

A. Incorrect: Expiration dates do not cause a collector set to stop. They stop new collections from starting when the expiration date has been reached.

B. Incorrect: To be running, the collector sets must be on a schedule; otherwise, they would stop when the user who created them logged off.

C. Correct: You must set a stop condition on each collector set to ensure that it stops.

D. Correct: You must set a duration on the collector set when you schedule it to run; otherwise, it will not stop.

2. **Correct Answers: A, B, C, and D**

A. Correct: Reliability Monitor will reveal whether any changes have been made to the server recently and whether those changes could be tied to performance bottlenecks.

B. Correct: Event Viewer, especially the System event log, will reveal any errors or warnings about performance on the system.

C. Correct: Task Manager will display a real-time view into resources and allow you to identify potential bottlenecks.

D. Correct: Performance Monitor, especially the role-based Data Collector Set templates, will help you quickly discover any performance issues with the current server configuration and make recommendations on possible changes to improve performance.

Case Scenario: Working with Lost and Found Data

Occasionally, especially in large forests, someone will delete a container at the same time that someone else creates or modifies an object in the same container. This can be on entirely different DCs, but when replication synchronizes data on the DCs, the newly created object no longer has a home. When this happens, AD DS automatically stores such objects within the LostAndFound container. This special container manages lost objects within the domain. Another special container, the LostAndFoundConfig container, manages lost objects for the entire forest. The LostAndFoundConfig container is in the forest root domain only.

Therefore, you should regularly review the LostAndFound and the LostAndFoundConfig containers for objects to determine whether these objects should be moved to new containers or simply deleted from the directory.

Use the following procedure to verify the LostAndFound container in a child domain:

1. Move to the Active Directory Users And Computers portion of Server Manager.

2. On the View menu, select Advanced Features, expand the tree, and then click the LostAndFound container.

3. Identify any objects located within this container. Decide whether they need to be moved to other containers or deleted.

Be careful when deleting objects. Make sure you review an object's properties before deleting it. Sometimes it is best to move the object and deactivate it while you communicate with your peers to determine whether it is a necessary object. Remember that once deleted, SIDs cannot be recovered.

Chapter 14

Lesson 1

1. **Correct Answer: C**

   A. **Incorrect:** Existing setup processes must complete before you can initiate another setup operation. It is also difficult to tell whether setup processes have completed when you use the command line unless you use the /w switch, which only returns the command prompt when an operation completes. After restarting the server, you will find that there are no processes currently in operation, yet you still cannot uninstall AD LDS.

   B. **Incorrect:** Using Server Manager does not solve the problem because you must remove AD LDS instances before you can remove the role.

   C. **Correct:** You must remove all existing AD LDS instances before you can remove the role from the server. After all instances have been removed, you can remove the AD LDS role. This is another example of the importance of AD LDS instance documentation.

   D. **Incorrect:** The oclist command gives you the names of all the roles and features to use with the ocsetup command. However, this must be a full installation of Windows Server 2008 R2 because you have access to Server Manager. The oclist command does not work on a full installation.

Lesson 2

1. **Correct Answer: D**

    A. Incorrect: All AD LCS instances have a schema and all instance schemas can be edited. This is one reason why you should use AD CS instead of AD DS to integrate applications.

    B. Incorrect: You can make modifications to the instance with the LDP.exe command, but Schema modifications should be performed through the AD Schema snap-in.

    C. Incorrect: You can make modifications to the instance with the LDIF files and the LDIFDE. exe command, but Schema modifications should be performed through the AD Schema snap-in.

    D. Correct: When you use AD LDS Setup to create instances with default port numbers, the first port used on member servers is port 389. For example, to connect to the first instance, you need to use Instance1:389. However, since your Active Directory Domain Services schema also uses port 389, and your server is a member of a domain, the AD Schema snap-in will not connect to the instance. This is one reason why you should never user port 389 for AD LCS instances in a domain.

Case Scenario: Determining AD LDS Instance Prerequisites

You look up AD LDS on the Microsoft TechNet Center for Active Directory technologies and come up with the following answers:

1. A data drive should be created for each server that will host AD LDS instances. Because these servers will host directory stores, you should place these stores on a drive that is separate from the operating system, and in separate folders so that they can be easily identified.

2. You should always use meaningful names to identify instances. For example, the name of the application that will be tied to this instance is a good candidate. Instance names are used to identify the instance on the local computer as well as to identify and name the files that make up the instance and the service that supports it. Names cannot include spaces or special characters.

3. Both AD LDS and AD DS use the same ports for communication. These ports are the default LDAP (389) and LDAP over the SSL, or Secure LDAP, (636) ports. AD DS uses two additional ports: 3268, which uses LDAP to access the Global Catalog, and 3269, which uses Secure LDAP to access the Global Catalog. Because AD DS and AD LDS use the same ports, you should make it a habit to use other ports, ports beyond the 50,000 range, for your AD LDS instances. This ensures that they are segregated from AD DS services, especially if the instance is installed within a domain. In addition, you should install PKI certificates on each AD LDS instance to use Secure LDAP for communication and management. This prevents tampering with or detection of AD LDS data.

4. Ideally, each AD LDS instance should make use of an application partition, even if no replication is required. Creating an application directory partition makes it easier to manage the instance through a variety of tools.

5. Instances should be run through the use of a service account. You can use the NetworkService account, but if you intend to run multiple instances, it may be best to use named or managed service accounts for each instance. This way, you know exactly when the instance performs operations because you can view the login operations of the specific service account in the Event Viewer.

Chapter 15

Lesson 1

1. Correct Answers: B and C

   A. **Incorrect:** Although you cannot install enterprise CAs on Windows Server 2008 Standard edition or Windows Server 2008 Web edition, you are actually running the Windows Server 2008 Enterprise edition of Windows Server because you verified this prerequisite at the beginning of the installation.

   B. **Correct:** If you are logged on with a local account, even an account with local administrative privileges, you cannot install an enterprise CA. You must use a domain account to install an enterprise CA.

   C. **Correct:** To install an enterprise CA, your server must be a member of the domain because enterprise CAs rely on the AD DS directory service to publish and issue certificates.

   D. **Incorrect:** Because of all the required components in an enterprise CA installation, you should use Server Manager to install this role.

Lesson 2

1. Correct Answer: B

   A. **Incorrect:** Although you can use Certutil.exe to load certificates, you should also be able to perform the same operation through the wizard.

   B. **Correct:** The certificate template access rights are not set properly. To load the certificate manually on the server, the user account must have the Allow::Enroll permission set. In addition, the server on which you load the certificate should have the Allow::Enroll permission. You must re-create the template and reissue it to correct its access rights.

   C. **Incorrect:** You should be able to load the OCSP certificate onto this server because it is an OR.

   D. **Incorrect:** Although the certificate should be able to load automatically if it has the Allow::Autoenroll permission set, there is no reason other than access rights that would stop you from loading it manually.

Case Scenario: Managing Certificate Revocation

You go to your superiors with the information. They need to undertake a police operation immediately to stop the two ex-employees from selling certificates with the Contoso name embedded in them. In addition, your sales personnel must initiate damage-control operations with your clients. Having software on the market that does not originate from Contoso, yet contains Contoso certificates, can be extremely damaging to your company's reputation.

For your part, you immediately move to block the use of the certificates. To do so, you must first bring the root CA online. Then you use the Certification Authority section of Server Manager to revoke the two stolen certificates. Fortunately, when you cancel these certificates, any certificates that were issued using these as a source are automatically invalidated.

Then you force publication of the Certificate Revocation List. To do so, you use the Revoked Certificates node of the Certification Authority console. Unfortunately, you realize that even if you publish this new CRL immediately, clients will not update their CRL until their next refresh cycle, which depends on the refresh configuration.

Finally, your organization should issue a public statement about the two lost certificates. All Contoso clients should know that they are at risk and must verify each certificate they receive in the Contoso name until the revocation has taken effect.

As you can see, root CA security is of the utmost importance in a PKI architecture.

Chapter 16

Lesson 1

1. **Correct Answer: D**

   A. Incorrect: The server is running AD RMS because the AD RMS node is available in Server Manager.

   B. Incorrect: The server certificate is validated during the installation process. At worst, you can always use a self-signed certificate. This cannot be the problem.

   C. Incorrect: To install AD RMS, your server must be a member of the domain because AD RMS relies on the AD DS directory service to publish and issue certificates.

   D. Correct: During the installation, your account is added to the AD RMS Enterprise Administrators group on the local computer. To update the privileges of your account, you must log off and then log on again. Without this procedure, your account will not have the required access rights to run AD RMS.

Lesson 2

1. **Correct Answer: B**

   A. Incorrect: To access HTTP over SSL, users must use a URL address in the HTTPS:// format.

   B. Correct: The server certificate is validated when users try to access the URL. If it is not from a trusted CA, it will not work. If you used a self-signed certificate, the URL would have worked when you accessed it from the server because the server trusts its own certificate, but it would not work from user browsers because they do not trust the self-signed certificate.

   C. Incorrect: To access AD RMS from outside the network, users do not need an AD DS account.

   D. Incorrect: The URL is correct because you verified it from the server you used to set it up.

Case Scenario: Preparing to Work with an External AD RMS Cluster

The best and easiest way to share policy infrastructures without putting federation trusts in place is to rely on cross-certificate publication. This means relying on trusted publishing domains. These domains enable your own AD RMS cluster to issue use licenses for content that was protected by another AD RMS cluster. To create a trusted publishing domain, you must import the publishing cluster's SLC as well as its private key into your own cluster.

To proceed, you must first export your Server Licensor Certificate, and then have it imported into your partner's root cluster. Your partner must also perform the same activity. After the two certificates are imported, both environments will be able to support the issuance of publishing and use certificates for each other.

Chapter 17

Lesson 1

1. **Correct Answer: B**

   A. Incorrect: All services can use a named service account to run.

   B. Correct: The named service account is automatically replaced by the Network Service account during installation. After the upgrade is complete, you must reset the service account for each AD FS service.

   C. Incorrect: Woodgrove's policies would affect servers in the Woodgrove network, not your own.

   D. Incorrect: Although the Network Service account has limited access rights to the local machine and is a good account to use for certain services, it is by no means a best practice, and Microsoft does not enforce its use.

Lesson 2

1. **Correct Answers: A, C, E, and F**

   A. Correct: You must communicate with your counterpart to determine how you will exchange policy files during the setup of the partnership.

   B. Incorrect: Contoso is the claims provider and does not manage extranet applications.

   C. Correct: Woodgrove Bank is the relying party and manages extranet applications.

   D. Incorrect: As the relying party, Woodgrove Bank does not need to configure its client computers.

   E. Correct: As the claims provider, Contoso needs to configure its client computers.

   F. Correct: Each partner must rely on an attribute store.

Case Scenario: Choosing the Right AD Technology

Answers may vary, but they should include all of the elements presented here.

You look over the requirements and decide that it is a good opportunity to rely on the five Active Directory technologies. You proceed as follows:

- Active Directory Domain Services (AD DS) will be used to upgrade the internal directory service.

- Active Directory Rights Management Services (AD RMS) will be implemented to protect your intellectual property. This means that when you create a partnership, your organization will be the resource organization because you host the AD RMS installation.

- To support the applications in the Extranet, you will need to implement identity federation with Active Directory Federation Services (AD FS) 2.0. You will implement the AD FS

Federated Web SSO design, and your organization will be the resource organization. In addition, the Web-based applications will be AD FS 2.0-enabled.

- The clients that access your applications will be supported by the AD FS 2.0 processes. Specifically, partner organizations, internal users, and the general public will rely on AD FS 2.0 to gain access to the applications.

- Communication security will be provided by your Active Directory Certificate Services (AD CS) implementation. To facilitate access to all applications and ensure that all partners can validate the certificates you generate, you will rely on a third-party commercial Trusted Certificate Authority as the root of your AD CS deployment. This way, all of your certificates will be trusted at all times because the root certificate is trusted by all.

This is a best practices implementation of the new AD technologies.

Index

Symbols and Numbers

A

C

G

About the Authors

DAN HOLME is a graduate of Yale University and Thunderbird with more than 17 years of experience as a consultant and trainer to Fortune-caliber clientele implementing Windows and SharePoint technologies. Among the highlights of his career is his role as Microsoft Technologies Consultant for NBC Olympics during the Olympic Games in Vancouver, Beijing, and Torino. In addition to penning best-selling books for Microsoft Press, Dan is a contributing editor for *Windows IT Pro* and *SharePoint Pro* magazines as well as the community lead of SharePointProMag.com. Each year, Dan reaches hundreds of thousands of IT professionals and business decision makers. His efforts have earned him the prestigious title of Microsoft MVP (Windows Server Directory Services, 2007, and SharePoint Server, 2008–2011). He has also been recognized as one of the top 50 SharePoint influencers and one of the top 10 partner MVPs in the world. As the Chief SharePoint Evangelist for AvePoint, Dan works tirelessly to solve customers' IT business challenges, educate the global community, and develop solutions that will set the standard for the next generation of collaboration platforms. When the work and travel stop, Dan can be found on his home base, Maui, with Wyatt, Keith, Maddie, Jack, and the entire *ohana*, to whom this book is dedicated.

DANIELLE RUEST and **NELSON RUEST** are technology futurists focused on infrastructure design and optimization as well as continued service delivery. They have been working with complex infrastructures for more than 20 years. Their systems designs include core application deployments such as email and collaboration. They have also been working with virtualization for more than 10 years. Their recent books include *MCITP Self-Paced Training Kit (Exam 70-238): Deploying Messaging Solutions with Microsoft Exchange Server 2007* (http://www.microsoft.com/learning/en/us/book.aspx?ID=10938&locale=en-us); *Virtualization: A Beginner's Guide* (http://www.amazon.com/Virtualization-Beginners-Guide/dp/007161401X/ref=bxgy_cc_b_img_a); a look at comprehensive virtualization infrastructure designs; and *MCTS Self-Paced Training Kit (Exam 70-652): Configuring Windows Server Virtualization* (http://www.microsoft.com/learning/en/us/Book.aspx?ID=13695&locale=en-us#tab1). They both work for Resolutions Enterprises Ltd. (www.reso-net.com).

JASON KELLINGTON, MCT, MCSE, MCITP, MCTS, is a consultant, trainer, and author living in beautiful, cold northern Canada with his wife and two boys. Jason has spent time as an engineer, developer, administrator, and educator during his 15+ years in IT. His consulting and training practice specialize in enterprise infrastructure deployment as well as data management and business intelligence. He has assisted in the development of several projects with Microsoft Press and Microsoft Learning.

Get Certified—Windows Server 2008

Ace your preparation for the skills measured by the Microsoft® certification exams—and on the job. With 2-in-1 *Self-Paced Training Kits*, you get an official exam-prep guide + practice tests. Work at your own pace through lessons and real-world case scenarios that cover the exam objectives. Then, assess your skills using practice tests with multiple testing modes—and get a customized learning plan based on your results.

EXAMS 70-640, 70-642, 70-646

MCITP Self-Paced Training Kit: Windows Server® 2008 Server Administrator Core Requirements

ISBN 9780735625082

EXAMS 70-640, 70-642, 70-643, 70-647

MCITP Self-Paced Training Kit: Windows Server 2008 Enterprise Administrator Core Requirements

ISBN 9780735625723

EXAM 70-640

MCTS Self-Paced Training Kit: Configuring Windows Server® 2008 Active Directory®

Dan Holme, Nelson Ruest, and Danielle Ruest

ISBN 9780735625136

EXAM 70-647

MCITP Self-Paced Training Kit: Windows® Enterprise Administration

Orin Thomas, et al.

ISBN 9780735625099

EXAM 70-642

MCTS Self-Paced Training Kit: Configuring Windows Server 2008 Network Infrastructure

Tony Northrup, J.C. Mackin

ISBN 9780735625129

ALSO SEE

Windows Server 2008, Administrator's Pocket Consultant, Second Edition

William R. Stanek

ISBN 9780735627116

EXAM 70-643

MCTS Self-Paced Training Kit: Configuring Windows Server 2008 Applications Infrastructure

J.C. Mackin, Anil Desai

ISBN 9780735625112

Windows Server 2008 Administrator's Companion

Charlie Russel, Sharon Crawford

ISBN 9780735625051

Windows Server 2008 Resource Kit

Microsoft MVPs with Windows Server Team

ISBN 9780735623613

EXAM 70-646

MCITP Self-Paced Training Kit: Windows Server Administration

Ian McLean, Orin Thomas

ISBN 9780735625105

Get Certified—Windows® 7

Desktop support technicians and administrators—demonstrate your expertise with Windows 7 by earning a Microsoft® Certification focusing on core technical (MCTS) or professional (MCITP) skills. With our 2-in-1 *Self-Paced Training Kits*, you get a comprehensive, cost-effective way to prepare for the certification exams. Combining official exam-prep guides + practice tests, these kits are designed to maximize the impact of your study time.

EXAM 70-680

MCTS Self-Paced Training Kit: Configuring Windows 7

Ian McLean and Orin Thomas

ISBN 9780735627086

EXAM 70-685

MCITP Self-Paced Training Kit: Windows 7 Enterprise Desktop Support Technician

Tony Northrup and J.C. Mackin

ISBN 9780735627093

EXAM 70-686

MCITP Self-Paced Training Kit: Windows 7, Enterprise Desktop Administrator

Craig Zacker and Orin Thomas

ISBN 9780735627178

GREAT FOR ON THE JOB

Windows 7 Resource Kit

Mitch Tulloch, Tony Northrup, Jerry Honeycutt, Ed Wilson, and the Windows 7 Team at Microsoft

ISBN 9780735627000

Windows 7 Inside Out

Ed Bott, Carl Siechert, Craig Stinson

ISBN 9780735626652

Windows 7 Administrator's Pocket Consultant

William R. Stanek

ISBN 9780735626997

microsoft.com/mspress

What do you think of this book?

We want to hear from you!
To participate in a brief online survey, please visit:

microsoft.com/learning/booksurvey

Tell us how well this book meets your needs—what works effectively, and what we can do better. Your feedback will help us continually improve our books and learning resources for you.

Thank you in advance for your input!